Development During Middle Childhood

The Years From Six to Twelve

CI.064557

W. Andrew Collins, *Editor*

Panel to Review the Status of Basic Research on
School-Age Children
Committee on Child Development Research and Public Policy
Commission on Behavioral and Social Sciences and Education
National Research Council

NATIONAL ACADEMY PRESS
Washington, D.C. 1984

National Academy Press   2101 Constitution Ave., NW   Washington, DC 20418

Library of Congress Cataloging in Publication Data

National Research Council (U.S.). Panel to Review the
   Status of Basic Research on School-Age Children.
   Development During Middle Childhood: The Years From Six to Twelve.

   Includes index.
   1. Child development—Addresses, essays, lectures.
2. Child psychology—Addresses, essays, lectures.
3. Elementary school children—Addresses, essays, lectures.
I.   Collins, W. Andrew, 1944–   II. Title.
HQ769.N312 1984   155.4'24   84-11457

ISBN 0-309-03478-7

Printed in the United States of America

PANEL TO REVIEW THE STATUS OF BASIC RESEARCH ON SCHOOL-AGE CHILDREN

W. ANDREW COLLINS (*Chair*), Institute of Child Development, University of Minnesota

THOMAS M. ACHENBACH, Department of Psychiatry, University of Vermont

EDGAR G. EPPS, Department of Education, University of Chicago

KURT W. FISCHER, Department of Psychology, University of Denver

WILLARD W. HARTUP, Institute of Child Development, University of Minnesota

ELEANOR E. MACCOBY, Department of Psychology, Stanford University

HAZEL J. MARKUS, Institute for Social Research, University of Michigan

JACK P. SHONKOFF, Department of Pediatrics, University of Massachusetts Medical School

THOMAS S. WEISNER, Department of Psychiatry and Department of Anthropology, University of California, Los Angeles

KIRBY A. HELLER, *Study Director*

CONTRIBUTORS

THOMAS M. ACHENBACH, Professor, Department of Psychiatry, University of Vermont

DANIEL BULLOCK, Assistant Professor, Department of Psychology, University of Denver

W. ANDREW COLLINS, Professor and Director, Institute of Child Development, University of Minnesota

EDGAR G. EPPS, Marshall Field IV Professor of Urban Education, Department of Education, University of Chicago

KURT W. FISCHER, Associate Professor, Department of Psychology, University of Denver

WILLARD W. HARTUP, Professor, Institute of Child Development, University of Minnesota

ELEANOR E. MACCOBY, Professor, Department of Psychology, Stanford University

HAZEL J. MARKUS, Associate Professor, Department of Psychology, and Associate Research Scientist, Institute for Social Research, University of Michigan

PAULA S. NURIUS, Doctoral Candidate, Department of Social Work and Department of Psychology, University of Michigan

JACK P. SHONKOFF, Assistant Professor of Pediatrics, Department of Pediatrics, and Codirector, Child Development Service, University of Massachusetts Medical School

SYLVIA F. SMITH, Research Assistant, Department of Education, University of Chicago

THOMAS S. WEISNER, Associate Professor of Anthropology, Department of Psychiatry and Department of Anthropology, University of California, Los Angeles

COMMITTEE ON CHILD DEVELOPMENT RESEARCH AND PUBLIC POLICY

WILLIAM A. MORRILL (*Chair*), Mathematica Policy Research, Inc., Princeton, New Jersey
WILLIAM KESSEN (*Vice Chair*), Department of Psychology, Yale University
EUGENE S. BARDACH, School of Public Policy, University of California, Berkeley
DONALD T. CAMPBELL, Department of Social Relations, Lehigh University
DORIS R. ENTWISLE, Department of Social Relations, The Johns Hopkins University
FRANK F. FURSTENBERG, Department of Sociology, University of Pennsylvania
JOEL F. HANDLER, School of Law, University of Wisconsin
SHEILA B. KAMERMAN, School of Social Work, Columbia University
JOHN H. KENNELL, School of Medicine, Case Western Reserve University, and Rainbow Babies' and Children's Hospital
LUIS M. LAOSA, Educational Testing Service, Princeton, New Jersey
FRANK LEVY, School of Public Affairs, University of Maryland
SAMUEL J. MESSICK, Educational Testing Service, Princeton, New Jersey
ROBERT H. MNOOKIN, Stanford Law School, Stanford University
JOHN MODELL, Department of History and Philosophy, Carnegie-Mellon University
JOHN U. OGBU, Department of Anthropology, University of California, Berkeley
T. M. JIM PARHAM, School of Social Work, University of Georgia

Contents

Preface   ix

Acknowledgments   xiii

1 Introduction   1

2 The Biological Substrate and Physical Health in
   Middle Childhood   24
   Jack P. Shonkoff

3 Cognitive Development in School-Age Children:
   Conclusions and New Directions   70
   Kurt W. Fischer and Daniel Bullock

4 Self-Understanding and Self-Regulation in Middle
   Childhood   147
   Hazel J. Markus and Paula S. Nurius

5 Middle Childhood in the Context of the Family . . .   184
   Eleanor E. Maccoby

6   The Peer Context in Middle Childhood   240
    Willard W. Hartup

7   School and Children: The Middle Childhood Years   283
    Edgar G. Epps and Sylvia F. Smith

8   Ecocultural Niches of Middle Childhood: A Cross-
    Cultural Perspective   335
    Thomas S. Weisner

9   The Status of Research Related to Psychopathology   370
    Thomas M. Achenbach

10 Conclusion: The Status of Basic Research on Middle
    Childhood   398
    W. Andrew Collins

Index.   422

Preface

In 1981 at the request of the W. T. Grant Foundation, the Committee on Child Development Research and Public Policy established the Panel to Review the Status of Basic Research on School-Age Children. The Grant Foundation's primary interest was to identify new and promising directions for basic research on human development during the early elementary years. Believing that development during the 6–12 age period has received less attention from the research community than the periods of infancy, the preschool years, and adolescence, the Foundation designated middle childhood health and development as a new priority for research support. To aid in its program planning efforts, the panel was asked (1) to identify significant aspects of social, emotional, cognitive, and physical development during this age period; (2) to review the current status of relevant basic research; (3) to highlight theoretical and methodological issues associated with the research; and (4) to suggest useful directions for future inquiry.

It was not the specific intention of our sponsors nor of the members of the committee that the panel should produce a traditional, comprehensive state-of-the-art review of all relevant research. The hope was that the report would reflect a degree of selectivity in the subtopics addressed, in the existing studies discussed, and in the types of future inquiry highlighted. We also hoped that the report would reflect the interdisciplinary process of review and synthesis that has become a hallmark of National Research Council studies. Reviews of research on child development have typically focused on the contributions of developmental psychology to understanding the nature of personal behavior and interactions, thought processes, and physical and emotional well-being at different ages. The panel's study was intended to integrate knowledge concerning these aspects of human development with a broader understanding of their relationship to the physical, social, cultural, and institutional factors that affect growth and behavior during middle childhood and that influence the longer-term progress of children following different developmental trajectories. In this way, the panel's study relied not only on the contributions of several specialized fields within developmental psychology but also on the contributions of clinical psychology, psychiatry, sociology, anthropology, education, and pediatrics.

As a starting point for the study, the members of the Committee on Child Development Research and Public Policy, along with W. Andrew Collins, the panel chair, designated significant aspects of development and factors affecting development in the 6–12 period to be addressed in the report:

• cognitive development, including learning processes, coordination and integration of knowledge acquisition, and planning functions;

• development of social concepts and skills, including children's understanding of social situations and events and appropriate behaviors as well as social concepts such as responsibility, intention, cooperation, and competition;

• development of concepts of self and social relations, including developmental changes in and environmental influences on self-concept, self-esteem, friendship, love, and loyalty;

• parent and family relations, including changes in interfamilial and extrafamilial relationships and interactions;

• peer relations, including the selection of friends, the formation of friendships, and the system of personal associations and relationships that develops among children in school and in other extrafamilial settings;

• social and cultural factors affecting development, including the influence of various social institutions such as the media, religious affiliations, and other formal and informal community organizations outside the family;

• educational/school factors affecting development, including the influence of curricular and extracurricular activities, school environment, and school structures as these interact with other dimensions of children's daily experiences;

• achievement and motivational factors affecting development, including emotion, motivation, and individual adaptation as they influence cognitive and social development as well as self-concept, self-esteem, and the range of social relations;

• deviance and psychopathology, including the range of problem behaviors and adjustments, ego processes, coping behaviors, and reactions to stress that occur in this age group as well as the antecedents in middle childhood of later deviant functioning; and

• health and physical growth, including the range of physical and physiological conditions and changes that occur during middle childhood and that influence social, emotional, and cognitive growth and development.

It is important to note the high degree of interrelation, and to some extent overlap, among these topical headings, which constituted the organizing framework for the study. In some cases they became the subjects of chapters of the report; in other cases they were addressed in the discussion in one or more chapters. With regard to each of these topics, however, special attention was given to the methodological problems of studying school-age children—for example, the settings in which they are available for study and the measurement of their skills and abilities as well as their potential reactions to many commonly used measurement procedures. Special attention was also given to the strength of the relevant theoretical underpinnings and to the extent of the empirical knowledge base. While these methodological problems exist, the panel found reasons for optimism about the potential for new knowledge. Equally important, the report lends credence to the hypothesis that there are important research issues to be pursued with regard to the development of 6- to 12-year-olds.

The panel members were selected for their expertise in these areas and for their willingness to undertake major responsibility for drafting the review chapters. Each member of the panel served as an author of this report and each as a critical sounding board for the written contributions of his or her colleagues. Moreover, each member contributed in a concrete way to the analytic and synthetic processes that yielded the insights about theoretical, empirical, and methodological issues that are the end result of this effort. Over the two-and-a-half-year course of the study, the panel met five times to conceptualize the relevant research issues, to review and critique the chapter drafts, and to develop the conclusions and recommendations that are presented throughout this report. This report is truly a product of the special commitment and hard work of the members of the panel themselves.

William A. Morrill, *Chair*
Committee on Child Development
Research and Public Policy

Acknowledgments

Special acknowledgment is due to W. Andrew Collins, who served as panel chair, editor of the report, and the author of the introductory and concluding chapters. His commitment of time, energy, and intellectual resources over the past two-and-a-half years has been extraordinary. Without him, this report would not have been possible.

Further acknowledgment is due to members of the staff of the Committee on Child Development Research and Public Policy for their contributions to the successful completion of the study. Cheryl D. Hayes, in her capacity as executive officer for the Committee on Child Development Research and Public Policy, assisted in the establishment of the panel, provided administrative direction and oversight throughout the study, and maintained liaison between the panel, the parent committee, the Commission on Behavioral and Social Sciences and Education, and the W. T. Grant Foundation. Kirby A. Heller served on a part-time basis as study director and played an important role in coordinating the work of the authors and the external review of the chapter drafts as well as assisting in drafting the introductory chapter. Susan Goff Timmer and S. Wayne Duncan were especially helpful in compiling the demographic information presented in the introductory chapter. Christine L. McShane, editor for the commission, edited the manuscript with a critical eye and managed the final production of the report. Marjorie B. Dahlin, staff member of the Committee on Child Development Research and Public Policy, assumed major responsibility for manuscript preparation and proofreading.

I would also like to acknowledge the special contribution of the numerous reviewers of the report. Several members of the Committee on Child Development Research and Public Policy as well as a number of invited external reviewers provided unusually detailed comments and critiques of the early drafts of the report. These careful and thoughtful reviews significantly influenced the final versions as they appear in this volume.

Finally, I would like to offer special thanks on behalf of the Committee on Child Development Research and Public Policy to Robert Haggerty, President of the W. T. Grant Foundation, for his advice and support throughout the study. But for his interest and initiative, this study would never have been done.

William A. Morrill, *Chair*
Committee on Child Development
Research and Public Policy

CHAPTER 1

Introduction

Children between the ages of 6 and 12 are in the age period commonly referred to as middle childhood. As an age group, 6- to 12-year-olds are less obviously set apart than infants, adolescents, and even preschool children are in most Western societies. Nevertheless, the implicit grouping of ages 6–12 appears to be neither an idiosyncratic invention of Western cultures nor merely a category by default among arbitrarily defined periods of human development. Rather, these years universally mark a distinctive period between major developmental transition points.

In diverse cultures the 5–7 age period is regarded as the beginning of the "age of reason" (Rogoff et al., 1975). Children are assumed to develop new capabilities at this age and are assigned roles and responsibilities in their families and communities. Middle childhood has also been differentiated from adolescence cross-culturally, largely by the onset of puberty. Recent emphasis on cognitive differences between 10- to 12-year-olds and relatively mature adolescents has also contributed to popular and scholarly distinctions between middle childhood and adolescence.

Historically, in many cultures the age of 6 or 7 was the time at which children were absorbed into the world of adults, helping shoulder family responsibilities and fill work roles alongside their elders. Only in recent centuries have changing concepts of the family and the advent of formal schooling removed children of this age from wide participation in adult society (Aries, 1962). Today and for most of this century, the ages of 6–12 have continued to be set apart from younger ages because they correspond

1

to the first 6 of the 12 compulsory school years. The segregation of children ages 6–12 in elementary schools provides a distinctive basis for the social definition of children and a social structure that constrains and channels development during this period.

Increasingly, however, the social norms and structures that determine the age grading of 6- to 12-year-olds are being blurred by secular trends toward earlier schooling and earlier puberty. Growing numbers of children younger than age 6 are beginning some kind of formal schooling, sometimes compulsory. The trend toward earlier puberty means that many 10-, 11-, and 12-year-olds are experiencing the physical changes traditionally associated with adolescence but out of synchrony with the transition into the teen years. The impact of this secular trend can be seen in experiments with school organizations in the past decade in an attempt to find workable age groupings for children whose physical, cognitive, and social characteristics are in transition. The term *preteen* has emerged to acknowledge this earlier advent of teenage characteristics.

As social structures for delineating ages 6–12 become less definite, it becomes more crucial to understand the nature of development in this period, including the ways in which it is—and is not—linked to particular social and cultural structures and demands on children. Toward this end, the chapters of this volume represent distillations of research findings from studies of children ages 6–12 and assessments of the status of knowledge in a number of areas.

The panel's primary goal was to assess what is known about the distinctive characteristics—physical, behavioral, social, and emotional—and development of children across the age span from 6 to 12. Although we have devoted considerable attention to the societal contexts of development in this period, including the social structures that shape and constrain the course of individual growth, of primary concern in our deliberations have been the implications for individual children—in particular, long-term individual outcomes of development.

In our view, developmental change is continuous and any segmentation into age periods is somewhat arbitrary. The widespread cultural demarcation of a period roughly corresponding to ages 6–12 raises important questions about the characteristics of children in this age group and, equally significant, the implications of segregation along these age boundaries for the developmental tasks, limitations, and possibilities encountered by individual children. The period is clearly not a static one developmentally, despite what has sometimes seemed to be a lack of concern among scholars about the significance of changes in middle childhood. We have viewed the middle childhood years as part of a continuous process as well as a period characterized by distinct abilities and age-related changes. Two questions recur in the chapters that follow:

1. What is known about characteristics that distinguish children in middle childhood from those in the preschool years?
2. What significant developmental changes ordinarily occur within these years?

During middle childhood, children gain access to new settings and encounter pressures that present them with distinctive developmental challenges. The widening world of middle childhood is marked especially by the entry into school of children from all strata of U.S. society. School entry signifies a new set of social contacts with both adults and other children as well as a wider variety of settings than those that characterize early childhood. Consequently, school experiences and influences were central considerations in the panel's deliberations, as was the role of peers both in and out of school. The implications of a widening social world for family relationships—and their continuing functions for children in middle childhood—also occupied a primary role in our discussions. Fundamental to the topics we have chosen is the problem of characterizing the environmental constraints and options for children in diverse settings across the society.

The developmental difficulties and subsequent dysfunctions associated with children ages 6–12 also were major issues in the panel's deliberations. Although a detailed assessment of evidence on problem behaviors such as delinquency, drug use, runaways, and the like could not be undertaken within the scope of the panel's work, we did address both psychological and physical health in middle childhood—in particular, what is known and what needs to be known about the long-term implications of development for physical and mental health.

In this introductory chapter we first outline some of the important theoretical views that have shaped research in middle childhood. We present a group portrait of children in middle childhood in this country in order to give a demographic and social context to the research that is covered in the remainder of the volume. Finally, we give a brief overview of each of the topics covered in the individual chapters.

THEORETICAL VIEWS OF MIDDLE CHILDHOOD

The body of research concerned with children ages 6–12 encompasses disciplines ranging from psychology and sociology to medicine and public health. Surprisingly, few theoretical formulations have included extensive treatments of this age group, in contrast to the amount of theoretical attention given to infancy, early childhood, and adolescence. The two major views of the child between 6 and 12—those advanced by Sigmund Freud and Jean Piaget—focus on some possible reasons for the common belief in middle childhood as a distinct developmental period.

Sigmund Freud assigned to the years between ages 5 or 6 and adolescence the vital tasks of skill development and the consolidation of psychosexual achievements from earlier periods. Freud's characterization of this period as one of latency has been widely misconstrued as indicating it is relatively insignificant, perhaps because the psychosexual events of earlier and later periods appear more dramatic in psychoanalytic thought. This aspect of Freud's formulation is also captured by Erik Erikson's emphasis on the development of a sense of industry and Harry Stack Sullivan's interpretation of the importance of interpersonal relationships during the same period. Although none of these three theorists has had a substantial impact on research on middle childhood, Sullivan's ideas have frequently been invoked in connection with research on social relations with peers in the elementary school years. All three, however, underscore the occurrence of significant psychological developments in middle childhood and the importance of recognizing the culturally defined tasks associated with the period.

The second major view, represented by Jean Piaget's theory of cognitive development, emphasizes the extent to which children in this age period become capable of logical thinking, reasoning, and problem solving in a variety of tasks. Whereas preschool children are inordinately tied to the concrete, readily perceptible characteristics of tasks, the thoughts of children ages 6–12 are more fully logical and more systematic. Thus, in Piaget's view the significant psychological accomplishments of middle childhood are in the realm of intellectual competence. The goal of most of the research emanating from Piaget's theory has been understanding the logical model of intellectual functioning; indeed, the major contribution of Piaget-inspired scholars has been an image of the child at every stage of development as an active, integrating organism in interaction with the environment. Cognitive-developmental formulations such as Piaget's undergird a core of studies of children ages 6–12 that have contributed substantially to knowledge of specific aspects of this age period; these include not only studies of cognitive development per se but also studies of concepts and understanding of the social and subjective worlds. In recent years research on self-concept, social interactions, family and peer relationships, school functioning, and health has been influenced by cognitive-developmental perspectives. In each of these domains the focus has been on differences between the intellectual capabilities of children in middle childhood and those of younger and older children.

Rich though these theoretical traditions are, they offer only part of the relevant background to a consideration of the status of research on middle childhood. Throughout this volume our focus on middle childhood encompasses a variety of factors in development and individual functioning that make up a broad consideration of the years 6–12.

DEMOGRAPHIC OVERVIEW OF CHILDREN IN MIDDLE CHILDHOOD

We begin with a sketch of children in middle childhood in the United States today. Our purpose is not an exhaustive demographic analysis of middle childhood but rather an impressionistic overview of the lives of such children. Through the presentation of data from large-scale data sources, the following sections serve as background to the analyses of children's development in the remainder of this report.

Several limitations on the type and scope of information presented should be made clear at the outset. First, despite repeated calls for an integrated system of childhood social indicators that tracks the welfare of children in this country, such a system has yet to be developed. Data based on sources with long histories, such as the Current Population Survey, are a major source of information about population trends, the types of families in which children are growing up, and the schools they attend. Less is known, at least from a national perspective, about the quality of children's lives and their perceptions of their worlds. Several recent studies, such as the National Survey of Children (Zill, in press), have begun to fill this gap. Nevertheless, we have only a rudimentary understanding of children's own views of their lives.

Besides the relative scarcity of certain types of information, other limitations mark these data. For our purposes the preferable unit of analysis is the child. The following sections reflect this preference, but in many cases information in which the family is the unit of analysis was the only kind available. In addition, data are most frequently reported in broad age categories that are not consistent across data sources or over time. Whenever possible, we report information on children between the ages of 6 and 12. Often, however, data were available only on expanded age groupings, such as 5–13 or 6–13.

A hallmark of these data is the diversity of the population of children in middle childhood. National averages often mask important differences between subgroups—racial differences and regional differences, for example— and national surveys often inadequately report information about minority groups (Zill et al., 1983). In this overview we focus on racial differences because of the frequently striking contrast between white and black children in our society. We recognize, however, that the presentation of data would be facilitated by further disaggregation into more finely differentiated subgroups. We also recognize the need for information on children ages 6–12 in other cultural and minority groups in the United States, particularly Asian-American, Hispanic, and Native American groups.

The Population of School-Age Children

In 1982 the population of U.S. children ages 6–12 was 23.6 million, representing slightly more than 10 percent of the total U.S. population of 232 million. This age group is approximately equally divided by sex (51 percent were boys, 49 percent were girls). Of the total number of children, 15 percent were black. Relative to children of all ages, a higher proportion of black children (12.6 percent) than white children (9.7 percent) were between the ages of 6 and 12.

Current data are not available for racial and ethnic group breakdowns of children ages 6–12. These data are published, however, for children ages 5–13 or 5–14 (see Table 1-1). Table 1-1 presents the number of children

TABLE 1-1   Racial and Ethnic Origins of
School-Age Children (numbers in thousands)

	Number	Percentage
Racial and Ethnic Origins of Children Ages 5–14 (1980)		
White	27,491	78.7
Black	5,163	15.8
American Indian, Eskimo, and Aleut	302	0.9
Asian and Pacific Islander	582	1.7
Other	1,400	4.0
Children of Hispanic origin[a]	3,012	8.6
Total	34,938	100.0
Children Ages 5–13 by Type of Hispanic Origin (1979)		
Mexican	1,575	—
Puerto Rican	404	—
Cuban	113	—
Central or South America	157	—
Other Hispanic	254	—
Total	2,500	—

[a]May be of any race.

in six racial and ethnic groups and their proportion in the population and provides additional data on children of Hispanic origin.

The proportion of all children in middle childhood has been steadily declining during the past two decades. In 1960 children ages 6–12, part of the postwar baby boom, represented slightly less than 16 percent of the population; by 1970 they represented 14.1 percent. With the simultaneous rise in the average life expectancy, the population on average has been gradually getting older.

Census Bureau projections estimate that the population of children ages 6–12 as well as the percentage of the population ages 6–12 will continue to decline through 1985. Their number will then gradually increase through the remainder of this century before once again declining in the beginning of the twenty-first century.

Children's Environments

The racial and cultural diversity of children ages 6–12 in the United States raises questions about how their lives are different and what components of the differences may be significant to their development. Although at present we can only speculate on the implications, we can see a number of dimensions on which children in this age group vary.

Children ages 6–12 were fairly well distributed across the country in 1981, but the geographical distribution varied by race (Table 1-2). More than half of black children, compared with less than a third of white children, live in the South. In contrast, white children are more likely than blacks to live in the Northeast and in the West.

Nearly half of all children live in a Standard Metropolitan Statistical Area (SMSA) with a population of at least 100,000 people (Table 1-3). Black children are more likely than white children to live in or near a city of 500,000 or more people. In contrast, white children are more likely to live outside the city limits and in areas defined as non-SMSAs (population less than 50,000). For example, while 44.1 percent of white children live in nonurban areas, only 27.5 percent of black children live outside central cities.

To further underscore the disparate environments of black and white children (Tables 1-4 and 1-5), 84 percent of white children live in single-family dwellings, and their families typically own the place in which they live. Black children are much less likely (61 percent) than white children to live in single-family dwellings and much more likely to live in an apartment, project, or two-family dwelling. Two-thirds of white children live in dwellings with six or more rooms, while two-thirds of black children live in dwellings with no more than five rooms.

TABLE 1-2   Region of Residence of Children Ages 6–12, 1981

	White	Black	Total
Northeast			
Weighted N	7,060	584	7,644
Unweighted N	204	43	247
Percentage	22.0%	12.2%	20.7%
North Central			
Weighted N	9,824	1,366	11,190
Unweighted N	307	141	448
Percentage	30.6%	28.5%	30.4%
South			
Weighted N	9,677	2,496	12,173
Unweighted N	346	506	852
Percentage	30.2%	51.1%	30.0%
West			
Weighted N	5,433	332	5,765
Unweighted N	177	52	229
Percentage	16.9%	6.9%	15.6%
Foreign Country			
Weighted N	72	16	88
Unweighted N	3	5	8
Percentage	0.2%	0.3%	0.2%

SOURCE: Unpublished data from Panel Study of Income Dynamics, Institute for Social Research, Ann Arbor, 1982.

Nearly one-third of all families with children ages 6–11 report that they live in a neighborhood in which street lighting is poor and where there is considerable street noise, and 25 percent live near heavy traffic, according to data from the 1977 Annual Housing Survey. Approximately 3.7 million children, 17.1 percent of the age group, live in neighborhoods in which street crime is common.

Family Environments

The majority of children ages 6–12 live in nuclear-type families—that is, with either one or two parents and children (see Table 1-6). But there are some differences between the family composition of white and black families. Black children are more likely than white children to live in extended families—families that contain other people related to the head of the household. The proportion for both groups is small, however. Furthermore, as Table 1-7 shows, there is a greater likelihood for black parents to have more children, spanning a wider range of ages. Black children ages 6–12 are likely to have more siblings in general and more siblings close to

TABLE 1-3 Size of Residence of Children Ages 6–12

SMSA[a] Size		White	Black	Total
SMSA: largest city is 500,000 or more	Weighted N	7,189	1,800	8,989
	Unweighted N	215	334	549
	Percentage	22.5%	37.7%	24.4%
SMSA: largest city is 100,000 to 499,999	Weighted N	7,481	1,121	8,602
	Unweighted N	251	156	407
	Percentage	23.4%	23.5%	23.4%
SMSA: largest city is 50,000 to 99,999	Weighted N	4,671	359	5,030
	Unweighted N	151	74	225
	Percentage	14.6%	7.5%	13.7%
Non-SMSA: largest city is 25,000 to 49,999	Weighted N	3,679	278	3,957
	Unweighted N	115	30	145
	Percentage	11.5%	5.8%	10.8%
Non-SMSA: largest city is 10,000 to 24,999	Weighted N	3,547	472	4,019
	Unweighted N	120	48	168
	Percentage	11.1%	9.9%	10.9%
Non-SMSA: largest city is under 10,000	Weighted N	5,427	745	6,175
	Unweighted N	182	100	282
	Percentage	17.0%	15.7%	16.8%

[a]Standard metropolitan statistical area.
SOURCE: Unpublished data from Panel Study of Income Dynamics, Institute for Social Research, Ann Arbor, 1982.

TABLE 1-4 Type of Dwelling of Children Ages 6–12, 1981

		White	Black	Total
Single-family dwelling	Weighted N	26,857	2,915	29,772
	Unweighted N	877	463	1,340
	Percentage	83.9%	60.9%	80.9%
Two-family unit; duplex	Weighted N	1,479	462	1,941
	Unweighted N	47	57	104
	Percentage	4.6%	9.6%	5.3%
Apartment; project	Weighted N	1,788	1,055	2,843
	Unweighted N	56	181	237
	Percentage	5.6%	22.0%	7.7%
Mobile home; trailer	Weighted N	1,364	204	1,568
	Unweighted N	43	33	76
	Percentage	4.3%	4.3%	4.3%
Other	Weighted N	504	152	656
	Unweighted N	12	12	24
	Percentage	1.6%	3.2%	1.8%

SOURCE: Unpublished data from Panel Study of Income Dynamics, Institute for Social Research, Ann Arbor, 1982.

TABLE 1-5   Status of Dwelling of Children Ages 6–12, 1981

		White	Black	Total
Dwelling owned by parent	Weighted N	23,724	2,034	25,758
	Unweighted N	759	297	1,056
	Percentage	74.0%	42.4%	69.9%
Dwelling rented by parent	Weighted N	7,652	2,591	10,171
	Unweighted N	256	416	672
	Percentage	23.9%	52.5%	27.6%
Dwelling neither owned nor rented	Weighted N	690	241	931
	Unweighted N	22	34	56
	Percentage	2.2%	5.0%	2.5%

SOURCE: Unpublished data from Panel Study of Income Dynamics, Institute for Social Research, Ann Arbor, 1982.

their own age. Black and white families also differ according to parents' marital status, parents' employment status, and financial resources. Hispanic families differ from both black and white families in that they appear likely to have more and younger children. Comparable information is lacking on other ethnic groups.

Most school-age children (about 80 percent overall) live with two parents, according to Census Bureau estimates and estimates from the Panel Study of Income Dynamics. There are sizable racial variations, however. Table 1-8 shows that, while 83 percent of white school-age children lived with two parents in 1981, only 51 percent of comparably aged black children

TABLE 1-6   Family Composition of Children Ages 6–12, 1981

Number of Children Who Live in Families:	Weighted	White	Black	Total
With head and immediate family only	N	30,313	4,081	34,394
	Percentage	94.5%	85.1%	93.3%
In which family unit includes other people related to head	N	928	413	1,311
	Percentage	2.9%	8.6%	3.6%
In which family unit includes people unrelated to head who pool resources	N	233	27	260
	Percentage	0.7%	0.6%	0.7%
Other	N	522	273	865
	Percentage	1.8%	5.7%	2.3%
Total	N	32,066	4,794	36,860

SOURCE: Unpublished data from Panel Study of Income Dynamics, Institute for Social Research, Ann Arbor, 1982.

TABLE 1-7 Characteristics of Families With Children (percentage)

	White	Black	Hispanic Origin[a]	Total
Families with children:				
Ages 6–17 only	56.7	55.4	45.5	56.3
Some ages 6–17, some under 6	19.2	23.8	27.2	19.2
Under 6 only	24.9	20.7	27.3	24.5
Families with:				
1 child 6–11	52.7	50.4	22.5	52.29
2 children 6–11	19.8	19.1	9.6	19.7
3 children 6–11	2.7	3.9	2.5	2.9
4 or more children 6–11	0.3	1.2	0.5	0.5
Average number of children per family with children	1.85	2.01	2.15	1.88

[a]May be of any race
SOURCE: Bureau of the Census (1982).

TABLE 1-8 Marital Status of Parents of Children Ages 6–12, 1981

		White	Black	Total
Married or permanently cohabiting	Weighted N	26,662	2,457	29,119
	Unweighted N	890	401	1,291
	Percentage	83.1%	51.3%	79.0%
Father absent; mother present, single, never legally married	Weighted N	256	720	976
	Unweighted N	7	113	120
	Percentage	0.8%	15.0%	2.7%
Widowed	Weighted N	164	215	379
	Unweighted N	5	11	16
	Percentage	0.5%	4.5%	1.0%
Divorced	Weighted N	3,538	607	4,145
	Unweighted N	87	98	185
	Percentage	11.0%	12.7%	11.2%
Separated	Weighted N	805	770	1,575
	Unweighted N	26	112	138
	Percentage	2.5%	16.1%	4.3%
Mother absent; father present	Weighted N	641	25	666
	Unweighted N	22	12	34
	Percentage	2.0%	0.5%	1.8%

SOURCE: Unpublished data form Panel Study of Income Dynamics, Institute for Social Research, Ann Arbor, 1982.

lived with two parents. Further differences emerge between the races among children living with only their mothers: 75 percent of white children who lived with their mothers in single-parent families did so because their parents were divorced, compared with 26 percent of black children. In contrast, one-third of black children lived with their mothers alone because they were single and never married and one-third because their parents were separated. According to Census Bureau estimates, approximately 72 percent of Hispanic children live with two parents (Bureau of the Census, 1981), a figure similar to that for white children.

Cumulative percentages of children who experience some form of family disruption (e.g., their parents divorce, and some then remarry) present a more long-term perspective on the changes that families undergo during their children's school-age years. Table 1-9 describes the likelihood that a child's family will be disrupted by the time he or she is 13. By the age of 6, 24 percent of children born between 1965 and 1967 and 29 percent of those born between 1968 and 1969 had experienced some change in their parents' marital status. By age 13 the percentages increase by 30 percent for each birth cohort.

TABLE 1-9 Cumulative Percentage of Children Experiencing Family Disruption

Child's Year of Birth	Child's Age							
	6	7	8	9	10	11	12	13
All children								
1965–1967[a]	16	18	20	21	22	23	25	26
1968–1969[a]	22	23	27	28	29	31	33	33
1965–1967[b]	24	23	27	28	29	30	32	33
1968–1969[b]	29	31	34	35	36	38	39	40
White children								
1965–1967[a]	15	16	17	18	20	21	21	22
1968–1969[a]	20	22	24	25	26	28	29	30
1965–1967[b]	18	19	20	21	23	24	24	25
1968–1969[b]	23	24	27	28	28	30	32	32
Black children								
1965–1967[a]	21	23	25	26	27	29	36	36
1968–1969[a]	33	33	47	48	50	50	51	51
1965–1967[b]	39	40	42	43	44	45	50	51
1968–1969[b]	58	58	67	68	69	69	70	70

[a]Includes only children born after their mother's first marriage who are currently living with one biological parent.

[b]Includes all children, except formally adopted children, regardless of where they are living or whether their mother ever married.

SOURCE: Furstenburg et al. (1983:660).

When the probability of marital disruption is examined separately by race, striking differences can be observed. By the age of 6, approximately 35 percent more black children born between 1968 and 1969 had experienced some family disruption. The difference in proportion does not change substantially over the middle childhood years for this cohort, although the percentage of black children experiencing family disruption climbs to 70 percent by the time they reach age 13. These figures are high in part because of the large number of black children born to single mothers. Still, a comparison of the figures in the rows of Table 1-9 that have a superscript *a* reveals that in the early 1980s half of black children and almost a third of white children, born after their parents were married, by the age of 13 were not living with both biological parents.

Labor Force Participation and Family Income

Not surprisingly, children ages 6–13 are more likely to have mothers in the labor force than children who are under 6. In 1982, approximately 14,835,000 children ages 6–13 had mothers in the labor force; this number represents 58 percent of children in this age group. In contrast, in 1970, 43 percent of children ages 6–13 had mothers in the labor force. (It should be noted that not all mothers in the labor force work full time; see Chapter 5.)

As Table 1-10 shows, mothers of black children ages 6–13 are much more likely to be in the labor force than mothers of white or Hispanic children. They are also more likely to be unemployed. Although children in single-parent families are also more likely to have mothers in the labor force than those in two-parent families, the mothers of black children in single-parent families and, to a lesser extent, mothers of Hispanic children, are less likely to be in the labor force than those in two-parent families.

The importance of the employment of black mothers to family income is seen in Table 1-11. In a two-parent family in which the father is employed, the mother's employment in a black family increases family income by two-thirds. In the same situation, a white mother's employment increases family income by an eighth, possibly because many of these women work only part time. The employment of Hispanic mothers falls between the two, increasing family income by 41 percent on average. Also clear in Tables 1-11 and 1-12 is the financial disadvantage of being a single mother, particularly a single black mother. The average income of single white, black, or Hispanic mothers is near or below the poverty level. Approximately half of white children and almost two-thirds of black and Hispanic children who live with single mothers have family incomes below $10,000 a year.

TABLE 1-10   Employment Status of Parents of Children Ages 6–13, March 1982 (numbers in thousands)

	White	Black	Hispanic Origin
Total children, ages 6–13	21,513	3,450	2,195
Children in married-couple families	17,811	1,692	1,582
% of total children	82.8%	49.0%	72.1%
Father unemployed	1,051	158	145
% of total in married-couple families	5.9%	9.3%	9.2%
Mother unemployed	788	146	96
% of total in married-couple families	4.4%	8.65	6.1%
Mother not in labor force[a]	7,754	554	828
% of total in married-couple families	43.5%	32.7%	52.3%
Father and mother unemployed	145	45	16
% of total in married-couple families	.08%	2.7%	1.0%
Father and mother employed[a]	8,265	812	593
% of total in married-couple families	46.4%	48.0%	37.5%
Children in female-headed families	3,331	1,694	578
% of total children	15.5%	49.1%	26.3%
Mother unemployed	220	190	42
% of total in female-headed families	6.6%	11.2%	7.3%
Mother employed	2,121	736	237
% of total in female-headed families	63.7%	43.4%	41.0%
Mother not in labor force	989	768	300
% of total in female-headed families	29.7%	45.3%	51.9%

[a]Excludes fathers in the armed forces.
SOURCE: Unpublished data, Bureau of Labor Statistics, March 1982.

In 1981, 15.1 percent of white children ages 6–13 and 43.8 percent of the same-age black children lived below the official poverty level ($9,287 in 1981 for a family of four). Comparable data were not available for children of single mothers. Among children ages 6–14 living with their single mothers, 40.8 percent of white children and 64.8 percent of black children had family incomes below the poverty level. The greater financial need of black families is also reflected in the amount of transfer monies they receive. According to data from the 1982 Panel Study of Income Dynamics, approximately 6 percent of white children ages 6–12 lived in families receiving AFDC (Aid to Families with Dependent Children) in 1981, compared with

TABLE 1-11   Mean Family Income for Families With Children Ages 6–13, March 1982

	White	Black	Hispanic Origin	Total
Lives with mother and father	$29,207	$22,978	$21,133	$28,731
Father employed and				
Mother employed	32,364	28,528	26,694	32,089
Mother unemployed	24,389	19,644	19,743	23,786
Mother not in labor force	28,704	17,456	18,978	28,246
Father unemployed and				
Mother employed	23,047	20,993	18,482	22,602
Mother unemployed	18,208	23,606	15,533	19,534
Mother not in labor force	16,249	10,869	10,524	15,757
Lives with mother only	9,829	8,067	8,969	10,604
Mother employed	14,387	11,252	11,990	13,642
Mother unemployed	8,254	7,920	7,945	8,249
Mother not in labor force	7,027	5,053	6,726	6,191

SOURCE: Unpublished data, Bureau of Labor Statistics, March 1982.

nearly 23 percent of black children. Black children represent 15 percent of the total population of children ages 6–12, but they represent 36 percent of all children in families that receive AFDC monies.

The population of children ages 6–12 thus is marked by physical, economic, and social variations that almost certainly constrain the nature of the experience and the course of the development of individual children. In the chapters that follow, a central theme is the incorporation of environmental diversity into research on development in middle childhood.

Education

Despite the diversity of children in middle childhood, there is one common factor in their lives: Nearly all (99 percent) children of elementary school age are enrolled in school. Public school enrollment statistics, which include about 89 percent of the population of children ages 6–12, have mirrored population statistics. By 1976, following the enrollment bulge produced by the baby boom, the number of children in school had fallen to the 1960 level of approximately 30.5 million (Bureau of the Census, 1981). Enrollment as of 1980 was approximately 26.7 million. On the basis of projections of the elementary school population (according to fertility expectations), enrollment is expected to continue its decline until 1985, at which point the number of school children should gradually increase. By 1988 they will reach the 1978 enrollment levels.

TABLE 1-12   Income Groups of Families of Children Ages 6–13, March 1982

	White	Black	Hispanic Origin	Total
Total children ages 6–13	21,513	3,450	2,195	25,781
Total children in married-couple families	17,811	1,692	1,582	20,180
% of total	82.8%	49.0%	72.1%	78.3%
Under $7,000	658	139	97	838
Percentage[a]	3.7%	8.2%	6.1%	4.2%
$7,000–$9,999	658	120	171	819
Percentage[a]	3.7%	7.1%	10.8%	4.1%
$10,000–$14,999	1,806	227	312	2,130
Percentage[a]	10.1%	13.4%	19.7%	10.6%
$15,000–$19,999	2,117	275	275	2,461
Percentage[a]	11.9%	16.3%	17.4%	12.2%
$20,000–$34,999	7,499	659	495	8,361
Percentage[a]	42.1%	39.0%	31.3%	41.4%
$35,000–$49,999	3,384	223	184	3,751
Percentage[a]	19.0%	13.2%	11.6%	18.6%
$50,000 and over	1,689	50	47	1,819
Percentage[a]	9.5%	3.0%	3.0%	9.0%
Total children in female-headed families	3,331	1,694	578	5,154
Percentage of total	15.5%	49.1%	26.3%	20.0%
Under $7,000	1,165	915	270	2,111
Percentage[b]	35.0%	54.0%	46.7%	41.0%
$7,000–$9,999	539	285	129	856
Percentage[b]	16.2%	16.8%	22.3%	16.6%
$10,000–$14,999	726	278	92	1,040
Percentage[b]	21.8%	16.4%	15.9%	20.2%
$15,000–$19,999	399	134	49	541
Percentage[b]	12.0%	7.9%	8.5%	10.5%
$20,000–$34,999	414	75	34	503
Percentage[b]	12.4%	4.4%	5.9%	9.8%
$35,000–$49,999	79	8	3	87
Percentage[b]	2.4%	0.5%	0.5%	1.7%
$50,000 and over	11	0	1	16
Percentage[b]	0.3%	0.0%	0.2%	0.2%

[a]Percentage of children in married-couple families.
[b]Percentage of children in female-headed families.

Private school enrollment, two-thirds of which is in Catholic schools, is less strongly tied to population growth than is public school enrollment. Private school enrollment reached a peak of 15 percent of school children in 1964 and 1965 and declined to about 11 percent in 1980. Black enrollment, however, has increased as white enrollment has decreased. In 1980, 12 percent of white children and 5 percent of black children were enrolled in private schools.

Educational achievement among elementary school students still varies substantially by race and age. Table 1-13 shows the percentage of students below modal grade of enrollment for students ages 6–9 and 10–13. The difference in the proportion of black and white students ages 6–9 below grade level is very slight, but among those ages 10–13 the percentages diverge. Black boys ages 10–13 are 60 percent more likely than white boys to be enrolled below their modal grade level, and black girls are 50 percent more likely than white girls to be enrolled below their modal grade level. The issue of disparities in educational achievement is clearly a factor in the experiences of children in the middle childhood years.

Children's Lives Out of School

According to 1981 data from the Panel Study of Time Use in American Households, approximately 60 percent of children's time during the week is spent in activities that, for the most part, they must do: sleeping, attending school, washing and dressing, and doing housework (Table 1-14). When these are accounted for, however, the average child has approximately 67 hours of discretionary time each week.

Two types of activities dominate this out-of-school discretionary time for most American children: television viewing and time "on their own," including time spent with peers in play and other activities without adult supervision or involvement. A recent major study of time use (Medrich et al., 1982) estimates that these two activities consume 70 percent or more of children's roughly 7 hours of out-of-school time daily. Time with parents and organized activities (including sports) constituted a relatively small per-

TABLE 1-13 Percentage of Children Ages 6–13 Below Modal Grade of Enrollment

Race	Boys	Girls
White		
Ages 6–9	17.9	13.2
Ages 10–13	23.7	16.3
Black		
Ages 6–9	18.2	16.0
Ages 10–13	37.7	24.4

SOURCE: Bureau of the Census (1982).

TABLE 1-14 Hours per Week Spent Doing Selected Primary Activities by Children Ages 6–12 (standard deviations in parentheses)

Activity	6–8 (N = 69)	9–10 (N = 59)	11–12 (N = 61)
Market work	1.4 (7.5)	1.3 (6.7)	.8 (2.3)
Household work	2.5 (2.7)	3.1 (3.0)	4.4 (5.2)
Personal care	5.7 (2.7)	4.9 (2.3)	5.6 (3.0)
Sleep	71.1 (7.8	67.4 (11.5)	62.3 (11.4)
School	24.4 (10.4)	28.1 (8.8)	25.7 (11.3)
Homework	.8 (1.8)	2.7 (3.8)	3.7 (5.1)
Sports	3.1 (5.0)	3.4 (5.3)	4.2 (6.6)
Other outdoor activities	1.7 (4.8)	1.9 (3.5)	2.6 (4.3)
Cultural arts	.6 (1.1)	.5 (1.1)	.6 (1.3)
Playing	14.1 (10.0)	9.1 (7.3)	5.1 (8.0)
Watching television	12.9 (10.4)	16.8 (12.2)	19.1 (11.4)
Listening to music	.5 (1.0)	.6 (1.4)	1.5 (4.3)
Reading	.8 (2.0)	1.3 (2.8)	1.5 (2.8)

SOURCE: Panel Study of Time Use in American Households, Institute for Social Research, Ann Arbor, 1981.

centage of children's daily time in the urban area in which the research was conducted.

For most children ages 6–12 in the United States, television viewing constitutes the largest single portion of free time on a typical weekday. Current estimates for school-age children put the amount of viewing at 3–4 hours daily (Comstock et al., 1980; Medrich et al., 1982), a larger figure than is reported for preschoolers and adolescents. Eleven- and twelve-year-olds, particularly boys, watch television more than any other age group. Viewing preferences show distinct shifts from children's fare toward general programming, such as action-adventure dramas and other programs that contain a wide range of realistic behavioral and role models. Economically disadvantaged children are three times more likely to be heavy television viewers than are more advantaged youngsters. Perhaps because of the confounding effect of socioeconomic status, black youngsters are more likely to view television heavily than are whites overall, although disadvantaged whites are also heavy viewers.

As children get older, more time is spent doing homework. Still, American children spend only an average of one-half hour per weekday studying, compared with the 2 to 3.5 hours a day that Japanese children, for example, spend studying (Nakanishi, 1982).

Table 1-14 also suggests that children spend little time reading, although older children spend more time reading than younger children. Data from the Panel Study of Time Use refute the assumption that children would spend more time reading if they did not watch so much television. Medrich et al. (1982) note little relationship between patterns of television use and reading, but they did find that children who read every day are more likely to be light viewers.

Organized activities also consume many hours of time for large numbers of American children. More than 8 million youngsters between 6 and 16 are involved in sports activities each year, and many participate in clubs, religious programs, and organized groups; take private lessons; attend camp; and so forth. Both the degree of participation in out-of-school activities and the contents of the programs in which children participate are strongly associated with social group and ethnic status. For example, black boys are more likely than boys in other ethnic groups to participate in team sports, while white boys are more likely to be involved in individualized sports, such as swimming or tennis (Medrich et al., 1982). Socioeconomic factors also affect whether activities that are available to children are primarily privately funded and organized or publicly supported. Nevertheless, children from all socioeconomic strata show some level of participation in organized activities. The impact of participation in out-of-school activities has been studied very little. Because of the increased number of children involved and the opportunities available, however, these activities should be considered a significant dimension in the expanding social worlds of children ages 6–12.

THEMES OF THE REPORT

In the chapters that follow, the status of knowledge on children in middle childhood is assessed within the framework of the three major foci that guided the panel's work:

1. the distinctive characteristics of children ages 6–12 compared with children in other developmental periods and the typical changes that occur during these years;

2. the impact of access to new settings and changing qualities of relationships, including the tasks, options, and limitations that are characteristic of the environments that school-age children encounter; and

3. the nature and long-term implications of developmental difficulties and the different developmental trajectories followed by individual children during middle childhood.

The distinctiveness of middle childhood development depends, in the first analysis, on the characteristics of children as they enter and traverse the period. Chapters 2, 3, and 4 focus on the child's physical and cognitive growth and the fundamental psychological processes of developing a sense of self and capabilities for self-regulation during middle childhood.

In Chapter 2, Jack P. Shonkoff addresses the nature of physical changes leading to puberty—a physical event that now occurs by age 12 for large numbers of American children. He devotes attention to research on neurotransmission processes and hormonal factors in behavior and their contribution to knowledge of the biological substrate of middle childhood development. Studies in these areas offer promising approaches to the understanding of gender differences as well as to a range of specific behavior patterns. Research on brain-behavior relations can facilitate better understanding of both basic intellectual and behavioral functioning and the various dysfunctions that are commonly grouped together as learning disabilities. Difficulties with school performance are a major social and psychological problem in the elementary school years, and the long-term problems associated with them are now well established.

The intellectual capabilities of children ages 6–12 have been extensively studied, and these studies are a major source of knowledge about the distinctiveness of middle childhood and its links to other developmental periods. In Chapter 3, Kurt W. Fischer and Daniel Bullock distill the major information that has emerged from this research. The impetus for much of this work has come from the Piagetian tradition, in which the more elaborate conceptual and reasoning skills of school-age children were attributed to a capacity for concrete operational thought. Fischer and Bullock also identify a major shift in cognitive functioning for Western children between ages 5 and 7 and another between ages 10 and 12. A primary theme in their review is the way in which children's environments and typical experiences "collaborate" in the process of cognitive change. They urge an approach to cognitive change and cognitive performance that focuses on the environmental supports for certain skills and approaches to tasks and problems that children develop. They also explore the linkages between these changes and other developmental changes, such as emotional knowledge and expression.

Hazel J. Markus and Paula S. Nurius (Chapter 4) extend the analysis of cognitive components to the school-age child's task of forming a self-concept from the diverse new sources of information about his or her characteristics and capabilities. Much new information derived from a wide range of settings must be incorporated into knowledge about the self in these years. This knowledge, together with knowledge about social norms and expectations and about strategies for managing one's own behavior, is crucial to the increasingly greater responsibilities that 6- to 12-year-olds can assume and fulfill. These authors, like Maccoby in Chapter 5, view middle childhood as a time when social controls become coregulatory in nature. In contrast to the extensive adult regulation of children's behavior in early childhood, children ages 6–12 must assume a larger share of responsibility for their own behavior in coordination with parents, peers, and others.

The impact of a dramatically shifting social context—transformations in relationships with parents, more extensive involvement with peers in terms of both time and the number of contacts, and entry into the traditional structures of schooling—is the topic of Chapters 5, 6, and 7. In Chapter 5, Eleanor E. Maccoby attempts to tie major developmental changes in school-age children to changes in parental roles and expectations and to issues that typically are dealt with in parent-child relationships. She addresses questions of the linkages between cognitive changes and the process of increasing coregulation between parent and child. She also reviews social-strata, subcultural, and ethnic-group differences in parent-child relationships and examines the currently limited information on variations in family structures such as single-parent and dual-career families. Her perspective acknowledges the systemic nature of family relationships, and she addresses the nature and distinctive influence of father-child and sibling relationships in middle childhood.

The increasing amount and variety of contact between school-age children and their peers are the focus of Willard W. Hartup's review in Chapter 6. Organizing the literature in terms of different types of peer contexts (e.g., interactions, relationships, groups), Hartup reviews the status of knowledge on the settings, tasks, and persons involved in children's experiences with other children. The functional significance of peer relationships for such issues as gender-role learning in the elementary school years and the regulation of behaviors such as aggression and cooperation is central to the review. Other topics of particular importance are the long-term implications of the quality of a child's peer relationships in middle childhood and the

nature of dysfunctions in middle childhood that may result in poor adjustment in adolescence and adulthood. Hartup reviews the small body of literature on interventions to improve children's skills for successful peer
relationships as well as the descriptive literature on the normal growth of
these skills between ages 6 and 12.

In Chapter 7, Edgar G. Epps and Sylvia F. Smith consolidate an extensive
body of literature on schools and schooling to assess the implications of
school experiences in middle childhood. They address both manifest (e.g.,
skill acquisition, achievement aspirations) and latent (e.g., social role learning, status expectations) functions of schooling. In this context they discuss
the implications of social changes in schools, such as desegregation, and the
implications of specific instructional approaches for eliminating educational
inequality. The linkages between school and other significant social contexts, particularly the family, are also reviewed in terms of their implications
for development.

These broader and constantly changing social contexts in middle childhood help determine the course of developmental changes and thus must
be considered in analyses of the middle childhood period. In Chapter 8,
Thomas S. Weisner outlines a perspective on the role of environmental
influences. Construing *environment* broadly, Weisner argues for incorporating
conceptually the cultural, social, and economic conditions that determine
the influences on communities, families, and individual children in middle
childhood. He identifies several dimensions of variations in environments
found in cross-cultural studies (e.g., responsibilities required of children in
middle childhood, caretaking systems, pressures for individualism versus
cooperation, definitions of "problem" behaviors) and suggests hypotheses
for study in Western societies. Since many Western nations include diverse
subcultural and socioeconomically varied groups, Weisner's approach should
be a useful framework for careful formulation of further research on children
ages 6–12 in their social contexts.

The health of school-age children and long-term implications for healthy
functioning are addressed by Thomas M. Achenbach in Chapter 9 and by
Jack P. Shonkoff in Chapter 2. Shonkoff examines the implications of middle
childhood for the development of healthful life-styles in adulthood. The
years 6–12 are a time of primary learning relevant to concepts of health,
illness, and disease. It is also a period of increasing responsibility for interacting with the health care system and for many specific practices that have
long-term health implications (e.g., physical exercise, eating patterns).
Shonkoff discusses the importance of approaches to health education that
take into account cognitive and psychosocial characteristics of children in
this developmental period. He also provides an illuminating discussion of

the problems of chronically ill and disabled children and their families and the special difficulties encountered by them in middle childhood.

Thomas M. Achenbach's concern in Chapter 9 is the nature of psychological health in middle childhood. He focuses on the difficulties of specifying the nature of dysfunctions in this period, because of the overuse of nosological disease categories to describe behavioral difficulties. He describes research approaches that will enable researchers to differentiate various conditions more precisely and to examine the long-term consequences of different patterns of problem behaviors in middle childhood.

Chapter 10 summarizes the conclusions of the panel. W. Andrew Collins describes what is known about children ages 6–12 and their development and attempts to characterize some general issues that face future research on middle childhood. The principal concern throughout is on identifying prospects for enhancing our knowledge of this period of life.

REFERENCES

Aries, P.
    1962   Centuries of Childhood. Translated by R. Baldick. New York: Knopf.
Bureau of the Census
    1981   Household and Family Characteristics: March 1981. Series P-20, No. 371. Washington, D.C.: U.S. Government Printing Office.
    1982   Characteristics of American Children and Youth: 1980. Current Population Reports, P-23, No. 114. Washington, D.C.: U.S. Department of Commerce.
Comstock, G., Chaffee, S., Katzman, N., McComb, M., and Roberts, D.
    1978   Television and Human Behavior. New York: Columbia University Press.
Furstenburg, F.F., Nord, C.W., Peterson, J.L., and Zill, N.
    1983   The life course of children of divorce: Marital disruption and parental contact. American Sociological Review 48: 656–668.
Medrich, E.A., Roizen, J.A., Rubin, V., and Buckley, S.
    1982   The Serious Business of Growing Up. Berkeley: University of California Press.
Nakanishi, N.
    1982   A report on "How Do People Spend Their Time?" survey in 1980. Studies of Broadcasting 18:93–113.
Rogoff, B., Sellers, M., Pirrotta, S., Fox, N., and White, S.
    1975   Age of assignment of roles and responsibilities in children: a cross-cultural survey. Human Development 18:353-369.
Zill, N.
    In   Happy, Healthy, and Insecure: A Portrait of Middle Childhood in the United States. New
    press   York: Cambridge University Press.
Zill, N., Sigal, H., and Brim, O.
    1983   Development of Childhood Social Indicators. Pp. 188–222 in Edward F. Zigler, Sharon Kagan, and Edgar Klugman, eds., Children, Families, and Government Perspectives in American Social Policy. New York: Cambridge University Press.

CHAPTER 2

The Biological Substrate and Physical Health in Middle Childhood

Jack P. Shonkoff

In industrialized societies, school-age children are generally the healthiest segment of the population. In general, they are not exposed to the nutritional deficiencies and infections that plague so many children in developing countries, and they have not yet experienced the myriad changes of adolescence or the increased risks of major diseases that adults face.

For children ages 6–12, health issues are best defined in the context of the developmental tasks of this period. Whereas acute illnesses are generally brief and followed by the resumption of normal routines, chronic impairments and catastrophic diseases demand sophisticated medical treatments in conjunction with attention to the child's personal and social development. Moreover, although more research is needed on socioeconomic class differences in health status and use of health services, and although poverty continues to pose a major threat to the physical and mental well-being of children in the United States, the most far-reaching basic research concerns from a public health perspective go beyond the domain of the organized health care system and involve the more pervasive matter of life-style. Accidents accounted for half the deaths of children ages 5–14 in the United States in 1978, and more than 50 percent of them were related to motor vehicles (Bureau of the Census, 1982). Multiple risk factors for the most common adult diseases have been shown to include a number of behaviors whose antecedents are germinated, if not sprouted, during middle childhood. Exercise and attitudes toward physical fitness, coping with stress, tobacco and alcohol abuse, and dietary habits are some of the life-style characteristics that appear to warrant particular preventive attention during this age period.

24

This chapter provides an overview of the current research regarding health and illness during middle childhood. It reviews existing knowledge of the biological substrate of human function during this period. It also explores the problem of conceptualizing health and illness and analyzes it in the context of the child's emerging life-style and sense of his or her own health status both during the school years and in the future. An agenda for further study is proposed.

THE BIOLOGICAL SUBSTRATE

Physical Maturation

Despite significant individual differences, the rate of increase in stature during middle childhood is generally similar and regular until the onset of puberty. Skeletal maturity, as measured by bone age, is the most useful biological indicator of overall physiologic maturation. Its determination is based on the predictable, ordered appearance of primary and secondary centers of ossification that develop in the growth regions (epiphyses) of bones. Although some variability related to ethnic factors has been documented, measured differences in maturity are primarily related to variations in rate and not sequence. Thus, the order of epiphyseal ossification is governed largely by genetic factors. The rate of skeletal maturation, however, is influenced by both nature and nurture; for example, lower socioeconomic status as well as a wide range of pathological processes have been shown to correlate with delays in bone age, and girls demonstrate a faster rate of maturation than boys by approximately 20 percent (Sinclair, 1978). In general, skeletal maturation parallels skeletal growth and, therefore, height, with both ending when hormonal influences cause the epiphyses to fuse in late adolescence.

The onset of puberty heralds the beginning of reproductive maturity and provides a useful biological marker for the onset of adolescence. Pubertal changes have been reported to occur earlier in children from higher socioeconomic groups, those living in urban rather than rural areas, and children living at lower altitudes (Benson and Migeon, 1975). A later onset of puberty has been documented for children who are malnourished, those living in larger families, and girls engaged in strenuous exercise such as competitive athletics and dance (Frisch et al., 1980). Generally speaking, however, genetic factors appear to have a greater effect than environmental influences on the onset of puberty, an event that is largely related to a child's overall level of maturation and body size and that correlates better with bone age than chronological age.

Although the sequence of pubertal changes is relatively predictable, their timing is extremely variable. The normal range of onset is ages 8–14 in females and ages 9–15 years in males, with girls generally beginning two years earlier than boys (Benson and Migeon, 1975). In girls, puberty begins with a growth spurt, usually the first noticeable event, and is soon accompanied by enlargement of breast tissue and generally followed by menarche two years later. The onset of puberty in boys is typically marked by an increase in testicular size followed by a growth spurt. The peak growth velocity for both sexes (10.3 cm per year for boys and 9.0 cm per year for girls) is achieved 2 to 3 years after the beginning of the pubertal process (Smith, 1977). In general, the rate of maturation of boys is slower and less predictable than that of girls, and their age at the onset of puberty is more variable. For both sexes, pubertal changes before the thirteenth birthday are not uncommon.

Growth and development studies over the past 200 years have demonstrated a so-called secular trend toward an earlier age of menarche in the industrialized world. Data also suggest larger increments of growth, greater size for age during childhood, and earlier final height attainment (Smith, 1977). Despite questions about the reliability of past data collection methods, these trends appear to be accurate and the differences statistically significant. The age of menarche occurred 2–3 months earlier per decade during the past 150 years in Europe and the United States, with a leveling off of growth and age of menarche as standards of living increased (Wyshak and Frisch, 1982). More equitable socioeconomic conditions have also resulted in the elimination of discrepancies associated with social class and urban-rural differences. The current average age of menarche in the United States of 12.8 years has been relatively stable since 1947.

The reasons for this secular trend are not well understood. The reduction of such growth-retarding factors as poor nutrition and chronic illness has been cited most often, and recently documented trends toward a later age of menarche in Bangladesh appear to support this hypothesis (Chowdhury et al., 1978). Whether this historical acceleration in the rate of general body maturation has been associated with comparable changes in the rate of brain development and level of performance of children growing up in industrialized societies is unknown. Preliminary data do suggest, however, that variations in age of onset of puberty may have developmental and behavioral consequences during adolescence. In a study of more than 5,000 white males and females ages 12–17 (Duke et al., 1982), late-maturing males scored lower on education-related variables and early-maturing males scored higher than those in the middle maturity groups. These differences were found to be independent of measured intelligence and weaker at age

12 than at older ages. No consistent and statistically significant differences related to maturational status were found among females. Other studies, reporting inconsistent findings that imply disadvantages for early-maturing girls as well as late-maturing boys, suggest that cultural context and social class may be important determinants of the influences on behavior of the differential timing of physical maturation (Clausen, 1975; Jones et al., 1971). Interactions among academic achievement, personal and social development, and physiologic maturity are not well understood. Further studies of these relationships, particularly regarding the early onset of pubertal changes in the middle childhood years, are needed.

Developmental Neurobiology

Although the biology of physical growth and maturation during the middle childhood years is generally understood, the basic development and regulation of the nervous system and its relationship to behavior remain a complex mystery. The bulk of our knowledge regarding the process of neuromaturation comes from gross and microscopic anatomical studies that have demonstrated the highly regulated progression of cell proliferation, migration, and differentiation that characterizes the early development of the central nervous system in a wide variety of animal species. The relatively invariant timing of this process and the intricate coordination of its multiple interacting cellular systems strongly supports the assumption that early neuromaturation is largely controlled by a genetically determined regulatory system. That environmental factors can influence this process has been documented by a substantial body of data showing reduced cell numbers during the proliferation stage and reduced cell size during the differentiation stage in the face of severe and prolonged undernutrition. Moreover, relationships between differential visual experiences in early infancy and subsequent morphological changes in the brain suggest that behaviorally mediated contingencies can also have a significant effect on this highly controlled biological process (Hubel et al., 1977).

Since the average human brain is 65 percent of its adult size at birth and 90 percent by age 2, it is not suprising that anatomical studies alone have provided relatively little insight into the neuromaturational process beyond infancy. Thus, further understanding has required a shift in focus from structure to function. Available data on the biochemical and physiological mediators of human behavior, however, are extremely primitive, and their clinical applicability remains obscure. Several areas of investigation, especially the concepts of neurotransmission and neuromodulation, appear worthy of examination in relation to the development of school-age children.

Neurotransmission, the process whereby individual nerve cells communicate, involves the highly specific synthesis, storage, release, uptake, and degradation of discrete chemical substances that cross synaptic clefts and relay excitatory or inhibitory messages to postsynaptic receptor sites. Neuromodulation refers to the process whereby a specific substance simultaneously affects large numbers of neurons, thereby modifying a number of neurotransmitter actions. Hormonal influences provide a classic example of this latter activity.

Hormonal Influences

Hormonal influences on the central nervous system have been studied in a wide variety of animal species. Accumulated data suggest that specific hormones may exert differential effects on the brain, depending on its maturational status. During the critical early stages of development, for example, the influence may be inductive or organizational. In the mature central nervous system, excitatory, activational, and inhibitory effects are noted. School-age children and comparable groups among other vertebrate species have been less well studied than the perinatal and adult organisms.

Among the studies of hormonal influences on animal behavior, data on androgen effects are of particular interest for human development in middle childhood. The secretion of adrenal androgens in children begins to increase between ages 7 and 8, well before the dramatic rise in their plasma levels that accompanies the onset of puberty. The developmental and behavioral influences of these prepubertal androgens deserve further investigation.

Studies in rats, chickens, and rhesus monkeys strongly suggest that the organization and maintenance of social rank is, at least in part, affected by gonadal hormones. Positive correlations among aggressive behavior, social rank, and plasma androgen levels in males, and perhaps in females, have been extensively documented for a wide variety of species (Flickinger, 1966; Kling, 1975; Lloyd, 1971; Rose et al., 1971). The degree to which experiential factors modify the physiological effects of sex hormones is still unclear. Edwards and Rowe (1975) acknowledge that the specific expression of behaviors is related to environmental circumstances, but they view aggressive urges themselves as hormonally mediated, internal events. The relative validity of such assertions for human behavior is unclear, although evidence suggests that the influence of social experience increases as one ascends the phylogenetic tree (Lloyd, 1975). Studies by Olweus et al. (1980) documented strong correlations between plasma testosterone levels in pubertal boys and the intensity of their aggressive responses to provocation and weak correlations with aggressive attitude for unprovoked aggression. They suggest that further investigation requires careful delineation of different aggressive dimensions as well as avoidance of omnibus measures.

The neuromaturational timing of androgen influences is particularly intriguing. In many animal species, androgens exert an early organizing effect on brain architecture as well as on subsequent patterns of function. Morphologic differences between male and female brains in rats and rhesus monkeys, for example, have been well described (Bubenik and Brown, 1973; Raisman and Field, 1971), In humans, gestational plasma levels of testosterone have been directly correlated with aggressive postnatal behavior for children of both sexes (Kling, 1975), and girls exposed to increased androgenic stimulation in utero (e.g., newborns with adrenogenital syndrome) have been noted to later demonstrate more tomboy behavior than average female children (Ehrhardt, 1975; Money, 1973). A recent study describing impaired spatial ability in men with idiopathic hypogonadotrophic hypogonadism (characterized by an isolated, severe pubertal androgen deficiency), normal spatial skills in men with hypogonadism acquired during or after an otherwise normal puberty, and the failure of exogenous androgens to reverse the deficits in the postadolescent idiopathic group suggests that androgens may have a permanent organizing influence on cognitive function before or during puberty (Hier and Crowley, 1982). Although a number of methodological questions were raised about the collection and analysis of these data (Kagan, 1982) and adult male superiority on tests of spatial reasoning has been well documented (Maccoby and Jacklin, 1974), the hypothesis that these sex differences are mediated by a specific androgen effect just before or during puberty requires further evaluation.

The classic paradigm for hormonal research with experimental animals has involved extirpation of the gland, subsequent replacement therapy, and evaluation of behavior under both conditions. Aside from the ethical restrictions imposed on human research, most studies have been flawed methodologically because they have excluded females and have failed to delineate potentially confounding factors in the physical and social environment. Despite the limitations of available data, a substantial body of evidence suggests that gonadal hormones, gonadotropins, and adrenal hormones influence and are affected by social interactions among groups of experimental animals and may play an important role in the regulation of human social behavior (Lloyd, 1975; Rose et al., 1971). Future research in this area will demand sophisticated multidisciplinary collaboration in order to adequately investigate levels of interaction between neurohormonal regulation and the social-emotional milieu.

In addition to their association with aggression and dominance, adrenal steroids have been shown to be mobilized in response to a variety of aversive social stimuli, including crowding and defeat (Lloyd, 1975). In fact, brain-mediated interactions between the endocrine and autonomic nervous systems appear to play a vital role in the physiological response of humans to stress. The most commonly reported consequences of a stressful stimulus include increases in serum corticosteroid, catecholamine (epinephrine), growth hormone, and prolactin, with a corresponding fall in serum testosterone (Rose, 1980). Although increased epinephrine release by the adrenal medulla shows no evidence of a habituation effect, even after the organism shows behavioral adaptation to a repeated stressor, the hypothalamic-mediated release of increased corticosteroid by the adrenal cortex diminishes with repetition of the stress stimulus. Recent neuropeptide research on hypothalamic-pituitary-adrenocortical system function (Sowers, 1980) and investigations of the stress-induced effects of the hypothalamic-limbic-midbrain circuits on endocrine and autonomic nervous system responses (Usdin et al., 1980) have contributed to the rapidly increasing body of data documenting the physiological reactions produced by a variety of stressors, including situations that elicit a sense of threat, alarm, or distress as well as novelty, uncertainty, or unpleasantness (Hennessy and Levine, 1979). These same neuroendocrine circuits have also been shown to be significantly involved in mediating adaptive functions of memory, appraisal, and motivational-emotional responses. The contribution of these hormones to specific patterns of reaction and adaptation to social pressures and stress, however, remains to be elucidated and may ultimately provide critical insight into individual differences in resilience displayed by school-age children. Possible implications of these findings for health in middle childhood are discussed later in this chapter.

Neurotransmission

Perhaps the most promising area in research on brain-behavior relations is the current focus on the identification and functional understanding of neurotransmitters. The study of these substances, some of which have probably not yet been discovered, directly addresses the question of how nerve cells communicate with each other and, therefore, how they produce such complex behaviors as coordinated ambulation, creative problem solving, and affective experiences.

Neurotransmitters are the mediators of a highly regulated biological system. Virtually every neuron and tract in the brain is believed to exert its action through the release of a neurotransmitter, and virtually every recipient neuron has neurotransmitter receptor sites. Moreover, neurotransmitter systems are continually reorganized during the development of the organism. Thus, whereas neuromaturation in the fetus and young infant may be demonstrated by observable changes in brain morphology, the maturational process in the older child may very well be characterized by significant modifications in neurotransmitter circuitry (Johnston and Singer, 1982). In fact, it is reasonable to hypothesize that the relative plasticity of an immature nervous system may be related to the degree to which production and receptor sites can be modified to accommodate to different neurotransmitters. This hypothesis has particular relevance for the issue of age changes in responsiveness to psychopharmacotherapy.

Chemical substances that have been identified as neurotransmitters (amino acids, peptides, and biogenic amines such as dopamine, norepinephrine, epinephrine, and serotonin) have been the object of preliminary investigations whose potential findings may ultimately illuminate some of the neurological enigmas and developmental vicissitudes of the school-age period. Research with adults, for example, has shown that circulating epinephrine plays an important role in the coping behavior of healthy persons exposed to a variety of psychosocial stressors (Rose, 1980). Under conditions of low and moderate behavioral arousal, a direct correlation has been reported between catecholamine secretion and efficiency of performance. Studies with children suggest that, among normal youngsters, those who secrete relatively more epinephrine tend to be socially and emotionally better adjusted than those with lower secretions (Frankenhaeuser and Johansson, 1975). Lambert et al. (1969) reported that 8-year-old children with higher secretions of epinephrine were judged as being quicker and livelier, more decisive, open, curious, playful, and candid than their peers with lower epinephrine output. This trend was more pronounced for boys than for girls. The implications of these data for understanding differences in vulnerability and resilience are discussed later in this chapter.

Preliminary evidence linking several neurological and functional disorders with abnormalities of specific neurotransmitter metabolism have provided the impetus for many clinical studies but no conclusive results. The report of elevated platelet serotonin in a subgroup of children with autism (Schain and Freedman, 1961), for example, and the recently described (though not replicated) improvement in behavior and cognitive function after pharmacologic reduction of elevated blood levels in three autistic youngsters (Geller et al., 1982) has renewed interest in the role of serotonin in the development of the central nervous system without clarifying the pathophysiology of autistic behavior.

The continuing search for the neurochemical bases of attention-deficit disorders is particularly illustrative of the frustrations that have plagued investigators in this area. The successful therapeutic use of dextroamphetamine and methylphenidate in appropriately selected children has been interpreted as indirect evidence for a catecholaminergic defect, inasmuch as these medications augment the function of catecholamines (Wender, 1971). Rodent studies in which the selective destruction of neurons rich in catecholamine was followed by clinical hyperactivity provided further support for this hypothesis (Shaywitz et al., 1976). However, the marked heterogeneity of the children clinically diagnosed as having attention deficits, the demonstration of decreased reaction time and improved performance on cognitive tests in "normal" prepubertal boys treated with dextroamphetamine (Rapoport et al., 1978), and the unavailability of a specific diagnostic test have thwarted attempts to characterize precisely the neurochemical basis of this developmental disability. Pathogenetic mechanisms for well-documented toxins, such as lead (Needleman et al., 1979), and objects of speculation, such as food additives (Denny, 1982), remain to be elucidated.

The neurophysiological mechanisms underlying the entire spectrum of learning disorders in school-age children are the subject of an extensive literature whose review is beyond the scope of this chapter. Although all learning is essentially mediated through brain function, the relevance of most available neuroscientific data for the practical management of school dysfunction is currently unclear. Repeated attempts to reliably link atypical electroencephalographic patterns and clinical signs of neuromaturational delay (so-called soft signs) with attention deficits and learning disabilities, for example, have yielded inconsistent results (Adams et al., 1974; Barlow, 1974; Lewis and Freeman, 1977; Touwen, 1972). Although voluminous data on cerebral lateralization and hemispheric dominance have clearly demonstrated the linear, sequential, analytic, and verbal characteristics of left-brain function and the spatial, simultaneous, holistic, and intuitive nature of processing on the right, the translation of such findings into effective strategies for educational intervention has not been achieved. Neuropsychological assessment offers a promising vehicle for elucidating the biological basis for differences in learning style and proficiency among school-age children. Its applicability for educational planning and curriculum design, however, is unlikely to be realized unless neuroscientists, clinicians, and educators cooperate in the design, implementation, and analysis of collaborative investigation.

The study of neurotransmission, neuromodulation, and neuropsychology is in its infancy. Attempts to study interactions among multiple biochemical systems and the phenomenon of localized instead of whole-brain effects underline the technical complexity of this research. New technologies, such as positron emission tomography (PET scanning), offer methods for examining neurotransmitter receptors in living patients (Wagner, 1980). Their utility awaits the test of time.

It is reasonable to expect that basic neurobiological research will ultimately elucidate the biochemical and physiological bases for a host of neurological disorders, specific learning difficulties, and behavioral dysfunctions that afflict children in middle childhood. Furthermore, it is perhaps not unthinkable that neurotransmitter and neuroendocrine profiles might ultimately provide insight into the biological bases for individual differences in temperament, coping style, and overall resilience and vulnerability throughout the life cycle. For the present and the near future, the application of neurochemical and neuropsychological assessment techniques to the study of the human nervous system is just beginning. In the more distant future, knowledge of brain-behavior relations might very well form the basis for a highly sophisticated system of diagnostic assessment and prescriptive intervention for the developmental and behavioral concerns of school-age children.

CONCEPTS OF HEALTH, ILLNESS, AND DISEASE

A consideration of health issues of school-age children must begin with a clarification of what is meant by the terms *health, illness,* and *disease.* Perhaps the most pervasive metaphor in the history of medicine has been the concept of health as a state of equilibrium or balance. This concept provided an organizing principle for Hippocratic medicine in the fifth and fourth centuries B.C. and formed the basis for Galen's second-century A.D. popularization of the interaction of the four body humors, which dominated medical theory for several hundred years (Mechanic, 1978). It is also clearly reflected in the ancient Chinese concepts of yin and yang (Wallnofer and Von Rottauscher, 1972) and in the traditional health beliefs of many native American groups who believe that physical and mental health are a reflection of one's harmony with the earth (Primeaux, 1977). The biological principle of homeostasis reflects the enduring influence of this concept of dynamic equilibrium in contemporary biomedical science.

Despite the persistence of this seemingly universal principle, a satisfactory operational definition of health or wellness has not been developed. Dubos (1968:67) described health as a "modus vivendi enabling imperfect men to achieve a rewarding and not too painful existence while they cope with an imperfect world." Parsons (1972:117) defined health as "the state of optimum *capacity* of an individual for the effective performance of the roles and tasks for which he has been socialized." The frequently quoted definition of the World Health Organization describes "a state of complete physical, mental, and social well-being and not merely the absence of disease or infirmity" (Constitution of the World Health Organization, 1958:459).

From the literary to the political, such definitions underscore the widespread agreement on the importance of viewing health as a social concept (Lewis, 1953). As noted by Mechanic (1978:53):

> [E]ven physical well-being is dependent on the context in which we live, our associations with others, and the physical and social assaults to which our living situation exposes us. . . . Moreover, even from a practical standpoint, we must come to appreciate that in the long run our well-being is less dependent on the elegance and sophistication of medical practice than on how we choose to live and what is done to the environment in which we live.

The implications of this model for the health and development of school-age children are discussed later in this chapter.

The phenomenon of sickness has been relatively easier to characterize. Its analysis has been significantly enhanced by those who have specified a differentiation between the concept of illness and that of disease. Eisenberg (1977:11) succinctly summarized this critical distinction by noting that "patients suffer 'illnesses'; physicians diagnose and treat 'diseases.' " That is to say, disease refers to abnormality in the structure and/or function of body organs, whereas illness refers to the human experience of an uncomfortable change in one's state of being with or without an undesirable impairment of social function (Fabrega, 1974; Kleinman et al., 1978). Thus, disease and illness do not always coexist. Half of all adult visits to a physician's office are for symptoms whose biological basis is not identified (Stoeckle et al., 1964). Many children with congenital heart disease never experience cardiac symptoms and therefore are not ill. Illness in any given individual is often distinct from the course of his or her disease. Among the many factors that contribute to these distinctions, the degree to which the human experience of poor health is affected by social and cultural influences has been extensively studied.

Cultural Influences

Physical illness implies a state of being that is undesirable, uncomfortable, or damaging in relation to the values and usual life situations characteristic of a given ecocultural niche. Thus, individual differences in perceptions, experiences, and coping patterns are significantly modified by systematic variations in the systems of meaning used to explain the phenomenon of sickness (Fabrega, 1972; Kleinman et al., 1978; Spector, 1979). A seizure disorder may be variably regarded as a simple disease, a stigmatizing defect, or a reflection of supernatural powers (Mechanic, 1978). In some societies, obesity is the object of envy and desire; others define it as a health risk or a frank disease. Scoliosis in a school-age girl is understood and experienced in dramatically different ways by an African believer in demons (Hughes and Bontemps, 1958) and a middle-class family in the United States. Many pathological conditions are not defined as illnesses in those societies in which their prevalence is almost universal (Dubos, 1965).

Studies of cultural variations in acknowledging symptoms and seeking medical assistance within the United States have documented important social class and ethnic differences (Beecher, 1956; Koos, 1954; Zborowski, 1952; Zola, 1966). Analyses of these findings, however, have not distinguished among differences in objective symptoms, varied interpretations of the same symptoms, variations in willingness to express concerns or to seek help, or the use of different vocabulary for expressing distress (Mechanic, 1972). Moreover, individual differences within apparently homogeneous groups have been shown to be "vast and impressive" (Mechanic, 1978:35).

The cultural context of health and illness and the particular dilemma of contemporary health care in the United States have been critically examined by Eisenberg (1976:186), who noted:

Illness experience is patterned by culture. Medical lore is integral to every existing human culture. Every human group has a body of beliefs about illness and healing. As culture evolves over time, folk knowledge becomes the special prerogative of healers. The shaman or healer in traditional societies does what the physician does in Western societies. He diagnoses; he prescribes ritual actions designed to overcome illness; he casts a prognosis; and he legitimates the mysteries of death. He names and explains just as we name and explain, although he and we employ very different explanatory systems.

The explanatory system of American medicine is the biomedical model of health and disease. Its benefits have been dramatic and far-reaching. Its boundaries, however, have become increasingly apparent, especially with regard to the salient health issues of middle childhood. A critical examination of the biomedical model, in contrast to the proposed enhancements of a biopsychosocial orientation, provides a method for taking a broad look at the physical health needs of school-age children.

The Biomedical Model

The biomedical model, which continues to dominate Western medicine, is governed by the philosophical traditions of reductionism and mind-body dualism. The former concept is manifested in the belief that all human illness, including complex behavioral dysfunction, can be explained ultimately by a disordered biochemical or neurophysiological process. Studies of neurotransmission and neuromodulation reflect this orientation. Mind-body dualism, which has its roots in the work of Descartes in the seventeenth century, separates somatic from mental and interpersonal functions and pays little attention to the psychological, social, and behavioral aspects of disease.

As a scientific framework for the study of the molecular biology of pathological processes, the biomedical model has been extraordinarily productive. Its contribution to our understanding of the etiology and pathogenesis of human disease, as well as to the development of rational therapeutic interventions, continues to strengthen the technical efficacy of Western medical care. A growing appreciation of the diversity of clinical signs and symptoms demonstrated by many well-defined diseases, however, highlights the incompleteness of the traditional biomedical model. Congenital cytomegalovirus, fetal alcohol syndrome, and lead intoxication, for example, are some of the many conditions whose organic etiology has been identified but whose developmental and behavioral manifestations are highly variable. The demonstration that a significant proportion of that variability may be attributed to psychosocial factors suggests the need for a reassessment of the traditional categorization of diseases solely according to their biological causes—the single cause:single disease illusion. Thus, Achenbach's discussion (in this volume) of the relative merits of nosological versus multivariate approaches for the classification of psychopathology has relevance for so-called physical disease as well.

Critics of the biomedical model have charged that it embodies a simplistic view of the human body as a machine and conceptualizes disease as the result of a defective part or overall mechanical breakdown. By forcing a dichotomous choice between disease and nondisease, it fails to acknowledge the continuum from optimal function through degrees of dysfunction that characterizes human well-being. Moreover, its relative disregard for the social and psychological determinants of human illness has stimulated the demand for a broader biopsychosocial model of health and disease (Engel, 1977).

The Biopsychosocial Orientation

The biopsychosocial approach provides a "framework within which can be conceptualized and related, as natural systems, all the levels of organization pertinent to health and disease from subatomic particles through molecules, cells, tissues, organs, organ systems, the person, the family, the community, the culture, and ultimately the biosphere" (Engel, 1979:266). In the tradition of viewing health as a state of relative balance and harmony, it provides a vehicle for analyzing the integrity of each component level as well as their reciprocal interactions within a dynamic hierarchical system that extends from molecule to culture.

Unlike the biomedical model, which restricts its factor analytic approach to the patient and his or her component parts, the biopsychosocial orientation is based on a general systems theory, which demands a sophisticated analysis of social and cultural levels of organization as well as the interacting systems linking each component in the overall hierarchy. The analytic techniques employed successfully at any given level are likely to differ, as will the approaches used to understand the collective system (Weiss, 1967). The obvious gain in comprehensiveness provided by this proposed model has been described by Engel (1979:266):

Health, disease, illness and disability thus are conceptualized in terms of the relative intactness and functioning of each component system on each hierarchical level. Overall health reflects a high level of intraand inter-systemic harmony. Such harmony may be disrupted at any level, that of the cell, the organ, the person, or the community. Whether the resulting disturbance is contained at the level at which it was initiated or whether other levels become implicated is a function of the capacity of that system to adjust to change. . . . Such contrasts between smooth functioning and disruption provide the bases upon which health, disease, illness and disability may be differentiated.

The potential richness of a biopsychosocial orientation is most compelling. Although the availability of sophisticated analytic techniques for the entire hierarchy as well as for each of its component levels is highly variable, the model itself represents a critical conceptual advancement over its more narrow predecessor. As Eisenberg (1976:186) observed: "Our worship of restricted disease models resembles a ritual or magical belief more than it does scientific logic." The biopsychosocial orientation demands the application of science to those aspects of health and disease that concern the patient as an individual and as a social being, dimensions that heretofore have been considered part of the more subjective art of medicine. It offers a far richer framework for studying the health of school-age children.

Developmental Considerations

The universality of illness and the clearly delimited nature of the "sick" role make these phenomena "a strategic arena in which to consider role learning, attitude formation, and other aspects of the process of acquiring general social orientation" (Campbell, 1975:92) during the school-age years. The diversity of opinion regarding concepts of health and illness among scholars and the lay adult public, however, raises a number of intriguing questions regarding middle childhood. How does an understanding of health and illness develop during this period? What are the cognitive and affective factors that determine the contents of children's beliefs? How are evolving concepts influenced by family, peers, school, media, and personal experiences with sickness? Simply stated, what do children think about health and illness, where do those thoughts come from, and how do they evolve into adult concepts?

The earliest attempts to address these questions were methodologically unsophisticated and without theoretical content beyond that provided by the psychoanalytic model. Most studies described children's feelings about their own illnesses and often focused on the emotional impact of associated experiences, such as hospitalization (Prugh et al., 1953). The most common observation reported by clinical researchers was that children often thought they were responsible for their own ill health and viewed disease as a punishment for wrongdoing (Beverly, 1936; Freud, 1952; Langford, 1948; Lynn et al., 1962). In a more recent study of 408 healthy children from first-, third-, and fifth-grade classes, however, Brodie (1974) confirmed this finding in only one-quarter of the sample. He found, rather, that nonanxious children frankly rejected the notion of illness as punishment.

With increasing interest in the development of health-related concepts, attention has shifted toward explorations of children's ideas about illness and not just their affective responses. Nagy (1951), one of the first investigators to explore children's theories of illness, found very little appreciation before age 12 of the multiplicity of causal factors of disease. More recently, Campbell (1975) devised a listing of 11 illness themes ranging from relatively immature somatic sensations ("feeling bad," "stomach ache") to more sophisticated levels concerned with dispositional states ("irritable," "unhappy") and role functioning ("don't want to go to school," "stay home from work"). Although greater precision in definition and greater emphasis on alterations in role performance and/or psychosocial disposition were found with increasing age, Campbell's data were still essentially descriptive and not articulated in terms of a unified theoretical model.

Current investigators, moving beyond a simple cataloging of responses, have begun to analyze children's explanations of illness within a framework that reflects the sequence and structure of the major stages of cognitive development as formulated by Jean Piaget and Heinz Werner (Bibace and Walsh, 1981; Perrin and Gerrity, 1981). Generally speaking, these studies demonstrate that kindergarten children display magical thinking, that fourth-grade children believe that illness is caused by germs without any insight into the issue of host susceptibility, and that eighth-grade children understand the concept of multiple interacting mechanisms for etiology and treatment. Concepts of illness causality were noted to lag behind but closely parallel the development of concepts of physical causality in the youngsters studied, with illness prevention appearing to be more difficult to understand than causation or treatment. Differences in patterns of decalage were not found to be related to sex or socioeconomic status (Perrin and Gerrity, 1981).

The most sophisticated theoretical formulation of developing concepts of illness currently available is that of Bibace and Walsh (1980, 1981). Through an analysis of the cognitive processes underlying children's ideas about illness at different ages, they have constructed a model consonant with Piaget's stages of cognitive development, which includes two subtypes of explanation within each of three major categories: *phenomenism* and *contagion* in the preoperational stage, *contamination* and *internalization* during the stage of concrete operations, and *physiological* and *psychophysiologic* conceptualization during the formal operations period. Consistent data from a series of studies confirmed the usefulness of this classification, and frequency distributions of the responses of normal children validated its ordered developmental sequence (Bibace and Walsh, 1981).

The development of concepts of health, compared with those of illness, has been less well studied, possibly because being well is more abstract and therefore more difficult for a child to define than is the idea of being hurt or sick (Neuhauser et al., 1978). Nevertheless, children as young as 6 have been found to articulate positive ideas about health. In a study of 264 elementary school students, for example, first graders tended to define health as a series of specific practices (e.g., "eating the right foods" and "getting enough exercise"), and fourth graders tended to focus more on themes related to being in good shape and feeling good. Seventh graders (12-year-olds) showed evidence of an emerging perception of health as "long-term—involving the body, mind, and in some cases, the environment" (Natapoff, 1978:999). Although available data regarding health (as opposed to illness) concepts are limited and largely descriptive—and further study in this area is clearly needed—it would appear reasonable to hypothesize that children's ideas about health are influenced in large part by their level of cognitive development. The implications of this hypothesis for the challenges of health promotion and education during middle childhood are considered later.

Available data on the degree to which the development of concepts of health and illness may be modified by environmental influences are inconclusive and contradictory. Although maternal attitudes and behavior regarding child health do influence children's patterns of illness behavior, the degree of variance in children's responses that can be explained by mothers' responses is often extremely small and therefore less influential than anticipated (Mechanic, 1964). Campbell (1975) concluded that children's concepts do not result from direct maternal teaching and noted that "a more casual learning process may be involved, one in which mother's perspectives may make a difference only insofar as they impinge on and thus modify children's relevant responses" (p. 99). In a subsequent study of short-term patients on a pediatric ward, however, Campbell (1978) attributed more weight to maternal influences, especially in the later childhood years, and noted that children's reports of their own illnesses were tied to age and sex roles and were significantly related to parental socioeconomic status. Although Natapoff (1978) found no significant socioeconomic differences in children's views of health, other data suggest that such influences may be relevant. For example, the prevalence of belief in health-related television commercials reported for poor children and their parents was 20 to 30 percent higher than that found among middleor upper-class families (Lewis and Lewis, 1974). The relative and interacting contributions of these and other relevant variables have not been studied adequately.

Personal experience with illness is another important variable whose impact has not been well delineated. In a study of chronically ill hospitalized children ages 5–13, Brewster (1982) compared performance on high-affect cognitive tasks (illness causality and ideas regarding the intent of medical procedures) with that on low-affect tasks (e.g., conservation, physical causality, etc.) and found no significant differences in the mean scores for any age group. Campbell (1975) interviewed an acutely hospitalized, essentially normal group of children ages 6–12 and found that past experience with sickness did affect the level of sophistication of children's concepts of illness but noted that the differences were contingent on age. That is to say, children under age 9.5 whose health was rated poorer than that of their parents had the least sophisticated concepts, while more mature responses were obtained from the older group. The influence of past experience with disease on conceptual development regarding health and illness clearly requires further investigation.

Relationships among concepts of health and illness, affective responses, and health-related behaviors are complex and not well understood. Radius et al. (1980) studied the health beliefs of 249 children ages 6–17 and found health issues to be a meaningful concern for the majority, regardless of age, sex, or participation in risk-taking behaviors. Gochman (1971) interviewed 108 children ages 7–18 and found health to be of relatively low salience. We know very little about the genesis of health beliefs. Our understanding of the conditions under which they are acquired and the factors that promote individual differences is severely limited. We know even less about how to change health beliefs at different ages. In fact, available data show them to be relatively well established and difficult to alter by the end of the school-age years (Weisenberg et al., 1980). Finally, we have little evidence that health beliefs are important determinants of health-promoting behaviors during middle childhood and the early adolescent period.

The study of the development of concepts of health and illness of school-age children is in its infancy. Its importance is best appreciated in the context of recent attitudinal and substantive changes in the delivery of medical care for children in the United States ages 6–12. Middle childhood is regarded increasingly as a significant period of transition toward independent interaction with the health care system. Routine well-child examinations are shifting from parent-physician dialogue to more extensive discussion with children about their own health maintenance. Youngsters with chronic diseases or handicapping conditions are encouraged to assume growing responsibility for decisions regarding their own care. For some children, increasing autonomy is beneficial; for others it may be premature and detrimental. Further investigation regarding individual differences in this process of transferring responsibility is needed.

Theoretical frameworks within which such matters can be facilitated and analyzed are being constructed. Greater understanding of the developmental unfolding of these issues will be particularly important in communicating more appropriately with school-age children, thereby enhancing our ability to meet the challenges of health promotion, education, and management of chronic illnesses and disabling conditions during this dynamic period of expanding self-understanding and self-regulation.

PHYSICAL HEALTH AND THE EMERGING SENSE OF SELF

The school-age years mark an important period of growing awareness of oneself. For the child between ages 6 and 12, the construction of the self-concept is both intimately private and intensely social. The intersection of this emerging sense of personal identity with issues related to physical health falls in the realm of what eventually becomes known as life-style.

The concept of life-style implies a pattern of behavior and values that extends over a period of time. Though hardly immutable, one's life-style tends to include habitual characteristics whose modifiability is presumed to be inversely related to age. Thus, as an organizing construct for thinking about health, the early development of life-style during the school-age years is particularly salient. Its association with the major causes of death in childhood (accidents) and in adult life (cardiovascular and malignant diseases) underlines its influence on both immediate and long-term health concerns.

Health Promotion and the Evolution of Personal Life-Styles

Increasing evidence suggests that the ways in which people live and the patterns of behavior and adaptation they exhibit play a major role in determining their health status throughout the life cycle. A recent Institute of Medicine report, based on the views of more than 400 leaders in the biomedical and social sciences, noted (Hamburg et al., 1982:1):

The heaviest burdens of illness in the United States today are related to aspects of individual behavior, especially long-term patterns of behavior often referred to as "life-style." As much as 50 percent of mortality from the 10 leading causes of death in the United States can be traced to lifestyle.

As public health initiatives have shifted emphasis from the treatment of acute illness to the prevention of chronic disease, the modification of detrimental behavior patterns has received growing attention. Difficulties in altering long-standing adult behaviors have led to a logical interest in expanded efforts on behalf of children. Physical exercise, eating patterns, and self-induced vulnerability are some of the life-style elements that have been targeted for such efforts.

Physical Exercise

Vigorous exercise on a regular basis, as a health-enhancing behavior, has gained considerable popular support. Although the often claimed salutary effects of exercise on emotional well-being have not been extensively studied, the association between physical activity and lowered risk of clinical complications secondary to atherosclerosis has been well documented (Dawber, 1980; Thomas et al., 1981).

The mechanism through which physical activity may affect morbidity and mortality from cardiovascular disease has not been well elucidated. Whether inactivity is an independent risk factor or whether it has multiple effects through interactions with other variables remains to be determined. Studies of serum lipid profiles in adults, for example, have demonstrated greater risk for coronary artery disease when low-density lipoproteins (LDL-cholesterol) are elevated and an apparent protective effect from high-density liproproteins (HDL-cholesterol) (National Heart, Lung, and Blood Institute, 1981). Elevations of serum HDL-cholesterol in association with physical exercise have been clearly demonstrated in adults and replicated in a controlled study of girls ages 8–10 (Gilliam and Burke, 1978; Glomset, 1980). The significance of this particular mechanism in the pathogenesis of cardiovascular disease is not known.

Although the cardiovascular benefits for adults of fitness from aerobic exercise have been established (Paffenbarger and Hyde, 1980), little is known about the long-term effects of physical training by children. Rowland (1981:7–8) noted:

The basic premise for the promotion of physical fitness rests upon the assumption that repeated aerobic exercise (training) will produce a series of physiologic changes (training effect or fitness), and that these alterations can be translated into objective benefits to the individual. That repeated aerobic exercise produces such changes in adults is well documented, but in children it remains controversial.

Whether the relatively high levels of fitness found in school-age children compared with adults are related to differences in activity level or genetically determined differences in physiological development is currently unclear (Hamilton and Andrew, 1976; Hovell et al., 1978). Although relevant physiological measures in competitive swimmers and track stars are advanced for age, the observed differences may not be secondary to training but rather a result of the fact that genetically endowed athletes are more likely to be successful in sports. In addition, although the process of atherosclerosis begins in early childhood and continues throughout the life cycle, it is not at all clear whether physical fitness during childhood has any effect on the rate of decline of cardiovascular function or the risk of coronary artery disease in later life. That physical activity during the adult years does appear to be important for cardiovascular health, however, highlights the importance of reinforcing it in the emerging life-style of the school-age child.

Most children naturally enjoy participation in physical exercise. Concerns have been voiced, however, that the sedentary influences of modern society are resulting in decreasing childhood fitness. Only one out of every three school children participates in a daily program of physical education (Select Panel for the Promotion of Child Health, 1981). Interest in organized sports for young people, however, has increased over the past 10 years and is now estimated to involve over 8 million American children (Goldberg et al., 1978). Participation in physical activity, nevertheless, dramatically declines with increasing age. One of six persons in the United States ages 10–17 was classified as physically underdeveloped by the standards of the President's Council on Physical Fitness and Sports (1977). In 1974 the President's Council estimated that almost half of adult Americans did not participate in any form of exercise (Apple and Cantwell, 1979). The growing popularity of both organized and informal efforts to promote physical fitness, however, has probably improved these statistics substantially.

The need to promote continued involvement in physical activity beyond the school-age years is clear. Critics have argued that the traditional system of recreation and school activities has focused on the athletically gifted or early-maturing child and has emphasized the acquisition of skills in such sports as baseball, basketball, and football, which have limited cardiovascular benefits and are less likely to be pursued in adulthood (Pate and Blair, 1978).

Concerns about overemphasis on performance in competitive athletics have also been raised regarding psychological stress and predisposition to injury (Rowland, 1981). Epiphyseal fractures in football players and little league pitchers (Adams, 1965), for example, with their potential risk of distorting subsequent long-bone growth, are some of the specific injuries that have stimulated the growth of sports medicine as a new pediatric specialty (Micheli and Smith, 1982). Increasing female participation in organized sports programs has raised additional questions for study. The well-known phenomenon of delayed menarche in young track stars and ballet dancers, for example, has been shown to be reversible after cessation of vigorous training, but ultimate fertility and endocrine status after many years of competition remain unknown (Warren, 1980; Frisch et al., 1980). The American Academy of Pediatrics' Committee on the Pediatric Aspects of Physical Fitness, Recreation and Sports (1975) specifically examined the issue of sex differences and subsequently endorsed coeducational sports programs in the prepubescent years, noting that young girls can effectively compete against boys in any sport when matched for weight, skills, size, and physical maturation.

Current knowledge regarding physical activity in childhood is limited. The long-term benefits and risks of a variety of activity profiles have not been described. The frequency, intensity, and duration of exercise necessary for fitness has been well defined for adults but not for children at different ages. The well-documented value of routine, vigorous aerobic exercise for adults, in conjunction with the decline in physical fitness often seen with advancing age, underscores the critical need for physical education programs during the school-age years that are oriented toward high-level activity involving sustained exercise of the large muscle groups, that place emphasis more on endurance than on speed, and that introduce the kinds of sports and aerobic activity that can be continued into the adult years. The differential benefits of individual sports, their specific impact on self-esteem and evolving attitudes toward recreational exercise among children of varying athletic abilities, and the developmental consequences of the competitive pressures of organized sports during middle childhood clearly require further study.

Eating Patterns

American eating patterns have changed dramatically over the past 30 years. In response to recommendations to decrease cholesterol and fat intake, our consumption of eggs and milk fats have each dropped 30 percent, the per capita consumption of lard has fallen by 80 percent, and that of butter by 55 percent (Page and Friend, 1978; Stamler, 1978). Conversely, the use of margarines and vegetable oils has increased markedly, and overall trends show a significant decrease in the proportion of calories in the average American diet contributed by fat (Rizek and Jackson, 1980). This shift in eating habits has been accompanied by a 7 percent drop in average serum cholesterol levels, with a greater decrease among the higher educated segment of the population (Levy, 1979). Over the past 20 years, however, food processing and refinement have grown, and the proliferation of "convenience" foods has dramatically increased, and sales by fast-food restaurants have increased 305 percent (Select Panel for the Promotion of Child Health, 1981).

Few available data specifically address the eating patterns of school-age children. A detailed survey of the diets of children under age 13 in the Bogalusa Heart Study, however, showed overall consumption of foods high in saturated fat, sucrose, and sodium, with snack foods high in fat, salt, and sugar accounting for approximately one-third of the total caloric intake. Moreover, although correlations between diet and serum lipid levels have not been demonstrated in adults, they were documented in the children studied in Bogalusa (Berenson et al., 1982). These findings clearly conflict with the total population data described above. Whether they are representative of other childhood samples requires further study.

The development of eating patterns is generally established in infancy and early childhood (Lowenberg, 1977) and heavily influenced by cultural and familial factors. Preliminary studies of the emergence of concepts of nutrition suggest that kindergarten children understand that "good" and "bad" foods can influence health and growth, but comprehension of how nutritional factors relate to later physical status is not apparent until the sixth grade (Wellman and Johnson, 1982).

The potential impact of television on this process is worthy of particular attention. One study of children's programs revealed that 68.5 percent of the commercial messages were for food, of which 25 percent were for cereal, 25 percent for candy and sweets, and 8 percent for snacks and other foods. Ten percent of the advertisements were for quick meals and eating places, and sugar cereals outnumbered unsugared cereals by a ratio of 3 to 1 (Barcus, 1975; National Science Foundation, 1977). Children ages 5–10 have been noted to attend more closely to commercials than those ages 11–12 (Ward et al., 1972), while older children are more likely to question commercials (Blatt et al., 1972). McNeal (1969) and Yankelovich (1970) found that children attempted to influence parental buying practices on the basis of what they heard on television commercials, and mothers were noted to be more likely to honor requests for food than for other products (Berey and Pollay, 1968). The excessive focus of television commercials on food products has been clearly documented. However, we know relatively little about the extent of their impact on eating patterns in middle childhood, nor have we adequately evaluated the potential usefulness of this medium for more nutrition education. A better understanding of these and other influences on food preferences in early and middle childhood requires further study.

A detailed review of the nutritional status of school-age children in the United States is beyond the scope of this paper. Owen and Lippman (1977), in reviewing three national surveys and a number of regional and local studies, found a low prevalence of clinical signs suggestive of significant nutritional deficits, although iron deficiency continues to be a major problem, and overall nutritional status consistently correlates directly with socioeconomic status or income. The developmental consequences of intrauterine and early childhood malnutrition have been studied extensively. Speculation regarding an association between chronic undernutrition and developmental vulnerability, including the possible effects of iron-deficiency anemia on scholastic achievement, suggests a need for further investigation (Webb and Oski, 1973).

Perhaps the most important health-related problem associated with eating behavior during the school-age years is obesity (Merritt, 1982). Although definitions of obesity vary, a weight that is 20 percent or more above average for a given age, height, and gender is a commonly accepted standard (Van Itallie, 1979). Despite the failure to elucidate the role of obesity as an independent risk factor for cardiovascular disease in adult life, obesity is closely associated with a number of well-documented vulnerabilities, including hypertension, hypercholesterolemia, and diabetes mellitus (Hamburg et al., 1982). In addition, overweight individuals are cosmetically handicapped and frequently victimized by social discrimination, which may have long-term psychological sequelae for a vulnerable school-age child (Nathan, 1973).

Although the differential diagnosis of obesity includes a long list of pathological conditions, more than 90 percent of obese children are fat because they consume more calories than they expend. Some inequality in energy balance may have major genetic determinants (Weil, 1981), but most obesity is caused by excessive eating. A greatly reduced activity level is another factor associated with obesity in children (Mayer, 1975; Rowland, 1981). Whether this correlation is a causal one—and, if so, in which direction it operates—is currently unclear. Some inactive children may be predisposed to obesity. Many obese children are secondarily inactive. In both cases the progressive decrease in activity level that often accompanies a weight increase results in lower energy needs, which then require even fewer calories per day. The importance of physical activity in the treatment of obesity is critical.

Relationships between childhood and adult obesity have not been clearly delineated. Charney et al. (1976) reviewed medical records from infancy through age 30 for an adult population in Rochester, New York, and reported a relative risk factor for obesity of 2.5 (chance of a fat infant becoming a fat adult) and an attributable risk value of 50 percent (chance of a fat adult having been a fat child). Few data are available on the factors that perpetuate or counteract the progression of obesity from childhood to adulthood. The central importance of two major life-style issues in its pathogenesis, eating patterns and activity level, suggests that successful intervention in the school-age years will contribute to improved health in adult life. The validity of this hypothesis, however, remains to be documented. The possible contribution of a range of underlying psychological disturbances (e.g., depression, anxiety) to both the initiation and the continuation of excessive weight gain during middle childhood requires extensive investigation.

Self-Induced Vulnerability

Cigarette smoking, excessive alcohol consumption, and drug abuse contribute to a significant percentage of adult disease and death. Although the prevalence of such behaviors is relatively low in the preadolescent years, school-age children provide a natural population for early prevention efforts. The problem of cigarettes is particularly compelling. Of all the major risk factors for serious illness, disability, and premature death in the United States, the U.S. Public Health Service (1979) noted that smoking may be the most important preventable one. Unfortunately, the process through which young people first become smokers has been inadequately studied (Blaney, 1981).

Cigarette smoking is a major contributor to the development of lung cancer and chronic bronchitis and accounts for nearly 50 percent of adult excess mortality from cardiovascular disease. Although an augmented risk of coronary artery disease is associated with the onset of smoking before age 20, large numbers of teenagers and young adults continue to adopt the habit, especially females. As noted by Blaney (1981:192):

Obviously, reaching children before they begin smoking, or at least reaching young adolescents before they become addicted smokers, is the most logical way to reduce the health risks from smoking. Yet it is for this period of early smoking onset where data are most lacking. In other words, we cannot readily explain why children start to smoke or what means are most effective in preventing or reducing their smoking.

Although cigarette smoking in adolescents and adults has been studied extensively, relatively few investigations have looked specifically at the school-age years. Moreover, most attitudinal studies are cross-sectional, generated inconsistent data on the stability and predictability of individual beliefs, and do not address questions regarding the genesis of observed differences (Downey and O'Rourke, 1976; Laoye et al., 1972). Investigations of peer and parental influences have largely focused on older adolescents, thereby precluding an examination of their differential impact and interaction with other variables at successive times in the process through which one changes from a school-age nonsmoker to an adolescent or young adult smoker (Banks et al., 1978; Levitt and Edwards, 1970). Evidence that sibling variables may be highly significant requires more systematic examination (Banks et al., 1978; Lanese et al., 1972).

The fact that knowledge of the health risks of tobacco neither deters people from smoking nor changes existing smoking habits has been consistently demonstrated for adolescents and adults (Allegrante et al., 1977; Laoye et al., 1972). Although children as young as 7 or 8 have been shown to understand the danger, their appreciation of its personal implications may not be clear (Bland et al., 1975; Schneider and Vanmastrigt, 1974). Suggestions that immediate and short-term risks be emphasized have not consistently led to a more effective impact on smoking by children (Bland et al., 1975; Bynner, 1970). The relevance of these findings for the design and implementation of health education programs for preadolescents is clear.

Despite a large body of literature on smoking prevention efforts, very few programs have been based on a firm theoretical framework and systematic evaluation has been sparse (Evans et al., 1979; Green, 1979). Recent attempts to directly address the issue of peer pressure have provided a potentially fruitful avenue for further study. Using the concept of psychological inoculation, high school students have been trained to teach behavioral techniques to junior high school students to help them resist temptations and pressures from their peers. Preliminary findings from a series of controlled studies demonstrate significant impact on reported smoking behaviors, with effects persisting for almost 3 years (McAlister et al., 1979; Telch et al., 1982). Data reflecting comparable influences on alcohol consumption and marijuana use suggest the need for replication and further analysis of this model of behavioral change (McAlister et al., 1980).

Persistent Impairment and the Challenge of Functional Adaptation

While most school-age children enjoy unparalleled good health, a significant minority suffer chronic illness or disability. Although the definition of a chronic disorder has varied, it generally refers to an illness that interferes with ordinary activity and that lasts for more than three months in a given year or requires one or more months of continuous hospitalization. In a large epidemiologic survey of more than 5,000 children in Great Britain, Pless and Douglas (1971) used these criteria and calculated a prevalence rate of 112 per 1,000, exclusive of mental deficiencies. Males were found to outnumber females by 1.4 to 1, and the distribution of illness severity was reported to be 54 percent mild, 34 percent moderate, and 12 percent severe. Other prevalence rates cited in the literature vary, depending on the sampling procedures or definitions used, and range from 5 to 20 percent, including such diverse disorders as asthma, diabetes mellitus, meningomyelocele, juvenile arthritis, seizure disorders, cystic fibrosis, and childhood malignancy. In a review of three epidemiologic surveys, Pless and Roghmann (1971) observed that "about one child in 10 will experience one or more chronic illnesses by the age of 15 and up to 30 percent of these children may be expected to be handicapped by secondary social and psychological maladjustments" (p. 357). The comprehensive management of the multiple needs of chronically impaired children and their families is now recognized as an increasingly important pediatric responsibility during the school-age years (Hobbs et al., 1983; Task Force on Pediatric Education, 1978).

A large number of studies have explored the developmental-behavioral impact of chronic disease on affected children. For the child between ages 6 and 12, who is frequently judged according to academic, athletic, and social competence, the psychological burden of a persistent disorder can be particularly weighty. Sperling (1978) noted that deficits in ability or diminished physical attractiveness cause profound threats to self-esteem and perpetuate an atmosphere of stress. A higher incidence of psychiatric problems and behavioral disorders among such children has been reported by many investigators (Mattson, 1972; McAnarney et al., 1974; Pless and Roghmann, 1971). Conversely, other studies have failed to document higher rates of emotional disturbance (Bedell et al., 1977; Gayton et al., 1977). Pless and Pinkerton (1975) summarized a large body of literature that revealed a higher incidence of maladjustment among chronically ill children as well as evidence of successful adaptation in a substantial number. Sex, age at onset of disease, its course and severity, the visibility and specific consequences of associated handicaps, individual coping styles, and the quality of the parent-child relationship are some of the many variables that have been correlated with overall adjustment (Hewett et al., 1970; Mattson and Gross, 1966). Major methodological limitations in many studies, including absence of control groups and subjective methods of data collection, have contributed to the inconclusive and contradictory nature of the currently available data.

The literature on family impact is more voluminous but no less equivocal. Increased stress, problems of diminished parental self-esteem, persistent anxiety, depressive feelings, and marital discord have been reported repeatedly (Aply et al., 1967; Boles, 1959; Holt, 1958; Marcus, 1977; Turk, 1964). Other studies have noted more adaptive outcomes (Gayton et al., 1977; Vance et al., 1980). In a review of more than 50 reports on the impact of a handicapped child on the family, Murphy (1982) found only 16 controlled analytical studies, 11 of which involved parents of moderately to profoundly retarded children. Moreover, only 8 of the studies included a control group of healthy children, while the others compared handicapped populations. Vance et al. (1980) reviewed the literature on the methodological and conceptual problems of families and placed particular emphasis on the appropriate selection of control groups and the formulation of interview questions. Despite their limitations, however, the available data suggest that a chronically impaired child is a stressor to which different families adapt with varying degrees of success. Recent attempts have been made to measure differential impacts with greater precision and reliability (Stein and Riessman, 1982). More studies are needed to identify those variables that predict specific outcomes.

Questions regarding the impact of childhood chronic illness on healthy siblings have received increased attention in recent years. Although some studies have reported positive effects, such as increased understanding of problems and favorable responses to increased responsibilities (Caldwell and Guze, 1960; Hunt, 1973), most investigators have found increased guilt, anxiety, resentment, feelings of rejection, somatic complaints, and maladjustment in school (Mattson, 1972; Tew and Laurence, 1973). Lavigne and Ryan (1979) reported siblings of children attending hematology, cardiology, and especially plastic surgery clinics to be more withdrawn socially and more irritable than children without chronically ill family members. In addition, although neither the age nor the sex of the healthy sibling appeared to correlate with adverse outcome, the interaction between the two was noted to be significant. By contrast, Breslau et al. (1981) studied the psychological functioning of siblings of children with cystic fibrosis, cerebral palsy, myelodyplasia, and multiple handicaps and found no relation to type or severity of disability but did find an interaction between age and sex that completely contradicted that reported by Lavigne and Ryan (1979). Furthermore, although global ratings of behavioral symptoms were not different from those of control subjects, subscales measuring interpersonal aggression with peers and within the school revealed significantly higher scores among siblings of disabled children. Breslau et al. (1981) highlighted this finding, pointing out the danger of overemphasizing mean differences in global ratings on behavior inventories without examining differences in specific behavioral domains. Although recent studies regarding sibling effects have demonstrated greater methodological sophistication, a great deal more work is needed to identify the factors that account for differences and similarities between siblings of disabled children and those with healthy brothers and sisters.

Perhaps the most exciting new conceptualization in the literature on chronic impairment is reflected in a recent monograph from the Carnegie Council on Children (Gliedman and Roth, 1980). In a sharp indictment of the use of normative models of development to study the adaptation of handicapped children and their families, Gliedman and Roth make the following observation (pp. 58–59):

[D]evelopmentalists have made a crucial oversight. They take it for granted that theories constructed for able-bodied children can correctly interpret the developmental significance of the handicapped child's behavior. The importance of this research shortcoming cannot be emphasized too much. Because of stigma and misunderstanding, handicapped children often live in a social world that is radically different from the one inhabited by their able-bodied peers, and their physical or mental disabilities often impose sharp constraints on the ways that they can obtain and analyze experience. These social and biological differences raise a fundamental theoretical question for the field of child development: *do some handicapped children develop according to a healthy logic of their own?* By ignoring this question developmentalists more than imperil the value of their research; they run the risk of sometimes perpetuating the traditional deviance analysis of disability in a more subtle and more socially acceptable form. It is simply not enough to apply mainstream developmental theories to disability. Psychologists must first assess the applicability of these theories to each of the many groups of children with handicaps.

Support for this challenge is derived from varied yet related literature dealing with issues ranging from ethnic biases in "standardized" developmental models (Labov, 1972) to the dysfunctional use of conventional male-derived theories of personality and moral development in women's studies (Gilligan, 1979) and the necessity of constructing alternative models of normative development for children who are congenitally blind (Fraiberg, 1977) or deaf (Klima and Bellugi, 1979). The need for a new family sociology or anthropology "to locate those factors of family life that correlate with an handicapped child's achieving independence and self-respect later in life" (Gliedman and Roth, 1980:61) was also emphasized.

Gliedman and Roth (1980) conceptualized the predicament of the developing handicapped child as a "cruel experiment of nature." They offer the intriguing suggestion that the social experiences of the disabled child be exploited as an opportunity to test the universality of theories of development, including the relative influences of nature and nurture, in a unique type of cross-cultural research (p. 64):

It is conceivable that the handicapped child may provide the investigator with an opportunity to study groups of children who do not pose such profound cross-cultural problems because they belong to his own culture, yet who are subjected to an array of socialization experiences that are even more alien to the norms of an able-bodied American childhood than those of a child who grows up in a non-Western culture. Should this prove to be the case, the implications for constructing meaningful tests of theories of child development would be staggering. For years psychologists have rushed off to faraway places in the hope of testing the relative importance of nature and nurture, the universality of Piaget's stages of cognitive development, Kohlberg's stages of moral development, and various psychodynamic theories of emotional development. Is it possible that all this time the best groups of children with whom to explore these and other crucial developmental issues have been quite literally staring us in the face? Is it possible that the study of the handicapped child represents the best way to deepen our understanding of how all children grow up?

It is clear that new and creative frameworks are needed to deepen our understanding of how chronically ill and handicapped children grow up. Particularly for those whose impairments are highly visible, normative criteria for examining social interaction and the development of self-concept preclude nondeviant judgments. The increasing body of literature regarding successful coping and positive adaptation among many handicapped children and their families suggests the possibility that alternative pathways of development may be operative for the disabled population. Gliedman and Roth have made a valuable contribution in raising these issues and in planting the seeds for what may be the ultimate cross-cultural study.

AN AGENDA FOR FURTHER INVESTIGATION

The salience of physical health as a developmental issue in the middle childhood years is both trivial and central. School-age children are among the healthiest members of American society, and their physical well-being is generally assumed. It is ironic, however, that this apparently uneventful interval in the life cycle may be the most sensitive period for the development of many of the functional patterns that significantly influence health status during the adult years. Moreover, for children with chronic impairments, the impact of diminished physical health may exert a pervasive influence on the developmental process.

This chapter has provided an overview of current knowledge regarding a selection of physical health issues for school-age children. The preliminary nature of available data and the significant number of conceptual and informational gaps were noted earlier in this chapter. This final section proposes avenues for additional investigation and suggests how the matter of physical health can be studied in the context of development during middle childhood. Three integrating themes will be addressed—childhood perspectives on health and disease, the phenomena of vulnerability and resilience, and the challenges of health education.

The Child's View of Health and Illness

During the years from 6 to 12, cognitive maturation, the development of literacy skills, and a host of social experiences facilitate children's acquisition of knowledge and growing sophistication about the world in which they live. At the same time, and perhaps of more importance, the school-age child is developing a concept of himself or herself as an individual and a sense of how and where he or she fits within that world. The degree to which perceptions of personal well-being and physical integrity are consciously incorporated into one's developing construction of self and the extent to which that process is influenced by a variety of constitutional and environmental variables remain largely unexplored. Further elucidation of these issues will provide critical data needed to guide the evolution of a personal health care system in which cross-generational communication succeeds and school-age children are guided to function as independent consumers.

We know very little about what the concept of health means to a school-age child who has never experienced serious illness. We know even less about those variables that contribute to the individual differences in belief patterns that have been described in the limited studies conducted thus far. While some investigators have suggested that basic values and perceptions regarding health and illness are fairly uniform among Western cultures, others have highlighted the importance of subgroup differences related to a number of demographic variables (Gochman and Sheiham, 1978; Wright, 1982). Several observers have characterized health beliefs as highly resistant to modification; others have examined the potent influences of such agents of change as parents and television.

Perhaps the greatest limitation of our current knowledge of children's ideas about health is its static nature. Currently available data have almost all been collected cross-sectionally. Rather than further documentations of significant correlations between already established views of health and specific demographic or experiential variables, there is a compelling need for well-designed longitudinal studies that employ multivariate analytic techniques and that demonstrate the differential impact and interactional effects of clusters of variables at different points in time. Only then, when we are able to better describe the formation of health concepts and the way in which specific factors influence their unfolding and manifestations, will we be able to communicate effectively with school-age children about the relevance to their health of particular behaviors and life-style issues.

For children with acute illnesses or chronic diseases, the need for further research on their views of health and sickness has both immediate and long-term importance. Not only is the existing literature on the influences of chronic health impairment on development during middle childhood inconclusive and frequently contradictory, but it has also only begun to provide the data needed to promote the kind of direct communication with children that will facilitate optimal comprehensive care. Common problems such as passive acceptance and poor compliance regarding treatment are characteristic of many children with chronic illnesses. Explanations of the etiologies of symptoms, the rationale for specific therapeutic interventions, and the reasons for particular diagnostic studies or hospitalizations are some of the many critical areas of physician-patient communication that require developmentally appropriate conceptualizations that are just beginning to be described and that demand extensive further study. A facilitation of increasing personal responsibility and involvement in decision making is highly dependent on an understanding of the developmental progession of a chronically ill child's ideas about his or her disorder.

In summary, investigators have just begun to explore children's views of health and illness in a systematic and theoretically guided fashion. The current scarcity of such data reflects a pediatric clinical tradition of information sharing with parents and less effective communication with children (Pantell et al., 1982). Changing trends toward viewing children as more active and informed participants in their own medical care have stimulated demands for a better understanding of how their health-related concepts mature. Increasing interest in the conscious promotion of healthful lifestyles as early as possible has similarly emphasized the need for guidelines on how to talk effectively with young children. The recently demonstrated inability of pediatricians to correctly discriminate typical illness concepts at different ages in the middle childhood years (Perrin and Perrin, 1983) underlines the need for a genetic epistemology of health and disease concepts. Practically speaking, we can neither raise health-promoting consciousness nor comprehensively manage persistent illnesses in school-age children until we can learn to speak and understand their language.

The Enigma of Resilience and Vulnerability

Individual differences in susceptibility to physical as well as psychiatric disease have been acknowledged clinically for a long time, and attempts to elucidate the mechanisms for these differences have been undertaken by both biomedical and social scientists. A great deal of research, most of it oriented toward studies of animals and adults, has specifically looked at the biology of stress responses as a vehicle for understanding the phenomenon of differential vulnerability to illness. A brief review of current knowledge in this highly active area of biobehavioral research, some of which was described earlier in this chapter, suggests a number of possible applications to the study of health in school-age children. The fact that stress has been implicated as a risk factor for a large number of physical diseases is well established for both adults and children (Elliot and Eisdorfer, 1982; Heisel et al., 1973; Meyer and Haggerty, 1962; Rahe and Arthur, 1978). The details of how certain stressors contribute to specific pathologies in a given individual, however, are far from being elucidated (Hamburg et al., 1982). Genetically determined variations in catecholamine or corticosteroid metabolism or neuroregulator activity in the brain, for example, might very well play a major role in individual differences in susceptibility to particular diseases (Vogel and Motulsky, 1979). Such differences could be mediated through differential perceptions of external or internal stimuli, variations in the responses of end organs to hormonal influences, or the actual nature of the hormones released (Hamburg et al., 1982). Correlations between stressors and pathology, however, almost never reflect simple cause-effect relationships. Rather, they are related to complex interactions among a variety of environmental influences and constitutional factors that mediate individual physiological responses to stress. Hamburg et al. (1982) noted that "the relations doubtless will be difficult to disentangle, but the problems are too important and the prospects too promising to justify neglect" (p. 74).

The assertion that individual variation in resistance to illness undoubtedly has a biological basis does not diminish the significance of environmental contributions to the pathogenesis of much organic morbidity, particularly in relation to socioeconomic variables. Poor children miss more school days because of illness and are hospitalized more frequently and for longer durations than other children (Egbuonu and Starfield, 1982). Children who live in crowded substandard housing have greater exposure to infectious diseases.

Black children ages 5–14 have higher mortality rates than their white peers and are 24 percent more likely to die in accidents. In 1976, 76 percent of white children were immunized against measles compared with 61 percent of nonwhites. Data collected from 1971 to 1974 revealed unfilled, decayed teeth in 42 percent of black children ages 6–11, in contrast to a rate of 29 percent among whites (Select Panel for the Promotion of Child Health, 1981). Many biological risk factors for mild mental retardation, such as malnutrition and increased body lead burden, are more prevalent in lower socioeconomic classes (Shonkoff, 1982).

For those interested in the nature-nurture dynamics of resilience and vulnerability regarding illness or disability in school-age children, efforts might be directed toward the elucidation of psychosocial protective factors that appear to facilitate more adaptive responses to stress. Recent studies suggest that social supports, such as a caring family and friends, provide a critical buffer against stressful experiences, perhaps by promoting effective coping strategies that help individuals defuse stressful stimuli and restore the state of physiological balance needed to maintain good health (Cobb, 1976; Haggerty, 1980; Rutter, 1981; Werner and Smith, 1982). Relations among life stresses, the availability of support systems, socioeconomic group differences in disease prevalence rates, and long-term health issues are particularly worthy of further investigation in this regard.

More careful study of potential stress reducers, their distribution in population groups, and their interactions with individual characteristics of children and environmental variables should lead to a richer understanding of the phenomena of resilience and vulnerability. The benefits and growth-promoting aspects of stress also demand critical analysis. The middle childhood period offers an extensive array of issues around which such investigations could be organized. A great deal remains to be learned about the relationships among stresses, such as family disruption or reorganization and school pressures regarding individual achievement, and health disturbances, such as persistent somatic complaints (e.g., headaches, recurrent abdominal pain) and psychosomatic disorders (e.g., asthma, chronic inflammatory bowel disease). Stresses accompanying important social changes in the family, school, and peer context are discussed extensively in several chapters of this volume. Studies of their impact on the physical health of school-age children will considerably expand our knowledge of human adaptation.

Whither Health Education?

The need for effective health education for school-age children is universally accepted. Successful efforts require prior consideration of a variety of issues, including precise definition of goals and objectives, specific identification of target groups, choice of dissemination modes, and design and implementation of strategies for evaluation. Most health education activities have not addressed all these concerns in a systematic manner.

Perhaps the most important issue from the perspective of basic research on school-age children is related to the need for reliable outcome data. Although the possibility of affecting health-related behavior in adult populations has been demonstrated (Maccoby et al., 1977; Puska, 1973), the efficacy of most childhood health education regarding behavior change has been disappointing (Berberian, 1976; Iammarino, 1980; Levy, 1980). Bartlett (1981:1387) noted:

Evaluation studies of even the best developed school health education curricula generally reveal that these programs are very successful in increasing knowledge, somewhat successful in improving attitudes, and infrequently successful in facilitating life-style changes. The effects of school health education on such pupil outcomes as decision-making and social interaction abilities have seldom, if ever, been measured. Additionally, limited evidence suggests the possibility that school health education programs are more likely to achieve significant improvement in health behaviors when they are directed toward diseases with high perceived susceptibility and severity, and/or include high involvement of students and parents.

A recently reported pilot test of a family-oriented cardiovascular risk reduction program based on social learning theory offers a promising model of a controlled, systematically evaluated behavioral intervention for families with school-age children (Nader et al., 1983). Preliminary data demonstrating significant differences in reported dietary choices support the need for further efforts to both implement and carefully measure such educational efforts.

The agenda for evaluating health education programs is a full one. Data are needed to identify "the tasks that are appropriate for learning about wellness at various points along the developmental continuum and those tasks that will enhance an individual's motivation to work toward wellness" (Ng et al., 1981:50). The likelihood that alternative formats and strategies will be variably effective at different ages demands a developmental approach to the establishment of goals and process and outcome measures. The fact that knowledge alone does not ensure appropriate behavior suggests that the conceptualization of health education in the school years must move beyond the domains of cognitive and educational psychology and into the realms of social psychology, anthropology, and sociology.

SUMMARY

Physical health in middle childhood is intimately related to interactions among a child's biological function, socioeconomic environment, and the evolution of his or her personal life-style. As such, it is determined by physiological mechanisms as well as the imperatives of the ecocultural niche. The importance of this interplay among constitutional, genetic, and psychosocial influences is equally critical for both the maintenance of well-being and the natural history of illness or disability.

In short, an understanding of health requires an understanding of the way people live. As it relates to adaptation and function, health can be viewed as a lens through which biological integrity and the negotiation of developmental tasks can be analyzed throughout the life cycle.

Middle childhood embodies a particularly rich host of transitions. From the perspective of traditional health care delivery needs, this period is relatively uneventful. As a stage of human development, however, the school-age years are rich in health-related issues. As our concepts of health and illness are broadened, the heretofore neglected years from 6 to 12 emerge as fertile ground for expanded basic research.

REFERENCES

Adams, J.
  1965   Little League shoulder: Osteochondrosis of the proximal humeral epiphysis in boy baseball pitchers. *California Medicine* 105:22.
Adams, R., Kocsis, J., and Estes, R.
  1974   Soft neurological signs in learning-disabled children and controls. *American Journal of Diseases of Children* 128:614–618.
Allegrante, J., O'Rourke, T., and Tuncalp, S.
  1977   A multivariate analysis of selected psychosocial variables on the development of subsequent youth smoking behavior. *Journal of Drug Education* 7:237–248.
American Academy of Pediatrics, Committee on the Pediatric Aspects of Physical Fitness, Recreation and Sports
  1975   Participation in sports by girls. *Pediatrics* 55:563.
Aply, J., Barbour, R., and Westmacott, I.
  1967   Impact of congenital heart disease on the family: Preliminary report. *British Medical Journal* 1:103.
Apple, D., and Cantwell, J.
  1979   *Medicine for Sport.* Chicago: Year Book Medical Publishers, Inc.
Banks, M., Bewley, B., Bland, J., Dean, J., and Pollard, V.
  1978   Long-term study of smoking by secondary school children. *Archives of Disease in Childhood* 53:12–19.
Barcus, F.
  1975   *Weekend Commercial Children's Television—1975.* Newtonville, Mass.: Action for Children's Television.
Barlow, C.
  1974   "Soft signs" in children with learning disorders. *American Journal of Diseases of Children* 128:605–606.
Bartlett, E.
  1981   The contribution of school health education to community health promotion: What can we reasonably expect? *American Journal of Public Health* 71:1384–1391.
Bedell, J., Giordani, B., Amour, J., Tavormina, J., and Boll, T.
  1977   Life stress and the psychological and medical adjustment of chronically ill children. *Journal of Psychosomatic Research* 21:237.
Beecher, H.
  1956   Relationship of the significance of wound to the pain experienced. *Journal of the American Medical Association* 161:1609–1613.
Benson R., and Migeon, C.
  1975   Physiological and pathological puberty, and human behavior. In B. Eleftheriou and R. Sprott, eds., *Hormonal Correlates of Behavior.* Vol. 1. New York: Plenum Press.

Berberian, R.
1976   The effectiveness of drug education programs: A critical review. *Health Education Monographs* 4:377–398.
Berenson, G., Frank, G., Hunter, S., Srinivasan, S., Voors, A., and Webber, L.
1982   Cardiovascular risk factors in children: Should they concern the pediatrician? *American Journal of Diseases of Children* 136:855–862.
Berey, L., and Pollay, R.
1968   The influencing role of the child in family decision making. *Journal of Marketing Research* 5:70.
Beverly, B.
1936   Effect of illness on emotional development. *Journal of Pediatrics* 8:533–543.
Bibace, R., and Walsh, M.
1980   Development of children's concepts of illness. *Pediatrics* 66:912–917.
1981   Children's conceptions of illness. In R. Bibace and M. Walsh, eds., *New Directions for Child Development: Children's Conceptions of Health, Illness, Bodily Functions*. No. 14. San Francisco: Jossey-Bass.
Bland, J., Bewley, B., Banks, M., and Pollard, V.
1975   Schoolchildren's beliefs about smoking and disease. *Health Education Journal* 34:71–78.
Blaney, N.
1981   Cigarette smoking in children and young adolescents: Causes and prevention. *Advances in Behavioral Pediatrics*. Vol. 2. Greenwich, Conn.: JAI Press.
Blatt, J., Spencer, L., and Ward, S.
1972   A cognitive developmental study of children's reactions to television advertising. In E. Rubinstein, G. Comstock, and J. Murray, eds., *Television and Social Behavior*. Vol. 4. *Television in Day to Day Life: Patterns of Use*. Washington, D.C.: U.S. Government Printing Office.
Boles, G.
1959   Personality factors in mothers of cerebral palsy children. *Genetic Psychology Monographs* 59:159.
Breslau, N., Weitzman, M., and Messenger, K.
1981   Psychologic functioning of siblings of disabled children. *Pediatrics* 67:344–353.
Brewster, A.
1982   Chronically ill hospitalized children's concepts of their illness. *Pediatrics* 69:355–362.
Brodie, B.
1974   Views of healthy children toward illness. *American Journal of Public Health* 64:1156–1159.
Bubenik, G., and Brown, G.
1973   Morphologic sex differences in primate brain areas involved in regulation of reproductive activity. *Experientia* 29:619.
Bureau of the Census
1982   Current Population Reports, P-23, No. 114, *Characteristics of American Children and Youth: 1980*. Washington, D.C.: U.S. Department of Commerce. Available from the U.S. Government Printing Office.
Bynner, J.
1970   Behavioral research into children's smoking. Some implications for anti-smoking strategy. *Royal Society of Health Journal* 90:159–163.
Caldwell, B., and Guze, S.
1960   A study of the adjustment of parents and siblings of institutionalized and non-institutionalized retarded children. *American Journal of Mental Deficiency* 64:845.

Campbell, J.
  1975   Illness is a point of view: The development of children's concepts of illness. *Child Development* 46:92–100.
  1978   The child in the sick role: Contributions of age, sex, parental status, and parental values. *Journal of Health and Social Behavior* 19:35–51.
Charney, E., Goodman, H., and McBride, M.
  1976   Childhood antecedents of adult obesity—Do chubby infants become obese adults? *New England Journal of Medicine* 295:6.
Chowdhury, A., Huffman, S., and Curlin, G.
  1978   Malnutrition, menarche, and marriage in rural Bangladesh. *Social Biology* 24:316–325.
Clausen, J.
  1975   The social meaning of differential physical and sexual maturation. In S. Dragstin and G. Elder, eds., *Adolescence in the Life Cycle*. New York: Halsted.
Cobb, S.
  1976   Social support as a moderator of life stress. *Psychosomatic Medicine* 38:300–314.
Constitution of the World Health Organization
  1958   In *The First Ten Years of the WHO*. Geneva: Palais des Nations.
Dawber, T.
  1980   *The Framingham Study: Epidemiology of Atherosclerotic Disease*. Cambridge, Mass.: Harvard University Press.
Denny, F.
  1982   Defined diets and childhood hyperactivity: Consensus conference. *Journal of the American Medical Association* 248:290–292.
Downey, A., and O'Rourke, T.
  1976   The utilization of attitudes and beliefs as indicators of future smoking behavior. *Journal of Drug Education* 6:283–295.
Dubos, R.
  1965   *Man Adapting*. New Haven, Conn.: Yale University Press.
  1968   *Medicine, Man and Environment*. New York: Praeger Publishers.
Duke, P., Carlsmith, J., Jennings, D., Martin, J., Dornbusch, S., Gross, R., and Siegel-Gorelick, B.
  1982   Educational correlates of early and late sexual maturation in adolescence. *Journal of Pediatrics* 100:633–637.
Edwards, D., and Rowe, F.
  1975   Neural and endocrine control of aggressive behavior. In B. Eleftheriou and R. Sprott, eds., *Hormonal Correlates of Behavior*. New York: Plenum Press.
Egbuonu, L., and Starfield, B.
  1982   Child health and social status. *Pediatrics* 69:550–557.
Ehrhardt, A.
  1975   Prenatal hormonal exposure and psychosexual differentiation. In E. Sachar, ed., *Topics in Psychoendocrinology*. New York: Grune & Stratton.
Eisenberg, L.
  1976   Medical ecology: The epidemiology of handicap. *Birth Defects: Original Article Series* 12(4):181–188.
  1977   Disease and Illness. *Culture, Medicine, and Psychiatry* 1:9–23.
Elliott, G., and Eisdorfer, C.
  1982   *Stress and Human Health*. New York: Springer.
Engel, G.
  1977   The need for a new medical model: A challenge for biomedicine. *Science* 196:129–135.
  1979   The biomedical model: A Procrustean bed? *Man and Medicine* 4(4):257–275.

Evans, R., Henderson, A., Hill, P., and Raines, B.
1979   Smoking in children and adolescents: Psychosocial determinants and prevention strategies. In *Smoking and Health: A Report of the Surgeon General.* Available from the U.S. Government Printing Office. DHEW Publication No. (PHS) 79-50066. Washington, D.C.: U.S. Department of Health, Education, and Welfare.

Fabrega, H.
1972   The study of disease in relation to culture. *Behavioral Science* 17:183–203.
1974   *Disease and Social Behavior.* Cambridge, Mass.: MIT Press.

Flickinger, G.
1966   Response of the testes to social interaction among grouped chickens. *General and Comparative Endocrinology* 6:89.

Fraiberg, S.
1977   *Insights From the Blind.* New York: Basic Books.

Frankenhaeuser, M., and Johansson, G.
1975   Behavior and catecholamines in children. In L. Levi, ed., *Society, Stress and Disease.* Vol. 2. *Childhood and Adolescence.* London: Oxford University Press.

Freud, A.
1952   The role of bodily illness in the mental life of children. In P. Eissler, ed., *Psychoanalytic Study of the Child.* New York: International Universities Press.

Frisch, R., Wyshak, G., and Vincent, L.
1980   Delayed menarche and amenorrhea in ballet dancers. *New England Journal of Medicine* 303:17–19.

Gayton, W., Friedman, S., Tavormina, J., and Tucker, F.
1977   Children with cystic fibrosis: I. Psychological test findings of patients, siblings, and parents. *Pediatrics* 59:888–894.

Geller, E., Ritvo, E., Freeman, B., and Yuwiler, A.
1982   Preliminary observations on the effect of fenfluramine on blood serotonin and symptoms in three autistic boys. *New England Journal of Medicine* 307:165–169.

Gilliam, T., and Burke, M.
1978   Effects of exercise on serum lipids and lipoproteins in girls, ages 8 to 10 years. *Artery* 4:203.

Gilligan, C.
1979   Woman's place in man's life cycle. *Harvard Education Review* 49(4).

Gliedman, J., and Roth, W.
1980   *The Unexpected Minority: Handicapped Children in American Society.* New York: Harcourt Brace Jovanovich.

Glomset, J.
1980   High-density lipoproteins in human health and disease. *Advances in Internal Medicine* 25:91.

Gochman, D.
1971   Some correlates of children's health beliefs and potential health behavior. *Journal of Health and Social Behavior* 12:148–154.

Gochman, D., and Sheiham, A.
1978   Cross national consistency in children's beliefs about vulnerability. *International Journal of Health Education* 21(3):189–193.

Goldberg, B., Veras, G., and Nicholas, J.
1978   Sports medicine: Pediatric perspective. *New York State Journal of Medicine* 78:1406.

Green, D.
1979   Youth education. In *Smoking and Health: A Report of the Surgeon General.* DHEW Publication No. (PHS) 79-50066. Washington, D.C.: U.S. Government Printing Office.

Haggerty, R.
1980   Life stress, illness and social supports. *Developmental Medicine and Child Neurology* 22:391–400.
Hamburg, D., Elliott, G., and Parron, D., eds.
1982   *Health and Behavior: Frontiers of Research in the Biobehavioral Sciences.* Report of a study from the Institute of Medicine. Washington, D.C.: National Academy Press.
Hamilton, P., and Andrew, G.
1976   Influence of growth and athletic training on heart and lung functions. *European Journal of Applied Physiology* 36:27.
Heisel, J., Ream, S., Raitz, R., Rappaport, M., and Coddington, R.
1973   The significance of life events as contributing factors in the diseases of children. III. A study of pediatric patients. *Journal of Pediatrics* 83:119–123.
Hennessy, J., and Levine, S.
1979   Stress, arousal, and the pituitary-adrenal system: A psychoendocrine hypothesis. In J. Srague and A. Epstein, eds., *Progress in Psychobiology and Physiological Psychology.* New York: Academic Press.
Hewett, S., Newson, J., and Newson, E.
1970   *The Family and the Handicapped Child.* Chicago: Aldine.
Hier, D., and Crowley, W.
1982   Spatial ability in androgen-deficient men. *New England Journal of Medicine* 306:1202–1205.
Hobbs, N., Perrin, J., and Ireys, H.
1983   *Summary of Findings and Recommendations. Public Policies Affecting Chronically Ill Children and Their Families.* Nashville: Center for the Study of Families and Children, Institute for Public Policy Studies, Vanderbilt University.
Holt, K.
1958   The influence of a retarded child upon family limitation. *Journal of Mental Deficiency Research* 2:28.
Hovell, M., Bursick, J., and Sharkey, R.
1978   An evaluation of elementary students' voluntary physical activity during recess. *Research Quarterly of the American Association of Health and Physical Education* 49:460.
Hubel, D., Wiesel, T., and LeVay, S.
1977   Plasticity of oculardominance columns in monkey striate cortex. *Philosophical Transactions of the Royal Society of London* 278:411.
Hughes, L., and Bontemps, A.
1958   *The Book of Negro Folklore.* New York: Dodd, Mead.
Hunt, G.
1973   Implications of the treatment of myelomeningocele for the child and his family. *Lancet* 2:1308.
Iammarino, N.
1980   The state of school heart health education: A review of the literature. *Health Education Quarterly* 7:298–320.
Johnston, M., and Singer, H.
1982   Brain neurotransmitters and neuromodulators in pediatrics. *Pediatrics* 70:57–68.
Jones, M., Bayley, N. and Macfarlane, J., eds.
1971   *The Course of Human Development.* Toronto: John Wiley & Sons.
Kagan, J.
1982   The idea of spatial ability. *New England Journal of Medicine* 306:1225–1227 (Editorial).
Kleinman, A., Eisenberg, L., and Good, B.
1978   Culture, illness, and care—Clinical lessons from anthropologic and cross-cultural research. *Annals of Internal Medicine* 88:251–258.

Klima, E., and Bellugi, V.
1979   *The Signs of Language.* Cambridge, Mass.: Harvard University Press.
Kling, A.
1975   Testosterone and aggressive behavior in man and non-human primates. In B. Eleftheriou and R. Sprott, eds., *Hormonal Correlates of Behavior.* New York: Plenum Press.
Koos, E.
1954   *The Health of Regionville.* New York: Columbia University Press.
Labov, W.
1972   *Language in the Inner City: Studies in the Black English Vernacular.* Philadelphia: University of Pennsylvania Press.
Lambert, W., Johansson, G., Frankenhaeuser, M., and Klachenberg-Larsson, I.
1969   Catecholamine excretion in young children and their parents as related to behavior. *Scandinavian Journal of Psychology* 10:306–318.
Lanese, R., Banks, R., and Keller, M.
1972   Smoking behavior in a teenage population: A multivariate conceptual approach. *American Journal of Public Health* 62:807–813.
Langford, W.
1948   Physical illness and convalescence: Their meaning to the child. *Journal of Pediatrics* 33:242–250.
Laoye, J., Creswell, W., and Stone, D.
1972   A cohort study of 1,205 secondary school students. *Journal of School Health* 42:47–52.
Lavigne, J., and Ryan, M.
1979   Psychologic adjustment of siblings of children with chronic illness. *Pediatrics* 63:616–627.
Levitt, E., and Edwards, J.
1970   A multivariate study of correlative factors in youthful smoking. *Developmental Psychology* 2:5–11.
Levy, R.
1979   Testimony before the Subcommittee on Nutrition of the Committee on Agriculture, Nutrition, and Forestry, United States Senate, 96th Congress, May 22.
Levy, S.
1980   Nutrition-education research: An interdisciplinary evaluation and review. *Health Education Quarterly* 7:107–126.
Lewis, A.
1953   Health as a social concept. *British Journal of Sociology* 2:109–124.
Lewis, C., and Lewis, M.
1974   The impact of television commercials on health-related beliefs and behaviors of children. *Pediatrics* 53:431–435.
Lewis, D., and Freeman, J.
1977   The electroencephalogram in pediatric practice: Its use and abuse. *Pediatrics* 60:324–330.
Lloyd, J.
1971   Weights of testes, thymi, and accessory reproductive glands in relation to rank in paired and grouped house mice. *Proceedings of the Royal Society of Experimental Biology and Medicine* 137:19.
1975   Social behavior and hormones. In B. Eleftheriou and R. Sprott, eds., *Hormonal Correlates of Behavior.* New York: Plenum Press.
Lowenberg, M.
1977   The development of food patterns in young children. In P. Pipes, ed., *Nutrition in Infancy and Childhood.* Saint Louis: C.V. Mosby.

Lynn, D., Glaser H., and Harrison, G.
   1962   Comprehensive medical care for handicapped children: III. Concepts of illness in children with rheumatic fever. *American Journal of Diseases of Children* 103:42–50.
Maccoby, E., and Jacklin, C.
   1974   *The Psychology of Sex Differences.* Stanford, Calif.: Stanford University Press.
Maccoby, N., Farquhar, J., Wood, P., and Alexander, J.
   1977   Reducing the risk of cardiovascular disease: Effects of a community-based campaign on knowledge and behavior. *Journal of Community Health* 3:100–114.
Marcus, L.
   1977   Patterns of coping in families of psychotic children. *American Journal of Orthopsychiatry* 47:388–395.
Mattson, A.
   1972   Long-term physical illness in childhood: A challenge to psychosocial adaptation. *Pediatrics* 50:801–811.
Mattson, A., and Gross, S.
   1966   Social and behavioral studies on hemophiliac children and their families. *Journal of Pediatrics* 68:952.
Mayer, J.
   1975   Obesity during childhood. In M. Winick, ed., *Childhood Obesity.* New York: John Wiley & Sons.
McAlister, A., Perry, C., Killen, J., Slinkard, L., and Maccoby, N.
   1980   Pilot study of smoking, alcohol and drug abuse prevention. *American Journal of Public Health* 70:719–721.
McAlister, A., Perry, C., and Maccoby, N.
   1979   Adolescent smoking: Onset and prevention. *Pediatrics* 63:650–658.
McAnarney, E., Pless, I.B., Satterwhite, B., and Friedman, S.
   1974   Psychological problems of children with chronic juvenile arthritis. *Pediatrics* 53:523–528.
McNeal, J.
   1969   An exploratory study of consumer behavior of children. In J. McNeal, ed., *Dimensions of Commercial Behavior.* New York: Appleton-Century-Crofts.
Mechanic, D.
   1964   The influence of mothers on their children's health attitudes and behavior. *Pediatrics* 39:444–453.
   1972   Social psychologic factors affecting the presentation of bodily complaints. *New England Journal of Medicine* 286:1132–1139.
   1978   *Medical Sociology.* Second edition. New York: Free Press.
Merritt, R.
   1982   Obesity. *Current Problems in Pediatrics* 12(11).
Meyer, R., and Haggerty, R.
   1962   Streptococcal infections in families: Factors altering individual susceptibility. *Pediatrics* 29:539.
Micheli, L., and Smith, A.
   1982   Sports injuries in children. *Current Problems in Pediatrics* 12(9).
Money, J.
   1973   Effects of prenatal androgenization and deandrogenization on behavior in human beings. In W. Ganong and L. Martini, eds., *Frontiers in Neuroendocrinology.* New York: Oxford University Press.
Murphy, M.
   1982   The family with a handicapped child: A review of the literature. *Journal of Developmental and Behavioral Pediatrics* 3(2):73–81.

Nader, P., Baranowski, T., Vanderpool, N., Dunn, K., Dworkin, R., and Ray, L.
1983 The Family Health Project: Cardiovascular risk reduction education for children and parents. *Journal of Developmental and Behavioral Pediatrics* 4:3–10.
Nagy, M.
1951 Children's ideas on the origin of illness. *Health Education Journal* 9:6.
Natapoff, J.
1978 Children's views of health: A developmental study. *American Journal of Public Health* 68:995–1000.
Nathan, S.
1973 Body image in chronically obese children as reflected in figure drawings. *Journal of Personality Assessment* 37:456–462.
National Heart, Lung, and Blood Institute
1981 *Arteriosclerosis, 1981*. DHHS Publication No. (NIH) 81-2034. Washington, D.C.: U.S. Department of Health, Education, and Welfare. Available from the U.S. Government Printing Office.
National Science Foundation
1977 *Research on the Effects of Television Advertising in Children: A Review of the Literature and Recommendations for Future Research*. Washington, D.C.: National Science Foundation.
Needleman, H., Gunnoe, C., Leviton, A., Reed, R., Peresie, H., Maher, C., and Barrett, P.
1979 Deficits in psychologic and classroom performance of children with elevated dentine lead levels. *New England Journal of Medicine* 300:689–695.
Neuhauser, C., Amsterdam, B., Hines, P., and Steward, M.
1978 Children's concepts of healing: Cognitive development and locus of control factors. *American Journal of Orthopsychiatry* 48:335–341.
Ng, L., Davis, D., Manderscheid, R., and Elkes, J.
1981 Toward a conceptual formulation of health and well being. In L. Eng and D. David, eds., *Strategies for Public Health*. New York: Van Nostrand Reinhold.
Olweus, D., Mattson, A., Schalling, D., and Low, H.
1980 Testosterone, aggression, physical, and personality dimensions in normal adolescent males. *Psychosomatic Medicine* 42:253–269.
Owen, G., and Lippman, G.
1977 Nutritional status of infants and young children: U.S.A. *Pediatric Clinics of North America* 24(1):211–227.
Paffenbarger, R., and Hyde, R.
1980 Exercise as protection against heart attack. *New England Journal of Medicine* 302:1026.
Page, L., and Friend, B.
1978 The changing United States diet. *BioScience* 28:192–197.
Pantell, R., Stewart, T., Dias, J., Wells, P., and Ross, W.
1982 Physician communication with children and parents. *Pediatrics* 70:396–401.
Parsons, T.
1972 Definitions of health and illness in the light of American values and social structure. In E. Jaco, ed., *Patients, Physicians, and Illness*. Second edition. New York: Free Press.
Pate, R., and Blair, S.
1978 Exercise and the prevention of atherosclerosis: Pediatric implications. In W. Strong, ed., *Atherosclerosis: Its Pediatric Aspects*. New York: Grune & Stratton.
Perrin, E., and Gerrity, P.
1981 There's a demon in your belly: Children's understanding of illness. *Pediatrics* 67:841–849.
Perrin, E., and Perrin, J.
1983 Clinicians' assessments of children's understanding of illness. *American Journal of Diseases of Children* 137:874–878.

Pless, I.B., and Douglas, M.
  1971   Chronic illness in childhood: Part I. Epidemiological and clinical characteristics. *Pediatrics* 47:405–414.
Pless, I.B., and Pinkerton, P.
  1975   *Chronic Childhood Disorder: Promoting Patterns of Adjustment.* London: Henry Klimpton Publishers.
Pless, I.B., and Roghmann, K.
  1971   Chronic illness and its consequences: Observations based on three epidemiologic surveys. *Journal of Pediatrics* 79:351–359.
President's Council on Physical Fitness and Sports
  1977   *The Physically Underdeveloped Child.* Washington, D.C.: U.S. Government Printing Office.
Primeaux, M.
  1977   American Indian health care practices: A cross-cultural perspective. *Nursing Clinics of North America* 12:57.
Prugh, D., Staub, E., Sands, H., Kirschbaum, R., and Lenihan, E.
  1953   A study of the emotional reactions of children and families to hospitalization and illness. *American Journal of Orthopsychiatry* 23:70–106.
Puska, P.
  1973   The North Karelia project: An attempt at community prevention of cardiovascular disease. *World Health Organization Chronicle* 27:55–58.
Radius, S., Dielman, T., Becker, M., Rosenstock, I., and Horvath, W.
  1980   Health beliefs of the school-aged child and their relationship to risk taking behaviors. *International Journal of Health Education* 23(4):227–235.
Rahe, R., and Arthur, R.
  1978   Life change and illness studies: Past history and future directions. *Journal of Human Stress* 4:3–15.
Raisman, G., and Field, P.
  1971   Sexual dimorphism in the preoptic area of the rat. *Science* 173:731.
Rapoport, J., Buchsbaum, M., Zahn, T., Weingartner, H., Ludlow, C., and Mikkelsen, E.
  1978   Dextroamphetamine: Cognitive and behavioral effects in normal prepubertal boys. *Science* 199:560–562.
Rizek, R., and Jackson, E.
  1980   *Current Food Consumption Practices and Nutrient Sources in the American Diet.* Hyattsville, Md.: Consumer Nutrition Center, Human Nutrition Science and Education Administration, U.S. Department of Agriculture.
Rose, R.
  1980   Endocrine responses to stressful psychological events. *Psychiatric Clinics of North America* 3:251–276.
Rose, R., Holaday, J., and Bernstein, I.
  1971   Plasma testosterone, dominance rank and aggressive behavior in rhesus monkeys. *Nature* 231:366.
Rowland, T.
  1981   Physical fitness in children: Implications for the prevention of coronary artery disease. *Current Problems in Pediatrics* (9).
Rutter, M.
  1981   Stress, coping and development: Some issues and some questions. *Journal of Child Psychology and Psychiatry* 22:323–356.
Schain, R., and Freedman, D.
  1961   Studies on 5-hydroxyindole metabolism in autistic and other mentally retarded children. *Journal of Pediatrics* 58:315–320.

Schneider, F., and Vanmastrigt, L.
1974 Adolescent–pre-adolescent differences in beliefs and attitudes about cigarette smoking. *Journal of Psychology* 87:71–81.

Select Panel for the Promotion of Child Health
1981 *Better Health for Our Children: A National Strategy.* DHHS (PHS) Publication No. 79-55071. Washington, D.C.: U.S. Department of Health and Human Services.

Shaywitz, B., Yager, R., and Klopper, J.
1976 Selective brain dopamine depletion in developing rats: An experimental model of minimal brain dysfunction. *Science* 191:305.

Shonkoff, J.
1982 Biological and social factors contributing to mild mental retardation. In K. Heller, W. Holtzman, and S. Messick, eds., *Placing Children in Special Education: A Strategy for Equity.* Panel on Selection and Placement of Students in Programs for the Mentally Retarded, Committee on Child Development and Public Policy, National Research Council. Washington, D.C.: National Academy Press.

Sinclair, D.
1978 *Human Growth After Birth.* Third edition. London: Oxford University Press.

Smith, D.
1977 *Growth and Its Disorders.* Philadelphia: W.B. Saunders.

Sowers, J., ed.
1980 *Hypothalamic Hormones.* Stroudsburg, Pa.: Dowden, Hutchinson and Ross.

Spector, R.
1979 *Cultural Diversity in Health and Illness.* New York: Appleton-Century-Crofts.

Sperling, E.
1978 Psychological issues in chronic illness and handicap. In E. Gellert, ed., *Psychosocial Aspects of Pediatric Care.* New York: Grune & Stratton.

Stamler, J.
1978 Introduction to risk factors in coronary artery disease. In H. McIntosh, ed., *Baylor College of Medicine Cardiology Series* (3). Northfield: Medical Communications.

Stein, R., and Riessman, C.
1980 The development of an impact-on-family scale: Preliminary findings. *Medical Care* 18:465–472.

Stoeckle, J., Zola, I., and Davidson, G.
1964 The quantity and significance of psychological distress in medical patients. *Journal of Chronic Disease* 17:959–970.

Task Force on Pediatric Education
1978 *The Future of Pediatric Education.* Evanston, Ill.: American Academy of Pediatrics.

Telch, M., Killen, J., McAlister, A., Perry, C., and Maccoby, N.
1982 Long-term follow-up of a pilot project on smoking prevention with adolescents. *Journal of Behavioral Medicine* 5:1–8.

Tew, B., and Laurence, K.
1973 Mothers, brothers, and sisters of patients with spina bifida. *Developmental Medicine and Child Neurology* 15 (Suppl. 29):69–76.

Thomas, G., Lee, P., Franks, P., and Paffenbarger, R., eds.
1981 *Exercise and Health: The Evidence and the Implications.* Cambridge, Eng.: Oelgeschlager, Gunn, and Hain.

Touwen, B.
1972 Laterality and dominance. *Developmental Medicine and Child Neurology* 14:747–755.

Turk, J.
1964 Impact of cystic fibrosis on family functioning. *Pediatrics* 34:67.

U.S. Public Health Service
1979   Smoking and Health: A Report of the Surgeon General. DHEW Publication No. (PHS) 79-
        50066. Washington, D.C.: U.S. Department of Health, Education, and Welfare. Avail-
        able from the U.S. Government Printing Office.
Usdin, E., Kvetnansky, R., and Kopin, I., eds.
1980   Catecholamines and Stress: Recent Advances. New York: Elsevier/North Holland.
Vance, J., Fazan, L., Satterwhite, B., and Pless, I.B.
1980   Effects of nephrotic syndrome on the family: A controlled study. Pediatrics 65:948–955.
Van Itallie, T.
1979   Obesity: Adverse effects on health and longevity. American Journal of Clinical Nutrition
        32:2723–2733.
Vogel, F., and Motulsky, A.
1979   Human Genetics: Problems and Approaches. Berlin: Springer-Verlag.
Wagner, H.
1980   Nuclear imaging: New developments. Hospital Practice 15:117.
Wallnofer, H., and Von Rottauscher, A.
1972   Chinese Folk Medicine. New York: American Library.
Ward, S., Levinson, D., and Wackman, D.
1972   Children's attention to television commercials. In E. Rubinstein, G. Comstock, and J.
        Murray, eds., Television and Social Behavior. Vol. 4. Television in Day-to-Day Life:
        Patterns of Use. Washington, D.C.: U.S. Government Printing Office.
Warren, M.
1980   The effects of exercise on pubertal progression and reproductive function in girls. Journal
        of Clinical Endocrinology and Metabolism 51:1150.
Webb, T., and Oski, F.
1973   Iron deficiency anemia and scholastic achievement in young adolescents. Journal of
        Pediatrics 82:827–830.
Weil, W.
1981   Obesity in children. Pediatrics in Review 3:180–189.
Weisenberg, M., Kegeles, S., and Lund, A.
1980   Children's health beliefs and acceptance of a dental preventive activity. Journal of Health
        and Social Behavior 21:59–74.
Weiss, P.
1967   1 + 2 = 2: When one plus one does not equal two. In G. Quarton, T. Melnechuk,
        and F. Schmidt, eds., The Neurosciences: A Study Program. New York: Rockefeller Uni-
        versity Press.
Wellman, H., and Johnson, C.
1982   Children's understanding of food and its functions: A preliminary study of the devel-
        opment of concepts of nutrition. Journal of Applied Developmental Psychology 3:135–148.
Wender, P.
1971   Minimal Brain Dysfunction in Children. New York: Wiley Interscience.
Werner, E., and Smith, R.
1982   Vulnerable But Invincible—A Study of Resilient Children. New York: McGraw-Hill.
Wright, E.
1982   Children's perceptions of vulnerability to illness and dental disease. Community Dentistry
        and Oral Epidemiology (10)1:29–32.
Wyshak, G., and Frisch, R.
1982   Evidence for a secular trend in age of menarche. New England Journal of Medicine 306:1033–
        1035.
Yankelovich, D.
1970   Mothers' Attitudes Toward Children's Programs and Commercials. Newton Center, Mass.:
        Action for Children's Television.

Zborowski, M.
   1952   Cultural components in responses to pain. *Journal of Social Issues* 8:16–30.
Zola, I.
   1966   Culture and symptoms: an analysis of patients' presenting complaints. *American Sociological Review* 31:615–630.

CHAPTER 3

Cognitive Development in School-Age Children: Conclusions and New Directions

Kurt W. Fischer and Daniel Bullock

W hat is the nature of children's knowledge? How does their knowledge change with development? In pursuing these fundamental questions in the study of cognitive development, researchers often expand their focus to include a range of children's behaviors extending far beyond the standard meaning of knowledge.

In the two primary cognitive-developmental traditions, the questions typically take different forms. In the structuralist tradition, influenced strongly by the work of Jean Piaget, Heinz Werner, and others, the questions are: How is behavior organized, and how does the organization change with development? In the functionalist tradition, influenced strongly by behaviorism and information processing, the question is: What are the processes that produce or underlie behavioral change? In this chapter we review major conclusions from both traditions about cognitive development in school-age children.

The study of cognitive development, especially in school-age children, has been one of the central focuses of developmental research over the last 25 years. There is an enormous research literature, with thousands of studies investigating cognitive change from scores of specific perspectives. Despite this diversity, there does seem to be a consensus emerging about (1) the conclusions to be reached from research to date and (2) the directions new research and theory should take. A major part of this consensus grows from an orientation that seems to be pervading the field: It is time to move beyond the opposition of structuralism and functionalism and begin to build a broader, more integrated approach to cognitive development (see Case, 1980; Catania, 1973; Fischer, 1980; Flavell, 1982a). Indeed, we argue that without such an integration attempts to explain the development of behavior are doomed.

The general orientations or investigations of cognitive development are similar for all age groups—infancy, childhood, and adulthood. The vast majority of investigations, however, involve children of school age and for those children a number of specific issues arise, including in particular the relationship between schooling and cognitive development.

This chapter first describes the emerging consensus about the patterns of cognitive development in school-age children. A description of this consensus leads naturally to a set of core issues that must be dealt with if developmental scientists are to build a more adequate explanation of developmental structure and process. How do the child and the environment collaborate in development? How does the pattern of development vary across traditional categories of behavior, such as cognition, emotion, and social behavior? And what methods are available for addressing these issues in research?

Under the framework provided by these broad issues, there are a number of different directions research could take. Four that seem especially promising to us involve the relationship between cognitive development and emotional dynamics, the relationship between brain changes and cognitive development, the role of informal teaching and other modes of social interaction in cognitive development, and the nature and effects of schooling and literacy. These four directions are taken up in a later section.

PATTERNS OF DEVELOPMENTAL CHANGE

One of the central focuses in the controversies between structuralist and functionalist approaches has been whether children develop through stages. Much of this controversy has been obscured by fuzzy criteria for what counts as a stage, but significant advances have been made in pinning down criteria (e.g., Fischer and Bullock, 1981; Flavell, 1971; McCall, 1983; Wohlwill, 1973). In addition, developmentalists seem to be moving away from pitting structuralism and functionalism against each other toward viewing them as complementary; psychological development can at the same time be stagelike in some ways and not at all stagelike in other ways. As a result of these recent advances in the field, it is now possible to sketch a general portrait of the status of stages in the development of children.

The General Status of Stages

Children do not develop in stages as traditionally defined. That is, (1) their behavior changes gradually not abruptly, (2) they develop at different rates in different domains rather than showing synchronous change across domains, and (3) different children develop in different ways (Feldman, 1980; Flavell, 1982b).

Cognitive development does show, however, a number of weaker stagelike characteristics. First, within a domain, development occurs in orderly sequences of steps for relatively homogeneous populations of children (Flavell, 1972). That is, for a given population of children, development in a domain can be described in terms of a specific sequence, in which behavior a develops first, then behavior b, and so forth. For example, with Piaget and Inhelder's (1941/1974) conservation tasks involving two balls or lumps of clay, there seems to be a systematic three-step sequence (see Hooper et al., 1971; Uzgiris, 1964): (1) conservation of the amount of clay (Is there more clay in one of the balls, even though they are different shapes, or do they both have the same amount of clay?), (2) conservation of the weight of clay (Does one of the balls weigh more?), and (3) conservation of the volume of clay (Does one of the balls displace more water?). The explanation and prediction of such sequences is not always easy, but there do seem to be many instances of orderly sequences in particular domains.

Second, these steps often mark major qualitative changes in behavior— changes in behavioral organization. That is, in addition to developing more of the abilities they already have, children also seem to develop new types of abilities. This fact is reflected in the appearance of behaviors that were not previously present for some particular context or task. For example, in pretend play the understanding of concrete social roles, such as that of a doctor interacting with a patient, emerges at a certain point in a developmental sequence for social categories and is usually present by the age at which children begin school (Watson, 1981). Likewise, the understanding of conservation of amount of clay develops at a certain point in a developmental sequence for conservation.

More generally, there appear to be times of large-scale reorganization of behaviors across many (but not all) domains. At these times, children show more than the ordinary small qualitative changes that occur every day. They demonstrate major qualitative changes, and these changes seem to be characterized by large, rapid change across a number of domains (Case, 1980; Fischer et al., in press; Kenny, 1983; McCall, 1983). Indeed, the speed of change is emerging as a promising general measure for the degree of reorganization. We refer to these large-scale reorganizations as *levels*. We use the term *steps* to designate any qualitative change that can be described in terms of a developmental sequence, regardless of whether it involves a new level.

Third, there seem to be some universal steps in cognitive development, but their universality appears to depend on the way they are defined. When steps are defined abstractly and in broad terms or when large groups of skills are considered, developmental sequences seem to show universality across domains and across children in different social groups. When skills of any specificity are considered, however, the numbers and types of developmental steps seem to change as a function of both the context and the individual child (Bullock, 1981; Feldman and Toulmin, 1975; Fischer and Corrigan, 1981; Roberts, 1981; Silvern, 1984). For large-scale (macrodevelopmental) changes, then, there seem to be some universals, but for small-scale (microdevelopmental) changes, individual differences appear to be the norm. The nature of individual differences seems to be especially important for school-age children and is discussed in greater depth in a later section.

Large-Scale Developmental Reorganizations

In macrodevelopment there seem to be several candidates for universal large-scale reorganizations—times when major new types of skills are emerging and development is occurring relatively fast. Different structuralist frameworks share a surprising consensus about most of these levels, although opinions are not unanimous (Kenny, 1983). The exact characterizations of each level also vary somewhat across frameworks. Our descriptions of each level, including the age of emergence, are intended to capture the consensus.

Between 4 and 18 years of age—the time when many children spend long periods of time in a school setting—there seem to be four levels. The first major reorganization, apparently beginning at approximately age 4 in middle-class children in Western cultures, is characterized by the ability to deal with simple relations of representations (Bickhard, 1978; Biggs and Collis, 1982; Case and Khanna, 1981; Fischer, 1980; Isaac and O'Connor, 1975; Siegler, 1978; Wallon, 1970). Children acquire the ability to perform many tasks that involve coordinating two or more ideas. For example, they can do elementary perspective-taking, in which they relate a representation of someone else's perceptual viewpoint with a representation of their own (Flavell, 1977; Gelman, 1978). Similarly, they can relate two social categories, e.g., understanding how a doctor relates to a patient or how a mother relates to a father (Fischer et al., in press).

The term *representation* here follows the usage of Piaget (1936/1952; 1946/1951), not the meaning that is common in information-processing models (e.g., Bobrow and Collins, 1975). Piaget hypothesized that late in the second year children develop representation, which is the capacity to think about things that are not present in their immediate experience, such as an object that has disappeared. He suggested that, starting with these initial representations, children show a gradual increase in the complexity of representations throughout the preschool years, culminating in a new stage of equilibrium called "concrete operations" beginning at age 6 or 7.

Research has demonstrated that children acquire more sophisticated abilities during the preschool years than Piaget had originally described (Gelman, 1978), and theorists have hypothesized the emergence of an additional developmental level between ages 2 and 6—one involving simple relations of representations. The major controversy among the various structural theories seems to be whether this level is in fact the beginning of Piagetian concrete operations or a separate reorganization distinct from concrete operations. Many of the structural approaches recasting Piaget's concepts in information-processing terms have treated this level as the beginning of concrete operations (Case, 1980; Halford and Wilson, 1980; Pascual-Leone, 1970).

For Piaget (1970), the second level, that of concrete operations, first appears at age 6–7 in middle-class children. In many of the new structural theories, concrete operations constitute an independent level, not merely an elaboration of the level involving simple relations of representations (Biggs and Collis, 1982; Fischer, 1980; Flavell, 1977). The child comes to be able to deal systematically with the complexities of representations and so can understand what Piaget described as the logic of concrete objects and events. For example, conservation of amount of clay first develops at this level. In social cognition the child develops the capacity to deal with complex problems about perspectives (Flavell, 1977) and to coordinate multiple social categories, understanding, for example, role intersections, such as that a man can simultaneously be a doctor and a father to a girl who is both his patient and his daughter (Watson, 1981).

The third level, usually called formal operations (Inhelder and Piaget, 1955/1958), first emerges at age 10–12 in middle-class children in Western cultures. Children develop a new ability to generalize across concrete instances and to handle the complexities of some tasks requiring hypothetical reasoning. Preadolescents, for example, can understand and use a general definition for a concept such as addition or noun (Fischer et al., 1983), and they can construct all possible combinations of four types of colored blocks (Martarano, 1977). Some theories treat this level as the culmination of concrete operations, because it involves generalizations about concrete objects and events (Biggs and Collis, 1982). Others consider it to be the start of something different—the ability to abstract or to think hypothetically (Case, 1980; Fischer, 1980; Gruber and Voneche, 1976; Halford and Wilson, 1980; Jacques et al., 1978; Richards and Commons, 1983; Selman, 1980). Recent research indicates that cognitive development does not stop with the level that emerges at age 10–12. Indeed, performance on Piaget's formal operations tasks even continues to develop throughout adolescence (Martarano, 1977; Neimark, 1975). A number of theorists have suggested that a fourth level develops after the beginning of formal operations—the ability to relate abstractions or hypotheses, emerging at age 14–16 in middle-class Western children (Biggs and Collis, 1982; Case, 1980; Fischer et al., in press; Gruber and Voneche, 1976; Jacques et al., 1978; Richards and Commons, 1983; Selman, 1980; Tomlinson-Keasey, 1982). At this fourth level, adolescents can generate new hypotheses rather than merely test old ones (Arlin, 1975); they can deal with relational concepts, such as liberal and conservative in politics (Adelson, 1975); and they coordinate and combine abstractions in a wide range of domains.

Additional levels may also develop in late adolescence and early adulthood (Biggs and Collis, 1980; Case, 1980; Fischer et al., 1983; Richards and Commons, 1983). At these levels, individuals may able to deal with complex relations among abstractions and hypotheses and to formulate general principles integrating systems of abstractions.

Unfortunately, criteria for testing the reality of the four school-age levels have not been clearly explicated in most cognitive-developmental investigations. There seems to be little question that some kind of significant qualitative change in behavior occurs during each of the four specified age intervals, but researchers have not generally explicated what sort of qualitative change is substantial enough to be counted as a new level or stage. Learning a new concept, such as addition, can produce a qualitative change in behavior; but by itself such a qualitative change hardly seems to warrant designation as a level. Thus, clearer specification is required of what counts as a developmental level.

Research on cognitive development in infancy can provide some guidelines in this regard. For infant development, investigators have described several patterns of data that index emergence of a new level. Two of the most promising indexes are (1) a spurt in developmental change measured on some continuous scale (e.g., Emde et al., 1976; Kagan, 1982; Seibert et al., in press; Zelazo and Leonard, 1983) and (2) a transient drop in the stability of behaviors across a sample of tasks (e.g., McCall, 1983). Research on cognitive development in school-age children would be substantially strengthened if investigators specified such patterns for hypothesized developmental levels and tested for them. Available evidence suggests that these patterns may index levels in childhood as well as they do in infancy (see Fischer et al., in press; Kenny, 1983; Peters and Zaidel, 1981; Tabor and Kendler, 1981).

In summary, there seem to be four major developmental reorganizations, commonly called levels, between ages 4 and 18. Apparently, the levels do not exist in a strong form such as that hypothesized by Piaget (1949, 1975) and others (Pinard and Laurendeau, 1969). Consequently, the strong stage hypothesis has been abandoned by many cognitive-developmental research- ers, including some Piagetians (e.g., Kohlberg and Colby, 1983). Yet the evidence suggests that developmental levels fitting a weaker concept of stages probably do exist.

Relativity and Universality of Developmental Sequences

One of the best-established facts in cognitive development is that per- formance does not strictly adhere to stages. On the contrary, developmental stages vary widely with manipulations of virtually every environmental factor studied (Flavell, 1971, 1982b). Developmental unevenness, also called hor- izontal decalage (Piaget, 1941), seems to be the rule for development in general (Biggs and Collis, 1982; Fischer, 1980). During the school years it may well become even more common than in earlier years. By the time children reach school age they seem to begin to specialize on distinct de- velopmental paths based on their differential abilities and experiences (Gard- ner, 1983; Horn, 1976; McCall, 1981). Some weak forms of developmental stages—what we have called levels—probably exist, as we have noted, but they occur in the face of wide variations in performance.

Since developmental unevenness has been shown to be pervasive, it seems inevitable that developmental sequences will vary among children and across contexts. Unfortunately, there have been few investigations testing for var- iations in sequence. Most of the studies documenting the prevalence of decalage are designed in such a way that they can detect only variations in the speed of development on a fixed sequence, not variations in the sequence itself. The dearth of studies testing for individual differences in sequence, apparently arises from the fact that cognitive developmentalists have been searching for commonalities in sequence, not differences.

Nevertheless, a few studies have expressly assessed individual differences, and their results indicate that different children and different situations do in fact produce different sequences (Knight, 1982; McCall et al., 1977; Roberts, 1981). A plausible hypothesis is that developmental sequences are relative, changing with the child, the immediate situation, and the culture.

To examine this hypothesis researchers must face an important hidden issue—the nature and generality of the classifications used to code successive levels or steps of behavioral organization. Indeed, when issues of classification are brought into the analysis, it becomes clear that universality and relativity of sequence are not opposed. With a general mode of analysis, children can all show the same developmental sequence in some domain, while with a more specific mode of analysis they can all demonstrate different sequences in the same domain.

Figure 3-1 helps show why. The arrows and solid boxes depict developmental paths taken by two children, boy X on the left and girl Y on the right. The letters in the boxes indicate the specific content of the behaviors at each step, and the hyphens connecting letters indicate that two contents have been coordinated or related. The word step is used to describe a specific point in a sequence without implying how that step relates to developmental levels such as those described above.

Depending on how these sequences are analyzed, they can demonstrate either commonalities or individual differences—that is, that both children move through the same sequences or that each child moves through a different sequence. When viewed in terms of the specific steps each child traverses, the figure shows different developmental sequences. At step 1, child X can control skill or behavior F, and at step 2 he can control skills F and M separately but prefers F. Finally he reaches step 3, where he can relate F to M. Child Y at step 1 can control skill M, and at step 2 she can control both M and F but prefers M. Finally she reaches step 3, where she

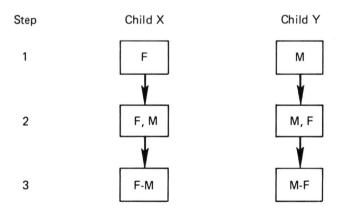

Step	Child X	Child Y
1	F	M
2	F, M	M, F
3	F-M	M-F

FIGURE 3-1 Two developmental sequences demonstrating both commonalities and individual differences.

can relate M to F. For example, in social play, F might represent the social category for father, M the social category for mother, F-M an interaction in which the father dominates, controlling what the mother does, and M-F an interaction in which the mother dominates, controlling what the father does. Thus, all three steps clearly differ for the two children.

Such plurality would seem to contradict the idea of a universal developmental sequence, since the two children are demonstrating different sequences for similar content. Yet when the specific steps are characterized more generally, it is possible to see these different paths as variations on a common theme. Analysis in terms of the social categories present, for instance, leads to the conclusion that steps 2 and 3 are the same in the two children: At step 2 both children comprehend the two separate categories of mother and father, and at step 3 they both understand how a mother and a father can interact.

In a still more general classification, the steps can be defined in terms of social category structure rather than the particular categories. Then, steps 2 and 3 remain equivalent for the children, and, in addition, step 1 becomes equivalent, since both children control similar structures, a single category (mother or father). In addition, skills that deal with markedly different contents can also be considered equivalent. An interaction between a doctor and a patient is equivalent structurally to the interaction between mother and father at step 3, since both interactions involve a social role relation between two categories.

When cognitive-developmental theorists posit general developmental levels, they are defining developmental sequences even more abstractly—in terms of highly general, structural classes of behaviors. For the level of concrete operations, for example, the conservation of amount of clay can be considered structurally equivalent to the intersection of social categories (Fischer, 1980). Conservation of clay involves the coordination of two dimensions (length and width) in two balls of clay, and the intersection of categories involves the coordination of two social categories for two people (such as doctor/father with patient/daughter).

These considerations lead to a reconceptualization of the controversy over whether developmental sequences are relative or universal. For highly specific classes of behavior, universality would seem impossible, relativity inevitable. At the extreme, even the social category of mother is not the same for the two children, since the behaviors and characteristics that each child includes in the category undoubtedly differ. As a result of such variations, no two randomly chosen children could be expected to show the same specific developmental sequences. Even identical twins exposed to, say, a common mathematics curriculum would follow developmental paths for mathematics that differed in detail. Thus, a useful analysis must distinguish irrelevant from relevant detail and generalize over the latter.

Of course, what counts as relevant detail depends on the researcher's purpose. And care must be taken to avoid trivialization of the issue of universality in a second way—by using overly general or ill-defined classes. It is important that what counts as an equivalent structure be specified with some precision. For example, all instances of two units of something cannot be counted as equivalent unless there is a clear rationale for classifying the units as equivalent. With social categories, it would seem unwise to treat "mother" as structurally equivalent to "corporation president." One of the primary tasks for cognitive developmentalists is to devise a system for analyzing structural equivalences across domains (Flavell, 1972, 1982a; Wohlwill, 1973).

Assuming an opposition between relativity and universality, then, is too simple, because at times individual differences may usefully be seen as variations on a common theme. Many of the current disagreements among researchers about universality and relativity in sequences could be clarified by consideration of the nature of the structural classifications being used. In practice, investigators can use a straightforward rule of thumb: They can construct their classes at an intermediate degree of abstraction—neither so specific as to miss valid generalization nor so general that they serve only the purpose of imposing order.

How the controversy about relativity and universality will be resolved rests in part on whether the structures and processes of developmental reorganization can be usefully regarded as similar across different domains of cognition and across children who differ in their achievements within domains. Can the growth of linguistic skill be usefully described in the same terms as the growth of mathematical skill? Or are there distinct linguistic and mathematical faculties whose development remains fundamentally dissimilar in any useful system for classifying sequences (Gardner, 1983)? Is the difference between a retarded child and a prodigy a difference of sequence or a difference in the speed of mastering what can usefully be considered the same sequence (Feldman, 1980)? These questions are just beginning to be addressed in a sophisticated manner.

Processes of Development

Many of the questions about the nature of developmental stages, their universality, and the extent of individual differences would be substantially clarified by a solid analysis of the processes underlying cognitive development. However, the best way to conceptualize the results of the extensive research literature on developmental processes is very much an open question. No emerging consensus is evident here, except perhaps that none of the traditional explanations is adequate. Three main types of models have dominated research to date.

The first type of model grows out of Piaget's approach. The developing organization of behavior is said to be based fundamentally in logic (Piaget, 1957, 1975). Developmental change results from the push toward logical consistency. Stages are defined by the occurrence of an equilibrium based on logical reversibility, and two such equilibria develop during the school years—one at concrete operations and one at formal operations.

Tests of this process model have proved to be remarkably unsuccessful. The primary empirical requirement of the model is that, when a logical equilibrium is reached, individuals must demonstrate high synchrony across domains. The prediction of synchrony arises from the fact that at equilibrium a logical structure of the whole (*structure d'ensemble*) emerges and quickly pervades the mind, catalyzing change in most or all of the child's schemes. Consequently, when a 6-year-old girl develops her first concrete operational scheme, such as conservation of number, the logical structure of concrete operations should pervade her intelligence in a short time, according to Piaget's model. Her other schemes should quickly be transformed into concrete operations.

Such synchrony across diverse domains has never been found. Instead, synchrony is typically low, even for closely related schemes such as different types of conservation (e.g., number, amount of clay, and length). Even if one allows that several concrete operational schemes might have to be constructed before the rapid transformation occurs, the evidence does not support the predicted synchrony (Biggs and Collis, 1982; Fischer and Bullock, 1981; Flavell, 1982b).

Efforts to study other implications of the logic model also have failed to support it (e.g., Braine and Rumain, 1983; Ennis, 1976; Osherson, 1974). Several attempts have been made to build alternative models based on some different kind of logic (e.g., Halford and Wilson, 1980; Jacques et al., 1978). But thus far there have been only a few studies testing these models, and it is therefore not yet possible to evaluate their success.

The second type of process model in cognitive-developmental theories is based on the information-processing approach. The child is analyzed as an information-processing system with a limited short-term memory capacity. In general, the numbers of items that can be maintained in short-term memory are hypothesized to increase with age, thereby enabling construction of more complex skills. The exact form of the capacity limitation is a matter of controversy, but in all existing models it involves an increase in the number of items that can be processed in short-term or working memory. The increase is conceptualized as a monotonic numerical increment from 1 to 2 to 3, and so forth, until some upper limit is reached. This memory model has been influential and has generated a large amount of interesting research, although it has not yet produced any consensus about the exact form of the hypothesized memory process (Dempster, 1981; Siegler, 1978, 1983). One of the primary problems with the model seems to be the difficulty of using changes in the number of items in short-term memory to explain changes in the organization of complex behavior. Although analysis of behavioral organization is always difficult, the distance between the minimal structure in short-term memory and the complex structure of a behavior such as conservation or perspective-taking seems to be particularly difficult to bridge. How can a linear numerical growth in memory be transformed into a change from, for example, concrete operational to formal operational perspective-taking skills (Elkind, 1974)? Although such a transformation may be possible, its nature has not proved to be transparent or simple (Flavell, 1984).

Moreover, how to conceptualize working memory is itself a controversial issue. Various investigators have challenged the traditional conceptualization that there is an increase in the size of the short-term memory store (Chi, 1978; Dempster, 1981; see also Grossberg, 1982: chs. 11 and 13). Fortunately, ever richer developmental models involving ideas about working memory capacity have continued to appear since Pascual-Leone's (1970) ground-breaking work (see Case, 1980; Halford and Wilson, 1980), and perhaps one of these will be successful in overcoming the problems mentioned.

The third common type of model assumes that development involves continuous change instead of general reorganizations of behavior like those predicted by the logic and limited-memory models. The fundamental nature of intelligence is laid down early in life, and development involves the accumulation of more and more learning experiences. Behaviorist analyses of cognitive development constitute one of the best-known forms of this functionalist model. A small set of processes defines learning capacity, such as conditioning and observational learning, and all skills—ranging from the reflexes of the newborn infant to the creative problem solving of the artist, scientist, or statesman—are said to arise from these same processes (Bandura and Walters, 1963; Skinner, 1969). Any behavioral reorganizations that might occur are local, involving the learning of a new skill that happens to be useful in several contexts.

Some information-processing approaches also assume that the nature of intelligence is laid down early and that development results from a continuous accumulation of many learning experiences: The child builds and revises a large number of cognitive "programs," often called production systems (Gelman and Baillargeon, 1983; Klahr and Wallace, 1976). Children construct many such systems, such as one for conservation of amount of clay and one for conservation of amount of water in a beaker. At times they can combine several systems into a more general one, as when conservation of clay and conservation of water are combined to form a system for conservation of continuous quantities. These reorganizations remain local, however. There are no general levels or stages in cognitive development—no all-encompassing logical reorganizations and no general increments in working memory capacity.

Researchers who believe in the continuous-change model tend to investigate the effects of specific types of processes or content domains on the development of particular skills. One of the processes emphasized within the continuous change framework has been automatization, the movement from laborious execution of a skill or production system to execution that is smooth and without deliberation. Several studies have demonstrated that automatization can produce what seem to be developmental anomalies. When school-age children are experts in some domain, such as chess, they can perform better than adults who are not experts (Chi, 1978). More generally, many types of tasks produce no differences between the performances of children and adults (Brown et al., 1983; Goodman, 1980).

In research on specific content domains, the general question is typically how the nature of a domain affects a range of developing behaviors. For example, the nature of language, mathematics, or morality is said to produce "constraints" on the form of development in relevant behaviors (Keil, 1981; Turiel, 1977). Development in domains that involve self-monitoring, such as knowledge about one's own memory processes (metamemory), is hypothesized to have general effects on many aspects of cognitive development (Brown et al., 1983; Flavell and Wellman, 1977).

Within the continuous-change, functionalist framework, investigators often assume that there is some intrinsic incompatibility between general cognitive-developmental reorganizations and effects of specific domains or processes. Yet it is far from obvious that any such incompatibility exists. The process of automatization can have powerful effects on developing behaviors, and at the same time children can show general reorganizations in those behaviors (Case, 1980). The domain of mathematics can produce constraints on the types of behaviors children can demonstrate, and at the same time those behaviors can be affected by general reorganizations. The reason for the assumption of incompatibility seems to be that developmentalists view the logic and limited-memory models as incompatible with the continuous-change model.

The assumption of incompatibility between reorganization and continuous change seems to stem from the fundamental starting points of the models: The logic and short-term memory models focus primarily on the organism as the locus of developmental change, whereas the continuous models focus on environmental factors. Several recent theoretical efforts have sought to move beyond this limit of the three standard models by providing a more genuinely interactional analysis, with major roles for both organismic and environmental influences (Fischer, 1980; Halford and Wilson, 1980; Silvern, 1984). Approaches that explicitly include both organism and environment in the working constructs for explaining developmental processes may provide the most promise for future research.

THE CENTRAL ISSUES IN THE FIELD TODAY

The differences among the traditional approaches to development are important to understand, but they seem much less significant today than they did 10 years ago. A pervasive change in orientation seems to be taking place among behavioral scientists—a shift away from emphases on competing theories toward integrating whatever tools are available to explain behavior in the whole person, in all of his or her complexity. The present era seems to be a time of integrating rather than splitting. Structuralism and functionalism, for example, are seen not as competing approaches but as complementary ones, emphasizing different aspects of behavior and development. This new orientation is evident throughout this volume.

In the study of cognitive development, this change in the field appears to be associated with attempts to go beyond certain fundamental limitations of previous approaches and to move toward a more comprehensive framework for characterizing and explaining cognitive development. At least three basic questions have arisen as part of this movement toward a new, integrative framework. All three involve efforts to avoid conceptual orientations that have proved problematic in past research. The most fundamental of the three questions is: How do child and environment jointly contribute to cognitive development? The other two questions involve elaborations of this question: How do developing behaviors in different contexts and domains relate to each other? What methods are appropriate for analyzing cognitive development? In a general way the answers to these questions apply to development at any age, but the answers apply in particular ways to school-age children.

The Collaboration of Child and Environment

The central unresolved issue in the study of cognitive development today seems to be the manner in which child and environment collaborate in development. As a result of the cognitive revolution, it is generally accepted that the child is an active organism striving to control his or her world. But this emphasis on the active child often seems to lead to a neglect of the environment. Contrary to the structural approaches of such theorists as Piaget (1975) and Chomsky (1965), it appears to be impossible to explain developing behavior without giving a central role to the specific contexts of the child's action, including those in the school environment (see Scribner and Cole, 1981; Flavell, 1982b).

Giving context a central role does not mean merely demonstrating once again that environmental factors affect assessments of developmental steps. Researchers have documented these effects in thousands of studies, thus pointing out the inadequacies of the Piagetian approach to explaining the unevenness of development. Surely Piaget, Kohlberg (1969, 1978), and other traditional structural theorists have failed to deal adequately with the environment. It is also true, however, that the functionalists have not produced a satisfactory alternative—an approach that both deals with the environment's roles in development and treats children as active contributors to their own development (Lerner and Busch-Rossnagel, 1981). An analysis of the collaboration of child and environment in development is just as unlikely to arise from a functionalist emphasis on the environment as from a structuralist emphasis on the child.

A Diagnosis

Why has the study of cognitive development repeatedly fallen back on approaches that focus primarily on either the child or the environment? Why have developmentalists failed to build approaches based on the collaboration of child with environment?

Historically, developmental psychology has been plagued by repeated failures to accept what should be one of its central tasks: to explain the emergence of new organization or structure. These failures have most commonly taken either of two complementary forms. In one form, nativism, the structures evident in the adult are seen as already preformed in the infant. These structures need only be expressed when they are somehow stimulated or nourished at the appropriate time in development. In the second form, environmentalism, the structures in the adult are treated as already preformed in the environment. These structures need only be internalized by some acquisition process, such as conditioning or imitation. Typically, structuralist approaches assume some form of nativism, and functionalist approaches assume some type of environmentalism.

Although it is common to focus on the difference between nativism and environmentalism, there is a fundamental similarity, a common preformism.

Both approaches reduce the phenomena of development to the realization of preformed structures. The mechanisms by which the structures are realized are clearly different, but in both cases the structures are present somewhere from the start—either in the child or in the world (Feffer, 1982; Fischer, 1980; Sameroff, 1975; Silvern, 1984; Westerman, 1980).

A mature developmental theory, we believe, must move beyond explanation by reduction to preexisting forms. It must build constructs that explain how child and environment collaborate in development, and one of the primary tasks of such constructs must be to explain how new structures emerge in development (Bullock, 1981; Dennett, 1975; Haroutunian, 1983).

If the future is not to be a reenactment of the past, it is important to ask why it has been so difficult to avoid drifting toward one or another type of preformism. Why has no well-articulated, compelling alternative to preformism been devised? Any compelling alternative to preformism must describe how child and environment collaborate to produce new structures during development. Constructing such a framework is an immensely difficult task. At the very least, the framework must make reference to cognitive structure, environmental structure, the interaction of the two, and mechanisms for change in structure. The scope of these issues makes such a framework difficult to formulate and difficult to communicate once formulated.

Unfortunately, even approaches that have explicitly attempted to move beyond preformist views have typically failed to do so. Piaget provides a case in point. He set out expressly to build an interactionist position, an approach that would deal with both child and environment and thus avoid the pitfalls of nativism and environmentalism (Piaget, 1947/1950). Yet the theory he eventually built placed most of its explanatory weight on the child and neglected the environment.

Consider, for example, his famous digestive metaphor for cognitive development. Just as the digestive system assimilates food to the body and accommodates to the characteristics of the particular type of food, so children assimilate an object or event to one of their schemes and accommodate the scheme to the object or event. Piaget seems to have chosen this metaphor expressly as a device to avoid preformist thinking, yet he still drifted back toward preformism. In practice, the focus for applications of the metaphor was the assimilation of experience to preexisting schemes. The other side of the metaphor—accommodation to experience—was systematically neglected. For example, Piaget (1936/1952, 1975) differentiated many different types of assimilation but generally spoke of accommodation in only global, undifferentiated terms.

Similarly, the structures behind Piaget's developmental stages—concrete operations and formal operations in school-age children—were treated as static characteristics of the child. The environment was granted an ill-defined role in supporting the emergence of the structures, but the structures themselves were treated as if they came to be fixed characteristics of the child's mind (Piaget and Inhelder, 1966/1969). In a genuinely interactionist position, these structures would have been attributed to the collaboration of the mind with particular contexts. Piaget's neglect of the environment became particularly evident when he was faced with a host of environmentally induced cases of developmental unevenness (termed horizontal decalage). His response was that it was simply impossible to explain them (Piaget, 1971:11). Because of Piaget's neglect of the environment, even supporters of his position have argued that it is essentially nativist (Beilin, 1971; Broughton, 1981; Flavell, 1971).

Toward a Remedy

If the foregoing diagnosis is accurate, any remedy must explicitly counteract the tendency to drift toward attributing cognitive structures to either the child or the environment. What is needed seems to be a framework providing constructs and methods that force researchers to explicitly deal with both child and environment when they characterize how new structures emerge in development.

What might such a framework look like? Many would recommend general systems theory, because it views the child as an active component in a larger-scale dynamic system that includes the environment. To date, however, systems theory does not seem to have been successful in promoting research explicating the interaction between child and environment in development. Many investigators appear simply to have learned the vocabulary of the approach without changing the way they study development. Apparently, the concepts of systems theory lack the definiteness needed to guide empirical research in cognitive development toward a new interactional paradigm. A few provocative approaches based on general systems concepts have begun to appear in the developmental literature (e.g., Sameroff, 1983; Silvern, 1984), but they seem to bring to bear additional tools that specifically promote interactional analyses.

It is in such practical tools that the proposed remedy lies. To promote interactional analyses, a framework needs to affect the actual practice of cognitive-developmental research. We would like to suggest that the concept of collaboration may provide the basis for such a framework.

The Collaborative Cycle

Human beings are social creatures, who commonly work together for shared goals. That is, people collaborate. Often when two people collaborate to solve a problem, neither one possesses all the elements that will eventually appear in the solution. During their collaboration, a social system (Kaye, 1982) emerges in which each person's behavior supports the other's behavior and thought in directions that would not have been taken by the individuals alone. Eventually a solution—a new cognitive structure—emerges. It bears some mark of each individual, yet it did not exist in either person prior to the collaboration, nor would it have developed in either one without the collaboration. Indeed, even after the structure has developed, the individuals may be able to access it only by reconstituting the collaboration. Of course, besides having the same two people collaborate again, it is also possible for one of them to collaborate with a different partner (Bereiter and Scardamalia, 1982; Brown et al., 1983; Maccoby and Hartup, in this volume).

Figure 3-2 shows this developmental process as a collaborative cycle. The two left circles represent, respectively, structures that are external and internal to an individual. Consider a girl engaged in solving a puzzle with her father. The father provides external structures to support or scaffold her puzzle solving by stating the goal of the task, lining up a puzzle piece to highlight how it fits in its particular place, providing verbal hints, and so forth (Brown, 1980; Kaye, 1982; Wertsch, 1979; Wood, 1980). The child's knowledge and skills for solving the puzzle constitute the core of the developing internal structures.

The collaboration of external and internal structures produces the behavioral episodes represented in the right circle. The girl and her father work at solving the puzzle, and, as a result of the collaboration, she can achieve a scaffolded mental state, which she could not achieve by herself as quickly or in the same form.

The feedback arrows running from the right circle to the left ones in Figure 3-2 show the dependence of developmental change on collaboration. By performing the task in a scaffolded interaction, the girl learns the goal of the puzzle and how to go about solving it without her father's help. She develops more sophisticated internal structures so that she is less dependent on the complex external structures provided by her father. Of course, the development of this ability takes many steps: The father constantly updates his scaffolding to fit the child's present knowledge and skill. In this way, developmental change occurs both inside the child and outside her—an often overlooked fact to which we will return.

In much human behavior there is indeed a collaboration between two or more individuals. Recent socially oriented analyses of development have emphasized this process. Sometimes the emphasis is on the joint contributions of collaborating individuals, and the process is called coregulation or something similar (see Feldman, 1980; Markus and Nurius, Maccoby, and Weisner, in this volume; Westerman and Fischman-Havstad, 1982). Some-

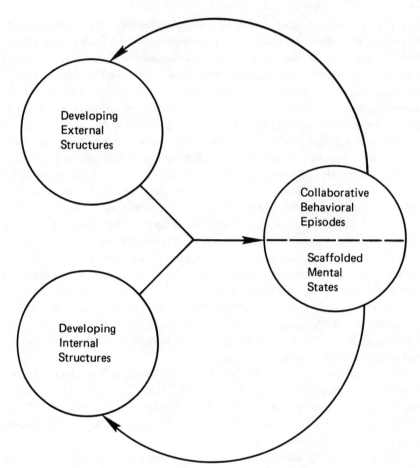

FIGURE 3-2   Development schematized as a collaborative cycle.

times the emphasis is on the role of the parent or older child in supporting and advancing the child's behavior, and the process is called scaffolding or something similar, as in Figure 3-2 (Bruner, 1982; Kaye, 1982; Laboratory of Comparative Human Cognition, 1983; Lock, 1980; Vygotsky, 1934/1978; Wertsch, 1979; Wood et al., 1976; Wood, 1980).

Even when a child is acting alone, collaboration can occur because the nonpersonal environment can play the role of collaborator. Because environments have structures, every environment supports some behaviors more than others. For example, a tree that has strong branches far down on its trunk provides strong support for climbing, a tree with only high branches provides less support, and a pole with no branches provides little support.

Of course, much about human environments is socially constructed. Consequently, the collaboration between child and environment often involves other people even when no other person is immediately present, because people have constructed the physical environment to correspond with mental structures that organize their activity. Good examples include a library with a spatial/topical organization of its many books and a classroom with its desks, chalkboards, and wall displays all designed to facilitate the types of interactions needed for schooling.

Implications for Research

Although the collaboration approach has not yet been fully articulated, it already seems to have straightforward implications for research practice. If child and environment are always collaborating to produce a behavior, explanations of that behavior must invoke characteristics of both. As a practical procedure to encourage such explanations, investigators can use research designs that vary important characteristics of both the child and the environment. With such designs, variations in both child and environment are likely to affect behavior (Fischer et al., in press; Hand, 1981).

A series of studies on the development of understanding social categories illustrates how this type of research design can lead to analyses of the collaboration between child and environment in cognitive development (Hand, 1982; Van Parys, 1983; Watson and Fischer, 1977, 1980). The studies were designed to test several predicted sequences for the development of social categories such as the social roles of doctor and patient and the social-interaction categories of "nice" and "mean." Each study was designed to include variations in both the child and the environment.

The main variable involving child characteristics was age. A wide age range was included in each study to ensure substantial variation in children's capacities to understand the social categories. Ages ranged from 1 to 12 and thus included the relevant periods for the major developmental reorganizations in preadolescent school-age children.

To determine the contribution of environmental characteristics, behavior was assessed under three different conditions, which were designed to provide varying degrees of support for advanced performance. In a structured condition—the elicited-imitation assessment—a separate task was administered to test each predicted step in the developmental sequence. The subject was shown a story embodying the skill required for that step and was asked to act out the story. Thus this condition provided high environmental support for performance at every step. The other two conditions provided less support and thus assessed more spontaneous behavior. In the free-play condition, each child played alone with the toys, acting out his or her own stories. In the best-story condition the experimenter returned to the testing room and asked the child to make up the best story he or she could.

The results showed a systematic effect of environmental support on the child's performance, but the effect varied as a function of the developmental level of the child's best performance. For the first several steps in the developmental sequence, virtually all children showed the same highest step in all three conditions. However, a major change occurred beginning with the first step testing the developmental level of simple relations of representations (which typically emerges at approximately age 4). At this step most children performed at a higher step in the structured assessment than in the two more spontaneous conditions, and that gap grew systematically in the later steps in the sequence. Figure 3-3 shows these results for the studies of the social roles of doctor and patient, and parallel results were

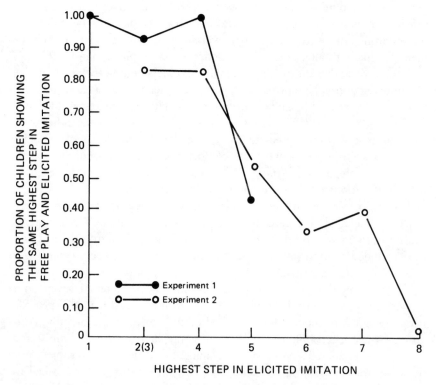

FIGURE 3-3   A systematic change in the proportion of children showing the same step in elicited imitation and free play. Adapted with permission from Watson & Fischer (1980). Copyright© American Psychological Association.

obtained in studies of the social interaction categories of nice and mean (Hand, 1982) and the self-related categories of gender and age (Van Parys, 1983).

A similar design and method was used to test for an analogous phenomenon in adolescents. The developmental sequence involved the moral concepts of intention and responsibility. It was predicted that at the cognitive-developmental level of formal operations (also called "single abstractions") subjects would show the same highest step in a structured assessment and in a spontaneous condition. However, when they became capable of performing at the next developmental level, relations of abstractions, a major gap would appear between performance in the structured and spontaneous conditions. The prediction was supported. Once again, the highest developmental step that the individual demonstrated varied systematically as a function of both the individual's capacity and the environmental condition (Fischer et al., 1983).

In analyzing results of this sort a proponent of a noncollaborative approach would ask which condition provides the best assessment of the child's true competence. The collaboration theorist replies, "You've missed the point. Competence as traditionally assessed is a joint function of child and environment." The child does not have any true competence independent of particular environmental conditions. Competence varies with degree of support.

Even for an individual child research can be designed to investigate variations in both the child and the environment. Cole and Traupman (1983), for example, assessed a learning disabled child's capabilities using a range of cognitive tests and examined his performance in settings outside the classroom. They found that, in settings involving social interactions with other people, his disabilities were hardly noticeable because he used his social skills to compensate for them. Thus, the portrait of the child in a standard testing situation was vastly different from the portrait in a real-life social setting.

It is surprising how few cognitive-developmental studies have systematically varied characteristics of both child and environment. Typically, studies examine either changes with age and ability or changes resulting from environmental factors. In the infrequent studies that include variations in both child and environment, the interpretations often neglect the interaction and instead focus on the child and the environment separately. For example, many studies criticizing Piaget's work demonstrate that variations in environmental conditions produce developmental unevenness (decalage), but they seldom deal with the variations as a function of children's ages or abilities. Fortunately, there are a growing number of exceptions to this characterization—studies that seriously consider the effects of both child and environment on performance. The results of these studies are already beginning to transform explanations of cognitive development (see O'Brien and Overton, 1982; Rubin et al., 1983; Tabor and Kendler, 1981).

The Transformation of Concepts of Ability and Competence

As these research examples illustrate, analyzing development as a collaborative process leads to a reconceptualization of many basic cognitive-developmental concepts. Since every behavior can be seen to depend on a collaboration between child and environment, it becomes impossible to analyze any behavior without including both organismic and environmental factors.

Cognitive developmentalists and psychometricians commonly speak of children's ability, or capacity, or competence, as if a child possessed a set of static characteristics that could be defined independently of any context: One child has the ability to understand conservation of water, and another child does not. As soon as the collaborative role of the environment is introduced, these concepts must be radically changed. Competence is not a fixed characteristic of the child but an emergent characteristic of the child in a specific context. It is not enough to make a distinction between competence and performance, because in standard usage this distinction begs the question. The assumption is made that children really do possess a set of competences, but they are somehow prevented from demonstrating them in their performance (Overton and Newman, 1982). If concepts such as ability and competence are to be consonant with a collaboration approach, they must be redefined in terms of the interaction of child with environment.

Within a collaboration approach, concepts of ability and competence retain their utility, because the child is part of the analysis, too. In certain contexts, children perform up to a certain level of complexity and not beyond it, thus demonstrating a certain competence for those contexts. At times children show partial knowledge of what is needed for a particular task (Brown et al., 1983; Feffer, 1982) and so demonstrate the competence for collaboration with a more knowledgeable partner. Also, children evidence large individual differences in the facility with which they can generalize an ability to new contexts, thus demonstrating variations in the competence to generalize. Upon the emergence of formal operation, for example, very bright children seem to be able to use their new capacity quickly in a wide range of tasks, whereas children of normal intelligence take much longer to extend the capacity to many tasks (Fischer and Pipp, 1984; Webb, 1974).

The collaboration orientation poses many new questions for the study of cognitive development. It is not enough to ask questions such as: How does the child's behavior change with age, or how does the child's behavior change as a function of experience? Instead, questions like the following need to be asked: Why do children often perform below capacity? How does context support or fail to support high-level performances that are known to be within the child's reach? How do specific collaborative systems support the acquisition of particular skills in different ways at different developmental levels? How is the nature of the child's experience jointly regulated by the child and by resources (human and other) available in the child's environment? Later, we examine several lines of research that show promise of contributing answers to such questions.

Integrating Across Traditional Research Categories

In the same way that scholars are coming to treat child and environment as collaborators in development they are recognizing the need to integrate the traditional categories for categorizing behavior. Cognition and emotion, for example, are not separate in the developing child. There seem to be at least three reasons for this changing orientation.

First, after decades of research, developmentalists have found that a child's behavior does not fit neatly into separate boxes labeled cognition, emotion, motivation, social skills, personality, and physical development (see, for example, Harter, 1982, 1983; Selman, 1980). Indeed, even behavior in more restricted, intuitively appealing categories such as perspective taking and conservation does not fit together coherently (see Hooper et al., 1971; Rubin, 1973; Uzgiris, 1964). Behavioral development has not proved to follow the "obvious" categories devised by developmentalists.

Second, the general movement toward integrating diverse approaches and dealing with the whole child leads not only to an emphasis on the collaboration of child and environment but also to the consideration of relations between behaviors in the traditional categories: How does emotional development relate to cognitive development? How does social development relate to cognitive development? Instead of one set of researchers studying a cognitive child, while another set studies a social child, and still another set studies an emotional child, the field is moving toward viewing the child as a whole—a cognitive, social, emotional, motivated, personal, biological child.

Third, during the last 20 years the cognitive-developmental orientation has become a dominant influence in the study of development, and it has provided a major impetus toward integration. The central questions in the study of cognitive development involve the organization of behavior and the processes underlying behavioral change. Because these questions are so general and fundamental, their applicability is not limited to the traditional domain of cognitive development—increments in knowledge about "cold" topics, such as objects, space, and scientific principles. All behavior, including that involving "hot" topics, such as emotions and social interaction, is organized in some way and undergoes developmental change.

The movement toward integration across behavioral categories has been promising, and many interesting results have come from research in this new tradition. But thus far progress has been limited by several conceptual difficulties.

Overcoming the Obstacles

One of the central conceptual problems has been the tendency to reify the traditional behavioral categories despite the lack of evidence that children's behavior fits the categories. Thus, the most common hypotheses about the relationship between, for example, cognitive development and social development have assumed the validity of cognition and social skills as separate categories. This assumption is especially clear when cognitive development is postulated as a prerequisite for social development.

One such hypothesis that has received much attention involves the relation between cognition and morality: Cognitive development is hypothesized to be a prerequisite for moral development (see Kohlberg, 1969). In practice, this proposition has been taken to mean that performance on Piagetian tasks is a prerequisite for performance on Kohlberg's moral dilemmas. Why should conservation of amount of clay, for instance, be a prerequisite for moral reasoning based on normative concepts of good and bad (Kohlberg's stage 3)? Is there any sense in which conservation is included in the concepts of good and bad? Or is there any way that conservation is more fundamental to mental functioning than concepts of good and bad? Isn't it just as reasonable (or unreasonable) to suggest that concepts of good and bad may be a prerequisite for conservation? If evidence does not support the division of behavior into separate categories of cognition about science problems and moral reasoning, it cannot be meaningful to suggest that such cognition is a prerequisite for moral reasoning (Rest, 1979, 1983).

A similar problem arises when investigators assume that the behaviors captured by the traditional categories are totally separate, showing no relation to each other at all. One of the most neglected topics for school-age children is emotional development, which is sometimes treated as if it is not related at all to cognitive development. Perhaps this assumption helps explain why cognitive developmentalists have omitted emotions from their research agenda. In a later section we suggest some guidelines for stimulating the study of emotional development in school-age children, especially as it relates to cognitive development.

A third, related conceptual problem has been the assumption that one variable can capture an entire behavioral category. Self-esteem as assessed by a questionnaire is treated as measuring the core of the developing self (Harter, 1983; Markus and Nurius, in this volume; Wylie, 1979). The stage of moral judgment, as assessed by reasoning about a set of moral dilemmas, is believed to assess the fundamental nature of moral development (Rest, 1983).

This mistaken assumption is at the heart of a recent controversy about the nature of brain-behavior relations. Several investigators have used measurements of the growth rate of children's heads as indexes of changes in the children's ability to learn (Epstein, 1978; Toepfer, 1979). Although no measures of learning were used, conclusions were drawn from the head-growth data about what children of different ages were able to learn. The relationship between brain growth and cognitive development is an exciting topic worthy of research, as we discuss later. It is important, however, that researchers differentiate what they are measuring from other developmental changes. Relationships between developments in different domains cannot be assumed; they must be assessed.

Implications for Research

Since the traditional categories for categorizing behavior do not seem to capture either the way behavior is organized or how its organization develops, it makes sense to analyze development across categories. More generally, the concern for explaining development in the whole child and for building a framework that emphasizes the collaboration of child and environment demands that researchers assess behavior in multiple contexts and with various methods. In doing such research, however, developmentalists need (1) to avoid allowing the categories to limit their thinking, as when cold cognition is considered to be a prerequisite for moral reasoning, and (2) to avoid assuming that a single variable will provide a valid index of overall cognitive functioning, as when head growth is treated as if it directly reflects cognitive changes.

In practice, doing research on development across traditional categories is closely related to doing research on the collaboration of child and environment in development. In both cases a number of variables must be measured in several settings, and the investigator must analyze not only each variable itself but also the relations among variables. Consider, for example, research on the effects of divorce on the school-age child. It would appear to be wise to assess (1) the child's understanding of family roles and the effects of divorce on that understanding, (2) the child's emotional reactions to the divorce, (3) the types of social interactions between parents and child and the changes in those interactions that resulted from the divorce, (4) the child's attitudes toward the parents, and so forth. On the basis of the collaboration argument, it may also be important to measure each of these factors under several different degrees of environmental support. Obviously, such research is difficult because it can quickly become unmanageably complex.

Despite this complexity it is possible to do research on patterns of development across categories without either being overwhelmed by complexity or becoming entangled in the conceptual problems that have plagued much past research. At least two helpful guidelines can be articulated: First, development should be analyzed in what promises to be a coherent domain of personal functioning. For example, an investigator might study the mastery of early skills involved in learning to read words (for example, Knight, 1982) or the relationship of divorce to a child's understanding and use of social roles in the family. Within such domains the investigator can examine development in different contexts while still keeping the project within a manageable scope. In addition, the coherence of the domain itself will often provide environmental support to guide the investigator's efforts.

Second, the researcher needs to use methods and measures appropriate to the questions being addressed. Of course, this admonition has been made often. In cognitive-developmental research, however, inadequate methods have been used repeatedly even when appropriate methods were available. In addition, recent innovations in developmental methodology have provided powerful methods for studying many fundamental developmental issues, including relationships between development in different contexts.

Methods of Assessing Development Change and Continuity

Cognitive-developmental research has not generally been distinguished by the sophistication of its methodology. One of the primary reasons has been that the traditional methods used in the behavioral sciences are not appropriate for studying such issues as developmental change and continuity (Wohlwill, 1973). Analysis of variance, for example, was originally constructed to test whether one or more factors made a difference in the outcomes of independent, equivalent groups. It was not constructed to examine questions about cognitive-developmental issues such as changes in the organization of behavior.

Children almost invariably become smarter as they grow older, and so it has been a simple matter in cognitive-developmental research to use analysis of variance to demonstrate differences between age groups and to use correlations to demonstrate relations between development and age. By themselves, such differences and relations can be uninteresting unless they help answer important questions such as the following: Do children show a systematic developmental sequence in a given domain? Does that sequence demonstrate reorganization of behavior? Are there differences in the speed of developmental change at different times in that domain? Across domains or contexts, are there systematic relations among sequences, reorganizations, changes in speed, or other developmental patterns?

Fortunately, there has recently been substantial progress in constructing designs, measures, and statistics for asking developmental questions (Applebaum and McCall, 1983; Bart and Krus, 1973; Coombs and Smith, 1973; Fischer et al., in press; Krus, 1977; Siegler, 1981; Wohlwill, 1973). Although we do not review all these methods here, we do sketch some of the important concepts behind them.

Developmental Sequences

Systematic change is clearly one of the fundamental concerns of developmental science in general. In cognitive development the tool used most often to describe and analyze systematic change has been the developmental sequence—a series of steps, levels, or stages that portray how behavior gradually changes from some starting point to some endpoint (Flavell, 1972). As a descriptive tool the sequence has been at the center of cognitive-developmental research, providing the core set of observations on which most cognitive-developmental theories are based, ranging from classical approaches (for example, Piaget and Inhelder, 1966/1969; Werner, 1957) to more recent ones (for example, Case, 1980; Siegler, 1981).

Developmental sequences demonstrate not only developmental change but also a form of developmental continuity. They describe how one type of behavior gradually changes into another, and scales based on sequences can be used to examine when change is relatively gradual and continuous and when it is relatively abrupt and discontinuous.

Since the developmental sequence is so important to the study of cognitive development, scaling should clearly be a central concern in research. Documenting that a description of a series of steps in fact forms a scale would seem to be integral to the research enterprise, yet very few investigations of cognitive development in school-age children demonstrate a basic concern with scaling.

The most common type of study in published cognitive-developmental research fits the following description. Children from a few different age groups are tested on several tasks. For example, 5-, 8-, and 11-year-olds are tested on three tasks: one task for conservation of number of plastic chips, one for conservation of amount of clay in a ball, and one for conservation of amount of water in a beaker. Performance on each task is scored on a three-step hypothesized sequence. Step 1 reflects a clear nonconservation response, such as a statement that the amount changes when the array is transformed. Step 2 indicates a transitional or ambiguous response, as when a child states that the amount stays the same but gives no satisfactory elaboration or explanation. Step 3 indicates an answer showing full conservation. An analysis of variance is then performed on the results, which demonstrate that, for each of the three tasks, performance improved across the three age groups and that performance for one or two tasks was significantly better than that for the other tasks. For example, children had significantly more advanced scores for conservation of number than for the other two tasks.

These analyses clearly demonstrate that the older groups performed better than the younger ones—hardly a surprise. The results document little else of interest, failing even to test directly for any developmental sequences. They do not adequately test the hypothesized three-step sequence, nor do they demonstrate that the three conservation tasks form a two-step sequence, with conservation of number developing before the other two.

To test a developmental sequence an independent assessment is required of each step in the hypothesized scale (Fischer and Bullock, 1981). With such an assessment it is possible to test directly whether one step comes consistently before or after another. Performance on the independent assessments should form a Guttman (1944) scale, in which every child passes all the steps prior to his or her highest step passed (and fails all the steps after the lowest step failed). Table 3-1 shows the possible performance profiles that are consistent with a simple eight-step Guttman scale. Scales can also be more complex, with two or more tasks at a single step, as for step 2 in Table 3-2. Indeed, methods are available for tracing highly complex scales, such as those that branch into multiple parallel paths (Bart and Krus, 1973; Coombs and Smith, 1973; Krus, 1977).

The design of the hypothetical study of conservation allows only one such direct test for sequence. Because of the independent assessment of the three types of conservation, a sequence involving those types can be tested. For example, consider a two-step sequence in which the first step is full under-

TABLE 3-1 Strong Scalogram Method: Profiles for an 8-Step
Developmental Sequence

Developmental	Tasks							
Step	A	B	C	D	E	F	G	H
0	–	–	–	–	–	–	–	–
1	+	–	–	–	–	–	–	–
2	+	+	–	–	–	–	–	–
3	+	+	+	–	–	–	–	–
4	+	+	+	+	–	–	–	–
5	+	+	+	+	+	–	–	–
6	+	+	+	+	+	+	–	–
7	+	+	+	+	+	+	+	–
8	+	+	+	+	+	+	+	+

NOTE: Correct performance of a task is indicated by +.

standing of conservation of number and the second is full understanding of either conservation of clay, water, or both. With that sequence every child should show one of the profiles for steps 0, 1, and 2 in Table 3-2. However, it is not possible to test directly the hypothesized three-step developmental sequence (from nonconservation to conservation with explanation) within each type of conservation, because with the specified design of the study the steps are not assessed independently.

There is another method that provides independent assessments without requiring a separate task for each step—the longitudinal design traditionally espoused for developmental research (Wohlwill, 1973). Longitudinal testing of children on the three conservation tasks would make it possible to determine whether for each task and every child, steps always occurred in the

TABLE 3-2 Profiles for a Measure With Two
Tasks at Step 2

Developmental	Tasks				
Step	J	K	L	M	N
0	–	–	–	–	–
1	+	–	–	–	–
2	+	+	–	–	–
2	+	+	+	–	–
2	+	–	+	–	–
3	+	+	+	+	–
4	+	+	+	+	+

NOTE: Correct performance of a task is indicated by +.

predicted order. From one testing to the next, children should either move to a higher step or remain at the same step. This design has been used very effectively in research on moral development to demonstrate that the stages hypothesized by Kohlberg do in fact form a developmental sequence (Colby et al., 1983; Kuhn, 1976; Rest, 1983). The use of scalogram assessments in longitudinal research would provide even greater power and precision, however. With separate tasks to assess each step, individual children's development could be traced in detail. We know of no studies of cognitive development in school-age children using scalograms with a longitudinal design.

Of course, longitudinal research is not needed to test a developmental sequence. With a cross-sectional design, powerful methods are available for rigorously testing a predicted developmental sequence, as suggested by Tables 3-1 and 3-2. Scalogram statistics can be used to test how well the data fit the predicted scale (Green, 1956), and measures approximating a developmental scale can be devised when a specific sequence cannot be predicted. A strong scalogram measure, in which a different task is constructed a priori to assess each predicted step in a sequence, can be especially useful because the theoretical interpretation of each task can be specified unambiguously. For the most part, however, researchers have not taken advantage of the obvious virtues of scalogram methods for testing sequences or other hypotheses about development.

In most published studies, scalability tests are not reported even when the design allows them. The apparent reason for the neglect of scalogram methods is that, when they were used to test some of the detailed developmental sequences inferred by Piaget from mean age differences between tasks, the scalability of the sequences was poor (Hooper et al., 1979; Kofsky, 1966; Wohlwill and Lowe, 1962). Instead of concluding that Piaget's sequences were incorrect, developmentalists seem to have shot the messenger that brought the bad news: They discarded scalogram methods, for the most part. Fortunately, this unwarranted neglect of a powerful method appears to be coming to an end.

The cognitive-developmental issues that can be addressed with scalogram methods include the following: (1) With independent assessments of each steps, the parallels and differences between developments in different contexts can be traced precisely (Corrigan, 1983). (2) Individual differences in developmental sequences can be directly tested, especially when separate assessments are used to detect hypothesized differences (Knight, 1982). (3) Changes in the speed of development can be detected.

The particular method will vary with the hypothesis, of course. For instance, to test for changes in the speed of development, such as spurts and plateaus, it is essential that subjects be sampled such that their ages are distributed evenly (Fischer et al., in press). If a developmental spurt is predicted at age 10, for example, it is necessary to sample children evenly throughout the age range between 9 and 11. If all children tested are at a few restricted ages, such as within a few months of age 9 or 11, it will be impossible to determine whether a difference between 9- and 11-year-olds reflects a developmental spurt, since the distribution of ages alone will produce a bunching of subjects at certain steps in the scale.

Several studies using appropriate designs to assess speed of development have found that speed does seem to accelerate at certain ages during the school years and to slow down at other ages (Jacques et al., 1978; Kenny, 1983; Tabor and Kendler, 1981). That is, there may be periods of discontinuity and periods of continuity as assessed by speed of development. Current data are consistent with the hypothesis that spurts are associated with the large-scale reorganizations or levels described earlier (Fischer and Pipp, 1984), although more research is necessary to fully test this hypothesis.

In general, research with infants and young children has used much more sophisticated scaling methods than has research with school-age children. For example, Seibert and Hogan (1983), Uzgiris and Hunt (1975), and others have devised a number of scales for infant cognitive development in which each step in a predicted sequence is assessed independently. These scales have been used by various investigators to examine developmental change with some precision (Hunt et al., 1976; Seibert et al., in press). Using methods that approximate a Guttman scale, McCall et al. (1977) analyzed a longitudinal study of performance on infant intelligence tests to assess both changes in the speed of development and individual differences in developmental sequences. We know of no large-scale research projects on school-age children that have used such sophisticated methods to assess developmental change.

Rule-Assessment Methods

Developmental sequences are a central concern in cognitive research, but an emphasis on the relations of behavior across contexts highlights the centrality of a second, related issue: the generality or breadth of applicability of a skill or scheme. A full analysis of the skill underlying a behavior should predict not only where that behavior will fall in a developmental sequence but also how the skill will be evident across a range of contexts.

In recent years several investigators have elaborated a set of methods for assessing the rules underlying a behavior and explaining how those rules apply across contexts (Klahr and Wallace, 1976; MacWhinney, 1978; Siegler, 1981). Siegler (1983) provides an especially clear statement of the logic of rule assessment and focuses on school-age children (as does most rule-assessment research).

Typically, "rule" refers to a mental procedure whose operation affects performance on many problems within a task domain. Virtually all of the various approaches to specifying rules derive from the theory of production systems (Newell and Simon, 1972), which analyzes human behavior in terms of systems of rules for generating actions. A rule is defined in terms of a condition-action pair, in which the condition for taking some action is specified abstractly. For example, in simple arithmetic tasks involving division, such as 13 divided by 3, a sequence of rules can be used to describe the division procedure. After an estimate has been made of the whole number required in the quotient, a rule applies for dealing with what is left over, the remainder: If the remainder is less than the divisor, a fraction is made, with the remainder as the numerator and the divisor as the denominator. The "if" clause specifies the condition, and the "then" clause gives the action to be followed. For 13 divided by 3 the estimated whole number is 4. Application of the rule leads to the following procedure: The remainder of 1 is less than the divisor of 3, and therefore the remainder is made into a fraction of 1/3.

To use this rule across division problems, the child must check the current situation to see whether it meets the condition specified in the rule. Such checking can be done only if the rule is represented in some general format. To start with, the child must be able to distinguish which number is currently serving as remainder and which as divisor. Neither remainder nor divisor can be specified in the rule in terms of particular numerical values, such as 1 and 3, respectively, because across problems all numbers can be in both categories.

Researchers can determine whether a child is using such a rule in some set of problems by testing him or her on a number of division problems. The child is said to be using the rule whenever the pattern of behaviors (answers or methods of solution) on some set of the problems fits the rule. The child does not have to state the rule explicitly.

Though the concept of "rule" was controversial two decades ago, today it provides a basis for one of the most promising approaches for exact specification of the cognitive structures underlying child performance. Indeed, it also promises more generally to provide a powerful tool for describing change and continuity in cognitive organization.

In practice, research based on the rule-assessment approach has been characterized by two prominent features. First, it has provided highly differentiated models of regularities in behavior across contexts, including not only correct performances but also errors. This research has articulated the Piagetian hypothesis that errors form coherent patterns that derive from developmentally immature procedures (see Roberts, 1981; Siegler, 1981, 1983). Thus, both errors and correct performances can serve as indexes of the current state of a child's rule system for a particular task domain.

Second, the rule-assessment approach has fostered what might be called a "particulate" view of the child's mind. The methods are designed to detect rules in specified, interrelated tasks, in which the rules are described in terms closely tied to the tasks. Changes in performance are typically explained in terms of modifications, additions, or deletions of particular rules. Just as the philosopher Hume was criticized for depicting the mind as a "bundle of perceptions," some researchers who use rule-assessment techniques might be criticized for depicting the mind as a bundle of rules. Although such localism avoids the postulation of global, vague cognitive metamorphoses, it is in danger of treating the child too narrowly—as merely a solver of division problems, for example.

This pull toward the particular seems to be necessary if researchers are to deal with the effects of specific environments, but there is no need to stop with the particular. In some work in this tradition, children's goals figure in the definition of every rule, and these goals can apply across situations. Moreover, the idea of a rule system seems to have within it the seeds of an approach that combines the particular with the general, because rules must articulate with one another in such a system (Anderson, 1982; Siegler and Klahr, 1982) and because the construction of rules must be determined in part by the general nature of the child's information-processing system.

What seems to be required is the construction of a framework that expressly integrates methods for examining large-scale developmental changes, such as the general developmental levels, with approaches for analyzing particular rule systems. Toward this end, a straightforward approach would combine the use of developmental scales to analyze broad-scale patterns with the use of rule-assessment methods to analyze particular sets of tasks included in those scales. Thus, developmentalists can move toward a richer, fuller portrait of the development of the child in context.

EXAMPLES OF PROMISING NEW DIRECTIONS

The three central issues in the study of cognitive development—the collaboration of child and environment, the relationship of development in traditional research categories, and the methods necessary to investigate developmental questions—lead naturally to a reorientation of research. In this emerging reorientation, as we see it, the study of knowledge defined narrowly is deemphasized, and the study of the organization of behavior in general becomes the focus of developmental inquiry. The analysis of behavioral organization requires topics and methods that directly involve the collaboration of child and environment in development. A number of topics could potentially fit this criterion, but four especially promising new directions that deal with school-age children seem to us to merit the attention of cognitive-developmental researchers: (1) emotional development and its relation to cognitive development; (2) the relation of brain changes to cognitive development; (3) the role of social interaction, especially informal teaching, in cognitive development; and (4) the nature of schooling and literacy and their effects on cognitive development.

Cognitive Development and Emotional Dynamics

Emotion is becoming a central research topic, not only in the study of development but also in behavioral science more generally. From the 1940s until the mid-1970s, so little research was done on emotional development that it was fair to say that emotions had virtually disappeared from developmental science.

In the last 10 years, interest in emotional development has clearly been stirring, and much of the resulting research has dwelt on the relationship between cognition and emotion in development. Researchers on infancy have led the way, with arguments that emotions show major developmental reorganizations that are closely related to cognitive changes (Campos et al., 1978; Emde et al., 1976), and now research on cognition-emotion relationships in childhood is beginning to appear.

Children's Conceptions of Emotions

The research that seems to have advanced farthest involves the development of conceptions of emotions in school-age children. During the school years, several major changes take place, as children become able to understand that a person can experience two distinct emotions at the same time and then to integrate emotions into abstract categories for interpreting behavior.

To study how children think about their emotions, Harter (1982) devised a series of interview tasks ingeniously adapted to avoid the usual problems that arise with interviewing young children. Her research demonstrated systematic changes in the organization of children's thinking about emotions in themselves and in other people. One of the central changes was that children gradually became able to conceive of themselves as experiencing two distinct emotions at the same time, as when a girl felt happy that her parents gave her a bicycle but sad that it was only a 3-speed not a 10-speed. Preschoolers were unable to think of experiencing two emotions simultaneously. The best they could do was to portray one emotion followed by another: The girl with the bicycle could first feel happy that she had been given a bicycle and later feel sad that it was not a 10-speed. The elementary school years marked the onset of the capacity to conceive of experiencing two emotions simultaneously, and not until age 9 or later was this ability fully consolidated across Harter's various interview tasks.

Hand (1982) found the same general developmental pattern with a different type of emotion category and a different methodology. The emotions dealt with social interaction categories such as "nice" and "mean." Her main measures required children to act out stories involving these categories, and the conditions for acting out the stories provided varying degrees of environmental support for advanced performance. She also employed a structured interview designed to provide a strong-scalogram test of the developmental sequences she had predicted.

Hand's findings strongly supported the conclusion that preschool children cannot conceive of two or more simultaneous emotions. One of her subjects provided a striking example of preschool children's difficulty in thinking about simultaneous emotions: A girl was shown a story in which one child acted nice and mean simultaneously to another child, and then she was asked to retell the story in her own terms. The girl changed the story, separating it into two distinct stories. First she told about the two children being mean to each other. Then she said, "And a long time later," and began an independent story about the two children being nice to each other. In the story the girl had seen, there was no separation of the nice and mean interactions; instead, they were intertwined and integrated. To understand how the child in the story could experience two emotions, the girl apparently had to distort the story by separating the emotions into two separate stories. Other preschool children showed similar distortions, altering the stories about simultaneous emotions by separating the positive and negative emotions into distinct stories.

Hand's various assessment conditions also demonstrated that the ability to understand that opposite emotions can be experienced simultaneously could appear as early as age 6–7 or as late as age 10–12, depending on the degree of environmental support provided. Thus, social conceptions of emotions seem to show the same pattern as nonsocial conceptions: Variations in both child and environment affect the child's competence.

Hand extended the developmental sequence for nice and mean interactions into the adolescent years (Hand, 1981; Hand and Fischer, 1981). Even under supportive environmental conditions, elementary school children do not seem to be able to integrate nice and mean interactions into general abstract categories, such as "Nice or mean intentions matter more than nice or mean actions."

Hand's categories did not deal with pure emotions but instead involved emotions in social interactions. Indeed, except perhaps for the few "pure" emotions proposed by researchers such as Ekman et al. (1972) and Izard (1982), most human emotions seem to be intimately connected with social situations. Categories for social interactions as well as those for personality descriptions, such as evil, kind, sincere, honest, and responsible are often heavily loaded with emotions. The development of categories for social interactions and personality descriptions appears to follow the same sequence outlined for emotions (Fischer et al., in press; Harter, 1982; Rosenberg, 1979; Selman, 1980):

1. Preschool children seem to be able to deal with only one concrete category at a time or with a simple relationship between closely related categories, such as that indicated in the statement, "If you are mean to me, I will be mean to you."

2. Elementary school children begin to be able to describe and use intersections of concrete social and personality categories. For example, by the third or fourth grade, a boy can describe how his best friend generally tries to be nice to him and to share things most of the time, even though he can be mean and stingy when he gets grumpy.

3. In adolescence, children begin to describe themselves and other people in terms like those of personality theories. They use trait names, such as responsible, introspective, and nonconformist, and eventually they even begin to use ideas similar to the Freudian notion of internal psychological conflict.

In general, then, substantial progress has been made toward describing the development of school-age children's conceptions of emotions and related social and personality categories. As valuable as this progress is, there is much more to emotional development than conceptions of emotions.

Emotional Reorganizations

One of the most straightforward implications of the organization approach to cognitive development is that each major reorganization or level of development should produce a significant change in emotions. This hypothesis has been pursued most explicitly in infancy, for which data and theory have suggested reliable emotional concomitants of general behavioral reorganizations (Campos et al., 1978; Emde et al., 1976; McCall et al., 1977;

Papousek and Papousek, 1979; Sroufe, 1979; Zelazo and Leonard, 1983). For example, the social smile, eye-to-eye contact, and the greeting response all seem to emerge at 2–4 months, which is also a time of major cognitive reorganization. Similarly, at 7–9 months, stranger distress, separation distress, and fear of heights appear to increase dramatically just as another cognitive reorganization is occurring.

Similar emotional reorganizations can be expected to occur for every new cognitive-developmental level during the school years, although virtually no research has examined such changes. Despite the dearth of research, the psychological literature suggests many possible examples of such reorganizations involving emotions.

With the emergence of simple relations of representations at approximately age 4, there appears to be a surge of new emotions accompanying the new understanding of social roles in the family. The emotions described in Freud's (1909/1962) analysis of the Oedipus conflict may well be a part of this reorganization (Fischer and Watson, 1981). The understanding of social roles may also lead to a change in the nature of friendships, since the child will now be able to understand the role relations in friendship (see Furman, 1982; Hartup, 1983). Any such change in important social relationships would seem almost inevitably to have emotional consequences.

For the development of concrete operations at age 6–7, a number of emotional changes have been suggested by Freud and others. At this point, children appear to develop a clear-cut conscience, with an accompanying surge in guilt (Freud, 1924/1961, 1933/1965). They develop the capacity for social comparison, so they can compare and contrast their own behavior with that of other people (Ruble, 1983). Presumably, this capacity can lead to a surge in both anxiety and pride about one's relative social standing. One component of this new ability for social comparison may also be a spurt in identification with parents and other significant adults, since identification requires the comparison of self with the adult (Kagan, 1958). Any change in how children understand themselves is likely to have emotional implications.

Formal operations and the ability to understand single abstractions emerge at age 10–12 with serious emotional consequences. The confusion and turmoil of early adolescence may result in part from this new capacity (Elkind, 1974; Inhelder and Piaget, 1955/1958; Rosenberg, 1979). With formal operations, children can construct new, general concepts about themselves and other people, but they remain unable to compare one such abstraction with another. Consequently, they have difficulty thinking clearly about abstract concepts. One 16-year-old, looking back on the time when he was 12–14, described it as a fog from which he was just now emerging (Fischer et al., 1983). Erikson (1974) has suggested that the formal operations level gives the ability to form an identity—another major change in the sense of self, with inevitable emotional concomitants. The development level that first appears at age 14–16, relations of abstractions, presumably has emotional consequences, too. The ability to relate abstractions would help the individual move out of the confusing fog of early adolescence. Likewise, it might lead to a substantial change in emotions about intimate relationships, because the person could begin to relate an abstraction about his or her own personality to an abstraction about the personality of a loved one (Fischer, 1980).

Such hypotheses about emotional reorganizations during childhood have been almost entirely unexplored. Plainly, this is a promising direction for research and one in which there is no lack of stimulating hypotheses to guide the investigator. The methods outlined above for studying developments in the organization of behavior can be used in the study of such emotional changes and will substantially enhance the usefulness of such research.

Freudian Processes

It is no accident that hypotheses suggested by Freud appear repeatedly in the section on emotional reorganizations. Psychoanalysis remains one of the most fertile sources of hypotheses about emotional development. Although researchers have generally neglected psychoanalytic ideas about emotional development, especially for the school-age child, a resurgence of interest is evident.

In fact, there are signs that a major conceptual breakthrough may be in progress. For years many scholars have been dissatisfied with Freud's model of the mind (Hartmann, 1939; Holt, 1976; Schafer, 1976). Repeatedly the suggestion has been made that the cognitive-developmental orientation might well provide the framework necessary to rebuild the psychoanalytic theory of the mind (Rapaport, 1951; Schimek 1975; Wolff, 1967). A group of neo-Freudians has been working to construct a position called "object relations" theory that makes signficant steps toward integrating the cognitive-developmental and psychoanalytic orientations (for example, Kernberg, 1976; Winnicott, 1971). More recently, Feffer (1982) has suggested a recasting of the distortions of primary process in cognitive-developmental terms.

These integrations of psychoanalysis and cognitive development have already led to a large number of interesting empirical claims. For example, it has been hypothesized that mechanisms of defense follow a developmental progression (A. Freud, 1966; Fischer and Pipp, in press; Haan, 1977; Vaillant, 1977). Repression appears to first develop at age 3–4, which is the approximate age of emergence of the ability to relate representations. Several sophisticated mechanisms of defense, such as sublimation, suppression, and mature humor, do not seem to emerge until after age 11 or 12, when formal operations are beginning. These are only a few of the many interesting hypotheses in the literature about emotional development in school-age children.

Despite the easy access of such hypotheses, there have been few studies testing them. Mahler et al. (1975) assessed the development of mother-child relationships in infants and preschool children, which supported several object-relations hypotheses about the early development of self. With school-age children it is difficult to find any systematic research. Clearly, this is another promising direction.

Research on Emotions

One of the reasons for the lack of research on emotional reorganizations and Freudian processes has been that it has proved to be difficult to determine how to investigate them. Research with seriously disturbed children is particularly difficult to do, and the induction of strong emotions in children for research purposes is unethical. As a result, scholars interested in pursuing these important questions have often had to approach them indirectly—studying, for example, the development of children's conceptions of defense mechanisms in other people (Chandler et al., 1978).

A straightforward solution to this dilemma may be available. Many issues in children's everyday lives naturally evoke emotions of various degrees and types. Such issues seem to provide natural avenues for studying the organization of behavior in a way that brings together cognition and emotion.

One set of candidates includes virtually any topic involving the self—identification, identity, self-control, attributions about one's successes and failures. Kernberg (1976) has suggested that one of the primary dimensions around which the psyche is organized is whether events are perceived as threatening to the self or as supportive of the self, and much social-psychological research with adults generally supports this hypothesis (Greenwald, 1980). The development of self in children and its relation to the organization of behavior is a promising avenue for studying cognition-emotion relations.

Another set of issues of special relevance to school-age children is family relations, including the emotional climate in the family. The Oedipus conflict is merely the most discussed of a wide-ranging set of family phenomena that are emotion laden.

Consider, for example, divorce. The proportion of children growing up in divorced families has risen sharply, and some projections place it at 40–50 percent in coming years. The experience of divorce is clearly emotional for many children, and systematic relations seem to exist between emotional problems in adulthood (such as loneliness and depression) and the ages of individuals when their parents were divorced (Shaver and Rubenstein, 1980). In addition, young children seem to seriously misunderstand the causes of their parents' divorce, often blaming themselves for the breakup (Longfellow, 1979; Wallerstein and Kelly, 1980). Research on how children understand and deal with divorce would seem a natural avenue for studying the development of emotion and cognition. How children understand what happened and how they conceive of the relationships in their family will probably relate in interesting ways to how they feel about themselves and their parents.

Children's reactions to illness provide another promising topic for the study of emotion-cognition relations. Virtually all children experience illnesses several times during the school years, and a substantial number of children suffer from chronic illnesses (Shonkoff, in this volume). Research on how children understand what happens during an illness and how they cope with it promises to illuminate cognition-emotion relations in development. Indeed, it would be surprising if mechanisms of defense and other emotional organizations could not be investigated in connection with divorce and illness.

A note about emotional development is in order. In our analysis we have focused on promising areas for study of how emotion relates to cognitive development. In doing so we have not differentiated the many components of emotions, including triggering, expression, suppression, interpretation, and communication. Clearly, a full analysis of emotional development will require study of these components (Campos et al., 1983).

Relations Between Brain Changes and Cognitive Development

It is a truism in developmental science that changes in the brain must be central to cognitive development, yet researchers have mostly neglected investigation of the relationship between brain and cognition in development. Recent research on development in animals has begun to illuminate relevant topics, such as the processes by which experience affects the development of the visual system in mammals (Movshon and Van Sluyters, 1981) and the mechanisms by which the brain adjusts to early damage (Goldman-Rackic et al., 1983).

Of course, the methods used to study brain development in animals cannot be applied to human beings, but the paucity of research on the relationship between brain changes and cognitive development in children is nevertheless remarkable. One reason for neglect of this topic seems to be that previous investigations searching for such relationships did not meet with much success. Another reason may be that scientists shy away from the topic because past findings have sometimes led to a simplistic form of reductionist thinking, in which any brain changes are assumed to have direct correlates in behavioral development.

A few investigators have studied the relationship between certain global changes in the brain and the cognitive-developmental levels occurring during the school years. They have uncovered evidence that brain or head growth may spurt on the average at ages 4–5, 6–7, 10–12, and 14–16 (Eichorn and Bayley, 1962; Epstein, 1974, 1980; Fischer and Pipp, 1984; Nellhaus, 1968). The primary data involve growth in head circumference and change in certain waves of the electroencephalogram. The data for head circumference tend to support the occurrence of spurts at the expected ages, but there is substantial inconsistency across studies (McQueen, 1982). Fewer studies exist on the electroencephalogram, but extant data appear to be more consistent across samples. For brain-wave characteristics that show consistent increases or decreases with age, children show spurts during the four predicted age periods.

Unfortunately, these data have been used to support unjustified conclusions about the nature of cognitive development and learning at various ages during the school years. Children can learn new skills during periods of brain growth spurts, it has been claimed, but they cannot learn during periods of slow growth (Epstein, 1978, 1980; Toepfer, 1979). Thus, for example, children between ages 12 and 14 are said to be unable to learn new skills, because brain growth shows a plateau rather than a spurt during that period. These conclusions have been based almost entirely on the brain growth data, with virtually no assessment of actual learning.

Despite the limitations of the data, some school systems have begun to base portions of their curricula on these unwarranted conclusions. Efforts are being made, for example, to build middle-school curricula around the assumption that children of middle-school age cannot learn very much because their brains are not undergoing a growth spurt. Clearly, no conclusions about learning ability or recommendations about educational practices can be supported by data on brain growth alone.

Several recent studies have tested the hypothesis that individual children undergo cognitive spurts when they show head-growth spurts and cognitive plateaus when they show head-growth plateaus (McCall et al., 1983; Petersen and Cavrell, in press). The results are clear: There was no correlation between head growth and cognitive growth. The most reasonable conclusion at this point seems to be that head growth and cognitive-developmental level are related for large samples but not for individual children.

Similar problems have arisen in research on the development of brain lateralization (Kinsbourne and Hiscock, 1983). From a few early findings on differences between the right and left hemispheres, some investigators have jumped to broad generalizations about the different natures of intelligence in the two hemispheres. Journalists and educators have gone further and drawn sweeping, unjustified conclusions about the nature of intelligence in general and cognitive development in particular. There seems to be an unfortunate tendency for people to repeatedly make the same unjustified leap from data on brain growth to conclusions about behavior.

This leap is apparently predicated on the assumption that brain developments appear before behavioral changes and then have an immediate, measurable impact on behavior. Based on research on the relationships between developments in other domains, the most reasonable hypothesis is that the relationship between brain changes and cognitive development will be highly complex. Indeed, behavioral changes are probably just as likely to precede brain changes as to follow them. For both head circumference and the electroencephalogram, for example, brain growth shows a spurt one to three years after the first cognitive changes reflecting concrete operations: Concrete-operational skills are first evident as early as age 5.5–6, but brain spurts do not usually appear until age 7–9. One reasonable hypothesis is that small behavioral changes typically precede any global brain changes of the type measured by head circumference and the electroencephalogram. Some animal research supports the argument that behavioral changes can precede major brain changes (Greenough and Schwark, in press).

The findings of correlations between brain growth and cognitive development may eventually lead researchers to examine seriously brain-behavior relationships in development. The research topic is both legitimate and important, and eventually it is likely to produce important scientific breakthroughs. However, the complexity of the topic means that legitimate applications leading to the solution of practical problems almost certainly will not be available for a long time (Shonkoff, in this volume).

Cognitive Development and Modes of Social Interaction

A third promising direction in the study of cognitive development addresses the question of how social interaction dynamically constitutes a favorable climate for the growth of the mind. In the past, psychologists' answers to related questions have often over- or underestimated the contribution of social interaction to normal cognitive development. Recently, renewed interest in the problem has produced a burst of naturalistic and seminaturalistic studies of parent-child and teacher-student interactions.

This new research has begun to chart a middle course between two extreme views of the role of social interaction in cognitive development. The first of these extremes can be called the social learning straw man. It holds that most cognitive development is a result of imitation, which is construed as mere mimicry rather than cognitive reconstruction. The second extreme can be called the little scientist straw man. This position holds that most cognitive development is a result of autonomous inventions, cognitive reconstructions in which social interaction plays no formative role. Both of these views are caricatures of human development. A minimal task for cognitive developmentalists is to portray the role of social interaction without resorting to either caricature.

The words that best depict the middle-course alternative emerging from recent research are *guided reinvention* (Lock, 1980; see also Karplus, 1981; Resnick, 1976), which acknowledges the social learning theorists' insistence that social guidance is ubiquitous, both within and outside the classroom. They also acknowledge, however, the Piagetian insight that to understand is to reconstruct. Thus, the guided reinvention perspective elaborates the theme that normal cognitive development must be understood as a collaborative phenomenon.

In classical writings on cognitive development, Vygotsky (1934/1962, 1934/1978) seems to have best anticipated the guided reinvention perspective. For Vygotsky, an analysis of modes of social interaction is essential for explaining cognitive development. In addition, he argued that an explanation of guided reinvention must use the historical-reconstructive method, which is similar to what Piaget called the "genetic" method. For Vygotsky, Piaget's "to understand is to reconstruct" was as apt a summary of the successful theorist's efforts as it was a summary of the child's efforts. Vygotsky argued that developmentalists need to study the dynamics of the developmental process directly, rather than continuing merely to draw inferences about the process from structural analyses of the products of development.

What would a reconstructive understanding of social interaction involve? One of Vygotsky's central tenets was that social interaction is organized on a number of planes and that each successive plane is associated with greater cognitive powers. One way of conceiving these planes is schematized in Table 3-3, adapted from a convergence rate hierarchy proposed in Bullock (1983) as a synthesis of both Vygotskyan and social learning (Bandura, 1971) principles.

The core ideas of the convergence rate hierarchy are simple. Cognitive development can be idealized as a process of converging, step by step, toward some higher plane of knowledge and skill. Such convergence must proceed at some rate, and that rate is affected by many factors. One basic factor is the plane of social interaction available to the young, e.g., whether the young participate in symbolic communication with elders. Table 3-3 presents a hypothetical ordering of some major steps along the road to the complexly

TABLE 3-3   A Hierarchy of Factors Affecting
Convergence Rate

1. Natural Selection (NS)
2. NS + Reflex Conditioning (RC)
3. NS + RC + Conditionable Goal-Directed Activity (CGDA)
4. NS + RC + CGDA + Affective Bonding/Communication (ABC)
5. NS + RC + CGDA + ABC + Constructive Imitation (CI)
6. NS + RC + CGDA + ABC + CI + Purposive Teaching (PT)
7. NS + RC + CGDA + ABC + CI + PT + Symbolic
   Communication (SC)
8. NS + RC + CGDA + ABC + CI + PT + SC + Writing (W)
9. NS + RC + CGDA + ABC + CI + PT + SC + W +
   Advanced Literacy (AL)

layered type of social interaction available to today's children. Each step is called a level, but this terminology is not meant to imply any special connection with the levels of cognitive reorganization suggested by cognitive-developmental theorists.

By hypothesis, each new level in the hierarchy produces an increase in the average convergence rate of offspring toward higher levels of knowledge and skill (see Bullock, 1983, for details). Beyond level 3, each level involves an innovation in the form of social interaction. Thus, the hierarchy synthesizes social learning theorists' observations about the effects of modeling on learning rate (Bandura, 1971) and Vygotsky's observations about the hierarchically layered nature of social interaction (see also Dennett, 1975; Premack, 1973).

The entire hierarchy might be taken as a schematic for assembling a system for guided reinvention. In this regard, special note should be made of levels 5 and 6, because they mark the crystallization of two complementary roles, i.e., child as reinventor and parent as guide. The words *constructive imitation*, which describe the social innovation at level 5, are meant to be a reminder of the reconstructive nature of imitation noted by all major students of imitation since Baldwin (1895; Bandura, 1971, 1977; Guillaume, 1926/1971; Kaye, 1982; Piaget, 1946/1951). Many imitative achievements are not mere mimicry; instead, they involve persistent reconstructive efforts on the part of the imitator. These efforts are a major source of developmental reorganizations, especially when complemented by the purposive teaching spontaneously provided by parents. Also, because constructive imitation engages a wide range of cognitive resources, there is no isolable imitative faculty, as some have supposed.

By hypothesis, constructive imitation by children and purposive teaching by parents are complementary components of an evolved system for guided reinvention. Moreover, when these components are seen as parts of the entire hierachy, a further hypothesis is suggested. When cognitive development is proceeding most rapidly, it will involve guided reinvention embedded within goal-directed activity that is jointly undertaken by an apprentice (the child) and an expert, who are tied together by positive affect. This would be true if the higher social-interactive levels are built on the lower, older ones and continue to depend on them for their own optimal functioning. For example, the developmental value of practices at the high end of the hierarchy, such as formal schooling, may depend on the modes of interaction at lower levels. A corollary to this hypothesis is that the large departures from the modes of interaction that evolved to support guided reinvention will create difficulties for children. The remainder of this section surveys research relevant to these ideas and traces possible implications for education.

Guided Reinvention Within Dyadic Goal-Directed Activity

The most intensive basic research on naturally occurring social-interactive modes as vehicles for guided reinvention (outside classrooms) has occurred in the field of language development (Brown, 1980; Bruner, 1983; Bullock, 1979; Cross, 1977; Kaye, 1982; Kaye and Charney, 1980; Lock, 1980; Moerk, 1976; Snow, 1977; Swensen, 1983; Wells, 1974). Most of this research involved children younger than school age. There are, however, a few notable studies of older children in domains of cognitive development other than language (Donaldson, 1978; Heber, 1977; Karplus, 1981; Wertsch, 1979; Wood, 1980). We briefly survey available results from the language development literature and use the results from studies of older children to demonstrate the generality of basic principles.

Both logical (Bruner, 1975; Macnamara, 1972; Wittgenstein, 1953) and empirical (Bullock, 1979; Cross, 1977; Snow, 1977; Swensen, 1983) analyses indicate that normal language development depends on social-cognitive coordination between the child and someone who uses language in a contextually appropriate way while interacting with the child. Other research has shown that mere exposure to television does not result in normal language development, apparently because its dynamic linguistic stimulation is provided without social-cognitive coordination. There is now ample evidence that an extraordinarily high degree of social-cognitive coordination can accelerate language development (Cross, 1977; Swenson, 1983).

Social-cognitive coordination is always a matter of degree. The degree of coordination increases with the amount of overlap between two individuals' understanding of the situation in which they jointly find themselves (e.g., the situation of playing a game). Thus, a high degree of social-cognitive coordination requires the achievement of many moments of shared understanding.

Shared understanding is such a critical factor because normal language development is a comprehension-driven process that involves much more than the learning of syntactic patterns (Curtis, 1981; Macnamara, 1972; Nelson, 1973; Wittgenstein, 1953), even though it is sometimes discussed as a pure exercise in pattern learning (Kiss, 1972). Comprehension involves both isolating new patterns and making sense of them by finding a way to articulate them with what is already understood (Clark and Clark, 1977; Schlesinger, 1982). In guided reinvention the child and adult share an understanding of their joint situation, and the adult's speech takes that understanding as a point of departure while heeding developmental and contextual constraints. As a result of this support, the child stands a good chance of being able to comprehend the adult's utterance the first time he or she hears it, even when it contains novel components (Bullock, 1979; Cross, 1977; Wells, 1974).

How do child and adult articulate new patterns with what the child already understands? The child seeks above all to discover the relevance of the adult's contributions to his or her own purposes and goals at the moment. The adult attempts to ensure that his or her acts are relevant to the child's activity in a way that the child is prepared to discover.

How is shared understanding dynamically maintained over long bouts of interaction? Parents of children who exhibit rapid language development actively work to maintain shared understanding over long stretches of interaction. They do this in several ways. They introduce objects to serve as bases for joint activities, and they closely monitor their child's apparent goals or intentions. During most of their interactive turns, they attempt to modulate, correct, or elaborate their child's behavior rather than redirect it. And they construct an internal model of their child's current preferences, skills, and world knowledge, which they continuously update and check (Brown, 1980; Kaye, 1982; Nelson, 1973; Snow, 1977).

Embedded Teaching and Formal Schooling

It would certainly be misleading to say that language is not taught, but the type of teaching uncovered in these naturalistic studies of language development is unlike that found in most formal schooling. Under normal conditions it seems that every child receives a steady diet of what might be called embedded teaching—elaborative and corrective acts responsively embedded by parents in the flow of joint goal-directed activity. As the child spontaneously and vigorously works to master a wide range of goals, his or her constructive efforts are constantly guided by the parent's embedded teaching efforts. Although such efforts do not obviate the need for inventive and inductive efforts by the child (Maratsos, 1983), they appear to be crucial if the child's efforts are to result in a course of development that is recognizably normal.

With preschool and school-age children, research has focused not on language learning but on cognitive tasks ranging from puzzle solving to classical Piagetian tasks such as seriation and conservation. Yet the results paint much the same picture (Heber, 1977; Sonstroem, 1966; Wertsch, 1979; Wood, 1980). In his survey of this small body of research, Wood (1980) concluded that "where instruction is contingent on the child's own activities and related to what he is currently trying to do, . . . considerable progress may be made" (p. 290). His survey also revealed that when instructional techniques depart from the embedded teaching mode the child's progress is markedly slowed. Finally, in research on the learning cycle or guided discovery approach to the instruction of mathematical reasoning, this embedded teaching method was very successful in a domain in which many students fail with more traditional classroom techniques (Karplus, 1981).

Much more research along these lines is needed, especially with school-age children. We expect that studies of embedded teaching with older children will show it to be superior to "disembedded" teaching, especially in the promotion of lasting changes in cognitive skills. Here, disembedded teaching means any teaching that departs significantly from guided reinvention. On the basis of available research, two characteristics of guided reinvention seem particularly critical: (1) any new information provided is relevant to furthering the child's current goal-directed activity, and (2) information is provided in a way that is immediately responsive and "proportionate" (Wood, 1980) to the child's varying information needs. Note that much classroom instruction departs from guided reinvention in both respects.

Recently a number of authors have tried to explain the difficulty many children have making the transition to school or the related difficulty they have in becoming engaged in certain school subjects (Bereiter and Scardamalia, 1982; Cook-Gumperz and Gumperz, 1981; Donaldson, 1978; Papert, 1980). All these analyses support the idea that many children fail not because of inability but because they are ill prepared for the mode of social interaction encountered in many classrooms. This ill preparedness—or to see it the other way, this ill adaptedness of some schooling modes to what many children naturally expect—has two consequences. First, many children fail to progress at an acceptable rate and fall progressively further behind their peers. Second, many children become disaffected with the classroom setting.

Obviously, these two results are closely linked. Failure to progress implies continual frustration, which leads to global disaffection. But several lines of research suggest a deeper relationship. In the literature on the development of affective relationships, responsiveness seems to play a crucial role in attachment formation (Ainsworth, 1979). At every level of the convergence rate hierarchy, the child's development depends on the contributions of others in immediate social interaction. In parametric research on what makes educational computer games attractive, contingency on the child's behavior in essential (Malone, 1981). And in informal research on how to make mathematics more appealing, Papert (1980) even speaks seriously of the child's affective relationship to the world of mathematics. Given the human ability to personify, there is no reason to dismiss Papert's usage as mere metaphor.

There is ample evidence that several qualities of dyadic social interaction contribute to a positive attitude toward instructional activities, what Malone (1981) calls their holding power: in particular, goal-directedness, responsiveness, novelty, and performance-contingent shifts in problem difficulty. Indeed, a classic study by Bowman (1959) showed that disaffected delinquents will regain interest in classroom work and markedly reduce their disruptive behavior when the classroom mode is restructured around goal-directed activities. Although Bowman failed to find larger academic gains in the embedded teaching group than in a control group, the study deserves replication with more sensitive cognitive outcome measures and with a better-designed "guided reinvention" curriculum.

We would like to raise another issue, although we cannot pursue it here. We noted earlier that the disembedded teaching that children encounter in many classroom settings does not meet their expectations. However, this statement is too weak because it presents too passive a picture of the student. We believe that children actively try to structure their interactions such that the type of teaching they receive is the embedded type. Children demand involvement as performers rather than as mere observers. (See Barker and Gump, 1964, for the classic treatment of this distinction.) A common childhood plea is "I want to be included and help you do it, not just watch." In this connection it is also interesting to note a convergence with Harter's (1978) revision of the concept of competence motivation. According to her reformulation, the child with high competence motivation actively resists excessive guidance in joint-task contexts.

Collaboration Not Conservation

As noted in the introduction to this section, history shows that it has been quite difficult to maintain a balanced view of the role of social interaction in cognitive development. Many seem to think of the problem according to the scheme of a "conservation" equation: Child's Contribution + Social Contribution = A Constant Amount of Knowledge. Given this scheme, the laws of algebra demand that if the child's contribution goes up the social contribution must go down, and vice versa. Any theorist who focuses on one factor is led by the scheme to downplay the other. But the scheme itself is plainly inappropriate. Not only is the amount of knowledge not conserved, but the evidence indicates that social factors contribute most when embedded within the child's own ongoing efforts at mastery. As Bullock (1983) noted when proposing the convergence rate hierarchy, higher cognitive potentials seem to arise with specific new types of social interaction. By emphasizing the concept of guided reinvention, we hope to have made it difficult for investigators to continue thinking in terms of the conservation scheme.

Because this treatment stands on the shoulders of Vygotsky's pioneering work and because the next section is devoted to the topic of literacy, it is fitting to round off this section with Vygotsky's (1934/1978:117–118) prescient remarks about the need for embedded teaching of literacy:

Reading and writing must be something the child needs. Here we have the most vivid example of the basic contradiction that appears in the teaching of writing not only in Montessori's school but in most other schools as well, namely, that writing is taught as a motor skill and not as a complex cultural activity. . . . Writing should be meaningful for children, . . . an intrinsic need should be aroused in them, and . . . writing should be incorporated into a task that is necessary and relevant for life. Only then can we be certain that it will develop not as a matter of hand and finger habits but as a really new and complex form of speech.

The Effects of Schooling and Other Literate Practices

One of the most promising new directions for cognitive-developmental research concerns the cognitive effects of literacy and formal schooling (Cole and Bruner, 1971; Cole and Griffin, 1980; Goody, 1977; Luria, 1976; Olson, 1976; Ong, 1982; Scribner and Cole, 1981; Vygotsky 1934/1978). This new area has live roots in anthropology, educational theory, historiography, philosophy, linguistics, and developmental and cross-cultural psychology. These roots give the area both a singular vitality and a special promise for promoting communication among relatively isolated academic disciplines (Ong, 1982). Moreover, literacy and schooling relate closely to the emphasis on the interaction between child and environment in cognitive develop- ment. The effects of literacy and schooling seem to arise from the environ- mental supports they provide for advanced cognitive functioning. To understand cognitive development in the child in school, scientists and educators need to understand how the teaching of literacy and schooling relates to the child's natural learning processes and how literacy and school- ing affect the child's mind.

Our treatment of literacy effects necessarily begins with the problem of definition, because there are many literacies and each may have distinctive cognitive-developmental effects. The range of literate practices is analyzed in terms of how each functions in mental life. This analysis leads to the specification of appropriate methods for assessing the cognitive effects of literate practices. The approach presented here represents what seems to be an emerging consensus about literacy and schooling.

Defining Literacy

What are the cognitive effects of literacy? According to recent research (Goody, 1977; Scribner and Cole, 1981), answering this question in a scientifically useful manner requires careful specification of what is meant by literacy. All literacies involve both (1) one or more conventionalized systems for external representation of ideas and (2) a set of cultural practices that use the systems. Literacies include all conventionalized representational systems, not just alphabetic writing. Any cognitive consequences can be expected to be determined jointly by the specific nature of a representational system and its associated practices. As a reminder of these points, we use the words *literate practices* rather than *literacy*.

Table 3-4 presents some literate practices that span a range from simple labeling (practice 1) to scientific theory construction (practice 9). To il- lustrate the vastness of this span, we discuss two extreme cases of literate practices: the use of a limited writing system by some men in West Africa and the use of multiple representational systems by modern scientists. The vast differences between these two cases suggest enormous differences in their cognitive consequences.

In the first case, men belonging to the rural Vai people in West Africa are taught a native script (Scribner and Cole, 1981). (Literate practices are virtually absent among Vai women.) The Vai script is a syllabary, a system for representing speech phonetically syllable by syllable. In this system a text consists of a continuous stream of symbols without any segmentation

TABLE 3-4   A Range of Literate Practices

A. Amplification
    1. Labeling containers to signify contents.
    2. Listing donations at a wedding feast.
    3. Writing status reports or orders.

B. Nonlocal Integration
    4. Compiling a chronology of events by piecing together
        fragmentary reports.
    5. Writing an essay by integrating research notes collected over a
        long interval.
    6. Summarizing the results of a long series of experiments recorded
        in a log.
    7. Checking a document for equivocal usage of key terms.

C. Systemic Analysis
    8. Comparing the properties of two closed representational systems
        (e.g., two alphabets or two taxonomies).
    9. Composing a formalism capable of expressing a set of critical
        theoretical distinctions.

markers such as blanks to indicate word boundaries. Also, homophonic syllables (such as *boar* and *bore* in English) are always represented by the same symbol. These characteristics make it virtually impossible to read Vai script rapidly with full comprehension. Because of this limitation as well as competition from other scripts, the Vai script is highly restricted in the range of practices it supports. The script is neither taught nor used in formal school settings, and its major use is letter writing (practice 3 in Table 3-3). Scribner and Cole report that letters written in Vai script are short and limited to expected themes. Because of the difficulty of reading the script, long texts on novel themes would overwhelm even the most accomplished Vai readers. Not one Vai occupation depends critically on the use of the script.

At the other extreme, consider a modern scientist working at the frontiers of the field of neural modeling of cognitive processes (Grossberg, 1982). A single paper published in this area may draw on a tool kit of conventionalized representations that includes (1) standard written English, including the modern Roman alphabet and numerous other conventions; (2) mathematical equations, including modern number systems and the Greek alphabet; (3) a biochemical symbol system; (4) labeled graphs that are a hybrid of iconic and more arbitrary representational devices; (5) a computer language used to write simulation programs; and (6) models of memory, cognitive development, and other psychological processes. All these resources are being used to compose a new formalism capable of expressing a set of critical theoretical distinctions (practice 9) for characterizing the design principles exhibited by the human brain.

Modern science has institutionalized the practice of inventing such new representational systems. This enterprise is critically dependent for its success on both the evolving representational systems already in the tool kit and the evolving tradition of scientific practices (e.g., techniques for studying nonlinear differential equations, computer simulation techniques, and so forth). Equally important, the whole enterprise would be inconceivable to anyone who was unschooled in similar literacy-based practices. Even for someone who knew some such practices but was not familiar with the specific tool kit, the enterprise would be difficult to conceive with any specificity. The scientific enterprise is thus much farther removed from the preliterate world than is the Vai practice of writing simple status reports or orders.

Consequently, it would be odd to expect the Vai male's literacy to have the same cognitive effects as the neural modeler's literacy. In fact, both persons differ in some way from nonliterates because of their shared encounter with an external, representational system in use. Yet that common difference pales in comparison with other intellectual differences arising from the distinctiveness of their literate practices.

A common question in research has been whether some specific cognitive effect should be attributed to literacy or to formal schooling. The definitional problems with such a question are similar to those with questions about the effects of literacy alone. The term *formal schooling* is just as ill defined as the term *literacy*. Moreover, posing a dichotomy between literacy and formal schooling obscures the fact that all types of formal schooling are literacy based. Though it is possible to have literate practices without formal schooling, it is not possible to have formal schooling without literate practices. In general, formal schooling and literate practices are closely linked. Many literate practices with distinctive cognitive effects were probably invented in an attempt to improve schooling (Goody, 1977), and many children encounter these practices for the first time in a school setting.

Characterizing the Range of Literate Practices

The literate practices in Table 3-4 are divided into three groups: amplification, nonlocal integration, and systemic analysis. These labels are meant to capture qualitative differences in how literate practices seem to function in the cognitive life of individuals and to suggest directions for research on literate practices.

In amplification, some human ability already exists in some form, and the literate practices simply magnify that ability (Cole and Bruner, 1971;

Cole and Griffin, 1980). For example, labeling of containers (practice 1) provides redundant cues for identifying contents and thus often increases the speed of identification. Listing donations (practice 2) duplicates a preliterate mnemonic achievement and supports more accurate recall. The writing of orders (practice 3) substitutes for speaking them in a way that allows the orders to affect people at greater distances. Note that these are all quantitative (amplifying) effects. They leave the structure of the activity largely unchanged.

A literate practice can do more than amplify. It can induce a qualitatively different ability (Cole and Griffin, 1980). Though the distinction between quantitative and qualitative is sometimes fuzzy, it is useful. Classical writings on cognitive development describe two pervasive functions of literate practices that involve qualitative effects: nonlocal integration and systemic analysis, as shown in Table 3-3 (e.g., Inhelder and Piaget, 1955/1958; Vygotsky, 1934/1978).

Many literate practices support nonlocal integration of materials that would otherwise remain separate. Under aliterate conditions, thoughts tend to shift from one content to the next on the basis of characteristics that are relatively obvious and that have already been recognized. Contents with similarities, complementarities, or other relationships that have not yet been recognized will rarely be juxtaposed in thought. As a result, the undiscovered relationships between them will rarely be discovered.

When writing, the writer has a device that supports the juxtaposition of such apparently disparate contents and thus raises the chances of discovering a new way of integrating experience. As a result, writing can accelerate the pace of conceptual innovation, forming the core of new types of cultural practices, including the scientific method. By overcoming a systematic limit of human memory, it opens up a new range of human practices. For example, in constructing the theory of evolution, Darwin had to put together widely disparate contents. Howard Gruber (1981) wrote of Darwin: "To understand what he had seen, and to construct a theory that would do it new justice, he had to re-examine everything incessantly from the varied perspectives of his diverse enterprises" (p. 113, italics added). Darwin wrote down observations and thoughts in a series of logs and notebooks to facilitate this process. Indeed, the experimentalist's practice of keeping a log is a particularly clear example of how writing can overcome the limitations of memory. The log supports simultaneous consideration of experiments that are temporally and conceptually remote.

Nonlocal integration is certainly not unique to literate practices. Under aliterate conditions it would seem to occur primarily in social interactions in which communicating individuals try to reconcile disparate schemes. It is probably common in language and cognitive development, when a child is trying to reconstruct integrative schemes underlying adult usage (Feldman, 1980; Horton and Markman, 1980; Laboratory of Comparative Human Cognition, 1983; Perret-Clermont, 1980). Among adults it can occur when individuals confront each others' disparate ways of organizing experience. At the same time, literacy practices themselves support a heterogeneity of adult perspectives unheard of in aliterate cultures. After the invention of literate practices, a language's stock of terms based on nonlocal integration explodes (Slaughter, 1982). Apparently, literacies support lifelong use of a type of integration that would otherwise be rarely exploited after the early years of development.

A third function of literate practices, systemic analysis, occurs whenever the focus of a thinker's concern is the adequacy of an entire representational system. Nonlocal integration promotes the building of conventionalized representational systems, and systemic analysis involves the evaluation of those systems. It seems that literate practices provide strong support for the ability to consider such systems and to analyze and compare them.

Consider the following historical examples. The ancient Greeks compared what is now known as the Greek alphabet with various other writing systems of the time. It was seen as an improvement over its competitors because it could represent vowel sounds as well as consonantal sounds (practice 8 in Table 3-4). Riemannian geometry was an improvement over Euclidean geometry because it provided a better representation of physical space under relativistic conditions (practice 8). Most behavioral scientists have joined the enterprise of trying to formulate a new cognitivist theoretical system for thought and behavior because the old behaviorist system appears to be inherently unequal to the task of modeling psychological phenomena (practice 9).

Systemic analysis is fundamental to the modern scientific enterprise. Modern scientists are acutely aware that at some future date their current systems for representing reality will probably prove inadequate. They take it as their task to contribute to a better, but never final, fit between data patterns and theoretical models (representational systems) (Goody, 1977; Toulmin, 1972). Such an attitude has led to ferment on many levels. Scholars of many stripes struggle with the problems of relativism, and school-age children are confused at the apparent lack of absolute truth in modern knowledge. To understand this attitude, children seem to require many years of experience, and they may be able finally to understand it only when they reach the highest levels of cognitive development (Kitchener, 1983).

This phenomenon seems to be tightly bound up with the development of literate practices (Goody, 1977; Ong, 1982). It seems to require at least four components: (1) possession of the concept of a representational system, (2) appreciation that the belief system accepted in one's day is one of many possible systems, (3) presumption that today's belief system will prove less adequate than some alternatives that have not yet been specified, and (4) institutionalized support of practices that have a history of producing improvements in representational systems. The second, third, and fourth components require historical studies and are therefore literacy dependent in a strict sense, because historical studies do not seem to be possible without written histories. The first component, possession of the concept of a representational system, seems at least to be greatly facilitated by literate practices. The development of this concept in school-age children certainly merits study (Feldman, 1980; Gardner, 1983).

Aliterate cultures seem to provide little environmental support for the concept of a representational system (Goody, 1977), but literacy provides open and direct support for the concept. Writing is permanent, and so language becomes subject to extended scrutiny. As a result, people can conceive the nature and shortcomings of the written system for language. For example, all alphabets are small systems that can be understood as a whole and that are manifestly imperfect in their ability to represent speech. They fail to capture even many of the vocal aspects of speech, such as timing and inflection. These limitations make it relatively easy for literate peoples to abstract the concept of a representational system.

Methods for Assessing the Cognitive Effects of Literate Practices

If this characterization of the functioning of literate practices in mental life is correct, most traditional methods for assessing literacy effects will need to be revised. Consider one assessment strategy used often in the past: The researcher constitutes a group with equal numbers of illiterates and literates and tests all of them on some cognitive task, such as recalling a long list of words. All subjects perform the task in the same way, with no access to literate tools such as pencil and paper. After statistically controlling for factors such as intelligence, age, and social background, the researcher assesses whether there is any residual effect of literacy on performance. To date, the results of such traditional studies have been disappointing, typically showing no, or only modest, effects of literacy (Scribner and Cole, 1981).

In hindsight this failure is not surprising because the studies do not assess the right skills. First, subjects performing the tasks are denied access to the literate tool kit during their performance. Unable to use the external tools of literacy, they are denied environmental support for their literate skills, which typically require operations with external representational devices.

As a result, the main effects of literacy are at best severely attenuated. Second, the research addresses basic cognitive abilities such as recall. Literacy effects that do not permanently amplify such basic abilities go undetected. Third, the major comparison treats illiterates and literates as homogeneous classes, ignoring the tremendous differentiation within the class of literates. In particular, many literates have little exposure to the literate skills most critical to the modern knowledge explosion—the practices that institutionalize nonlocal integration and systemic analysis.

Figure 3-4 shows the range of conditions needed to assess the cognitive effects of literate practices in children or adults. Subjects need to be differentiated according to their literacy status, as shown in the top row. Preliterates are members of cultures that lack any literate practices, while illiterates are aliterate members of cultures rich in literate practices. This distinction permits assessment of whether some cognitive effects of literate practices diffuse within a culture to those who have not actually learned enough to be literate. Nominal literates have learned the basics about using an external representational system but not the practices that promote nonlocal integration and systemic analysis, while advanced literates have mastered some of those practices. This distinction allows assessment of the effects of the advanced literacy skills related to the modern knowledge explosion.

Individuals should be tested with or without access to the external tool kit of literacy, as shown in the second row of the figure. Testing both ways is critical so that researchers can determine whether literacy effects depend on the environmental support of the tool kit. Most past assessments of

		Person's Literacy Status						
		Preliterate		Illiterate		Nominal Literate		Advanced Literate	
Access to Tools		Present	Absent	Present	Absent	Present	Absent	Present	Absent
Type of Task	Basic Ability								
	Nonlocal Integration								
	Systemic Analysis								

FIGURE 3-4   A matrix of contrasts for the assessment of literacy effects.

literacy effects have denied access to the tools (Scribner and Cole, 1981) and thus have tested only for the residual effects of prior engagement in literate practices. Also, subjects should be tested on a range of types of task, as shown in the left column. Many of the effects of literate practices will remain obscure if only basic cognitive abilities are assessed.

An Emerging Consensus

The approach outlined here represents an emerging consensus about the effects of literacy (Bullock, 1983; Cole and Griffin, 1980; Goody, 1977; Scribner and Cole, 1981; Slaughter, 1982; Tannen, 1982; Vygotsky, 1934/ 1978; Zebroski, 1982). This consensus includes an appreciation of at least four major characteristics of the functioning of literate practices:

1. Literate practices are highly diverse.
2. The diversity includes differences not only in the tools of literacy but also in the cultural practices related to the tools.
3. Many literacy effects depend on long exposure to organized use of literate tool kits, and the most interesting literacy effects are probably not automatic products of learning to read, write, or count. Literate practices have their effects via a long developmental process beginning in the school years and extending into adulthood.
4. Different literate practices play different roles in mental life, and some of the most important roles seem to involve providing support for functioning at levels of cognitive development that emerge in the late school years and beyond.

Of course, the consensus is not complete. Two of the remaining controversies are especially relevant here. First, do literate practices have a pervasive effect on thinking and consciousness, or are their effects highly specific and localized? Second, are literate practices fundamental to the most advanced forms of human thinking, as Vygotsky (1934/1978) believed, or can such advanced skills develop without literacy?

Although firm answers to these questions will not be available until more of the blank cells in Figure 3-4 are filled in, we hazard two predictions. On general theoretical grounds (Fischer, 1980; Fischer and Bullock, 1981) and on the basis of available research on literacy effects (see Scribner and Cole, 1981), we expect that some form of the specificity hypothesis will survive the test of time. But along with specificity there can also be some generality. Literacy is itself a vehicle for partially overcoming the natural tendency for skills to remain localized.

Regarding the role of literate practices in advanced forms of thought, we have already proposed that modern scientific enterprises are literally inconceivable to preliterates because they involve explicit attempts to revise entire conceptual systems. It remains to be seen whether other examples of such systemic analysis can be found among preliterates (Goody, 1977).

Literate Practices and Schooling

We noted earlier that the mode of teaching in traditional schooling departs substantially from the natural teaching mode children experience in everyday life. Instead of being embedded in the course of joint goal-directed activity, teaching is disembedded and organized around domains of knowledge (Slaughter, 1982).

This property of formal schooling appears to be a product of literate practices. In all likelihood the very idea of a domain of knowledge and the disembedded teaching it encourages are two sides of a coin that could only be minted in a literate culture. Only with literacy are words or statements disembedded from the evanescent stream of human action and given the spatial permanence of things. Only with literacy are large bodies of such statements sorted into separate places that are internally organized according to the taxonomic schemes associated with domains of knowledge.

Based on the concept of domains of knowledge, teaching can be disembedded from the world of human purposes and reconceptualized as the transfer of a body of knowledge from one depository (books) to another (children). As Ong (1982:175–177) suggested, the message transfer model of communication appears to be a distortion based in literate educational practice. Fortunately, teachers can reembed their teaching in several ways and reintroduce the natural strategy of guided reinvention. They can show children how what they learn is relevant to everyday goals, and they can introduce the new goals related to domains of knowledge. Children can learn such goals as adding newly encountered facts to the appropriate domain, trying to find and fill gaps in existing domains, trying to reorganize or reconceptualize domains of knowledge, and trying to transfer organizational schemes from one domain to another. An important topic for research is how schooling practices can be organized to help children make such practices their own.

Modern science could in some ways serve as a model for such research, since it seems to be the epitome of a collaborative, literacy-based enterprise (Toulmin, 1972). Goody, one of the most insightful theorists of literacy effects, made the following argument (1977:46–47, emphasis added):

It is not so much scepticism itself that distinguishes post-scientific thought as the accumulated scepticism that writing makes possible; it is a question of establishing a cumulative *tradition of critical discussion*. It is now possible to see why science, in the sense we usually think of this activity, occurred only when writing made its appearance and why it made its most striking advances when literacy became widespread. Here, the cumulative tradition of critical discussion provides a milieu within which scientific advances can occur rapidly. It is only within this milieu that scientists have the ability to construct new insights so rapidly. Goody noted the implication of this fact for the traditional competence-performance distinction (p. 18):

[Studies of literacy effects] can be taken to indicate . . . that while cognitive capacities remain the same, access to different skills can produce remarkable results. Indeed, I myself would go further and see the acquisition of [literate] means of communication as effectively transforming the nature of cognitive processes, in a manner that leads to a partial dissolution of the boundaries erected by psychologists and linguists between abilities and performance.

SUMMARY AND CONCLUSIONS

Cognitive development in school-age children has been one of the most active areas of research in developmental science. Yet the range of issues investigated has been relatively narrow and based primarily on Piaget's theory of cognitive development, school-related concerns about the testing of intelligence and achievement, and behaviorist theories of conditioning and learning and, more recently, information-processing theories.

Today many cognitive-developmental scholars are moving toward a broader, more integrative orientation, emphasizing relationships among the traditional categories for behavior (cognition, emotion, social behavior, personality, and so forth) and constructs that highlight the interaction or collaboration of child and environment. There has also been a growing emphasis on constructing and using methods and statistics that allow direct tests of cognitive-developmental hypotheses, in place of traditional methods and statistics, which often do not allow appropriate tests.

A Portrait of the Capacities of the School-Age Child

The cognitive capacities that develop during the school years do not develop in stages as traditionally defined. Instead, children's abilities seem to cumulate gradually and to show wide variations as a function of environmental support. Certain components of children's capacities do show weakly stagelike characteristics, however. At specific periods a wide range of children's abilities appear to undergo rapid development. These spurts may be particularly evident in children's best performances.

When the various neo-Piagetian theories are compared, there seems to be a consensus, with substantial empirical support, that four of these large-scale reorganizations occur between ages 4 and 18. At approximately age 4, middle-class children develop the capacity to construct simple relationships of representations, coordinating two or more ideas. The capacity for concrete operations emerges at age 6–7, as children become able to deal with complex problems about concrete objects and events. The first level of formal operations appears at age 10–12, when children can build general categories based on concrete instances and when they can begin to reason hypothetically. Abilities take another leap forward at age 14–16, when children develop the capacity to relate abstractions or hypotheses.

Cognitive developmentalists have often assumed that all children move through the same general developmental sequences, but research suggests that such generality occurs at best only for the most global analytic categories, such as concrete and formal operations. With more specific analyses, it seems that children will demonstrate important differences in developmental sequences. Only with research on these differences will a full portrait of school-age children's capacities be possible.

Little consensus exists on the specific processes underlying the cognitive changes that occur during the school years. Most characterizations of these processes fall into two opposing frameworks: an emphasis on changes in organization, usually conceptualized in terms of either logic or short-term memory capacity, versus an emphasis on continuous accumulation of independent habits or production systems. Progress is not likely to arise from continuation of arguments based on this assumption of opposition. The most promising direction for resolution would seem to lie in attempts to determine when abilities show reorganization and when they show continuous accumulation.

What Is Not Known

The new integrative orientation in cognitive-developmental science has led to wide recognition of the need for framing questions in ways that avoid the traditional oppositions that have typified behavioral science. Most centrally, questions have traditionally been formulated in ways that led to answers focusing on either the child or the environment as the main locus of developmental change. What many researchers are striving for today are ways of building constructs that combine the child and the environment as joint determiners of development. A promising direction for this enterprise is a focus on the collaboration of child and environment. The child is seen as always acting in some particular context that supports his or her behavior to varying degrees. One result of this focus is that concepts of ability, capacity, and competence are radically altered. They are no longer fixed characteristics of a child but emergent characteristics of a child in a context. How to recast these concepts is a major unresolved question in cognitive development.

To do research based on the integrative, collaborative orientation, investigators need to assess behavior in multiple contexts and with various methods. It cannot be assumed that a single variable provides a valid index of overall cognitive functioning in any domain or that behavior is truly divided into neat boxes labeled cognition, social behavior, emotion, and so forth. Within this reorientation toward research, investigations naturally cross traditional category boundaries and examine variations in the child and the environment simultaneously. We have focused on four topics consistent with this reorientation that have been generally neglected in research on cognitive development in school-age children.

Emotion has traditionally been treated as distinct from cognition, but some recent research suggests that in many ways the two may develop hand in hand. Some research has shown that school-age children make major advances in their ability to conceptually integrate diverse emotions. Other major topics that demand investigation include emotional reorganizations that appear to accompany the general cognitive reorganizations of the school years and Freudian, psychodynamic processes, which seem to flower during these years. A promising approach to studying emotion-cognition relationships is to choose issues in children's daily lives that naturally evoke strong emotions, such as the self, divorce, and illness.

Brain development is a major topic in the neurosciences today, but there has been little research on the relationships between brain development and cognitive development. Such research is especially difficult to do, and it has an unfortunate history. Preliminary results have often been overgeneralized and distorted, and unjustified claims have been made about practical implications for education or other socially important endeavors. Nevertheless, research on brain growth and cognitive development promises to provide important scientific breakthroughs, even though it will be a long time before legitimate practical applications will be possible.

Social development and cognitive development have typically been treated as distinct categories, and there has been little research on the contributions of social interaction to cognitive development. The few studies in recent years on this topic suggested that social interaction plays a central role in cognitive development in the school years. Much of the course of normal cognitive development seems to involve a process of guided reinvention, in which the child constructs new skills with the help of constant support and guidance from the social environment, especially from dyadic interactions. Analysis of this process has been almost completely neglected in school-age children, despite the fact that many of the failures of school-based education seem to result from the ways that classroom procedures diverge from the norm of guided reinvention.

Schooling and the literate practices associated with it seem to produce major extensions of human intelligence. Not only are basic cognitive abilities amplified, but the scope of intelligence broadens greatly, and a new capacity arises to conceive of representational systems and to analyze them. The scientific revolution appears both to have resulted from these extensions of human intelligence and to be producing further extensions. These effects of schooling and literate practices illustrate the central role of the environment in supporting cognitive growth. Unfortunately, research has been sparse on these effects, epsecially in school-age children, even though the school years appear to be the period during which these new types of intelligence are built.

The present epoch is an exciting time in the history of developmental science in general and the study of cognitive development in particular. With the new emphasis on relating the parts of the child and on placing the child firmly in a context, we expect to see major advances in the understanding of cognitive development in school-age children.

ACKNOWLEDGMENTS

We thank Richard Canfield for his help in the preparation of this chapter. We also thank the following people for their contributions: Helen Hand, Susan Harter, Marilyn Pelot, Kathy Purcell, Phillip Shaver, Louise Silvern, Helen Strautman, and Michael Westerman. Preparation of the chapter was supported by a grant from the Carnegie Corporation of New York and from the National Institute of Mental Health, grant number 1 RO3 MH38162-01. The statements made and views expressed are solely those of the authors.

REFERENCES

Adelson, J.
    1975   The development of ideology in adolescence. In S.E. Dragastin and G.H. Elder, Jr.,
            eds., Adolescence in the Life Cycle. Washington, D.C.: Hemisphere Publishing Corp.

Ainsworth, M.D.S.
    1979   Attachment as related to mother-infant interaction. In J.S. Rosenblatt, R.A. Hinde, C. Beer, and M. Busnel, eds., *Advances in the Study of Behavior*. Vol. 9. New York: Academic Press.
Anderson, J.R.
    1982   Acquisition of cognitive skill. *Psychological Review* 89:369–406.
Applebaum, M.I., and McCall, R.B.
    1983   Design and analysis in developmental psychology. In W. Kessen, ed., *Handbook of Child Psychology*. Vol. 1. *History, Theory, and Methods*. New York: John Wiley & Sons.
Arlin, P.K.
    1975   Cognitive development in adulthood: A fifth stage? *Developmental Psychology* 11:602–606.
Baldwin, J.M.
    1895   *Mental Development in the Child and the Race*. New York: Macmillan.
Bandura, A.
    1971   Analysis of modeling processes. In A. Bandura, ed., *Psychological Modeling: Conflicting Theories*. Chicago: Atherton.
    1977   *Social Learning Theory*. Englewood Cliffs, N.J.: Prentice-Hall.
Bandura, A., and Walters, R.H.
    1963   *Social Learning and Personality Development*. New York: Holt, Rinehart & Winston.
Barker, R.G., and Gump, P.V.
    1964   *Big School, Small School*. Stanford, Calif.: Stanford University Press.
Bart, W.M., and Krus, D.J.
    1973   An ordering-theoretic method to determine hierarchies among items. *Educational and Psychological Measurement* 33:291–300.
Beilin, H.
    1971   Developmental stages and developmental processes. In D.R. Green, M.P. Ford, and G.B. Flamer, eds., *Measurement and Piaget*. New York: McGraw-Hill.
Bereiter, C., and Scardamalia, M.
    1982   From conversation to composition: The role of instruction in a developmental process. In R. Glaser, ed., *Advances in Instructional Psychology*. Vol. 2. Hillsdale, N.J.: Erlbaum.
Bickhard, M.H.
    1978   The nature of developmental stages. *Human Development* 21:217–233.
Biggs, J.B., and Collis, K.F.
    1982   *Evaluating the Quality of Learning: The SOLO Taxonomy (Structure of the Observed Learning Outcome)*. New York: Academic Press.
Bobrow, D.G., and Collins, A.
    1975   *Representation and Understanding*. New York: Academic Press.
Bowman, P.H.
    1959   Effects of a revised school program on potential delinquents. *Annals* 322:53–62.
Braine, M.D.S., and Rumain, B.
    1983   Logical reasoning. In J.H. Flavell and E.M. Markman, eds., *Handbook of Child Psychology*. Vol. 3. *Cognitive Development*. New York: John Wiley & Sons.
Broughton, J.M.
    1981   Piaget's structural developmental psychology, III. Function and the problem of knowledge. *Human Development* 24:257–285.
Brown, A.L., Bransford, J.D., Ferrar, R.A., and Campione, J.C.
    1983   Learning, remembering and understanding. In J.H. Flavell and E.M. Markman, eds., *Handbook of Child Psychology*. Vol. 3. *Cognitive Development*. New York: John Wiley & Sons.

Brown, R.
1980   The maintenance of conversation. In D.R. Olson, ed., *The Social Foundations of Language and Thought*. New York: Norton.
Bruner, J.S.
1975   From communication to language: A psychological perspective. *Cognition* 3:255–287.
1982   The organization of action and the nature of adult-infant transaction. In M. Cranach and R. Harre, eds., *The Analysis of Action*. New York: Cambridge University Press.
1983   *Child's Talk*. New York: Norton.
Bullock, D.
1979   Social Coordination and Children's Learning of Property Words. Unpublished doctoral dissertation, Stanford University.
1981   On the current and potential scope of generative theories of cognitive development. In K.W. Fischer, ed., *Cognitive Development*. New Directions for Child Development, No. 12. San Francisco: Jossey-Bass.
1983   Seeking relations between cognitive and social-interactive transitions. In K.W. Fischer, ed., *Levels and Transitions in Children's Development*. New Directions for Child Development, No. 21. San Francisco: Jossey-Bass.
Campos, J.J., Hiatt, S., Ramsay, D., Henderson, C., and Svejda, M.
1978   The emergence of fear on the visual cliff. In M. Lewis and L. Rosenblum, eds., *The Origins of Affect*. New York: Wiley.
Campos, J.J., Barrett, K.C., Lamb, M.E., Goldsmith, H.H., and Stenberg, C.
1983   Socioemotional development. In M.M. Haith and J.J. Campos, eds., *Handbook of Child Psychology. Vol. 2. Infancy and Developmental Psychobiology*. New York: John Wiley & Sons.
Case, R.
1980   The underlying mechanism of intellectual development. In J.R. Kirby and J.B. Biggs, eds., *Cognition, Development, and Instruction*. New York: Academic Press.
Case, R., and Khanna, F.
1981   The missing links: Stages in children's progression from sensorimotor to logical thought. In K.W. Fischer, ed., *Cognitive Development*. New Directions for Child Development, No. 12. San Francisco: Jossey-Bass.
Catania, A.C.
1973   The psychologies of structure, function, and development. *American Psychologist* 28:434–443.
Chandler, M.K., Paget, K.F., and Koch, D.A.
1978   The child's mystification of psychological defense mechanisms: A structural and developmental analysis. *Developmental Psychology* 14:197–205.
Chi, M.T.H.
1978   Knowledge structures and memory development. In R.S. Siegler, ed., *Children's Thinking: What Develops*. Hillsdale, N.J.: Erlbaum.
Chomsky, N.
1965   *Aspects of the Theory of Syntax*. Cambridge, Mass.: MIT Press.
Clark, H.H., and Clark, H.H.
1977   *Psychology and Language*. New York: Harcourt Brace Jovanovich.
Colby, A., Kohlberg, L., Gibbs, J., and Lieberman, M.
1983   A longitudinal study of moral judgment. *Monographs of the Society for Research in Child Development* 48(1, Serial No. 200).
Cole, M., and Bruner, J.S.
1971   Cultural differences and inferences about psychological processes. *American Psychologist* 26:867–876.

Cole, M., and Griffin, P.
1980   Cultural amplifiers reconsidered. In D.R. Olson, ed., *The Social Foundations of Language and Thought*. New York: Norton.
Cole, M., and Traupman, K.
1983   Comparative cognitive research: Learning from a learning disabled child. In W.A. Collins, ed., *Minnesota Symposium on Child Psychology*. Vol. 15. Hillsdale, N.J.: Erlbaum.
Cook-Gumperz, J., and Gumperz, J.J.
1981   From oral to written culture: The transition to literacy. In M.F. Whiteman, ed., *Writing: The Nature, Development, and Teaching of Written Communication*. Vol. 1. Hillsdale, N.J.: Erlbaum.
Coombs, C.H., and Smith, J.E.K.
1973   On the detection of structure in attitudes and developmental processes. *Psychological Review* 80:337–351.
Corrigan, R.
1983   The development of representational skills. In K.W. Fischer, ed., *Levels and Transitions in Children's Development*. New Directions for Child Development, No. 21. San Francisco: Jossey-Bass.
Cross, T.G.
1977   Mothers' speech adjustments: The contributions of selected child listener variables. In C.E. Snow and C.A. Ferguson, eds., *Talking to Children: Language Input and Acquisition*. Cambridge, England: Cambridge University Press.
Curtis, S.
1981   Dissociations between language and cognition: Cases and implications. *Journal of Autism and Developmental Disorders* 11:15–30.
Dempster, F.N.
1981   Memory span: Sources of individual and developmental differences. *Psychological Bulletin* 89:63–100.
Dennett, D.C.
1975   Why the law of effect will not go away. *Journal for the Theory of Social Behaviour* 5:169–187.
Donaldson, M.
1978   *Children's Minds*. New York: Norton.
Eichorn, D.H., and Bayley, N.
1962   Growth in head circumference from birth through young adulthood. *Child Development* 33:257–271.
Ekman, P., Friesen, W.V., and Ellsworth, P.
1972   *Emotion in the Human Face*. New York: Pergamon Press.
Elkind, D.
1974   *Children and Adolescents*. Second ed. New York: Oxford University Press.
Emde, R., Gaensbauer, T., and Harmon, R.
1976   Emotional expression in infancy: A biobehavioral study. *Psychological Issues, 10*. New York: International Universities Press.
Ennis, R.H.
1976   An alternative to Piaget's conceptualization of logical competence. *Child Development* 47:903–919.
Epstein, H.T.
1974   Phrenoblysis: Special brain and mind growth periods. *Developmental Psychobiology* 7:217–224.
1978   Growth spurts during brain development: Implications for educational policy and practice. In J.S. Chall and A.F. Mirsky, eds., *Education and the Brain*. Yearbook of the NSSE. Chicago: University of Chicago Press.
1980   EEG developmental stages. *Developmental Psychobiology* 13:629–631.

Erikson, W.H.
1974   Youth: Fidelity and diversity. In A.E. Winder and D.L. Angus, eds., *Adolescence: Contemporary Studies*. New York: American Book Company.
Feffer, M.H.
1982   *The Structure of Freudian Thought: The Problem of Immutability and Discontinuity in Developmental Theory*. New York: International Universities Press.
Feldman, C.F., and Toulmin, S.
1975   Logic and the theory of mind. *Nebraska Symposium on Motivation* 23:409–476.
Feldman, D.H.
1980   *Beyond Universals in Cognitive Development*. Norwood, N.J.: Ablex.
Fischer, K.W.
1980   A theory of cognitive development: The control and construction of hierarchies of skills. *Psychological Review* 87:477–531.
Fischer, K.W., and Bullock, D.
1981   Patterns of data: Sequence, synchrony, and constraint in cognitive development. In K.W. Fischer, ed., *Cognitive Development*. New Directions for Child Development, No. 12. San Francisco: Jossey-Bass.
Fischer, K.W., and Corrigan, R.
1981   A skill approach to language development. In R. Stark, ed., *Language Behavior in Infancy and Early Childhood*. Amsterdam: Elsevier-North Holland.
Fischer, K.W., Hand, H.H., and Russell, S.
1983   The development of abstractions in adolescence and adulthood. In M.L. Commons, F.A. Richards, and C. Armon, eds., *Beyond Formal Operations*. New York: Praeger.
Fischer, K.W., Hand, H.H., Watson, M.W., Van Parys, M., and Tucker, J.
In   Putting the child into socialization: The development of social categories in the preschool
press   years. In L. Katz, ed., *Current Topics in Early Childhood Education*. Vol. 6. Norwood, N.J.: Ablex.
Fischer, K.W., and Pipp, S.L.
1984   Processes of cognitive development: Optimal level and skill acquisition. In R.J. Sternberg, ed., *Mechanisms of Cognitive Development*. San Francisco: W.H. Freeman.
In   Development of the structures of unconscious thought. In K. Bowers and D. Meichen-
press   baum, eds., *The Unconscious Reconsidered*. New York: John Wiley & Sons.
Fischer, K.W., Pipp, S.L., and Bullock, D.
In   Detecting discontinuities in development: Method and measurement. In R.N. Emde and
press   R. Harmon, eds., *Continuities and Discontinuities in Development*. Norwood, N.J.: Ablex.
Fischer, K.W., and Watson, M.W.
1981   Explaining the Oedipus conflict. In K.W. Fischer, ed., *Cognitive Development*. New Directions for Child Development, No. 12. San Francisco: Jossey-Bass.
Flavell, J.H.
1971   Stage-related properties of cognitive development. *Cognitive Psychology* 2:421–453.
1972   An analysis of cognitive-developmental sequences. *Genetic Psychology Monographs* 86:279–350.
1977   *Cognitive Development*. Englewood Cliffs, N.J.: Prentice-Hall.
1982a   On cognitive development. *Child Development* 53:1–10.
1982b   Structures, stages, and sequences in cognitive development. In W.A. Collins, ed., *Minnesota Symposium on Child Psychology*. Hillsdale, N.J.: Erlbaum.
1984   Discussion. In R.J. Sternberg, ed., *Mechanisms of Cognitive Development*. San Francisco: W.H. Freeman.
Flavell, J.H., and Wellman, H.M.
1977   Metamemory. In R.V. Kail, Jr., and J.W. Hagen, eds., *Perspectives on the Development of Memory and Cognition*. Hillsdale, N.J.: Erlbaum.

Freud, A.
1966   *The Ego and the Mechanisms of Defense*. Translated by C. Baines, New York: International
        Universities Press.
Freud, S.
1924/   The dissolution of the Oedipus complex. In *The Complete Psychological Works of Sigmund*
1961   *Freud*. J. Strachey, trans. Vol. 19. London: Hogarth. (Original work published 1924.)
1909/   Analysis of a phobia in a five-year-old boy. In J. Strachey, ed. and translator, *The*
1962   *Standard Edition of the Complete Psychological Works of Sigmund Freud*. Vol. 10. London:
        Hogarth. (Original work published in 1909.)
1933/   *New Introductory Lectures on Psychoanalysis*. J. Strachey, trans. New York: Norton. (Orig-
1965   inal work published in 1933.)
Furman, W.
1982   Children's friendships. In T.M. Field, A. Huston, H.C. Quay, L. Troll, and G.E. Finley,
        eds., *Review of Human Development*. New York: John Wiley & Sons.
Gardner, H.
1983   *Frames of Mind: The Theory of Multiple Intelligence*. New York: Basic Books.
Gelman, R.
1978   Cognitive development. *Annual Review of Psychology* 29:297–332.
Gelman, R., and Baillargeon, R.
1983   A review of some Piagetian concepts. In J.H. Flavell and E.M. Markman, eds., *Handbook*
        of Child Psychology. Vol. 3. *Cognitive Development*. New York: John Wiley & Sons.
Goldman-Rakic, P.S., Iseroff, A., Schwartz, M.L., and Bugbee, N.M.
1983   The neurobiology of cognitive development. In M.M. Haith and J.J. Campos, eds.,
        Handbook of Child Psychology. Vol. 2. *Infancy and Developmental Psychobiology*. New York:
        John Wiley & Sons.
Goodman, G.S.
1980   Picture memory: How the action schema affects retention. *Cognitive Psychology* 12:473–
        495.
Goody, J.
1977   *The Domestication of the Savage Mind*. New York: Cambridge University Press.
Green, B.F.
1956   A method of scalogram analysis using summary statistics. *Psychometrika* 1:79–88.
Greenough, W.T., and Schwark, H.D.
In   Age-related aspects of experience effects upon brain structure. In R.N. Emde and R.J.
press   Harmon, eds., *Continuity and Discontinuity in Development*. New York: Plenum.
Greenwald, A.G.
1980   The totalitarian ego: Fabrication and revision of personal history. *American Psychologist*
        35:603–618.
Grossberg, S.
1982   *Studies of Mind and Brain*. Boston Studies in the Philosophy of Science. Vol. 70. Dor-
        drecht, Holland: D. Reidel.
Gruber, H.E.
1981   *Darwin on Man*. Second ed. Chicago: University of Chicago Press.
Gruber, H., and Voneche, J.
1976   Reflexions sur les operations formelles de la pensée. *Archives de Psychologie* 64(171):45–
        56.
Guillaume, P.
1926/   *Imitation in Children*. Chicago: University of Chicago Press. (French edition published
1971   in 1926.)
Guttman, L.
1944   A basis for scaling qualitative data. *American Sociological Review* 9:139–150.

Haan, N.
1977   Coping and Defending. New York: Academic Press.
Halford, G.S., and Wilson, W.H.
1980   A category theory approach to cognitive development. Cognitive Psychology 12:356–411.
Hand, H.H.
1981   The relation between developmental level and spontaneous behavior: The importance of sampling contexts. In K.W. Fischer, ed., Cognitive Development. New Directions for Child Development, No. 12. San Francisco: Jossey-Bass.
1982   The Development of Concepts of Social Interaction: Children's Understanding of Nice and Mean. Unpublished doctoral dissertation, University of Denver. Available from Dissertation Abstracts International.
Hand, H.H., and Fischer, K.W.
1981   The Development of Concepts of Intentionality and Responsibility in Adolescence. Paper presented at the Sixth Biennial Meeting of the International Society for the Study of Behavioral Development, August. Toronto.
Haroutunian, S.
1983   Equilibrium in the Balance. New York: Springer-Verlag.
Harter, S.
1978   Effectance motivation reconsidered: Toward a developmental model. Human Development 21:34–64.
1982   A cognitive-developmental approach to children's use of affect and trait labels. In F. Serafico, ed., Socio-Cognitive Development in Context. New York: Guilford Press.
1983   Developmental perspectives on the self-system. In E.M. Hetherington, ed., Handbook of Child Psychology. Vol. 4. Socialization, Personality, and Social Development. New York: John Wiley & Sons.
Hartmann, H.
1939   Ego Psychology and the Problem of Adaptation. New York: International Universities Press.
Hartup, W.W.
1983   Peer relations. In E.M. Hetherington, ed., Handbook of Child Psychology. Vol. 4. Socialization, Personality, and Social Development. New York: John Wiley & Sons.
Heber, M.
1977   The influence of language training on seriation of 5-6-year-old children initially at different levels of descriptive competence. British Journal of Psychology 68:85–95.
Holt, R.R.
1976   Freud's theory of the primary process. Psychoanalysis and Contemporary Science 5:61–99.
Hooper, F.H., Goldman, J.A., Storck, P.A., and Burke, A.M.
1971   Stage sequence and correspondence in Piagetian theory: A review of the middle-childhood period. In Research Relating to Children. Bulletin 28. Urbana, Ill.: Educational Resources Information Center.
Hooper, F.H., Sipple, T.S., Goldman, J.A., and Swinton, S.S.
1979   A cross-sectional investigation of children's classificatory abilities. Genetic Psychology Monographs 99:41–89.
Horn, J.L.
1976   Human abilities: A review of research and theory in the early 1970s. Annual Review of Psychology 27:437–486.
Horton, M., and Markman, E.M.
1980   Developmental differences in the acquisition of basic and superordinate categories. Child Development 51:708–719.
Hunt, J. McV., Mohandessi, K., Ghodssi, M., and Akiyama, M.
1976   The psychological development of orphanage-reared infants: Interventions with outcomes (Tehran). Genetic Psychology Monographs 94:177–226.

Inhelder, B., and Piaget, J.
1955/ *The Growth of Logical Thinking from Childhood to Adolescence.* A. Parsons and S. Seagrim,
1958 trans. New York: Basic Books. (Original work published in 1955.)
Isaac, D.J., and O'Connor, B.M.
1975 A discontinuity theory of psychological development. *Human Relations* 29:41–61.
Izard, C.E.
1982 *Measuring Emotions in Infants and Children.* London: Cambridge University Press.
Jacques, E., Gibson, R.O., and Isaac, D.J.
1978 *Levels of Abstraction in Logic and Human Action.* London: Heinemann.
Kagan, J.
1958 The concept of identification. *Psychological Review* 65:296–305.
1982 *Psychological Research on the Human Infant: An Evaluative Summary.* New York: W.T. Grant Foundation.
Karplus, R.
1981 Education and formal thought—A modest proposal. In I.E. Sigel, D.M. Brodzinsky, and R.M. Golinkoff, eds., *New Directions in Piagetian Theory and Practice.* Hillsdale, N.J.: Erlbaum.
Kaye, K.
1982 *The Mental and Social Life of Babies.* Chicago: University of Chicago Press.
Kaye, K., and Charney, R.
1980 How mothers maintain "dialogue" with two-year-olds. In D.R. Olson, ed., *The Social Foundations of Language and Thought.* New York: Norton.
Keil, F.
1981 Constraints on knowledge and cognitive development. *Psychological Review* 88:197–227.
Kenny, S.L.
1983 Developmental discontinuities in childhood and adolescence. In K.W. Fischer, ed., *Levels and Transitions in Children's Development.* New Directions for Child Development, No. 12. San Francisco: Jossey-Bass.
Kernberg, O.
1976 *Object Relations Theory and Clinical Psychoanalysis.* New York: Jason Aronson.
Kinsbourne, M., and Hiscock, M.
1983 The normal and deviant development of functional lateralization of the brain. In M.M. Haith and J.J. Campos, eds., *Handbook of Child Psychology. Vol. 2. Infancy and Developmental Psychobiology.* New York: John Wiley & Sons.
Kiss, G.R.
1972 Grammatical word classes: A learning process and its simulation. In G.H. Bower, ed., *The Psychology of Learning and Motivation.* New York: Academic Press.
Kitchener, K.S.
1983 Cognition, metacognition, epistemic cognition: A three level model of cognitive monitoring. *Human Development* 4:222–232.
Klahr, D., and Wallace, J.G.
1976 *Cognitive Development: An Information-Processing View.* Hillsdale, N.J.: Erlbaum.
Knight, C.C.
1982 Hierarchical Relationships Among Components of Reading Abilities of Beginning Readers. Unpublished doctoral dissertation, Arizona State University.
Kofsky, E.
1966 A scalogram study of classificatory development. *Child Development* 37:191–204.
Kohlberg, L.
1969 Stage and sequence: The cognitive-developmental approach to socialization. In D.A. Goslin, ed., *Handbook of Socialization Theory and Research.* Chicago: Rand McNally.
1978 Revisions in the theory and practice of moral development. In W. Damon, ed., *New Directions for Child Development: Moral Development.* San Francisco: Jossey-Bass.

Kohlberg, L., and Colby, A.
1983   Reply to Fischer and Saltzstein. In A. Colby, L. Kohlberg, J. Gibbs, and M. Lieberman, A longitudinal study of moral judgment. *Monographs of the Society for Research in Child Development* 48(1-2, Serial No. 200).
Krus, D.J.
1977   Order analysis: An inferential model of dimensional analysis and scaling. *Educational and Psychological Measurement* 37:587–601.
Kuhn, D.
1976   Short-term longitudinal evidence for the sequentiality of Kohlberg's early stages of moral judgment. *Developmental Psychology* 12:162–166.
Laboratory of Comparative Human Cognition
1983   Culture and cognitive development. In W. Kessen, ed., *Handbook of Child Psychology. Vol. 1, History, Theory, and Methods.* New York: John Wiley & Sons.
Lerner, R.M., and Busch-Rossnagel, N.A., eds.
1981   *Individuals as Producers of Their Own Development: A Life Span Perspective.* New York: Academic Press.
Lock, A.
1980   *The Guided Reinvention of Language.* New York: Academic Press.
Longfellow, C.
1979   Divorce in context: Its impact on children. In G. Levinger and O.C. Moles, eds., *Divorce and Separation: Context, Causes, and Consequences.* New York: Basic Books.
Luria, A.S.
1976   *Cognitive Development: Its Cultural and Social Foundations.* Cambridge, Mass.: Harvard University Press.
Macnamara, J.
1972   Cognitive basis of language learning in infants. *Psychological Review* 79:1–13.
MacWhinney, B.
1978   The acquisition of morphophonology. *Monographs of the Society for Research in Child Development* 43(1-2, Serial No. 174).
Mahler, M.S., Pine, F., and Bergman, A.
1975   *The Psychological Birth of the Human Infant: Symbiosis and Individuation.* New York: Basic Books.
Malone, T.W.
1981   Toward a theory of intrinsically motivating instruction. *Cognitive Science* 4:333–369.
Maratsos, M.
1983   Some current issues in the study of the acquisition of grammar. In J.H. Flavell and E.M. Markman, eds., *Handbook of Child Psychology. Vol. 3. Cognitive Development.* New York: John Wiley & Sons.
Martarano, S.C.
1977   A developmental analysis of performance on Piaget's formal operations tasks. *Developmental Psychology* 13:666–672.
McCall, R.
1981   Nature-nurture and the two realms of development. *Child Development* 52:1–12.
1983   Exploring developmental transitions in mental performance. In K.W. Fischer, ed., *Levels and Transitions in Children's Development.* New Directions for Child Development, No. 12. San Francisco: Jossey-Bass.
McCall, R.B., Eichorn, D.H., and Hogarty, P.S.
1977   Transitions in early mental development. *Monographs of the Society for Research in Child Development* (3, Serial No. 171).
McCall, R.B., Meyers, E.D., Jr., Hartman, J., and Roche A.F.
1983   Developmental changes in head-circumference and mental-performance growth rates: A test of Epstein's phrenoblysis hypothesis. *Developmental Psychobiology* 16:457–468.

McQueen, R.
1982   Brain Growth Periodization: Analysis of the Epstein Spurt-Plateau Findings. Multnomah County Education Service District Education Association, Portland, Oregon.
Moerk, E.L.
1976   Processes of language teaching and training in the interactions of mother-child dyads. Child Development 47:1064–1078.
Movshon, J.A., and Van Sluyters, R.C.
1981   Visual neural development. Annual Review of Psychology 32:477–522.
Neimark, E.D.
1975   Longitudinal development of formal operational thought. Genetic Psychology Monographs 91:171–225.
Nellhaus, G.
1968   Head circumference from birth to eighteen years: Practical composite of international and interracial graphs. Pediatriacs 41:106–116.
Nelson, K.
1973   Structure and strategy in learning to talk. Monographs of the Society for Reseach in Child Development 38(1-2, Serial No. 149).
Newell, A., and Simon, H.A.
1972   Human Problem Solving. Englewood Cliffs, N.J.: Prentice-Hall.
O'Brien, D.P., and Overton, W.F.
1982   Conditional reasoning and the competence-performance issue: A developmental analysis of a training task. Journal of Experimental Child Psychology 34:274–290.
Olson, D.
1976   Culture, technology, and intellect. In L. Resnick, ed., The Nature of Intelligence. Hillsdale, N.J.: Erlbaum.
Ong, W.J.
1982   Orality and Literacy: The Technologizing of the Word. New York: Methuen.
Osherson, D.N.
1974   Logical Abilities in Children. Vol. 1. Organization of Length and Class Concepts: Empirical Consequences of a Piagetian Formalism. Hillsdale, N.J.: Erlbaum.
Overton, W.F., and Newman, J.L.
1982   Cognitive development: A competence-activation/utilization approach. In T.M. Field, A. Huston, H.C. Quay, L. Troll, and G.E. Finley, eds., Review of Human Development. New York: John Wiley & Sons.
Papert, S.
1980   Mindstorms: Children, Computers, and Powerful Ideas. New York: Basic Books.
Papousek, H., and Papousek, M.
1979   Early ontogeny of human social interaction: Its biological roots and social dimensions. In M. von Cranach, K. Foppa, W. Lepenies, and D. Ploog, eds., Human Ethology. London: Cambridge University Press.
Pascual-Leone, J.
1970   A mathematical model for the transition rule in Piaget's developmental stages. Acta Psychologica 32:301–345.
Perret-Clermont, A.N.
1980   Social Interaction and Cognitive Development in Children. London: Academic Press.
Peters, A.M., and Zaidel, E.
1981   The acquisition of homonymy. Cognition 8:187–207.
Petersen, A.C., and Cavrell, S.M.
In   Cognition during early adolescence. Child Development.
press

Piaget, J.
  1941   Le mecanisme du developpement mental et les lois du groupement des operations. *Archives de Psychologie, Geneve* 28:215–285.
  1949   *Traite de Logique: Essai du Logistique Operatoire.* Paris: A. Colin.
  1947/   *The Psychology of Intelligence.* M. Piercy and D.E. Berlyne, trans. New York: Harcourt
  1950   Brace. (Original work published in 1947.)
  1936/   *The Origins of Intelligence in Children.* Translated by M. Cook. New York: International
  1952   Universities Press. (Original work published in 1936.)
  1957   Logique et equilibre dans les comportements du sujet. *Etudes d'Epistemologie Genetique* 2:27–118.
  1946/   *Play, Dreams, and Imitation in Children.* New York: Norton. (Original work published in
  1951   1946.)
  1970   Piaget's theory. In P.H. Mussen, ed., *Carmichael's Manual of Child Psychology.* Vol. 1. New York: John Wiley & Sons.
  1971   The theory of stages in cognitive development. In D.R. Green, M.P. Ford, and G.B. Flamer, eds., *Measurement and Piaget.* New York: McGraw-Hill.
  1975   L'equilibration des structures cognitives: Probleme central du developpement. *Etudes d'Epistemologie Genetique* 33.
  1983   Piaget's theory. In W. Kessen, ed., *Handbook of Child Psychology. Vol. 1. History, Theory, and Methods.* New York: John Wiley & Sons.
Piaget, J., and Inhelder, B.
  1941/   *The Child's Construction of Quantities: Conservation and Atomism.* Translated by A.J.
  1974   Pomerans. London: Routledge & Kegan Paul. (Original work published in 1941.)
  1966/   *The Psychology of the Child.* Translated by H. Weaver. New York: Basic Books. (Original
  1969   work published in 1966.)
Pinard, A., and Laurendeau, M.
  1969   "Stage" in Piaget's cognitive-developmental theory: Exegesis of a concept. In D. Elkind and J.H. Flavell, eds., *Studies in Cognitive Growth: Essays in Honor of Jean Piaget.* New York: Oxford University Press.
Premack, D.
  1973   Concordant preferences as a precondition for affective but not symbolic communication (or how to do experimental anthropology). *Cognition* 1:251–264.
Rapaport, D.
  1951   *Organization and Pathology of Thought.* New York: Columbia University Press.
Resnick, L.B.
  1976   Task analysis in instructional design: Some cases from mathematics. In D. Klahr, ed., *Cognition and Instruction.* Hillsdale, N.J.: Erlbaum.
Rest, J.R.
  1979   *Development in Judging Moral Issues.* Minneapolis: University of Minnesota Press.
  1983   Morality. Pp. 556–629 in J.H. Flavell and E.M. Markman, eds., *Handbook of Child Psychology. Vol. 3. Cognitive Development.* New York: John Wiley & Sons.
Richards, F.A., and Commons, M.L.
  1983   Systematic and metasystematic reasoning: A case for stages of reasoning beyond formal operations. In M.L. Commons, F.A. Richards, and C. Armon, eds., *Beyond Formal Operations: Late Adolescent and Adult Cognitive Development.* New York: Praeger.
Roberts, R.J., Jr.
  1981   Errors and the assessment of cognitive development. In K.W. Fischer, ed., *Cognitive Development.* New Directions for Child Development, No. 12. San Francisco: Jossey-Bass.
Rosenberg, M.
  1979   *Conceiving the Self.* New York: Basic Books.

Rubin, K.H.
1973   Egocentrism in childhood: A unitary construct? *Child Development* 44:102–110.
Rubin, K.H., Fein, G.G., and Vandenberg, B.
1983   Play. In E.M. Hetherington, ed., *Handbook of Child Psychology. Vol. 4. Socialization, Personality, and Social Development.* New York: John Wiley & Sons.
Ruble, D.N.
1983   The development of social comparison processes and their role in achievement-related self-socialization. In E.T. Higgins, D.N. Ruble, and W.W. Hartup, eds., *Social Cognition and Social Development: A Socio-Cultural Perspective.* New York: Cambridge University Press.
Sameroff, A.J.
1975   Transactional models in early social relations. *Human Development* 18:65–79.
1983   Developmental systems: Contexts and evolution. In W. Kessen, ed., *Handbook of Child Psychology. Vol. 1. History, Theory, and Methods.* New York: John Wiley & Sons.
Schafer, R.
1976   *A New Language for Psychoanalysis.* New Haven, Conn.: Yale University Press.
Schimek, J.G.
1975   A critical examination of Freud's concept of unconscious mental representation. *International Review of Psychoanalysis* 2:171–187.
Schlesinger, I.M.
1982   *Steps to Language.* Hillsdale, N.J.: Erlbaum.
Scribner, S., and Cole, M.
1981   *The Psychology of Literacy.* Cambridge, Mass.: Harvard University Press.
Seibert, J.M., and Hogan, A.E.
1983   A model for assessing social and object skills and planning intervention: Testing a cognitive stage model. In R.A. Glow, ed., *Advances in Behavioral Measurement of Children.* Greenwich, Conn.: JAI Press.
Seibert, J.M., Hogan, A.E., and Mundy, P.C.
In   Mental age and cognitive stage in very young handicapped children. *Intelligence.*
press
Selman, R.L.
1980   *The Growth of Interpersonal Understanding: Developmental and Clinical Analyses.* New York: Academic Press.
Shaver, P., and Rubenstein, C.
1980   Childhood attachment experience and adult loneliness. *The Review of Personality and Social Psychology* 1:42–73.
Siegler, R.S.
1978   The origins of scientific reasoning. In R.S. Siegler, ed., *Children's Thinking: What Develops?* Hillsdale, N.J.: Erlbaum.
1981   Developmental sequences within and between concepts. *Monographs of the Society for Research in Child Development* 46(2, Serial No. 189).
1983   Information processing approaches to development. In W. Kessen, ed., *Handbook of Child Psychology. Vol. 1. History, Theory, and Methods.* New York: John Wiley & Sons.
Siegler, R.S., and Klahr, D.
1982   When do children learn? The relationship between existing knowledge and the acquisition of new knowledge. In R. Glaser, ed., *Advances in Instructional Psychology.* Vol. 2. Hillsdale, N.J.: Erlbaum.
Silvern, L.
1984   Emotional-behavioral disorders: A failure of system functions. In G. Gollin, ed., *Malformations of Development: Biological and Psychological Sources and Consequences.* New York: Academic Press.

Skinner, B.F.
    1969   Contingencies of Reinforcement: A Theoretical Analysis. New York: Appleton-Century-Crofts.
Slaughter, M.M.
    1982   Universal Languages and Scientific Taxonomy in the Seventeenth Century. Cambridge, England: Cambridge University Press.
Snow, C.E.
    1977   The development of conversation between mothers and babies. Journal of Child Language 4:1–22.
Sonstroem, A.M.
    1966   On the conservation of solids. In J.S. Bruner, R.R. Olver, and P.M. Greenfield, eds., Studies in Cognitive Growth. New York: John Wiley & Sons.
Sroufe, L.A.
    1979   Socioemotional development. In J.D. Osofsky, ed., Handbook of Infant Development. New York: John Wiley & Sons.
Swensen, A.
    1983   Toward an ecological approach to theory and research in child language acquisition. In W. Fowler, ed., Potentials of Childhood. Vol. 2. Lexington, Mass.: D.C. Heath.
Tabor, L.E., and Kendler, T.S.
    1981   Testing for developmental continuity or discontinuity: Class inclusion and reversal shifts. Developmental Review 1:330–343.
Tannen, D.
    1982   The myth of orality and literacy. In W. Frawley, ed., Linguistics and Literacy. New York: Plenum.
Toepfer, C.F., Jr.
    1979   Brain growth periodization: A new dogma for education. Middle School Journal 10:20.
Tomlinson-Keasey, C.
    1982   Structures, functions, and stages: A trio of unresolved issues in formal operations. In S. Modgil and C. Modgil, eds., Piaget 1896–1980: Consensus and Controversy. New York: Praeger.
Toulmin, S.
    1972   Human Understanding. Vol. 1. The Collective Use and Evolution of Concepts. Princeton, N.J.: Princeton University Press.
Turiel, E.
    1977   Distinct conceptual and developmental systems: Social convention and morality. Nebraska Symposium on Motivation 25:77–116.
Uzgiris, I.C.
    1964   Situational generality in conversation. Child Development: 35:831–842.
Uzgiris, I.C., and Hunt, J. McV.
    1975   Assessment in Infancy: Ordinal Scales of Psychological Development. Urbana, Ill.: University of Illinois Press.
Vaillant, G.E.
    1977   Adaptation to Life. Boston: Little, Brown.
Van Parys, M.M.
    1983   Understanding and Use of Age and Sex Roles in Preschool Children. Unpublished doctoral dissertation, University of Denver.
Vygotsky, L.S.
    1934/   Thought and Language. Cambridge, Mass.: MIT Press. (Original work published in 1934.)
    1962
    1934/   Mind in Society: The Development of Higher Psychological Processes. Cambridge, Mass.:
    1978   Harvard University Press. (Original work published in 1934.)

Wallerstein, J.S., and Kelly, J.B.
1980   *Surviving the Breakup: How Children and Parents Cope With Divorce*. New York: Basic Books.

Wallon, H.
1970   *De l'Acte a la Pensée*. Paris: Flammarion.

Watson, M.W.
1981   The development of social roles: A sequence of social-cognitive development. In K.W. Fischer, ed., *Cognitive Development*. New Directions for Child Development, No. 12. San Francisco: Jossey-Bass.

Watson, M.W., and Fischer, K.W.
1977   A developmental sequence of agent use in late infancy. *Child Development* 48:828–835.
1980   Development of social roles in elicited and spontaneous behavior during the preschool years. *Developmental Psychology* 16:483–494.

Webb, R.A.
1974   Concrete and formal operations in very bright 6- to 11-year-olds. *Human Development* 17:292–300.

Wells, G.
1974   Learning to code experience through language. *Journal of Child Language* 1:243–269.

Werner, H.
1957   The concept of development from a comparative and organismic point of view. In D.B. Harris, ed., *The Concept of Development*. Minneapolis: University of Minnesota Press.

Wertsch, J.V.
1979   From social interaction to higher psychological processes: A clarification and application of Vygotsky's theory. *Human Development* 22:1–22.

Westerman, M.
1980   Nonreductionism in Mainstream Psychology: Suggestions for Positive Hermeneutics. Paper presented at the convention of the American Psychological Association, September, Montreal, Canada.

Westerman, M.A., and Fischman-Havstad, L.
1982   A pattern-oriented model of caretaker-child interaction, psychopathology, and control. In K.E. Nelson, ed., *Children's Language*. Vol. 3. Hillsdale, N.J.: Erlbaum.

Winnicott, D.W.
1971   *Playing and Reality*. New York: Basic Books.

Wittgenstein, L.
1953   *Philosophical Investigations*. New York: Macmillan.

Wohlwill, J.F.
1973   *The Study of Behavioral Development*. New York: Academic Press.

Wohlwill, J.F., and Lowe, R.C.
1962   An experimental analysis of the development of conservation of number. *Child Development* 33:153–167.

Wolff, P.H.
1967   Cognitive considerations for a psychoanalytic theory of language acquisition. In R.R. Holt, ed., *Motives and Thought: Psychoanalytic Essays in Honor of David Rapaport*. Psychological Issues 5(2-3, Serial No. 18/19). New York: International Universities Press.

Wood, D.J.
1980   Teaching the young child: Some relationships between social interaction, language, and thought. In D.R. Olson, ed., *The Social Foundations of Language and Thought*. New York: Norton.

Wood, D.J., Bruner, J.S., and Ross, G.
1976   The role of tutoring in problem-solving. *Journal of Child Psychology and Psychiatry* 17:89–100.

Wylie, R.C.
    1979   The Self Concept. Vol. 2. Theory and Research on Selected Topics. Rev. ed. Lincoln:
            University of Nebraska Press.
Zebroski, J.T.
    1982   Soviet psycholinguistics: Implications for teaching of writing. In W. Frawley, ed., Lin-
            guistics and Literacy. New York: Plenum.
Zelazo, P.R., and Leonard, E.L.
    1983   The dawn of active thought. In K.W. Fischer, ed., Levels and Transitions in Children's
            Development. New Directions for Child Development, No. 12. San Francisco: Jossey-Bass.

CHAPTER 4

Self-Understanding and Self-Regulation in Middle Childhood

Hazel J. Markus and Paula S. Nurius

Theoretical work in both psychology and sociology accords self-concept a critical role in organizing past behavior and in directing future behavior. Self-concept is viewed broadly as the meeting ground of the individual and society and represents the individual's efforts to find personal meaning and understanding. Self-concept has been studied with respect to virtually every conceivable domain of behavior, including such diverse concerns as cognitive ability and competence, moral behavior, occupational choice, delinquency and deviance, friendship patterns, family relations, and health and adjustment. The implicit view of many of these studies, and the one proposed here, is that self-concept is not incidental to the stream of behavior but functions to mediate and regulate the stimuli provided by the environment. Self-concept is not the only psychological structure implicated in guiding behavior, but it is a central one. In this chapter we explore the development of self-concept during middle childhood, focusing on both the content of self-concept—what children understand about themselves—and the function of self-concept—how it may control or regulate behavior.

Self-understanding and self-regulation have nearly always been treated as independent, and virtually no research relates the two. Each is important for middle childhood, and each could have been the focus of a separate chapter. We discuss them together to highlight the idea that the two areas are interdependent. This interdependence is particularly evident during middle childhood.

147

fforts to understand the self and to link it to the regulation
t is connected with a hyphen to an ever-increasing set of
There are studies not only of self-concept, self-esteem, and
but also self-understanding, self-awareness, self-evaluation,
self-monitoring, self-presentation, self-consciousness, self-control, and self-management. This recent surge of interest in the self is reflected in several thorough collections of empirical and theoretical work, including Bandura (1978), Craighead et al. (1978), Damon and Hart (1982), Flavell and Ross (1981), Harter (1983b), Lynch et al. (1981), Rosenberg (1979), Rosenberg and Kaplan (1982), Suls (1982), and Wegner and Vallacher (1980).

For the most part these efforts are not integrative reviews that critically evaluate the state of research but rather are chapters or collections of papers summarizing the empirical and theoretical results of the recent interest in the self. They provide a clear picture of what is known, suggest some promising directions for further effort, and reveal issues that are not yet appropriately understood. Taken as a whole, they examine many important concerns, but a unified consideration of both the content and the behavioral function of the self-concept is yet to be made. Moreover, the research specifically relevant to middle childhood is scattered throughout these works and constitutes only a small fraction of the total. Compared with research on adults, the range of self-concept research specific to school-age children has been extremely limited. In addition, most empirical research on the self-concept has been decidedly atheoretical, especially with regard to school-age children. The vast majority of the studies have investigated only a single aspect of the self-concept: self-esteem (how good or bad children feel about themselves). The premise underlying almost all research on the self is that self-concept is not just reflective or incidental to the ongoing behavior but is importantly engaged in mediating and regulating behavior. Whether one focuses on the recent surge of empirical work on the self or on some of the earlier theoretical statements about self-concept (e.g., Adler, 1972; Comb and Snygg, 1959; Horney, 1953; Kelly, 1955; Rogers, 1951; Sullivan, 1953), one idea is clear: self-concept is critically implicated in behavior. Moreover, if one is interested in significant behavior change, one must change self-concept.

Four features of middle childhood mark this period as especially significant in shaping the content and function of a child's self-concept. Between the ages of 6 and 12, most children begin having extensive contact with society and must intensify their efforts to come to terms with both their own needs and goals and those of others in their social environments (e.g., parents, teachers, peers). They become less egocentric and are thus better able to empathize and take the perspective of another person. As a result, they are increasingly sensitive to the views of others and to social, as opposed to material, reinforcers. Also, during middle childhood, their repertoire of concepts and skills continues to grow at a rapid rate. The acquisition of a variety of intellectual, social, artistic, and athletic skills provides new do-mains for self-definition.

The influence of these characteristics of middle childhood on the devel-opment of self-understanding and self-regulation are dealt with by the major developmental theorists, although their views are somewhat inconsistent. Freud (1956) viewed middle childhood as a period of latency when, in contrast to earlier periods of development, children are relatively free from domination by the id. It is the age of the ego, the time at which the child can, in a relatively unconflicted manner, turn away from the family to the outside world. This allows the child to become rapidly socialized—to develop both the self and the social knowledge necessary to become a member of society.

Cooley (1902) and Mead (1934) stressed that the basis of the self-concept is the individual's perception of the reactions of others. Middle childhood, as the time when individuals become most intensely aware of the evaluation of others, can thus been seen as a critical period for the development of the social self. According to Erikson (1959), middle childhood is the stage of self-development that can best be characterized by the conviction "I am what I learn." The child's increasing interest in learning and developing new skills culminates in a personal "sense of industry"—a basic sense of competence (in contrast to one of inferiority) that is relevant both to the mastery of more sophisticated learning tasks and to cooperation. Depending on the experience of this period, children develop views of themselves as industrious and productive or as inferior and inadequate. Piaget (1952), focusing on children's cognitive development, characterized middle child-hood as a time when children become less egocentric and much more re-sponsive to the views of others. The development of self-concept, then, is marked by a growing appreciation of the self as a social object.

Regulation of Behavior: The Self-System and the Social System

Like most researchers, we view self-concept as an essentially social phe-nomenon. To develop a concept of the self, a child must take the self as an object and view it as others do. From the child's point of view, then, constructing a self-concept involves the integration of self-perception with other people's perceptions. The child's self-concept builds on itself as each new item of information is chosen, interpreted, and absorbed into the con-text of previous self-knowledge. The self-concept is not a fixed or a static entity; it is a dynamic structure. Some aspects of it change continually in response to the current interplay of individual and social forces.

From a social-psychological perspective, children's behavior can be regulated by their own needs, desires, goals, knowledge, skills, and expectations (self-system forces) or by what other people need, desire, know, expect for them (social-system forces). Under some circumstances, behavior may seem inordinately regulated by the social system (e.g., when a 10-year-old, saving for a bike, is required to buy his sister a birthday present). Under other circumstances, behavior may appear as regulated solely by the individual at the expense of certain social-system constraints or conventions (e.g., when the 10-year-old disregards the gift-giving convention in favor of keeping the money for his bike).

Coregulation refers to a coordination and interdependence of these personal and situational forces. Such mutual and reciprocal regulation can be seen as the goal of socialization. When such coregulation occurs, behavior does not seem to be regulated by the social situation, nor does it seem to be personally determined or completely controlled by individual needs and desires. Rather, coregulation stems from internalized norms and values— those that were originally imposed on the child by the social system but that have since been incorporated into the child's self-system and are now maintained by individual desires and goals. When this occurs, the self-system and the social system can be seen as interdependent.

As they participate in more activities and settings and as an increased number of people attempt to regulate their behavior, school-age children develop more sophisticated strategies for controlling their own behavior. Increased self-regulation occurs as children work to control their own behavior in whatever domains are available (clothes, eating, hobbies, or free-time activities). At the same time, the social system places ever greater demands and constraints on them. Many school-age children, for example, are required to care for younger children, to participate in household chores, to do homework, and to obey a variety of playground and classroom rules.

As they mature and are socialized, children's own needs, desires, goals, knowledge, skills, and expectations overlap or become the same as those of society, and coregulation occurs. As a consequence, children begin to complete homework, to help others, or to obey rules because they themselves desire to do so. Thus, in middle childhood, children become acutely aware of the social forces on behavior and of the benefits of behaving in accordance with them. Children learn that their own needs can often be met by regulating behavior according to the demands of the larger social system.

Children of different ages, of different backgrounds, or of different cultures vary with respect to how much of their behavior is a result of their own goals, knowledge, skills, and expectations and how much is controlled by the constraints provided by others. For some children the coordination of self and social-system pressures on behavior is not always successful, and the individual and social forces create an inordinate struggle that continues during most of middle childhood and perhaps throughout life. Only by locating children within their relevant social environments can we begin to make reasoned speculations about the processes of self-definition and self-understanding and the likely role of the resulting self-concept in regulating behavior.

Self-Concept Tasks of Middle Childhood

As children enter middle childhood and strive to become members of society, they are faced with a number of social tasks or problems. These tasks are present throughout life, but effort with respect to them is particularly evident during middle childhood. These tasks shape self-concept in major ways, and growth in the content and function of the self-concepts of school-age children is critically dependent on how these tasks are approached and completed. Four of these tasks are described below.

1. *Developing a relatively stable and comprehensive understanding of the self.* At the most general level, this involves an increasing differentiation of what is "me" from what is "not me" and an understanding, in Goffman's (1959) terms, of what the "territories of the self" are. In earlier periods of development, self-understanding is likely to be based on ascribed characteristics (e.g., name, boy, brother) and on an understanding of one's own capacities and abilities. In middle childhood, self-understanding expands to reflect other people's perceptions. A key feature of this period is an increasing sensitivity to the needs and expectations of others and to the knowledge of the self that comes from them. A majority of the child's efforts may be directed toward belongingness (particularly with respect to their peers) and developing a social identity through the world of achieved roles to which they have now been introduced (e.g., becoming a friend, a student, a girl scout, a baseball team member). Self-understanding now also includes some awareness of more achieved characteristics, such as values, norms, enduring goals, ideals, future plans, and strategies.

2. *Refining one's understanding of how the social world works.* During middle childhood, children move beyond simple social-role categorization to the more complex coordination of several social or behavioral roles. They begin to identify the rules governing appropriate social conduct with respect to these more complex role discriminations. A child can understand, for example, that a parent can also be someone else's child or that the one person can be both nice and mean (Fischer et al., in press).

In acquiring a better understanding of the relationships among people, children begin to appreciate more fully the concepts of fairness, power, equality, and status and to further differentiate their early notions of friendship and trust. Their social understanding is very often facilitated by a best friend, typically a same-sex peer with whom the child creates a private social world. This private world can be critical for self-concept development because it serves as a training ground for social, emotional, and moral development. As children interact with peers who don't always share their view of the world, they develop an understanding of the limits of their own perspective.

3. *Developing standards and expectations for one's own behavior.* Children must internalize the standards of their society so that their needs and goals better coincide with those of society. A child increasingly reflects on and incorporates norms not only to please others but also to please the self as well. For the school-age child the task of developing standards is often complicated by having two relevant societies to function within—the society of children and the child's larger adult society.

The standards and expectations that are incorporated into self-concept are the basis for self-evaluation and self-criticism. A child's self-esteem will depend on whether the outcome of these evaluations leads to self-doubt or to self-confidence. Moral development, consisting of more advanced moral reasoning and increased motivation to behave morally, is an especially important aspect of the acquisition of standards and expectations for the self. Essential to moral development is the growing ability to "decenter" and to take another's point of view (Flavell, 1975). This involves not only being able to differentiate one viewpoint from another but also controlling one's own viewpoint when making inferences about others (Higgins, 1981). Moreover, the school-age child becomes able to hold and integrate multiple and not always congruent views of the self. For example, both the "good" self and the "bad" self can now be identified and to some extent understood.

4. *Developing strategies for controlling or managing one's behavior.* As children enjoy increasing freedom and participation in the social worlds, they must assume an increasingly greater responsibility for the control of their behavior. Impulse control strategies are now complemented by the child's motives for learning, mastery, and accomplishment. School-age children must also learn to contend with conflicting goals and expectations (e.g., their own and those of adults, peers) and to cope with the way in which goals, values, and expectations may differ among individuals and situations.

This task requires that children develop a behavioral repertoire of self-monitoring, self-presentation, and self-control strategies and skills. It further requires that they believe in their ability to be efficacious and to bring their behavior into line with personal or social standards. A particularly important aspect of managing one's behavior involves learning to realistically assign and accept responsibility and blame.

In the course of solving these four tasks, a child generates a substantial amount of knowledge that increases self-understanding and affects self-regulation. The rate and the extent to which children approach these tasks are not uniform; they vary among children and contexts or situations, depending on factors in the self-system and the social system. The resultant self-knowledge includes descriptive information about physical, demographic, and trait characteristics as well as knowledge about one's behavioral capacities. Perhaps even more important, however, the base of self-knowledge now includes representations of one's needs and motives, both those given by society and those that are relatively more individual and idiosyncratic. Moreover, it contains one's goals, plans, rules, and behavioral strategies for meeting personal and social standards. In this sense self-concept can be seen as both a product of past social behavior and an impetus for future social behavior. It is this rich and dynamic nature of self-concept that has not been sufficiently appreciated in previous research and that is increasingly the focus of recent studies.

In the following sections, we review what is currently known about the nature of self-concept and its role in the regulation of behavior in school-age children. The empirical literature can be roughly organized into two broad categories: research that has focused on the content of self-understanding and self-knowledge and research that has focused on the function of self-concept by investigating such processes as self-regulation and self-control. Throughout we highlight the unanswered questions and suggest research to achieve a richer understanding of the content and function of the self-concept of the school-age child. We also examine a number of important social variables that are likely to be associated with variation in the nature of self-understanding and to influence behavioral regulation.

RESEARCH ON SELF-UNDERSTANDING

Self-Description: From Concrete to Abstract

Virtually all of the empirical work on the development of self-understanding has examined children's self-descriptions to determine what they reveal about the self as an object of thought. In James's (1910) terms, they have focused on the self as "me" and typically have not been concerned with the self as "I"—that aspect of the self that is active and ongoing and that contains the processes of thinking and knowing. The generally held view in the developmental literature is that a concept of self has its early roots in children's abilities to recognize themselves. This rudimentary self-concept is further elaborated and differentiated throughout development as the individual develops an understanding of those aspects of self that are regarded as significant.

The empirical studies on the development of self-knowledge provide a reasonably consistent picture. With increasing age a child's conception of the self becomes increasingly abstract (Bannister and Agnew, 1977; Lively and Bromley, 1973; Montemayor and Eisen, 1977; Rosenberg, 1979). Young children describe themselves in objective, concrete terms, noting their appearance, their address, and their toys. In contrast, adolescents are much more likely to describe themselves in terms of personal beliefs, characteristics, and motivations. For example, a 9-year-old might say, "My name is Bruce, I have brown eyes, I'm 9 years old, I have 7 people in my family," whereas a 17-year-old girl might say, "I am a human being, I am a girl, I am an individual" (Montemayor and Eisen, 1977).

Exactly how the concrete, somewhat shallow self-concept of the 6- or 7-year-old evolves into a more complex pattern is unclear. Nor do we understand why children select particular categories to use in describing themselves at particular times. McGuire et al. (1978) and McGuire and Padawer-Singer (1976) reported that children, like all others, were likely to think about themselves in terms of those dimensions on which they are distinctive or on which they stand out from others. Thus, young children in classrooms filled with older children were likely to mention their age when asked to "Tell us about yourself." Similarly, the relatively small number of children with red hair were more likely to mention hair color. Black and Hispanic children attending a school that was predominantly white were much more likely to mention their race or ethnic group than were white students.

Although these findings about developmental changes in self-knowledge are plausible, Harter (1983b) draws attention to a potential difficulty in using an adult category system to analyze the "Who am I?" responses of children at different developmental levels. The meanings of certain terms used by children take on very different meanings at different ages. Harter noted that when a 10-year-old describes himself or herself as a "person," the term is likely to be used in a very concrete fashion to indicate that "Now I am a person who is quite separate or distinct from others." When an 18-year-old uses the word *person*, it may be in terms of its more abstract metaphysical sense of "I am a human, I am like all other people." Similarly, the mention of *girl* by a 6-year-old may reflect the realization of gender constancy, while the mention of *girl* by an 11- or 12-year-old may be in reference to thoughts about her social or sexual self.

The research on self-understanding could be productively elaborated and extended by focusing on knowledge about the self that is not based solely on physical and psychological traits or categories. By relying on the unstructured "Who am I?" format, researchers may fail to generate information about other critical aspects of self-knowledge, such as a child's rules, standards, goals, plans, and strategies for maintaining behavior. While children may not have the verbal ability to describe or report efficiently these aspects of self-knowledge, they represent a significant component of their growing self-understanding. Some amount of in-depth, semistructured interviewing may be necessary to elicit these other aspects of self-understanding from school-age children.

Guardo and Bohan (1971) successfully used a semistructured interview with children ages 6–9 to evaluate each child's sense of constancy. They found that most children have a sense of self-identity and did not believe, for example, that they could change into an animal, a child of the opposite gender, or even a different child of the same gender. Yet the reasons underlying the children's beliefs varied across age levels. Young children thought they could not change because of overt physical or behavioral factors; older children thought they could not change into another child because of differences in thoughts and feelings.

In a study designed to study children's "naive epistemologies," Broughton (1978) confirmed these general findings on self-constancy. While young children are quite likely to confuse the terms *body, self, mind,* and *brain,* the 8-year-old child begins to appreciate that a mind is separate from the body and has control over behavior. When a sense of the subject self is achieved, the child can begin to monitor his or her own thoughts and to develop internal personal standards for behavior. At this point, issues of personal regulation and their potential conflict with social regulation are decidedly more apparent for the child.

Selman (1980) suggested that even 6- or 7-year-olds can appreciate the distinction between a subjective self and an objective self. Others (e.g., Flavell et al., 1978) have found the emergence of this differentiation around age 3, suggesting that it may bear an important relationship to language development. One sure indicator that a child has differentiated the objective self from the subjective or mental self is an understanding of the concept of self-deception. At about age 8, children appreciate the idea that the self can fool the self—that you can talk yourself into saying or doing one thing while thinking another (Selman, 1980). The processes underlying such self-understanding deserve intensive empirical and conceptual scrutiny, for they are at the heart of how children develop a will or a sense of individual purpose and of how they become aware of both their separateness and connection to the social world.

Beyond Self-Description

Some research using methods other than simple self-descriptions suggests that school-age children may have a much more elaborate and extensive system of self-knowledge than has typically been assumed. Damon and Hart (1982), for example, concluded that some aspects of what they distinguish as the four major senses of self—physical self, active self, social self, and psychological self—are evident in some form at nearly every age. During middle childhood, they claim, the physical self includes activity-related physical attributes; the active self includes capabilities relative to others; the social self includes activities that are considered in light of others' reactions (approval or disapproval); and the psychological self includes knowledge, learned skills, motivation, or activity-related emotional states.

Harter's (1983b) model of developmental change in self-concept combines a focus on both content and structure. Hypothesizing an increasing differentiation as well as an integration of the self-concept, she suggests five dimensions—physical attributes, observable attributes, emotions, motives, and cognitions—that progress through four states paralleling Piagetian stages, from simple descriptions to trait labels to single abstractions to higher-order abstractions.

Future research on self-understanding should concentrate on several aspects that have yet been fully considered and explored: self-knowledge of emotions, of motives and goals, of skills and abilities, and of social roles. Very little is understood, for example, about children's understanding of emotional states, their origins, or their consequences. Anecdotal evidence suggests that during middle childhood children have some of their most intense emotional experiences. They can be devastated when they are rejected by a desired peer group, club, or team, and they can be enormously proud of themselves when they get a perfect score on a test or win an athletic event. The function of these experiences in generating enduring self-knowledge and in producing an overall level of self-esteem is also not well understood. The empirical work on self-esteem documents that children vary in their sense of goodness or worth and that most children have some understanding of what constitutes a good self and a bad self. Yet for the most part self-esteem has been analyzed separately from the content of self-knowledge; it is therefore difficult to determine the exact antecedents of feelings of pride or shame in the self or, reciprocally, the manner in which these feelings may influence the nature and extent of self-knowledge.

Children's understanding of their abilities and skills also should be examined. The theoretical work on self and identity formation claims that in middle childhood children develop a sense of their competence and an initial sense of themselves as valued members of society. The adult's global feelings of self-confidence can often be traced to particular events and experiences of this period. Yet little is known about these aspects of self-concept and how they develop. Higgins and Eccles (1983), for example, suggested that one's enduring self-concept of academic ability is dependent on one's experiences in elementary school. A variety of studies on self-esteem in middle childhood also indicate that a child's general feeling of self-worth may be linked to academic experiences (see Epps and Smith, in this volume) and that efforts in other nonacademic areas may not compensate for the feelings of inferiority that can accompany, for example, the disheartening experience of a failure in school.

The self-concept also encompasses representations of motives, goals, and potential selves—selves that are hoped for or aspired to (ideal selves) and selves that are feared. We know that children vary in their motives for achievement and affiliation (Atkinson and Birch, 1978; Kohn, 1977), but we are unaware of the specific antecedents or consequences of these motives. In a study of possible selves, Markus and Nurius (1983) suggested that the development of various competencies and abilities may be fostered by social environments that allow individuals to develop a variety of possible selves— the capable self, the productive self, the useful self, the nice self, the important self. In retrospect, it is hardly surprising that there is relatively little empirical work on the dynamic aspects of self—on goals, motives, or possible selves. These elements of self-concept often do not have natural language labels, as do behavioral characteristics or qualities; studying them therefore requires a departure from some of the standard self-descriptive techniques.

A final, relatively neglected aspect of school-age children's self-understanding is what they know about their social selves and their place in the social world. Work by McGuire and McGuire (1982) suggests that, by age 8, children derive self-knowledge from social comparisons of all sorts. Ruble (in press) found that young children (less than 7 years old), when asked to describe their performance on a task, used an absolute statement, telling how well they did on a particular task. Older children based their self-evaluations, at least in part, on a comparison of their own behavior with that of other children. Lively and Bromley (1973) also documented the use of social comparisons around the age of 7.

As a child's awareness of others is refined, he or she becomes capable of self-criticism. Some research indicates that children ages 9–10 evidence a temporary drop in self-esteem, perhaps because of their emerging self-critical abilities. Self-criticism is obviously linked to the internalization of standards, and both are key factors in developing self-control and self-management (see the section below).

School-age children also take on a variety of new social roles—student, team member, friend. This type of self-knowledge is particularly important because it reflects knowledge of one's self in achieved rather than ascribed roles (Higgins and Eccles, 1983). In general, however, the self-knowledge that accompanies social roles is not well understood by researchers and requires the in-depth study of children in the appropriate contexts. For example, some research (Blumenfeld et al., 1979) suggests that acquiring self-knowledge of the student role may be as important as acquiring academic skills.

We know relatively little about these additional aspects of self-knowledge in part because self-concept is most often investigated in highly artificial situations. Assessing self-concept in meaningful contexts (play situations, competitive/cooperative situations, frustrating or rewarding situations) may activate some of these other aspects of self-knowledge and allow investigators to have access to them. Self-descriptions also should be elicited under a variety of task constraints. As children begin to appreciate the discrepancies between the subjective and the objective self, the settings in which descriptions are elicited may affect their reports. Thus, children may describe themselves in one way to their teacher and in quite another way to a potential friend or a stranger.

The Self-Concept in Information Processing

There is consensus in most of the recent research on self-understanding that self-concept is not a unitary, monolithic structure but is a multifaceted phenomenon, some aspects of which are continually changing. In viewing self-concept as an active, dynamic structure that is involved in mediating the social environment, self-concept has been viewed as an organized set of cognitive structures. Building on cognitive personality theory (Epstein, 1973; Kelly, 1955), Markus (1977, 1980) defined the self as a set of cognitive schemas. Self-schemas are knowledge structures about the self that derive from past experiences and that organize and guide the processing of the self-relevant information contained in the individual's social experiences. The individual is thought to actively construct both generalizations and hypotheses about the self from ongoing life events (e.g., "I am independent," "I get along well with all types of people," "I am shy," "I am a good mother, teacher, volleyball player"). Self-schemas develop around those aspects of the self that become personally significant in the course of social interactions, and they reflect domains of enduring salience, investment, or concern.

Self-schemas provide the individual with a point of view, an anchor, or a frame of reference. As mechanisms of selectivity, they guide the individual in choosing the aspects of social behavior to be regarded as relevant and function as interpretive frameworks for understanding this behavior. The information-processing consequences of self-schemas have been discussed at length elsewhere (see Markus and Sentis, 1982; Markus and Smith, 1981, for reviews). With respect to the self, individuals with self-schemas in particular domains (1) can process information about the self efficiently (make judgments with relative ease and certainty, (2) are consistent in their responses, (3) have relatively better recognition memory and recall for information relevant to this domain, (4) can predict future behavior in the domain, (5) can resist information that is counter to a prevailing schema, and (6) can evaluate new information for its relevance to a given domain.

The self-schemas of children have not yet been explored, but Markus (1980) hypothesized that during middle childhood some of the most powerful and enduring self-schemas take shape. Self-schemas of academic ability, of popularity with peers, and of athletic ability are particularly likely to be generated during the elementary school years. Self-schemas define a past self, but even more important, because they contain representations of goals, plans, and behavioral strategies, they help define a future possible self.

A schematic view of the self does not make it any more accessible to direct observation, yet a view of the self as a knowledge structure (or a set of structures) does divest it of some of its mystical properties. Investigators may ask some relatively more focused questions about the active role of the self and the self as a process. Such questions include: How is the self represented in memory? How does it influence the way we process information about the social world? Is the self-structure just one of many structures that may be engaged to handle incoming information, or is it unique in some ways? And where in the information-processing sequence is it implicated—at encoding, at retrieval, or at inference?

In the social-psychological research on self-concept, other recent developments might be productivly applied to understand the self-concept of the school-age child. Greenwald (1980), for example, has analyzed the self as a totalitarian state with some built-in biases that function to preserve its organization. These include egocentricity, beneffectance (a view of the self as responsible for the desired but not the undesired), and conservatism (resistance to cognitive change). All of these cognitive biases surely begin to develop very soon in an individual's experience of self and contribute to the total self-concept. Other theoretical ideas on self-presentation, self-monitoring, and self-awareness are also analyses of self-concept processes that could be usefully explored with children (see Wegner and Vallacher, 1980, for a review).

RESEARCH ON SELF-REGULATION

Self-regulation can best be described as a set of components (e.g., self-monitoring, self-evaluation, self-reinforcement, and self-control) constituting a dynamic process rather than as a single act or state. The disparate attempts to specify this complex process can be organized under four major headings: (1) ego control theories, (2) social learning theories, (3) cognitive/behavior modification theories, and (4) component models of self-regulation. The degree to which the self is centrally implicated by these theoretical perspectives varies, but they have all generated research that is potentially important for understanding the role of the self-concept in behavioral regulation during middle childhood.

Implications From Ego Psychology

With respect to self-management skills and motives, the psychodynamic model focuses on the internal drives and familial influences involved in adaptation, self-preservation, and mastery as well as on the conflicts and complications involved with each. In this tradition, Freud (1922) envisioned self-management as stemming both from the drive for self-preservation and from the management functions of the ego and the superego. The influence of the superego comes through the conscience as the moderating moral agent and through the ego ideal as the internalization of positive values and aspirations from significant family members (or, according to Shibutani, 1961, from a wider social network). Middle childhood is viewed as a period of latency wherein the superego has become strong enough to keep the disruptive forces (impulses) of the id under control, thus allowing the ego to develop. Through development of the ego, coregulation of self and social forces increasingly supplants the more fundamental regulation based on impulse (self as id) gratification. By its very definition as a period of latency, this ego development is not viewed as consciously involving intense conflict or struggle on the part of the individual. Furthermore, while some degree of external influence is acknowledged, traditional ego control theorists view self-control as a relatively stable personality characteristic deriving predominantly from forces within the self.

Loevinger's (1966; Loevinger and Wessler, 1970) theory of ego development, which expands on Kohlberg's (1969) well-known stages of moral development, incorporates many elements of the early ego theorists. Her model postulates a fixed sequence of developmental stages of impulse control and character development. With each stage the child is better able to control his or her behavior and to understand both internal and external sources of conflict and reward. Increasing self-control is first motivated by fear of reprisal, followed by a sense of moral obligation to obey rules, and finally by a sense of moral principle and personal integrity. This last stage best characterizes middle childhood. While developmental progress certainly varies, children in later middle childhood tend to be less rigid and self-centered in their moral reasoning.

From a developmental point of view, several questions about this and similar general stage models arise. While the stages are assumed to be broadly applicable, empirical validation of them as a measure of individual differences has been achieved only for adults. Whether the sequential nature of these stages can be generalized to children, however, is unclear. The extent to which such variables as intelligence and verbal fluency (Hauser, 1976) may mediate or be influenced by stage development is also unclear. And the extent to which the ego developmental levels can be used to predict and explain situation- or domain-specific behavior needs further investigation.

A somewhat different line of research involving impulse control has been that of Block and Block (1971, 1980). Their view of ego functioning draws heavily on Lewin's (1935, 1936, 1938, 1951) theory of motivational dynamics in a bounded psychological system of needs and forces. The major focus of their work has been identifying the components of ego control and ego resiliency, and their work is especially pertinent to middle childhood because it links the concept of ego control to the self-regulation patterns and skills of the individual.

In their investigation of antecedents leading to individual differences in ego control, Block and Block found considerable evidence of particular parental characteristics and child-rearing techniques associated with lack of impulse control (undercontrollers) and excessive control (overcontrollers). For example, undercontrollers as children tended to have neglectful parents who typically made little effort to encourage achievement or to teach age-appropriate skills. Family dynamics were often tense and unpredictable, with punishment often being more an expression of the parents' own anger than a consequence of the child's behavior that could be controlled. In short, the extent to which and the manner in which parents taught or imposed regulation on their children was predictive of the children's subsequent patterns of self-regulation. Even though the ego-control perspective highlights the role of the individual disposition, this research also implicates the potentially powerful influence of the salient environment—the family—and the importance of attending to it in the study of self-regulation.

The empirical investigation of many ego-centered constructs with children has required adjustments to make them more meaningful and appropriate to various age levels. What is lacking in the ego psychology literature is a thorough analysis of the ways in which ego control, ego resiliency, and other ego-related skills or states may be manifested differently at different developmental stages. Also needed is an assessment of the complementary nature of other theoretical explanations of self-regulation with those of ego development.

Social Learning Theory and Self-Management

While ego-control theorists view self-control as a stable dispositional (personality) characteristic, social learning theorists focus on the discriminative, situationally specific qualities of self-control. For example, a child's perception of how rewarding or punishing a model or a course of action is perceived to be will greatly influence his or her behavior. The basic self-control processes that have been explored from a social learning perspective also have centered around the functional control of impulses. By and large, these pursuits have involved resistance of temptation in the absence of surveillance, self-imposed delay of gratification or expression of impulses for the sake of future consequences, the tolerance of self-initiated frustration, and delay of self-imposed rewards (see Harter, 1983b, for an extensive review).

Although recent work on social learning has begun to address the role of cognitive mediators in the self-control process, traditional approaches focused on environmental sources of behavioral control and viewed the individual in a largely reactive position. From this perspective, behavior that appears to be under control through self-reinforcement can, under close examination, be shown to be caused by near or distant external contingencies. Those who relax these traditional assumptions have tended to highlight the interactive relationship between the individual and the environment.

Two areas that have been studied from a social learning perspective are especially relevant to the self-concept tasks of middle childhood: (1) the effects of punishment and (2) the effects of modeling on self-regulation and self-control. Considerable support now exists for the general effectiveness of punishment in a child's development of internalized control (i.e., values and norms incorporated into the self-system) (see Johnston, 1972 and Parke,

1977, for reviews). Both the affective and cognitive aspects of self-concept play a role in self-regulation. For example, Aronfreed (1968, 1969, 1976) built a strong case for the importance of affect (particularly anxiety) in promoting the internalization of self-control standards. In his view a child will strive to avoid such negative affects as guilt, anxiety, or fear that become associated with the cognitive representations that co-occur with the punishment of certain behaviors. By reducing the occurrence of these negative affects, the child will avoid or reduce the associated cognitions and, thus, the related behavior.

Although a variety of potentially negative consequences are associated with punishment, there is evidence that punishment is particularly effective if accompanied by an explicit verbal rationale or moral evaluation. The relative effectiveness of different types of rationales tends to vary with the developmental stage of the child. For example, rationales emphasizing the rights of others as well as those based on empathy and an appreciation for others' feelings are more effective with children age 7 or older than with preschoolers. Pressley (1979) and Parke (1970, 1974, 1977) attribute these results to increased cognitive sophistication and more developed moral reasoning (and, thus, a better defined self-system).

Because of their greater self-awareness and astuteness at observing and inferring from others, school-age children are particularly vulnerable to influence through social modeling. Investigation of the effects of modeling in shaping and eliciting desirable behavior or suppressing undesirable behavior in children indicates the importance of situational and model characteristics. For example, the extent to which models are perceived as powerful and rewarding (Mischel and Grusec, 1966; Mischel and Liebert, 1966, 1967) or as behaving consistently with a child's moral or performance standards (e.g., Mischel and Liebert, 1966; Rosenhan and White, 1967) is significantly related to the likelihood of the child's emulating them and adopting their standards. Children are also more likely to inhibit behavior that they have observed being punished (Bandura, 1973; Bandura et al., 1963), particularly when the relevant contingencies are clearly communicated (Ross and Ross, 1976) and the child has an opportunity to practice the self-regulatory response (White, 1972).

Cognitive/Behavior Modification

Based on experimental clinical evidence with adults (e.g., Bandura, 1977; Mahoney, 1974) and with children (Craighead et al., 1976), social learning theories have expanded to incorporate an emphasis on cognitive mediation. These broader models highlight the role of social cognition (structures and processes) and developmental variables in self-regulation. The inclusion of active internal (self-system) variables and their dynamic, interactive relationships with external (social-system) variables represents an attempt at more integrative theorizing and more effective applications (Craighead et al., 1978).

Recent work by Mischel and his colleagues, for example, has focused on the mediating influence of attentional and cognitive-representational processes on children's ability to delay gratification and to resist temptation. Their empirical work suggests that it is the nature of the cognitive representation of rewards (e.g., thinking of a marshmallow as being white and puffy like clouds versus thinking of it as sweet and chewy) that appears to be the major determinant of young children's ability to wait for a larger reward. Furthermore, cognitive transformations that serve to minimize motivational arousal (i.e., that minimize the desire for immediate gratification) are likely to be most effective in promoting self-control (Mischel, 1974; Mischel and Baker, 1975; Mischel and Moore, 1973, Moore et al., 1976). Building on a greater awareness of his or her own motives and the conflicts they engender, the school-age youngster begins to develop an array of self-control strategies for managing difficult tasks and for overcoming "hot" (affect-laden) temptations (Mischel, 1979). This phenomenon exemplifies the manner in which the major developmental tasks in middle childhood build on each other as children become more and more accomplished and sophisticated in their self-control efforts.

In investigating children's ability to use self-instructional plans, Mischel and Patterson (1976, 1978) found that both the nature of the content or substance (e.g., temptation inhibiting, reward oriented, task facilitating) of the plan used, as well as its structure or organization (e.g., detailed or not), influenced the effectiveness of its use. More recent investigations into children's knowledge about the self-control process have suggested that lack of knowledge and lack of a repertoire of relevant strategies partly explain young children's failure to employ effective self-control strategies (Glucksberg et al., 1975; Patterson and Kister, in press).

Meichenbaum's (1976, 1977) research on self-instructional training, grounded in the early formulations of Luria (1959, 1961) and Vygotsky (1962), represents another important contribution to the study of self-regulation. Meichenbaum applied a developmental framework in assessing the influence of cognitive and linguistic processes over voluntary motor behaviors. In his three-stage model, behavior is initially controlled primarily through the speech of others (usually adults). In stage two the child's overt speech becomes an increasingly effective behavior regulator, and in stage three the child's covert or inner speech aids in effective self-regulation. Meichenbaum and others have used this cognitive behavior/linguistic model to develop treatment programs for children with a variety of impulse-control problems. [For reviews of the treatment efficacy of these and other cognitive behavior modification procedures, see Craighead et al. (1978), Karoly (1977), Kendall (1977), Kendall and Finch (1979), Mash and Dalby (1978), Meichenbaum and Goodman (1971).] Camp and her colleagues have extended this approach by emphasizing the importance of alternative, socially desirable behaviors to replace the inappropriate ones (Camp, 1980; Camp and Bush, in press; Camp and Ray, in press; Camp et al., 1977).

Distinctions between these various theoretical orientations are often not clear, and, as is evident here, considerable overlap exists among the avenues of research. Nevertheless, these efforts all highlight the cognitive behavior link and emphasize the growing awareness of the need to include such internal and "mediational" constructs as self-concept as well as other cognitive structures.

Component Models of Self-Regulation

Component models of self-regulation specify the processes that trigger self-regulation and the sequence in which they occur. Like the cognitive behavior formulations of self-regulation, these models emphasize the importance of cognitive mediating processes to understand the relationship between cognition and behavior. While originally formulated for application to adults, the study of their application to children is growing.

While the various-component models differ in their specification of the critical processes involved (e.g., Bandura, 1977, 1982; Carver and Scheier, 1982; Kanfer, 1980; Kanfer and Phillips, 1970), all emphasize the importance of monitoring or observing one's own behavior, comparing ongoing performance to previously formed standards of values, and modifying behavior to reduce the perceived discrepancy between ongoing behavior and standards of comparison. Under the Kanfer model, for example, the child may develop new behaviors as well as regulate previously learned ones.

For example, in learning to write the letters of the alphabet, children may carefully monitor their writing behaviors, compare their work with former efforts or with an ideal model, and either modify their writing to more closely approximate their goals or feel satisfied with their accomplishments and leave them as is. A more complex and more social example is the reaction of the child who impulsively takes a favorite toy away from a playmate. The chain of quiet play behavior has been broken. The child sees the friend's unhappiness, evaluates his or her behavior against the value of "nice boys and girls share," experiences guilt, and adjusts his or her behavior by returning the toy and resuming play.

The models also share an emphasis on self-knowledge as primary in self-regulation. Carver and Scheier explicitly implicate self-understanding in their description of the function and salience of self-monitoring and self-anchored reference standards or values (Carver et al., 1981; Carver and Scheier, 1981a, 1981b; Scheier and Carver, in press). Attention or focus on the self serves an important mediating role in self-regulation. Directing attention to the self increases the tendency to compare one's present state with relevant and salient reference values and results in increased conformity to these standards.

Within Bandura's (1981) model, perceived self-efficacy is critical to effective self-regulation. While initial efficacy experiences are centered in the family, peers assume an increasingly important role in the school-age child's developing self-knowledge of his or her capacities. It is through peer interactions that children broaden the scope of or make finer distinctions as to their capacities and subsequent efficacy. The relationship between peer affiliations and efficacy development is viewed as reciprocal and as capable of working to the benefit or the detriment of the child.

The Need for Integrative and Developmental Perspectives

Research on self-management has been characterized by a diversity of theoretical approaches. Unfortunately, advances in one school of thought are rarely considered by another, and the result has been minimal theoretical integration. As a consequence, much of the work has served to explain only pieces of the phenomenon. Many are too global to be of practical utility (e.g., many of the stage models); others are too factor or situation specific to be generalizable across circumstances or to be meaningful to theorists of different perspectives. To gain a more comprehensive understanding of self-management and the range of intervening variables, a streamlining and integration of major findings from the fields of self-theory, cognitive psychology, social learning theory, ego development, and developmental psychology will surely be necessary.

Self-management is a crucial concern of middle childhood, yet much of the research is not couched within a developmental perspective. This omission partly reflects the difficulty of reliably measuring and understanding the various components and processes of self-management given the accelerated changes that characterize normal growth during this period. For example, are the various components of self-regulation equally important at all ages?

At a minimum, the cumulative and age-related nature of children's learning must be acknowledged (Staats, 1975).

Scaled-down models of self-regulation based on adult behavior may be not only insufficient but also inaccurate. Harter (1983b) suggests that the order of acquisition of critical components of the self-regulation process (i.e., self-monitoring, self-evaluation, and self-reinforcement) may be the reverse of the order in which they are postulated as operating in adulthood. Moreover, constructs and components of the self that are central and meaningful to the adult's self-definition may not be relevant to the child's self-definition or may be relevant in very different ways. Similarly, the manner and sequence of information processing and decision making changes with age as the child's cognitive skills (such as viewing the self as an object and reinforcing the self without external supports) increase.

Following this line of thought, Harter (1982) has pressed for the need to distinguish between the self as knower (active agent engaging in the processes of self-management) and the self as object (cognitive construction to which these processes are applied). Differentiating ontogenetic changes within these two realms should provide a more comprehensive understanding of self-observation, self-evaluation, and self-response and of the linkage between self-knowledge and self-management. In short, differentiation among the various dimensions (e.g., situational, perceptual, cognitive, behavioral, attitudinal, and emotional) of self-management from a development perspective is needed if meaningful and useful applications relevant to children are to be established.

In one attempt at synthesizing the relevant speculative and empirical literatures, Karoly (1977) presented a tentative four-component model that describes self-regulatory efforts. The first three steps—problem recognition and appraisal, commitment (choice), and extended self-management (self-control)—are capable of reciprocal influence; the fourth step involves habit reorganization. The model assumes some sort of novel or dramatic change recognized by the actor, which interrupts automatic chains of response or regulation and provokes a shift to "manual control."

Admittedly, models such as this one require considerably more detailed operationalization and evidence of applicability across situations and individuals. Karoly's model is exemplary, however, in its attention to skills that change during development, such as the ability to recognize a behavior management problem and to appreciate the potential value of self-management procedures. Step two, commitment, is also of particular importance for self-management by children, for the child must prefer self-management over perceived alternatives. The dimensions of perception, understanding, and motivation are often overlooked by researchers, theorists, and clinicians concerned with self-regulation in children. More recently, Karoly (in press) offered a more finely differentiated specification of the skill components requisite for acquiring and maintaining a repertoire of functional self-regulation responses. Efforts such as these, refined with regard to developmental differences and to means of utilization (e.g., assessment, prediction, intervention), have considerable promise.

MODERATING VARIABLES: SELF-SYSTEM AND SOCIAL SYSTEM

The framework outlined in the beginning of the chapter suggests a number of variables that may potentially influence the self-system and the social system as well as the resulting processes of self-understanding and self-regulation. Different social environments may be associated with very different self-concepts. Most obviously perhaps, children may differ in the ratio of social-system to self-system sources of regulation that characterize their behavior.

In some environments, children are enthusiastically encouraged to develop means for regulating their own behavior. They are also taught the importance of developing a separate, differentiated, or unique sense of self, and they soon develop strategies for protecting this unique self and for evaluating, monitoring, and presenting it to others. Children who have not been encouraged to develop autonomous selves may have proportionately more socially regulated reactions as a basis for self-understanding. When children are always surrounded by a similar set of others or have little privacy, it may be unnecessary and perhaps impossible to forge a differentiated sense of self.

Variation in the Self-System

Some societies encourage the development of a well-differentiated, autonomous self that is forcefully and willfully in control of all the important aspects of individual behavior. This self is also required to be a special or even unique self that is quite different from others, despite the obvious behavioral similarity that is required by the social environment. Such a view encourages what appears to be two selves—one that is private and one that is manipulated or presented to the public. Individuals are likely to vary, however, in how they meet these requirements.

Self-Awareness

Some people are more aware of their private selves or internal states than others. Researchers have explored differences in self-awareness of internal states under the label of self-consciousness (Buss and Scheier, 1976; Scheier and Carver, 1977). Those high in private self-consciousness are very aware of their beliefs, moods, and feelings and are highly reflective. In contrast, persons high in public self-consciousness are more aware of the self as a social object. They are highly concerned with their appearance and with the impression they are likely to make on others. To date, no investigations of this phenomenon have been conducted with children, but it is likely that marked differences in the self-consciousness of adults have their roots in strategies developed in middle childhood. One could hypothesize, for example, that those highest in public self-consciousness might have been most adept at early regulation of their behavior to meet the behavioral standards of others.

Snyder (1974, 1979) studied another aspect of self-awareness, that of self-monitoring. Self-monitoring refers to how much attention and value an individual accords to standards that are suggested by the environmental context. Snyder (1979) demonstrated significant differences in the social behavior of high and low self-monitors. Again, this phenomenon has not been explored specifically with children, but the origins of this individual difference could be examined by combining Snyder's ideas with the extensive theorizing on self-monitoring in the literature on self-regulation.

Self-Presentation

Jones and his colleagues (Jones and Berglas, 1978; Jones and Pittman, 1982) studied differences among individuals in the strategies they use to present the self to others. Self-presentation strategies involve individuals shaping their behaviors to create desired impressions of themselves in specific persons within the social environment. These strategies can be of either a self-enhancing or a self-handicapping nature. They might be aimed at maintaining a particular self-image or at changing one's own or another's image of the self. The ultimate goal is to control others' impressions or attributions of oneself.

This sometimes may take maladaptive forms. Research regarding self-handicapping, for example, suggests that some people regulate their behavior by selecting those circumstances for action that are most likely to render performance feedback ambiguous, which protects their private views of themselves from unequivocal negative feedback. Such stages may have their origins in middle childhood and may be particularly important in explaining scholastic underachievement. Children who are concerned about their own competence but whose view of their competence is uncertain or low may be more likely to deliberately underachieve than are their self-assured peers. The outcome is a less-than-best effort that invites failure but that also provides an attributional "out" ("I didn't try hard enough") regarding the question of competence. Again, however, both the theoretical and the empirical support undergirding these notions are adult based and devoid of developmental specification.

Variations in the Social System

With respect to potential variation in the nature of the social system, a number of factors have received empirical attention. For the most part, variables that influence the nature of the social environment experienced by the child (including social status, gender, family configuration, and child-rearing practices) have been analyzed primarily with respect to their influences on self-esteem. Their influence on all other aspects of the self-concept is yet to be investigated.

Social Class

Researchers who have focused on the relationship between social class and self-concept have been uniformly impressed with the potential for this variable to have a powerful infuence on the self. Social class is a critical determinant of experiences and expectations. Social class can moderate the content of one's self-understanding; the nature of one's knowledge about the social world; and the content and nature of the particular rules, standards, and strategies that an individual develops in the course of socialization. This is due in part to the tendency of children to base their self-concepts on comparisons with others in terms of possessions, skills, and accomplishments. Lower-income children have fewer possessions. They also have less opportunity to develop their abilities (Berger, 1980); are less likely to feel that they are efficacious or have control over their futures (Bartel, 1971); and may be less likely to try hard, thus accomplishing less (Maehr, 1974).

Despite its origin in the social system, the meaning and importance of social class to a child must be assessed from the perspective of the child. Rosenberg (1979:147) provides one of the most compelling statements of this view:

One cannot understand the significance of a social structural variable for the individual without learning how this variable enters his experiences and is processed within his own phenomenal field. . . . If we hope to appreciate the meaning of social class (or, for that matter, the meaning of any social identity element, such as race, gender, or religion) for the child, it is essential to see social class from his viewpoint, to adopt the child's eye view of stratification, to understand how it enters his experiences and is internally processed. To the sociologist, social class means differential prestige, respect, possessions, and power, with obvious self-esteem implications. But from the viewpoint of the child, the matter appears entirely different.

Unfortunately, virtually all the research on the effects of social class has been concerned not with the child's view of stratification but almost exclusively with self-esteem. The vast majority of the research has focused on the relationship between academic achievement and self-esteem (see Epps and Smith, in this volume). Purkey (1970), for example, has shown a consistent relationship between these two variables as well as a relationship between social class and academic achievement.

In one of the most systematic studies of social class and the self (conducted in Baltimore and Chicago), Rosenberg (1979) explored the relationship between socioeconomic status and global self-esteem and attempted to see if children actually perceived their social-class standing. No association was found between social class and self-esteem among 8- to 11-year olds, a modest association was found among adolescents, and a somewhat stronger one was seen among adults. The lack of relationship between social status and self-esteem in middle childhood is probably explained by the fact that children at this age are seldom exposed to class-related social experiences, such as occupational discrimination (Kohn, 1969).

Issues surrounding social class may not be as important in middle childhood as they are later in life. This view holds that children of this age are relatively protected from categorizations and judgments based on social-class standing, particularly if the child grows up in a relatively homogeneous social environment. As Rosenberg (1979) pointed out, the individuals in the environment of the school-age child and the ones most likely to affect the child's self-esteem are usually of the same social standing as the child. Under most conditions these individuals do not stress social class in their interactions with the child. In contrast, the reflected appraisals received by adults position them squarely in social space.

Ethnicity

What happens when a child's social world includes both a minority and a majority group, thereby increasing the salience of ethnicity and social class for the child? Viewing oneself as different from the majority group could conceivably lead to low self-esteem, especially when the minority group is the object of intense discrimination within the larger society. This notion was taken as self-evident by early investigators of the problem and received some support (Clark, 1965; Clark and Clark, 1947; Proshansky and Newton, 1968). Yet many recent investigations of the relationship between minority-group status and self-esteem, including a comprehensive review by Wylie (1979), do not support this conclusion.

Nonetheless, ethnicity remains a controversial and contested area of research (see McCall and Simmons, 1978; St. John, 1975; Cohen, 1972). Rosenberg (1979), for example, concluded that the self-esteem of blacks will suffer only in those circumstances in which blacks actually use whites as comparison groups. His study indicates that black students who interacted primarily with whites and compared themselves unfavorably with whites experienced reduced self-esteem. Most black children, however, interact primarily with other black children, and their self-evaluations, based on comparisons with their relevant social group, do not create in them a minority or low-status view of themselves.

Research in this area, as in that on the effects of social class, needs to focus on the child's perceptions of his or her social environment and go beyond studies that center on self-esteem. While self-esteem may not be influenced by either ethnicity or social class, it is indeed plausible that these factors will be reflected in the content of self-knowledge and in the nature of children's motives, goals, plans, and strategies.

Other Social System Variables

A number of studies have investigated the relationships between a variety of other aspects of the social system and the content and function of the self-concept during middle childhood but, again, not in any systematic or comprehensive fashion. Little is known, for example, about the relationship between styles of parenting and the nature of self-concept. The work on understanding contingencies and acquiring behavioral rules stresses the importance of consistency in the behavior of others in the social environment and the clarity with which the goals are modeled or presented (Mischel et al., 1978; Patterson, in press; Yates and Mischel, 1979). Unpredictability and inconsistency appear to cause some anxiety and confusion in the child, but the mediating links have not been specified. Similarly, poor supervision and parenting have been related to behavior problems in middle childhood. Specifying the relationship between these types of variables and compliance as well as the internalization of behavior standards creates a number of intriguing problems for researchers.

The relationship between other social-system variables, such as gender and family configuration, and self-concept could be further examined. Family configuration (birth order, family size, and sex composition) provides the child's most meaningful social environment for a substantial period of his or her life. Many aspects of the self-system, particularly those regarding strategies for managing one's own behavior in relationship to others and modes of social comparison, may be influenced by whether one is the first-born or a later-born child or whether one lives in a small or a large family. Zajonc (1976) emphasized the potential importance of family configuration as a social-environmental variable, but he explored it only in relation to intellectual performance.

METHODOLOGY

Many of the methodological and measurement issues involved in studying self-understanding and self-regulation have been interwoven throughout our discussion of substantive concerns. In many cases, what appears as deficient and inadequate methodology is a direct function of ill-defined constructs and the lack of a comprehensive theoretical context.

The use of more delimited, more precise constructs is necessary. The grand theories that have undergirded previous research are no longer sufficient. More integrated and comprehensive theories must clearly define each structure and process in terms of patterns of development. One proposed framework for cognitive development focuses on (1) sequence (What is the order in which developments occur?); (2) synchrony (Which developments occur at the same time as others?); and (3) constraint (Of all the possible developments, which are most likely to occur?) (Fischer and Bullock, 1981).

Efforts to formulate theoretical paradigms that reflect the dynamic inter-dependence between self-system and social system also would be particularly useful. Karoly's (1977) four-stage model and her more recent efforts (in press) at further discrimination among the various influences and skill components constituting self-management represent noteworthy examples.

A further point follows from one general limitation of many self-concept theories that have stressed the importance of the individual's internal processes while neglecting other objectively measurable variables. Such variables include the individual's previous experience, his or her objective characteristics/individual differences, and differences in significant features of the social environment (e.g., family configuration). While the effect of environmental factors on cognitive development has received considerable attention, developmental theorists must now specify how these effects contribute to change in the organization of behavior (Fischer, 1980).

We reiterate the case for more innovative study design emphasized throughout this volume. To adequately chart developmental progress, longitudinal designs are useful. This necessitates, among other things, developmental models and measures that are appropriate to the abilities children of different ages possess. Closely related to this is the need for designs that can better accommodate the dynamic interaction between the self-system and the social system. Admittedly, this is a major dilemma for psychology in general and one that requires considerable ingenuity as well as methodological sophistication. Studies conducted within the natural contexts of middle childhood that more closely approximate the child's natural life experience would be a potentially useful addition to the research. More detailed methodological suggestions and guidelines can be found in the work of Karoly (1977), which addresses the measurement needs of research on children's self-management, and in research by Wylie (1979), which explores difficulties in assessing self-concept.

CONCLUSION

This chapter reviews the major efforts concerned with the content and function of self-concept in children ages 6–12. We have combined two previously disparate literatures—one on self-understanding and self-knowledge and one on self-regulation and have tried to demonstrate that the study of what children know about themselves becomes most useful when it is linked with past behavior and perceptions and its role in ongoing and future behavioral regulation. Conversely, we have stressed that a complete understanding of the processes of behavioral regulation will require an understanding of what children know about themselves—what rules, standards, values, or goals they have for themselves—and how this knowledge is used to control behavior. An interweaving of these two areas—self-understanding and self-regulation—will result in a richer, more dynamic, and more interactive formulation of self-concept, one in which self-concept can be analyzed as both a social consequence and as a social force.

In outlining the theoretical and empirical work on self-concept, we have emphasized the importance of viewing self-concept as being determined by both individual and social-system needs and goals. At any point in the individual's life, the current self-concept reflects an organization and integration of the salient self-perceptions. Many of these self-perceptions are determined by the reactions of others. The result is that the content of self-knowlege and the way this knowledge is invoked to regulate behavior are likely to be continually changing as children mature and their social environments change or expand. In middle childhood the development of self-concept requires that children develop a relatively stable and comprehensive understanding of themselves, that they refine their understanding of how the social world works, that they develop standards and expectations for their own behavior, and that they develop strategies for controlling or managing their behavior. Changes in the child (e.g., cognitive development) and changes in the social environment (e.g., going to school) can be analyzed for their likely impact on these various components of self-concept.

As indicated by our review of the literature on self-understanding, much is known about the content of self-concept. What is missing, however, is a broader perspective on self-understanding, one that includes an examination of children's knowledge of their motives, goals, standards, and strategies for self-regulation. The role of emotional content in self-concept and the relationship between knowledge of affective states and behavioral regulation are also in need of greater specification. Understanding these additional aspects of self-knowledge will enable us to specify more fully the role of self-concept in the regulation of behavior and to understand how self-concept changes in response to the social environment.

With respect to behavioral regulation, a number of theoretical perspectives, many quite similar, attempt to explain how children gain control of their behavior. These general approaches to self-management have been quite global in their analysis of self-control. More detailed empirical work on particular self-management tasks is clearly needed. Moreover, research on self-management should be more closely tied to the research on self-knowledge. Finally, the research on self-regulation should be expanded beyond studies concerned solely with achievement and performance.

Despite some significant gaps, our understanding of the role of the individual in regulating his or her own behavior is considerable compared with our understanding of the role of the social system. Research that has implicated the social system in behavior has seldom been systematic. In part this is due to the lack of good conceptual models relevant to the problem. From the work of behaviorists and cognitive behaviorists on self-control, we have some knowledge of how minor changes in a very constrained environment influence behavior. With respect to the larger social environment, much less exists. Rosenberg's (1979) work involving social-class differences is an exception, but it has been confined to self-esteem. In developing better models of social-system influence on behavior, the range of links between cognitive developments in the child and social developments should be extensively explored. For example, it is often asserted that children will not engage in social comparison or self-criticism before they are cognitively able to take the perspective of another. The configuraton of the social environment, however, may markedly facilitate or impair this cognitive development. For example, a child in a family with three other children may be required to take the perspective of another much sooner than an only child.

In general, the social environment should not be construed as a monolithic external factor that impinges on a fairly stable self. Instead it can be more productively viewed as shaping or creating the social self and, in turn, as being structured by the individual. More models of the mutual and reciprocal influences between the self-system and the social system should provide an understanding of how coregulation between the two systems is achieved and of how individuals become members of society or social beings. While we have some understanding of how the school-age child gains a coherent and stable view of self, we know much less about how the child gains social knowledge and develops interpersonal standards and individual strategies for the control of behavior.

Above all, we have stressed in this chapter the need to locate children within their broader social contexts regardless of the particular phenomenon being analyzed and the value of studying self-concept in relation to the regulation of behavior. Quite simply, our review suggests that the nature or content of self-concept should not be studied apart from its social origins or its specific behavioral functions for the individual.

REFERENCES

Adler, A.
1927   The Practice and Theory of Individual Psychology. New York: Harcourt, Brace and World.
Aronfreed, J.
1968   Conduct and Conscience: The Socialization of Internal Controls Over Behavior. New York: Academic Press.
1969   The concept of internalization. In D.A. Goslin, ed., Handbook of Socialization Theory and Research. New York: Rand McNally.
1976   Moral development from the standpoint of a general psychological theory. In T. Lickona, ed., Moral Development and Behavior. New York: Holt, Rinehart & Winston.
Atkinson, J.W., and Birch, D.
1978   An Introduction to Motivation. Rev. ed. New York: Van Nostrand.
Bandura, A.
1973   Aggression: A Social Learning Analysis. Englewood Cliffs, N.J.: Prentice-Hall.
1977   Self-efficacy: Toward a unifying theory of behavioral change. Psychological Review 84:191–215.
1978   The self system in reciprocal determinism. American Psychologist 33:344–358.
1981   Self-referent thought: The development of self-efficacy. In J.H. Flavell and L.D. Ross, ed., Social Cognitive Development: Frontiers and Possible Futures. Cambridge, England: Cambridge University Press.
1982   The self and mechanisms of agency. In J. Suls, ed., Psychological Perspectives on the Self. Hillsdale, N.J.: Lawrence Erlbaum.
Bandura, A., Ross, D., and Ross, S.A.
1963   Vicarious reinforcement and imitative learning. Journal of Abnormal and Social Psychology 67:601–607.
Bannister, D., and Agnew, J.
1977   The child's construing of self. In J. Cole, ed., Nebraska Symposium on Motivation. Lincoln: University of Nebraska Press.
Bartel, N.R.
1971   Locus of control and achievement in middle- and lower-class children. Child Development 42:1099–1107.

Berger, K.S.
    1980   *The Developing Person.* New York: Worth Publishers.
Block, J.
    1971   *Lives Through Time.* Berkeley, Calif.: Bancroft Books.
Block, J.H., and Block, J.
    1980   The role of ego-control and ego-resiliency in the organization of behavior. In W.A. Collins, ed., *Minnesota Symposium on Child Psychology.* Vol. 13. Hillsdale, N.J.: Lawrence Erlbaum.
Blumenfeld, P., Bossert, S., Hamilton, U.L., Wesselo, C., and Meece, J.
    1979   Teacher Talk and Student Thought: Socialization Into the Student Role. Paper presented at the Conference on Teacher and Student Perceptions of Success and Failure, Pittsburgh, Pa.
Broughton, J.
    1978   Development of concepts of self, mind, reality, and knowledge. *New Directions for Child Development* 1:75–100.
Buss, D.M., and Scheier, M.F.
    1976   Self-consciousness, self-awareness, and self-attribution. *Journal of Research on Personality* 10:463–468.
Camp, B.W.
    1980   Two psychoeducational treatment programs for young aggressive boys. In C.K. Whalen and E. Henker, eds., *Hyperactive Children: The Social Ecology of Indentification and Treatment.* New York: Academic Press.
Camp, B.W., and Bush, M.A.
    In   *The Think Aloud Program: Background Research and Program Guide.* Champaign, Ill.:
    press   Research Press.
Camp, B.W., and Ray, R.S.
    In   Aggression. In A. Meyers and W.E. Craighead, eds., *Cognitive Behavior Therapy With*
    press   *Children.* New York: Plenum Press.
Camp, B., Bloom, G., Hebert, F., and Van Doorninck, W.
    1977   "Think Aloud": A program for developing self-control in young aggressive boys. *Journal of Abnormal Child Psychology* 5:157–169.
Carver, C.S., and Scheier, M.F.
    1981a   *Attention and Self-Regulation: A Control-Theory Approach to Human Behavior.* New York: Springer-Verlag.
    1981b   A control-systems approach to behavioral self-regulation. In L. Wheeler, ed., *Review of Personality and Social Psychology.* Vol. 2. Beverly Hills, Calif.: Sage.
    1982   Control theory: A useful conceptual framework for personality-social, clinical, and health psychology. *Psychological Bulletin* 92(1):111–135.
Carver, C.S., Ganellen, R., Froming, W.J., and Chambers, W.
    1981   Are Many Acts of Modeling "Accessibility" Phenomena? Unpublished manuscript.
Clark, R.B.
    1965   *Dark Ghetto: Dilemmas of Social Power.* New York: Harper & Row.
Clark, K.B., and Clark, M.P.
    1947   Racial identification and preference in Negro children. In T.M. Newcomb and E. Hartley, eds., *Readings in Social Psychology.* New York: Holt.
Cohen, E.G.
    1972   Interracial interaction disability. *Human Relations* 25:9–27.
Combs, A., and Snygg, D.
    1959   The development of the phenomenal self. In A. Combs and D. Snygg, eds., *Individual Behavior.* Second ed. New York: Harper & Row.
Cooley, C.H.
    1902   *Human Nature and the Social Order.* New York: Scribner.

Craighead, W.E., Kazdin, A.E., and Mahoney, M.J.
1976   Behavior Modification: Principles, Issues, and Applications. Boston: Houghton Mifflin.
Craighead, W.E., Wilcoxon-Craighead, L., and Meyers, A.W.
1978   New directions in behavior modification With Children. In M.Herson, R.M. Eisler, and P.M. Miller, eds., *Progress in Behavior Modification*. Vol. 6. New York: Academic Press.
Damon, W., and Hart, W.
1982   The development of self-understanding from infancy through adolescence. *Child Development* 53:841–869.
Epstein, S.
1973   The self-concept revisited or a theory of a theory. *American Psychologist* 28:405–416.
Erikson, E.H.
1959   *Identity and the Life Cycle.* New York: International Universities Press.
Fischer, K.F.
1980   A theory of cognitive development: The control and construction of hierarchies and skills. *Psychological Review* 87(6):477–531.
Fischer, K.W., and Bullock, D.
1981   Patterns of data: Sequence, synchrony, and constraint in cognitive development. In K.W. Fischer, ed., *Cognitive Development.* San Francisco: Jossey-Bass.
Fischer, K.W., Hand, H.H., Watson, M.W., Van Parys, M.M., and Tucker, J.L.
In   Putting the child into socialization: The development of social categories in preschool
press   children. In L. Katz, ed., *Current Topics in Early Childhood Education.* Vol. 6. Norwood, N.J.: Aflex.
Flavell, J.H.
1975   *The Development of Role-Taking and Communication Skills in Children.* Huntington, N.Y.: Krieger. (Originally published by Wiley in 1968.)
Flavell, J.H., and Ross, L.
1981   Social and cognitive development: Frontiers and possible future. New York: Cambridge University Press.
Flavell, J.H., Shipstead, S.G., and Croft, K.
1978   What Young Children Think You See When Their Eyes Are Closed. Unpublished manuscript, Stanford University.
Freud, S.
1922   *Beyond the Pleasure Principle.* London: Hogarth Press.
1956   Formulations in the two frames of mental functioning. In J. Strachy and A. Freud, eds., *The Standard Edition of the Complete Psychological Works of Sigmund Freud.* Vol. 12. London: Hogarth. (Originally published in 1911.)
Glucksberg, S., Krauss, R.M., and Higgins, E.T.
1975   The development of referential communication skills. In F.D. Horowitz, ed., *Review of Child Development Research.* Vol. 4. Chicago: University of Chicago Press.
Goffman, E.
1959   *The Presentation of Self in Everyday Life.* Garden City, N.Y.: Doubleday.
Greenwald, A.G.
1980   The totalitarian ego: Fabrication and revision of personal history. *American Psychology* 35:603–613.
Guardo, C.J., and Bohan, J.B.
1971   Development of a sense of self-identity in children. *Child Development* 42:1909–1921.
Harter, S.
1982   A developmental perspective on some parameters of self-regulation in children. In P. Karoly and F.H. Kanfer, eds., *Self-Management and Behavior Change.* New York: Pergamon Press.

1983a Competence as a dimension of self-evaluation: Toward a comprehensive model of self-worth. In R. Leahy, ed., *The Development of the Self.* New York: Academic Press.
1983b Developmental perspectives on the self-system. In M. Hetherington, ed., *Carmichael's Manual of Child Psychology. Volume on Social and Personality Development.* New York: John Wiley & Sons.
Hauser, S.
1976 Loevinger's model and measure of ego development: A critical review. *Psychological Bulletin* 83:928–955.
Higgins, E.T.
1981 Role-taking and social judgment: Alternative developmental perspectives and processes. In J.H. Flavell and L. Ross, eds., *Social Cognitive Development: Frontiers and Possible Futures.* New York: Cambridge University Press.
Higgins, E.T., and Eccles, J.
1983 Social cognition and the social life of the child: States and subcultures. In E.T. Higgins, D.N. Ruble, and M.W. Hartup, eds., *Social Cognition and Social Behavior: Development Issues.* New York: Cambridge University Press.
Horney, K.
1953 *Neurosis and Human Growth.* New York: Norton.
James, W.
1910 *Psychology: The Briefer Course.* New York: Henry Holt and Co.
Johnston, J.M.
1972 Punishment of human behavior. *American Psychologist* 27:1033–1054.
Jones, E.E., and Berglas, S.
1978 Control of attributions about the self through self-handicapping strategies: The appeal of alcohol and the role of underachievement. *Personality and Social Psychology Bulletin* 4(2):200–206.
Jones, E.E., and Pittman, T.S.
1982 Toward a general theory of strategic self-presentation. In J. Suls, ed., *Psychological Perspectives of the Self.* Vol. 1. Hillsdale, N.J.: Lawrence Erlbaum.
Kanfer, F.H.
1970 Self regulation: Research, issues, and speculations. In C. Neuringer and J.L. Michael, eds., *Behavior Modification in Clinical Psychology.* New York: Appleton-Century-Crofts.
1980 Self-management methods. In F.H. Kanfer and A.P. Goldstein, eds., *Helping People Change: A Textbook of Methods.* Second edition. New York: Pergamon Press.
Kanfer, F.H., and Phillips, J.S.
1970 *Learning Foundations of Behavior Therapy.* New York: John Wiley & Sons.
Karoly, P.
1977 Behavioral self-management in children: Concepts, methods, issues, and directions. In M. Hersen, R.M. Eisler, and P.M. Miller, eds., *Progress in Behavior Modification.* Vol. 5. New York: Academic Press.
In Self-management problem in children. In E.J. Mas and L. Terdal, eds., *Behavioral Assessment of Childhood Disorders.* New York: Guilford Press.
press
Kelly, G.A.
1955 *The Psychology of Personal Constructs.* New York: Norton.
Kendall, P.
1977 On the efficacious use of verbal self-instructional procedures with children. *Cognitive Therapy and Research* 1:331–341.
Kendall, P.C., and Finch, A.
1979 Developing non-implulsive behavior in children: Cognitive behavioral strategies for self-control. In P.C. Kendall, and S.D. Hollon, eds., *Cognitive-Behavioral Interventions: Theory, Research, and Procedures.* New York: Academic Press.

Kohlberg, L.
   1969   Stage and sequence: The cognitive-developmental approach to socialization. In D.A.
          Gossin, ed., *Handbook of Socialization Theory and Research*. Chicago: Rand McNally.
Kohn, M.
   1969   *Class and Conformity: A Study in Values*. Homewood, Ill.: Dorsey.
   1977   *Social Competence, Symptoms, and Underachievement in Childhood: A Longitudinal Per-*
          spective. New York: Halsted Press.
Lewin, K.
   1935   *A Dynamic Theory of Personality*. New York: McGraw-Hill.
   1936   *Principles of Topological Psychology*. New York: McGraw-Hill.
   1938   *The Conceptual Representation and the Measurement of Psychological Forces*. Durham, N.C.:
          Duke University Press.
   1951   *Field Theory in Social Science*. New York: Harper & Row.
Lively, W.J., and Bromley, D.B.
   1973   *Person Perception in Childhood and Adolescence*. London: John Wiley & Sons.
Loevinger, J.
   1966   The meaning and measurement of ego development. *American Psychologist* 21:195–206.
Loevinger, J., and Wessler, R.
   1970   *Measuring Ego Development*. Vol. 1. San Francisco: Jossey-Bass.
Luria, A.
   1959   The directive function of speech in development. *Word* 15:341–352.
   1961   *The Role of Speech in the Regulation of Normal and Abnormal Behaviors*. New York: Liveright.
Lynch, M.D., Norem-Hebeisen, A.A., and Gergen, K., eds.
   1981   *Self-Concept: Advances in Theory and Research*. Cambridge, Mass.: Ballinger.
Maehr, M.L.
   1974   Culture and achievement motivation. *American Psychologist* 29:887–896.
Mahoney, M.J.
   1974   *Cognition and Behavior Modification*. Cambridge, Mass: Ballinger.
Markus, H.
   1977   Self-schemata and processing information about the self. *Journal of Personality and Social*
          Psychology 35:63–78.
   1980   The self in thought and memory. In D.M. Wegner and R.R. Vallacher, eds., *The Self*
          in Social Psychology. New York: Oxford University Press.
Markus, H., and Nurius, P.S.
   1983   Possible Selves. Unpublished manuscript, University of Michigan.
Markus, H., and Sentis, D.
   1982   The self in social information processing. In J. Suls, ed., *Psychological Perspectives on the*
          Self. Hillsdale, N.J.: Lawrence Erlbaum.
Markus, H., and Smith, J.
   1981   The influence of self-schemas on the perception of others. In N. Cantor and J.F. Kihls-
          trom, eds., *Personality, Cognition, and Social Interaction*. Hillsdale, N.J.: Lawrence Erl-
          baum.
Mash, E., and Dalby, J.
   1978   Behavioral interventions for hyperactivity. In R. Tries, eds., *Hyperactivity in Children:*
          Etiology, Measurement and Treatment Implications. Baltimore, Md.: University Park Press.
McCall, G.J., and Simmons, J.L.
   1978   *Identities and Interaction*. Rev. ed. New York: Free Press.
McGuire, W.J., and McGuire, C.V.
   1982   Significant others in self-space: Sex differences and developmental trends in the social
          self. In J. Suls, ed., *Psychological Perspectives on the Self*. Vol. 1. Hillsdale, N.J.: Lawrence
          Erlbaum.

McGuire, W.J., McGuire, C.V., Child, P., and Fujioka, T.
1978   Salience of ethnicity in the spontaneous self-concept as a function of one's ethnic distinctiveness in the social environment. *Journal of Personality and Social Psychology* 36:511–520.
McGuire, W., and Padawer-Singer, A.
1976   Trait salience in the spontaneous self-concept. *Journal of Personality and Social Psychology* 33:743-754.
Mead, G.H.
1934   *Mind, Self, and Society.* Chicago: University of Chicago Press.
Meichenbaum, D.
1976   Toward a cognitive theory of self-control. In G.E. Schwartz and D. Shapiro, eds., *Consciousness and Self-Regulation: Advances in Research.* Vol. 1. New York: Plenum Press.
1977   *Cognitive Behavior Modification.* New York: Plenum Press.
Meichenbaum, D., and Goodman, J.
1971   Training impulsive children to talk to themselves: A means of developing self-control. *Journal of Abnormal Psychology* 77:115–126.
Mischel, W.
1974   Processes in delay of gratification. In L. Berkowitz, ed., *Advances in Experimental Social Psychology.* Vol. 7. New York: Academic Press.
1979   On the interface of cognition and personality: Beyond the person-situation debate. *American Psychologist* 34(9):740–754.
Mischel, W., and Baker, N.
1975   Cognitive appraisals and transformations in delay behavior. *Journal of Personality and Social Psychology* 31:254–261.
Mischel, W., and Grusec, J.
1966   Determinants of the rehearsal and transmission of neutral and aversive behaviors. *Journal of Personality and Social Psychology* 3:197–205.
Mischel, W., and Liebert, R.M.
1966   Effects of discrepancies between observed and imposed reward critieria on their acquisition and transmission. *Journal of Personality and Social Psychology* 3:45–53.
1967   The role of power in the adoption of self-reward patterns. *Child Development* 38:673–683.
Mischel, W., and Moore, B.
1973   Cognitive Transformations of the Stimulus in Delay of Gratification. Unpublished manuscript, Stanford University.
Mischel, W., and Patterson, C.J.
1976   Substantive and structural elements of effective plans for self-control. *Journal of Personality and Social Psychology* 34:942–950.
1978   Effective plans for self-control in children. In W.A. Collins, ed., *Minnesota Symposium on Child Psychology.* Vol. 11. Hillsdale, N.J.: Lawrence Erlbaum.
Mischel, W., Mischel, H.N., and Hood, S.Q.
1978   The Development of Knowledge of Effective Ideation to Delay Gratification. Unpublished manuscript, Stanford University.
Montemayor R., and Eisen, M.
1977   The development of self-conceptions from childhood to adolescence. *Developmental Psychology* 13:314–319.
Moore, B., Mischel, W., and Zeiss, A.
1976   Comparative effects of the reward stimulus and its cognitive representation in voluntary delay. *Journal of Personality and Social Psychology* 34:419–424.

Parke, R.D.
1970   The role of punishment in the socialization process. In R.A. Hoppe, G.A.. Milton, and E.C. Simmel, eds., *Early Experiences and the Process of Socialization*. New York: Academic Press.
1974   Rules, roles, and resistance to deviation in children: Explorations in punishment, discipline, and self-control. In A. Pick, ed., *Minnesota Symposium on Child Psychology*. Vol. 8. Minneapolis: University of Minnesota Press.
1977   Punishment in children: Effects, side effects, and alternative strategies. In H.D. Hom, Jr., and P.A. Robinson, eds., *Psychological Processing in Early Education*. New York: Academic Press.
Patterson, C.J.
In   Self-control and self-regulation in childhood. In T. Field, A. Huston-Stein, et al., eds.,
press   *Review of Human Development*. New York: John Wiley & Sons.
Patterson, C.J., and Kister, M.C.
In   Development of listener skills for referential communication. In W.P. Dickson, ed.,
press   *Children's Oral Communication Skills*. New York: Academic Press.
Piaget, J.
1952   *The Origins of Intelligence in Childhood.* Translated by Margaret Cook. New York: International Universities Press.
Pressley, G.M.
1979   Increasing children's self-control through cognitive interventions. *Review of Educational Research.*
Proshansky, H., and Newton, P.
1968   The nature and meaning of Negro self-identity. In M. Deutsch, I. Katz, and A.R. Jensen, eds., *Social Class, Race, and Psychological Development*. New York: Holt, Rinehart and Winston.
Purkey, W.W.
1970   *Self-Concept and School Achievement.* Englewood Cliffs, N.J.: Prentice-Hall.
Rogers, C.R.
1951   *Client-Centered Therapy.* Boston: Houghton.
Rosenberg, M.
1979   *Conceiving the Self.* New York: Basic Books.
Rosenberg, M., and Kaplan, H.B., eds.
1982   *Social Psychology of the Self-Concept.* Arlington Heights, Ill.: Harlan Division.
Rosenhan, D.L., and White, G.M.
1967   Observation and rehearsal as determinants of prosocial behavior. *Journal of Personality and Social Psychology* 35:424–431.
Ross, D.M., and Ross, S.A.
1976   *Hyperactivity: Research, Theory, and Action.* New York: John Wiley & Sons.
Ruble, D.
In   The development of social comparison processes and their role in achievement-related
press   self-socialization. In E.T. Higgins, D. Ruble, and W.W. Hartup, eds., *Social Cognition and Social Behavior: Development Perspectives.*
St. John, N.H.
1979   *School Desegregation: Outcomes for Children.* New York: John Wiley & Sons.
Scheier, M.F., and Carver, C.S.
1977   Self-focused attention and the experience of emotion: Attraction, repulsion, elation and depression. *Journal of Personality and Social Psychology* 35:624–626.
In   Self-directed attention and the comparison of self with standards. *Journal of Experimental*
press   *Social Psychology.*

Selman, R.
1980   *The Growth of Interpersonal Understanding.* New York: Academic Press.
Shibutani, T.
1961   *Society and Personality.* Englewood Cliffs, N.J.: Prentice-Hall.
Snyder, M.
1974   The self-monitoring of expressive behavior. *Journal of Personality and Social Psychology* 30:526–537.
1979   Self-monitoring processes. In L. Berkowitz, ed., *Advances in Experimental Social Psychology.* Vol. 12. New York: Academic Press.
Staats, A.W.
1975   *Social Behaviorism.* Homewood, Ill.: Dorsey.
Sullivan, H.S.
1953   *The Interpersonal Theory of Psychiatry.* New York: Norton.
Suls, J., ed.
1982   *Psychological Perspectives on the Self.* Vol. 1. Hillsdale, N.J.: Lawrence Erlbaum.
Vygotsky, L.
1962   *Thought and Language.* New York: John Wiley & Sons.
Wegner, D.M., and Vallacher, R.R., eds.
1980   *The Self in Social Psychology.* New York: Oxford University Press.
White, G.M.
1972   Immediate and deferred effects of model observation and guided and unguided rehearsal of donating and stealing. *Journal of Personality and Social Psychology* 21:139–148.
Wylie, R.
1979   *The Self-Concept.* Rev. ed. Lincoln: University of Nebraska Press.
Yates, B.T., and Mischel, W.
1979   Young children's preferred attentional strategies for delaying gratification. *Journal of Personality and Social Psychology* 37:286–300.
Zajonc, R.B.
1976   Family configuration and intelligence. *Science* 192:227–236.

CHAPTER 5

Middle Childhood in the Context of the Family

Eleanor E. Maccoby

Between the time when children enter school and the time they reach adolescence, the family plays a crucial role in socialization, although its role is not so predominant as in the early childhood years. In middle childhood, teachers, peers, coaches, and others outside the family have more contact with the child than in early childhood, and they exercise varying degrees of influence. During this time, parents negotiate on behalf of the child with these other socialization agents, but their parenting functions are still exercised mainly through interaction with the child.

Psychological research on parent-child interactions has heavily emphasized infancy and the preschool period rather than later periods. In compiling a recent review of research on this topic, Maccoby and Martin (1983) located more than three times as many studies on children under age 6 as on school-age children. Although the research on certain aspects of family-based socialization in the school-age period is thin, studies on family characteristics and their relationship to children's current or future deviance—e.g., alcoholism, drug addiction, aggression, delinquency, depression—present substantial information on the school-age years (Farrington and West, 1981; McCord, 1979; McCord and McCord, 1960; Pulkkinen, 1982; Robins, 1974; Robins and Ratcliff, 1980; Rutter, 1982). This chapter reviews some of the major themes of existing work, identifies promising themes that appear in more recent writings, and suggests gaps that additional research might help to fill.

Most research on socialization within the family has been concerned with individual differences, explaining why children vary in their personal attributes. The major hypothesis has been that such variation stems at least in part from differences in parental socialization of children. Many studies have looked for dimensions in which parents differ and have then examined the relationship between these variations among parents and the characteristics of their children.

The early work was essentially linear in concept, having its origins in a view of socialization wherein parents, by means of reinforcement and discipline, trained their children to carry out certain behaviors and avoid others. In addition, some researchers studied the development of children's motivation to pattern themselves after their parents' values and behaviors via the process of identification. While the concept of identification gave children a somewhat more active role in their own socialization than did simple reinforcement theories, socialization was still conceptualized primarily as a flow of influence from parents to children, with children acquiring sets of behavioral tendencies in the form of habits or motives.

The characteristics of parents and children that were studied varied from narrow and specific to broad and abstract. The child outcome measures ranged from highly specific responses (e.g., the frequency of smiling) to global characteristics, such as intelligence or competence. On the parental side, specific characteristics—such as the frequency with which parents rewarded or punished a given behavior—were studied; at the opposite extreme, such general characteristics as warmth or permissiveness were assessed. Although the work did not deny that individuals' behavior varies from one situation to another the focus was to identify individual characteristics of both parent and child that had some stability across time and situations and to look for functional relationships between the parental characteristics as antecedents and the child characteristics as outcomes.

A major refinement of this point of view has been the study of behavioral patterns, in both parents and children. The assumption underlying the study of parental patterns or clusters has been that the effect of a parental practice depends on the context of other parenting characteristics with which it occurs (see Baumrind, 1967, 1971; Becker, 1964). Investigation of child behavioral patterns occurs in studies of attachment, in which it is argued that children's attachment is adequately characterized not by counting the frequency of specific behaviors, but only by studying clusters of behaviors taken in context (Sroufe and Waters, 1977). This point of view has been applied primarily to infants and toddlers, while the trait approach remains predominant in studies that examine how parental practices influence the characteristics of preschool children.

In recent years, a more interactive, less linear point of view has emerged. Researchers increasingly examine the effects of children on parents, the effects of parents on children, and cyclical processes. Little of this work, however, is developmental in concept. Researchers are only beginning to ask: How does parent-child interaction change with the developmental level of the child? Does a particular child-rearing style have a different impact on children of various ages? How much does the impact of parental treatment of a school-age child depend on the relationship established with that child at earlier periods of development? How much are parents limited or facilitated in the relationship they can have and the child-rearing methods they can use with a school-age child by the characteristics that the child has developed during the first 6 years of life?

The major contention of this chapter is that the process of child-rearing undergoes important changes as children develop, and that middle childhood, with regard to parent-child relationships, has its own distinctive features. The chapter presents developmental changes that normally occur as children enter the middle childhood years, some of the concomitant changes in parents' child-rearing roles, and some of the more traditional socialization findings—those concerned primarily with individual differences among school-age children and their parents. The chapter goes on to describe how parents differ from one another, then summarizes some of the major findings for this age period concerning the way parental variations relate to the variations among children in their personalities and social behavior. It takes up some of the differences among groups of parents (e.g., social class, ethnic, and family-structure groups) and considers some of the conditions that might bring these differences about.

CHILD-REARING AND DEVELOPMENTAL CHANGE

Issues and Processes of Socialization

Amount of Parent-Child Interaction

As children enter the school-age years, there is a great decline in the amount of time they spend in their parents' presence and in the total amount of time their parents devote to them. Hill and Stafford (1980) reported in a time-use study that parents spend less than half as much time in caretaking, teaching, reading, talking, and playing with children ages 5–12 as they do with children of preschool age. The drop in interaction time is more precipitous and occurs earlier with a lower parental education level. Other studies concur in finding this strong decline in interaction rates with the increasing age of the child (e.g., Baldwin, 1955).

Parent-Child Issues

There are important changes, too, in the kind of issues parents deal with in their day-to-day interactions with their children. Interactions with preschoolers focus on modesty, bedtime routines, control of temper tantrums, fighting with siblings or other children, eating and table manners, getting dressed by themselves, and attention seeking (Newson and Newson, 1968; Sears et al., 1957). Some of these issues carry over into the school-age years (e.g., fighting, children's reactions to discipline). New issues emerge by age 7 (Newson and Newson, 1976): whether to require chores and how to enforce standards of performance; whether children should be paid for household work; how they can be encouraged to entertain themselves rather than relying on parents for activity planning; how to support them in their relationships with peers and whether to monitor their friendships and discourage or encourage contact with specific children.

An important parental issue in middle childhood is how to keep track of children's whereabouts and activities now that they are spending more time away from home. With varying degrees of success, parents teach their children to inform them of their whereabouts at all times; parents often require either that children come directly home from school to discuss what they propose to do or that they check in by phone.

An issue entirely new to middle childhood is how parents deal with the child's problems at school—e.g., a child's unwillingness to go to school or a child's report of an encounter with the teacher (Newson and Newson, 1977). Parents also become concerned about how much to become involved in the child's schoolwork. Roberts and colleagues (1981), working with an American longitudinal sample of children studied at ages 3 and 12, reported increasing parental emphasis on children's achievement during this period, a trend related primarily to their performance in school.

Although there is reason to believe that the issues arising between parents and children change significantly as children enter and progress through the middle childhood period, data on these changes are limited, and many issues have been studied only minimally. We know little, for example, about what moral or ethical matters come up in family exchanges or how they are dealt with.

We should be aware that the above discussion of issues proceeds from a rather culture-bound perspective. Weisner's chapter in this volume shows that in non-Western societies, in which most of the world's children live, the 6–12 age period is when children enter the work world, contributing to the necessary survival functions of families—e.g., care of younger children, agricultural work, care of animals. In such societies, the issues that preoccupy Western parents may have little relevance.

Techniques of Discipline

Parents report that interactions with school-age children are in some respects easier than with preschoolers; for example, it may be possible to use reasoning rather than discipline. The children's increasing ability to discuss issues with their parents, however, is a mixed blessing; parents often weary of extended arguments and regret their children's increasing skill in catching their parents' inconsistencies.

Studies consistently show a decline in the use of physical punishment as children get older (Clifford, 1959; Fawl, reported in Patterson, 1982; Newson and Newson, 1976). Parents also decreasingly use distraction and physically moving the child away from forbidden or dangerous activities. At the same time, there is evidence of an increase, as children move from the preschool into the school-age years, in parents' using deprivation of privileges, appeals to the child's self-esteem or sense of humor, arousal of the child's sense of guilt, and reminders that children are responsible for what happens to them (Clifford, 1959; Roberts et al., 1981). Threatening, ignoring, and isolating appear to decline from the time of school entrance to the later middle childhood years.

Changes in Affectional Relationships

If we assume that the issues and techniques of discipline change with children's development, as well as the nature of the parent-child relationship itself, we are on thin ground as far as research evidence is concerned. The work that is available does not reveal a consistent picture. Consider for example the role of affect in the relations between parents and children, taking positive affect first. Newson and Newson (1968) reported that, at age 4, the question of open displays of affection did not appear to be problematic. In a majority of cases, both parents and children seemed to accept and value cuddling. By age 7 (Newson and Newson, 1976), many of the children were becoming circumspect, avoiding affectionate displays with their parents whenever a peer was present, although they still sought physical affection at private moments such as bedtime. From the parents' standpoint, mothers expressed continued readiness for physical contact with their children. The implication of this descriptive account is that it is primarily the children, rather than the parents, who pull away from physical affection and provide the impetus for whatever decline in such displays occurs with age.

Shows of physical affection, of course, are only one aspect—and a fairly narrow one—of the affectional relationship between parent and child. The detailed work on attachment that is now available in infancy and the early childhood years has no counterpart in research on middle childhood. While a few writers (Bowlby, 1969; Marvin, 1977) have studied the transition that occurs at about age 3 from proximity-seeking to more distal forms of attachment, few have examined transitions that occur beyond this point.

Some years ago, Baldwin (1946), working with families in the Fels longitudinal study, compared the relationships between parents and 3-year-olds with those between parents and 9-year-olds. At the younger age, higher levels of parental warmth were recorded on all the relevant measures: child centeredness, approval, acceptance, affection, and rapport. Parents of 9-year-olds were less warm in all these ways and more severe and critical. Lasko (1954), working with the same data but reporting on more age levels and differentiating the sample by birth order, reported that the decline in parental warmth was found primarily for firstborn children. She indicates that later-borns have an affectional relationship with their parents that is more stable over time.

A recent report from another longitudinal study presents a different picture. Roberts et al. (1981) reported a decrease, between the ages of 3 and 12, in displays of physical affection, but there was little change in the reported mean levels of enjoying parenting, having positive regard for the child, and having respect for the child's opinions and preferences. Thus it appears that although parental warmth is shown in different ways with older children, it may not shift downward, as Baldwin claimed. A third study (a cross-sectional one by Armentrout and Burger, 1972) asked children in grades 4 through 8 to describe certain aspects of their parents' child-rearing practices. The parental acceptance-rejection balance changed with the ages studied. For boys, acceptance by parents increased from the fourth to fifth grade, then declined; for girls, the peak was reached in the sixth grade and declined thereafter.

The trends in displays of negative affect between parents and children are somewhat clearer than the trends for displays of positive affect. Generally, anger between parents and children declines as children move into the school years. Goodenough (1931) reported that the frequency of angry outbursts by children declined after the age of 18–24 months. Patterson (1982) reported a steady decline, between ages 2 and 15, in the frequency of coercive behavior directed by children toward other family members (whining, yelling, hitting, ignoring others' overtures), and Newson and Newson showed a decrease in the frequency of temper tantrums between the ages of 4 and 7. Concomitantly, a steady decrease occurred, from age 3 to age 6 to age 9, in the frequency of disciplinary encounters (Clifford, 1959); that is, in conflictual incidents in which the parent directed the child to do something or to stop doing something and the child failed to comply. Such conflicts, especially when they culminate in physical punishment, often involve angry emotions for both parents and children. The finding that physical punishment is much less frequent with school-age than preschool children indicates that parents and school-age children either have fewer conflicts or have learned to deal with them without letting them escalate into highly emotional encounters. When school-age children do become angry, however, they do not recover from it as quickly as they did when younger (Clifford, 1959), and this means their parents must deal with the aftereffects of emotional outbursts—sulkiness, depressed mood, avoidance of parents, or passive noncooperation.

Information on the displays of positive and negative affect between parents and children gives us only a partial picture of their affective relationship. Attachment bonds within families presumably have more generalized manifestations and, with respect to such bonds, a number of important questions remain unanswered. What is the capacity of children in middle childhood to form strong bonds with new caretakers? What is the impact of disruption at this age of earlier-formed bonds? To what extent do the reactions of children at this age to disruption of bonds depend on the nature of interpersonal ties formed at earlier ages? When disruptions of bonds occur at this age, what are the implications for the child's functioning at subsequent age periods? I discuss these issues briefly below but must note that they are still open questions.

Changes in Control Processes

It is a usual assumption that a major accompaniment of children's developmental change is the gradual shift of controlling functions from parent to child. In fact, this assumption is largely unverified. We have little information concerning changes that occur in the degree and kind of parental control between the preschool and school-age periods.

Baldwin's (1946) reports from the Fels longitudinal study in some ways run counter to a transfer-of-power trend. Comparing the behavior of a group of parents toward their 3-year-olds with the behavior of the same parents when their children were 9, Baldwin reported that the parents were more restrictive, more coercive, stricter, and even somewhat less democratic with the children when older. The parental attitude toward 3-year-olds was predominantly indulgent and protective, while much more was expected of older children, who were thought to be capable of conforming to nearly adult norms of behavior.

In a cross-sectional study with more age groups (each half-year or year from ages 6 to 10), Emmerich (1962) questioned parents concerning their child-rearing. He extracted two dimensions: one running from nurturant (positive, facilitating reactions) to restrictive (negative, interfering reactions), and the other, a power scale, reflecting the amount of active control exerted by the parent, which included rewards as well as punishment. Neither factor showed any consistent increase or decrease over the 6–10 age period.

The more recent study by Armentrout and Burger (1972) covered an older age range (10–14). These children reported a considerable decline in the amount of psychological control (possessiveness, intrusiveness, arousal of guilt) exercised by their parents. On the firm-lax dimension, however, there was an increase in parental firmness up to the age of 12, then a decline.

In a study of preadolescents and adolescents, Dornbusch et al. (1983) analyzed the responses of youth to questions concerning how decisions were made regarding: how they should spend their money, how they should dress, how late they might stay out, and what peers they should associate with. Over the age range 12–17, an increasing proportion of youth reported that they make such decisions alone, and a decreasing proportion reported that their parents made them alone. The proportion reporting that such decisions were made jointly remained constant. The findings would be consistent with a shift in the locus of decision making from parent-alone, to joint, to youth-alone.

Taken together, these studies suggest that, at least in some respects, the transfer of power from parent to child occurs somewhat more slowly than had been supposed, with the major shift to genuine child autonomy beginning to occur at about age 12. The information to support this suggestion is meager, however, and it is obvious that children ages 6–12 already are participating in the controlling and managing processes. This participation is a simple necessity that stems in part from the decrease in time that parent and child are together. I suggest that the original conception of parents transferring control directly to their children may be an oversimplified one— that a better conceptualization involves an intermediate process that may be called *coregulation*. That is, before they relinquish control of a given aspect of their children's lives, parents continue to exercise general supervisory control, while children begin to exercise moment-to-moment self-regulation.

This phase is paramount for many aspects of children's behavioral development during the 6–12 age period. The process of coregulation, if it is to be successful, must be a cooperative one, with clarity of communication between parent and child of paramount importance. The parental tasks during this period are threefold: First, they must monitor, guide, and support their children at a distance—that is, when the children are out of their presence; second, they must effectively use the times when direct contact does occur; and third, they must strengthen in their children the abilities that will allow them to monitor their own behavior, to adopt acceptable standards of good and bad behavior, to avoid undue risks, and to know when they need parental support or guidance. Children must be willing to inform parents of their whereabouts, activities, and problems so that parents can mediate and guide when necessary; parents must keep informed about events occurring outside their presence and must coordinate agendas that link the daily activities of parent and child.

Parents seem to have some, although not explicit, knowledge that different methods are needed for out-of-sight control than for face-to-face control of children. Grusec and Kuczynski (1980) found that most parents use a variety of methods in attempting to influence their children's behavior, and that the method chosen depends in part on whether infractions occur in or out of the parents' presence. For in-presence infractions (e.g., quarreling among siblings, excessively noisy behavior, or throwing a ball in the living room), parents tend to use power-assertive methods. For infractions not directly observed, however, (e.g., stealing money, teasing an old man, running into the street) parents are more likely to use reasoning and explanation. In an unpublished study, Kuczynski compared methods of parental influence when the parents either (1) knew they would be absent or (2) did not know they would be absent at the time of the child's compliance with parental instructions. When the child was out of parental sight, parents were more likely to use inductive reasoning and character attribution—e.g., "You are certainly nice and helpful." With boys, they also used less power assertion if they needed out-of-sight compliance. With the child's increasing age, we should expect an increase in parents' fostering out-of-sight compliance.

These changes in child-rearing occur concurrently with a variety of normative developmental changes that occur in all children during middle childhood, albeit at somewhat different rates. We turn now to a consideration of these changes—what they are and how they might be linked to the ontogeny of the parent-child relationship. Because there is little research focusing on how changes in child-rearing are related to the developmental level of the child, this section is necessarily speculative. It will point to some gaps in our theorizing and knowledge and suggest some promising approaches.

Normative Developmental Changes in Children

Developmental changes occurring in early childhood, such as the shift from crawling to walking and running or the acquisition of language, are dramatic and universally acknowledged. The developmental advances that occur in middle childhood are less obvious but nonetheless important. A review of the developmental changes in middle childhood follows (for a fuller exposition, see Maccoby, 1984).

Social Cognition and Social Competence

Between ages 6 and 12 children's ability to adopt the perspectives of others and to recognize other people's purposes and probable reactions substantially increases (Selman and Byrne, 1974). Partially as a consequence of this improved understanding, school-age children also improve considerably in their referential communication skills (Krauss and Glucksberg, 1969). That is, they are more able to select and convey the crucial information necessary for a partner to understand the message that the child wants to convey.

A second social-cognitive gain has to do with the child's increasing understanding of social roles—their requirements and how they intersect. The acquisition of sex-role knowledge has been more extensively studied than most other aspects of role concepts, but it is reasonable to believe that in middle childhood there is considerable expansion of children's understanding of other roles as well—e.g., teacher and pupil, leader and follower. Some aspects of role learning that affect peer interaction are discussed by Hartup (in this volume).

Some changes in children's conceptions of parent-child roles may affect family interactions. Specifically, there is a shift in children's conceptions about authority and the basis for parents' rights to exercise it (Damon, 1977). While preschoolers tend to think that parental authority rests on the power to punish or reward, the beginning of an exchange relationship can be seen with the onset of the middle childhood period. Children of this age begin to say that they ought to obey because of all the things their parents do for them. Some time after the age of 8, children also begin to give weight to their parents' expert knowledge and skill as a reasonable basis for parental authority. We may assume that parental appeals based on fairness, the return of favors, or reminders of the parents' greater experience and knowledge would be increasingly persuasive as the child progresses through this period, so that parents would less often feel compelled to resort to promises of reward or threats of punishment.

There are many other components of the social competence acquired in middle childhood. Some (e.g., entry skills that facilitate a child's joining peer group activities) have been studied primarily in the context of peer interaction. We know little about the role of other family members in children's acquisition of the social skills that they employ outside the family, although there is reason to believe that their behavior with siblings does generalize to peers (Dunn, 1983). It would be useful to know more about the transfer of social skills, not only from the family to other contexts, but also in the reverse direction; it is reasonable to believe that social skills acquired during peer interaction are sometimes brought to bear in a child's negotiations with family members.

Self-Concepts

About the time of entrance into school, children begin to acquire the ability to view the self from an outside (other-person) perspective. At about the same time or a little later, children also begin to define themselves more in terms of such attributes as appearance, possessions, or activities (see Markus and Nurius, in this volume). Perhaps in part as a consequence of these changes, children become more susceptible to attributional appeals. Grusec and Redler (1980) found, for example, that the generalized altruism of 5-year-olds was not enhanced when the experimenter responded to their generosity by an attribution such as "I can see that you are the kind of person who likes to help." Eight-year-olds, however, showed increased helpfulness in an unrelated situation a week or two later as a result of such treatment.

Although to our knowledge the point has not been tested, it seems likely that during the school-age years children would become more responsive to parental reminders that other people will not think well of them if they behave in certain ways. That children are beginning to see themselves as others see them, however, does not necessarily mean that they will become more tractable. When children realize that they can tailor their behavior and emotional expressiveness to what they think are the expectations and values of a given audience, they become more self-conscious and less open, even with their parents. Some parents (see Newson and Newson, 1976) complain that when their children have entered the school-age period, it is no longer so easy to know what their children are thinking and feeling; this renders the task of monitoring and guidance more difficult.

Impulsivity

Impulsivity declines fairly steadily from early childhood into the school-age years. As we have already noted, the frequency of angry outbursts declines, and children are more able to endure frustration and accept delays in gratification. Although not clearly demonstrated in research, it is probably also true that children improve in their ability to regulate their bodily activity according to the demands of the situation they are in, so that they exhibit less restless motion and wild running about as they grow older.

What are some of the implications of these changes for parents? Probably less parental power assertion is required. Halverson and Waldrop (1970) reported that mothers of impulsive preschool children used more negative, controlling statements than did the mothers of less impulsive children. (Of course, we do not know from this correlation whether the mothers' autocratic treatment caused the children's impulsiveness or vice versa. Perhaps both effects occurred.) An elegant set of studies by Barkley and colleagues (Barkley and Cunningham, 1979; Barkley, 1981) provides a clearer picture of the causal directions. These studies show that when the hyperactive behavior of diagnosed children is brought under control through drug therapy, maternal directiveness decreases and supportive responses increase. Whalen et al. (1980, 1981) have shown similar decreases in controlling behavior by teachers following drug therapy with hyperactive boys. Informal experience in dealing with young children suggests that when children are angry, distracted, or highly excited they cannot listen to reason; in order to get a message through to them at such times, parents must raise their voices, become peremptory, and perhaps resort to physical restraints. The decline in the use of physical punishment as the child gets older is well documented, and we may assume that one of the factors underlying this change is the decrease in the number of occasions on which the child has lost control.

With children's increasing control over their emotionality and hyperactivity that they achieve with age, parents become progressively more able to engage their children in problem-solving dialogues that may require time and sustained attention from both parent and child. Clifford (1959) noted with children ages 3 and 6 disciplinary encounters were more common when the children were tired or hungry; by the age of 9, this correlation had disappeared. This finding suggests that older children are more able to maintain self-control under the stresses of moderate hunger or fatigue; they do not become so restless or demanding that they require parental power-assertive controls.

Another aspect of impulse control is children's increasing ability to focus their attention on task-relevant information and carry out exhaustive searches for needed information without being distracted by irrelevant information and events (see Lane and Pearson, 1982, for a review). There is some indication that when a parent is trying to get a child to do an onerous task and the child becomes distracted, the parent becomes more peremptory— uses shorter sentences and, at least with boys, more often resorts to giving direct commands (Chapman, 1979). Perhaps older children's greater ability to sustain their attention during conversation with parents permits parents to use longer sentences and fewer imperatives than they use for younger children (Chapman, 1979).

Cognitive Executive Processes

Many developmental changes occur in cognitive processes as children enter and traverse the school-age period. These are reviewed elsewhere in this volume (see Fischer and Bullock). For purposes of this chapter, the changes that appear most relevant to parent-child interaction are those reflecting growth in the so-called executive functions (Sternberg and Powell, 1983). When children are asked to solve a problem, there is a regular increase with age in the extent to which they adopt a plan or goal for their activity. They become more efficient in the use of their memory capacity, in part because many subroutines are automated (Brown and DeLoache, 1978). Thus children can make more and better use of previously stored information. In addition, they become progressively more able to monitor their own knowledge and their progress toward goals; they can determine what information is necessary in order to carry out a plan. School-age children are increasingly able to coordinate goals and subgoals into action hierarchies— deciding which of a set of subroutines is to be run off first, which second, and so on. When an initial set has not been productive, they are increasingly able to break off the subroutine and adopt a new problem-solving strategy. The sheer accumulation of knowledge is important too, particularly knowledge concerning social scripts. That is, children store prototypic representations of the sequences in which events usually occur and the roles that various actors play in these sequences.

Clearly, these cognitive changes among school-age children must have profound implications for parent-child interaction. Children's increasing knowledge of social scripts and their ability to govern their own actions must mean that they need fewer cues from their parents to keep them on a planful track; furthermore, they should be more able to coordinate their activities with those of their parents. Consequently, parents can drop some of their monitoring activities. Such activities as bathing and brushing teeth will become fully automated and will require no monitoring. For other activities the child can assume some portion of the monitoring; however, how the checking processes are divided between parent and child is something we know little about.

To our knowledge, no studies have focused on changes in the locus and content of monitoring with children's increasing age, and this is a serious gap. We can only assume that there is a transition stage, during which moment-to-moment monitoring by parents is replaced by a joint monitoring process, so that with older children parents intervene only at the higher modes of action hierarchies, while children self-monitor the subroutines. A second serious gap in our knowledge is the degree to which parents and children share social scripts and what the consequences of discrepancies are.

Vulnerability to Stressors

There is no reason to believe that children in the middle childhood period are any more or any less vulnerable to stress than they are at any other age (Maccoby, 1983). The particular stressors to which they are vulnerable, however, are different from those at earlier or later ages, and the nature and duration of the stress effects are probably also different, although evidence on this point is inconclusive.

The complexity of this issue is shown in the research on attachment, separation, and bereavement. Much of the work has been done with infants, toddlers, and preschoolers, but some studies include older children and yield interesting comparisons. Although children ages 6–12 are clearly less distressed by relatively short-term separations from their parents than are younger children, they grieve more intensely and for a longer time over the death of a parent (see Rutter, 1983, for a review of evidence). It is not known, however, whether the long-term effects of bereavement and separation are greater or less when they occur during middle childhood than at other times (Garmezy, 1983:63; Rutter, 1983:18–19).

Part of the problem in making strong inferences about a child's degree of stress at the time of a separation or bereavement is that the effects of a child's age are usually confounded by the length of separation, the nature of alternative care during separation or bereavement, and the nature and duration of living conditions prior to the stressful event. Wallerstein and Kelley (1980) report that children's reactions to their parent's divorce varies with the children's age (see section on single parents below). In Wallerstein and Kelly's study, however, the numbers of children in each age group are low and there is no comparison group of children from nondivorced families; therefore, replication is needed.

Important questions remain: the effects of separation and bereavement depend not only on how much distress children experience at the time these events occur, but also on how quickly the children form secure bonds with new caretakers. Do children in middle childhood not only grieve longer but also find it more difficult to form new relationships with a stepparent or adoptive parent? Do school-age children benefit more than younger children from maintaining a relationship with the noncustodial parent after divorce?

Important though the issues of separation and bereavement are, other vulnerabilities to stress occur during middle childhood. School-age children show greater sensitivity to insults or other attacks on their rights or competence; to disruptions in intimate friendships with peers; and to unfavorable comparisons with the academic or athletic achievements of other children. At the same time, there is decreased vulnerability to many stressors that plague younger children, such as having to wait for an expected treat or having to adapt to household demands and routines.

Thus far in this section, developmental change has been presented as a relatively autonomous process—one that is largely independent of the history of the parent-child relationship but that has an impact on the relationship. For such changes as physical growth, this is a reasonable picture. For other aspects of development, age-related changes are a joint product of organismic development and the cumulative effects of earlier experience, with prior parent-child interaction being a significant portion of that experience. How the two forces are weighted in bringing about developmental change is an important research issue in itself, one about which we cannot generalize at present.

Clearly, however, the sequence of developmental events is more complex than would be implied by either a simple parent-shapes-child formulation or one that views developmental change as inherent in the child and changes in parental behavior as mainly a reflection of children's development. Children's developmental changes emerge, in part, from prior socialization efforts by their parents. Presumably, a child who is developing new skills in self-regulation will employ these skills quite differently, depending on whether a relationship of trust, open communication, and mutual willingness to accept influences from the partner was previously established between parent and child. And, presumably, some children develop self-regulatory skills faster than others, depending in part on their parents' prior effectiveness.

To date, however, research on the family almost totally lacks work on how parental effectiveness in socializing school-age children is related to the earlier phases of interaction. What is needed is longitudinal research that looks for sequential phases in the parent-child relationship, each phase being a joint product of the relationship that existed earlier and the new capabilities of the child.

The Role of Mutual Cognitions

Another gap in our knowledge of parent-child relationships concerns the way parents and children label one another and the attributions they make concerning one another's motives (see Hess, 1981; Maccoby and Martin, 1983). Presumably such cognitions play a larger role in middle childhood than they did when the child was younger. Parents and children do not react to one another solely on the basis of the partner's immediately prior behavior. They react on the basis of how this behavior is interpreted and what they think the behavior signals in the way of a sequence of actions that will probably follow.

As children grow older, parents and children accumulate experience with one another and develop expectations of the other's probable reactions. It appears inevitable that each must begin to label the other in terms of broad stereotypes and that these codified expectations must influence the inter-action between parent and child. It seems likely that parents with more than one child would label their children differentially, selecting a given child as more moody or more cooperative or more argumentative or less bright than other members of the family. Parents' demands of and responses to this child's behavior would be tailored accordingly—e.g., a child iden-tified as especially bright might get more explanations. The labels given to a specific child, then, would presumably reflect not only that child's own behavior, but how it compared with that of siblings.

To our knowledge, there has been no research that directly studies (1) the degree of agreement among family members in the labels applied to individual family members or (2) the way in which parental stereotypes or labels affect their interaction with each child. Several studies, however, do suggest a role for cumulative expectations. Halverson and Waldrop (1970) observed adults' reactions to boys who varied in hyperactivity. Women interacting with unfamiliar boys did not tailor their controlling behaviors to the level of the child's hyperactivity, even though hyperactive boys did display hyperactive behavior during the observational session. When mothers were observed interacting with their own sons, however, maternal behavior was related to the child's hyperactivity as independently assessed. Thus, the mothers must have been reacting to their accumulated knowledge of their child's hyperactive characteristics, rather than to the details of the behavior that occurred during the observational session.

This interpretation is consistent with a report by Paton (cited in Bell, 1977) that when the impulsive behavior of hyperactive children is brought under control by medication, their mothers do not immediately change their style of dealing with the child. Instead, in a period as long as several months, mothers reorganize their reactions toward, and presumably their perceptions of, their changed child. In a similar vein, Chapman (1979) noted that when a distracting stimulus was introduced during the task-oriented interaction of a mother and son, mothers increased their use of commands; the commands, however, were not contingent on specific instances of the child's loss of attention. Rather, the mothers seemed to be reacting to their anticipation of attention lapses. That this maternal reaction occurred with boys but not with girls may reflect either an expectation that boys are more likely to be distracted or a cumulative experience that commands are more effective for controlling distraction with boys than with girls.

The role of mutual cognitions has recently become the focus of some interesting research on peer interactions. Dodge (1980) showed that an ambiguous action by a school-age child is interpreted differently by other children depending on whether the actor has a reputation for being aggressive. Furthermore, aggressive children are more likely than other children to interpret peers' behavior toward them as having aggressive intent. The two sets of perceptions conjoin to increase the likelihood of agonistic encounters when interactions involve children with an aggressive history.

We can only assume that mutual cognitions play a similar role between parents and children, and that their history of experience with one another leads each to make assumptions concerning the intentions that lie behind the other's overt acts. This is only an assumption, however, and many questions remain unanswered: How flexible are parents in changing their expectations and conceptions about their children as they undergo the kind of developmental changes outlined earlier? How can one interrupt cycles of self-fulfilling prophecies once they gather momentum? As children change with age, what are the changes in labels they give to their parents, in their differentiation between the two parents, and in the way their labels affect their reactions to parental inputs? These questions deserve a place on the agenda of future research on parent-child interaction in the school-age years.

Thus far we have considered primarily the developmental changes that almost all children undergo during the 6–12 age period and how these changes may affect parent-child interaction. Parents also undergo life-span developmental changes. For example, they become more experienced child-rearers, especially if more children are born. They may undergo occupational changes. As child-rearing demands are reduced, many mothers return to work, and one or both parents may take on more responsibilities outside the home. In some families, new responsibilities for the care of elderly grandparents are assumed. The spousal relationship will almost inevitably change, and as their children reach the middle childhood years, parents must renegotiate their respective roles in the child-rearing process. Furthermore, it is likely that parents' child-rearing values change as well, especially if the parents change occupation, residence, or marital status. We discuss below the impact of several changes that often occur in the lives of parents of school-age children—marital disruption, mothers working—but note here that the experiences of children in the middle childhood years have almost never been conceptualized in terms of the life-cycle stage that their parents have entered at the same time.

We move away from a description of normative developmental change and consider the fact that children change at different rates and along somewhat different developmental trajectories. Parents of school-age children also differ considerably from one another in the ways they deal with the issues of middle childhood and the degree to which they can enter effectively into the process of coregulation.

VARIATIONS AMONG FAMILIES

Dimensions of Parental Variation

Most parents use a variety of child-rearing techniques, depending on their goals and the situation in which the child's behavior is an issue. As we noted earlier, parents control infractions occurring in their presence in other ways than they control actual or potential infractions occurring away from home. Parents also vary from day to day in the way they react to their children's behavior and in the demands they make on children. Thus when parents are differentiated as to their permissiveness or warmth or strictness, these designations reflect only average tendencies. Some parents are biased in one direction, others in another, but for any parent, considerable variation in behavior occurs from time to time. A parent may also interact quite differently with different children in the same family. It is known that children within a family differ from one another nearly as much as they differ from children in other families (Rowe and Plomin, 1981; Scarr et al., 1981), and this fact suggests considerable within-family variability in parental as well as child behavior. It should be understood, therefore, that the research described below deals with between-family variability that may be large or small, relative to the amount of variation that occurs in a given parent from time to time and when dealing with different children in the same family.

Parents differ in terms of the sheer amount of interaction they have with their children; in the kinds of behavior they regard as acceptable or unacceptable; in the aspirations they have for their children and the demands they make for accomplishment; in the kinds of disciplinary and motivating techniques they use to influence their children; in the amount of control they attempt to exercise; and in the affective quality of their relationships with their children.

Early factor analysis of parents' reports concerning their child-rearing yielded two major dimensions of variation (Schaefer, 1959). One dimension concerned warmth or acceptance and reflected the fact that some parents characteristically feel and express considerable affection for their children—

taking pride in them and enjoying interacting with them—while other parents express a cold, rejecting attitude, experiencing the child as burdensome and unrewarding. Most parents fall toward the warm end of this continuum. The second major dimension, unrelated to the first, reflected the amount of control exercised, with some parents being highly restrictive and others highly permissive; most fall between the two extremes. A third dimension in which parents differ emerged in some studies: the openness of their communication with their children (Baumrind, 1967). Early research (Baldwin et al., 1945) stressed democratic child-rearing, which included the element of permissiveness. It also implied that parents felt the obligation to explain their requirements and disciplinary actions and that they allowed the child to participate in family decision making as much as possible.

Efforts to relate these dimensions of child-rearing to children's personality and social development had rather inconsistent results. Tight controls exercised by parents sometimes were associated with the child's being inhibited and fearful, sometimes with anger and aggression, and sometimes with competent, mature functioning. It became apparent that the effect of firm controls depended on how parental demands were selected and imposed and on the affective context in which they occurred. Parental strictness that involves power assertion on the basis of their authority and power to punish has a different effect than strictness that is a consistent enforcement of rules grounded in discussion and explanation.

Parental warmth—generally a positive factor in development—was also found to be variable in its effects, depending on whether it was accompanied by indulgence, overprotection, intrusive and anxious involvement in all aspects of the child's life, or reasonable rules firmly enforced. In addition, it mattered how contingent the parental behavior was—whether parents' warm reactions occurred in response to something the child had done— reflecting sensitivity to the child's states and activities—or occurred merely as an expression of the parent's mood. A number of studies also indicated that it was not sufficient merely to describe parents in terms of how frequently they used reasoning or explanation. The content of the reasoning was shown to be related to outcomes.

In the next section, findings on the relationship between parent's child-rearing attitudes or behaviors and the characteristics of their school-age children are briefly summarized.

Effects of Parental Variation

Parent-child interaction studies involving young children tend to stress the effects of parental variations on the child's attachment to parents, cooperativeness with parents, and social interactions with peers. As children grow into the middle childhood years, these aspects of their development continue to be important, but new outcome variables especially relevant to this age are added: self-concepts, internalization of moral values, social perception, prosocial and antisocial behavior.

The discussion below summarizes studies that deal with preadolescent school-age children (see also Maccoby and Martin, 1983). The reader is warned that almost all of the research represents correlations between characteristics of parents and characteristics of children measured at the same time. Such studies tell us little about the direction of the influence processes that occur between parent and child but do serve to connect the parent-child relationship with school-age children's individual characteristics. For convenience, these characteristics are called "effects" or "outcomes" because they have been conceived that way in the literature. Some of the aspects of children's functioning discussed below are also discussed in other chapters in this volume; the focus here is on the way these child characteristics are related to the functioning of the families in which the children are reared.

Aggression, Other Antisocial Behavior, and Undercontrol

In a longitudinal study in Finland, Pulkkinen (1982) studied children in families when the children were ages 8, 14, and 20. She reported that predelinquent, and subsequently delinquent, behavior in the children was more probable in families in which the parents were relatively uninvolved with the children—seldom talked with them, had little information about their activities and associates away from home, and were uninterested in the children's school progress. These parents tended not to listen to the children's opinions when formulating rules or making demands. In short, the parents were indifferent and unresponsive—or, to use Pulkkinen's term, "parent-centered."

The longitudinal study of children's development of ego controls by Block and Block (1980) has only begun to be reported. Their earlier findings on adolescents (Block, 1971) are consistent with the view that uninvolved, self-centered parenting is associated with undercontrolled, impulsive behavior in children. Thus far, few additional data are available concerning the middle childhood period.

Studies of the interaction patterns in the families of aggressive and predelinquent or delinquent children (e.g., Patterson, 1982) indicate that there are high rates of mutually coercive behaviors between parents and all the children in the family, but especially with the child who has been identified by the school, parents, or correctional authorities as out of control. Families of these children seem to lack mechanisms for shutting off cycles of hostile interaction among family members, so that hostility escalates to high levels. Family members avoid one another when possible, have few joint activities, and are ineffective in their efforts to solve day-to-day problems. The quality of interaction in the family and in the aggressive child's extrafamilial behavior has improved by teaching parents to state clear expectations of the child, to monitor the child's compliance, to use firm and consistent—but nonviolent—means of enforcing their requirements, to give praise and rewards for good behavior, and to engage in problem-solving discussions of unresolved issues that lead to anger and depression.

Studies of adolescent delinquents and young adult criminals consistently show that such persons have high rates of conduct problems during their middle childhood years. Furthermore, the incidence of conduct disorders is associated with pathology in the families of the deviant children: family discord, poor supervision of children, family instability that involves placing the children in nonfamily care for periods of time, and parental mental illness or criminality (Farrington and West, 1981; McCord, 1979; Robins, 1974; Rutter et al., 1975). To a considerable extent, then, the antisocial forms of adult deviance have their roots in family dysfunction during middle childhood. Perhaps some of the dysfunction can also be traced back to early childhood.

It has been shown that antisocial children tend to be deficient in social perspective taking; that is, they do not empathize with others' distress and tend not to consider how others will view their actions (Chandler, 1973; Chandler et al., 1974). Such findings suggest that parenting techniques that foster children's acquisition of social-cognitive skills may be instrumental in helping children to regulate their aggressive impulses. There is very little research on the relationship of child-rearing practices to children's social cognitions and empathic responses, but there is some evidence that other-oriented induction—that is, consistently reminding children of how their behavior looks to others and how it will affect others—is important (see Bearison and Cassell, 1975).

Self-Concepts

Two aspects of children's self-concepts have been studied in relationship to parental practices. The first is the child's self-esteem, and at first glance the results do not appear to be consistent. When parents are strict in the sense of imposing many restrictions, their children's self-esteem tends to be low. When parents are strict, however, in the sense of exercising firm control—monitoring their children's behavior and following through on requirements—the children's self-esteem tends to be high. The critical factor appears to be whether parental strictness is accompanied by emotional support, commitment to the children's welfare, and an open interchange of ideas between parent and child. Parental warmth is consistently associated with children's self-esteem (Loeb et al., 1980), while physical punishment and psychological punishment—withdrawal of love—are associated with low self-esteem.

A second aspect of parental influence on school-age children's self-concepts concerns the children's "inner locus of control"—their sense of being in control of the events affecting their lives. When parents of inner-locus children are observed attempting to teach or help their children with a task, their approach is to make suggestions that improve the child's chances of arriving at a solution, while parents of children who have an external locus of control are likely to issue specific directives or take the task out of the child's hands.

Internalization of Moral Values

Children tend to show signs of conscience—confess misdeeds, feel guilt—and make relatively mature moral judgments when their parents seldom use direct, unqualified power assertion. Parents of more morally mature children, when training and directing their children, stress the consequences of the children's actions for others. When these parental techniques are accompanied by withdrawal of love and arousal of the child's guilt feelings, the child's internalized moral values tend to be fairly rigid and rule oriented. When they are accompanied by firm follow-through on parental demands and low guilt induction, however, the child's moral orientation tends to be more flexible (M.L. Hoffman, 1970; Salzstein, 1976).

Prosocial Behavior

Prosocial behavior includes helpful and emotionally supportive acts directed toward others. Parents' use of other-oriented induction has been found to be associated with prosocial behavior in school-age children (see Radke-Yarrow et al., 1983, for a review). In addition, experimental studies in which nonparental adults have tried to train children in prosocial behavior have found that emphasizing a victim's distress, and the victim's relief when helped, effectively fosters children's prosocial behavior. This training is most effective if the teacher has previously established a nurturant relationship with the child (Yarrow et al., 1973). Effective helping of others depends somewhat on children's ability to take the perspective of others—to understand others' situations and feelings. As noted earlier, parents foster this ability by using other-oriented induction rather than authoritarian, directive techniques (Bearison and Cassell, 1975).

Competence

Baumrind (1973), in a longitudinal study of the development of competence in children, stressed three aspects of competence: cognitive abilities, social assertiveness, and social responsibility, i.e., effective cooperation with others, self-regulation of antisocial behavior. In a brief prepublication summary of findings on the interactions of parents with their 8- to 9-year-old children, Baumrind reported that, in both boys and girls, social responsibility is associated with parents' responsiveness to their children's needs and bids for parental attention. For boys, social responsibility is enhanced if the parents make fairly strict requirements for proper behavior. Cognitive competence is associated in both sexes with high parental demands; in boys, however, parental responsiveness contributes as well. Social assertiveness in boys is not associated with either demanding parents or responsive parents; girls with demanding parents, however, tend to be socially assertive. Baumrind suggested that each sex needs to be pushed by parents in order to develop a characteristic that is outside stereotypic sex roles: social assertiveness in girls, social responsibility in boys.

Many of the correlations emerging from the studies reported above are small. Much of the variance in children's characteristics cannot be attributed to parents' behavior as measured thus far. Furthermore, some inconsistent themes have emerged from the work summarized above. One theme is that the development of competencies in children requires the firm exercise of parental control. For example, in Patterson's (1982) interventions with parents of antisocial children, parents were taught to closely monitor their children's behavior, clearly require certain conforming behaviors from them, and consistently punish infractions. Thus, the pattern of behavior that was encouraged for parents was fairly power assertive.

The second theme is that power-assertive parenting is counterproductive—it promotes neither the internalization of adult values nor self-control. Indeed, some studies indicate that power-assertive pressure toward a particular value or behavioral goal causes children to devalue that behavior (Lepper, 1983). Can both themes be correct? Some researchers have attempted to reconcile them, but more work is needed.

At present, it appears that parents foster optimum development in middle childhood by teaching, guiding, and emotionally supporting their children.

Children ages 6–12 do not usually learn competence and self-sufficiency by fending for themselves. At this age, parental guidance in the form of power assertion is less effective than firm control combined with warm responsiveness and the exhortation that children's actions have consequences for themselves and others. Perhaps, however, we should consider the possibility that different patterns of change are optimal for families with different initial interaction patterns; that is, perhaps lax parents need to acquire power-assertive skills, and power-assertive parents need to acquire internalization-fostering skills. We can only assume that the desirable balance between the two themes is linked to the age of the child.

GROUP DIFFERENCES IN CHILD-REARING

Historically, researchers have compared parents from different socioeconomic levels or ethnic groups with respect to their child-rearing values and their characteristic modes of interacting with their children. In recent years, interest has focused on family structure with regard to the following comparisons: single-parent and two-parent families; families with two employed parents and those with one employed parent; families with high versus low father involvement in child-rearing; and reconstituted, i.e., stepparent, families versus families with two biological parents. We will focus first on the demographic comparisons, then on family structural ones.

Socioeconomic Status

Child-Rearing in Different Social Classes

When parents are grouped by income, education, or occupation—or indexed by a combination of these—average group differences in child-rearing consistently appear, although the overlap between groups is great (for reviews see Bronfenbrenner, 1958; Hess, 1970; Laosa, 1981; for studies providing data on specific issues, see Bee et al., 1969; Hill and Stafford, 1980; Newson and Newson, 1976; Shipman et al., 1976; Stafford, 1980; Yankelovich et al., 1977; Zill, in press). Major contrasts that have emerged with some consistency are that middle-class parents, compared with working- or lower-class parents:

• Have higher rates of interaction with their children and are more responsive to their children's bids for attention. Shipman and coworkers (1976) showed that higher-income and better-educated mothers of 8.5- to 9.5-year-old children were more likely than their lower-status counterparts to give informative-interactive responses to children's difficult questions; to know the child's teacher by name; and to take the child on outings outside the home.

• Use more elaborated language in talking with their children.

• Are more permissive toward sexual behavior and more accepting of children's displays of parent-directed anger; they are also less restrictive about the range of activities allowed the child. At the same time, they place somewhat greater demands on the child for maturity, achievement, and independence.

• Place less value on obedience and respect for authority and more value on the child's happiness, curiosity, creativity, and eagerness to learn.

• Are less power assertive and more democratic; that is, they are more likely to allow the child a voice in family decision making, more willing to listen to the child's point of view, less likely to give direct orders, and more likely to orient and motivate the child when tasks are undertaken. These differences are reflected also in disciplinary techniques: middle-class parents less often use physical punishment and more often use reasoning and explanation. Their reasoning more frequently takes the form of drawing children's attention to the effects of their behavior on others.

• Show a lower incidence of clearly hostile or rejecting attitudes toward their children. The large majority of parents, regardless of education and income, are reasonably warm and accepting, and scores on summary measures of warmth or affection are frequently not significantly different for the social class groups. The differences appear at the lower end of the distribution.

It seems clear that the sociocultural milieu in which parents function does affect their child-rearing. It is not clear, however, at what point along the continuum the greatest shifts in child-rearing occur. Various cutoff points have been used in different studies that compared groups. Some reports suggest that the major differences are between upper-middle-class parents and everyone else. It may be that with respect to several important aspects of child-rearing, such as the amount of affection expressed to the child, upper middle-, middle-, and working-class families are much alike, while it is the disorganized, multiproblem families (sometimes called the "underclass") who deviate in these aspects. Although the underclass represents a small proportion of all families, it is large enough to affect the means of any lower-class or working-class group in which it is included. We do not know, however, whether there are sharp transition points along the socioeconomic continuum in terms of how parents relate to their children. It remains to be discovered whether such sharp breaks exist, and if they do, where they occur with respect to various aspects of parenting.

Another question is: What aspect of socioeconomic status is most closely linked with what aspects of child-rearing? Laosa (1982) found that education carries far more weight than income in predicting the teaching styles of Chicano mothers, while others emphasize the importance of affluence or economic deprivation in influencing parental behaviors. This question alerts us to a point that has been stressed by a number of writers: that social class is not a meaningful variable in itself; rather it is a convenient index for variations in the life experiences of parents and children. These writers urge that we delve beneath the mere facts of parental education, income, and occupation, and investigate the processes whereby these demographic facts are translated into family life. We need to ask two questions: What are some hypotheses concerning why the child-rearing methods and values of parents are linked to their social class? And given that the linkages exist, what are their implications for children?

Some Models of Socioeconomic Differences in Child-Rearing

Socioeconomic differences in child-rearing can be conceptualized in a number of ways. A first point of view, the *cultural lag* model, comes primarily from cross-cultural studies and argues that when simple, preliterate societies undergo modernization, parents will begin to teach children some of the skills and values they will need for functioning in a complex socioeconomic system (e.g., increased orientation to time). Within a society, families differ in the degree to which they are subject to modernization pressures. Hence, group differences in child-rearing emerge (Inkeles, 1960). In advanced industrialized societies there are presumably subcultural pockets that continue to resemble simpler levels of social organization.

A second model may be called the *role-status transmission* model. From this point of view parents who are in occupations that call for self-regulation and initiative and whose work involves symbols rather than materials are likely to value and foster independence and self-direction in their children, while parents who are in subordinate roles in authority structures will value and foster obedience and be less concerned with their children's inner motivations and autonomy (Kohn, 1963, 1977). A variant of this view is that a lower-class position in society implies powerlessness in many spheres of life, not only the workplace, and that parents who feel powerless transmit to their children the message that they too are powerless (Sennett and Cobb, 1982). This is done in a variety of ways, including low mutuality in communication (i.e., less negotiation). When poverty is chosen as an alternative life-style, however, so that it does not imply powerlessness, it is not accompanied by the child-rearing styles that usually characterize lower-class parents (Weisner, 1982).

Another model, called the *expanded functioning* model, emphasizes the skills that are acquired through education. Education improves parents' vocabularies, improves their knowledge about issues, and promotes advanced styles of thinking and communicating with others. In particular, it brings about a shift from restricted to elaborated communicative codes (Bernstein, 1961; Hess and Shipman, 1967). Education also motivates parents to take an interest in their children's intellectual development, as manifested in more frequent reading to the child and the teaching of literacy skills (Laosa, 1982).

The *stress-interference* model emphasizes the destabilizing nature of lower-class life. Major and minor crises (an unexpected bill, a bounced check, trouble with the car, accidents, something lost or stolen, loss of a job, divorce) function as stressors and, at least for some parents, directly affect the way they deal with children. Typically, parents under stress reduce their interaction with the children and become impatient, irritable, and peremptory. These parental reactions exacerbate the irritable behavior of the children, which adds to parental stress; thus, a cycle of deteriorating parent-child relationships is set in motion (Hetherington et al., 1982; Patterson, 1982). Many kinds of crises are considerably more common in impoverished families. In those families stressors may have a multiplicative, rather than additive, effect. (Rutter, 1981:209). Many, though not all, impoverished families appear to live close to the point at which additional external stressors would produce disorganization of family functioning—loss of routines, abusiveness, or some degree of neglect or indifference toward children. Social-class differences in child-rearing, then, may be viewed as a reaction to the differential levels of stress impinging on parents in different social classes (Maccoby and Martin, 1983).

Still another view is that what appear to be social-class differences in child-rearing are actually products of other demographic and ecological conditions with which socioeconomic status is correlated. Thus, Burrows (1981) reported that while substantial social-class differences exist in Mexican families in the ways that parents deal with their children and children react to their parents, these differences are accounted for by the large family size and crowded living conditions of lower-class families, and once these variables are entered into a predictive equation, socioeconomic status produces no significant variance.

We must not overlook the possibility of reverse-order effects; that is, families may have drifted into the lower socioeconomic levels of society because of some pathology in the family members. Individuals who suffer from mental illness, alcoholism, drug addiction, etc., have difficulty holding jobs and maintaining an adequate income; as young people, they have difficulty meeting the demands of a school regime, complete fewer years of schooling, and are disadvantaged by these deficits in their life chances later on. Hence, the disorganized and distressed quality of family life and the deficits in parenting that are found in a subgroup of lower-status families appear to be a manifestation, in some cases, of the same intrapersonal factors that led them into their lower status rather than an outcome of being poor or uneducated. No doubt there are circular processes at work: being poor or uneducated increases the risk of various pathologies; these pathologies increase the risk of being poor and uneducated.

Socioeconomic Differences in Child-Rearing and Their Possible Implications for Children

Given that child-rearing varies in some respects according to the socioeconomic status of parents, what are the implications of such variations? Historically, researchers examined such differences in an effort to explain behavioral differences among children of different socioeconomic backgrounds. In particular, researchers asked whether certain aspects of child-rearing by lower-status parents are conditions that underlie the higher rates of delinquent and predelinquent behavior and the higher risk of poor academic performance among lower-status children. A central idea here is that parental behavior serves as the functional mediator between a family's social status and those aspects of children's behavior that are linked to social class. That is, parents' education or position in the social structure has an impact on how they raise their children—via some of the mechanisms listed above—and these class-linked variations in child-rearing produce differential behavior patterns in children, some of which adapt children to the social situation in which they have been reared or maladapt them to other social milieus. Thus a conservative cycle may be set in motion, tending to produce in children the characteristics that will keep them in the same social class occupied by their parents. Laosa (1982) argued, for example, that the teaching style employed by poorly educated mothers with their preschool children is dissimilar to the style the children encounter from teachers when they enter school; thus these children are poorly adapted to the school environment. We suspect, too, that the themes of child-rearing wherein the major social-class groups differ (see listing above) are such that middle-class families more effectively achieve the parent-child cooperation that is needed for the coregulation processes of middle childhood. If this is so, we have a tentative explanation for higher rates of out-of-control, antisocial behavior in lower-status children.

We must ask, however, if variations in parental behavior are indeed the main conduits whereby socioeconomic milieu is translated into meaningful experiences for children. Zill (in press), in a cautionary note, reports that maternal education is an independent and more powerful predictor of various child outcomes in his study than are the measured child-rearing variables through which maternal education presumably manifests itself. Of course, the problem may be that Zill's child-rearing measures were too narrow or too unreliable. But the question remains: What are the linkages between a social indicator such as mother's education, her child-rearing practices, and children's class-linked characteristics?

We cannot attempt to generate a quantitative estimate of the variance in child-rearing that is accounted for by socioeconomic factors. All we can say is that it is large (see Newson and Newson, 1976) and surprisingly consistent across samples and measures. If it is true, in addition, that socioeconomic factors continue to account for a substantial portion of child outcomes after the class-linked variations in child-rearing practices have been partialled out, then serious consideration would have to be given to the possibility that parents are not the main channels whereby sociocultural influences are transmitted to children, but that the transmission occurs directly (e.g., through TV, neighborhoods, etc.) to both parents and children, producing class-linked characteristics in both parents and children that have little or no functional connection. Researchers have rarely attempted to unravel these causal complexities, no doubt because small sample sizes or samples lacking socioeconomic range preclude employing the multivariate analyses that might be useful.

One way to approach the problem is through some form of multiple regression in which socioeconomic status is taken out first, so that it can be seen whether parental behavior makes any additional contribution to a child outcome, and then to reverse the procedure, determining whether socioeconomic status makes an independent contribution once parental behavior variations have been partialled out. These procedures, rarely used, examine the relative contributions of within-class versus between-class variations in parental behavior. Hess and Shipman (1967) have used multivariate analysis in their work with a sample of black mothers and children from several social classes; they found first-order relationships between socioeconomic status and maternal teaching styles. Furthermore, child outcome variables were related to both socioeconomic status and maternal teaching styles. Multivariate analysis showed that significant variation in child outcomes was still accounted for by maternal teaching styles, even after socioeconomic status had been taken out, while the reverse was not true. Such results support the view that socioeconomic status had its primary effect via mother-child interaction.

In general, however, there is scant information in the literature on middle childhood that reveals whether this pattern is a general one. By the pre-adolescent years, many children begin to understand what their own family's position in the social structure is and develop attitudes about what this position implies in the way of opportunities and probabilities of success. Such cognitions clearly could contribute to children's task motivations, among other things, over and above the effects of their class-linked experiences with their parents.

Ethnic Group Differences

We have limited information concerning how parents in ethnic cultures and subcultures differ from their mainstream counterparts in their interactions with their school-age children or concerning the effects, if any, these differences have on child development. The problems of identifying the links between ethnicity, parenting, and child outcomes are similar to those noted above with socioeconomic factors. Ethnic groups show great variability in the conditions of family life. Young, unmarried black mothers living on welfare payments in urban ghettos—so poignantly described by Carol Stack (1974)—have life situations utterly different from middle-class, two-parent black families with stable jobs and residences. Much parental behavior, such as maternal teaching styles, shows great variation within ethnic groups along socioeconomic lines (Hess and Shipman, 1967; Laosa, 1982). Apart from socioeconomic factors, ethnic groups that may be perceived by outsiders as homogeneous subcultures in fact are not so. Hispanic families, for example, differ in their life-styles depending on whether their origins are Cuban, Puerto Rican, Central American, or Mexican, and although they presumably share the same language and many of the problems of bilingualism, even their linguistic usages differ considerably (Laosa, 1982). Researchers sometimes aggregate such subgroups in the interests of obtaining adequate sample sizes for ethnic comparisons, but in doing so they run the risk of obscuring important variations and relationships.

Considering the great socioeconomic and other variation within ethnic groups, the dangers are obviously great that simple comparisons between black and white families or Hispanic and Anglo families will be confounded with these other variables. As is well known, black and Hispanic families typically have low average levels of income and parental education. An excellent example of how these differences may generate what appear to be ethnic differences is provided by Laosa's reports (1981, 1982) on the teaching behavior of Mexican-American mothers. Observations of the mothers' teaching styles revealed that Chicano mothers, on the average, tended to use demonstration and directives in teaching their children to perform a manual task, while Anglo mothers tended to use questioning and praise. There were, however, no differences between Chicanos and Anglos in their teaching style when comparisons were made for subgroups matched on education. Laosa (1982) noted that education rather than level of occupation is the crucial factor determining Chicano-Anglo differences in the aspects of child-rearing analyzed so far. Zill (in press) similarly found that a number of ethnic differences in child-rearing attitudes and values are a function of socioeconomic factors. When these are controlled, only a few distinctive ethnic characteristics remain.

Family structure is another source of confounding in comparisons between ethnic groups. Single-parent families constitute a considerably larger proportion of black than white families, and it is rare to find studies in which comparisons have been made between minority and majority families who have been equated for both socioeconomic and family structural characteristics.

Ethnicity and Family Influence in Middle Childhood

The limited research on families in minority subcultures focuses primarily on infants and preschool children. Only two large-scale interview studies with carefully selected representative samples provide some data on the middle-childhood period: the national survey by Zill (in press) of 2,301 children ages 7–11 in 1976–1977 and the more limited General Mills American Family study (Yankelovich et al., 1977) of 1,230 families with children under the age of 13, also conducted in 1976–1977. In addition, data are now available from a study of 764 sixth-grade children and their families in Oakland, California, the majority of whom were black (Medrich et al., 1982). The latter study found lower levels of interaction between parents and children in black than white families; that is, black families had a lower incidence of all family members eating together, sharing hobbies, going places together, and parents facilitating the children's activities—e.g., taking children to lessons or sports practice sessions. Black children in this study spent more time watching TV. These differences persisted after equating for education and income. We should note that this study was conducted in an urban area with a comparatively high proportion of educated, stable middle-income families. We do not know whether the same picture would emerge in an inner-city ghetto or among rural families.

The General Mills study (Yankelovich et al., 1977) reported that black parents place a higher value on achievement—in both school and sports—than do white families and that their children, reporting their awareness of this pressure, concur. From the Zill (in press) study we learn that, with socioeconomic factors equated, Hispanic families place greater emphasis on such traditional values as respect for authority than do other ethnic groups, while black families are more likely to use physical punishment. The latter finding echoes themes that emerged from a variety of early studies that used both observational and interview data and showed black parents to be more restrictive and punitive than white parents, and in some instances more overprotective (see Peters, 1981, for a review).

Interpreting Ethnic Group Differences

The use of physical punishment provides illustration of a more general issue: the same child-rearing variable may not have the same meaning in different cultures or subcultures. For example, Baumrind reported (1973) that authoritarian child-rearing was associated with positive outcomes in the small group of black girls in his study, while the reverse was true for white girls. Some studies have indicated (Peters, 1976; Young, 1970) that, while the frequent use of physical punishment is associated with a number of adverse outcomes in mainstream children, it may not have these correlates in black children. Is physical punishment part of a different cluster of parenting practices in black families? Does its greater frequency make it part of a cultural norm so that it is experienced as less punitive by the children involved? We do not know. We are merely alerted by this example to the dangers of generalizing the findings of mainstream-sample studies of child-rearing to minority cultures.

Important issues are posed by the question of how to interpret ethnic differences in child-rearing patterns. Debates over the deficit versus the pluralistic interpretations continue (see Laosa, 1982; Peters, 1981). The dangers of the ethnocentric imposition of middle-class white values on minority cultures are frequently pointed out and need no further elaboration here. In the larger context of cross-cultural differences in child-rearing, LeVine (1979) argued that cultural groups develop a pattern of parental functioning that is adapted to the cultural, economic, and ecological niche in which the group functions. LeVine stressed that, by and large, such patterns are successful adaptations. It is only under conditions of sociocultural change that they may become maladaptive. Perhaps in the long run this point of view will enable us to arrive at some reasonable interpretations of subcultural differences in child-rearing. It is too early, however, to embark on this enterprise. As far as middle childhood is concerned, we lack the necessary basic data on ethnic variations in child-rearing or their relationship to child outcomes. And analyses have not been performed that would allow us to understand the complex interweaving of such factors as income, education, ethnicity, family size, urban residence, and single parenthood.

Single-Parent Families

We turn now to variations in family structure and will consider both the current changes in family structures and the implications for school-age children. At the time of this writing, approximately one-fifth of American children ages 6–12 are living with only one parent, and as many as 40 percent will probably live in a single-parent household at some time during their childhood (see Chapter 1; see also Glick, 1979). The number of single-parent households has more than doubled in the last 20 years, and the majority of children in single-parent households (over 90 percent) live with their mothers. About three-quarters of the single-parent households result from the divorce or separation of married couples, although a growing minority are composed of never-married mothers and their children. The ethnic differences in the incidence of single-parent households are extreme: in 1977, the percentage of children under 18 living in such households was 11.9 for whites, 19.5 for Hispanics, and 41.7 for blacks. Typically, single-parent families are poor. Writers have recently begun to point to the feminization of poverty (Pearce and McAdoo, in press); that is, increasingly, families below the poverty line are headed by a single female parent. The number of such families is increasing: 38 percent of white mother-only families and 86 percent of black mother-only families fall below the official poverty line, compared with 16 percent and 46 percent, respectively, of two-parent families (Hill, 1983). The average income of single-parent households is much lower than two-parent households.

Single-parent families are heterogeneous in a number of ways. Eiduson and colleagues (1982) described three kinds of never-married single mothers: a group of *nest builders*, well-educated and self-supporting women who have elected to raise a child alone; a group of *post hoc adapters* who are not so well off as the nest builders but are possessed of sufficient personal and economic resources to manage their unplanned parenthood adequately; and a group of *unwed mothers* who did not welcome the pregnancy and are young, impoverished, poorly educated, and lacking in job skills. This last group turns either to welfare or parental assistance for economic support. Predictably, the Eiduson group reported considerable variation among these subgroups in values and coping styles. Nevertheless, when the subgroups were combined as a composite of single parents, they differed from traditional families and other alternative life-style families in that they experienced more residential moves and other forms of stress than any other group, were less satisfied with their lives, and had more disorganized households.

Single parents suffer from task overload. They must carry out alone the parenting responsibilities that are shared between two parents in intact households. In most cases, single mothers work full time; therefore, they have less time for parenting functions than the part-time employed mothers in dual-parent households. For the majority of single parents, the stress imposed by these realistic burdens is exacerbated by the emotional turmoil that attends and follows marital disruption. A number of studies of divorcing families (Hetherington et al., 1982; Wallerstein and Kelly, 1980; Zill, 1978) document what happens to the quality of parenting and the adjustment of children after families move from dual-parent to single-parent status. These studies include preschoolers and adolescents, but a substantial portion of the data deals with the middle-childhood period. From these and other sources, several consistent themes emerge:

1. Marital separation usually entails major emotional distress for children and disruption in the parent-child relationship. During the several years following separation, single parents —when compared with their own earlier patterns of behavior and with parents in intact families—typically show diminished parenting; that is, they tend to be self-preoccupied, less attentive and responsive to their children, less consistent, and more irritable. They spend less time with the children and tend to neglect such household routines as laundry, cleaning, regular meals, bedtimes, and baths. For many single parents, parenting functions return to a more organized and child-centered pattern as the stress of separation diminishes; this is more likely to happen when the parent forms new intimate ties and is no longer "single." As the custodial family stabilizes over time, contact with the noncustodial parent usually diminishes, so that the outside parent becomes peripheral in the lives of most children of divorce (Furstenberg et al., 1983).

2. The effect of marital disruption on children depends on the child's age at the time of the breakup. According to Wallerstein and Kelly (1980), the primary reaction of children ages 6–8 is marked grief and fear and an intense longing for the reconciliation of the parents; these reactions may continue into the later school-age years. By ages 9–12, children express a greater sense of shame over the divorce and more open anger toward one or the other of their parents—usually the parent deemed responsible for the divorce; they are thus vulnerable to being drawn into alliances by one parent against the other. Furthermore, children of this age are more likely to reject a stepparent. At both ages, deterioration of the children's behavior at home

and at school may be seen: increases in aggression; difficulties in maintaining friendships with peers; resistance or excessive dependency toward teachers; deterioration of school work; and in some children, a drift toward predelinquent activities and groups.

3. We know more about short-term effects of family disruption than we do about long-term effects. A remedy for this gap is long-term follow-ups of individuals whose families were disrupted during their childhood, although simple comparisons between such persons and persons from intact homes are likely to be confounded by socioeconomic status or ethnic differences. Some studies indicate that the long-term effects of broken homes may be modest for many of the children involved (Kulka and Weingarten, 1979), while other studies show continuing effects. A recent study of college students showed that students from intact homes have closer relationships with both parents—but particularly fathers—at this young adult period than students whose parents were divorced at an earlier time (Fine et al., 1983). In addition, there is evidence for an intergenerational transmission effect— that is, for individuals from broken homes to have higher rates of disruption in their own marriages and to show deficits in parenting (see Rutter, 1979, for a review). The effects of early disruption may depend on the concurrence of other risk factors. Thus Rutter (1981) reported that broken homes are associated with children's later delinquency and criminality in inner-city London but not on the Isle of Wight and attributed the difference to the fact that the restoration of harmonious family relations following divorce is more likely to occur on the Isle of Wight than in inner-city London.

The outcome measures in the existing studies of long-term effects did not include some of the effects that, from a theoretical standpoint, may be especially likely. Specifically, studies of early separation from attachment figures suggested that one of the sequelae of such separations might be increased vulnerability to disturbance over subsequent separations. General measures of happiness or the number of worries an individual has may not be fine-grained enough to pick up such specific effects.

When studies simply compare the children of single-parent families with other children, the reasons for any differences are unclear. For example, Yankelovich et al. (1977) reported that single mothers are more likely than other mothers to say that they have sometimes lost control and punished their children more than they deserve. Children of single mothers are more likely to argue with their mothers and have more difficulty getting along with other children. We do not know whether such problems are most likely to appear in divorced families, in families where the mother has never married, or in families where the father is dead. We also learn from the

Oakland study (Medrich et al., 1982) that single parents were less likely to register their children for out-of-school activities or spend time taking them to such activities; however, we do not know which subgroup of single parents—widowed, divorced, separated, or never-married—was responsible for the lower facilitation scores.

The Zill (1978) report provides a more differentiated picture. In the case of a widowed single parent, the mental health of the mother and children is very similar to that in two-parent families with reasonably happy marriages. This finding strongly suggests that the distinctive characteristics of single-parent families are not solely the result of the absence of an adult male in the household. Nor can we make the case that two parents are in all respects better than one, although in terms of time pressures, they usually are. Are the characteristics of single-parent families primarily a result of the stress of marital disruption? To some extent they are, but it should be noted that the indicators of family distress are as great for the never-married mothers as for the divorced and separated ones. The loss of a parent, therefore, may not be the primary factor. Do the higher levels of distress in single-parent families stem primarily from their poverty? Again, in part, yes, but Zill (1978) showed that after scores were adjusted for income and education, distress remained relatively high in all the groups of single-parent families except the widowed ones.

An unresolved issue concerns whether single-parent families suffer more difficulties in parent-child interaction than do discordant intact families experiencing much parental quarreling. Zill (1978) and Rutter (1982) both reported that signs of disturbance in children and distortions in parental behavior are as great in disharmonious two-parent families as they are in divorced or separated ones. In the study by Hetherington and colleagues (1982) and that by Wallerstein and Kelly (1980), however, the separation itself appears to have added considerable distress to all parties concerned, with the critical event being the departure of one parent from the household. Children often seem unaware of how serious their parents' dissension is and tend to be unprepared for the breakup. The split in living arrangements calls for the formation of a new kind of relationship with the noncustodial, visiting parent and for adaptation to a custodial parent who may be more vulnerable after the departure of the spouse.

There is great variability among single parents in the effectiveness with which they cope with the special demands of their situation. Some function well, better than they did in unsatisfactory marriages. Many do not. Little is known about the factors that underlie these variations. Studies of divorce indicate that continued involvement by the former spouse in child care and economic support considerably eases the burdens of single-parenthood, as does the formation of new intimate ties. Other kinds of support systems are valuable, particularly kin relationships in low-income minority communities. Minority families tend to have a larger number of kin living nearby, even though the number of nonparental adults living in the household may not be unusually high. While it is true, however, that minority single parents have considerable contact with kin, the nature of the contact is highly variable. Sometimes these contacts are supportive; in other cases they create additional strains and pressures (Stack, 1974).

Working Mothers

The second major social change that has occurred in recent years in addition to the increase in single parenthood has been the substantial increase in the number of married women with school-age children who work outside the home. Reviews are now available that summarize what is known about the impact of maternal employment on family life and on the development of children (Hayes and Kamerman, 1983; Hoffman, 1979; Kamerman and Hayes, 1982; Lamb, 1982; Moen, 1982). For the purposes of this chapter, there are several limitations on much of the research. The majority of studies examine the impact of maternal employment on infants and preschool children. Furthermore, a number of studies merely record whether a mother is working or not, without specifying whether the employment is full time or part time. In fact, although at least one-half of married American women with school-age children are now working, less than one-third work full time, and there is reason to believe that this is an important distinction with respect to the socialization of school-age children.

Does the employment of a mother place her children at any sort of risk? On the whole, the answer would appear to be no, but this answer must be qualified with "it depends." It depends, for one thing, on the socioeconomic situation of the family. If the mother is single, impoverished, and poorly educated, in many cases the children appear to benefit from the mother's employment, partly because of the increased income, but also because of the mother's improved morale and sense of competence. Possibly, too, the children benefit from their experiences in day care while their mothers are working. The impact of maternal employment also depends on the sex of the child. In poor families, there is evidence that the sons of employed mothers are somewhat less well adjusted than when the mother is not employed; and in middle-class families the sons of employed mothers may perform more poorly in school than they otherwise would. The daughters of working mothers, however, fairly consistently display higher achievement motivation than the daughters of nonemployed mothers.

In the majority of homes with two working parents, the mother still assumes major responsibility for household management and care of children. She is the one who usually takes the child to the doctor or dentist, to after-school lessons, or for outings on weekdays. And she also does most of the shopping, cooking, cleaning, and laundry. When she works full time in a 9 to 5 job, particularly when any other adults in the household are away from home at the same time, considerable task overload ensues. Working mothers report that time is their most precious and most scarce resource. They feel they have too little time to spend with their children; their school-age children echo this feeling, complaining that their parents spend too little time with them (Yankelovich, 1977).

Recent studies of children at risk for delinquency highlight the importance, for the avoidance of antisocial behavior, of parental monitoring of children's activities and whereabouts (Patterson, 1982; Pulkkinen, 1982). An understudied issue concerns the methods whereby working parents monitor their children's after-school activities and the effectiveness with which they can do so. Typically, infants, toddlers, and preschoolers are placed in formal or informal day care while their parents work. Thus, there is an adult formally responsible for their supervision. When children enter school, parents feel that the need for such formal arrangements is greatly reduced, since school serves a major baby-sitting function. Furthermore, as children enter and progress through the school-age years, the supervision they require changes dramatically. Even during the hours when they are not in school, they are often away from the house, playing with other children or attending a variety of after-school activities. Thus, as we have noted earlier, the parent's task is no longer one of monitoring a child who is within sight or immediate call. In the task of coregulation, the parent and child must cooperate in exchanging information about their plans and whereabouts. The child must take some responsibility for checking in, and the parent must be skillful in determining whether the child has told the truth, kept the parent adequately informed, and lived up to agreements. Parents differ significantly in how well informed they are about where their school-age children are, who they are with, and what they are doing.

The flexibility of the mother's working hours may make a considerable difference in the extent of parental monitoring. The Oakland study of sixth-grade children (Medrich et al., 1982) reported the following group differences with respect to the percentage of families in which neither parent was at home after school: when the mother works full time, 66 percent; when she works part time, 20 percent; when she does not work, 12 percent. A possible implication of such differences comes from the study by Dornbusch et al. (1983), in which it was shown that in the age range 10–14, children began heterosexual dating earlier when they lived in households in which no adult was at home after school.

We know little about how parents monitor their children's activities during out-of-school hours when parents are working and no adult is at home. Most schools do not provide after-school programs, and even when they do, children may choose not to attend. While a neighbor or relative may agree to "keep an eye" on a child after school and provide a place where the child can check in, we do not know whether these arrangements result in as effective monitoring of the child's activities as would be managed by the child's parents. We know that there are "latchkey" children (how many?) who are instructed to go home and remain at home until their parents return from work and whose mothers check on their whereabouts by phone; not all parents have easy access to telephones at the workplace. We can only speculate that in some undetermined proportion of cases, supervision is loose and the children are allowed to drift toward activities and companions that parents would disapprove. For example, the General Mills study (Yankelovich et al., 1977) showed that children of working mothers are more likely than children of nonworking mothers to have friends or acquaintances who have played hookey, gotten into trouble with police, run away from home, or experimented with drugs. Such predelinquent companionship has been shown to be a factor in the onset of delinquent or predelinquent behavior. Unfortunately, in the General Mills study the comparison between the children of working and nonworking mothers was not controlled for socioeconomic or family structural variables; therefore, it is not possible to determine what the independent contribution of the mother's work status is when it is uncomplicated by these other factors.

This brief review of some of the group differences in child-rearing patterns indicates that family function is related to the cultural and ecological niche in which the family is located (see Weisner, in this volume). Undoubtedly there are other aspects of family life—such as rural or urban living, the nearness of relatives, the presence of physical hazards in the neighborhood, or the degree of crowding—that affect the child directly but also indirectly through their impact on parents and their children-rearing practices (Bronfenbrenner, 1979). To a considerable extent, parents determine their children's physical environments—the nature of the house and neighborhood in which they will live, the objects with which the house is provided—but the parents are themselves constrained in making these choices by economic and cultural factors over which they often have little control. We have seen that sociocultural factors do not act singly. Family income, ethnicity, parental education and employment, and family structure are intricately linked.

To date, children's environments have been conceptualized mainly as forces impinging on them from the outside, which act on children but are not acted on by children. As children enter the middle childhood period, however, they begin to exercise some selection with respect to the settings they will enter and their social companions. Furthermore, it begins to matter to them how they conceive of the environmental and interpersonal situations in which they find themselves, and the competencies that they believe they can bring to bear in coping with them.

FAMILY ROLES AND SYSTEMS

Much of the research that has been summarized so far has dealt with parent-child interactions as though the parent-child dyad were the central functional unit through which families influence the development of children. We know, however, that the reality is much more complex. The relationship of a parent to a child is influenced by how the two parents relate to each other. One parent may function as an executive for the other; some parents provide support for one another's child-rearing, with positive effects; discord between parents has been shown to weaken the child-rearing effectiveness of either or both parents (see Maccoby and Martin, 1983, for a review). There is some evidence that the presence of a normal parent with whom the child has a good relationship will moderate or even cancel out the disruptive influence of a pathological or highly distressed parent (Hetherington et al., 1982; Rutter, 1971). The number of children in the family as well as their sexes and spacing also affects the functioning of the family as a whole.

There have been efforts to analyze the functioning of families as systems. For example, Bell and Harper (1977) discussed the upper and lower bounds that families set for the behavior of family members and the ways in which the family as a whole will move to redress the balance if the behavior of a member exceeds these bounds. Samaroff (1982) considered the family as a self-stabilizing system that can adapt to perturbations in the environment. In addition, clinicians have been concerned with the way in which therapeutic interventions with one family member may affect the functioning of other family members, for better or worse. Thus far, however, these conceptualizations have seldom entered the mainstream of research on the family, and little consideration has been given to whether there are changes in the family as a system when the developmental level of the children in the family changes. In the remainder of this chapter I focus on two aspects of the functioning of families that have been relatively neglected so far: the distinctive role of fathers and the role of sibling relationships in the functioning of families in the middle childhood years.

Fathers' Roles

The changes in women's roles—particularly their increasing participation in work outside the home—have been accompanied by ideological changes concerning fathers' roles in child-rearing. The movement toward a legal presumption of joint custody of children following divorce is one expression of the growing emphasis on the importance of fathers' playing a continuing role in the lives of their children. In intact families, at least among the current and recent college generation, fathers are expected to assume a larger share of day-to-day child-rearing duties. Increasingly, fathers are present at the birth of their children—reflecting both parental wishes and the adaptation of medical practice to accommodate the changes in views about fathering.

A body of research on fathers has grown up in recent years (see Lamb, 1981, and Parke and Tinsley, 1983, for reviews). One question that has been of considerable interest to researchers is: To what extent are the recent changes in attitudes about the role of fathers reflected in the day-to-day lives of families? First, a distinction should be made between competence and performance. Research with infants and young children has shown that fathers can perform competently all the child care activities that have traditionally been part of the maternal role, beyond childbearing and breastfeeding, of course. There is no reason to believe that fathers' competency does not extend to the middle-childhood period, although this question has not been studied. The frequency, however, with which fathers actually engage in child care activities seems largely unaffected by the changes in ideology and women's work patterns outlined above. Results from studies of fathers' participation in families with working compared with nonworking mothers are not entirely consistent, but the overall picture is one of very small increases—only a few minutes per day—if any, in the amount of fathers' time spent caring for children when mothers work. When modest increases do occur, they are likely to be confined to the period when there is at least one child under age 3. Some literature suggests that fathers begin to exercise a more equal role in child care only when they take over some of the executive—planning and management—functions, and these appear to be difficult to divide between the parents. Furthermore, the traditional styles of interaction characteristic of the two parents remain remarkably unchanged even in the relatively rare cases in which fathers do take on a fairly equal share of the child care responsibilities (Lamb et al., 1982).

The care-taking activities that loom large with infants and preschoolers diminish in importance as children enter the school-age period. We know little about the distinctive contribution of fathers at this time. Research has focused on a relatively narrow range of issues—e.g., the changes in fathers' functioning following divorce, the impact of father availability on sex-role development in boys and girls, and occasionally the father's role in motivating children for school achievement. Clearly, there are many other things we would like to understand, such as how mothers and fathers function or fail to function to support one another's child-rearing activities. It seems likely that both parental teamwork and division of labor are necessary for maintaining the coregulation processes with school-age children. This question leads to a larger one: Do fathers function mainly as a parallel parent influencing children in the same degree and in the same way as mothers? Or do the two parents have distinctively different influences on the children, by virtue of their gender and their differentiated extrafamilial activities?

There has been some work on nontraditional families in which the fathers take on an equal or even primary role in child care (see Parke and Tinsley, 1983, for a summary). Though these studies deal with families with very young children, some results are relevant to older children. For one thing, shared caretaking arrangements may not be stable. In a study of families in which fathers took at least an equal caretaking role with mothers during the child's early years (Russell, 1982), the follow-up study showed that within only 2 years after the initiation of the study, three-quarters of the families had returned to a traditional pattern of greater maternal than paternal involvement in child care. The fathers, however, who had formerly taken a large share of the child care responsibilities but no longer took this role, had a closer relationship with their children than fathers who had not been similarly involved. Longer-term follow-ups are needed to determine whether the early division of labor in child care has an impact on father-child relationships in middle childhood.

Sibling Relationships

The body of research on siblings and their role in the lives of children during middle childhood is sparse indeed. A recent review by Dunn (1983) concentrated on sibling relationships in early childhood, in part because more information was available for this age, but a number of points emerged from the review that have relevance for the middle childhood period.

1. The affective relationship between siblings is usually both intense and ambivalent. The relationship of older to younger siblings has some of the

elements of the parent-child relationship, in that the older child performs some caretaking, teaching, helping, dominating, and occasionally punishing. There is some evidence that older siblings age 6 or 7 are more effective in teaching a structured task to their younger siblings than are unrelated persons (Cicirelli, 1972). Further evidence of the role complementarity between siblings is evidenced by younger siblings who do more imitating and show more attachment behavior toward the older sibling than vice versa. At the same time there is considerable reciprocity in the relationship: intense pleasure in joint play, mutual empathy, and fairly frequent interchanges of reciprocated anger and teasing. In the families of hyperaggressive children, the amount of quarreling with siblings is especially marked (Patterson, 1982).

2. By the age of school entry, children who have siblings are spending considerably more time with them than they spend with their parents (Bank and Kahn, 1975).

3. Poor sibling relationships during the preschool years predict both continued poor sibling relationships by the age of school entry (Stilwell, 1983) and more antisocial behavior toward others outside the family in 8- or 9-year-old children (Richman et al., 1982).

4. The relationship between siblings is related to the mother's interaction with the children. In a study of fourth- and fifth-grade girls interacting with their mothers and with sisters two or three years younger than themselves, Bryant and Crockenberg (1980) found that mothers who are above average in responsiveness to their daughters' needs have children who show more prosocial and less hostile behavior toward their siblings than the children of less responsive mothers; furthermore, intersibling hostility is greater if the mother shows favoritism to one of the siblings. These findings are consistent with the research on younger children, which has underscored the important role played by the mother in shaping sibling relationships (Dunn and Kendrick, 1982). The findings also point strongly to the importance of considering the family as a system rather than as a collection of dyadic relationships.

5. Sibling relationships do not always lead to sibling similarities. Indeed, one of the major things that older siblings learn after the birth of a younger sibling is the ways in which they are different from the younger child. Mothers stress the differences: "You used to do that [drink from a bottle; soil your diapers], but now you're a big girl"; "the baby is too little to sit up at the table with us; isn't it nice that you can have dinner with Mommy and Daddy?" Despite occasional regression after the birth of a younger sibling, older siblings frequently show sudden gains in social maturity. Dunn (1983:801) stated: "Studies of middle childhood report that an age-gap of 2–4 years heightens the differences between sibling pairs." In general, however, research is only beginning to explore how the presence of siblings fosters

processes of differentiation and individuation, as distinct from mutual iden-tification.

We have noted above that siblings are frequently dissimilar with respect to various personality and intellectual attributes. One source of this differ-entiation may lie in the family dynamics that lead different children to take up different roles and that cause parental reactions toward one child to be influenced by and differentiated from their relationship with another child. There are many things we do not know: Do parental reactions exaggerate sibling differences? How do the dynamics of same-sex and cross-sex familial relationships play themselves out at this period of the children's lives?

The existence of substantial sibling differences provides an interesting counterweight to the earlier emphasis on socioeconomic factors and family structures. I have argued that a family's sociocultural milieu has important implications for the way the family functions. Siblings share their family's socioeconomic status, and they live together in either a single- or two-parent family with the same working or nonworking mother. Presumably, if stressful conditions impinging on the parents make them less responsive to their children, the impact of this change also falls on all children in the same family. Can the differences in the way parents treat different children in the same family be so great as to outweigh and affect each child more than do the common elements of the general family environment? A clue comes from the work of Elder (1974, 1979), who found that the economic stresses experienced by families during the Great Depression of the 1930s had neg-ative consequences for young children at the time of their fathers' unem-ployment but generally positive ones for adolescent children. Unemployed fathers tended to behave in arbitrary and punitive ways toward their children; older children could escape from these intrafamily tensions to some degree, while younger children could not. Furthermore, the older children could get part-time jobs and make positive contributions to the family economy. The Elder research highlights the fact that family characteristics may have profoundly different effects on children of different developmental levels. Some of the research on divorce, cited earlier, makes the same point.

These considerations return us full circle to the main theme of the first part of this chapter: it is time for researchers to give more serious thought to the developmental status of children and the way in which this devel-opment affects both parents' child-rearing methods and the more general sociocultural milieu in which the family functions.

METHODOLOGY

We have noted that the direction of effects in parent-child interactions has not been established. This problem is probably of greater importance in middle childhood than at earlier periods, because by middle childhood children have developed considerable skill in putting pressure on their socializers to achieve their own goals and in moderating or deflecting the socialization pressures that reflect the socializers' goals. Methods for identifying the direction of effects are currently under active development and debate. Experimental interventions, in which either the parent's behavior or the child's behavior is changed and changes in the partner noted, provide the most solid foundation for causal inference, although the strength of the conclusions will depend, among other things, on sample size, random assignment of cases to experimental and control groups, the use of placebos, and the blindness of observers. Pharmacological interventions (e.g., Barkley, 1981; Barkley and Cunningham, 1979; Barkley et al., 1983) provide excellent examples of such an approach. Interventions with clinical populations involving the training of a group of parents to improve their child-rearing skills are potentially powerful but often involve great difficulties in the selection of suitable control groups and the maintenance of observer blindness.

For ethical and practical reasons, however, experimental interventions are not possible for the study of many aspects of family functioning. In such cases, sequential data are of special value in unravelling causal sequences; such data can take the form of either (1) time-series or event-series coding of segments of ongoing parent-child interaction or (2) longitudinal data in which comparable variables are measured for both parent and child at successive points in time (see Maccoby and Martin, 1983; and Martin et al., 1981, for detailed discussion of these issues).

Perhaps the most difficult problem in designing a longitudinal study so that it will permit such analyses is deciding what behaviors are to be considered the same or even comparable from one age to another, because many behavioral systems change their form radically with children's development. Longitudinal work on the sequelae of early secure or insecure attachment, for example, has had to select outcome measures at preschool age quite different from the ones that indexed attachment at 12 or 18 months. And while change may not be so rapid between ages 6 and 12 as it was earlier, it is still great enough to create serious problems in longitudinal study. Age changes in the definition and measurement of a given attribute render questionable the methods of longitudinal analysis that call for the partialling out of autocorrelations. Such techniques have been used most successfully over relatively short age spans for which the same measures can be used through the life of the study. We suspect that these issues of developmental change constitute one reason why using structural models for time-sequential data analysis has trickled only slowly into child development research.

Nevertheless, the time is ripe for a wider application of the sophisticated multivariate analysis techniques that have been developed in recent years for nonexperimental data. These techniques require large samples and multiple measures of single constructs. Hence they are not likely to be feasible for studies calling for the kind of intensive assessments that can only be done with small samples. Nevertheless, when the number of variables is relatively small and it is possible to plan for a large sample, structural modeling procedures have begun to prove their power. An example comes from the work of Entwisle and Hayduk (1982). These investigators took note of the correlation between children's school achievement and their level of expectations for their achievement in school-related tasks. The study sought to determine which way the causal arrow pointed; by estimating alternative models, it showed that first-grade children's expectations determine their achievement rather than the reverse—a result that runs counter to findings with older children.

In the section on child-rearing characteristics of parents from different ethnic groups, we noted that ethnicity as a variable is often confounded with other characteristics of these groups, notably education and economic level. We implied that ethnic groups should be matched for these characteristics in order to obtain valid comparisons. The same kind of reasoning applies to comparisons of other groups. We need to introduce some cautions, however, concerning either planned or ex post facto matching. Selecting a subgroup of, say, single white mothers who match single black mothers with respect to other demographic variables results in the selection of a group of single white mothers who are unrepresentative of their own population. For longitudinal studies, this fact raises the issue of regression effects. Serious questions are being raised concerning the legitimacy of partialling out confounding variables in attempts to isolate the effect of single variables in "causal" analyses of samples in which it has not been possible to assign cases randomly to groups. These problems do not render group comparisons useless for some purposes, of course, but they do call for a reconsideration of how to analyze nonexperimental studies (Cronbach, 1982). The utility of causal models is currently being hotly debated. Clearly, there are trade-offs. Further application of these techniques in a variety of studies is needed before we will understand the limits of their applicability and can identify the kinds of studies in which the techniques will lead to different and more valid conclusions than would otherwise be possible.

Interviews with teachers, parents, and children; Q-sorts by parents and teachers; and paper and pencil assessment procedures (e.g., personality assessment batteries, moral dilemma stories) have been used extensively in studies of school-age children. The self-report measures take advantage of the fact that children of this age—at least those beyond third grade—are old enough to read questions, write out answers, and fully enter into conversations with interviewers. Measures derived from child reports and parent reports, however, are fraught with problems of halo effects, inaccurate recollections, and biases that reflect the subjects' wish to present themselves or their children in a favorable light. In recent years, these methods have been increasingly supplemented by observations of parent-child interaction. Observational data are valuable, expanding our knowledge beyond what was available from the interview and paper and pencil measures. Observational methods, however, have hazards. One-shot observations are of doubtful value; to get stable scores on the characteristics of parents or children, it is necessary to sample behavior across time and situations, and this is expensive. In addition, in some respects it is more difficult to conduct naturalistic observations of school-age children than with infants and preschoolers. M. Radke-Yarrow (personal communication) reported that when mothers have been trained as observers and dictate into a tape recorder brief summaries of disciplinary encounters with their children, children age 6 or 7 sometimes insist on dictating their own version of the episode, indicating their high level of awareness of being observed. Similar problems are encountered by those attempting to make inconspicuous observations on school playgrounds. It is difficult to prevent children from knowing they are observed. Furthermore, much of the free-play interaction of school-age children occurs in settings and at times that preclude observation.

In-home observations of older children are similarly susceptible to distortion. It is unnatural to require family members to remain in the same room for periods of observation or to set other constraints that may be desirable to researchers (e.g., family members should not read or watch television). Most observational studies have turned to structured problem-solving or teaching-learning kinds of interaction. It may be, however, that direct observations of any sort necessarily lose their ecological validity with the increasing age of the child. It appears that consideration of other assessment methods, and ways to improve them, is in order.

Some recent data, as yet unpublished, by Jacques Wright indicate that when observational scores are aggregated across a considerable number of occasions or situations or both, the aggregate scores correspond well (correlations in the 70s or higher) with the ratings on comparable dimensions made by adults who are familiar with how the children behave in a variety of settings. The ratings by familiar peers are also highly related to aggregated observational scores that reflect how the children actually behave; this relation is particularly strong with respect to antisocial behavior (see also Epstein, 1980, on the importance of aggregation). Thus, for research that seeks to identify children's stable individual characteristics, it may be both necessary and defensible to rely more heavily on ratings, Q-sorts, and nomination procedures rather than behavioral observations that are restricted in frequency and cross-situational scope (see also Cairns and Green, 1979). Peer nominations are important in assessing the social behavior of school-age children, but their use is constrained by ethical considerations. Researchers must not exacerbate the tendency of school-age children to negatively label their peers. Considering that each method has known strengths and weaknesses, researchers more often are turning to multimethod assessment batteries for both parent and child.

CONCLUSION

The first major theme of this chapter is that research on socialization has not been sufficiently developmental in concept. I have argued that the middle childhood period has its distinctive patterns of parent-child relationships and its distinctive socialization agenda, both of which need to be understood in terms of the developmental level children have reached by the time they enter this period and the normative developmental changes they undergo as they traverse it. I have traced some of these changes and suggested how they might be implicated in the patterns of parent-child interaction that characterize middle childhood. I have suggested that some of the traditional variables chosen by students of socialization, such as the frequency of reward or punishment, may not be as appropriate for the middle childhood period as they are for younger ages, and that we must be alert for the emergence of significant new parent-child interaction variables as children progress through the developmental timetable. Specifically, I have suggested that child-rearing shifts as children enter the school-age period, changing from largely face-to-face control, management, and teaching to more distal processes. These processes call for complex cooperation—coregulation—between parent and child. I have urged that research should focus on how these coregulation functions are carried out and how they change as children become more competent participants.

The second major theme concerns individual differences—differences among families in the way they rear their children during the middle childhood years and the possible effects of these variations. I have considered the evidence concerning differences in the way families in different social groups function and have discussed a number of viewpoints concerning how these group variations have evolved. While there are some replicable relationships between socioeconomic status and child-rearing, much less is known concerning how child-rearing is influenced by other aspects of the sociocultural niche in which families function. That we could list many alternative explanations for the known variations in child-rearing underscores our ignorance about the causal chain leading from the social and environmental conditions of family life to the functioning of parents to the various developmental paths taken by children. I have argued that these causal networks become more complex as children enter the age period when they begin to have some control over the selection and modification of their own environments. Longitudinal research is needed to clarify the effect of early family interaction patterns on later ones in the development of individual differences.

REFERENCES

Armentrout, V.A., and Burger, G.K.
    1972   Children's reports of parental child-rearing behaviors at five grade levels. *Developmental Psychology* 7:44–48.
Baldwin, A.L.
    1946   Differences in parent behavior toward three- and nine-year-old children. *Journal of Personality* 15:143–165.
    1955   *Behavior and Development in Childhood.* New York: Dryden Press.
Baldwin, A.L., Kalhorn, J., and Breese, F.H.
    1945   Patterns of parent behavior. *Psychological Monographs* 58:1–75.
Bank, S., and Kahn, M.D.
    1975   Sisterhood-brotherhood is powerful: Sibling subsystems and family therapy. *Family Process* 14:311–337.
Barkley, R.A.
    1981   The use of psychopharmacology to study reciprocal influences in parent-child interaction. *Journal of Abnormal Child Psychology* 9:303–310.
Barkley, R.A., and Cunningham, C.C.
    1979   The effects of methylphenidate on the mother-child interaction of hyperactive children. *Archives of General Psychiatry* 36:201–208.
Barkley, R.A., Cunningham, C.E., and Karlsson, J.
    1983   The speech of hyperactive children and their mothers: Comparison with normal children and stimulant drug effects. *Journal of Learning Disabilities* 16:105–110.
Baumrind, D.
    1967   Childcare practices anteceding 3 patterns of preschool behavior. *Genetic Psychology Monographs* 75:43–88.
    1971   Current patterns of parental authority. *Developmental Psychology Monographs* 4(1):part 2.
    1973   The development of instrumental competence through socialization. In A.D. Pick, ed., *Minnesota Symposium on Child Psychology.* Vol. 7. Minneapolis: University of Minnesota Press.
Bearison, D.J., and Cassell, T.Z.
    1975   Cognitive decentration and social codes: Communication effectiveness in young children from differing family contexts. *Developmental Psychology* 11:29–36.
Becker, W.C.
    1964   Consequences of different kinds of parental discipline. In M.L. Hoffman and L.W. Hoffman, eds., *Review of Child Development Research.* Vol. 1. New York: Russell Sage Foundation.

Bee, H.L., Van Egeren, L.F., Streissguth, A.P., Nyman, B.A., and Leckie, M.S.
1969   Social class differences in maternal teaching strategies and speech patterns. *Developmental Psychology* 1:726–734.
Bell, R.Q.
1977   Research strategies. In R.Q. Bell and L.V. Harper, eds., *Child Effects on Adults*. Hillsdale, N.J.: Lawrence Erlbaum.
Bell, R.Q., and Harper, L.V.
1977   *Child Effects on Adults*. Hillsdale, N.J.: Lawrence Erlbaum.
Bernstein, B.
1961   Social class and linguistic development: A theory of social learning. In A.H. Halsey, J. Flavell, and C.A. Anderson, eds., *Education, Economy, and Society*. New York: Free Press.
Block, J.
1971   *Lives Through Time*. Berkeley: Bancroft Books.
Block, J.H., and Block, J.
1980   The role of ego-control and ego-resiliency in the organization of behavior. In W.A. Collins, ed., *Minnesota Symposium on Child Psychology*. Vol. 13. Hillsdale, N.J.: Lawrence Erlbaum.
Bowlby, J.
1969   *Attachment*. New York: Basic Books.
Bronfenbrenner, U.
1958   Socialization and social class through time and space. In E.E. Maccoby, T.M. Newcomb, and E.L. Hartley, eds., *Readings in Social Psychology*. New York: Holt.
1979   *The Ecology of Human Development*. Cambridge, Mass.: Harvard University Press.
Brown, A.L., and DeLoache, J.S.
1978   Skills, plans and self-regulation. In R. Siegler, ed., *Children's Thinking: What Develops?* Hillsdale, N.J.: Lawrence Erlbaum.
Bryant, B., and Crockenberg, S.
1980   Correlates and dimensions of prosocial behavior: A study of female siblings with their mothers. *Child Development* 51:529–544.
Burrows, P.B.
1981   Parent-Child Behavior as a Function of Socio-economic Level and Family Size in Mexican Families. Paper presented at the biennial meeting of the Society for Research in Child Development, Boston, April.
Cairns, R.B., and Green, J.A.
1979   How to assess personality and social patterns: Observations or ratings? In R.B. Cairns, ed., *The Analysis of Social Interactions*. Appendix A. Hillsdale, N.J.: Lawrence Erlbaum.
Chandler, M.
1973   Egocentrism and anti-social behavior: The assessment and training of social-perspective taking skills. *Developmental Psychology* 9:326–336.
Chandler, M., Greenspan, S., and Barenboim, C.
1974   Assessment and training of role-taking and referential communication skills in institutionalized emotionally disturbed children. *Developmental Psychology* 10:546–553.
Chapman, M.
1979   Listening to reason: Children's attentiveness and parental discipline. *Merrill-Palmer Quarterly* 25:251–263.
Cicirelli, V.G.
1972   Concept learning of young children as a function of sibling relationships to the teacher. *Child Development* 43:282–287.
Clifford, E.
1959   Discipline in the home: A controlled observational study of parental practices. *Journal of Genetic Psychology* 95:45–82.

Cronbach, L.J.
1982   Designing Evaluations of Educational and Social Programs. San Francisco: Jossey-Bass.
Damon, W.
1977   The Social World of the Child. San Francisco: Jossey-Bass.
Dodge, K.
1980   Social cognition and children's aggressive behavior. Child Development 51:162–171.
Dornbusch, S.M., Carlsmith, J.M., Bushwall, S.J., Leiderman, H., Hastorf, A.H., Gross, R.T., and Rutter, P.
1983   Single Parents, Extended Households and the Control of Adolescents. Paper read at the Pacific Sociological Meetings, San Jose, Calif., April.
Dunn, J.
1983   Sibling relationships in early childhood. Child Development 54:787–811.
Dunn, J., and Kendrick, C.
1982   Siblings: Siblings, Love, Envy and Understanding. Cambridge, Mass.: Harvard University Press.
Eiduson, B., Kornfein, M., Zimmerman, I., and Weisner, T.
1982   Comparative socialization practices in traditional and alternative families. In M.E. Lamb, ed., Non-Traditional Families: Parenting and Child Development. Hillsdale, N.J.: Lawrence Erlbaum.
Elder, G.H.
1974   Children of the Great Depression. Chicago: University of Chicago Press.
1979   Historical changes in life patterns and personality. In P.B. Baltes and O.G. Brim, eds., Life Span Development and Behavior. Vol. 2. New York: Academic Press.
Emmerich, W.
1962   Variations in the parent roles as a function of parents' sex and the child's sex and age. Merrill Palmer Quarterly 8:1–11.
Entwisle, D.R., and Hayduk, L.
1982   Early Schooling. Baltimore: Johns Hopkins University Press.
Epstein, S.
1980   The stability of behavior II. Implications for psychological research. American Psychologist 35:790–806.
Farrington, D.P., and West, D.J.
1981   The Cambridge study in delinquent development. In S.A. Mednick and A.E. Baert, eds., Prospective Longitudinal Research. Oxford, England: Oxford University Press.
Fine, M.A., Moreland, J.R., and Schwebel, A.I.
1983   Long-term effects of divorce on parent-child relationships. Developmental Psychology 19:703–713.
Furstenberg, F.F., Nord, C.W., Peterson, J.L., and Zill, N.
1983   The life course of children of divorce: Marital disruption and parental contact. American Sociological Review 48:656–668.
Garmezy, N.
1983   Stressors of childhood. In N. Garmezy and M. Rutter, eds., Stress, Coping and Development in Children. New York: McGraw-Hill.
Glick, P.C.
1979   The children of divorced parents in demographic perspective. Journal of Social Issues 35:170–182.
Goodenough, F.L.
1931   Anger in Young Children. Minneapolis: University of Minnesota Press.
Grusec, J.E., and Kuczynski
1980   Direction of effect in socialization: A comparison of the parents' versus the child's behavior as determinants of disciplinary techniques. Developmental Psychology 16:1–9.

Grusec, J.E., and Redler, E.
1980 Attribution reinforcement and altruism: A developmental analysis. *Developmental Psychology* 16:525–534.
Halverson, C.F., and Waldrop, M.F.
1970 Maternal behavior toward own and other preschool children: The problem of "ownness." *Child Development* 41:838–845.
Hayes, C.D., and Kamerman, S.B., eds.
1983 *Children of Working Parents: Experiences and Outcomes.* Panel on Work, Family, and Community, Committee on Child Development Research and Public Policy. Washington, D.C.: National Academy Press.
Hess, R.D.
1970 Social class and ethnic influences on socialization. In P.H. Mussen, ed., *Carmichael's Manual of Child Psychology.* Vol. II. New York: John Wiley & Sons.
1981 Approaches to the measurement and interpretation of parent-child interaction. In R.W. Henderson, ed., *Parent-Child Interaction: Theory, Research and Prospects.* New York: Academic Press.
Hess, R.D., and Shipman, V.C.
1967 Cognitive elements in maternal behavior. In J.P. Hill, ed., *Minnesota Symposium on Child Psychology.* Vol. 1. Minneapolis: University of Minnesota Press.
Hetherington, E.M., Cox, M., and Cox, R.
1982 Effects of divorce on parents and children. In M. Lamb, ed., *Non-Traditional Families: Parenting and Child Development.* Hillsdale, N.J.: Lawrence Erlbaum.
Hill, C.R., and Stafford, F.P.
1980 Parental care of children: Time diary estimate of quantity, predictability and variety. *Journal of Human Resources* 15:219–239.
Hill, M.S.
1983 Trends in the economic situation of U.S. families and children. In R. Nelson and F. Skidmore, eds., *American Families and the Economy.* Committee on Child Development Research and Public Policy. Washington, D.C.: National Academy Press.
Hoffman, L.W.
1979 Maternal employment. *American Psychologist* 34:859–865.
Hoffman, M.L.
1970 Moral development. In P.H. Mussen, ed., *Carmichael's Manual of Child Psychology.* Vol. 2. New York: John Wiley & Sons.
Inkeles, A.
1960 Industrial man: The relation of status to experience, perception and value. *American Journal of Sociology* 66:1–31.
Kamerman, S.B., and Hayes, C.D., eds.
1982 *Families That Work: Children in a Changing World.* Panel on Work, Family, and Community, Committee on Child Development Research and Public Policy. Washington, D.C.: National Academy Press.
Kohn, M.L.
1963 Social class and parent-child relationships: An interpretation. *American Journal of Sociology* 68:471–480.
1977 *Class and Conformity; A Study in Values.* Second edition. Chicago: University of Chicago Press.
Krauss, R.M., and Glucksberg, S.
1969 The development of communication: Competence as a function of age. *Child Development* 40:255–266.
Kulka, R.A., and Weingarten, H.
1979 The long-term effects of parental divorce in childhood on adult adjustment. *Journal of Social Issues* 35:50–78.

Lane, D.M., and Pearson, D.A.
1982   The development of selective attention. *Merrill-Palmer Quarterly* 28:317–337.
Laosa, L.M.
1981   Maternal behavior: Sociocultural diversity in modes of family interaction. In R. W. Henderson, ed., *Parent-Child Interaction: Theory, Research and Prospects*. New York: Academic Press.
1982   School, occupation, culture and family: The impact of parental schooling on the parent-child relationship. *Journal of Educational Psychology* 74:791–827.
Lamb, M., ed.
1981   *The Role of the Father in Child Development*. Second edition. New York: John Wiley & Sons.
1982   *Non-Traditional Families: Parenting and Child Development*. Hillsdale, N.J.: Lawrence Erlbaum.
Lamb, M.E., Frodi, A.M., Hwang, C.P., and Frodi, M.
1982   Varying degrees of paternal involvement in infant care: Attitudinal and behavioral correlates. In M.E. Lamb, ed., *Non-Traditional Families: Parenting and Child Development*. Hillsdale, N.J.: Lawrence Erlbaum.
Lasko, J.K.
1954   Parent behavior toward first- and second-born children. *Genetic Psychology Monographs* 49:97–137.
Lepper, M.R.
1983   Social control processes and the internalization of social values: An attributional perspective. In E.T. Higgins, D.N. Ruble, and W.W. Hartup, eds., *Social Cognition and Social Development*. London and New York: Cambridge University Press.
LeVine, R.A.
1979   Cross Cultural Research on Child Development. Invited address presented at the meeting of Society for Research in Child Development, San Francisco, March.
Loeb, R.C., Horst, L., and Horton, P.J.
1980   Family interaction patterns associated with self-esteem in pre-adolescent girls and boys. *Merrill Palmer Quarterly* 26:203–217.
Maccoby, E.E.
1983   Social-emotional development and response to stressors. In N. Garmezy and M. Rutter, eds., *Stress, Coping and Development in Children*. New York: McGraw-Hill.
1984   Socialization and developmental change. *Child Development*. April.
Maccoby, E.E., and Martin, J.A.
1983   Socialization in the context of the family: Parent-child interaction. In E.M. Hetherington, ed., *Manual of Child Psychology*. Paul Mussen, general ed. Vol. 4, fourth edition. New York: John Wiley & Sons.
Martin, J.A., Maccoby, E.E., Baran, K.W., and Jacklin, C.N.
1981   Sequential analysis of mother-child interaction at 18 months: A comparison of microanalytic methods. *Developmental Psychology* 17:146–157.
Marvin, R.S.
1977   An ethological-cognitive model for the attenuation of mother-child attachment behavior. In T. Alloway, P. Pliner and L. Krames, eds., *Attachment Behavior*. New York: Plenum Press.
McCord, J.
1979   Some child-rearing antecedents of criminal behavior in adult men. *Journal of Personality and Social Psychology* 37:1477–1486.
McCord, W., and McCord, J.
1960   *Origins of Alcoholism*. Stanford, Calif.: Stanford University Press.

Medrich, E.A., Roizen, J., and Rubin, V.
1982   *The Serious Business of Growing Up.* Berkeley: University of California Press.
Moen, P.
1982   The two-provider family: Problems and potentials. In M.E. Lamb, ed., *Non-Traditional Families: Parenting and Child Development.* Hillsdale, N.J.: Lawrence Erlbaum.
Newson, J., and Newson, E.
1968   *Four Years Old in an Urban Community.* Chicago: Aldine.
1976   *Seven Years Old in the Home Environment.* New York: John Wiley & Sons.
1977   *Perspectives on School at Seven Years Old.* Winchester, Md.: Allen & Unwin.
Parke, R.D., and Tinsley, B.R.
1983   Fatherhood: Historical and contemporary perspectives. In K.A. McCluskey and H.W. Reese, eds., *Life Span Developmental Psychology: Historical and Cohort Effects.* New York: Academic Press.
Patterson, G.R.
1982   *Coercive Family Processes.* Eugene, Oreg.: Castalia Press.
Pearce, D., and McAdoo, H.P.
In   *Women and Children: Alone and in Poverty.*
press
Peters, M.F.
1976   Nine Black Families: A Study of Household Management and Child Rearing in Black Families with Working Mothers. Ph.D. dissertation, Harvard University.
1981   Parenting in black families with young children. In H. P. McAdoo, ed., *Black Families.* Beverly Hills: Sage Publications.
Pulkkinen, L.
1982   Self-control and continuity from childhood to adolescence. In P.B. Baltes and O.G. Brim, eds., *Life-Span Development and Behavior.* Vol 4. New York: Academic Press.
Radke-Yarrow, M., Zahn-Waxler, C., and Chapman, M.
1983   Children's prosocial dispositions and behavior. In E.M. Hetherington, ed., *Manual of Child Psychology.* Paul Mussen, general ed. Vol. 4, fourth ed. New York: John Wiley & Sons.
Richman, N., Graham, P., and Stevenson, J.
1982   *Preschool to School: A Behavioural Study.* London: Academic Press.
Roberts, G.C., Block, J.H., and Block, J.
1981   Continuity and Change in Parents' Child-Rearing Practices. Paper presented at meetings of the Society for Research in Child Development, Boston.
Robins, L.N.
1974   *Deviant Children Grow Up.* Huntington, N.Y.: Robert Krieger.
Robins, L.N., and Ratcliff, K.S.
1980   Childhood conduct disorders and later arrest. In L.N. Robins, P.J. Clayton, and J.K. Wing, eds., *The Social Consequences of Psychiatric Illness.* New York: Brunner/Mazel.
Rowe, D.C., and Plomin, R.
1981   The importance of non-shared environmental influence in behavioral development. *Developmental Psychology* 17:517–531.
Russell, G.
1982   Shared-caregiving families: An Australian study. In M.E. Lamb, ed., *Non-Traditional Families: Parenting and Child Development.* Hillsdale, N.J.: Lawrence Erlbaum.
Rutter, M.
1971   Parent-child separation: Psychological effects on the children. *Journal of Child Psychology and Psychiatry* 12:233–260.
1979   Maternal deprivation, 1972–1978: New findings, new concepts, new approaches. *Child Development* 50:283–305.

1981   *Maternal Deprivation Reassessed.* Second edition. Harmondsworth, England, and New York: Penguin Books.
1982   Epidemiological-longitudinal approaches to the study of development. In W.A. Collins, ed., *The Concept of Development.* Vol. 15: *Minnesota Symposium on Child Psychology.* Hillsdale, N.J.: Lawrence Erlbaum.
1983   Stress, coping and development: Some issues and some questions. In N. Garmezy and M. Rutter, eds., *Stress, Coping and Development in Children.* N.Y.: McGraw-Hill.
Rutter, M., Yule, B., Quinton, D., Rowlands, O., Yule, W., and Berger, M.
1975   Attainment and adjustment in two geographical areas III. Some factors accounting for area differences. *British Journal of Psychiatry* 126:520–533.
Salzstein, H.D.
1976   Social influence and moral development: A perspective on the role of parents and peers. In T. Lickona, ed., *Moral Development and Behavior: Theory, Research and Social Issues.* New York: Holt, Rinehart & Winston.
Samaroff, A.J.
1982   Development and the dialectic: The need for a system approach. In W.A. Collins, ed., *Minnesota Symposium on Child Development.* Vol. 15, Hillsdale, N.J.: Lawrence Erlbaum.
Scarr, S., Webber, P.L., Weinberg, R.A., and Wittig, M.A.
1981   Personality resemblance among adolescents and their parents in biologically related and adoptive families. *Journal of Personality and Social Psychology* 40:885–898.
Schaefer, E.S.
1959   A circumplex model for maternal behavior. *Journal of Abnormal and Social Psychology* 59:226–235.
Sears, R.R., Maccoby, E.E., and Levin, H.
1957   *Patterns of Child Rearing.* Evanston, Ill.: Row, Peterson.
Selman, R.L., and Byrne, D.F.
1974   A structural developmental analysis of levels of role-taking in middle childhood. *Child Development* 45:803–806.
Sennett, R., and Cobb, J.
1982   *The Hidden Injuries of Class.* New York: Random House.
Shipman, V.C., McKee, J.D., and Bridgeman, P.
1976   *Stability and Change in Family Status, Situational and Process Variables and Their Relation to Children's Cognitive Performance.* Princeton, N.J.: Educational Testing Service.
Sroufe, L.A., and Waters, E.
1977   Attachment as an organizational construct. *Child Development* 48:1184–1199.
Stack, C.B.
1974   Sex roles and survival strategies in an urban black community. In M.Z. Risaldo and L. Lamphere, eds., *Women, Culture and Society.* Stanford, Calif.: Stanford University Press.
Sternberg, R.J., and Powell, J.S.
1983   The development of intelligence. In J. Flavell and E. Markman, eds., *Cognitive Development,* Vol. 3. *Manual of Child Psychology,* fourth edition. Paul Mussen, general ed. New York: John Wiley & Sons.
Stilwell, R.
1983   *Social Relationships in Primary School Children as Seen by Children, Mothers, and Teachers.* Unpublished Ph.D. dissertation, University of Cambridge.
Wallerstein, J.S., and Kelly, J.B.
1980   *Surviving the Breakup: How Children and Parents Cope With Divorce.* New York: Basic Books.
Weisner, T.S.
1982   As we choose: Family life styles, social class, and compliances. In J.G. Kennedy and R. Edgerton, ed., *Culture and Ecology: Eclectic Perspectives.* A special publication of the American Anthropological Association, No. 15.

Whalen, C.K., Henker, B., and Dotemoto, S.
1980   Methylphenidate and hyperactivity: Effects on teacher behaviors. *Science* 208:1280–1282.
1981   Teacher response to the methylphenidate (Ritalin) versus placebo status of hyperactive boys in the classroom. *Journal of Child Development* 52:1005–1014.
Yankelovich, D., Clark, R., and Martire, G.
1977   *General Mills American Family Report.* Minneapolis, Minn.: General Mills, Inc.
Yarrow, M.R., Scott, P.M., and Waxler, C.Z.
1973   Learning concern for others. *Developmental Psychology,* 8:240–260.
Young, V.
1970   Family and childhood in a southern Negro community. *American Anthropologist* 72:269–288.
Zill, N.
In   *Happy, Healthy and Insecure.* New York: Cambridge University Press.
press
1978   Divorce, Marital Happiness, and the Mental Health of Children: Findings from the FCD National Survey of Children. Paper prepared for NIMH Workshop on Divorce and Children, Bethesda, Md., February.

CHAPTER 6

The Peer Context
in Middle Childhood

Willard W. Hartup

Socialization in the peer context varies from culture to culture, with considerable variation existing in the onset of a child's earliest experiences with other children. In most societies, children begin to socialize with one another in early childhood; sustained and coordinated social interaction becomes evident in the years between 3 and 6. Both quantitative and qualitative changes occur in middle childhood, and, between the ages of 6 and 12, socialization in the peer context becomes a central issue in children's lives.

The peer system can be represented as a matrix of contexts and components (see Figure 6-1). The vertical axis of this matrix consists of a hierarchical ordering (Hinde, 1976) of various social contexts. The most basic of these are interactions, i.e., meaningful encounters between two or more individuals. Relationships are interactions between individuals (known to each other) that persist over time and that involve expectations, affects, and characteristic configurations of interactions. Groups, subsuming both interactions and relationships, possess structural and normative dimensions that are not evident in either of the other contexts; most commonly, groups are polyadic rather than dyadic. Macrostructures are higher-order social contexts, including entities that we commonly call institutions or societies. These macrostructures consist of dynamic interrelationships among the interactions, relationships, and groups that constitute them.

Peer contexts involve specific objects and events occurring in specific times and locations. Three situational components can be identified: the

240

Components

Contexts	Setting	Problem	Actors
Interactions			
Relationships			
Groups			
Macrostructures			

FIGURE 6-1   The peer system.

setting, the "problem," and the actors. Settings consist of the milieux in which social activity occurs. Problems consist of the challenges existing in these settings that activate or energize the individuals involved. The actors are the individuals with whom the target child interacts.

Using this matrix we can describe the structure, content, affects, and diversity of the peer system—in each case as a function of context and component. This matrix is not a model of the peer system or a theory of social dynamics; it is a simple schematic that can be used to describe the peer system as it has been examined empirically. Less a theoretical statement than a pragmatic device, this matrix focuses attention on the various levels of the individual's commerce with other children.

Accordingly, in the various sections of this chapter, peer relationships in middle childhood are discussed with an emphasis on child-child interactions and their changes with age; close relationships and their significance; group formation and functioning; and interconnections between the peer system and two macrostructures—the family and the school. Peer interaction and the socialization of the individual child are examined in relation to conditions of the setting and the identity of the individuals with whom children interact. Methodological issues are discussed, especially the problems encountered in obtaining naturalistic data.

PEER CONTEXTS

Interactions

Child-child interaction differs from adult-child interaction in many ways. Barker and Wright (1955) observed that children's actions toward adults are weighted mainly with appeals and submissive acts; actions of adults toward children consist mainly of dominance and nurturance. These interactions are thus concentrated in two complementary issues: the child's dependency on the adult and the adult's need to control the child. In contrast, the most common actions of children toward child associates are sociability and assertiveness/aggression.

Cross-cultural observations (Whiting and Whiting, 1975) are consistent with these results, as are recent interviews with American schoolchildren (Youniss, 1980). Children see themselves as recipients of adult actions rather than vice versa. In contrast, child-child interactions are seen as revolving around equal exchanges between the actors. Concordantly, "kindnesses" in adult-child interactions are conceived as actions confirming complementary expectations, whereas kindnesses in child-child interactions consist of actions confirming more egalitarian expectations. Close relationships (e.g., friendships or parent-child relationships) usually involve mixtures of complementary and equal interactions, but this does not negate the thesis that children differentiate between adult-child and child-child relationships mainly in terms of this dichotomy.

The time that children spend together and the nature of their interactions when they are on their own are not well documented. Patterns of interaction have been most extensively examined in ad hoc settings, mainly schools, and it is largely on an anecdotal basis that we have concluded that more and more time is devoted to child-child interactions in middle childhood. Observations of 8 children, each covering an entire day (Barker and Wright, 1955), revealed that approximately 85 percent of the children's activities were social and that the proportion spent with child associates rose from 10 percent at age 2, to 20 percent at age 4, to slightly over 40 percent between ages 7 and 11. The school-age children engaged in an average of 299 behavior episodes (i.e., interactive segments marked by constant direction and intent) with other child associates in a typical school day, 45 of these with siblings and the remainder with friends. Detailed records based on observations of one of these children (Barker and Wright, 1951) indicate that most of these episodes consisted of play or "fooling around" and that the interactions consisted mainly of sociability and dominance exchanges. Although these measures are difficult to translate into time units, it can nevertheless be concluded that time spent with child associates consumed hours rather than minutes.

More recent time-use studies clarify, to some extent, what children do with one another on their own. Even so, the frequencies of their activities and the structures of the social interactions remain unstudied. Using interviews with 764 sixth graders in Oakland, California, Medrich et al. (1982) asked the children to enumerate "what you like to do when you are with your friends." Responses covered a range indicating that, in contrast to time spent alone, children spend their time with their friends engaged in physically active or "robust" interactions. Team sports accounted for 45 percent and 26 percent of the enumerations of boys and girls, respectively, although other types of robust interactions such as "general play," "going places," and "socializing" were more commonly mentioned by girls than by boys. These interactions occurred most often outside the home, although close to home and more often in private than in public places (e.g., parks and playgrounds), and were segregated by sex.

Overall, it appears that a substantial portion of the schoolchild's daily existence is spent in peer interaction and that the content of this interaction consists mainly of play and socializing. Children in many cultures also share work experiences in which they take turns and substitute for one another to a greater extent than when they work with adults (Weisner, 1982). The proportion of child-child interactions spent in work and in play thus varies from culture to culture, but the nature of this interaction seems universally to be more egalitarian than the interaction that occurs between children and adults.

The two classes of child-child interaction most extensively studied in developmental terms are aggression and prosocial activity. Overall, aggression decreases in middle childhood, although both mode and content change (Parke and Slaby, 1983). Physical aggression (more common among boys than among girls) and quarreling decrease, although abusive verbal exchanges increase. Schoolchildren typically engage in instrumental aggression (directed toward retrieving objects and the like) less frequently than younger children, although person-directed hostile aggression is more common among older ones. Increasingly salient in middle childhood are insults, derogation, and other threats to self-esteem (Hartup, 1974). Between ages 6 and 12, aggressive boys are more ready to attribute hostile intent to others than are nonaggressive boys. In addition, their associates more often attribute hostile intentions to aggressive than nonaggressive boys, and the former are more often targets of aggression (Dodge, 1980; Dodge and Frame, 1982). Individual differences in aggression among school-age males thus come to be associated with social cognitive biases (a willingness to perceive hostility in others), negative experiences with others, and "bad" social reputations.

Certain studies indicate that sharing and other forms of altruism increase in middle childhood; others suggest that these growth functions are more complex (Radke-Yarrow et al., 1983). In one investigation, for example, no relationship was found between age and the amount of sharing among kindergarten and second and fourth grade students, but among the older children more individuals shared, more individuals shared in "complex" situations, and more advanced reasoning was used to rationalize the altruism (Bar-Tal et al., 1980). Still other evidence suggests that age differences in altruism vary according to context. Kindergarten children were found to intervene directly in assisting another child with a difficult task, but third graders differentiated their assistance according to the situation—the older children would usually offer suggestions or assistance before actually giving it, and sometimes intervention would be withheld altogether (Milburg, McCabe, and Kobasigawa, unpublished data). Thus, there is evidence that complex attributions become increasingly involved in prosocial interactions as well as aggressive interactions in middle childhood.

Competition, in contrast to cooperation, increases with age when rewards are allocated in proportion to the number of points accumulated in a game (Avellar and Kagan, 1976) or when points are tallied (McClintock, 1974). These age gradients occur more clearly in some cultures (the United States, Japan) than in others (Mexico, Kenya). With outcome controlled, competitive preferences are not as clearly evident, and in some tasks cooperation increases with age (Kagan et al., 1977; Skarin and Moely, 1976). Chronological age and goal structure thus seem to interact in children's cooperative and competitive choices.

Studies of American children reveal that increases in competition under winner-takes-all conditions occur mainly in the preschool years; cooperation under shared reward conditions increases mainly between ages 6 and 8; and age differences in individualistic (proportional reward) conditions vary according to the manner in which a child's gains are linked to the gains of others (McClintock and Moskowitz, 1976; McClintock et al., 1977). With time, children differentially use strategies that coincide with the goal structures associated with obtaining valued outcomes. Children do not simply become more competitive or cooperative as they grow older. They become sensitive to the contingencies controlling the incentives that are important to them. Again, cognitive and social factors seem to determine the nature of child-child interactions in middle childhood.

More detailed studies, including direct assessment of the attributions made by children in distress or conflict situations, are relatively rare. We know that (a) the social cues used in interactions (e.g., facial expression, vocal intonation) are encoded with increasing accuracy between ages 6 and 10 (Girgus and Wolf, 1975); (b) visual attention is increasingly utilized in conversation (Levine and Sutton-Smith, 1973); (c) increases occur in speakers' abilities to transmit information about simple problems to listeners and to respond appropriately to queries from their listeners, and listeners' utilization of feedback improves (see, e.g., Karabenick and Miller, 1977); (d) abilities to infer motivation and intent in simulated social situations increase in middle childhood, although these trends are most evident in cognitively complex situations (see Shantz, 1983); and (e) increases occur in children's abilities to integrate two sources of information as opposed to one (Brady et al., 1983). These results suggest that a variety of cognitive constraints on social interaction become less evident in middle childhood. These constraints appear to involve the coding, storage, and retrieval of information as well as the integration and application of information in social situations. Existing studies thus provide a general characterization of child-child interactions between ages 6 and 12. First, time spent with child associates increases. Second, children become more adept at sending and receiving messages, in utilizing information from a variety of sources to determine their actions toward other children, in making causal attributions, and in coordinating their actions with those of others. We are only beginning, however, to understand the manner in which changes in the content and structure of child-child interactions reflect changes in cognitive functioning (Hartup et al., 1983).

Relationships

Social Attraction

Sociometric techniques have been used to examine the characteristics that make children attractive to one another. Usually, sociometric interviews are administered concurrently with personality and intelligence tests or with behavioral ratings made by teachers, children, or observers, and the various scores are correlated. We know three things.

First, social attractiveness is associated with sociocultural conditions. Social class is positively correlated with attractiveness (Grossman and Wrighter, 1948), and recent studies indicate that socioeconomic variations may exist in the values concomitant with sociometric status. For example, popularity in middle-class schools is correlated with the use of positive verbal overtures among children, whereas status in working-class schools is associated with the use of nonverbal overtures. Middle-class children who engage in nonverbal interactions, even though positive, are actually rejected more often than children who do not use these techniques (Gottman et al., 1975).

Second, characteristics of the child are correlated with social attraction. Being liked is associated with being physically attractive, socially outgoing, and supportive of others; achievements in school and in sports are also positively associated with social attractiveness. Being rejected is associated with being unattractive, immature, disruptive, and aggressive in indirect ways. Rejected children, however, are not necessarily more aggressive in general than their nonrejected peers (see Hartup, 1983).

Third, children's reputations mirror these differences. Sociometric "stars" and "average" children have social reputations that are accepting and that allow them considerable flexibility in dealing with their companions (Newcomb and Rogosch, 1982). These children are regarded by their associates as cooperative, supportive, and attractive (Coie et al., 1982). Rejected children are restricted by their reputations and the negative expectations of their companions. They tend to be perceived as disruptive and indirectly aggressive (Coie et al., 1982).

The causal connections underlying these results are presumably bidirectional. That is, the well-liked child appears to possess a repertoire of effective social skills and a positive social reputation—conditions associated with a high probability that other children will behave supportively. This support in turn maintains the competent behaviors and the child's social reputation. Similarly, negative attributes seem to undergird negative social reputations, nonsupportive feedback from one's associates, and in turn a continuation of the negative behaviors (see Coie and Kupersmidt, 1983; Dodge and Frame, 1982).

Certain side effects of these conditions have been documented. Popular and rejected children, for example, are members of distinctive social networks. Rejected children, compared with popular children, socialize on the playground in small groups and more frequently interact with younger and/or unpopular companions. The social networks of popular children are more likely to be composed of mutual friends and to be characterized as cliquish (Ladd, 1983). These distinctive networks suggest the existence of a self-maintaining cleavage between popular and rejected children. Social attraction thus seems to involve a nexus of social skills, social reputations, the extent to which one socializes with friends, and the extensiveness of one's social world.

Most likely this nexus is mediated through an intricate set of self-attitudes and emotions. To date, studies of self-esteem, self-conceptions, and social acceptance have not been convincing. Several investigators have noted small correlations between self-esteem and popularity (Horowitz, 1962; Sears and Sherman, 1964), but other results suggest that any correlation is curvilinear. Reese (1961) found that children with moderately high self-esteem were better accepted by their peers than were children with either low or very high self-esteem. Sixth graders with high self-esteem have been shown to make more extreme statements about the likability of others than their low self-esteem counterparts; the extent to which these children believe their evaluations of others are reciprocal is also positively related to self-esteem (Cook et al., 1978). But the self-system is involved in social relationships in very complex ways. Dodge and Frame (1982), for example, found that aggressive boys were characterized by hostile attribution biases only when the provocation was directed toward themselves. These biases were not evident in situations involving provocations directed at someone else.

Developmental changes in social attraction have been examined relatively rarely. For one thing, the characteristics associated with sociometric status do not appear to change with age. Friendliness is as strongly associated with popularity among older children as among younger children; indirect aggression is as strongly associated with rejection. Nevertheless, recent investigations reveal that more of the variance in social preferences can be predicted by fewer variables among young children than among older children. Social impact, too, rests on fewer attributes among younger children than among older ones (Coie et al., 1982). The results thus seem to indicate that person perception becomes more differentiated as children grow older—a conclusion that is consistent with the results of other investigations in which children's descriptions of one another were examined in relation to chronological age (Livesley and Bromley, 1973). Also, certain sociometric dimensions may become increasingly stable in the years between 6 and 12. For example, rejection status was observed to be stable over a 5-year span when assessment was initiated in the fifth grade but only over 3 years when initiated in the third grade (Coie and Dodge, 1983). These results suggest that a "crystallization" may occur in social relationships toward the end of middle childhood.

Friendship Selection

Children and their friends usually live in the same neighborhood, a condition that prevails in both early and middle childhood (Epstein, in press; Fine, 1980). Young children depend on their caretakers to put them in contact with other children more than school-age children do, and classroom proximity becomes salient in friendship selection in middle childhood. Conditions within classrooms, including seating arrangements and classroom organization, are also reflected in friendship selection.

Children select their friends mainly from among children their own age. When classroom conditions favor mixed-age choices (as in a one-room school), more than 67 percent of children in the first 6 grades have one or more friends of some other age (Allen and Devin-Sheehan, 1976). Nevertheless, the tendency for children and their friends to be similar in age is very strong. Whether this concordance derives from the age segregation that marks most schools and children's institutions or from children's own preferences is not certain. Moreover, there may be no way to resolve this issue, since age grading is pervasive in Western cultures.

Children and their friends are most commonly of the same sex (Tuma and Hallinan, 1977). This concordance peaks between ages 6 and 12, even though same-sex choices are more common than other-sex choices from the preschool years through adolescence. Since sex segregation is not common in schools except in sports activities, the concordance may derive from norms generated by children themselves rather than from the normative expectations of adults.

Fewer cross-race friendship selections occur in integrated classrooms than would be expected on the basis of chance, and this cleavage increases between ages 6 and 12—as determined by longitudinal studies (Singleton and Asher, 1979). Racial differentiations are not as strong in children's selection of playmates or work companions as in friendship choices, and age differences are not as evident (Asher et al., 1982).

Behavioral similarities and their role in mutual attraction in middle childhood have not been well studied. Kandel (1978), on the basis of one study of a large sample of adolescents, concluded that these similarities are not especially important in the selection of associates, except for similarities in significant nonnormative attitudes (e.g., about drug use). Given the importance to children of "doing things together" with their friends, it is difficult to believe that behavioral concordances are irrelevant in these selections (Smollar and Youniss, 1982). Nevertheless, except for a small number of investigations using global measures such as IQ, school achievement, or sociometric status, which show very modest concordance between children and their friends, this issue has not been closely examined. This state of affairs is unfortunate, since it has been known for some time that school-age children, like adults, demonstrate greater attraction for peers with whom they share many attitudes than for individuals with whom they share relatively few (Byrne and Griffitt, 1966).

Acquaintances

Friendship formation begins with acquaintanceship. As two individuals become familiar with each other, attraction seems to increase (Berscheid and Walster, 1978). Mere exposure (Zajonc, 1968) may account for these effects, and familiarization may also establish a secure base for social interaction; moreover, as individuals become acquainted with one another, their social repertoires become better meshed and more efficient. Various studies (mostly with younger children) support these ideas. To date, however, these hypotheses have not been used to any great extent in investigations with school-age children.

To investigate children's notions about the manner in which two individuals become friends, Smollar and Youniss (1982) asked three questions of subjects between ages 6 and 13: "What do you think might happen to make X and Y become friends?" "Not become friends?" "To become best friends?" The children's responses differed according to their ages. Younger children indicated that strangers would become friends if they did something together or did something special for one another. Children would become best friends, according to the younger children, if they could spend increased amounts of time together, especially outside school. In contrast, the older children emphasized getting to know each other ("talk and talk and find out if they like the same things"); discovering similarities between themselves was considered necessary to becoming best friends. Not becoming friends was associated among the younger children with negative or inequitable interaction. This condition was identified among the older children with the discovery that two individuals are different. What is interesting in these findings is the revelation that concordance was viewed as essential in friend-ship formation at all ages; it was mainly the expression of these concordances that differed with age. Younger children emphasized concrete reciprocities, while older children emphasized psychological similarities (e.g., in person-ality, likes, and attitudes).

Microanalytic studies of acquaintance interactions do not extend more than to the first few encounters between children. Virtually no develop-mental studies have been executed. First encounters differ with respect to a number of conditions, including the sociometric status of the children involved. When both children are of high status, information giving and seeking are more frequent than when both children are of low status. Dis-cussions about school, sports, the children themselves, and their acquaint-ances are common. Pairs of third- and fourth-grade children that include one high-status and one low-status child are virtually identical in these respects to those of two high-ranking children, presumably because the interaction is driven by the high-status member (Newcomb and Meister, 1982). A second investigation revealed that "stars" and sociometrically "average" third-grade children engaged in more introductory activity and information exchange, earlier onset of affective communication, and game-playing than "isolate" or "rejected" dyads. In contrast, isolates and rejected children attempted to initiate games more frequently but engaged in more inappropriate interactions than did stars or average dyads (Newcomb et al., 1982). These analyses thus indicate that a major function of the early encounters between children is assessment of interests and similarities.

Other studies indicate that synchronization is an outcome of the early encounters between strangers. Brody et al. (in press) observed triads of first- and third-grade children from different classrooms before and after a series of five play sessions. Postfamiliarization measures revealed more verbal in-teraction and improved task performance than among control subjects, in-dicating better meshing of individual contributions to task solution. Since mere exposure seems to have variable effects on social attraction among children (Cantor and Kubose, 1969), early social encounters seem mainly to provide a basis for interaction via the sharing of information and behavioral coordination. Beyond this, no clear picture of acquaintanceship processes emerges, and the features of acquaintance interaction that favor the continuance of an association are unknown.

Friends

School-age children have, on the average, five best friends—a number that is a bit higher than the number of friends acknowledged by preschool children and adolescents (Hallinan, 1980). In addition, relatively few (2 percent) have no friends when choosing in sociometric interviews, although a somewhat larger number (between 6 and 11 percent) are not chosen themselves. These frequencies do not change from age 6 to 12, although age differences have never been studied adequately (Epstein, in press). School-age children and their friends tend to be linked in twosomes rather than in the larger interlocking networks known as cliques or crowds. Relatively few cliques are observed in most elementary school classrooms, in contrast to junior and senior high school (Hallinan, 1976). Considerable interest is now evident among investigators in the social interaction of friends. Most of the recent work draws heavily from the theories of Harry Stack Sullivan (1953), who argued that friendships are hallmarks of the "juvenile era," reflecting new needs for interpersonal intimacy and new contexts for their expression. Recurrent themes in contemporary research are reciprocity, equity, fairness, mutuality, and intimacy as these mark both children's conceptions of their friends and their behavior with them. Presumably, these themes become more and more important in middle childhood, so that the need for developmental studies is especially acute.

Cross-sectional studies confirm that friendship expectations among school-children revolve around these issues. Development does not involve a change from the absence of reciprocity expectations among younger children to their presence. Reciprocity norms are evident among kindergartners (Berndt, 1977). Interviews (Youniss, 1980) and written essays (Bigelow, 1977) confirm that "reward-cost" reciprocities figure prominently in children's expectations of their friends at all ages. Bigelow's work suggests a progression from expectations among second and third graders that are based on common activities to sharing of rewards and other equities to mutual understanding, self-disclosure, and the sharing of interests among fifth and sixth graders. Youniss's studies suggest that young friends "match" each other's contributions to the interaction; older friends evidence equality and equal treatment in their relationships with one another; and young adolescents stress interpersonal intimacy. Thus, the case can be made that the major changes in children's friendship expectations occur in the way children use notions about reciprocities in social relationships rather than in the emergence de novo of generalized notions about fairness and mutuality. Individual differences in these understandings are largely unexplored except for the work of Selman (1980), and a connection between these social cognitive changes and behavior with friends has not been established.

Observational studies confirm that friendships are based on reciprocity and mutuality, but age changes in the behavioral manifestations of these reciprocities have been difficult to document. (Presumably, this derives from the difficulty of measuring the subtle affective and instrumental components of intimacy via direct observation.) Laboratory studies reveal that in cooperative settings friends are more interactive, affective, attentive to equity rules, mutually directive, and explore the materials more extensively than nonfriends (Foot et al., 1977; Newcomb and Brady, 1982; Newcomb et al., 1979). Changes in these differences with age are not dramatic in middle childhood (Newcomb et al., 1979). Berndt (1981b) found that fourth-grade friends assisted their partners and were more willing to share rewards with each other than were first graders. These changes are not striking until early adolescence, however, and then they occur most commonly when children have a choice between cooperation or competition in the task.

Competitive settings change the interaction between friends. In these situations, males are more competitive and less generous with their friends than with nonfriends (Berndt, 1981a). Competition also occurs more commonly between friends than between nonfriends when property rights are clearly understood (Staub and Noerenberg, 1981). Thus, under certain circumstances, friendship may furnish a basis for competition, even though in others it furnishes a basis for equity considerations and generosity. Studies of adults indicate that close relationships may maintain a basis for hostile, aggressive interaction as well as supportive, affectionate interaction. What evidence we have suggests that children also manifest these complexities, even though these elements are not well understood. Future investigations must concentrate not only on the documentation of fairness norms in friendship interactions in middle childhood but also on a complex array of attributions that make for distinctive interactions between children according to context.

More and more, the contemporary evidence stresses the importance of close relationships in childhood. Much remains to be documented, however, about children and their friends. Especially needed are studies addressing four issues: (1) the temporal course of friendships, including the accommodations made by friends to stress that comes from both inside and outside the relationship; (2) developmental vicissitudes, including the manner in which expectations and attributions among friends are connected to social interactions and the manner in which these relationships cycle through time; (3) individual differences among friendship pairs in the structure of these relationships, the use of reciprocity rules, the content of interactions, and their affective qualities; and (4) the socializing consequences of friendships, i.e., their role in increasing similarities between children, the developmental implications of having a best friend, and the value of friendships as protective factors in times of stress. The research agenda is formidable.

Groups

Groups exist when social interaction occurs over time among three or more children, values are shared, the members have a sense of belonging, and a structure exists to support the activities of the collective. Empirical studies have concentrated on three issues: group formation, norms, and structures.

Formation

Group formation has been understudied since the investigations 20 years ago by Sherif et al. (1961). That work confirmed the ubiquity of social structures based on power relations, the individual attributes associated with social power, and the emergence of group norms. Group formation has not been studied with children in the early school years, so developmental changes are undocumented. Only two studies have ever been conducted that chart changes in group interaction as a function of the age of the group members (A. Smith, 1960; H. Smith, 1973), and no longitudinal studies document the connections between norms and structures as they cycle through time. Processes in group formation among girls have been described less well than those among boys. Little is known about group formation among children from minority subcultures. And we know little about the impact of the macrostructure (e.g., schools) on the emergence of children's groups. Again, the research agenda is formidable.

Norms

Standards of conduct, called *norms*, govern the actions of group members. Certain norms governing children's interactions with one another emanate from the core culture and presumably derive from earlier socialization—e.g., sex-role stereotypes as well as attitudes about authority, equity, and reciprocity. Other norms emanate from group interaction, and these are the norms that adults associate with the peer culture. The existence of these normative frameworks is not in doubt, but the processes through which they emerge are. Knowing more about these processes is essential, however, since these norms may be salient in the development of health behaviors, antisocial activities, and discordance in parent-child relationships in middle childhood and adolescence.

On the basis of observations of little league baseball teams, Fine (1980) asserted that five conditions must exist for norms to become established: (1) someone must "know," i.e., possess a bit of social information and introduce it; (2) members must find the information usable; (3) new norms must satisfy some common need; (4) norms must support group structure and vice versa; and (5) circumstances must exist that trigger the normative activity. This framework seems valuable for examining the introduction, maintenance, and cessation of normative activities among children of various ages; these notions have not yet, however, been used extensively in empirical investigations.

One's own appearance, drinking, drug use, or popularity may determine the selection of one's associates (Dembo et al., 1979; Ladd, 1983). Longitudinal studies suggest that, in addition, one's behavior influences the behavior of those individuals selected as associates (Britt and Campbell, 1977; Kandel, 1978). Similarities among group members thus derive from both normative selection and normative socialization. Once again, the connections between these processes in middle childhood are not well understood, despite their obvious significance.

Especially understudied are normative constellations as they vary from one enclave to another. Drug users, for example, tend to congregate with one another, although the weight of the evidence suggests that children do not form subcultures that are distinguishable from others except in drug use (Huba et al., 1979). Ordinarily, though, it is assumed that smoking and drug use are especially common in groups of alienated or incompetent children. Which is correct? What "mixtures" of core-culture and counterculture norms predict antisocial behavior most successfully? So few intergroup comparisons have been made that it is impossible to answer these questions.

Structures

Group members differentiate among themselves in terms of social power, i.e., their effectiveness at directing, coordinating, and sanctioning the activities of other members. These differentiations are the basis for the social structures that are visible in every group. Group structures emerge in social interactions in early childhood, and these are relatively well studied. Relatively few investigations, however, have documented the existence of hierarchical social organizations in middle childhood (Sherif et al., 1961; Strayer and Strayer, 1976).

In some instances these structures seem to be based on dominance interactions, although social structures may also be based on being good at games, knowing how to organize activities, and social competence. In general, individual differences in attributes that facilitate the group's objectives are the basis for the social order; structures based on dominance interactions do not always vary concordantly. Leaders are not necessarily tough or mean, nor are they necessarily the most popular children. Leaders are the ones who know what to do.

Our notions about group structures have been derived mainly from observations of children in classrooms and summer camps. Classroom observations are notably constrained in providing us with a clear picture of those structures that exist in informal groups. The social structure of the classroom is dominated by an adult (the teacher), and normative activity revolves around academics. Camp settings are not as heavily constrained but have their own limitations. One of the most severe gaps in our knowledge of the social psychology of middle childhood is information about the structure and functioning of informal groups.

Omitted from most studies is a consideration of the connections between norms and the social organization. Sherif et al. (1961) documented the intimate relationship between structure and function in social groups, but current investigations have been dominated by the notion that social structures exist mainly to reduce the amount of aggression among group members (Savin-Williams, 1979; Strayer and Strayer, 1976). Separate considerations of normative functions and social organization have not been wise, however, since this strategy has reduced the interest of investigators in group-to-group variations. These variations need to be better understood, not only to document the diversity of the social environment but also to better understand the conditions under which children are attracted to membership in certain groups.

SITUATIONAL COMPONENTS

Setting Conditions

The conditions of settings constrain child-child interactions (Barker and Wright, 1951). Nevertheless, we have no clear idea about where children spend time when they are on their own, let alone what social experience is like in these places. Enough has been accomplished to demonstrate that child-child interactions vary according to conditions of the setting, but no "ecology of the peer context" emerges from this material.

Playthings constrain the amount and maturity of child-child interactions, as examination of the protocols from *One Boy's Day* (Barker and Wright, 1951) shows. Other than the documentation that physical activities promote "robust" interactions and that nonphysical activities are especially associated with helping behaviors (Gump et al., 1957), little is known about playthings and play situations as constraints on social interactions in middle childhood.

The availability of resources and the space with which to use them bear on social interactions. Crowding effects have been studied mainly with younger children, and methodological flaws mar many of the studies with school-age children. Space variations apparently do not affect either positive social interaction or aggression in a linear mode. Only when space per child is severely limited is positive interaction reduced and negative interaction increased. With severe crowding, children experience emotional arousal and increased competitiveness (Aiello et al., 1979). But there is also evidence that access to resources may be more important in determining the nature of child-child interactions than the amount of space available (Smith and Connolly, 1977).

The number of children congregated together is also salient even though, in the primary grades, children tend to interact in dyads rather than in larger sets. Three-child (and larger) enclaves become more common during middle childhood on playgrounds and in parks (Eifermann, 1971), but dyadic interaction, with its concentration of social attention, remains evident. Interaction is more intense and cohesive in smaller enclaves than in larger ones. Consensus in group discussions is easier to reach and leaders exert more extensive influence, even though the members of small enclaves have a sense of self-importance and coalitions are less common (Hare, 1953). Given that children remain committed to dyadic interactions throughout middle childhood, it is to be regretted that we do not know whether the nature of these exchanges varies according to the size of the groups in which they are embedded.

Problems

Every social situation contains some element of challenge, something to be done, something to activate or energize the actors. Multiple challenges exist in most social situations, and these may form a hierarchy according to their relative importance. Different challenges may be important at different times. In some instances the main tasks are externally imposed and evident to everyone; in others the tasks are not well defined, and the participants must construct the task as they go along. Only recently has there been much interest in tasks and their role in child-child relationships. Illustrations can be selected, however, that demonstrate (a) the effects of a task on social interaction, (b) changes that occur with age in the tasks children consider important, and (c) individual differences in the tactics children use in certain situations.

The strategic demands of a social situation vary according to context. Children usually understand, for example, that when a child is being teased by a number of children the most appropriate way to assist the victim is through ordering and commanding the teasers (Ladd and Oden, 1979). When encountering a solitary child who has been teased, however, appropriate assistance is understood to include consolation, instruction, and suggestions of alternative actions. Children who do not endorse these strategic norms but instead endorse idiosyncratic social strategies turn out to be relatively low in the sociometric hierarchy. Thus, a child's endorsement of normative strategies in certain task situations seems to be central in social effectiveness.

When social situations are not well structured, children construct their own goals, and to some extent these change between ages 6 and 12. Renshaw and Asher (1983) showed third- and sixth-grade children four hypothetical social situations (social contact with strange children, group entry, a friendship issue, and an instance of conflict) and conducted interviews about the goals and strategies the children considered important. Both the third and the sixth graders recognized "friendly" goals as most appropriate in each of these social situations, but, when asked to mention their own goals, the older children mentioned friendly ones more often and the younger children were more often concerned with defending their rights. Endorsed social strategies also differed according to age. The older children, in contrast to the younger ones, more often were outgoing and accommodative, indicating more sophisticated adjustment to the social task.

One task that has received considerable recent attention is group entry. Results indicate that children vary in the extent to which they view entry as important as well as in the tactics they use to enter a group (Dodge et al., 1983; Putallaz and Gottman, 1981). As it turns out, successful entry usually involves sequences of tactics that progress from the use of low-risk ones (e.g., waiting and hovering on the edges of a group) to high-risk ones (e.g., statements and requests). Moreover, the child must then use high-risk tactics that maintain the group's frame of reference (e.g., calling attention to what the group is doing) rather than disrupting it (e.g., calling attention to oneself). The effectiveness of these strategies has been demonstrated among children interacting with familiar associates as well as unfamiliar ones and in naturalistic as well as laboratory settings. Some evidence suggests that the high-risk tactics that work are more consistently used by children toward the end of middle childhood than at the beginning (Lubin and Forbes, 1981). Furthermore, their use differentiates popular, neglected, and rejected children (Dodge et al., 1983; Putallaz and Gottman, 1981).

There is every reason to believe, then, that tasks interact with developmental and clinical status in determining the social strategies that children use with their associates. Even a child's understanding of what the social task is may index relevant individual differences in social functioning. Clearly, additional work in this important new area should be encouraged.

Actors

Age

Children's associates vary widely in age, with as much as 65 percent of social contacts occurring with others who are more than 12 months younger or older (Barker and Wright, 1955). Mixed-age contacts among adolescents occur more commonly in shopping malls and parks than in schoolyards (Montemayor and Van Komen, 1980). Similar data are not available, however, to show where mixed-age experiences are especially common among school-age children. Nevertheless, two conclusions emerge from recent studies of mixed-age interactions compared with same-age interactions: mixed-age interactions are less egalitarian than same-age interactions, and social accommodations are made in mixed-age circumstances that are not evident under same-age conditions.

Children are more nurturant and directive with younger children and more dependent with older children (Graziano et al., 1976; Whiting and Whiting, 1975); similar role asymmetries are evident between siblings who differ in age by 2–3 years (Brody et al., 1982). Same-age interaction, in contrast, is marked by "sociable" and "aggressive" interactions (i.e., equal exchanges) to a greater extent than mixed-age interactions (Whiting and Whiting, 1975). These differences are concordant with differences in attributions made to same- and mixed-age associates. Power attributions are more commonly made to older associates ("smart," "best," "bossy") and their reciprocals to younger associates ("weak," "dumb"). In these comparisons, attributions to same-age associates are more likely to resemble those made to younger associates than to older ones (Graziano et al., 1980).

Three omissions, however, mark our data base. First, the differences between mixed and same-age interactions that emerge in early childhood and extend to the early school years have not been explored among older schoolchildren. The developmental course of the complementarities existing in mixed-age interactions is thus not well documented. Second, little is known about these complementarities as a function of the age differences of children. Most investigators have examined mixed-age interactions between children who differ by two years in chronological age. One-year differences seem to affect children's efficacies as role models (Thelen and Kirkland, 1976), but little else is known about these smaller differences. No investigator has examined the complementarities that may exist across greater differences in age. Third, little is known about the role of attributions in generating the differences between mixed- and same-age interaction in various setting conditions. The existing data derive mainly from observational studies in cooperative atmospheres.

Sex

Children's societies are segregated by sex. Within these male and female cultures, boys interact in outdoor public places more commonly than girls do and come under the supervision of adults less frequently. Boys interact in larger groups than do girls, and mixed-age contacts are more frequent in male interactions. Play among boys is rougher and includes more frequent instances of fighting than play among girls (Lever, 1976; Thorne, 1982). In addition, social speech seems to serve different functions in male and female societies. Girls use speech more extensively than boys to create and maintain relationships, to criticize others in acceptable ways, and to clarify the speech of others. Boys use words to assert social position, to attract and maintain an audience, and to assert themselves when other speakers have the attention of the audience (Maltz and Barker, in press).

Mixed- and same-sex interactions have seldom been compared. Sgan and Pickert (1980) examined assertive bids in a cooperative task with triads of kindergarten, first-grade, and third-grade children. With age, boys made proportionally fewer cross-sex assertive bids in mixed-sex triads and girls made more; concomitantly, same-sex assertions increased among girls but decreased among boys. These trends result in mixed-sex interactions becoming more egalitarian with age, but whether these trends are evident in competitive or individualistic tasks is not known. Coalition formation differs according to gender composition, with same-sex coalitions formed more frequently in mixed-sex triads than cross-sex coalitions, especially when children of the same sex occupy positions of relatively low social power (Leimbach and Hartup, 1981). Gender and power relationships thus may interact in the emergence of cross-sex social organizations. Developmental trends in these outcomes have not been charted.

Despite the sex cleavage in middle childhood, sex segregation is not complete. Rather, this segregation seems to have a "with-then-apart" structure in which the sexes congregate separately but also come together in many situations, especially schoolyards and city streets. Using the techniques of participant observation in school hallways, cafeterias, and playgrounds, Thorne (1982) established, first, that sex segregation derives from both inclusion and exclusion and, second, that cross-sex exclusions are based mainly on sex typing and the "riskiness" of romantic involvement. Even so, "borderwork" (i.e., ritualized "invasions" resulting in cross-sex interaction) are common. Some of these, for example, "chasing," and "kiss and chase," have sexual overtones. Others involve stigmatization (boys referring to the girls as cootie queens). Still others involve territorial invasions. But cross-sex interactions also occur, in which the children merge easily into interactions with the opposite sex. Common examples include the inclusion of girls in team sports, especially tomboys (see Lever, 1976). As adolescence approaches, the taboo against romantic involvement begins to break down, and occasionally boys and girls will consider themselves as going together. And when tasks and resources are absorbing and adults legitimate cross-sex interactions, more harmonious cross-sex contacts occur.

These observations indicate that much can be learned from naturalistic investigations about the forces that support sex segregation in middle childhood and, more important, the forces that instigate and maintain cross-sex interactions in these years. The developmental implications of cross-sex interactions are especially significant. Indeed, it may be their highly ritualized nature that represents their significance in development.

Race

Racial awareness increases in middle childhood, although the contemporary evidence is not extensive concerning the foundations of the race cleavage that marks children's societies. Prowhite/antiblack biases are evident among white children, but in many instances the choices of black children do not depart from chance (Banks, 1976). "Eurocentric" prowhite/antiblack choices decline among school-age black children (Spencer, 1981), although there is considerable variation in the existence of problack biases. Associative contacts are more likely to be of the same sex than of the same race (Asher et al., 1982), but assortments in cafeterias, playgrounds, and hallways are notably segregated by race. School integration has changed these patterns somewhat, although friendship interactions among adolescents are strongly constrained by race (see above).

These segregations in child-child interactions are undoubtedly based on both inclusive and exclusive processes. The salience of racial similarities has seldom been explored as a basis for inclusion; in contrast, considerable

thought has been given to racial biases as sources of exclusion. The borderwork and other conditions that instigate mixed-race interactions are not
well established except that cooperative activities in the service of superordinate goals seem to promote it (Aronson, 1978). Microanalytic studies of
mixed-race interactions compared with same-race interactions are virtually
nonexistent. Among younger adolescents in mixed-race conditions, white
children are more likely to initiate social interaction than are black children,
and white children have stronger influence on group decisions. No evidence
establishes the precursors of these patterns in middle childhood or the conditions that might modify them.

Comment

Presumably many other "actor attributes" determine the nature of child-
child interactions in middle childhood. The source of a leader's authority
and his or her personal attributes determine social effectiveness among adolescents, but the emergence of these conditions in middle childhood is
unstudied. The status of handicapped children in mainstreamed classrooms
is generally not good, and observational studies are now being addressed to
the attributions and attitudes that may be responsible (see Hartup, 1983).
Overall, though, we know relatively little about the implicit personality
theories of schoolchildren and scarcely more about these matters in early
adolescents. Recent work indicates the significance of these implicit theories
in interactions among adults, however, so concentrated work with children
is urgently needed.

PEER RELATIONSHIPS AND THE INDIVIDUAL CHILD

Poor peer relationships in middle childhood are characteristic of children
who are at risk for emotional and behavioral disturbances in adolescence
and adulthood. Early childhood assessments are not strong predictors of social
difficulties in middle childhood (Richman et al., 1982), but individual differences during the school years are correlated with subsequent adjustment.
Negative reputations and social rejection among elementary school children,
for example, are prognostic indicators of continuing rejection by schoolmates
(Coie and Dodge, 1983) as well as poor mental health and psychosexual
difficulties in adolescence and young adulthood (Cowen et al., 1973; Roff,
1963; Sundby and Kreyberg, 1968). Prediction of schizophrenic breakdown
from peer status in middle childhood has not been demonstrated since social
withdrawal and isolation are themselves not stable through this time (Coie
and Dodge, 1983). Beginning in early adolescence, however, irritability,

aggressiveness, and negativistic behavior in peer interactions are character-istic of premorbid individuals (Watt and Lubensky, 1976). Consistent as these results are, it is difficult to interpret them. Childhood indicators of later maladjustment include somatic disturbances, family dif-ficulties, and school failure as well as difficulties with contemporaries. Peer problems, then, may simply reflect general difficulties in development and not be direct determinants of emotional disturbance. Whatever the child-hood antecedents of behavior disorders, difficulties with contemporaries may contribute, on their own, to negative self-attitudes, alienation, and reduc-tions in social effectiveness. Poor peer relationships are among the most consistently reported "problems" in the referral of children to mental health clinics (Achenbach and Edelbrook, 1981). Consequently, the connections between family and peer relationships across time, as these involve self- and other attributions, social isolation, and social competence, need to be ex-amined (following the example of one investigation, in which social isolation among 5-year-olds was found to be predictive of social cognitive difficulties a year later and which at that point were linked to peer rejection and withdrawal—Rubin et al., in press). New documentation connecting peer adjustment in middle childhood to later negative outcomes is not needed. Rather, the studies needed should be multidimensional examinations over time of social development and life events culminating in undesirable out-comes.

Similar comments can be made about peer relationships and crime. In middle childhood, "delinquents to be" have difficulties getting along with others and in treating others courteously, tactfully, and fairly. These children are also less well liked by their contemporaries (Conger and Miller, 1966; West and Farrington, 1973). Concordantly, self-evaluations in early ado-lescence indicate that delinquents to be do not enjoy close personal rela-tionships with others, are less interested in organized activities, and are immature. Middle childhood, then, may be a time in which precursors of criminal behavior are established, including negative self-attitudes and alien-ation. Delinquency is not a well-differentiated construct, however. These notions deserve examination in carefully designed longitudinal studies.

Studies centered on the processes of peer socialization have been con-ducted mainly with preschool children. The evidence indicates that mod-eling and reinforcing events are used in this context with increasing deliberation in middle childhood (Hartup, 1983). What children learn and how much they learn through these contingencies are difficult to specify and may remain so, although it is clear that peer interactions involve prosocial as well as aggressive experiences. Since more aggression occurs in child-child inter-actions than in other contexts, and since endorsement of antisocial norms countenanced by other children increases in middle childhood (Berndt, 1979), fine-grained analyses should be extended to naturalistic situations. These studies are needed to specify the conditions associated with the emergence of individual differences in assertiveness and aggression. Children do not become uniformly more "conforming" in middle childhood (see Hartup, 1983), but other conditions encouraging the development of antisocial behavior within the peer context may exist in these years—for example, the combination of a negative reputation among one's peers and one's own disposition to attribute hostile intentions to others (Dodge and Frame, 1982).

Sexual socialization in middle childhood is understudied, mainly because of the difficulty of conducting relevant studies. Early childhood studies make it clear that child-child interactions extend the sex typing of the individual; playground observations of schoolchildren support this thesis (see above). But sexual knowledge and experimentation also derive from contacts with other children (Kinsey et al., 1948). The scarcity of information on this subject, however, is disturbing—consider, for example, the need to determine the circumstances contributing to sexual socialization as antecedents of adolescent pregnancy.

Several investigators (see Thorne, 1982) have commented on the sexual character of children's play, especially in the robust, physical interactions of boys. Sexual concomitants in child-child interactions are common and explicit in conversations on the playground. It is difficult to discount the normative significance of these events or to ignore their possible contributions to sexual socialization. Close examination of sexuality in child-child interactions could illuminate many critical issues. Same-sex contacts in middle childhood, for example, may contribute both sexual knowledge and normative "stylistic" elements to the child's repertoire, e.g., braggadocio among boys. Opposite-sex encounters may constitute sexually neutralized introductions to the complementarities needed in heterosexual communication.

Moral relativism was believed by Piaget (1932) to arise within child-child interactions in middle childhood. Recent studies demonstrate that children's conversations modify their moral judgments (Berndt et al., 1980), but it has been difficult to connect peer interaction in the natural context with the maturity of the child's moral orientation. Preadolescents who belong to clubs and social organizations receive higher scores on moral judgment than do those who belong to relatively few organizations (Keasey, 1971), but the correlational nature of this evidence reduces its significance. Children's conversations about moral issues need closer examination, and content analyses centered on moral interaction in natural settings should be encouraged. Whether the child's moral orientation is tied especially closely to peer interactions may not be the most relevant issue. More important, we need to better understand those processes in child-child interactions that have moral implications. Along with knowing what children do when they are on their own, this information could contribute greatly to knowledge about the role of child-child relationships in moral socialization.

FAMILY AND PEER RELATIONSHIPS

Familial Correlates of Peer Competence

In early childhood, secure attachments between a child and his or her caretakers promote exploration of the environment, including the other children who inhabit it. Mothers arrange contacts between their young children and other youngsters, believing this to be desirable. In addition, social interactions within the family promote individuation and the growth of self-esteem—conditions that maximize the chances of success once peer interaction begins. Consistent with these notions are empirical studies showing secure attachments in the first 2 years to be antecedents of sociability, empathy, and effectiveness in child-child relationships at ages 3 and 4 (Waters et al., 1979).

The connections between family and peer relationships extending into middle childhood are not well documented. One would expect parent-child relationships marked by emotional support and appropriate demands for compliance to continue to be associated with positive outcomes in child-child relationships. And, indeed, cross-sectional studies reveal that mothers and fathers of well-liked children are emotionally supportive, infrequently frustrating and punitive, and discouraging of antisocial behavior in their children (Winder and Rau, 1962).

Other investigators (Hoffman, 1961) have observed the antecedents of self-confidence, assertiveness, and effectiveness with other children to include (a) among boys, affection from both mothers and fathers accompanied by dominance from fathers but not mothers, and (b) among girls, affection from both parents accompanied by dominance from mothers but not fathers. In addition, sociometric status is known to be positively correlated with parental affection and the absence of family tension (Cox, 1966) as well as with parents' satisfaction with their children (Elkins, 1958). No evidence suggests that the child-rearing correlates of social competence in middle childhood differ in any substantive way from their correlates in early childhood, even though specific exchanges between parents and their children that can be called supportive or dominant undoubtedly change.

Assuming that family and peer relationships are interactive in individual development, one would expect disturbance in one context (e.g., the family) to disturb the child in the other (e.g., child-child relationships). For example, unemployment, terminal illness within the family, and family conflict would be expected to affect the child's functioning with other children. Scattered evidence is consistent with this notion. Girls ages 10–13 whose fathers were unemployed for a substantial time during the depression reported more strain in their relationships with age-mates, less self-confidence, and more concern about having friends than did girls from less deprived families (Elder, 1974). Time spent with peers and popularity, however, did not differ between girls in these two types of families. Perturbations traced to the father's unemployment were not evident among boys. The data suggest that the earlier maturing of the girls and their greater concern with grooming and attractiveness may underlie these findings. In addition, boys may have been buffered from the impact of their father's unemployment by their own increased work activities.

Divorce and its impact on socialization in the peer context have not been examined extensively with children ages 6–12. Studies of younger children (e.g., Hetherington, 1979) indicate that age-mate relationships suffer initially with the occurrence of divorce and that "recovery" coincides with stabilization of interpersonal relationships within the family. Young boys are more at risk for peer difficulties in the aftermath of divorce than young girls are—the latter apparently receiving more frequent emotional support from their teachers and mothers.

One interesting notion is that in middle childhood friends and other associates assist in the amelioration of the anxiety associated with divorce, in the resolution of loyalty conflicts, and in coping with the economic and practical exigencies deriving from the divorce. One investigation suggests these dynamics among boys but not girls (Wallerstein and Kelly, 1981). In this instance, school-age boys were able to turn to friends, seemingly to put distance between themselves and the troubled household. Girls, however, entered into friendships only when their relationships with their mothers were supportive. Otherwise, girls felt it necessary to abstain from interacting extensively with other children and were constrained from entering friendships. This sex difference was not evident among preschool children nor among adolescents in this investigation. Thus, the peer concomitants of divorce in middle childhood need further examination. The extent to which children use their friends instead of or in addition to their families for emotional and social support in middle childhood is an interesting question, especially since those adaptations may be sex linked.

Parents Versus Peers: The Issue of Cross-Pressures

The conventional wisdom stresses that the carryover from peer relationships to family relationships in middle childhood is mainly in the form of increased opposition between children and their parents. According to this argument, exposure to age-mates erodes the child's orientation to the family and establishes normative opposition. The evidence, however, does not suggest that these oppositions are especially intense before puberty; the opposition revolves mainly around antisocial norms. From one investigation (Berndt, 1979) with children in grades 3, 6, 9, and 11, the most striking results were (a) small decreases in conformity on prosocial issues with both parents and friends, (b) a gradual decline in conformity with parents in neutral situations but little change in conformity to peers, and (c) an increase in peer conformity to antisocial norms between grades 3 and 9 but not beyond. Children thus continue to use their parents as well as their friends as anchors for prosocial activity, disengaging from their parents mainly as normative anchors in antisocial activity. Other investigators have observed that peer-endorsed standards of misconduct become increasingly salient from grade 3 to 6 and from grade 6 to 8 but not beyond (Bixenstine et al., 1976). The major age changes occurring in response to cross-pressures thus involve antisocial norms; normative opposition increases as puberty approaches.

Changes in the general attitudes of children toward parents and peers are similar: (a) attitudes toward both parents and peers are more favorable than unfavorable at all ages, (b) the number of children reporting positive attitudes toward parents declines somewhat during middle childhood and an increase occurs again in middle adolescence, and (c) there is no general increase in the favorability of attitudes toward peers (Harris and Tseng, 1957). Other than a slight dip in the popularity of parents in preadolescence, there is thus no indication that parents are increasingly rejected nor peers increasingly accepted during middle childhood, although individual differences may be wide. By early adolescence, most individuals are able to synthesize their understandings and expectations of their parents and their peers.

Taken together, the literature connecting family and peer relationships is narrowly focused. We know the dimensions in child-rearing that predict sociometric status in middle childhood but little about changes in the family as these may bring about changes in child-child relationships. We know that normative concordance and discordance change with age, but we know little about the conditions that bring about these changes. We know little about the strategies that parents use for knowing where their children are, arranging contacts with other children, and coaching them in social skills. What attention is given by parents to children's thinking about their companions? Do parents contribute to the child's increasingly differentiated and "psychological" perceptions of their associates? Are there similarities between the theories of personality and attributional conventions used by parents with their children and those used by children with their associates? In what ways does intimacy within family relationships carry forward into the close relationships emerging between children and their friends? These issues cannot be addressed without concurrent studies in both the family and the peer contexts.

THE PEER CONTEXT AND THE SCHOOL

Classrooms are social units of major significance in Western cultures. Teachers establish the climate in these contexts, setting the conditions for social interactions and relationships. Child-child relationships, however, may constitute the "social frontier" in the classroom (Minuchin and Shapiro, 1983). In addition, child-child relationships within the classroom and the school are learning contexts; children teach things to one another, and these interactions contribute to children's growing understanding of the conditions under which people work and achieve.

Classroom Conditions and Peer Interactions

Numerous classroom conditions influence child-child interactions. The number of students, the physical arrangements, open versus traditional classroom structures, curriculum content, and teaching style are known to be correlated with variations in children's interactions with one another. Studies of these setting conditions are not easy to design, however, owing to the common confounding of these conditions with one another. For example, friendships and cliques are more numerous in large classes than in smaller ones (Hallinan, 1976) and group activity is more frequent. And these effects depend on the extent to which teachers organize small classes differently from larger ones (Smith and Glass, 1979).

Social interactions in open and traditional classrooms are not the same. Child-child contacts are more numerous in open classrooms, involving both work-oriented and social matters (Minuchin, 1976), and cross-sex and cross-age contacts are more frequent. Cooperative interactions are more common in open classrooms, since cooperative work opportunities are scheduled more often than in traditional settings. Cooperation in out-of-class situations, however, is also more common among children enrolled in open than in traditional classrooms. The induction of generalized cooperative expectations may thus be one outcome of experience in these situations. Nevertheless, the extent to which children create a cooperative ethic on their own in open classrooms is not known. Open classrooms provide a basis for friendship selection that differs from conditions in traditional classrooms. Hallinan (1976) found relatively rigid sociometric hierarchies in traditional classrooms along with clear-cut consensus concerning the identities of popular and isolated children. More diffuse social organizations were observed in open classrooms, with unreciprocated choices occurring less commonly and persisting over a shorter time than in traditional settings. Other investigators (Epstein, 1983) report that more students are selected and fewer are neglected as best friends in open than in traditional situations, with sociometric choices that are more commonly reciprocal. Open settings thus seem to encourage the continuing reorganization of close relationships to a greater extent than traditional settings do.

Curriculum Content

Curricular interventions centered on socialization consist of four main types: moral education, affective education, cooperative learning, and social skills training. Moral education has been studied in numerous variations ranging from the use of lessons that emphasize appropriate moral attitudes and behavior to the creation of "moral schools." Sometimes moral education consists of discussions about moral principles among the children themselves; other times it consists of the incorporation of moral issues into the curriculum in social studies or literature courses. Lockwood (1978) considered many of these studies to be poorly executed, although well-designed investigations demonstrate that (a) the direct discussion of moral dilemmas results in small advances in the maturity of moral reasoning among children; (b) these advances are more common among younger children than older ones, although individual differences are considerable; and (c) questions remain about the persistence of these advances and their manifestations in behavior. There has been little systematic evaluation of "moral schools" and virtually no effort to document the effects of moral education on child-child interactions. Many unresolved issues remain in evaluating moral education, including the effects of these interventions on children's interactions with one another. Moreover, these issues have been recognized for some time. It is nevertheless curious why we know so little about the effects of moral education on children's relationships with one another.

Model programs of affective education have been used with elementary school children, including the Human Development Program (Bessell and Palomares, 1970), the Affective Education Program (Newberg, 1980), and the Empathy Training Project (Feshbach, 1979). These and other models emphasize group dynamics, social values, and personal adjustment. Affective education has spread widely through U.S. schools, although definitive evaluation of the impact of these programs on child-child relationships is scarce. Again, Lockwood (1978) evaluated the evidence as showing positive effects on classroom behavior but inconsistent effects on self-esteem, self-concept, personal adjustment, and social values. The Empathy Training Project demonstrated decreases in rated aggression among children in the program and cognitive gains among those children showing the greatest gains in prosocial behavior and the greatest decreases in aggression. Further work with this program is needed, since its effects in nonexperimental settings have not been documented.

Cooperative learning environments promote friendly conversation, sharing, and helping among children, with the reverse being the case in competitive settings (Stendler et al., 1951). Peer tutoring occurs more frequently under cooperative than competitive conditions (DeVries and Edwards, 1972), and altruism occurs more frequently following cooperative than competitive experience (Johnson et al., 1976). In addition, attitudes toward oneself and one's coworkers are more positive as a consequence of cooperative rather than competitive experience. Cooperative classrooms are also more cohesive social units than competitive ones. Cohesiveness in racially integrated classrooms is evident when cooperative experiences prevail, although it is necessary for the contributions of minority children to be recognized as essential to class success in cooperative tasks in order for this to occur (Aronson, 1978).

Social skills training has been used with schoolchildren mainly in an effort to improve the status of isolated and withdrawn children. Numerous interventions have been tried, most based on the hypothesis that such children have difficulties in peer relationships because of their inadequate social skills, e.g., communication skills. Some of these interventions have been based on modeling; others have involved "unprogrammed" opportunities for withdrawn children to interact with better skilled companions. Coaching, which is an intervention that combines direct instruction, opportunities for rehearsal, and corrective feedback, has been used extensively.

The efficacy of modeling and unprogrammed socialization strategies has been demonstrated most thoroughly with preschool children. One investigation revealed that modeling techniques are effective in improving the social status of third- and fourth-grade children (Gresham and Nagle, 1980). Coaching studies have been variable in their outcomes (Combs and Slaby, 1977; Conger and Keane, 1981), but these techniques do seem to be effective in improving the sociometric status of isolated children and in some cases increase the frequency of the child's social contacts. Long-term maintenance of these outcomes has been assessed (Oden and Asher, 1977), although effects outside the school are unknown and effects on measures other than sociometric tests and classroom observations are not well documented. More serious, however, is the scarcity of developmental studies in this area. We know that training in social skills can be effective, but the extent to which outcomes are generalized outside the classroom and the extent to which developmental modifications need to be made in the interventions themselves remain to be evaluated.

Children as Teachers

Believed to benefit both tutor and tutee, peer tutoring has been viewed as a cost-effective instructional supplement in classrooms and as a basic element of socialization in certain cultures—e.g., the USSR. Empirical studies have mostly concerned the outcomes of the tutoring experiences—either for the child doing the teaching or for the child being taught. Benefits to the tutor are believed to include increases in motivation and task involvement that lead to gains in school achievement. Enhancement of self-esteem, prosocial behavior, and attitudes toward school are also cited as tutor benefits. The evidence is not entirely consistent in relation to these outcomes, and there is no obvious reason for the inconsistencies (Hartup, 1983). Tutee benefits are more clear-cut. The training of tutors must be carefully accomplished to maximize tutee outcomes, and maintenance regimes must be closely monitored (see Allen, 1976). Nevertheless, children clearly can teach one another a variety of subjects.

Very little effort has been made to determine the techniques that children use to teach one another. We know that children prefer to teach younger children and, conversely, to be taught by older children. Same-sex tutors and nonevaluative instructional conditions are also preferred (Lohman, 1969). Little is known about the strategies that children use in teaching one another or how strategies vary according to setting. The weight of the evidence suggests that peer teaching resembles adult pedagogics. Cooper et al. (1982) observed that issuing directives, describing the task, and making evaluative comments were the techniques most commonly used in classrooms; demonstration, labeling, pointing, questioning, praise, and criticism were common, too. Kindergarten children were more directive and intrusive than were second graders (especially when the children were asked to assumed a tutor role), but, since these observations were conducted in same-age situations, it is not clear whether the age differences were a function of the developmental status of the tutors, the tutees, or a combination of the two.

As it turns out, school-age children make a variety of instructional accommodations to the age of their tutees. Children instructing younger children use repetitions, strategic advice, progress checkups, direct assistance, and praise more frequently than children who instruct same-age tutees (Ludeke and Hartup, 1983). Children seem to possess "implicit theories" of teaching that assume younger children to require more cognitive structuring and more supportive and corrective feedback than same-age children. These theories have been studied only in relation to the actions of older children with younger associates, not vice versa; nothing is known about "upward" accommodations. Again, information is not available concerning these accommodations in relation to the magnitude of the age difference between children. Tutoring strategies are more elaborate when the difference between tutor and tutee is 4 years rather than 2 years, but nothing else is known.

Peer and Teacher Norms

Some investigators (Coleman, 1961) have regarded cross-pressures between peer and teacher norms as major sources of tension and dysfunction in schools. Certain evidence is consistent with this notion. Peer standards of misconduct are more readily endorsed by children when these endorsements will be secret than when they will be revealed to parents and teachers (Devereux, 1970). It is also clear that friends are sources of significant variance in the use of leisure time and decisions about whether to smoke or use drugs. But the issue is more complex. Surveys and questionnaires do not reveal that either middle childhood or adolescence is a stormy period of normative dissonance. The notion that adult-child relationships are understood by children to require self-control while peer relationships are based on self-indulgence and unbridled instinctual activity is not substantiated (Emmerich et al., 1971).

A small number of studies tell us about the tacit rules that children use to govern their behavior in the classroom and their notions about the manner in which classrooms work. These studies are largely normative and not addressed to the manner in which children acquire these rules. Nucci and Turiel (1978) observed social transgressions in nursery schools, interviewing the children about these incidents. Their distinctions between conventional transgressions (e.g., playing in the wrong place) and moral transgressions (e.g., taking something that belongs to someone else) agreed most of the time with the distinctions made by adults. Second, fifth, and seventh graders also make these distinctions (Nucci and Nucci, 1979), reacting to conventional transgressions with comments about the rules and to moral transgressions with arguments about the intrinsic implications of these events. Moreover, school rules are seen by children according to these same distinctions; for example, rules about harming others are distinguished from conventions about dress. Most children believed that rules about doing harm are necessary.

Teachers do not always react consistently to conventional and moral transgressions; conventional transgressions are sometimes treated as moral issues and vice versa (Nucci, 1979). The extent of these incongruities and their effects on children (especially their effects on the teacher's credibility) are unknown. And, more broadly, we know little about the effects of different patterns of school authority and organization on children's understanding of social rules and the internalization of responsibility norms.

Missing, too, is information about the child's distinctions between parent-endorsed norms and teacher-endorsed norms. Most of our attention has been given to the differentiation occurring in middle childhood between adult-endorsed (i.e., parents and teachers combined) and peer-endorsed norms. Nevertheless, parents are not teachers. Compliance demands, conduct expectations, and the contingencies involved in the expression of affection and support differ in families and classrooms. Consequently, a differentiated examination of children's reactions to adult authorities needs to be undertaken in order to understand the connections between the family and the peer system, on one hand, and between the peer system and the school, on the other. Investigations focused explicitly on concordance and discordance between teacher-child and parent-child interactions are essential.

METHODOLOGICAL ISSUES

Socialization in the peer context confronts the investigator with numerous difficulties in data gathering. Neither as open to surveillance as preschool children nor as articulate as adolescents, school-age children are elusive quarry. Trained observers are an alien presence in the peer context; children bar them from access to activities with their companions, and observers respect the child's rights to privacy. Moreover, the intrusion of observers into the peer context unquestionably alters the events that occur there.

Nevertheless, one can argue that we have not been as creative as we might be in examining child-child relationships outside the school. First, more effective use can be made of those individuals whom we select as informants. Children themselves can be involved in many ways other than to complete *Guess Who* tests, sociometric nominations, checklists, and questionnaires. Recent studies (Youniss, 1980) suggest that the child interview has been underused as a means of gathering data on a variety of timely and theoretically relevant issues; children between ages 6 and 12 can be articulate about many issues. The nuances of sexual socialization may never be revealed in response to questioning by adult examiners, but the structure of the child's theories of interpersonal relationships might be.

Children can be used as observers of their own actions and the actions of their companions. One cannot expect children to carry clipboards and stopwatches to their hideouts or their playgrounds, but child observations can be accumulated in other ways. For example, the telephone can be used to obtain information about recent events, the circumstances under which the events occurred, their content, and their outcomes. One would expect these observations not to be as "clean" as those of trained observers, but no one knows the exact strengths and weaknesses of this strategy. Telemetric techniques can be used, too—both to gather time-use information and to gather information about the attributions and affects experienced in social interactions. To be sure, these technologies do not solve the issues of access and privacy that were mentioned, but their use would extend the range of settings in which we work, thereby justifying an increased effort to use them.

Parents are underused observers of child-child relationships. Restricted to the events that they can observe and to what their children tell them, parents nevertheless accumulate a considerable fund of information about the activities of their children and their companions. Diary records, an ancient and underused technique, are once again being utilized in studies of social development (see Radke-Yarrow et al., 1983). Electronic modes of data collection can supplement the written record in these efforts. Also, interviews should not be written off as data-gathering devices.

What about the scientist as observer or experimenter? Participant observation may be feasible in studying informal groups of adolescents, especially if the observer is sufficiently youthful (see Sherif and Sherif, 1964). No 20-year-old graduate student, however, can pass as a 10-year-old. Only more creative (and ethical) uses of "lurking" can be encouraged. New work suggests that we have not exhausted the possibilities (see, for example, Thorne's 1982 ethnographic observations centered on cross-sex borderwork occurring in playgrounds, hallways, and school cafeterias). Shopping malls and other sites have been used for observations of adolescents. Why not use similar observational settings to capture certain aspects of peer interaction among school-age children? These strategies are labor-intensive, but there is little choice. "Quick-test" classroom assessments must give way to more complex and time-consuming assessments of child-child interactions outside the classroom.

A recurrent theme throughout this chapter is the need for developmental studies, either through cross-sectional or longitudinal analysis. Unfortunately, more is involved in this effort than the assessment of children at different ages or tracking the necessary cohorts over time. The construction of age-appropriate measures is a continuing need and a complicated business. Sufficient attention is almost never given to psychometric issues and the appropriateness of research designs for conducting developmental work in this area (see Fischer and Bullock, in this volume). Investigators cannot avoid these issues, however, any more than they can avoid the other complexities inherent in developmental research.

CONCLUSION

Middle childhood is a time of consolidation and extension of peer relationships rather than a time of beginnings. Children make their initial contacts with other children in early childhood; commerce with them, however, increases dramatically between ages 6 and 12. Younger children understand certain things about the intentions and motives of other children, but these are elaborated and used with increasing effectiveness in middle childhood. Similarly, communication and the coordination necessary for engaging in cooperation and competition are established in the preschool years, but new integrations emerge among schoolchildren. Within the peer context, new content (e.g., sex) enters into child-child interactions, but these issues are integrated into normative structures whose precursors trace back to early childhood. Preschool children possess nascent notions about friendships and their implications, whereas the capacities for engaging in intimate interactions seem to emerge between 6 and 12. Younger children interact distinctively with adults as contrasted with age-mates, but more elaborate differentiations emerge in middle childhood within the social networks of the family, the peer context, and the school. Parent-child interactions change to some extent as children increase their activities with other children. Certain normative oppositions arise between parents and their children; issues connected with supervision and compliance change. But parents and children work out accommodations to these differences without changing the basic nature of their relationships and usually without detachment from one another.

Middle childhood is a distinctive time. The years between 6 and 12 present new and insistent demands for working out accommodations with other children—i.e., individuals who are similar to the child in cognitive capacities, knowledge, and social experience. Children must construct arrangements for working and playing with similar individuals governed by rules that differ, in many ways, from the rules that govern their exchanges with dissimilar individuals. Children must construct interactions with others on an equal basis and sustain them across situations and across time. No theme, issue, or corner to be turned may thus be evident in child-child relationships during middle childhood, but children must construct a wider and more varied range of accommodations that "work" with age-mates. In short, coming to terms with the peer context is itself a major challenge in the years between 6 and 12.

REFERENCES

Achenbach, T.M., and Edelbrock, C.S.
  1981   Behavioral problems and competencies reported by parents of normal and disturbed children aged 4 through 16. *Monographs of the Society for Research in Child Development* 46(1, Entire No. 188).

Aiello, J.R., Nicosia, G., and Thompson, D.E.
  1979   Physiological, social, and behavioral consequences of crowding on children and adolescents. *Child Development* 50:195–202.

Allen, V.L.
  1976   *Children as Teachers: Theory and Research on Tutoring.* New York: Academic Press.

Allen, V.L., and Devin-Sheehan, L.
  1976   *Cross-Age Interaction in One-Teacher Schools.* Madison: University of Wisconsin, Research and Development Center for Cognitive Learning.

Aronson, E.
  1978   *The Jigsaw Classroom.* Beverly Hills, Calif.: Sage.

Asher, S.R., Singleton, L.C., and Taylor, A.R.
  1982   Acceptance Versus Friendship: A Longitudinal Study of Racial Integration. Paper presented at the meeting of the American Educational Research Association, New York.

Avellar, J., and Kagan, S.
  1976   Development of competitive behaviors in Anglo-American and Mexican-American children. *Psychological Reports* 39:191–198.

Banks, W.C.
  1976   White preference in blacks: A paradigm in search of a phenomenon. *Psychological Bulletin* 83:1179–1186.

Barker, R.G., and Wright, H.F.
  1951   *One Boy's Day.* New York: Harper Brothers.
  1955   *Midwest and Its Children.* New York: Harper & Row.

Bar-Tal, D., Raviv, A., and Leiser, T.
  1980   The development of altruistic behavior: empirical evidence. *Developmental Psychology* 16:516–524.

Berndt, T.J.
  1977   The effect of reciprocity norms on moral judgment and causal attribution. *Child Development* 48:1322–1330.
  1979   Developmental changes in conformity to peers and parents. *Developmental Psychology* 15:608–616.
  1981a   Age changes and changes over time in prosocial intentions and behavior between friends. *Developmental Psychology* 17:408–416.
  1981b   Effects of friendship on prosocial intentions and behavior. *Child Development* 52:636–643.

Berndt, T.J., Caparulo, B.K., McCartney, K., and Moore, A.
  1980   Processes and Outcomes of Social Influence in Children's Peer Groups. Unpublished manuscript, Yale University.

Berscheid, E., and Walster, E.H.
  1978   *Interpersonal Attraction.* Second ed. Reading, Mass.: Addison-Wesley.

Bessell, H., and Palomares, V.
  1970   *Methods in Human Development: Theory Manual.* Revised ed. San Diego, Calif.: Human Development Training Institute.

Bigelow, B.J.
  1977   Children's friendship expectations: A cognitive developmental study. *Child Development* 48:246–253.

Bixenstine, V.E., DeCorte, M.S., and Bixenstine, B.A.
1976   Conformity to peer-sponsored misconduct at four grade levels. *Developmental Psychology* 12:226–236.

Brady, J.E., Newcomb, A.F., and Hartup, W.W.
1983   Context and companion as determinants of cooperation and competition in middle childhood. *Journal of Experimental Child Psychology* 36:396–412.

Britt, D.W., and Campbell, E.Q.
1977   Assessing the linkage of norms, environments, and deviance. *Social Forces* 56:532–550.

Brody, G.H., Graziano, W.G., and Musser, L.M.
In   Familiarity and children's behavior in same-age and mixed-age peer groups. *Developmental*
press   *Psychology*.

Brody, G.H., Stoneman, Z., and MacKinnon, C.E.
1982   Role asymmetries in interactions among school-aged children, their younger siblings, and their friends. *Child Development* 53:1364–1370.

Byrne, D., and Griffitt, W.B.
1966   A developmental investigation of the law of attraction. *Journal of Personality and Social Psychology* 4:699–702.

Cantor, G.N., and Kubose, S.K.
1969   Preschool children's ratings of familiarized and non-familiarized visual stimuli. *Journal of Experimental Child Psychology* 8:74–81.

Coie, J.D., and Dodge, K.A.
1983   Continuities and changes in children's social status: A five-year longitudinal study. *Merrill-Palmer Quarterly* 29:261–282.

Coie, J.D., and Kupersmidt, J.B.
1983   A behavioral analysis of emerging social status in boys' groups. *Child Development* 54:1400–1416.

Coie, J.D., Dodge, K.A., and Coppotelli, H.
1982   Dimensions and types of social status: A cross-age perspective. *Developmental Psychology* 18:557–570.

Coleman, J.S.
1961   *The Adolescent Society.* New York: Free Press.

Combs, M.L., and Slaby, D.A.
1977   Social skills training with children. In B. Lahey and A. Kazdin, eds., *Advances in Clinical Child Psychology.* Vol. 1. New York: Plenum Press.

Conger, J.D., and Keane, S.P.
1981   Social skills intervention in the treatment of isolated or withdrawn children. *Psychological Bulletin* 90:478–495.

Conger, J.J., and Miller, W.C.
1966   *Personality, Social Class, and Delinquency.* New York: John Wiley & Sons.

Cook, T.P., Goldman, J.A., and Olczak, P.V.
1978   The relationship between self-esteem and interpersonal attraction in children. *Journal of Genetic Psychology* 132:149–150.

Cooper, C.R., Ayers-Lopez, S., and Marquis, A.
1982   Children's discourse during peer learning in experimental and naturalistic situations. *Discourse Processes* 5:177–191.

Cowen, E.L., Pederson, A., Babijian, H., Izzo, L.D., and Trost, M.A.
1973   Long-term follow-up of early detected vulnerable children. *Journal of Consulting and Clinical Psychology* 41:438–446.

Cox, S.H.
1966   Family Background Effects on Personality Development and Social Acceptance. Unpublished doctoral dissertation, Texas Christian University.

Dembo, R., Schmeidler, J., and Burgos, W.
1979   Factors in the drug involvement of inner city junior high youths: A discriminant analysis. *International Journal of Social Psychology* 25:92–103.
Devereux, E.C.
1970   The role of peer-group experience in moral development. In J.P. Hill, ed., *Minnesota Symposia on Child Psychology*. Vol. 4. Minneapolis: University of Minnesota Press.
DeVries, D.L., and Edwards, K.J.
1972   *Learning Games and Student Teams: Their Effects on Classroom Processes*. Report no. 142. Baltimore, Md.: Center for School Organization of Schools, Johns Hopkins University.
Dodge, K.A.
1980   Social cognition and children's aggressive behavior. *Child Development* 51:162–170.
Dodge, K.A., and Frame, C.L.
1982   Social cognitive biases and deficits in aggressive boys. *Child Development* 53:620–635.
Dodge, K.A., Schlundt, D.C., Schocken, I., and Delugach, J.D.
1983   Social competence and children's sociometric status: The role of peer group entry strategies. *Merrill-Palmer Quarterly* 29:309–336.
Eifermann, H.R.
1971   *Determinants of Children's Game Styles*. Jerusalem: Israel Academy of Sciences.
Elder, G.
1974   *Children of the Great Depression*. Chicago: University of Chicago Press.
Elkins, D.
1958   Some factors related to the choice status of ninety eighth-grade children in a school society. *Genetic Psychology Monographs* 58:2076–2272.
Emmerich, W., Goldman, K.S., and Shore, R.E.
1971   Differentiation and development of social norms. *Journal of Personality and Social Psychology* 18:323–353.
Epstein, J.L.
1983   Selection of friends in differently organized schools and classrooms. In J.L. Epstein and N. Kareweit, eds., *Friends in School: Patterns of Selection and Influence in Secondary Schools*. New York: Academic Press.
In   Choice of friends over the life-span: Developmental and environmental influences. In
press   E. Mueller and C. Cooper, eds., *Peer Relations: Process and Outcomes*. New York: Academic Press.
Feshbach, N.D.
1979   Empathy training: A field study in affective education. In S. Feshbach and A. Frazek, eds., *Aggression and Behavior Change: Biological and Social Processes*. New York: Praeger.
Fine, G.A.
1980   The natural history of preadolescent friendship groups. In H. Foot, A. Chapman, and J. Smith, eds., *Friendship and Social Relations in Children*. New York: John Wiley & Sons.
Foot, H.C., Chapman, A.J., and Smith, J.R.
1977   Friendship and social responsiveness in boys and girls. *Journal of Personality and Social Psychology* 35:401–411.
Girgus, J.S., and Wolf, J.
1975   Age changes in the ability to encode social class. *Developmental Psychology* 11:118.
Gottman, J., Gonzo, J., and Rasmussen, B.
1975   Social interaction, social competence, and friendship in children. *Child Development* 45:709–718.
Graziano, W., French, D., Brownell, C., and Hartup, W.W.
1976   Peer interaction in same and mixed-age triads in relation to chronological age and incentive condition. *Child Development* 47:707–714.

Graziano, W., Musser, L.M., and Brody, G.H.
1980   Children's Social Cognitions and Preferences Regarding Younger and Older Peers. Unpublished manuscript, University of Georgia.
Gresham, F.M., and Nagle, R.J.
1980   Social skills training with children: Responsiveness to modeling and coaching as a function of peer orientation. *Journal of Consulting and Clinical Psychology* 48:718–729.
Grossman, B., and Wrighter, J.
1948   The relationship between selection-rejection and intelligence, social status, and personality among sixth-grade children. *Sociometry* 11:346–355.
Gump, P., Schoggen, P., and Redl, F.
1957   The camp milieu and its immediate effects. *Journal of Social Issues* 13:40–46.
Hallinan, M.T.
1976   Friendship patterns in open and traditional classrooms. *Sociology of Education* 49:254–265.
1980   Patterns of cliquing among youth. In H.C. Foot, A.J. Chapman, and J.R. Smith, eds., *Friendship and Peer Relations in Children*. New York: John Wiley & Sons.
Hare, A.P.
1953   Small group discussions with participatory and supervisory leadership. *Journal of Abnormal and Social Psychology* 48:273–275.
Harris, D.B., and Tseng, S.
1957   Children's attitudes towards peers and parents as revealed by sentence completions. *Child Development* 28:401–411.
Hartup, W.W.
1974   Aggression in childhood: Developmental perspectives. *American Psychologist* 29:226–341.
1983   Peer relations. In P.H. Mussen, ed., *Handbook of Child Psychology*. Vol. 4, E.M. Hetherington (Vol. ed.), *Socialization, Personality and Social Development*. New York: John Wiley & Sons.
Hartup, W.W., Brady, J.E., and Newcomb, A.F.
1983   Social cognition and social interaction in childhood. In E.T. Higgins, D.N. Ruble, and W.W. Hartup, eds., *Social Cognition and Social Development*. New York: Cambridge University Press.
Hetherington, E.M.
1979   Divorce: A child's perspective. *American Psychologist* 34:851–858.
Hinde, R.A.
1976   On describing relationships. *Journal of Child Psychology and Psychiatry* 17:1–19.
Hoffman, L.W.
1961   The father's role in the family and the child's peer-group adjustment. *Merrill-Palmer Quarterly* 7:97–105.
Horowitz, F.D.
1962   The relationship of anxiety, self-concept, and sociometric status among fourth, fifth and sixth grade children. *Journal of Abnormal and Social Psychology* 65:212–214.
Huba, G.J., Wingard, J.A., and Bentler, P.M.
1979   Beginning adolescent drug use and peer and adult interaction patterns. *Journal of Consulting and Clinical Psychology* 47:265–276.
Johnson, D.W., Johnson, R.T., Johnson, J., and Anderson, D.
1976   Effects of cooperative versus individualized instruction on student prosocial behavior, attitudes toward learning, and achievement. *Journal of Educational Psychology* 68:446–452.
Kagan, S., Zahn, G.L., and Gealy, J.
1977   Competition and school achievement among Anglo-American and Mexican-American children. *Journal of Educational Psychology* 69:432–441.

278   DEVELOPMENT DURING MIDDLE CHILDHOOD

Kandel, D.B.
1978   Similarity in real-life adolescent friendship pairs. *Journal of Personality and Social Psychology* 36:306–312.
Karabenick, J.D., and Miller, S.A.
1977   The effects of age, sex, and listener feedback on grade school children's referential communication. *Child Development* 48:678–683.
Keasey, C.B.
1971   Social participation as a factor in the moral development of preadolescents. *Developmental Psychology* 5:216–220.
Kinsey, A.C., Pomeroy, W.B., and Martin, C.E.
1948   *Sexual Behavior in the Human Male.* Philadelphia: W.B. Saunders.
Ladd, G.W.
1983   Social networks of popular, average, and rejected children in school settings. *Merrill-Palmer Quarterly* 29:283–308.
Ladd, G.W., and Oden, S.
1979   The relationship between peer acceptance and children's ideas about helpfulness. *Child Development* 50:402–408.
Leimbach, M.P., and Hartup, W.W.
1981   Forming cooperative coalitions during a competitive game in same-sex and mixed-sex triads. *Journal of Genetic Psychology* 139:165–171.
Lever, J.
1976   Sex differences in the games children play. *Social Problems* 23:479–487.
Levine, M.H., and Sutton-Smith, B.
1979   Effects of age, sex, and task on visual behavior during dyadic interaction. *Developmental Psychology* 9:400–405.
Livesley, W.J., and Bromley, D.B.
1973   *Person Perception in Childhood and Adolescence.* New York: John Wiley & Sons.
Lockwood, A.
1978   The effects of values clarification and moral development curricula on school age subjects: A critical review of recent research. *Review of Educational Research* 48:325–381.
Lohman, J.E.
1969   Age, Sex, Socioeconomic Status and Youths' Relationships With Older and Younger Peers. Unpublished doctoral dissertation, University of Michigan.
Lubin, D., and Forbes, D.
1981   Motivational and Peer Culture Issues in Reasoning-Behavioral Reactions. Paper presented at the meetings of the Society for Research in Child Development, Boston, April.
Ludeke, R.J., and Hartup, W.W.
1983   Teaching behaviors of nine- and eleven-year-old girls in same- and mixed-age situations. *Journal of Educational Psychology* 75:908–914.
Maltz, D.N., and Barker, R.A.
In   A cultural approach to male-female miscommunication. In J.A. Gumperz, ed., *Com-*
press   *munication, Language, and Social Inequality.*
McClintock, C.G.
1974   Development of social motives in Anglo-American and Mexican-American children. *Journal of Personality and Social Psychology* 29:348–354.
McClintock, C.G., and Moskowitz, J.M.
1976   Children's preferences for individualistic, cooperative, and competitive outcomes. *Journal of Personality and Social Psychology* 34:543–555.
McClintock, C.G., Moskowitz, J.M., and McClintock, E.
1977   Variations in preferences of individualistic, competitive, and cooperative outcomes as a function of age, game class, and task in nursery school children. *Child Development* 48:1080–1085.

Medrich, E.A., Rosen, J., Rubin, V., and Buckley, S.
1982   *The Serious Business of Growing Up.* Berkeley: University of California Press.
Minuchin, P.
1976   Differential Use of the Open Classroom: A Study of Explanatory and Cautious Children. Final Report, National Institute of Education.
Minuchin, P.P., and Shapiro, E.K.
1983   The school as a context for social development. In P.H. Mussen, ed., *Handbook of Child Psychology.* Vol. 4, E.M. Hetherington (Vol. ed.), *Socialization, Personality, and Social Development.* New York: John Wiley & Sons.
Montemayor, R., and Van Komen, R.
1980   Age segregation of adolescents in and out of school. *Journal of Youth and Adolescence* 9:371–381.
Newberg, N.
1980   Affective Education Addresses the Basics. Paper presented at the meetings of the American Education Research Association, Boston.
Newcomb, A.F., and Brady, J.E.
1982   Mutuality in boy's friendship relations. *Child Development* 53:392–395.
Newcomb, A.F., Brady, J.E., and Hartup, W.W.
1979   Friendship and incentive condition as determinants of children's task-oriented social behavior. *Child Development* 50:878–881.
Newcomb, A.F., Junenemann, A., and Meister, N.
1982   Acquaintanceship Formation Among Popular and Rejected Children. Unpublished manuscript, Michigan State University.
Newcomb, A.F., and Meister, N.
1982   Acquaintanceship Processes as a Function of Sociometric Status in School-Age Children. Unpublished manuscript, Michigan State University.
Newcomb, A.F., and Rogosch, F.
1982   The Influence of Social Reputation on the Social Relations of Rejected and Isolated Children. Unpublished manuscript, Michigan State University.
Nucci, L.
1979   Conceptual Development in the Moral and Social-Conventional Domains: Implications for Social Education. Paper presented at the meetings of the American Educational Research Association, San Francisco.
Nucci, L., and Nucci, M.S.
1979   Social Interactions and the Development of Moral and Societal Concepts. Paper presented at the meetings of the Society for Research in Child Development, San Francisco.
Nucci, L.P., and Turiel, E.
1979   Social interactions and the development of social concepts in preschool children. *Child Development* 49:400–407.
Oden, S., and Asher, S.R.
1977   Coaching children in social skills for friendship making. *Child Development* 48:494–506.
Parke, R.D., and Slaby, R.G.
1983   The development of aggression. In P.H. Mussen, ed., *Handbook of Child Psychology.* Vol. 4, E.M. Hetherington (Vol. ed.), *Socialization, Personality, and Social Development.* New York: John Wiley & Sons.
Piaget, J.
1932   *The Moral Judgment of the Child.* Glencoe, Ill.: Free Press.
Putallaz, M., and Gottman, J.M.
1981   An interactional model of children's entry into peer groups. *Child Development* 52:986–994.

Radke-Yarrow, M., Zahn-Waxler, C., and Chapman, M.
1983   Children's prosocial dispositions and behavior. In P.H. Mussen, ed., *Handbook of Child Psychology*. Vol. 4, E.M. Hetherington (Vol. ed.), *Socialization, Personality and Social Development*. New York: John Wiley & Sons.
Reese, H.W.
1961   Relationship between self-acceptance and sociometric choice. *Journal of Abnormal and Social Psychology* 62:472–474.
Renshaw, P.D., and Asher, S.R.
1983   Children's goals and strategies for social interaction. *Merrill-Palmer Quarterly* 29:353–374.
Richman, N., Stevenson, J.E., and Graham, P.J.
1982   *Preschool to School: A Behavioral Study*. London: Academic Press.
Roff, M.
1963   Childhood social interaction and young adult psychosis. *Journal of Clinical Psychology* 19:152–157.
Rubin, K.H., Daniels-Beirniss, T., and Bream, L.
In   Social isolation and social problem-solving: A longitudinal study. *Journal of Consulting*
press   *and Clinical Psychology*.
Savin-Williams, R.C.
1979   Dominance hierarchies in groups of early adolescents. *Child Development* 50:442–454.
Sears, P.S., and Sherman, V.S.
1964   *In Pursuit of Self Esteem*. Belmont, Calif.: Wadsworth.
Selman, R.L.
1980   *The Growth of Interpersonal Understanding*. New York: Academic Press.
Sgan, M.L., and Pickert, S.M.
1980   Cross-sex and same-sex assertive bids in a cooperative group task. *Child Development* 54:928–934.
Shantz, C.U.
1983   Social cognition. In P.H. Mussen, ed., *Handbook of Child Psychology*. Vol. 3, J.H. Flavell and E.M. Mankman (Vol. eds.), *Cognitive Development*. New York: John Wiley & Sons.
Sherif, M., and Sherif, C.W.
1964   *Reference Groups*. New York: Harper & Row.
Sherif, M., Harvey, O.J., White, B.J., Hood, W.R., and Sherif, C.W.
1961   *Intergroup Conflict and Cooperation: The Robbers Cave Experiment*. Norman: University of Oklahoma Press.
Singleton, L.C., and Asher, S.R.
1979   Racial integration and children's peer preferences: An investigation of developmental and cohort differences. *Child Development* 50:936–941.
Skarin, K., and Moely, B.E.
1976   Altruistic behavior: An analysis of age and sex difference. *Child Development* 47:1159–1165.
Smith, A.J.
1960   A developmental study of group processes. *Journal of Genetic Psychology* 97:29–39.
Smith, H.W.
1973   Some developmental interpersonal dynamics through childhood. *American Sociological Review* 38:543–352.
Smith, M.L., and Glass, G.V.
1979   *Relationship of Class Size to Classroom Processes, Teacher Satisfaction and Pupil Affect: A Meta-Analysis*. San Francisco: Far West Laboratory for Educational Research and Development.

Smith, P.K., and Connolly, K.J.
1977   Social and aggressive behavior in preschool children as a function of crowding. *Social Science Information* 16:601–620.
Smollar, J., and Youniss, J.
1982   Social Development Through Friendship. In K.H. Rubin and H.S. Ross, eds., *Peer Relationships and Social Skills in Childhood*. New York: Springer-Verlag.
Spencer, M.B.
1981   Personal-Social Adjustment of Minority Children. Emory University, Final report, Project No. 5-Ro1-Mh 31106.
Staub, E., and Noerenberg, H.
1981   Property rights, deservingness, reciprocity, friendship: The transactional character of children's sharing behavior. *Journal of Personality and Social Psychology* 40:271–289.
Stendler, C.B., Damrin, D., and Haines, A.C.
1951   Studies in cooperation and competition: I. The effects of working for group and individual rewards on the social climate of children's groups. *Journal of Genetic Psychology* 40:271–289.
Strayer, F.F., and Strayer, J.
1976   An ethological analysis of social agonism and dominance relations among preschool children. *Child Development* 47:980–989.
Sullivan, H.S.
1953   *The Interpersonal Theory of Psychiatry*. New York: Norton.
Sundby, H.S., and Kreyberg, P.C.
1968   *Prognosis in Child Psychiatry*. Baltimore: Williams and Wilkins.
Thelen, M.H., and Kirkland, K.D.
1976   On status and being imitated: Effects on reciprocal imitation and attraction. *Journal of Personality and Social Psychology* 33:691–697.
Thorne, B.
1982   Girls and Boys Together . . . But Mostly Apart: Gender Arrangements in Elementary Schools. Unpublished manuscript, Michigan State University.
Tuma, N.B., and Hallinan, M.T.
1977   The Effects of Similarity and Status on Change in School-Children's Friendships. Unpublished manuscript, Stanford University.
Wallerstein, J.S., and Kelly, J.B.
1981   *Surviving the Breakup: How Children and Parents Cope With Divorce*. New York: Basic Books.
Waters, E., Wippman, J., and Sroufe, L.A.
1979   Attachment, positive affect and competence in the peer group: Two studies in construct validation. *Child Development* 50:821–829.
Watt, N., and Lubensky, A.
1976   Childhood roots of schizophrenia. *Journal of Consulting and Clinical Psychology* 44:363–375.
Weisner, T.S.
1982   Sibling interdependence and child caretaking: A cross-cultural view. In M.E. Lamb and B. Sutton-Smith, eds., *Sibling Relationships*. Hillsdale, N.J.: Lawrence Erlbaum.
West, D.J., and Farrington, D.P.
1973   *Who Becomes Delinquent?* London: Heinemann.
Whiting, B.B., and Whiting, J.W.M.
1975   *Children of Six Cultures*. Cambridge, Mass.: Harvard University Press.
Winder, C.L., and Rau, L.
1962   Parental attitudes associated with social deviance in preadolescent boys. *Journal of Abnormal and Social Psychology* 64:418–424.

Youniss, J.
    1980   Parents and Peers in Social Development: A Sullivan-Piaget Perspective. Chicago: University
            of Chicago Press.
Zajonc, R.B.
    1968   Attitudinal effects of mere exposure. Journal of Personality and Social Psychology Monographs
            9(2, Pt. 2), 1–27.

CHAPTER 7

School and Children: The Middle Childhood Years

Edgar G. Epps and Sylvia F. Smith

This chapter is primarily concerned with the effects of schools and schooling on children ages 6–12. However, because formal schooling in the United States and many other nations frequently begins between ages 4 and 5, some of the research and theory reviewed encompasses this earlier period as well.

Throughout the world the most widely recognized function of elementary schools is to provide opportunities for children to acquire at least basic competencies in reading, writing, and computation. Less frequently discussed by educators, but of equal importance, is the fact that schools serve other less obvious societal functions, including (1) providing custodial care while parents work or pursue personal interests; (2) delaying children's entrance into the work force; (3) encouraging the development of social competencies; and (4) sorting and selecting for the purpose of impeding or maintaining established social roles, organizations, and institutions (Goodlad, 1973). Thus, the schooling process has a significant impact on the development of children both academically and societally.

The effects of schooling on children may not be obvious in societies in which the vast majority attend school. However, in countries in which smaller proportions of the population attend school, the effects are striking (Stevenson et al., 1978). World Bank (1980) records indicate that 64 percent of the children ages 6–11 in developing countries attended school in 1977, compared with 94 percent of the same-age children in developed countries. Substantial differences in literacy and other cognitive skills appear[1] when persons who have attended at least elementary school are compared with those who have not been exposed to formal education (Sharp et al., 1979; Stevenson et al. 1978). In developing nations a major concern is expanding access to formal education to reach a larger proportion of school-age children.

In cross-national comparisons of science achievement, secondary-level American students do not perform as well as students from Japan, Hungary, Australia, New Zealand, and the Federal Republic of Germany. However, data from the International Association for the Evaluation of Educational Achievement (Walberg, 1981) indicate that American 10-year-olds are achieving at approximately the average level for developed nations (although still far behind Japan). There is some evidence that parental expectations may account for the achievement advantages of Japanese students (Hess et al., 1980).

During these important middle childhood years, children are thought to be functioning developmentally at what Piaget termed the concrete and formal operational stages (see Fischer and Bullock, in this volume). During this phase, basic literacy as well as computational and conceptual skills are acquired. Children also develop relatively permanent attitudes about schools and learning, including study habits. A child's academic and social self-concepts develop incrementally with age (Benham et al., 1980), and the pressures of peer influence begin to emerge during the early school years (Hartup, in this volume; Minuchin and Shapiro, 1983).

Although varying in content and purpose across countries, the most universally recognized function of schools is to impart knowledge and skills that will enable the learner to participate successfully in the society's institutions. At this level schools are concerned with the development of reading, writing, speaking, and computational skills. In most instances teachers instruct children in groups at a given age or grade level, using a specified set of instructional materials, and the academic outcomes of this overt function are assigned highest priority.

With regard to socialization, schools by virtue of their structure also facilitate normative outcomes (Dreeben, 1968; Jackson, 1968). Dreeben contends that schools provide children with the psychological capacities needed for participation in societal institutions by fostering independence, achievement, universalisms, and specificity. Bowles (1975) sees the school's function as more allocative and argues that its main purpose is to perpetuate society's economic and class structures. These themes recur throughout this chapter.

Schooling occurs in the context of the society at large; therefore, its academic and normative functions are not independent of other societal institutions. The interaction between the home or family and the school is the most obvious example of social-system interaction, especially because for children of this age much of the parents' monitoring and control functions is taken over by the school during the main part of the day, and even before and after school in some areas.

This chapter discusses the school environment, the cognitive and affective effects of schooling, both manifest and latent, and schools and children in the context of family influence (socioeconomic background, home background, and the like). Issues related to school desegregation and bilingualism are also discussed. Wherever possible, we point out methodological weaknesses in the existing research and list issues for future investigation. We do not cover the literature on teaching methods in any detail, although instructional approaches that appear to be important conceptually and methodologically (e.g., Barr and Dreeben, 1983; Bloom, 1976) are discussed. And an issue of great current interest, mainstreaming of handicapped children, is not discussed (see Heller et al., 1982, and Johnson et al., 1983).

THE SCHOOL ENVIRONMENT

In this section we briefly discuss issues related to children's lives in the context of the school, especially school climate and teacher expectations, from a number of research perspectives.

Input-Output Analysis

The work of Coleman et al. (1966) and Jencks et al. (1972), which are examples of input-output formulations, have generally been interpreted to mean that differences in school environments are minimal at best and largely ineffective in influencing outcomes. These conclusions are based primarily on research with secondary school students. Other studies of the same genre suggest that elementary schools do have differential effects on student outcomes (Brookover et al., 1979; Edmonds, 1979; Entwisle and Hayduk, 1982; Murnane, 1975; Rutter, 1983; Rutter et al., 1979; Summers and Wolfe, 1977).

Alternative interpretations have been suggested. For example, Heyns (1978) and McPartland and Karweit (1979) suggested that the findings on school environments can be interpreted to mean that school environments provide similar educational experiences for all students and that schools are for the most part equally effective in influencing most learning outcomes.

At any rate, school effects at the elementary level have been studied much less than those at the secondary level, although the organization and locations of the two levels of schools differ in the extreme. In contrast to secondary schools, in elementary schools children often remain in one classroom with one teacher for most of the day. And in the United States, elementary schools are most often neighborhood schools, a circumstance that, for middle-class white students, leads to a high degree of concordance between home and school environments—perhaps potentiating effects of both. For lower-class and minority students, however, there is frequently a lack of congruence between home and school environments (see the section below on race and ethnicity).

Social-System Variables

From another perspective the school can be seen as a "cultural system of social relationships among family, teachers, students and peers" (Anderson, 1982:382). Studies with this focus examine how the various components in the "cultural system" of school interact to influence both cognitive and normative outcomes. Focal variables include ability grouping, classroom organization, and teacher-student relationships.

The effect of ability grouping on achievement remains debatable. While some studies report that no significant relationship exists, Brookover et al. (1979), Edmonds and Fredericksen (1978), McDill and Rigsby (1973), Sörensen (1970), and Weber (1971) indicate that the more homogeneous the group the higher the achievement.

Barr and Dreeben (1983) studied the ways teachers organized first-grade classrooms for reading instruction. They found that the number of instructional groups and the size of the groups were determined by such characteristics as class size and number of low-aptitude students in a classroom. Barr and Dreeben also observed that teachers moved children from group to group during the school year largely on the basis of how well they performed. The primary determinant of an individual's group placement was aptitude (reading readiness in this study). The average aptitude of the instructional group was a major determinant of how much material was covered in reading texts and ultimately how much the children learned.

Beckerman and Good (1981) found that the ratio of high- to low-aptitude students in a classroom affected the achievement of both. High- and low-aptitude third- and fourth-graders had greater achievement gains in classrooms in which more than one-third were high aptitude. Barr and Dreeben (1983) contend, however, that the number of low-aptitude students in a classroom is more important than the proportion. Studies by Eder (1981), Leiter (1983), and Rowan and Miracle (1983) also indicate that grouping strategies and the distribution of abilities have profound effects on student achievement. This topic deserves much more attention.

The degree and type of teacher-student interaction and the extent to which students interact in school activities and share in the decision-making process are related to positive effects. Despite these findings, Goodlad (1983) noted that "above the primary level, students experience few classroom activities that involve their own goal setting, problem solving, collaborative learning, autonomous thinking, creativity, and the like" (p. 305). This absence of student-initiated learning tasks may provide one explanation for Harter's (1981) finding that children's mastery motivation declines from grade 3 to grade 9.

Milieu Variables

Other research indicates that strong relationships, both positive and negative, apparently exist between the values and beliefs of various groups within a school and its climate and between values and student outcomes. Teacher commitment to and emphasis on students' academic achievement, rewards and praise, clear goal definition, peer norms, and group cooperation influence both school climate and student outcomes (Brookover et al., 1979; Edmonds, 1979; Rutter et al., 1979). Teacher characteristics (McDill and Rigsby, 1973; Rutter et al., 1979), teacher morale (Brookover and Lezotte, 1979; Ellett et al., 1977), student body characteristics (Brookover et al., 1979; Rutter et al., 1979), and student morale (Edmonds, 1979) are likely to act individually and in combination.

While research denies significant relationships between teacher characteristics, such as teacher preparation or salary and student outcomes, positive correlations have been noted between school climate as perceived by elementary children (Ellett et al., 1977) and student attendance and achievement at both the elementary and secondary levels. Likewise, Brookover et al. (1979) and Edmonds (1979) found positive relationships between student morale and achievement and between student morale and academic self-concept. Brookover et al. (1979) also reported that such student characteristics as race and socioeconomic status account for a smaller proportion of the variance in achievement than is accounted for by climate variables.

The Ecological Perspective

Ecological studies combine ecological elements from the input-output economists with social-system, culture, and milieu variables. Effects of both school (its physical characteristics) and schooling (the process) are at issue in such investigations.

In general, studies investigating the effect of ecological variables on student outcomes have produced low or inconsistent correlations. Rutter et al.

(1979) reported a positive relationship between decoration and care of the building and student achievement, but no relationship was found between the age of the building and achievement.

Findings with respect to effects of class and school size are mixed. As expected, small schools have been found to have better student behavior (Anderson, 1982). Although contrary to McDill and Rigsby (1973) and Rutter et al. (1979), Anderson (1982) reported that neither class nor school size affected learning outcomes. This could be due to a lack of agreement over the definitions of size terms (e.g., what constitutes small or large) and inconsistencies in measurement. Glass and Smith (1978), from a statistical research synthesis of a large number of studies, concluded that differences in achievement are greatest in a range of class sizes between 10 and 20. Glass et al. (1982) reviewed and critiqued the literature on class size and provided recommendations for research and policy.

Other important considerations include investigating the possibility of threshold effects for specific subgroups of students (e.g., those of lower ability) and possible connections between class size and instructional methods. Rutter (1983) and Summers and Wolfe (1977) contend that it is likely that less-able students will benefit from significant reductions (classes consisting of fewer than 20 pupils) in class size. Further investigation into effective ways of making such changes without detrimentally affecting average and above-average students is needed.

Teacher Behaviors and Expectations

Teacher behaviors and expectations, although not always systematically included, can be classified under the ecological approach. Although this research has a number of conceptual and methodological weaknesses, this continues to be an important line of investigation. During the 1960s and early 1970s, studies focusing on the influences of teacher behaviors and expectations on children's academic achievement and self-concept began to take shape. Studies such as those undertaken by Leacock (1969), Rist (1970), and Rosenthal and Jacobson (1968) suggested that teacher expectations can strongly influence both the cognitive and the affective development of children. On the basis of observing a single classroom of black children, Rist noted that by the eighth day of kindergarten the teacher had assigned the children to tables that reflected social-class groupings. These groupings persisted into second grade, and throughout this period teachers tended to favor the more advantaged children.

Much of the early expectancy research is thought to be flawed (see, for example, Elashoff and Snow, 1971), and a number of later studies have focused on whether teachers behave differently toward high- and low-achieving students (e.g., Brophy and Good, 1974). Although differential behavior is often observed, its precise relationship to student achievement remains unclear.

With a sample of 17,163 students representing 38 schools ranging in grade levels from elementary through high school, Goodlad et al. (1979) found that positive teacher behavior, such as praise, guidance, and encouragement, were strongest in the elementary years. By the senior year of high school, these encouraging behaviors declined as much as 50 percent in comparison to the early elementary school years (Benham et al., 1980).

Entwisle and Hayduk (1982) examined teacher, student, and parent expectations in three elementary schools (one middle-class and two lower-class schools). Their results raise many questions that should lead to further research. For example, they found that initial expectations of lower-class children were higher than those of middle-class children and that lower-class parents as well had overoptimistic expectations for their children's performance. There was a striking mismatch between lower-class parents' and children's expectations and the children's performance as assessed by teachers' marks. Furthermore, both parents and children in the middle-class school were more likely to change their expectations on the basis of feedback in the form of children's marks than were parents and children in the lower-class schools. The authors noted that far too little attention has been paid to what actually happens when marks are assigned. How do parents and children react? What is the effect on subsequent expectations and behaviors?

Research on social climate and teacher behavior suffers from many problems, especially a failure to conceptualize variables in terms of testable theory. Anderson (1982) made a number of recommendations with which we concur: more longitudinal research, improved statistical analysis, a focus on variables that are causally relevant to outcomes, and consideration of multiple outcomes and their interrelationships, since nonacademic outcomes may be important in mediating the outcome of achievement. In general, a diversity of research methods is called for. The use of in-depth observation, for example, could compensate for the fragmentary evidence on school climate typically yielded by surveys. Experimental methods, when feasible, are of course optimal. As Rutter et al. (1979:180) noted, "The only way to be sure that school practices actually influence children's behavior and attainments is to alter those practices and then determine if this results in changes in the children's progress."

EFFECTS OF SCHOOLING

Research on the effects of schooling has been approached from several distinct perspectives that overlap those identified in the previous section on school environment. Because subtle differences in conceptualization are important, a few of the predominant perspectives are mentioned for the sake of clarity.

Research on school production focuses on the relationship between the workings of schools and individual learning (Barr and Dreeben, 1983). More specifically, an attempt is made to identify what in the organization of schools leads to increments in individual learning outcomes. Such analyses generally reflect an economist's formulation of productivity. Formulations predicated on this theoretical approach suffer several limitations, including disagreement among researchers on whether the productive unit is the educational organization or the individual and at what level in the organization production takes place. Other conceptual weaknesses in this approach include (1) confusion over who or what the productive unit is; (2) failure to explain details of the schooling process and, as a result, failure to show how various parts of the school as an organization are integrated; (3) little if any integration of the processes that may occur at different levels (district, school, classroom, or individual); and (4) perhaps most important, failure to take into consideration characteristics of the learner.

The study of individual status attainment represents a second approach to research on the effects of schooling, very similar to school production studies but with some subtle differences (Barr and Dreeben, 1983). Research in this tradition focuses on educational attainment as the penultimate, or often ultimate, endogenous variable. Because researchers on social mobility became involved in studies of educational attainment indirectly, only recently has attention been given to students' earlier histories of attainment. As noted in the section on input-output analysis earlier, there are serious problems in trying to apply findings from this body of research to children ages 6–12.

Research classified under the process-product heading is concerned with instructional effectiveness. Studies are typically focused on identifying teaching behaviors and activities that increase learning outcomes. Brophy and Evertson (1974), Dunkin and Biddle (1974), Gage (1972, 1978), and Rosenshine (1971) are major contributors to this approach. The process variables include teaching behaviors, activities, and such characteristics as teacher explanation, demonstration, maintaining order, housekeeping, planning, and years of experience as well as classroom and pupil contextual variables. As mentioned, the findings from such studies are largely inconclusive or ungeneralizable. This is due to (1) the inclusion of an extensive number and range of teacher behaviors; (2) little agreement on which teacher behaviors are important; (3) failure to conceptualize adequately the instructional process and, therefore, how these variables operate to affect learning;

(4) the overly simplistic univariate analysis of the relationship between these teaching variables and educational outcomes; and (5) failure to consider children's characteristics and initiatory behavior in the process.

Recently researchers have attempted to deal with some of the inadequacies of this research by developing more sophisticated conceptual formulations, in which learning outcomes are purported to be influenced by intervening student characteristics, environmental variables, and instructional time. In his theory of educational productivity, Walberg (1981) specified the following variables: student ability and motivation, home environment and age, quality of instruction, quantity of instruction, and class environment. Formulations of this type are significant because they acknowledge that events occur simultaneously within the classroom that might influence learning outcomes, thus permitting us to study the possible interactive and mediating effects. The work of Bloom (1976), Carroll (1963), Fisher et al. (1978), and Wiley and Harnischfeger (1974) also bears on instructional time schemes as a significant variable.

Although most research on the effects of schooling has been confined to academic outcomes, some researchers have explored the influence of process variables on self-esteem and locus of control (Marjoribanks, 1979; Weiss, 1969) or academic expectations for the self (Entwisle and Hayduk, 1982). These efforts have tried to analyze and explain the development of self-esteem and locus of control considered as both an antecedent and a consequence of cognitive school outcomes.

Achievement

During middle childhood, children's ability to use images, symbols, concepts, and rules increases, as does their vocabulary. Middle childhood covers most of what Piaget termed the stage of concrete operations and the beginning of the stage of formal operations. It is a period when the child is expected to acquire a wide range of academic skills and to develop the ability to solve increasingly complex problems. Fischer and Bullock (in this volume) note that "competence is not a fixed characteristic of the child but an emergent characteristic of the child in a specific context." It is evident that the environment significantly affects cognitive development; however, there is a paucity of information on how the environmental context interacts with individual child characteristics to either facilitate or constrain development. Fischer and Bullock recommend an investigation into the collaboration between the child and the environment; we concur.

Children's preschool experiences in the home, nursery school, and playground provide them, to some extent, with the cognitive and social skills required for success in school. Children from different social-class and ethnic backgrounds typically differ in the degree to which their preschool experiences prepare them for schoolwork. We discuss some of these differences in greater detail later. Here we note that early school ability (e.g., reading readiness), which is highly predictive of later school achievement, is strongly related to family background characteristics. As Barr and Dreeben (1983) noted, reading readiness determines reading group placement, and group placement determines pace of instruction and, therefore, reading achievement. Reading achievement in first grade is highly predictive of reading achievement in second grade ($r = .84$).

For children in traditionally organized classrooms, achievement is remarkably stable during the school years. This is partly attributable to the high correlation between school achievement and general intelligence, which is usually between .50 and .60 (Lavin, 1965). Cognitive competencies assessed by intelligence tests overlap with the competencies measured by achievement tests. Bloom (1976) estimated that about 75 percent of subsequent achievement is accounted for by general intelligence. Achievement measures are usually highly correlated with one another. For example, reading comprehension correlates about .70 with tests of language skills and literature. Within domains, test scores are even more highly correlated (e.g., .80 for prior and subsequent tests of the same type). In summarizing results of longitudinal studies, Bloom reported that measures of achievement after grade 3 yield a median correlation with achievement at grade 12 of .70. Maruyama et al. (1981) reported correlations of .75 to .79 for verbal achievement between ages 12 and 15 and of .67 to .72 for verbal achievement between ages 9 and 12. In traditional instruction the best predictor of achievement at the end of the school year is achievement at the beginning of the year. A typical correlation is .80.

Bloom (1976) reported that studies using high-quality instruction (tutoring, mastery learning) have been able to substantially reduce the correlation between prior and later achievement in specific subjects. Anania (1981) reported a correlation of only .11 between prior achievement and final achievement in a course under tutorial conditions of instruction. More typical are the results reported by Froemel (1980). For students undergoing conventional instruction, the correlation between general intelligence and later achievement in a course was .45. For students in a mastery learning class, the correlation between measures of intelligence and measures of achievement at the beginning of the study was .46; after 3 months the correlation fell to .21; and after 6 months it was .11. Similar, though not always as dramatic, patterns of results have been consistent in studies of students from elementary grades through college (Bloom, 1976).

The stability described above is based on the persisting effec differences on achievement. Rutter (1983) contended that a ferences in academic achievement cannot be reduced without most advantaged pupils but did not provide any empirical sur assertion. Bloom (1976), however, cited the results of research. indicating that by using mastery learning techniques the achievement levels of the slowest pupils can be improved without impairing the progress of the more able students.

The stability between earlier and later achievement is not inevitable but is a pattern that, according to Bloom, is associated with schooling as it is traditionally organized. While Bloom and his associates have focused on tutoring and mastery learning, perhaps other organized instructional approaches could also reduce this stability substantially, especially computer-assisted or other individualized modes of instruction. Subsequent research in this area is warranted.

School-Related Affect

There has been a proliferation of research on general self-esteem and academic self-concept during the past two decades. Yet numerous methodological and conceptual problems continue to perplex researchers (see reviews by Wylie, 1974, 1979). There is little agreement on the meaning of the terms self-esteem and self-concept, and there is a paucity of knowledge about how a child's self-image changes during the middle childhood years (Markus and Nurius, in this volume). There is also a need to understand the dimensions or domains of self-concept (e.g., physical self, academic self, social self). Finally, the tendency to rely almost exclusively on self-report measures of self-evaluation is a major weakness of research in this area.

Self-esteem and academic self-concept are both positively correlated with academic achievement (Dolan, 1978; Hare, 1980; Maruyama et al., 1981; Purkey, 1970). However, there is little direct evidence that either self-esteem or academic self-concept has a direct causal influence on achievement. After reviewing research on primary-grade children and older students, Scheirer and Kraut (1979) concluded that the evidence does not support the view that positive changes in self-concept result in improved achievement. Rather, it is more likely that positive change in academic self-concept is an outcome of improved achievement (e.g., Kifer, 1975). Entwisle and Hayduk (1982), however, found this relationship to be reversed in the first grade, i.e., before children have much experience in school.

Educational and psychological researchers have shown considerable interest in the relationship of locus of control to achievement. For example,

Findley and Cooper (1983), from a synthesis of 98 such studies involving students ranging from first grade through college, concluded that more internal beliefs are associated with higher academic achievement but at a modest level ($r = .18$). The strength of the association was greatest at junior high school age ($r = .35$), was somewhat lower at grades 4 through 6 ($r = .24$), and weakest at the primary level (for grades 1–3, $r = .04$). These results are consistent with those of other reviews (e.g., Walden and Ramey, 1983). Walden and Ramey also reported that an experimental group of socially disadvantaged children who had participated in a 5-year preschool educational day care program had perceptions of control over academic successes equal to those of the middle-class comparison group and, like the middle-class children, scored relatively low on perceptions of control over general outcomes. Control beliefs predicted achievement for the experimental and middle-class comparision children but were unrelated to achievement for the socially disadvantaged children who had not had the benefits of preschool intervention. The small sample ($N = 65$) and the typically low reliability of locus of control measures at this age lead us to view these results as suggestive only.

Stipek and Weisz (1981) argued that new measures of children's perceptions of locus of control are needed that would yield subscores for different reinforcement domains. They also recommend studies of developmental changes in locus of control, including information on when children develop beliefs regarding locus of control in achievement situations, how this developmental process is affected by school experiences, and how attributions of failure affect mastery motivation. Harter (1978) suggested that failure perceived to be caused by a lack of competence could lead to anxiety, which interferes with subsequent performance.

Harter and Connell (in press) report the development of several instruments that address some of the concerns expressed by Stipek and Weisz. Among these are a perceived competence scale (Harter, 1982) that measures self-perceptions in the cognitive, social, and physical domains and a perceived control scale that assesses the extent to which children attribute their successes and failures to "unknown" causes or to internal or external causes. These instruments have been administered to hundreds of students in grades 3 through 9, and early analyses are beginning to shed light on developmental patterns. Harter (1981) also developed a scale that assesses intrinsic versus extrinsic mastery motivation in the classroom. Instruments for use with first and second graders are still badly needed, however, in part because these earliest years may be just the time when relationships among locus of control, academic expectations, and attributions are being worked out.

Miller (1982), in a review of studies of children in grades K–3, found that self-esteem declines between kindergarten and the third grade. When Miller interviewed subjects in December of first grade and reinterviewed the same children 1 year later ($N = 94$) on measures of self-concept of attainment, children who were immature overused the very top self-ranking and showed little stability over the 1-year period. At the second interview, fewer children were immature, and there was a significant decline in self-esteem. Whether the reported decline in self-esteem was due to developmental changes in cognition, as Miller suggested, or to negative experiences in school is equivocal. (See Markus and Nurius, in this volume, for a more detailed discussion of the development of self-evaluation and self-regulation.)

Teacher behaviors may be related to changes in self-esteem (Anderson, 1982; Goodlad et al., 1979; McDill and Rigsby, 1973; Miller, 1982), although the identification of the specific behaviors and how they produce positive or negative changes remains murky.

Anxiety in school settings, a concern of researchers since the 1950s (Sarason et al., 1960), also may contribute to changes in children's self-esteem. For students at all grade levels through college, high anxiety is almost always associated with impairment in cognitive functioning (Gaudry and Speilberger, 1971). Anxious students apparently spend part of the total task time on irrelevant behaviors, which result in performance decrements. There is little consensus on the origins of school-related anxiety (e.g., the extent to which anxiety is developed at home before the child enters school), but there is general agreement that school learning and evaluation processes affect the level and stability of children's school-related anxiety. More research in naturalistic settings is needed to determine the aspects of the teaching/learning/evaluation process that increase or reduce anxiety.

Harter and Connell (in press) contend that children's understanding of the contingencies that govern success and failure is critical. Children in grades 3 to 9 who attribute control to "unknown" sources tend to have lower levels of achievement than children who accept personal responsibility for their successes and failures (Connell, 1980). Harter and Connell identified a predictive sequence that flows from perceived control to actual achievement to competence evaluation to competence affect—and then to motivation to engage in further mastery attempts.

Social Roles

The role of the schools in preparing children to function appropriately as adults is an active area of research, mainly at the secondary level. To participate effectively in school and in societal institutions, children must learn (i.e., be socialized), to be independent achievers, to accept universal standards, and to function well as group members (Dreeben, 1968).

While instruction takes place in groups, rewards are allocated on the basis of individual competition. Children enter school with different capacities and with different levels of preparation for the school experience. Social class and ethnic differences in values and linguistic styles may be reflected in children's behaviors and attitudes and in the way teachers respond to them (Leacock, 1982). Children from middle-class families typically exhibit values and behaviors that are relatively consistent with the norms of the school. Children from working-class backgrounds, especially if they are members of a racial or ethnic minority group, frequently display behaviors and values that are in conflict with those of the school. These initial differences in school "survival" skills are thought to be translated into instructional group placement differences, which lead to differences in reading achievement. Since reading achievement is reflected in nearly all school subjects, this early placement has a lasting effect on achievement and subsequent attitudes toward school and educational attainment. Grouping in the primary grades and tracking in the intermediate grades and secondary school result in children being identified as academic winners or losers. These (unofficial) designations are associated with rates of staying in or dropping out of school, enrollment in academic or low-level classes, and going to college or entering the world of work. One might say that the process begins in the home, but it is institutionalized in the school (Rutter, 1983).

The opposing view emphasizes allocation. As Bowles and Gintis (1976) pointed out, children's experiences of segregation by group or track (or school) and of differential rewards in an educational setting with a meritocratic reward system could allocate them by preparing them to accept the reality of an adult work world characterized by hierarchical segmentation and unequal rewards. The outcome of school socialization in this view is a cohort of workers who believe that their place in society, either high or low, is deserved and is a function of their own abilities and efforts. In other words, one of the normative outcomes of schooling, resulting from a process that begins in elementary school, could be internalization of the meritocratic myth. The debate between these views continues.

The school's reinforcement of traditional societal roles may also occur in the different experiences of male and female pupils. Small-scale studies suggest that boys receive more attention, both positive and negative, from teachers than girls (Brophy and Good, 1974), that teachers react differently to black and white boys and girls (Grant, 1981), and that black teachers differ less in their treatment of girls and boys than do white teachers (Simpson and Erickson, 1983). Dweck et al. (1978) reported that teachers criticize boys more than girls, that criticism of boys is directed toward conduct and neatness, and that teachers are six times more likely to attribute academic failure to a lack of motivation or effort for boys than for girls. This pattern of differential feedback may help explain sex differences in achievement expectations. These results have not been supported by recent studies (for a comprehensive review, see Meece et al., 1982). There is a clear need for additional research on how classroom experiences affect girls' achievement expectations.

The role models provided by elementary school personnel may contribute to the reinforcement of traditional gender role expectations. Most elementary school teachers are women, but most administrators are men. Thus, there is a sex-ranked hierarchy among school personnel that may reinforce traditional notions of male superiority. Research is needed on the effects of different types of leadership roles held by women on girls' achievement expectations. For example, how does it make a difference in girls' expectations of achievement if the principal is a woman rather than a man? Another interesting research question is the nature of the interaction between maternal work roles, school leadership patterns, and girls' achievement expectations. The role of peers in maintaining or changing stereotypes should also be explored.

SOCIAL BACKGROUND AND SCHOOLING

This section discusses the effects of socioeconomic status, home environment, and race and ethnicity on educational outcomes for children. The discussion includes the interface between families and schools.

Unfortunately, most of the literature treats the learner conceptually as contributing little if anything to the schooling process. As a result, what is covered focuses largely on how families and schools influence the learner. Although our stated purpose is to uncover effects, further investigation is needed into the nature of the learner as producer and beneficiary of learning.

Family Influence and Educational Outcomes

In the past several decades, researchers have studied questions related to the relationship of family life to educational outcomes. These investigations have focused primarily on the effects of parental involvement, socioeconomic status, and home environment on children's cognitive and affective functioning.

Socioeconomic Status and Achievement

One of the most frequently studied aspects of the relationship between family and school as socializing environments is the effect of family background on school achievement. In most of this research the measure of family background is occupation, education, or income of the head of household, both parents, or some combination of these. The consistent finding is that the higher the family's social status, the more likely the child is to have high scores on achievement tests. Correlations between measures of socioeconomic status and standardized achievement test scores for individuals average between .20 and .25, while correlations based on aggregated scores (e.g., school or class means) average between .70 and .80 (Hess, 1970; White, 1982). In multivariate analyses, social class has been found to be primarily implicated through its relationship to ability as measured by intelligence tests (e.g., Maruyama et al., 1981). Socioeconomic status is associated with school grades in much the same fashion: the higher the status, the higher the grades.

These relationships vary in strength for different populations and for different types of tests. For example, the relationship of father's occupation to achievement is typically weaker for minority group students than for whites (DeBord et al., 1977; Epps, 1969). Interestingly, the correlation of socioeconomic status and achievement has been found to be consistent among developed countries; results similar to those in the United States have been found in England, France, Germany, and other European nations and in Japan and Israel. However, in developing nations, such as Uganda, the advantage of socioeconomic status does not appear to exist (Heyneman, 1976).

Correlational data, however, cannot speak to the processes by which families inculcate differential preparation or motivation for school learning or performance. What are the specific characteristics of the home environment that are associated with achievement?

Home Environment

Studies of home environments typically yield average correlations with intelligence for individuals of about .55 (Bloom, 1976; White, 1982). Even when students live in comparable neighborhoods and do not differ on traditional measures of socioeconomic status, home environment variables still explain a significant amount of achievement variance (Levine et al., 1972). (See Maccoby, in this volume, for a discussion of family interaction patterns.) Dave (1963) examined the relationship between the family environment and academic achievement of children at age 11. He identified six process variables as characterizing the educational "press" of the family environment: (1) achievement press, (2) language models, (3) academic guidance, (4) activeness of the family, (5) intellectuality in the home, (6) work habits of the family. These indicators have now been widely used in this country, in Trinidad (Dyer, 1967), and in Dublin (Kellaghan, 1977) to assess the degree of parental influence on academic achievement of children ages 8 and 11, respectively (Marjoribanks, 1979). The press variables accounted for much of the variance in achievement in academic subject areas and to a lesser degree were positively associated with measures of intelligence.

R. Clark (1982) used a case study approach to distinguish between surface structure of families (traditional socioeconomic indicators such as income, occupation, and education as well as family intactness and ethnicity) and internal structure of families (personality characteristics, communication patterns, and learning opportunity structures). Three types of home activities seemed especially relevant for school achievement: (1) explicit literacy-nurturing activities, which include studying, reading, writing, topical dialogues, and explicit social etiquette practices; (2) cultural literacy-enhancing activities that serve leisure needs, e.g., watching television, word games, and hobbies; and (3) home and personal health maintenance activities, e.g., chores, caring for children and other household members, and attending to one's own personal upkeep and well-being. Other important aspects of supportive family systems include interactive communication systems that provide opportunities for direct instruction, feedback opportunities, and reinforcement opportunities. If this type of qualitative research can be replicated, an explanation may be closer of why some families provide better support for school achievement than others.

There is some disagreement over the extent and direction of the interactive influences of home environment variables and individual child characteristics on achievement outcomes. How much influence does a child's intellect itself have on the nature of the home environment? Mercy and Steelman (1982) suggested that it is possible that bright children select intellectually stimulating activities or encourage their parents to provide such experiences. It is also possible that parents' aspirations for their child, parental concern for academic achievement, and other achievement "press" variables are based on parents' perceptions of their child's ability or potential. It is unlikely that the home environment effect represents a one-way flow from parent to child. The interactive approach seems to be more plausible and is consistent with the thrust of current research efforts, as detailed throughout this volume. Continued investigation following interactive formulations and using improved methodologies appears warranted in this area.

Maternal Influence

Among the maternal socialization variables, maternal educational background is thought to be the strongest predictor of achievement (Hess and Shipman, 1967; Laosa, 1982), and, of the many effects, the impact on linguistic development appears to be the greatest (Carew, 1980; Clarke-Stewart, 1973; Slaughter, 1983).

Hess et al. (1980) reported that maternal behaviors such as reading to children and providing them with opportunities for verbal expression are positively related to early reading skills (e.g., letter recognition at age 5). Using a measure of maternal press for achievement that attempts to assess the mother's efforts to motivate her child to achieve in school, they found that both the mother's pressure to achieve and her tendency to request verbal statements from her child are significantly and positively related to 5-year-olds' letter recognition scores. A measure of the verbal environment of the home correlated at a significant level with IQ at age 6.

The early work of Brophy (1970), Hess and Shipman (1965, 1967), and Stodolsky (1965) conceptualized the influence of maternal behaviors as representative of cognitive and affective structures that evoke certain intellectual and affective processes. These behaviors are thought to serve as models that strongly influence children's acquisition of specific cognitive and affective modes, which affect their subsequent learning and affective responses. Hess and Shipman stated (1967:58–60) that:

The mother's strategies are likely to have consequences for the child's ability to grasp a concept or learn a lesson in any specific teaching situation. The mother's strategies also have consequences for the cognitive structures (preferred response patterns) that emerge in the child and for his eventual educability in more formal, institutional instruction. . . . The styles of learning established at home interfere with subsequent learning and teaching processes in school. . . . This view . . . suggests that the role of the school in disadvantaged areas is not only to fill in deficits of language and specific cognitive skills but also to *resocialize* the child into more adaptable styles of learning.

In direct contradiction to Clark's argument in *Dark Ghetto* (1965), which held teachers responsible for underachievement, Hess and Shipman placed the burden of academic deprivation on maternal socialization. This position has critical implications for determining educational policy. One interpretation is that this deprivationist rationale relieves schools of the responsibility for change (Slaughter, 1983). Unfortunately, the deprivationist position is thought to have resulted in many minority and lower-status students being labeled uneducable (Baratz and Baratz, 1970; Leacock, 1982; Rist, 1973; Tulkin, 1972).

Parental Involvement

There is general agreement that children of parents who are more involved in their children's education adapt better to the demands of school than do the children of less-involved parents. However, as Epstein and Becker (1982) pointed out, not all forms of parental involvement are equally effective or equally welcomed by school personnel. Participation in PTA councils and as classroom volunteers typically involve relatively few parents, but nearly all parents can be involved in educational activities at home: "Of all types of parent involvement, supervision of learning activities at home may be the most educationally significant" (Epstein and Becker, 1982:111). And there is some evidence that intervention programs based on the principle of parental involvement, either as home educators of their own children or as teacher aides or tutors, have been relatively successful (Bronfenbrenner, 1974).

In an effort to assess the impact of a number of home background variables on the reading ability of 7- and 8-year-olds, Hewison and Tizard (1980) and Tizard et al. (1982) found a strong effect for parental assistance with reading. Children of parents who regularly heard their children read aloud ("coaching") had higher reading achievement scores than children whose parents did not listen to their oral reading on a regular basis.

Child-parent centers that stress parental involvement have been particularly effective in enhancing the achievement of low-income inner-city minority children (Fuerst, 1977). Combining a warm, supportive home atmosphere with a warm, supportive schooling setting was found to enhance the achievement of children in Project Head Start (Shipman et al., 1976). Comer (1980) also stressed the importance of parental involvement in contributing to effective student outcomes.

What of the interface between home and school? It is not clear that being active in school affairs has positive achievement outcomes for children unless parents are also providing the type of home environment that enhances achievement. Lightfoot (1979) pointed out that mothers and teachers may compete with each other in their efforts to influence children's development. If race and social-status differences are involved, these conflicts may take on chauvinistic characteristics. Lightfoot suggested that in cases in which parents and teachers, despite their differences, work cooperatively on behalf of the children, a creative tension may develop that will enhance their growth. Promising work on how teachers involve parents in the educational process is currently under way at Johns Hopkins University (Epstein and

Becker, 1982), but the issue of how different types of parental involvement affect children's adaptation to school is one that requires additional research.

Family and School Authority Patterns

Educational researchers have devoted considerable attention to studies of person-environment interactions or interactions of aptitude (trait) and treatment (e.g., Corno et al., 1981; Janicki and Peterson, 1981). While few consistent interaction effects have been reported (see Cronbach and Snow, 1977), the search for better statistical analysis strategies (Hedges, 1981) and better conceptual strategies continues. Epstein (1983) pointed out that, while psychologists have focused on person-environment interaction effects, sociologists and political scientists have studied environment-environment interaction effects. She advocates a merging of the two approaches into a person-environment-environment model: "Is there one best organization for educating, or do different approaches optimize development on particular outcomes for different students?" (p. 105).

Epstein's model was applied to a study of the relationship of family and school authority structures (two environments) to junior high and high school students' satisfaction with school (the students varied on measures of independence and locus of control). The two environments could be congruent or incongruent with each other, and each environment could be congruent or incongruent with a particular student's background. The results indicate that "school environments were especially important for students from families that do not emphasize participation in decisions at home" (p. 121). This was especially true for students who were initially high in independence and internal control orientation. Although the students in Epstein's study were beyond the elementary school level, it is reasonable to assume that the patterns exhibited by these students developed during the early school years. Additional research on the relationship of family decision-making structures and school decision-making structures in the early grades may help us understand how student characteristics, home environment, and school environment affect student adjustment to school.

Family Variables and Student Personality Dimensions

Investigations into the relationship and influences of the family on learning outcomes have not been confined to the cognitive-intellectual domain. Some research has focused on structural differences in childhood experiences that result in different achievement values, aspirations, and motivations. Conceptually, the achievement values here are much like the attitudes of "modernism" discussed by Inkeles (1968), self-direction versus conformity as identified by Kohn (1969), and three achievement values identified by Strodtbeck (1958): (1) a belief that the world is orderly and amenable to rational mastery, (2) a willingness to leave home to make one's way in life, and (3) a preference for individual rather than collective credit for work accomplished. Strodtbeck found that these values were a function of the balance of power between fathers, mothers, and sons within the family (mothers' dominance of their sons rather than father dominance).

Major gaps in this research exist. One issue is whether it is valid to apply an Anglo-American definition of achievement motivation on the basis of individualistic achievement efforts to those racial or ethnic groups that may place greater emphasis on group or family expressions of achievement and approval (e.g., Ramirez and Price-Williams, 1976). Laosa (1977) also pointed out that ethnic groups differ in the attributes that define optimal development or social competence in childhood.

The evidence on the issue is somewhat inconsistent. Ruhland and Feld (1977) found that black and white working-class children did not differ in autonomous achievement motivation, which is presumably learned at home prior to school age; however, white students scored significantly higher than blacks on social comparison motivation, which is acquired during the elementary school years. (Autonomous standards define excellence in relation to one's own past performance; social comparison standards are based on comparisons of one's own performance and that of others.) In contrast, a study (Moore, 1981) of black children adopted by black families and white families, found that black children adopted by white families were significantly more likely than black children adopted by black families to have high autonomous achievement motivation scores. The two groups did not differ on social comparison motivation scores.

The differences may be attributable to the fact that the children in Moore's study were all living in middle-class families, while the children in the Ruhland and Feld study attended working-class schools. Moore's results call into question Banks and McQuater's (1976) contention that the roots of low achievement motivation among blacks are not located in family and early socialization experiences.

One key intervening factor may be different determinants of locus of control in the home and at school. Neither the role of the family nor the role of teachers in determining locus of control has received sufficient research attention. Buriel (1981) found for grade-school Chicano children (but not for Anglo children) a positive relationship between students' perceptions of teachers' controlling behavior and internal control for success and a positive relationship between students' perceptions of teachers' supporting behavior and internal control for failure. Anglo and Chicano students were not different in levels of internal locus of control. Similarly,

Holliday (1984) compared 44 black 9- and 10-year-olds on mother's reports of children's competencies at home and in the neighborhood and teacher's reports of school competencies. The two sets of competencies were not related at a statistically significant level. Neither school self-esteem (Coopersmith scale) nor locus of control (Bialer-Cromwell scale) were significantly related to either set of competencies. Only teacher-reported competencies were significantly related to school grades and achievement test scores.

Holliday reported that teachers, in rating black students, tended to assign higher ratings to social activity than to academic activity. She suggested that teacher expectations may contribute to learned helplessness patterns in black children's academic behavior, similar to patterns of learned helplessness described by Dweck et al. (1978) for girls. Evidence from several studies suggests that black students are less accurate than whites in estimating their own achievement levels (Brookover et al., 1979; Busk et al., 1973; Massey et al., 1975), although Entwisle and Hayduk (1982) did not observe this in their sample in which children of the two races were of comparable socioeconomic level. The type of teacher feedback may also contribute to the development of patterns among minority students that cause them to be slower than whites in developing a logical approach to the inference of ability from outcome and effort cues.

Research on the relationship of home environment to social affect has concentrated on children ages 11–12, although one study of 8-year-olds in Dublin is reported (Kellaghan, 1977). There is a need to study younger children in order to study developmental patterns. If the methodology could be developed, it would be of interest to know what type of achievement values children bring from home upon entry in school. It would then be possible to determine how home-produced achievement values are enhanced or discouraged by the schooling process. Student achievement values measured at entry into the ninth grade change very little by graduation from high school. It thus appears that high schools have little impact on students' values. Is this also true for elementary schools? Additional work is needed on the effects of various educational practices on parents' and students' expectations and the relationship of these to achievement and affective outcomes. The work of Entwisle and Hayduk (1978, 1982) is a good beginning and should stimulate additional research.

Race and Ethnicity

Since the publication of *Equality of Educational Opportunity* (Coleman et al., 1966), the racial and ethnic compositions of schools have been important variables both empirically and conceptually. Most studies find that achievement varies negatively with the percentage of minority students in the school population. To a large extent, this is attributable to the fact that minority students are likely to come from poverty-level homes with all of the stresses typically associated with poverty (see Maccoby, in this volume). However, Ogbu (1978) noted that low achievement is not found among all racial minorities in American schools. For example, Asian-American students' achievement is usually higher than that of Anglo-Americans. According to Ogbu (1978), immigrant minorities (Chinese, Filipinos, and Japanese) do not exhibit the patterns of school failure found among castelike minorities (blacks, American Indians, Mexican Americans, and Puerto Ricans); Coleman et al. (1966) also reported this finding.

Comparative research in six countries confirms the general pattern: immigrant minorities did relatively well in school; nonimmigrant minorities experienced a high proportion of school failure. Ogbu (1983) suggested that the differences in minority-group performance in schools are attributable to differences in perceptions of schooling in relation to the opportunity structure, on one hand, and cultural inversion, on the other. The argument for perception of opportunity structure is more plausible for secondary school students than for elementary pupils, who are less likely to have well-formed ideas about societal barriers to social mobility. However, perceptions of the opportunity structure may influence how parents motivate their children for school achievement. Cultural inversion may result in linguistic, cognitive, and behavioral styles that conflict with the expectations of school staff.

Slaughter (1969, 1977) examined the relationship between selected home background variables and achievement development for a sample of Head Start children followed from nursery school through grade 6. Perhaps more important, she studied the interactions of parent, teacher, and student perceptions of children's abilities and potential for development. While Slaughter found several maternal socialization variables to be related to children's preschool IQ scores and reading-readiness scores, by grade 4 nearly all of these were nonsignificant. Slaughter (1977:128) concluded that "for this population the schooling experience is discontinuous with early childhood development." She also reported (1983:26) that "regardless of teacher feedback differentiating mother and child perceptions of the child's achievement effort and performance between grades kindergarten through 5, the school's own criteria of academic success indicated no differences among the children: academic performances were almost uniformly substandard." There is a strong indication that neither children nor mothers were aware that the children's performance was substandard. This pattern of inaccurate feedback has been reported by others (e.g., Massey et al., 1975).

Some researchers contend that there are ethnic differences in "theories of success" that prepare children to develop different sets of competencies (Ogbu, 1981). While social status as traditionally measured probably mediates these ethnic differences, it is likely that some ethnic "survivals" remain even when social status is controlled. Ogbu contends that the study of "native theory of success" provides important clues about what instrumental competencies people stress and what kinds of adults they want their children to be. It will also provide information on people's notions about how to succeed and about what constitutes a successful person.

In a provocative article entitled "Afro-American Cognitive Style: A Variable in School Success?" Barbara J. Shade (1982:238) wrote:

A review of the literature suggests that successful functioning within the current school context requires the cognitive strategies that are described as sequential, analytical, or object-oriented. An examination of the culture or lifestyle and world view of Afro-Americans, however, portrays strategies designed to foster survival and therefore tends to be rather universalistic, intuitive, and more than that, very person-oriented. It is postulated that an enhanced ability in social cognition may work to the detriment of the individuals within an object-oriented setting such as the school. To verify these assumptions requires strong and methodologically rigorous empirical studies.

These concerns about culturally different socialization goals and culturally specific cognitive styles require empirical verification, but in the meantime they should serve as cautions to theorists and researchers involved with universal developmental schema and stages. An early approach to studying the educational implications of cultural differences in learning patterns has not been followed up (see Lesser et al., 1967; Stodolsky and Lesser, 1967), and new investigations of this type may prove fruitful.

Research based on the Kamehameha Early Education Program (KEEP), a long-term research and development project designed to improve the school performance of educationally at-risk Hawaiian children, indicates that the performance of poor and minority children could be greatly enhanced if the home competence/school incompetence paradox could be resolved. These reseachers contend that nonmainstream children develop school-relevant cognitive strategies in the home environment before they enroll in school, but the school environment provides different types of cues for generating the use of these strategies. The children therefore exhibit a widespread inconsistency in the use of school-successful cognitive strategies. The KEEP reading program improved the reading achievement of Hawaiian children by providing "a bridging experience which encouraged and taught the children to perform at school at a level consistent with their home performance" (Gallimore and Au, 1979:34). While the specific elements of the KEEP program may not generalize to other ethnic groups, the process by which the program was developed should prove useful (Tharp and Gallimore, 1982).

The basic assumption of the KEEP project is a two-cultural model. For the Hawaiian children, there is a highly organized culture of the home, the community, and the child. The school culture and the child/home/community culture do not interact advantageously for effective teaching and learning. This circumstance is found among other poor minority-group children when they encounter the culture of the school. To develop school programs that capitalize on the child's cultural learning, a careful knowledge of both cultures is required. In the KEEP project this involved several years of ethnographic and sociolinguistic research with Hawaiian adults and children to acquire knowledge of the children's culture. To acquire knowledge of the school culture the researchers created and operated a school in which intensive observations could be made. Only after several years of multidisciplinary research and repeated efforts at educational innovation was an effective mix of cultural accommodations developed.

There is a need for additional work on the interface of family and school environments in the education process. How can education programs be designed so as to take advantage of the cultural values of students while still achieving the goals of literacy and computational competency as well as preparing young people for successful lives as adults? Slaughter (1981) discussed three societal changes that have educational implications for the 1980s: the movement of mothers into the labor force, the quest for high-quality day care, and the increase in the number of dependent families. Research on how schools can best serve children encountering these new circumstances is needed. More qualitative studies of family life and school life are needed.

SCHOOL DESEGREGATION

The research generated by legal efforts to desegregate public schools has typically focused on three questions: (1) Do minority children have higher achievement in integrated schools than in segregated schools? (2) Do children's racial attitudes become more positive after desegregation? (3) Does the self-esteem of minority students improve following desegregation? Reviewers of this research (e.g., St. John, 1975; Stephan, 1978) have concluded that most of the studies have been so poorly designed that it is nearly impossible to draw reliable inferences from them. The results of the research have been inconsistent, contradictory, and frequently null. Given the wide range of settings and conditions under which desegregation has occurred, it should not be surprising that it is difficult to assess the effect of desegregation as a "treatment." Despite the weak methodology and the differences in samples and measures used, a few generalizations are possible about the effects of desegregation on majority and minority children.

Racial Attitudes and Peer Relationships

Several reviews of the research (Cohen, 1975; St. John, 1975; Mc-Conahay, 1978) on racial attitudes have found that there are few true experiments, relatively few well-designed quasi experiments and longitudinal studies, and too much reliance on cross-sectional samples and correlational techniques. Nevertheless, there is general agreement that the existing research provides strong support for the "contact hypothesis." Allport (1954) contended that contact between groups will result in improved intergroup relations only if the contact occurs in a setting that provides equal status for minority- and majority-group members as well as strong institutional support for positive intergroup interaction. The likelihood of positive intergroup relations is improved when there is cooperative interaction involving the achievement of shared goals. While few school settings incorporate all of the conditions that foster equal-status interaction, results are most positive for schools that provide approximations of these conditions. Gerard et al. (1975) found that very little positive change in elementary school children's sociometric choices occurred during 4–6 years of desegregation, but this can be explained by the fact that few classrooms approximated the equal-status conditions advocated by Allport. These authors found teacher and student prejudice to be positively correlated. It is not likely that prejudiced teachers would establish equal-status situations in their classrooms. One would therefore not expect contact to foster positive interracial attitudes and behaviors under their leadership. It was noted by Gerard et al. (1975), however, that a favorable social climate in the classroom appeared to have a positive influence on the well-being of the higher-achieving minority children.

There is a need for additional research on school practices that improve racial attitudes and behaviors. Slavin and Madden (1979) found that having high school students of different races work together had positive effects but that few effects were found for teacher workshops or the use of multiethnic texts. Studies of this type at the elementary level would add considerably to our knowledge in this area. Schofield (1979), in an observational study of an integrated junior high school, found evidence that tracking students into different classrooms on the basis of ability or prior achievement resulted in resegregation and that resegregation leads to reduced cross-racial social interaction. Studies of the effects of ability grouping on interracial contacts and attitudes at the elementary school level would help clarify the effects of such school practices on children's attitudes and behaviors. There is promising work on team learning (Slavin and DeVries, 1979) and cooperative learning strategies (Johnson and Johnson, 1979).

Several additional issues need to be clarified by further resear[ch]
little about gender and age differences in response to desegr[egation]
study (St. John and Lewis, 1975) suggested that black girls l[ose]
after desegregation but that white girls and boys of both races do not suffer
such declines. Other research (Schofield and McGivern, 1978) found that
black boys and white girls were more positive about the experience of desegregation than either white boys or black girls. While it is generally accepted that results are more favorable if desegregation takes place early in
the school years, Scott and McPartland (1982) found age to be positively
related to racial tolerance. The nature of contextual and developmental
effects on changes in racial attitudes awaits future research.

Self-Esteem, Academic Self-Concept, and Racial Self-Identity

Efforts to determine the impact of school desegregation on the self-image
and motivation of black children have been hampered by the use of many
different self-esteem measures and by differences in the conditions under
which desegregation has taken place. In addition, many studies are cross-
sectional rather than longitudinal and attempt to assess effects after relatively
short periods of time. To add to the confusion, there is little agreement on
the meaning of such terms as *self-image, self-concept,* and *self-esteem* (for a
detailed discussion of such issues, see Markus and Nurius, in this volume).
In this chapter, self-esteem refers to global self-evaluation; academic self-
concept refers to self-evaluation with regard to schoolwork; and racial self-
identity refers to racial self-evaluation.

Several comprehensive reviews of research on the impact of desegregation
on self-esteem have been published (Epps, 1975, 1978, 1981; St. John,
1975; Stephan, 1978; Weinberg, 1977). The results have been mixed. Some
studies have found black student self-esteem to be enhanced by desegregation, others have found it to be reduced, and still others have found no
effects. Several recent studies (Cicirelli, 1977; Hare, 1977, 1980; Hunt and
Hunt, 1977) indicated that the self-esteem of black students in desegregated
schools is equal to or higher than that of white students. However, some
research (e.g., Hunt and Hunt, 1977) found black students' self-esteem to
be higher in segregated schools than in desegregated schools, and a longitudinal study by Gerard and Miller (1975) found that both before and after
desegregation black and Mexican-American children scored significantly
lower on self-attitudes than Anglo children. Changes in self-esteem following
desegregation seem to be relatively modest, and there is little support for
the contention that desegregation enhances minority self-esteem. Most studies report minority students scoring equal to whites in self-esteem.

Work on academic self-concept is also hampered by the limitations of the assessment instruments. The most frequently used measure is some variation of Brookover et al.'s (1962) self-concept of academic ability scale. This measure asks students to rate themselves on ability and grades compared with others in their classrooms or schools. Several general self-esteem scales include a school subscale (e.g., Coopersmith, 1967; Hare, 1980), which asks students how they feel about their schoolwork and their school experiences. Considering the typical gap between minority and white achievement, one would expect academic self-concept to decline following desegregation.

Green et al. (1975) used a measure called "need for school achievement" to assess a dimension similar to school self-esteem. They found that black and Mexican-American elementary school pupils scored lower than whites on this measure before desegregation and that scores declined for all three groups during their years of desegregated schooling. The authors noted that the changes are not attributable to ethnicity. Brookover et al. (1979) noted the surprisingly high academic self-concept scores of black students. There are at least three possible explanations for this phenomenon. First, black students may compare themselves only with other black students when responding to items such as "Compared to others in your class in ability, would you say you are among the best, above average, or below average?" Second, black students many not receive accurate feedback from teachers concerning their relative performance levels (see Massey et al., 1975, for evidence on this point). Third, children of relatively low socioeconomic level, irrespective of race, may have unrealistic self-concepts of ability (Entwisle and Hayduk, 1978, 1982). This issue should be the focus of further research.

Research on racial self-identity has attempted to determine the extent to which black children or other nonwhite minority children develop racial self-hatred, dominant-group preference, or rejection of their own group. The most extensive study of racial identity in the context of desegregation was conducted in Riverside, California (Goodchilds et al., 1975). This study used photographs of black, Mexican-American, and Anglo girls and boys to assess ethnic identity. The researchers found that a child's ethnic identity and self-attitude are not closely linked (nonsignificant correlations). McAdoo (1977) studied racial attitudes and self-esteem among black children in Michigan, Mississippi, and Washington, D.C. The Michigan children lived in a segregated neighborhood but attended biracial schools; the children in the other locations were racially isolated in the neighborhood and at school. While community setting is an important confounding factor, at age 10 only the desegregated Michigan children exhibited relatively high in-group preference as well as positive self-esteem. The other groups maintained high self-esteem but were less problack in their racial preferences. This study, like the Riverside one, seems to support the generalization that identification with one's own race increases with experience in interracial schools. The results of these studies also support Spencer's (1976) finding that racial self-identity and self-esteem are not related (see Spencer, 1982, for a critique of research on racial self-identity and self-esteem among black children).

Academic Achievement

Much attention has been given to the effects of desegregation on academic achievement (see the reviews by Bradley and Bradley, 1977; St. John, 1975). Despite the weak methodology of most of these studies, a few results seem to be fairly well supported.

There is consensus among researchers that, with few exceptions, white children's achievement is not affected either positively or negatively by desegregation. However, some studies have found that black achievement is higher in schools and classrooms in which the staff's racial attitudes are more positive (Coulson et al., 1977; Crain et al., 1981; Forehand et al., 1976). There is little support, however, for the hypothesis that the number of white friends or the amount of interracial contact enhances minority achievement (e.g., Singer et al., 1975). Similar results have been found for secondary school students (Patchen, 1982).

Reviews using statistical research synthesis techniques have found a general positive effect of desegregation on minority achievement (Crain and Mahard, 1982, 1983; Krol, 1978). Crain and Mahard (1982) reported that methodology had a strong effect on outcomes. "Eighteen of 21 samples (86 percent) taken from studies based on random assignment showed positive results, while at the other extreme, over half the studies that compared black performance with white performance or with national norms showed negative results of desegregation" (p. 15).

The Crain and Mahard study is the most extensive to date, covering 93 research reports that included 323 samples of black students. Among other important findings they noted that (1) studies of children who were desegregated at kindergarten or first grade are most likely to show positive results; (2) the typical study finds greater gains for IQ than for achievement test scores; (3) where achievement gains from desegregation are substantial, reading comprehension and language arts subtest scores show a greater increase than do other subtest scores; (4) where achievement gains are slight, the effect is lower for reading comprehension and language arts than for other subtest scores; and (5) metropolitan desegregation plans that result in classroom ratios of 10–30 percent black students are more likely to show achievement gains than are other types of plans.

The need for additional research syntheses as well as closer attention to experimental design is clear. While the "lateral transmission" hypothesis has not been supported, it is not known why desegregation is beneficial. That the teaching of reading comprehension and language arts is a key factor in minority achievement clearly warrants further exploration.

Most studies of desegregation have involved black students. However, many recent desegregation plans have been implemented in areas in which the Hispanic population is relatively large. Some locales also include substantial numbers of Asians and American Indians among their populations. Future researchers should attempt to provide additional information on how other minorities are affected by desegregation. In fact, simultaneous examination of three or more racial/ethnic groups would help untangle some of the perplexing strands in this area.

SECOND-LANGUAGE LEARNING AND BILINGUALISM

In areas where there are a substantial number of children whose proficiency in English is limited, school districts are required to provide some form of linguistic assistance (see Fernandez and Guskin, 1981, for a discussion of implementation problems). This assistance may take the form of teaching English as a second language, or it may be provided through a bilingual or multicultural approach. The relative effectiveness of the different approaches is the subject of considerable controversy. In this section we examine some of the issues and research in the area of second-language learning and bilingualism and discuss the implications of the research findings.

Bilingual Instruction and Intellectual Development

The majority of the studies conducted before 1962 found strong evidence for the contention that bilingual children, compared with monolingual children, were deficient in vocabulary, articulation, written composition, and grammar (Diaz, 1983:25). Thus, it was widely believed that bilingualism was detrimental to children's intellectual and cognitive development. However, the early studies suffered from many methodological weaknesses. Researchers frequently failed to control for socioeconomic status, degree of bilingualism, age at which the second language was learned, whether the second language was learned formally or acquired "naturally" or whether the child's first language had high or low status in the community.

Peal and Lambert's (1962) study of 75 monolingual and 89 balanced bilingual 10-year-old Canadian children produced the first strong evidence that bilingualism was positively associated with cognitive development. In this study, bilingual children performed better than monolingual children on tests of both verbal and nonverbal abilities. The bilingual children were superior in concept formation and cognitive flexibility and had a more diversified pattern of abilities than the monolingual children. While superior in methodology to most early studies, the results of the Peal and Lambert research may have been affected by sample selection bias. In attempting to ensure that their sample included only balanced bilingual children (those with age-appropriate abilities in both languages), less intelligent bilingual children with less English proficiency may have been eliminated from the sample, thereby creating an intellectual bias favoring the bilingual sample. Nevertheless, their focus on degree of bilingualism prompted later researchers to select bilingual samples with greater care, to measure respondents' actual degree of bilingualism, and to be alert to the possibility of situational influences that might enhance or deter bilingual children's cognitive and intellectual development.

Diaz (1983) concluded his review by noting that recent studies have presented evidence that bilingualism has a positive influence on children's cognitive and linguistic abilities. This evidence comes from studies of balanced bilingual children. "When compared to monolinguals, balanced bilingual children show definite advantages on measures of metalinguistic abilities, concept formation, field independence, and divergent thinking skills" (p. 48). Cummins (1979) proposed a "threshold" hypothesis that emphasizes the importance of the child's level of competence in both languages. When the child has low levels of competence in both languages, bilingualism is usually associated with negative cognitive effects. When the child has age-appropriate competence in one language but is less competent in another, bilingualism has little or no effect on cognitive development. It is in those instances in which the child has at least age-appropriate competence in two languages that positive effects of bilingualism, such as those described by Diaz, are most likely to be found.

Bilingualism and Achievement

It has consistently been reported that bilingualism among middle- and upper-class children is not associated with educational problems. Bilingualism among lower-class ethnic minority children, however, is frequently associated with low levels of academic achievement. Recent research suggests that "semilingualism" may be implicated in the relatively low academic achievement of bilingual minority children in the United States. Cummins (1979) described semilinguals as children who have low levels of competence in both their first and second languages. They tend to perform poorly on tests that measure such cognitive aspects of language usage as understanding the meaning of abstract concepts and synonyms. Diaz (1983) described semilinguals as "children whose second language gradually replaces the native tongue. Therefore, at a given point, these children are neither fluent speakers of the first language nor have mastered the second language with age-appropriate ability" (p. 33). Cummins (1979) also contended that the level of second-language competence that a child attains is partially a function of the type of competence the child has developed in his or her first language at the time that second-language learning takes place. This thesis is supported by research on English-speaking Canadian children attending French-language schools (Macnamara et al., 1976; Swain, 1978, cited in Cummins, 1979). These studies reported that by grade 6, English-speaking children attending French-medium schools did not differ in English achievement when compared with English-speaking children attending English-medium schools, although children attending French-medium schools received no English instruction before the third or fifth grade. Children in immersion programs also acquire second-language skills equal to those of native speakers by the end of elementary school. Cummins concluded: "These data suggest that (i) the prerequisites for acquiring literacy skills are instilled in most middle-class majority-language children by their linguistic experience in the home; (ii) the ability to extract meaning from printed text can be transferred easily from one language to another" (p. 234).

Cummins (1979) also noted that, compared with middle-class children, lower-class minority-language children do not enter school with adequate linguistic skills. He contended that "some children may have limited access to the cognitive-linguistic operations necessary to assimilate [a second language] and develop literacy skills in that language" (p. 236). Thus, lower-class minority-language children may be more dependent on the school to provide the prerequisites for the acquisition of literacy skills. However, Cummins also contended that such children's linguistic and academic growth is handicapped only when their functional literacy skills upon entry to school are translated into deficient levels of first- and second-language competence by inappropriate forms of educational treatment. Cummins hypothesized that "submersion" educational programs, which make no concessions to the child's native language or culture, are least likely to lead to positive achievement or motivational outcomes. Transitional bilingual programs, which use the native language as an instructional medium in the early grades while the child acquires proficiency in the second language, should result in the child's developing age-appropriate skills in the second language while competence in the native language fades away. Maintenance bilingual programs that provide instruction in two languages throughout the child's school career should produce an additive linguistic effect, leading to high levels of achievement in both languages. Cummins's hypotheses have yet to be tested by empirical research; however, he does provide a conceptual model that could be used as a framework for future research.

Most researchers agree that there is little hard evidence that one form of bilingual instruction is more effective than another. Many attempts to evaluate bilingual programs in the United States are plagued by methodological weaknesses that could invalidate their results. Commenting on the American Institutes of Research (1977) evaluation of Title VII bilingual programs, Cummins (1979) pointed out that "the AIR findings are uninterpretable since students whose language abilities are extremely varied and who have received a variety of educational treatments are aggregated for the purposes of data analyses" (p. 243). Cummins contends that bilingual education is a research area in which the interaction of background characteristics and treatment effects should be explored in an effort to ascertain which types of programs are most appropriate for children with different levels of functional linguistic skills.

Diaz (1983) noted two relatively neglected areas of research. He stated that there is a need for research on the effects of bilingualism on nonbalanced bilingual children (those with little knowledge of English). How many of these children (in which types of programs) will attain an effective balance between their two languages? How many will develop age-appropriate proficiency in either or both languages? A second area identified by Diaz as requiring additional research is that of information processing among young bilingual children. There is a need to develop a process model of how bilingualism affects children's cognitive development.

A recent survey (O'Malley, 1982) estimated that only one-third of all children of limited English proficiency in the United States are receiving some form of bilingual education or English as a second language instruction. Most of the children receiving bilingual instruction are in the early elementary grades. This suggests that most programs are not attempting to help children maintain their first language.

A number of politically sensitive questions may be answered by future research. For example, at what age should bilingual instruction begin? Is achievement more likely to be enhanced when instruction is begun in preschool, kindergarten, the primary grades, or the intermediate grades? What is the effect on the English achievement of bilingual children of including English-dominant or monolingual children in bilingual classes? How important is the cultural aspect of bilingual education for English achievement, self-concept, and attitudes toward school of minority-language children? Can maintenance bilingual programs for low-income minority-language children yield positive results similar to those reported for majority-language children in immersion programs?

Snow (1983) contends that children must acquire the ability to use language in a decontextualized manner if they are to be successful in school. Middle-class children acquire decontextualization in the home, but many lower-class homes do not provide the types of linguistic experiences that lead to the development of decontextualized language usage. This suggests that lower-class minority-language children may need preschool bilingual instruction to prepare them for school tasks. Curriculum development efforts at the preschool level show promise (Sandoval-Martinez, 1982), and additional developmental and evaluation research should be continued.

The areas of bilingual education and second-language acquisition have many research needs. The combination of strong political support for bilingual education from minority-language groups and support for improved foreign language instruction for English speakers should provide a climate conducive to vigorous research activity on language learning in the next decade.

INSTRUCTIONAL APPROACHES TO REDUCING EDUCATIONAL INEQUALITY

The primary objective of our education system is to assist children in realizing their maximum potential. Achieving this goal is in many ways contingent on the instructional method employed. In an effort to identify ways to maximize achievement and affective outcomes for the greatest number of children, we discuss instructional approaches that seem to offer promise. We provide a description of three alternative approaches to traditional instruction, discuss research findings from studies assessing their effectiveness, and comment on areas that warrant further investigation.

Open Education

Open education, in contrast to traditional education, involves greater flexibility in the use of space, more student choice of activity, a greater variety of learning materials, and more individual and small-group learning. Compared with traditional instruction, there is more emphasis on encouraging children's development of a sense of responsibility for their own learning and a sense of honesty and respect in interpersonal relationships.

Stallings (1975) studied first- and third-grade Follow Through classrooms representing "open" and "structured" models. She reported that teachers conformed to the instructional procedures prescribed by the sponsors and that the more structured approaches contributed to higher reading and math scores. However, she stated that "children taught by these methods tend to accept responsibility for their failures but not for their successes" (Stallings, 1975:106). The more open and flexible approaches are associated with lower absence rates and higher scores on a nonverbal problem-solving test of reasoning. The different approaches, according to Stallings, thus bring different strengths to their pupils. Cohen and De Avila (1983), citing Stallings, pointed out that structured or direct instruction approaches tend to contribute to achievement on a mathematics computation subtest to a greater extent than to achievement on a concepts and problem-solving subtest. Cohen and De Avila suggested that direct instruction contributes to the learning of tasks requiring memorization (e.g., computational skills) but that conceptual learning and problem-solving skills may be more effectively enhanced by other approaches (e.g., an approach that uses peer interaction and focuses on the teaching of problem-solving skills).

Recent reviews of research on open education (Hedges et al., 1981; Marshall, 1981) have found that programs labeled open education produce a variety of effects (Giaconia and Hedges, 1982:580):

Some open education programs produced particularly large, positive effects for student outcomes such as self-concept, reading achievement, creativity, locus of control, mathematics achievement, and favorable attitude toward school. Yet other open education programs yielded larger negative effects for these same student outcomes.

Differences in outcomes are attributable to differences in the specific components of open education that are implemented in different classrooms. The programs that produce superior effects on nonachievement outcomes have the following characteristics: (1) an active role for the child in guiding the learning process, (2) diagnostic evaluation rather than norm-referenced evaluation, (3) the presence of diverse materials to stimulate student exploration and learning, and (4) individualized instruction. It should be noted, however, that the programs that produce superior nonachievement outcomes tend to produce smaller than average effects on academic achievement (Giaconia and Hedges, 1982:586). However, traditional education appears to be only marginally more effective than open education for the traditional academic achievement measures. Giaconia and Hedges reported that "for many student outcomes, there are near zero differences between open and traditional education" (p. 586).

Additional research on open education should attempt to further explain the features that produce different achievement and nonachievement outcomes. There is also a need to look at differential effectiveness for student populations of different social compositions.

Lazar and Darlington (1982) conducted a study of the long-term effects of early childhood intervention programs. They did not address the structured versus open instruction controversy but rather assessed the average effect of program participation across the various models or programs. They concluded that "programs can be structured in a variety of ways, responding to complex and diverse needs of local communities, and still be potentially effective" (p. 65). Specifically, this research showed that children who attended programs were significantly more likely to meet their school's basic requirements. For example, they were less likely to have been retained in grade or to have been placed in special education classes than nonparticipants. Early education programs had a positive effect on IQ scores that lasted for 3 or 4 years, and program graduates did somewhat better on achievement tests than control subjects. In addition, program graduates had more positive attitudes toward achievement and school at the time of the follow-up. Finally, early education programs appear to have had a positive effect on children's families: Mothers of participants were more satisfied with their children's school performance than were mothers of controls, and they had high occupational aspirations for their children. Perhaps the most important lesson to be gained from this study is that instructional philosophies that differ drastically along the dimensions of openness and directedness can in the long run enhance children's educational competencies.

Cooperative Small-Group Instruction

The typical classroom goal structure is either competitive or individualistic. Classrooms organized on these principles encourage students to view their peers either as competitors for scarce rewards (teacher praise or grades) or as persons whose actions are unrelated to their own achievement. Most educators view cooperation as a desired outcome of schooling, but few efforts are made to organize instruction in ways that foster cooperation. Johnson and Johnson (1979) have undertaken research on cooperative goal structures, which foster interdependence among students. Students achieve their goals only if other students with whom they are linked achieve their goals.

According to these authors, cooperative goal structures can be set up in classrooms without great difficulty. The research results promise both achievement gains and more positive attitudes toward teachers, peers, school, and self. The major obstacle to the implementation of such strategies is currently parental, teacher, administrator, and political leadership attitudes.

Slavin and DeVries (1979) presented considerable evidence that learning in teams can produce the type of cooperative learning effects described by Johnson and Johnson (1979); however, these authors make a distinction between the games approach and the cooperative technique used with experimental groups at the University of Minnesota (Johnson and Johnson, 1979). The cooperative experimental groups have not demonstrated greater effects on achievement than standard techniques used with control groups. The team techniques that have been most successful in increasing academic performance require individual accountability on the part of students (e.g., Teams-Games-Tournaments; Jigsaw).

To raise the achievement levels of minority children, therefore, it is not enough to set up a cooperative reward and task structure and wait for achievement to increase. One reason for this is subcultural differences in response to different learning structures. For example, Lucker et al. (1976) found that Anglo children performed equally well in interdependent (using games) and traditional classes, but black and Mexican-American children performed significantly better in the interdependent classes. In interdependent classes the achievement level for minorities and Anglos did not differ; in traditional classes, however, Anglo children performed significantly better than minority children. Compared with those in traditional classrooms, students in interdependent learning groups increased in self-esteem, decreased in preference for competitive behavior, and viewed their classmates as learning resources.

A second constraint on the effectiveness of cooperative learning structures for increasing minority students' achievement has been noted by Cohen (1980) and Schofield and Sagar (1979). The reservations are based on observed effects of status differences in socioeconomic background and reading ability on patterns of interaction in interracial classroom groups. Since these status differences usually favor whites, patterns of dominance and friendship selection usually favor whites as well. Consequently, careful attention must be paid to organizing classroom learning groups so that they do not reinforce already existing patterns of status association and competence expectations. Cohen stated that "combining racial groups with similar levels of academic achievement makes it much easier to produce equal status relationships" (1980:273). Cohen also recommended reorganizing classrooms so as to minimize the continued use of reading competence as the major source of students' expectations about competence in general. This involves attention to multiple skills in the curriculum and the use of small groups in instruction. As Slavin and DeVries (1979:136–137) concluded:

If a school wants to promote positive race relations, to increase students' academic performance, to encourage mutual concern, and to develop self-esteem, team techniques may be a means to accomplishing those goals. They are practical and inexpensive, require no special training, and generate enthusiasm. Further, they have been extensively researched and field-tested in hundreds of classrooms.

There is ample evidence that school environments are often less congenial to minority children than to middle-class white children. For example, Mercer et al. (1974) found that third- and sixth-grade teachers rated Anglo children as significantly more competent and sociable than black or Mexican-American children. As long as these kinds of teacher attitudes exist, we are a long way from achieving the goal of effective integrated education. Restructuring schools so that they use cooperative learning structures and team techniques should help to overcome some of these problems. It will also be necessary, however, to change teachers' and administrators' attitudes about instructional processes as well as about the learning potential of minority students.

Mastery Learning

Mastery learning is an instructional technique based on Bloom's theory of school learning (1976). This technique is purported to ensure that 80–90 percent of the students receiving instruction under this method can achieve as high as the top 10 percent of the students in conventional classes. One of the most salient aspects of mastery learning is a corrective feedback procedure. It makes provisions for students to receive corrections and thus to some extent achieve mastery prior to proceeding to the next level or skill.

Findings from studies designed to assess this method's effectiveness support this claim. Block and Burns (1977) reported that 89 percent of the time mastery learning classes achieve at higher levels than students in classrooms using traditional methods. Bloom (1976) reported that the average student in mastery learning classes realized a level of achievement as high as students ranked at the 80th percentile in conventional classes. Furthermore, variation in achievement also tends to decline under the mastery learning technique.

Although Bloom estimated that the mastery learning approach is second only to tutoring in increasing educational achievement, it is not without problems. It is difficult to convince teachers and administrators that ability is not distributed along a normal bell-shaped curve. Bloom construes ability in terms of the amount of time it takes the student to learn a given unit, rather than in terms of how much a student can eventually learn. Consequently, Bloom (1982:13) urges researchers to spend less time classifying and predicting humans and more time and energy on the variables, processes, and concepts that can make a vast difference in teaching and learning. Bloom also contends that human potential for learning is best estimated under optimal conditions for learning. Therefore, the limits of human potential for learning should not be bound by estimates based on traditional methods.

Research Needs

Research on improving the quality of instruction is important and should continue to be a major force. The work of "master developers" (Rosenshine, in press), such as Bloom (mastery learning) and Slavin (student team learning), promises to have a direct effect on instructional practice. Implementation processes as well as theoretical developments should be stressed in future research on such instructional programs. In particular, there is a need for careful studies of the effects of various forms of within-class ability grouping on student achievement, attitudes, and behavior. There are no experimental studies of this critical dimension of classroom organization. Research of this type has been proposed by Slavin and Karweit. In addition, instructional pacing (Barr, 1974) has been found to have an important effect on learning. The emphasis of research should be on how pacing interacts with grouping to enhance or impede learning for different types of students (e.g., of high or low ability).

The use of statistical research synthesis (Burstein, 1980; Glass, 1978; Hedges, 1982; Lazar and Darlington, 1982) is increasing and should help clarify research results in areas in which a substantial body of research has conflicting conclusions. There is still a need, however, for studies that go beyond comparisons of program effects or the effects of student and teacher characteristics. A major focus of research should be on the processes of teaching and learning as they take place under specific conditions. Direct observations of classroom processes in conjunction with well-designed experiments are needed to improve our understanding of educational processes. The research should be guided by carefully constructed causal models that can be tested empirically in classrooms and schools. The emphasis should be on alterable variables that are amenable to manipulation by educators and policy makers (see Bloom, 1980).

CONCLUSION

This review has many gaps. For example, gender differences have been discussed primarily in the context of studies of other phenomena, yet a large portion of this chapter could have been devoted to that topic. Issues such as school desegregation and bilingual education, which appear to be fertile areas for research, are treated in greater detail. We chose to focus on what we perceive as the cross-cutting issues: the role of schooling, models of research on the effects of schooling, what happens to children in schools, and societal influences on schooling.

Children ages 6–12 exhibit tremendous physical growth and cognitive and emotional development. The graded structure of the schools attempts to provide learning settings and tasks appropriate to the children's developmental levels. The match is often less than perfect because knowledge of developmental progressions is at best fragmentary, and developmental progression itself is not static. As with other institutions, schools are slow to change.

Next to spending time with the family, children ages 6–12 spend most of their time in school. The type of learning and affective environment provided by the school can have a profound impact on children's intellectual and social development. Ecological research in classrooms suggests that children from different socioeconomic backgrounds experience schooling in different ways. There is lack of agreement among researchers with regard to the effects of different patterns of classroom organization and the way teacher attitudes and student characteristics interact to influence learning. We need to know more about how students perceive their classroom experiences and how these perceptions influence their achievement, attitudes, and behavior. It is probable that students perceive teacher behavior and instructional practices in different ways. We do not know much about how student perceptions interact with teacher behavior to produce motivation to learn or to avoid learning.

Student diversity continues to be a major issue. Not much is known about the relationship of various classroom management strategies to outcomes for students with different personal and social characteristics. There is a need to focus research on the quality of instruction and study the way students of different levels of ability and students from different cultural backgrounds react to different ways of presenting instruction.

There is much current activity involving children ages 6–12 in the school setting. Some of this research promises to expand our understanding of the impact of school on children. The linguistic approach to studying teaching-learning processes may help to explain how language is used to construct contexts of education and the meanings within those constructs. Integrating new developments from the study of cognition into research on classroom instruction may also increase our understanding of how schools influence children. Finally, far too little attention has been paid to outcomes of education other than academic achievement. To gain a better perspective on school influences, researchers should also focus on social development, attitudes, and values.

REFERENCES

Allport, G.
1954   *The Nature of Prejudice.* Reading, Mass.: Addison-Wesley.
American Institutes of Research
1977   Evaluation of the Impact of ESEA Title VII Spanish/English Bilingual Education Programs. Palo Alto, Calif.: American Institutes of Research.
Anania, J.
1981   The Effects of Quality of Instruction on the Cognitive and Affective Learning of Students. Unpublished doctoral dissertation, University of Chicago.
Anderson, C.S.
1982   The search for school climate: A review of the research. *Review of Educational Research* 52:368–420.
Banks, C., and McQuater, G.
1976   Achievement motivation and black children. *IRCD Bulletin* 11:4 (entire issue).
Baratz, J., and Baratz, S.
1970   Early childhood intervention: The social science base of institutional racism. *Harvard Educational Review* 40:29–50.
Barr, R.C.
1974   Instructional pace differences and their effect on reading acquisition. *Reading Research Quarterly* 9:526–554.
Barr, R., and Dreeben, R.
1983   *How Schools Work.* Chicago: University of Chicago Press.
Beckerman, T., and Good, T.
1981   The classroom ratio of high- and low-aptitude students and its effect on achievement. *American Educational Research Journal* 18:317–327.
Benham, B.J., Giesen, P., and Oakes, J.
1980   A study of schooling: Students' experiences in schools. *Phi Delta Kappa* 61:337–340.
Block, J., and Burns, R.
1977   Mastery learning. In L. Schulman, ed., *Review of Research in Education.* Vol. 4. Itasca, Ill.: Peacock.
Bloom, B.S.
1976   *Human Characteristics and School Learning.* New York: McGraw-Hill.
1980   The new direction in educational research: Alterable variables. *Phi Delta Kappa* 61:382–385.
1982   The future of educational research. *Educational Researcher* 11:6, 11–19.
Bowles, S.
1975   Unequal education and the reproduction of the social division of labor. In M. Carnoy, ed., *Schooling in a Corporate Society.* Second ed. New York: David McKay.
Bowles, S., and Gintis, H.
1976   *Schooling in Capitalist Society: Educational Reform and the Contradictions of Economic Life.* New York: Basic Books.
Bradley, L., and Bradley, G.
1977   The academic achievement of black students in desgregated schools. *Review of Educational Research* 47:399–499.
Bronfenbrenner, U.
1974   Is early intervention effective? *Teachers College Record* 76:279–303.
Brookover, W.B., and Lezotte, L.W.
1979   Changes in School Characteristics Coincident with Changes in Student Achievement (Executive Summary). Occasional Paper No. 17, Michigan State University, Institute for Research on Teaching, May.

Brookover, W.B., Patterson, A., and Thomas, S.
1962   Self-Concept of Ability and School Achievement. U.S. Office of Education, Cooperative
        Research Project No. 845. East Lansing : Office of Research and Publications, Michigan
        State University.
Brookover, W., Beady, C., Flood, P., Schweitzer, J., and Wisenbaker, J.
1979   School Social Systems and Student Achievement: Schools Can Make a Difference. New York:
        Praeger.
Brophy, J.
1970   Mothers as teachers of their own preschool children: The influence of socioeconomic
        status and task structure on teaching specificity. Child Development 41:79–94.
Brophy, J.E., and Evertson, C.M.
1974   Process Product Correlations in the Texas Teacher Effectiveness Study. Report No. 74-4.
        Austin: University of Texas Research and Development Center for Teacher Education.
Brophy, J., and Good, T.
1974   Teacher-Student Relationships: Causes and Consequences. New York: Holt, Rinehart &
        Winston.
Burstein, L.
1980   The analysis of multilevel data in educational research and evaluation. In D.C. Berliner,
        ed., Review of Research in Education. Vol. 8. Washington, D.C.: American Educational
        Research Association.
Buriel, R.
1981   Relation of Anglo- and Mexican-American children's locus of control beliefs to parents'
        and teachers' socialization practicies. Child Development 52:104–113.
Busk, P., Ford, R., and Schulman, J.
1973   Effects of schools' racial composition on the self-concept of black and white students.
        Journal of Educational Research 67:57–63.
Carew, J.
1980   Experience and the development of intelligence in young children at home and in day
        care. Monographs of the Society for Research in Child Development 45(6–7, Serial no. 187).
Carroll, J.G.
1963   A model of school learning. Teachers College Record 64:723–733.
Cicirelli, V.
1977   Relationship of socioeconomic status and ethnicity to primary grade children's self-
        concept. Psychology in the Schools 14:213–215.
Clark, K.
1965   Dark Ghetto. New York: Harper & Row.
Clark, R.
1982   The Quality of Family Pedagogic Life: What Is That? Unpublished paper presented at
        the annual meeting of the American Educational Research Association, New York.
Clarke-Stewart, K.A.
1973   Interactions between mothers and their young children: Characteristics and conse-
        quences. Monographs of the Society for Research in Child Development 38(6–7, Serial no.
        153).
Cohen, E.
1975   The effects of desegregation on race relations. Law and Contemporary Problems 39:271–
        299.
1980   Design and redesign of the desegregated school: Problems of status, power, and conflict.
        In W. Stephan and J. Fegin, eds., School Desegregation: Past, Present and Future. New
        York: Plenum Press.
Cohen, E., and De Avila, E.
1983   Indirect Instruction and Conceptual Learning. Unpublished paper, Stanford University.

Coleman, J.S., Campbell, E.Q., Mabson, C.J., McPartland, J., Mood, A., Weinfeld, F.D., and York, R.L.
   1966   *Equality of Educational Opportunity.* 2 vols. Washington, D.C.: Office of Education, U.S. Department of Health, Education and Welfare.
Comer, James P.
   1980   *School Power.* New York: Free Press.
Connell, J.P.
   1980   A Multidimensional Measure of Children's Perceptions of Control. Unpublished master's thesis, University of Denver.
Coopersmith, S.
   1967   *The Antecedents of Self-Esteem.* San Francisco: W.H. Freeman.
Corno, L., Mitman, A., and Hedges, L.
   1981   The influence of direct instruction on student self-appraisals: A hierarchical analysis of treatment and aptitude-treatment interaction effects. *American Educational Research Journal* 18:39–61.
Coulson, J., Hanes, S., Ozene, D., Bradford, C., Doherty, W., Duck, G., and Hemenway, J.
   1977   *The Third Year of Emergency School Aid Act (ESAA) Implementation.* Santa Monica, Calif.: System Development Corp.
Crain, R., and Mahard, R.
   1982   *Desegregation Plans That Raise Black Achievement: A Review of the Research.* Santa Monica, Calif.: Rand Corp.
   1983   The effect of research methodology on desegregation-achievement studies: A meta-analysis. *American Journal of Sociology* 88:839–854.
Crain, R., Mahard, R., and Narot, R.
   1981   *Making Desegregation Work: How Schools Create Social Climates.* Cambridge, Mass.: Ballinger.
Cronbach, L., and Snow, R.
   1977   *Aptitude and Instructional Methods.* New York: Irving Productions.
Cummins, J.
   1979   Linguistic interdependence and the educational development of bilingual children. *Review of Educational Research* 49:222–251.
Dave, R.
   1963   The Identification and Measurement of Environmental Process Variables That Are Related to Educational Achievement. Unpublished doctoral dissertation, University of Chicago.
DeBord, L., Griffin, L., and Clark, M.
   1977   Race and sex influence in the schooling process of rural and small town youth. *Sociology of Education* 50:85–102.
Diaz, R.
   1983   Thought and two languages: The impact of bilingualism on cognitive growth. In E. Gordon, ed., *Review of Research in Education.* Vol. 10. Washington, D.C.: American Educational Research Association.
Dolan, L.
   1978   The affective consequences of home support, instructional quality, and achievement. *Urban Education* 13:323–344.
Dreeben, R.
   1968   *On What Is Learned in School.* Reading, Mass.: Addison-Wesley.
Dunkin, M.J., and Biddle, B.J.
   1974   *The Study of Teaching.* New York: Holt, Rinehart & Winston.
Dweck, C., Davidson, W., Nelson, S., and Enna, B.
   1978   Sex differences in learned helplessness: II. The contingencies of evaluative feedback in the classroom. III. An experimental analysis. *Developmental Psychology* 14:268–276.

Dyer, P.
  1967   Home Environment and Achievement in Trinidad. Unpublished doctoral dissertation, University of Alberta.
Eder, D.
  1981   Ability grouping as a self-fulfilling prophecy: A micro-analysis of teacher-student interaction. *Sociology of Education* 54:151–161.
Edmonds, R.
  1979   Some schools work and more can. *Social Policy* (March/April):28–32.
Edmonds, R.R., and Fredericksen, J.R.
  1978   *Search for Effective Schools: The Identification and Analysis of City Schools That Are Instructionally Effective for Poor Children.* Cambridge, Mass.: Harvard University, Center for Urban Studies.
Elashoff, J., and Snow, R.
  1971   *Pygmalion Reconsidered.* Worthington, Ohio: Jones.
Ellett, C.D., Payne, D.A., Master, J.A., and Pool, J.E.
  1977   The Relationship Between Teacher and Student Assessments of School Environment Characteristics and School Outcome Variables. Paper presented at the twenty-third annual meeting of the Southeastern Psychological Association, Hollywood, Fla., May.
Entwisle, D.R., and Hayduk, L.A.
  1978   *Too Great Expectations: The Academic Outlook of Young Children.* Baltimore, Md.: Johns Hopkins University Press.
  1982   *Early Schooling Cognitive and Affective Outcomes.* Baltimore, Md.: Johns Hopkins University Press.
Epps, E.
  1969   Correlates of academic achievement among northern and southern urban Negro students. *Journal of Social Issues* 25(3):55–70.
  1975   Impact of school desegregation on aspirations, self-concept, and other aspects of personality. *Law and Contemporary Problems* 39:300–313.
  1978   The impact of school desegregation on the self-evaluation and achievement orientation of minority children. *Law and Contemporary Problems* 42:57–76.
  1981   Minority children: Desegregation, self-evaluation, and achievement motivation. In W. Hawley, ed., *Effective School Desegregation: Equity, Quality, and Feasibility.* Beverly Hills, Calif.: Sage.
Epstein, J.
  1983   Longitudinal effects of family-school-person interactions on student outcomes. In A. Kerckhoff, ed., *Research in Sociology of Education and Socialization.* Vol. 4. Greenwich, Conn.: JAI Press.
Epstein, J., and Becker, H.J.
  1982   Teachers' reported practices of parent involvement: Problems and possibilities. *Elementary School Journal* 83:103–113.
Fernandez, R., and Guskin, J.
  1981   Hispanic students and school desegregation. In W. Hawley, ed., *Effective School Desegregation: Equity, Quality, and Feasibility.* Beverly Hills, Calif.:Sage.
Findley, M., and Cooper, H.
  1983   Locus of control and academic achievement: A literature review. *Journal of Personality and Social Psychology* 44:419–427.
Fisher, C.W., Filby, N.N., Maliave, R., Cohen, L.S., Dishaw, M.M., Moore, J.E., and Berliner, D.C.
  1978   Teaching Behaviors, Academic Learning Time and Student Achievement. Final report of Phase III-B, Beginning Teacher Evaluation Study. Far West Laboratory for Educational Research and Development, San Francisco.

Forehand, G., Ragosta, M., and Rock, D.
1976   *Conditions and Processes of Effective School Desegregation.* Princeton, N.J.: Educational Testing Service.

Froemel, J.
1980   Cognitive Entry Behaviors, Instructional Conditions, and Achievement: A Study of Their Interrelationships. Unpublished doctoral dissertation, University of Chicago.

Fuerst, J.
1977   Child parent centers: An evaluation. *Integrated Education* (May-June):17–20.

Gage, N.L.
1972   *Teacher Effectiveness and Teacher Education.* Palo Alto, Calif.: Pacific.
1978   *The Scientific Basis of the Art of Teaching.* New York: Teachers College Press.

Gallimore, R., and Au, K.
1979   The competence/incompetence paradox in the education of minority culture children. *The Quarterly Newsletter of the Laboratory of Comparative Human Cognition* 1(3):32–37.

Gaudry, E., and Spielberger, C., eds.
1971   *Anxiety and School Achievement.* Sydney, Australia: John Wiley & Sons.

Gerard H., and Miller, N.
1975   *School Desegregation.* New York: Plenum Press

Gerard, H., Jackson, T., and Conolley, E.
1975   Social contact in the desegregated classroom. In H. Gerard and N. Miller, eds., *School Desegregation.* New York: Plenum Press.

Giaconia, R.M. and Hedges, L.V.
1982   Identifying features of effective open education. *Review of Educational Research* 52:579–602.

Glass, G.V.
1978   Integrating findings: The meta-analysis of research. In L.S. Shulman, ed., *Review of Research in Education.* Vol. 5. Itasca, Ill.: Peacock.

Glass, G.V., and Smith, M.
1978   *Meta-Analysis of Research on the Relationship of Class Size and Achievement.* San Francisco: Far West Laboratory for Educational Research and Development.

Glass, G., Cohen, E., and Smith, M.
1982   *School Class Size: Research and Policy.* Beverly Hills, Calif.: Sage.

Good, T.L.
1983   Classroom research: A decade of progress. *Educational Psychologist* 18:127–144.

Goodchilds, J., Green, J., and Biksen, T.
1975   The school experience and adjustment. In H. Gerard and N. Miller, eds., *School Desegregation.* New York: Plenum Press.

Goodlad, J.I.
1973   The elementary school as a social institution. In J. Goodlad and H. Shane, eds., *The Elementary School in the United States.* Seventy-second Yearbook of the National Society for the Study of Education, Part II. Chicago: University of Chicago Press.
1983   Individuality, commonality, and curricular practice. In G. Fenstermacher and J. Goodlad, eds., *Individual Differences and the Common Curriculum.* Eighty-second Yearbook of the National Society for the Study of Education, Part I. Chicago: University of Chicago Press.

Goodlad, J.I., Sirotnik, K.S., and Overman, B.C.
1979   An overview of a study of schooling. *Phi Delta Kappa* 61:174–178.

Grant, L.
1981   Race, Sex, and Schooling: Social Location and Children's Experiences in Desegregated Classrooms. Unpublished dissertation, University of Michigan.

Green, D., Miller, N., and Gerard, D.
1975   Personality traits and adjustment. In H. Gerard and N. Miller, eds., School Desegregation. New York: Plenum Press.
Hare, B.
1977   Racial and socioeconomic variation in preadolescent area-specific and general self-esteem. International Journal of Intercultural Relations 1:31–51.
1980   Self-perception and academic achievement: Variations in a desegregated setting. American Journal of Psychiatry 137:683–689.
Harter, S.
1978   Effectance motivation reconsidered: Toward a developmental model. Human Development 1:34–64.
1981   A new self-report scale of intrinsic versus extrinsic orientation in the classroom: Motivational and informational components. Developmental Psychology 17:300–312.
1982   The perceived competence scale for children. Child Development 53:87–97.
Harter, S., and Connell, J.P.
In   A model of the relationship among children's academic achievement and their self-
press   perceptions of competence, control, and motivational orientation. In J. Nicholls, ed., The Development of Achievement Motivation. Greenwich, Conn.: JAI Press.
Hedges, L.V.
1981   Appendix note: Illustrating two-aptitude treatment interactions: A methodological note. American Educational Research Journal 18:57–61.
1982   Estimating effect size from a series of independent experiments. Psychological Bulletin 92:490–499.
Hedges, L.V., Giaconia, R.M., and Gage, N.L.
1981   Meta-Analysis of the Effects of Open and Traditional Instruction. Stanford University Program on Teaching Effectiveness Meta-Analysis Project, Final Report, Vol. 2.
Heller, K., Holtzman, W., and Messick, S., eds.
1982   Placing Children in Special Education: A Strategy for Equity. Panel on Selection and Placement of Students in Programs for the Mentally Retarded, Committee on Child Development Research and Public Policy. Washington, D.C.: National Academy Press.
Hess, R.
1970   Social class and ethnic influences on socialization. In P. Mussen, ed., Carmichael's Manual of Child Psychology. Vol. 2. New York: John Wiley & Sons.
Hess, R., and Shipman, V.
1965   Early experience and the socialization of cognitive modes in children. Child Development 36:869–886.
1967   Cognitive elements in maternal behavior. In J. Hill, ed., Minnesota Symposia on Child Psychology. Vol. 1. Minneapolis: University of Minnesota.
Hess, R., Holloway, S., Price, G., and Dickson, W.
1980   Family environments and the acquisition of reading skills. In L. Laosa and I. Sigel, eds., Families as Learning Environments for Children. New York: Plenum Press.
Hewison, J., and Tizard, J.
1980   Parental involvement and reading attainment. The British Journal of Educational Psychology 50:209–215.
Heyneman, S.
1976   A brief note on the relationship between socioeconomic status and test performance among Ugandan primary school children. Comparative Education Review 20:42–47.
Heyns, B.
1978   Summer Learning and the Effects of Schooling. New York: Academic.
Holliday, B.G.
1984   Towards a structural model of teacher-child transactional processes affecting black children's academic achievement. In M. Spencer, G. Brookings, and W. Allen, eds., Be-

ginnings: *The Social and Affective Development of Black Children.* Hillsdale, N.J.: Lawrence Erlbaum.

Hunt, J., and Hunt, L.
1977   Racial inequality and self-image: Identity maintenance as identity diffusion. *Sociology and Social Research* 61:539–559.

Inkeles, A.
1968   Social structure and the socialization of competence. In *Socialization and Schools.* Reprint Series No. 1, *Harvard Educational Review.*

Jackson, P.W.
1968   *Life in Classrooms.* New York: Holt, Rinehart & Winston.

Janicki, T., and Peterson, P.
1981   Aptitude-treatment interaction effects of variations in direct instruction. *American Educational Research Journal* 18:63–82.

Jencks, C., Smith, M., Acland, H., Bane, M., Cohen, D., Gintis, H., Heyns, B., and Michelson, S.
1972   *Inequality: A Reassessment of the Effect of Family and Schooling in America.* New York: Basic Books.

Johnson, D.W., and Johnson, R.T.
1979   Cooperation, competition, and individualization. In H.J. Walberg, ed., *Educational Environments and Effects.* Berkeley, Calif.: McCutchan.

Johnson, D.W., Johnson, R.T., and Maruyama, G.
1983   Interdependence and interpersonal attraction among heterogeneous and homogeneous individuals: A theoretical formulation and a meta-analysis of the research. *Review of Educational Research* 53:5–54.

Kellaghan, T.
1977   Relationships between home environment and scholastic behavior in a disadvantaged population. *Journal of Educational Psychology* 69:754–760.

Kifer, E.
1975   Relationship between academic achievement and personality characteristics: A quasi-longitudinal study. *American Educational Research Journal* 12:191–220.

Kohn, M.
1969   *Class and Conformity: A Study in Values.* Second ed. Chicago: University of Chicago Press.

Krol, D.F.
1978   A Meta-Analysis of School Desegregation and Achievement. Unpublished doctoral dissertation, Western Michigan University.

Laosa, L.
1977   Socialization, education, and continuity: The importance of the socioculture context. *Young Children* 32:21-27.
1982   School, occupation, culture and family: The impact of parental schooling on the parent-child relationship. *Journal of Education Psychology* 74:791–827.

Lavin, D.E.
1965   *The Prediction of Academic Performance: A Theoretical Analysis and Review of Research.* New York: Russell Sage Foundation.

Lazar, I., and Darlington, R.
1982   Lasting effects of early education: A report from the consortium for longitudinal studies. *Monographs for Research in Child Development* 47 (2–3, Serial no. 195.)

Leacock, E.
1969   *Teaching and Learning in City Schools.* New York: Basic Books.
1982   The influence of teacher attitudes on children's performance: Case studies. In K. Borman, ed., *The Social Life of Children in a Changing Society.* Hillsdale, N.J.: Lawrence Erlbaum.

Leiter, J.
1983   Classroom composition and achievement gains. *Sociology of Education* 56:126–132.
Lesser, G., Fifer, G., and Clark, D.
1967   Mental abilities of children in different social and cultural groups. In J. Roberts, ed., *School Children in the Urban Slum*. New York: Free Press.
Levine, D., Lachowicz, H., Oxman, K., and Tangeman, A.
1972   The home environment of students in a high achieving inner-city parochial school and a nearby public school. *Sociology of Education* 45:435–445.
Lightfoot, S.
1979   Families and schools. In H. Walberg, ed., *Educational Environment and Effects*. Berkeley, Calif.: McCutchan.
Lucker, G., Rosenfeld, D., Sikes, J., and Aaronson, E.
1976   Performance in the interdependent classroom: A field study. *American Educational Research Journal* 68:588–596.
Macnamara, J., Svarc, J., and Horner, S.
1976   Attending a primary school of the other language in Montreal. In A. Simoes, Jr., ed., *The Bilingual Child*. New York: Academic Press.
Marjoribanks, K.
1979   Family environments. In H. Walberg, ed., *Educational Environments and Effects*. Berkeley, Calif.: McCutchan.
Marshall, H.H.
1981   Open classrooms: Has the term outlived its usefulness? *Review of Educational Research* 51:182–192.
Maruyama, G., Rubin, R., and Kingsbury, G.
1981   Self-esteem and educational achievement: Independent constructs with a common cause. *Journal of Personality and Social Psychology* 40:962–975.
Massey, G., Scott, M., and Dornbusch, S.
1975   Racism without racists: Institutional racism in urban schools. *The Black Scholar* 7:2–11.
McAdoo, H.P.
1977   The development of self-concept and race attitudes in black children: A longitudinal study. In *Report of the Third Conference on Empirical Research in Black Psychology*. Washington, D.C.: National Institute of Education.
McConahay, J.
1978   The effects of school desegregation upon students' racial attitudes and behavior: A critical review of the literature and a prolegomenon to future research. *Law and Contemporary Problems* 42:77–107.
McDill, E.L., and Rigsby, L.C.
1973   *Structure and Process in Secondary Schools: The Academic Impact of Educational Climates*. Baltimore, Md.: Johns Hopkins University Press.
McPartland, J.M., and Karweit, N.
1979   Research on educational effects. In H.J. Walberg, ed., *Educational Environments and Effects*. Berkeley, Calif.: McCutchan.
Meece, J.L., Parsons, J.E., Kaczala, C.M., Goff, S.B., and Futterman, R.
1982   Sex differences in math achievement: Toward a model of academic choice. *Psychological Bulletin* 91:324–348.
Mercer, J., Coleman, M., and Harloe, J.
1974   Racial/ethnic segregation and desegregation in American public education. In C. Gordon, ed., *Uses of the Sociology of Education*. 73rd Yearbook of the National Society for the Study of Education, Part II. Chicago: University of Chicago Press.
Mercy, J.A., and Steelman, L.C.
1982   Familial influence on the intellectual attainment of children. *American Sociological Review* 47:532–542.

Miller, A.
1982 Changes in Self-Esteem in Early School Years: Cognitive Development or Declining Self-Affect. Paper presented at the annual meeting of the American Educational Research Association, New York, March.
Minuchin, P.P., and Shapiro, E.K.
1983 The school as a context for social development. In P.H. Mussen, ed., *Handbook of Child Psychology*. Fourth ed. E.M. Hetherington, ed., *Social Development*, Vol. 3. New York: John Wiley & Sons.
Moore, E.G.
1981 Ethnicity as a Variable in Child Development. Unpublished paper, Arizona State University.
Murnane, R.J.
1975 *The Impact of School Resources on the Learning of Inner City Children*. Cambridge: Ballinger.
Ogbu, J.U.
1978 *Minority Education and Caste: The American School System in Cross-Cultural Perspective*. New York: Academic Press.
1981 Origins of human competence: A cultural-ecological perspective. *Child Development* 52:413–429.
1983 Crossing Cultural Boundaries: A Comparative Perspective on Minority Education. Unpublished paper for a Symposium on Race, Class, Socialization, and the Life Cycle, University of Chicago, October 21–22.
O'Malley, J.M.
1982 Instructional services for limited English proficient children. *NABE Journal* 7:21–35.
Patchen, M.
1982 *Black-White Contact in Schools: Its Social and Academic Effects*. West Lafayette, Ind.: Purdue University Press.
Peal, E., and Lambert, W.
1962 The relation of bilingualism to intelligence. *Psychological Monographs* 76(546):1–23.
Purkey, W.
1970 *Self-Concept and School Achievement*. Englewood Cliffs, N.J.: Prentice-Hall.
Ramirez, M., and Price-Williams, D.
1976 Achievement motivation in children of three ethnic groups in the United States. *Journal of Cross-Cultural Psychology* 7:49–60.
Rist, R.C.
1970 Student social class and teacher expectations: The self-fulfilling prophecy in ghetto education. *Harvard Educational Review* 40:411–451.
1973 *The Urban School: A Factory for Failure*. Cambridge, Mass.: MIT Press.
Rosenshine, B.V.
1971 *Teaching Behaviors and Student Achievement*. London: National Foundation for Educational Research in England and Wales.
In The master teacher and the master developer. In M. Wang and H. Walberg, eds.,
press *Adapting Instruction to Student Differences: A Synthesis of Theory, Research and Practice*. Berkeley, Calif.: McCutchan.
Rosenthal, R., and Jacobson, L.
1968 *Pygmalion in the Classroom*. New York: Holt, Rinehart & Winston.
Rowan, B., and Miracle, A.W., Jr.
1983 Systems of ability grouping and the stratification of achievement in elementary schools. *Sociology of Education* 56(July):133–144.
Ruhland, D., and Feld, S.
1977 The development of achievement motivation in black and white children. *Child Development* 48:1362–1368.

DEVELOPMENT DURING MIDDLE CHILDHOOD

Rutter, M.
  1983   School effects on pupil progress: Research findings and policy implications. *Child Development* 54:1–29.
Rutter, M., Maughn, B., Mortimore, P., Ouston, J., and Smith, A.
  1979   *Fifteen-Thousand Hours: Secondary Schools and Their Effects on Children.* Cambridge, Mass.: Harvard University Press.
Sandoval-Martinez, S.
  1982   Findings from the Head Start bilingual curriculum development effort. *NABE Journal* 7:1–12.
Sarason, S., Lighthall, F., Waite, R., and Ruebush, B.
  1960   *Anxiety in Elementary School Children.* New York: John Wiley & Sons.
Scheirer, M., and Kraut, R.
  1979   Increasing educational achievement via self-concept change. *Review of Educational Research* 49:131–150.
Schofield, J.
  1979   The impact of positively structured contact on intergroup behavior: Does it last under adverse conditions? *Social Psychology Quarterly* 42:280–284.
Schofield, J., and McGivern, E.
  1978   Who Likes Desegregated Schools? The Effect of Sex and Race on Students' Attitudes. Paper presented at the meeting of the American Educational Research Association, Toronto, March.
Schofield, J., and Sager, A.
  1979   The social context of learning in an interracial school. In R. Rist, ed., *Desegregated Schools: Appraisals of an American Experiment.* New York: Academic Press.
Scott, R., and McPartland, J.
  1982   Desegregation as national policy: Correlates of racial attitudes. *American Educational Research Journal* 19:397–414.
Shade, B.
  1982   Afro-American cognitive style: A variable in school success. *Review of Educational Research* 52:219–244.
Sharp, D., Gale, M., and Lave, C.
  1979   Education and cognitive development: The evidence from experimental research. *Monographs of the Society for Research in Child Development* 44(1–2, Serial no. 178).
Shipman, V., Boroson, M., Bridgemen, B., Gant, J., and Mikovsky, M.
  1976   *Disadvantaged Children and Their First School Experiences: Notable Early Characteristics of High and Low Achieving Black Low-SES Children.* (PR-76-21) Princeton, N.J.: Educational Testing Service (ERIC Document Reproduction Service No. ED 138–340).
Simpson, A., and Erickson, M.
  1983   Teachers' verbal and nonverbal communication patterns as a function of teacher race, student gender, and student race. *American Education Research Journal* 20:183–198.
Singer, H., Gerard, H., and Redfern, D.
  1975   Achievement. In H. Gerard and N. Miller, eds., *School Desegregation.* New York: Plenum Press.
Slaughter, D.
  1969   Maternal antecedents of the academic achievement behaviors of Afro-American Head Start children. *Educational Horizons* (Fall):24–28.
  1977   Relation of early parent-teacher socialization influences to achievement orientation and self-esteem in middle childhood among low-income black children. In J. Glidewell, ed., *The Social Context of Learning and Development.* New York: Gardner.
  1981   Social policy issues affecting infants. In B. Weissbourd and J. Musich, eds., *Infants: Their Social Environments.* Washington, D.C.: National Association for the Education of Young Children.

1983   Education and family. In B. Bloom and C. Mathis, eds., The Schools, Schools of Education and Major Changes Affecting Education: The Crises of Our Time. Unpublished manuscript.

Slavin, R.E., and DeVries, D.L.
1979   Learning in teams. In H.J. Walberg, ed., *Educational Environments and Effects*. Berkeley, Calif.: McCutchan.

Slavin, R., and Madden, N.
1979   School practices that improve race relations. *American Educational Research Journal* 16:169–180.

Snow, C.E.
1983   Literacy and language: Relationships during the preschool years. *Harvard Educational Review* 53:165–189.

Sörensen, A.B.
1970   Organizational differentiation of students and educational opportunity. *Sociology of Education* 43:355–376.

Spencer, M.B.
1976   The Social-Cognitive and Personality Development of the Black Pre-school Child: An Exploratory Study of Developmental Process. Unpublished doctoral dissertation, University of Chicago.
1982   Personal and group identity of black children: An alternative hypothesis. *Genetic Psychology Monographs* 106:59–84.

St. John, N.H.
1975   *School Desegregation: Outcomes for Children*. New York: John Wiley & Sons.

St. John, N., and Lewis, R.
1975   Race and the social structure of the elementary classroom. *Sociology of Education* 48:346–368.

Stallings, J.
1975   Implementation and child effects of teaching practices in Follow Through classrooms, with commentary by M. Almy, L.B. Resnick, and G. Leinhardt. *Monographs of the Society for Research in Child Development* 43(165).

Stephen, W.
1978   School desegregation: An evaluation of predictions made in *Brown* v. *Board of Education*. *Psychological Bulletin* 85:217–237.

Stevenson, H.W., Parker, T., Wilkinson, A., Bonneveux, B., and Gonzalez, M.
1978   Schooling, environment, and cognitive development: A cross-cultural study. *Monographs of the Society for Research in Child Development* 43(3, Serial no. 175).

Stipek, D.J., and Weisz, J.R.
1981   Perceived personal control and academic achievement. *Review of Research in Education* 51:101–137.

Stodolsky, S.
1965   Maternal Behavior and Language and Concept Formation in Negro Pre-school Children: An Inquiry Into Process. Doctoral dissertation, University of Chicago.

Stodolsky, S., and Lesser, G.
1967   Learning patterns in the disadvantaged. *Harvard Educational Review* 37:546–593.

Strodtbeck, F.
1958   Family interaction, values and achievement. In D. McClelland et al., eds., *Talent and Society*. New York: Van Nostrand.

Summers, A.A., and Wolfe, B.L.
1977   Do schools make a difference? *American Economic Review* 67:639–652.

Swain, M.
  1978   French immersion: Early, late or partial? *The Canadian Modern Language Review* 34:557–585.
Tharp, R., and Gallimore, R.
  1982   Inquiry process in program development. *Journal of Community Psychology* 10:103–118.
Tizard, J., Schofield, W.N., and Hewison, J.
  1982   Collaboration between teachers and parents assisting children's reading. *British Journal of Educational Psychology* 52:1–15.
Tulkin, S.
  1972   An analysis of the concept of cultural deprivation. *Developmental Psychology* 6(2):326–339.
Walberg, H.J.
  1981   A psychological theory of educational productivity. In F. Farley and N. Gordon, eds., *Psychology and Education: The State of the Union*. Berkeley, Calif.: McCutchan.
Walden, T., and Ramey, C.
  1983   Locus of control and academic achievement: Results from a preschool intervention program. *Journal of Educational Psychology* 75:347–358.
Weber, G.
  1971   *Inner City Children Can Be Taught to Read: Four Successful Schools*. Occasional paper 18. Washington, D.C.: Council for Basic Education.
Weinberg, M.
  1977   *Minority Students: A Research Appraisal*. Washington, D.C.: National Institute of Education.
Weiss, J.
  1969   The Identification and Measure of Home Environmental Factors Related to Achievement Motivation and Self-Esteem. Unpublished dissertation, University of Chicago.
White, K.R.
  1982   The relation between socioeconomic status and academic achievement. *Psychological Bulletin* 91:461–481.
Wiley, D.E., and Harnischfeger, A.
  1974   Explosion of a myth: Quality of schooling and exposure to instruction, major educational vehicles. *Educational Researcher* 3:7–12.
World Bank
  1980   Education Sector Policy Paper. Third ed. W.D. Haddad, A. Habte, and M. Hultin. Washington, D.C.: World Bank.
Wylie, R.
  1974   *The Self-Concept*. Rev. ed. Lincoln: University of Nebraska Press.
  1979   *The Self-Concept: Theory and Research on Selected Topics*. Vol. 2. Lincoln: University of Nebraska Press.

CHAPTER 8

Ecocultural Niches of Middle Childhood: A Cross-Cultural Perspective

Thomas S. Weisner

I magine a satellite that could randomly sample the culture areas of the world. This imaginary satellite can focus on households with children ages 6–12 and can take audio and video recordings of their daily routines. The satellite can record with whom children associate; how far they venture from home; what work they do at what ages; the nature and difficulty of the tasks; with whom they work and how that work is shared; and the characteristics of the play group, household, and domestic group surrounding them. From the recordings we can assess the sources of child stimulation; how children explore the settings within their community; and with whom they talk and their topics of discourse and interaction. Children and adults in the sample communities could interpret the recordings and add to our understanding of settings and environments by bringing their subjective meanings to our interpretations. Together, the objective and subjective data would provide a systematic assessment of the social ecologies of childhood and development around the world. For any group of children we would be able to define their ecocultural niche (Super and Harkness, 1982).

The term *ecocultural niche* defines what Bronfenbrenner (1979) called the ecology of child development, going back to the tradition of Barker and Wright (1954). In comparative and cross-cultural studies (e.g., Berry, 1979:121–125; Konner, 1977; LeVine, 1977; Ogbu, 1981; Super and Harkness, 1980; B. Whiting and J. Whiting, 1975; J. Whiting and B. Whiting, 1978; and others), the ecocultural niche describes the sociocultural environment surrounding the child and family. The term *niche* implies that this context has evolved through time and has adapted to the constraints imposed by the subsistence base, the climate, and the political economy of the region.

The term *niche* connotes a somewhat different view of the environment than is implied by the proximal home learning environment or the social structure, although it includes these. Parents, children, and families adapt to a niche and shape it to some extent as well. The niche includes the features of the environment, as conventionally defined, and also the scripts, plans, and intentions of the actors. Thus, the ecocultural niche includes variables inside as well as outside the person. Its most important elements are the relationships between participants in organized behavior settings or activity units—actors with goals and intentions in a context. The study of the niches of childhood, then, includes the study of the actions, motivations, and goals or purposes shaped by those niches. As Super and Harkness (1982) emphasized, these contexts, or scaffolds, for children's development change over time, just as individuals change and develop. Thus, the goals of a developmental analysis include not only the study of individual and group differences but also the study of changes in the scaffolding surrounding children over time.

Many features of the niche have been shown to affect children directly, or indirectly through the child's participation in the family or community. Whiting et al. (in press) developed an inventory of cultural features that influence child development. Their list, which appears below, is derived from cross-cultural as well as American studies and so includes some domains and activities that are not relevant to American children. The domains themselves, however—the work cycle, health status, children's work and chores—probably represent pancultural features that affect all children:

1. The characteristics of the *subsistence work cycle* and the economic and technological system that produces it, including wage work, tending crops or animals, distance from the home, migration, etc.

2. The *health status and demographic characteristics* of the community, including mortality risks, availability of health care, birth control, family size, etc.

3. Overall *community safety* other than health and mortality, such as dangers from motor vehicles, intra- and intercommunity violence and warfare, etc.

4. The *division of labor* by age and sex and perhaps other criteria like caste or race in childhood, adolescence, and adulthood, including the relative importance of various activities for subsistence and prestige.

5. The *work that children are expected to do* beginning as a toddler through adolescence.

6. Child-rearing and *child care tasks* in particular, including the personnel available and used for caretaking.

7. The *role of the father and older siblings* in child care as a special issue of nonmaternal child care.

8. The composition of *children's play groups* by age, sex, and kinship category (siblings, cousins, relatives, and nonrelatives).

9. The autonomy, independence, and *role of women in the community*.

10. Institutionalized *women's support groups*, both formal and informal, such as work groups, church clubs, mutual aid societies, etc.

11. Various sources of child stimulation; more generally, the *available sources of cultural influence* on children from both literate and oral sources, including the child's contact with the media, the outside world, and toys.

12. *Parental sources of information* concerning child health, nutrition, new methods of subsistence activities, and new methods of child care; the availability of novel or contrastive beliefs about childhood in the community.

13. Measures of *community heterogeneity and change*, including the presence of subethnic communities, bilingualism, subcastes, social-class differences and social solidarity; the role of minorities; group oppression and lack of community commitment among some subgroups; information on migration; and the number of generations that families have lived in the community.

Ecocultural variables like these have been developed from some basic ideas about how the econiche has been formed; they are influenced by their functions for community adaptation and by the overall level of cultural complexity.

The domains in this list, for example, can be grouped into five clusters on the basis of how they help children and families to adapt and survive. One cluster influences health and mortality (health and community demography, safety, defense and protection). Another affects provision of food and shelter (the subsistence work cycle, chores). Another influences the personnel likely to be around children and what those people are likely to be doing (daily routines, division of labor, child care system, play groups). A fourth focuses more specifically on the role of women and mothers in the community as the primary responsible caretakers (support, women's status, fathers' and siblings' roles). A fifth assesses cultural alternatives available in the community (heterogeneity, outside influence and information).

Cultural complexity is another widely used summary dimension that influences econiche constraints and opportunities. Cultural complexity includes an extensive cash economy, technological specialization, permanent urban settlement patterns, a centralized political and legal system, a priesthood and other specialized religious roles, literacy, hierarchical status distinctions (such as a caste organization or social classes), and a diversity of alternative cultural models in the community (such as in bicultural or multilingual settings) (Murdock and Provost, 1981). Complexity does not necessarily imply a more elaborate, ritual/symbolic world, nor an easier, more effort-free or stress-free life; but the size of the population and the scale of activities is greater.

American children, of course, grow up in one of the most complex cultures in the world, in this sense of hierarchy, stratification, technology, and alternative choices available. The score for an American family on nearly every niche feature is affected by that fact. Complex environments appear to promote increased nonaffiliative, individual achievement striving in children's social behavior and in parental goals (Gallimore, 1981); more personalized competition between children (Seymour, 1981); more egoistic and dominant social behaviors in children (B. Whiting and J. Whiting, 1975); lower rates of nurturant and prosocial behaviors, which are emphasized later in childhood (B. Whiting and J. Whiting, 1975); less sex-role segregation in family roles; a less shared-function, more specialized family role system; a more democratic family (J. Whiting and B. Whiting, 1975); and a general decline in the use of nonparental care by kin, especially sibling caretaking (Weisner and Gallimore, 1977).

Adaptation and complexity are also related to the ability to accumulate and store food and other resources for family use. In modern, complex societies, year-long, stable availability of food and many other resources is taken for granted, although the ability of families to purchase these resources is problematic. In much of the world, however, families face regular uncertainty in this matter. For example, early and strict responsibility and compliance training and high peer affiliation orientation appear more frequently as socialization goals and as child-rearing practices in societies that emphasize the accumulation of resources (Barry et al., 1959). Berry (1976) contrasted "loose" societies (low accumulation, often based on a hunting economy, high mobility, dispersed settlement patterns, unstratified, and egalitarian) with "tight" ones (high accumulation, dense settlement, stratified, etc.). He suggested that psychological differentiation and field independence characterize low food accumulating, low-density, migratory peoples.

Regardless of the different ways to generate and cluster the variables that make up the niche description, certain dimensions recur as powerful ecocultural determinants of child development: (1) the personnel available in the family—which individuals, ages, sexes, kin; (2) the goal requirements, or tasks, to be done, which provide the reasons for children and others to be there; and (3) the cultural scripts, plans, and schemata that give meaning, create people's motivation, and give cues to intentions and purposes.

Many studies in developmental psychology use home learning environment or microsystem as the unit of analysis to study the effects of niche influences. The ecocultural niche includes the proximal home learning environment but is broader. The ecocultural niche helps to account for the existence of a particular home learning environment in the first place. It accounts for the limited child caretaking personnel available to assist American parents, for instance. It explains why the timing of bedtime and meals is so problematic for many American families. It identifies the source of the varying cultural ideas that appear in popular books on child stimulation or on television (Beekman, 1977; Wertz and Wertz, 1977). The immediate home environment, then, is a result of the interaction between family goals and ideals, child characteristics, and constraints and opportunities within the ecocultural niche.

Developmental research already uses econiche measures, such as social class or socioeconomic level, level of formal education, race, ethnicity, religion. These kinds of measures lump together many disparate features of the niche, drawn from different domains and functions, into a single packaged variable (B. Whiting, 1976). Econiche variables decompose global descriptors like socioeconomic level into a much more complex set of measures. In addition, measures derived from ecocultural niche domains are more likely to reveal the mechanisms by which class or education produce their effects on children. One reason for this is that the niche features outlined here each have specific links to the daily routine of the child and the family. The daily routine of a child includes all the varied activity settings, with their personnel, cultural scripts, and plans and tasks, that the child experiences (Cole, 1981; B. Whiting, 1980). The use of the ecocultural niche model depends on an analysis of these activity settings, for they are the immediate situational circumstances that provide the social scaffold for assisting children to think, speak, and act (see Fischer and Bullock, in this volume).

These scaffolds have their own developmental course in every culture. The developmental course of the individual is paralleled by the development of familial scripts and activity settings. These settings change with maturation, just as the child is changing. Children's behavior between 6 and 12 results from the interplay between the child's development, on one hand, and the development of a culture's activity settings or scaffolds, on the other (see Super and Harkness, 1982). Thus, the ecocultural model has a theoretical and a comparative implication. For theory, research is needed on the development of activity settings that will parallel studies of individual differences in children's development. For comparative research, the range of activity settings available for American children must be viewed in the context of the range of such settings for children around the world.

Child development studies done in Western cultures rarely compare the data collected to data from other cultures around the world. Weisner et al.

(1983) studied American parents who were attempting to be more "natural" and emotionally expressive in child-rearing practices with their infants and young children or who were voluntarily poor and emphasized loose, flexible discipline and compliance patterns (Weisner, 1982a). Although pronatural and voluntarily poor parents did differ in a number of child care practices from a comparison group, interactional styles often did not. More importantly, the practices on which innovative families differed (such as more frequent breastfeeding, later weaning, or sleeping with the child) did not differ very much when compared to the range of such practices around the world. Thus American parents who weaned "late" did so by the time the child was 18 months; however, most cultures and mothers around the world do not even begin the weaning process until after age 18 months.

Although strictness of discipline and the extent of immediate compliance to parental requests varied in the American sample, the cross-cultural evidence indicates that our culture is unusually flexible and permits children more autonomy and latitude in negotiations with parents over compliance than do most cultures around the world (Minturn and Lambert, 1964; Lambert et al., 1979). The absolute amount of delayed compliance or negotiated requests is high in American samples, compared with comparable samples from Africa, for instance (Weisner, 1979).

Many statistically significant differences between Western samples may be of a similar character: they may produce only very small substantive differences in behavior, which are of small magnitude, with outcomes that are not sustained for very long. One powerful reason may be the fact that on a pancultural scale the magnitudes of the intracultural differences are not very large. The only way to test this would be to systematically and routinely compare developmental data collected within our own niche, with data collected from a wide range of econiches and cultures around the world. Such a practice would, I expect, have the same importance in interpreting developmental data as the currently routine expectation in scientific studies of reporting test and instrument norms or statistical variance within a sample.

The influence of the niche is subject to empirical test, as are features of the child or parents, such as gender, age, and temperament. This point is important to emphasize because culture is so often treated in just the opposite way—as an untested, packaged variable. The ecocultural niche approach must not assume what is often exactly what needs to be proven: that cultural factors indeed have important effects. Culture must be used as a set of variables like others whose specific character and effects can be measured and tested.

The same point is true for determining which aspects of the econiche have the strongest effect—ethnic or cultural membership itself or subsistence and environmental constraints. For instance, Edgerton (1971) systematically tested values and personality characteristics in adults from four tribal cultures in East Africa. Within each culture, some individuals lived primarily as pastoralists and others as horticulturalists. Edgerton was thus able to compare the effects of cultural membership versus subsistence adaptation—pastoral or horticultural—for each of eight sample groups (four cultures × two subsistence modes). Results showed that both cultural group membership and subsistence modes differentiated between dependent variables in his study. Pastoralists were more concerned with displays of affection, direct aggression, divination, and independence than were farmers. Farmers emphasized disrespect for authority and favored conflict avoidance, indirect aggression, emotional constraint, and other values, compared with pastoralists. Tribal membership, however, was the best overall predictor of these sample differences, and subsistence mode was next best.

In brief, the ecocultural niche defines the contexts for development; these contexts represent evolved, adapted family responses to opportunities and constraints of the environment; the activity settings that result are the measurable, visible features that can influence children and families. The study of child development, then, should include the study of the relationships between the activity settings provided for children within the niche, on one hand, and the maturational uniformities and individual differences children and parents bring to these activity settings, on the other. Basic research on the 6–12 age period should pursue new knowledge regarding the development and influence of activity settings of children at these ages and study a far broader range of such settings in American society and around the world.

Finally, I believe that high-quality description of the lives of children in other cultural settings is in and of itself of basic scientific value in providing a mirror for ourselves. Lambert (1971:61) commented on the intrinsically valuable character of cross-cultural data—its ability to awaken us to new alternatives:

Since no one culture has managed to achieve a monopoly of all the "good" or "bad" conditions for parent-child relations, then we are going to be delighted as we travel about the world. We are always going to find some facet of human personality or personality organization which glows with a serene excellence that we have never met before. And lying below the fact of that fresh, though partial and perhaps even fleeting, excellence, is new knowledge about how to make some future generation (and its parents) better, more happy, or more free.

Although comparative work is widely accepted in principle or as a programmatic need, it is not being done. LeVine (1980) reviewed every article and research note published over a 5-year period in four developmental journals and six anthropology journals. These represented the ten major journals in the two disciplines. Only 9.3 percent of the articles in the developmental journals included any data on subcultural variations in the United States, Europe, Israel, or anywhere else (171 of the 1,843 articles). Of these 171, 75 percent reported data from other Western industrial societies, leaving only 42 articles (2.3 percent of the total) with any data from Latin America, Asia, or Oceania. Similarly, the six anthropology journals published 911 articles during this 5-year period, of which only 70 (7.7 percent) gave any consideration to child care or development. The situation is even worse than this implies, since one of the anthropology journals, *Ethos,* by itself published almost one-third of all the articles on children in the anthropology articles reviewed. The regions of the world are also very unevenly represented; Latin America, for example, is far more frequently mentioned than other parts of the world.

WESTERN AND NON-WESTERN CULTURES

In the discussion of ecocultural niches of middle childhood in this chapter, American children ages 6–12 are often lumped with Western children or those living in complex societies. This is a gross oversimplification and of course does not mean that there are not large differences in the experience of children across Western societies. Similarly, children in non-Western cultures are often lumped together to contrast with American children. This is an even grosser oversimplification, since the range of cultures is even greater within this category. References to non-Western societies should be understood as referring primarily to middle-range horticultural and simple agricultural societies, unless otherwise noted. Most examples are drawn from Polynesia (Tahiti, Hawaii) and sub-Saharan Africa (East Africa, Ghana, Botswana).

It is not possible or appropriate to present an ethnographic overview of the patterns of child care during the 6–12 age period around the world. The emphasis on broad, cross-cultural contrasts in this chapter is not intended to homogenize the rest of the world, nor to imply that there are not enormous social-class, racial, and ethnic differences in Western societies, nor to suggest that non-Western societies are uniform. To the contrary, the point is to search for the niche and activity settings that influence child development and that are the result of just such class and ethnic differences.

The chapters in this volume reflect many of the central themes of middle childhood: caretaking patterns, schooling, health, cognition, and self-understanding. Cross-cultural perspectives are especially important in the study of cultural conceptions of the person and the self; children's own theories of their development and roles; the differing structures for child caretaking during this period, particularly nonparental care; the socialization of appropriate emotional expression; the influence of deviance and psychopathology in middle childhood; the influence of schooling and literacy; the effects of urbanization and modernization; sex-role and gender-identity development; the transition to adolescence; and others. I have selected four of these themes to illustrate a comparative niche approach: the structure of caretaking; development of the self; troublesomeness in children; and schooling effects. Each of these domains is covered in the next four sections, followed by a discussion of methods.

A goal of this volume is to suggest areas for new basic research. The topics covered in this chapter are those that are not already covered in other cross-cultural reviews, such as the *Handbook of Cross-Cultural Human Development* (Munroe et al., 1981); that do not as yet have extensive comparative research but look promising; that appear to be important during the 6–12 age period; and that are emphasized in the other chapters in this volume.

PATTERNS OF CARETAKING OF CHILDREN

A central issue in American families with children ages 6–12 is the gradual shift in direct control of the child's behavior and activity settings from parents to the world of the school and peers. Medrich et al. (1982:102–103) reported that parents in Oakland, California, feel they need to devote less of their time to either direct physical care or nonphysical care of their children during this period. The papers by Maccoby and Markus and Nurius in this volume emphasize that an important general developmental task for American children in this period of life is to accomplish a gradual change in processes of control and regulation. Children appear to gradually move from coregulated activities to self-regulated ones. Parents retain overall managerial influence, but children are increasingly capable of self-regulation of their activities for long periods of the day. American parents encourage individuation and self-control during this period but also attempt to negotiate with children and withhold resources in order to retain overall managerial control within the family.

The developmental task or agenda that faces parents and children in many non-Western cultures is related to but different in many ways from the American one of individuation and separation from the parent as an exclusive controller. Rather, the task involves children gradually moving from under the responsibility of older children and other nonparental members of the household (e.g., grandparents or aunts) to becoming a responsible caretaker, in charge of younger siblings and cousins. Children ages 6–12 take on increasingly responsible family roles, including those relating to child care. Parents' roles include the managerial and disciplinary ones familiar in American families, but child care is more diffused and shared. This caretaking pattern has as its goal to produce an interdependent, responsible child, rather than an independent, self-directed, highly individuated child.

Many cultures also share the belief that between age 5 and age 7 children begin to acquire reason or sense, the ability to understand cultural rules and to carry out directions. Rogoff et al. (1975), Super (1981), and J. Whiting and B. Whiting (1960) identified this age period from cross-cultural samples, and Nerlove et al. (1974) did so with data from Guatemala. Nerlove et al. identified two natural indicators of cognitive skill that develop before or during this period, which are both important in shared child management activities: self-managed sequencing of activity and voluntary social activities. Self-managed sequencing refers to the child's ability to follow a precise sequence or series of acts autonomously—e.g., washing clothes, which entails gathering up a basket, clothes, and soap, putting the clothes in a basket, going to water or the river, etc. These tasks require, in correct order, "a scanning of the model and mapping of that model onto alternatives, remembering what one had already tried and how well it fit" (Nerlove et al., 1974:287). Voluntary social activities involve self-directed, shared activity with others, which assumes a shared goal and rule understandings. For language-related voluntary social activities, learning "to name, recognize, and verbally relate functions or attributes of objects" to others (p. 287) is crucial, including learning kinship rules and cultural and family standards. Voluntary social activities thus include understanding and storing multiple roles and social scripts as well as the ability to lead and direct them. Sibling caretaking exemplifies the application of both of these skills to an important family function.

Rogoff et al. (1980) extended their cross-cultural work to the 8–10 age period, suggesting that children appear to be developing skills at performing more complex tasks, which require more elaborate understanding of context-appropriate behaviors and more complex understanding of causality and intent—which increase the child's ability to consolidate and integrate the separately acquired skills learned in the 5–7 transition period.

Effective performance of child care, as a part of the competencies needed to perform domestic chores and even manage the domestic routine, requires a minimum level of both these kinds of skills in childhood, and in turn domestic duties help train children in more general skills. Thus the age of greatest involvement in and responsibility for shared child and domestic task management corresponds to the 6–12 developmental period, when these social and cognitive skills become available to children.

The contrasts between coregulation and self-regulation and between interdependence and independence are certainly expressed as cultural goals and emphasized in parental talk and metaphor. The degree to which children's and parents' behavior in fact reflects these metaphors seems to vary widely. The role of socialization and internalized behavioral tendencies, in addition to differences in activity settings as influences on metaphor and behavior, needs new research. There is a sense in which all children are interdependent within their family and community and a sense in which autonomous self-regulation is more of a Western cultural myth than a behavioral reality. The differences, however, between Western and non-Western children in nurturance, prosocial responsibility, and affiliative orientations have been well established (e.g., B. Whiting and J. Whiting, 1975).

Sibling Caretaking

Barry and Paxson (1971) surveyed 186 societies in the cross-cultural sample of the Human Relations Area Files and concluded that mothers were considerably less frequently the primary caretaker of children than either siblings, older children, or female adults other than the mother. Thus, children ages 6–12 in most of the non-Western world continue what already has been a common experience for them earlier in life: They participate in peer and sibling caretaking systems and are not usually under the direct, personal care and supervision of their mothers.

Gallimore et al. (1974), Leiderman and Leiderman (1973; 1977), Levy (1973), Mead (1961), Minturn and Lambert (1964), Weisner and Gallimore (1977), B. Whiting and J. Whiting (1975), and J. Whiting and B. Whiting (1973) have all recorded comparative data and developed theories about sibling care. Sibling care is associated with the following ecocultural conditions: horticultural, pastoral, and simpler agricultural societies in which the family workload is high; mothers are responsible for work outside the home; residence patterns establish sets of neighboring, extended family groups with children available for shared care; and shared work roles and task allocations within families promote joint care of younger children. *Shared functioning* is a useful term for describing such flexible, nonexclusive family work roles and child care responsibilities (Gallimore et al., 1974). Children ages 6–12 are cared for by older children; then, through participation in pivot roles (Levy, 1973), they move to caretaking supervision of still younger children. Mothers' roles are as indirect managers of the sibling and family group—assigning duties, overseeing the senior sibling caretaker, jointly doing chores and activities with children, providing discipline and occasional instruction, or simply modeling correct behavior.

Children ages 6–12 are also sent away from their own natal home, for years at a time or permanently, to live with others. In many West African societies, for instance, fostering is common (Goody, 1982). In such systems, children are sent away to live with other kin; to live with kin or nonkin to whom parents owe a debt (debt fosterage); to live as apprentices and work for a craftsman; to work for an important personage or chief as a means of developing a political alliance; or to be fostered for educational advantage or service obligations. In many societies, including East African, children are sent to live with their kin to assist elderly grandparents or the child's mother's sister during difficult times (Weisner, 1982c). In Polynesia, adoption is frequent (some 23 percent of children in one Hawaiian community were adopted) and can extend throughout childhood (Levy, 1973; Ritchie and Ritchie, 1979). Such practices are seen by parents as a necessary and expected reallocation of an important family resource—their children. The institutions of fostering and adoption when children are ages 6–12 encourage socialization practices similar in many ways to those involved in sibling caretaking: diffusion of affect, attachment to community, early expectations of prosocial, mature behaviors, strong compliance and deference expectations, work and responsibility expectations imposed early in life, and others.

Weisner and Gallimore (1977) suggested a number of child outcomes that might be predicted to differ in settings with extensive peer or sibling care socialization systems of this kind. For example, *polymatric* systems (Leiderman and Leiderman, 1973, 1977), or multiple caretaking of infants and young children, may diffuse early attachment. It can also increase the child's secure sense that others in the community will care for him or her. There appears to be a balance between the insecurity of diffused and variable attachment to several caretakers and security in *having* several reliable alternative caretakers. Children in polymatric caretaking systems become responsible, active participants in their wider community during the 6–12 age period. This early maturity may be in part the result of more exposure to the security of wider nonparental community care and obligations.

Children's play groups also depend on caretaking obligations: Child caretakers pool their younger charges, and they do chores along with them. Children ages 6–12 frequently divide into groups of mixed-age girls and younger boys; younger boys are usually separated from older boys, who are off in small packs (Weisner, 1979).

This diffusion of child care responsibilities through the sibling hierarchy and among other kin relieves the parent of the constant monitoring characteristic of many Western domestic care situations. Children can be out of sight and out of hearing among peers and still be considered safe and acting responsibly. Of course mischief, teasing, and worse certainly occur.

But the generalized, expectable cultural climate for compliance in tasks and child care seems to constrain most children during middle childhood (see section on troublesomeness below).

Caretakers also learn responsibility, nurturance, and prosocial behavioral styles—girls more so than boys (Edwards and Whiting, 1980; J. Whiting and B. Whiting, 1973). Sibling care may reduce the strength of the internalized parental role model and increase the influence of community constraints based on shared function. It has also been suggested that individual differences across children are reduced as a result (Levy, 1973; Mead, 1961). Shared caretaking systems have also been linked to differences in cognitive style in children, such as field dependence and increased social empathy. Such children emphasize affiliation and cooperation rather than individual achievement in their play styles and in responses to standardized tasks (Gallimore et al., 1974; Madsen, 1971; Madsen and Shapira, 1970). Children in these kinds of caretaking settings may also differ in their classroom learning styles and in the ways they interact with teachers and peers—having fewer verbal interactions with teachers or directing help seeking away from the teacher and towards peer learning in the classroom (Jordan and Tharp, 1979; Weisner, 1976).

Dunn (1983), Gottman (1983), and Hartup (in this volume) review, the evidence on the development of peer friendships and associations, from acquaintanceship through the various stages of friendship. North American studies emphasize dyadic themes of reciprocity, equity, fairness, mutuality, and intimacy in children's choosing and developing friendships. There is no question that making and retaining friends is crucial in the school-age period for American children. In the North American niche, this process occurs among strangers for the most part. The task for the American child involves entering new and strange settings (primary schools, sports teams, churches, new neighborhoods) and selecting, with parental monitoring and influence to some degree, others to play with from among these groups of children. The American friendship relationship usually involves the creation of new, personal, independent alliances.

Contrast this with the task of the 6- to 12-year-old in more kin-based, shared-function, sibling care cultures. There are very few activity settings in which other children who are strangers would ever be present. If so, older children or adults would almost certainly be there to carefully monitor what could be a potentially dangerous, uncertain situation. For most children in such societies, the task and activity setting are quite different than for the American child: Children already are participating in established, probably permanent relationships with cousins, clan-mates, or village-mates. The task is not to construct a new acquaintance, but rather, first, to learn precisely who the other child is and how he or she is related (e.g., kinship ties, parents' status vis-à-vis one's own parents, the family's reputation, etc.) and, second, to observe carefully how others in one's own sibling and courtyard cousin group relate to that child. Thus the first steps do not require the child to personally initiate interaction, then display such personal skills as mutuality and verbal appropriateness. Rather, the child first must understand how the culture has already classified him or her into a preexisting set of alliances and feuds; second, the child must incorporate the acquaintance into his or her immediate sibling group. In addition, children ages 6–12 will very early have to consider what work, tasks, and chores must be done along with this child as a friend. Friendship will require much more than play, games, and childhood intimacy.

The childhood relationships formed in the sibling care system will persist throughout the life span. The same groups of children who are involved in shared care and not-always-benevolent authoritarianism in their families will in turn become adults who must cooperate in managing land, cattle, businesses, and other family resources. For example, these children will soon engage in extensive marriage negotiations. Thus the shared responsibilities of children ages 6–12 anticipate the subsequent adaptations of siblings to their adult-life roles.

Nonmaternal sibling care systems should not be seen simply as a big, cooperative, shared-play group. Fierce feuds, bitterness, and competition can characterize sibling relationships in childhood and adulthood. Teasing, benign neglect, and the domination by older children of younger ones are frequent. These experiences create rivalries and competition as well as cooperation in shared defense and survival needs of the community.

New basic research on the development of friendship and childhood intimacy in the Western econiche, compared with those of non-Western societies, probably would be especially fruitful. All children probably share the developmental task during this period of learning how to sustain shared intimacy with peers. In much of the world, however, this task is undertaken by relatives and child acquaintances who are already known and by groups of children who are going to be lifelong sources of support for each other or lifelong opponents or both.

Sibling caretaking may assume increasing importance in this culture, and American children ages 6–12 will probably participate in shared responsibility even more than they have in the past. American mothers of children ages 6–12 are steadily increasing the number of hours they work outside the home in wage employment. And Bane et al. (1978) have pointed out that American parents utilize kin and in-home shared care more frequently and prefer it to nonhome, nonparental care. An important issue for new basic research on school-age children in American society will be to assess the effects of shared and sibling caretaking in the American context.

Father Roles

There is an apparent secular trend in the United States for fathers to take on a greater role in domestic work, including more involvement in direct child care (Lamb, 1981). Although the degree of such change may be less than what some parents and others hope for (Pleck, 1979; Weisner, 1982a), there is nonetheless a persistent and growing expectation for increased participation by fathers. American white middle-class fathers, however, are already actively involved in the domestic routine and in supplemental child care, compared with fathers in most other cultures. Many features of our ecology and culture already encourage this relatively high involvement. The features of the ecocultural niche that have been identified in other cross-cultural studies (Katz and Konner, 1981; Weisner, 1982b) as associated with higher father involvement include:

• nuclear or conjugal family model, not stem, extended, or joint families;
• neolocal residence customs (couples live apart from their own kin);
• relatively high geographical mobility of parents;
• a high expectation of intimacy between couples (emotional, interpersonal, sharing of information, sharing resources);
• relatively low availability of support from kin for assistance and support;
• relatively low neighborhood solidarity and support for parents;
• relatively low threat of violence to the home or community; and
• infrequent use of sibling caretaking, adoption, fosterage, child lending, or other institutions for sharing children.

Some of these features affect the availability of different kinds of caretakers (e.g., fathers, siblings, nonparental caretakers). Other cultural features influence the quality of parent's involvement with their spouse and with their children; for example, greater sharing and intimacy between American couples may translate into more shared activities and emotional involvement between fathers and children.

There are surprisingly few cross-cultural studies of fathers using direct, naturalistic observation with quantitative methods for description and analysis of paternal behavior. (There are relatively few such studies of families in the cross-cultural literature to begin with.) The reason usually given for this is that the base rate for occurrence of father-child interaction is typically very low compared with interaction rates for peers, siblings, and mothers. For example, Weisner (1979) and B. Whiting et al. (in press) dropped father-child dyads (children ages 2–11) from statistical analyses for this reason. Fathers were present only between 3 and 14 percent of the time (in New England the figure was 9 percent) in the Six Cultures study (B. Whiting and J. Whiting, 1975:45). Only 1 percent of the interaction of boys and girls ages 3–11 was with fathers, compared with 10 percent with mothers, 54 percent with peers, and 15 percent with infants and toddlers (p. 153); limited data on father interaction prevented direct comparisons between mothers and fathers.

Konner (1975) observed !Kung infants and children ages 2–6 throughout the year during daylight hours. Fathers interacted with infants in 13.7 percent of the observations compared with an equivalent 99 percent for mothers. !Kung fathers were present in 30 percent of the observations of children ages 2–6. In contrast, Blurton-Jones and Konner (1973) reported fathers present 19 percent of the time during similar observations made in London. Fathers' participation in infant care expressed as a percentage of mothers' care is only between 2.3 percent and 6.3 percent for children ages 2–6.

Although these studies find fathers home much less than mothers and find fathers interacting relatively infrequently with infants and young children when they are home, these studies do not demonstrate the true proportions of father involvement with older children. Relatively few studies have included older children, and observations are not made at times when fathers are most likely to be home: early mornings, evenings, weekends, and holidays. Most settings for observational work focus on the home and its surroundings and perhaps a school—but these are not the places where fathers are likely to be found during much of the day. Field observational work should be designed to include the times and places where fathers and children are most likely to be together.

Basic research on new fathering styles among American families (Lamb, 1982; Radin, 1982; Weisner, 1982b) has also shown that children are experiencing a wide variety of father roles. Some fathers appear to truly share active management of the home and domestic routine with the mother. Others have increased their shared involvement and support of what remains primarily a maternal responsibility. Other fathers are largely absent, involved in careers that take them away from either shared support or true equal management. Still other children divide their time between parents who share their custody but are no longer living together. Similar data need to be collected on the diversity of actual patterns of involvement of fathers with children ages 6–12 elsewhere in the world. The simple assessment of task or chore responsibilities of fathers or their presence in the home needs to be replaced with a more complex picture of the types of emotional involvements and coregulation of activities that fathers share with their sons and daughters during middle childhood.

Conclusion

The ecocultural niche of middle-range societies (those based on horticulture or simple agriculture with family groups as important primary subsistence producers and consumers) frees mature, adult working-age women from exclusive child care responsibility. The niche also provides many of the essential conditions that encourage the sharing of caretaking and other work roles with children ages 6–12 (such as larger family size, joint and stem family patterns). Children ages 6–12 experience an active participatory role in family survival tasks in such settings, and they are important participants (although still lowly in status and power) in the tasks of the wider community outside the family. The activity settings for such children in these kinds of middle-range societies expose them to a wider circle of kin and community members and to greater responsibility and expectations for prosocial behavior than is the case for American children. Coregulation is also encouraged, while autonomy and individualism are discouraged. Obedience and compliance are expected, rather than being the subject of continual negotiation between parents and children regarding work or free time.

Basic research on nonmaternal care of children more generally should begin by mapping the true range of kinds of such care provided for children ages 6–12 around the world and the niches in which these occur. A number of plausible outcomes of nonmaternal care (such as emotional or attachment differences and affiliation motives) have been suggested, but these have rarely been measured directly or concurrently with direct measures of caretaking patterns and styles. In addition, the importance of shared, conjoint caretaking, with both adults and children participating, needs closer study. Descriptions of mutually exclusive types of caretaking (maternal; polymatric) often do not capture the variability in the strategic use of conjoint caretaking so characteristic of many societies, including the United States.

SELF-CONCEPTIONS AND ECOCULTURAL VARIATIONS

Markus and Nurius (in this volume) emphasize that the study of the self in children ages 6–12 includes the study of self-regulation in children—that is, how children monitor and manage their behavior in ongoing interaction. Understanding how children acquire their skills at self-regulation in turn will require new basic research on the activity settings that surround them.

American cultural goals emphasize egalitarian ideals and universalistic moral convictions regarding sharing and fairness. But the day-to-day activity settings in which American children typically find themselves (e.g., classrooms, sports, individual homework) in fact encourage individualism, autonomy, competitiveness, self-direction, and self-regulation. In contrast, while many non-Western cultures have public overt beliefs emphasizing differences between clans, castes, religious groups, or regions, in their daily routines, these children participate in activity settings that emphasize shared functioning, coregulation of behavior, compliance to adults and older children and that discourage exploration or private self-aggrandizement. It is argued in this section that different kinds of activity settings produce differing patterns of self-regulation, self-understanding, and conceptions of personhood. The same contrasts between Western and non-Western activity settings described above for the consequences of caretaking are also relevant in shaping the development of the self.

Individuation and Individualism

Franz Boas (cited in Miller, 1963:280) reported in 1911 that "the three personal pronouns—I, thou, and he—occur in all human languages. . . . The underlying idea of these pronouns is the clear distinction between the self as speaker, the person or object spoken to, and that spoken of." Every child, then, learns to distinguish between him- or herself, the dyad, and others separate from the self or the immediate group. In this sense, individuation is a universal process.

Shweder and Bourne (1981) distinguished between individuation and individualism; between the development of the I or me and egoism; between a sense of uniqueness as a person and a claim of personal autonomy from others. Individuation seems to be a universal process, but individualism, egoism, and autonomy from others seem far more characteristic of Western self-conceptions during the 6–12 age period and throughout life. The idea of the individual self as contained inside a private mind, within "a bag of skin," looking out on the world, seems not to be universal (Shweder and Bourne, 1981). Children in many non-Western cultures certainly do learn about themselves as unique individuals, but without the accompanying egoism, self-aggrandizement, autonomy, or concerns over invidious comparisons and esteem that seem to characterize the relatively few available Western reports of children's self-concepts.

Levy, for example, described a typical man, called Poria, in a Tahitian village, Piri (Levy, 1973:217); Poria is a unique individual, but neither autonomous nor part of an autonomous group:

In Piri he is simply Poria, a unique individual with his own ways of getting on with others and of organizing his life. He is one of a large number of different kinds of individuals in the world of Piri, and he feels himself to be not "of the same measurements" as the others. People in Roto [an urban area] have, perhaps, more occasion to identify themselves as "types," Tahitians, in contrast with the many non-Tahitians surrounding them, or to solidify themselves with others.

Tahitians emphasize the role of shared life stages in accounting for their behaviors much more than Americans would. They are likely to describe whole periods of their life, especially adolescence and the early years of marriage or later childhood by saying "I was in the _____ period at that time." Shared life stage categories or kinship groupings, rather than nonshared categories, are used to compare people. The intimate, face-to-face, small-scale character of such societies seems to promote shared, nonprivate self-concepts in children. Typological descriptions or labeling of others in the village context is infrequent except in terms of shared categories like life stages.

Hallowell (1955) described the Ojibwa Indian self as part of a world of individuals seeking power over each other, beset by fears and anxieties concerning magic or sorcery. Ojibwa worry about giving offense to others and seek power from supernatural spirits who operate in the world only through men. The spirits are largely beneficent, but the men and women sometimes are not. For Hallowell, each cultural environment must be studied anew to search for the particulars that define self-conceptions. The self in this view is formed as a part of the larger construction of cultural meaning, which is a universal process in Hallowell's view. Hallowell's approach is at once pancultural and universal with regard to processes of self-understanding, but highly particularistic with regard to the content and substance of self-identity. This view reflects a relativistic position on development of the self and emphasizes the importance of the content of ideas within a specific cultural-historical period, or behavioral environment.

Shweder (1981) also saw self-concepts acquired in childhood to be part of the larger cultural solutions to the problem of meaning, but he proposed in addition a set of specific topics for self-understanding in a local niche. He presented a list of 10 themes about social existence, which (a) resolve moral dilemmas; (b) are possibly universal problems of meaning; and (c) appear to be taught to all children as they acquire their self/cultural/moral understandings of their world (1981:8):

1. the problem of personal boundaries—what's me versus what's not me;
2. the problem of sex identity—what's male versus what's female;
3. the problem of maturity—what's grownup versus what's childlike;
4. the problem of cosubstantiality—who is of my kind and thus shares food or blood or both with me versus who is not of my kind;
5. the problem of ethnicity—what's our way versus what's not our way;

6. the problem of hierarchy—why do people share unequally in the burdens and benefits of life?;

7. the problem of nature versus culture—what's human versus what's animal-like;

8. the problem of autonomy—am I independent, dependent, or interdependent?;

9. the problem of the state—what I want to do versus what the group wants me to do; and

10. the problem of personal protection—how can I avoid the war of all against all?

There are as yet far too few cross-cultural data on children's self-concepts and identity formation to support even descriptive generalizations about each of these issues for children ages 6–12. These themes, however, are surely widespread and take comparative research beyond the occasional collection of interesting but nongeneralizable case studies. Shweder's (1981) topical domains provide a framework for comparative data collection on the content of children's ideas about the self and social personhood in Western and non-Western settings.

What are some of the features of activity settings for children ages 6–12 that might be linked to differences in self-conception? These characteristics are probably related to Damon and Hart's (1982) listing of proposed universal mechanisms in the acquisition of self-knowledge (internalization of cultural standards and scripts; development of schemata for the self; modeling; and identity formation). And they should also be linked to differences in children's processes of self-regulation, following Markus and Nurius (in this volume). One niche difference with possible consequences for self-conceptions concerns the degree of privacy, or separation of role performances, available to children ages 6–12 in American versus non-Western activity settings. Non-Western children do not seem to experience the degree of privacy that American children do during this period. A second major difference has already been considered: the degree to which coregulated, shared functioning is expected of children ages 6–12 in non-Western settings. The next section briefly considers some basic research issues regarding the interrelationships between niche features, such as privacy and shared functioning, and self-conceptions.

Private and Public Selves

Western children live in a remarkably private culture. Most cultures are vastly more public than is ours in their geography, architecture, and daily routine. The opportunity to be private is so much greater in the West, and we encourage such privacy early in children's lives by giving them their own rooms and spaces, their own toys and other possessions. We allow children some degree of choice over their food, playmates, TV shows, clothes. We negotiate with children over space and possessions and make children at least partly coequal interlocutors concerning these and other matters. American children learn how to make behavior and possessions private or at least capable of being kept private as a matter of their choice.

Self-presentation in activity settings without privacy of these kinds is like being on a social stage with no private dressing rooms, where the stage wings are visible to nearly all of the audience, and where the same audience and cast comes to every show. The formation of social character in children ages 6–12 in such public cultures occurs in contexts in which nearly all the behaviors a child displays are potentially known to everyone else.

The public character of life extends to the sharing of resources. Food, knowledge, child care responsibilities, and material possessions are shared in order to survive. Stinginess is one of the profoundly negatively sanctioned traits. "Visualize the kind of sharing that occurs around the dinner table in a Western household but expanded in scale to include a group of 15–30 people, and you have some idea of the nature of sharing in a !Kung camp" (Lee, 1981:98). Foraging peoples like the !Kung exemplify, albeit in extreme form, other fundamentals of the development of the self in non-Western settings: far more aspects of life are public; roles and settings are perpetually undermanned due to the small scale of village life; relationships are multiplex and face-to-face; and children participate in or observe most of adult life from age 6 on.

The !Kung also illustrate how public are the most intimate details of life. The private, separated self—undramatized, carrying secrets one intends to reveal to no one or to only a few selected intimate others—is relatively undeveloped in children given the way !Kung foragers deal with personal troubles (Lee, 1981:99):

Daily life goes on in full view of the camp. People rarely spend time alone, and to seek solitude is regarded as a bizarre form of behavior. Even marital sex is carried on discreetly under a light blanket shared with the younger children around the family fire. It is considered bad manners for others to look. Sullen, withdrawn behavior is regarded with concern and not allowed to continue. The person showing it is pestered and goaded until he or she loses his temper and the anger that follows helps to clear the air and reintegrate the outsider. When people are depressed or their feelings are hurt, they express it by awaking at night to compose sad songs, which they play for themselves on the thumb piano. These poignant refrains form a counterpoint to the night sounds of the crackling sleeping fires and the calls of the night-jars, and no one tells the players to pipe down or shut up.

This is not to say that private self-reflection does not occur in shared-function, non-Western settings (Shostak, 1981). But public debate, shared conversations, and family negotiations about children's personal life course, viewed apart from the child's role in the family and community, are not common in the non-Western world for children ages 6–12. In contrast, first graders in Los Angeles are asked to describe themselves, to tell why they are different from everyone else, and to think of good things about themselves—including drawing pictures, writing stories, and speaking in public to their classmates. They come home and ask their parents for pictures of themselves to bring to school and put up on the wall; they make an outline of their hand and print their name to go up on the board with the picture. Children 6–12 in much of the non-Western world do not engage in these kinds of self-contemplation and public displays. If these activities occur at all, they come much later in life than in the West.

Langness and Frank (1981:101–105) confirmed this view of cultural presumptions about private selves in their review of self-conceptions as revealed in non-Western life histories, biographies, and autobiographies. The Western conception of biography sees the self and the life course as a unified, continuous progress, as the stories of lives viewed or reviewed. This seems inevitable to us: Clues to later life are to be found in childhood experiences; life is a chronology through time; a person's own feelings, perceptions, and life events are the central things; there is a search for causes and effects of one's actions that depend on the contrast between an inner and an outer world. Yet most cross-cultural biographical accounts seem largely concerned with the public self: one's role in public affairs; a sense of community integrity; one's role in family activities; the esteem with which one is viewed in the community. For example, Geertz (1973) described the Balinese as presenting the social and public self as the real self; that self is what is of personal importance, providing the focus of efforts toward self-expression, and it is reported to others as one's true self.

It is worth emphasizing the point made at the beginning of this chapter: neither the Western nor the non-Western generalized patterns I have outlined are meant to exclude the obvious diversity in the acquisition of an individualistic sense of self. There are boastful, self-aggrandizing childhood socialization patterns in the non-Western world (e.g., the Northwest Coast), and there are many cultures and subcultures in the Western world without the pressures for individualism that I have described. Religion, ethnicity, local patterns of class or cultural dominance, and other features clearly modify the development of the individualistic self during the 6–12 age period. And individual differences within every community produce variations in self-esteem and egoism, apart from any general effect of the local ecocultural setting. The goal of new basic research on self-acquisition should be to disentangle these features wherever possible and to put them to systematic, comparative test.

Ecocultural Origins of Differences in Self-Regulation

Differing patterns of self-concepts and self-regulation have their origins, in part, in the demographic facts that so profoundly separate the Western and non-Western worlds. In non-Western cultures, family size is large; child mortality is high; a child's own parents, and some nonparental caretakers as well, may die before the child reaches marriage age; dangers from raiding, feuds, or outright warfare are all vivid realities for children in many parts of the world. In such circumstances, the unstated presumptions about the life course that buttress the Western focus on personal self-investment may not hold—namely, the assumption that one's family and neighbors and the child himself or herself will survive to adulthood. A child's concern for self-expression, and parental searches for behavioral evidence of it, in part may be a modern luxury of safe, healthy, low-mortality environments.

Family survival also involves putting children ages 6–12 into the public world of work. These children are subject to strong, early compliance and discipline training (Minturn and Lambert, 1964); the use of stern discipline and physical punishment for transgressions; low warmth and positive affect in child care (Rohner, 1975); relatively little direct parental involvement with children during this period; and infrequent direct praise. In contrast, research on American child care environments, which encourage positive self-esteem; self-confidence; egoism; individualism; and an open, exploratory demeanor in new social situations, shows the opposite pattern. American family settings promoting such a pattern in self-concept include parental warmth, personal attention to children, family democracy and negotiation, and an absence of overcontrol in family discipline styles (Maccoby, in this volume).

S. LeVine's (1979) description of the socialization of Gusii girls illustrates the difference. The Bantu Gusii are a patrilineal, patrilocal, horticultural society in Western Kenya. Children are strictly controlled and punished and expected to assist in family subsistence and in child care (p. 384):

If a girl is taught to fear the unknown from infancy, required to be an obedient worker in the family labor force from early childhood, given no praise for conformity or accomplishment, provided no parental approval for play or noninstrumental activities, and punished for deviation from parental command, she will become wary from calling attention to herself. Having learned that displaying good behavior does not result in positive attention, whereas misdemeanors—particularly seeking fun with friends instead of performing chores—inevitably result in punishment if discovered, she will adaptively develop the "low-profile strategy" of social interaction.

These child-rearing practices do appear to produce a child who is non-egoistic, not given to self-aggrandizement, and who functions by accommodating to shared family obligations.

Conclusion

Children's self-conceptions are infrequently studied in cross-cultural research. Similarly, how the self is shaped by constraints of the ecocultural niche is not a common way to study the self in Western research. But it is precisely at the intersection of these two domains that new research on the self should be done with children ages 6–12. Clearly, the development of self-understanding is central during this period; for this reason, despite the dearth of comparative research on the subject, I have included some material on the self in this chapter. I have focused on the public nature of self-presentation and the effects of shared functioning, coregulation, and strict compliance training on the development of the self in non-Western settings. New research is needed on what other aspects of community ecology may be related to self-concepts.

Children's own views and ideas about themselves and their community are especially needed. Children's own voices are infrequent in the cross-cultural record. This is true in many respects of Western research as well, to the extent that this work has relied exclusively on paper-and-pencil tests or formalized procedures. In addition, the dimensions of high and low self-esteem or coregulation versus self-regulation will perhaps need to be revised. Children in non-Western settings are not always well described by "low self-esteem" or "shared" functioning. More elaborated, empirically based descriptions of the development of self in children of these ages in a variety of econiches are needed.

TROUBLESOMENESS IN CHILDREN

As American children enter schools, they come to the attention of teachers and others in public institutions. Shonkoff (in this volume) and Achenbach (in this volume) review the process of referral, diagnosis, and labeling for physical, mental, and learning-related problems associated with this period. When children are in need of treatment or consultation of some kind, American parents intervene directly themselves or seek outside professional services or both. The American goal is to change the child and the situation: if the child is having troubles in school, then improve his or her school skills; if the child has behavior problems, provide counseling or special medical help. There seem to be many aspects of behaviors inside and outside school that do worry parents of children ages 6–12. Achenbach and Edelbrock (1981) identified 118 such behavior problems and 20 social competence items in their Child Behavior Checklist. Items ranged from truancy to cannot concentrate; refuses to talk; nervous; disobedient at home; feels unloved; and many others. Thus, many American children ages 6–12 have difficulties adjusting to outside institutions; they are the target of individually focused treatments; and there seem to be many areas of children's behavior during this period that are potentially troublesome.

The non-Western contrasts to the American child's experience provide a final example of the potential usefulness of ecocultural and comparative research for the study of children ages 6–12. It seems to be the case that: (1) children ages 6–12 in many non-Western settings are integrated smoothly (perhaps a better description is, without question) into the world of work, schooling, and community life outside the home; (2) a widely used mode for dealing with troublesomeness in children when it does occur is to change the child's family situation or activity setting rather than to focus on trying to change the individual child; and (3) compared with the large number of reported American parental concerns about their children, there are far fewer such troublesome behaviors either reported or observed in non-Western studies of children ages 6–12. That is, children do not appear to be nearly as troublesome and/or their parents report far fewer behavioral troubles than do American parents and school or medical personnel.

Unfortunately, there has been very little basic research done in cross-cultural samples on the naturally occurring behavioral problems that appear in children ages 6–12 (see Edgerton, 1976). Similarly, it is startling to discover that there is no systematic account in the comparative literature— of which I am aware—that compares cross-cultural treatments of children who are identified as troubled in some way. The suggestion that there is relatively less troublesome behavior among children ages 6–12 in non-Western societies depends in part on the negative evidence that little is reported in the available literature.

Some of the problems reported for American children depend on what definition the culture provides for a particular behavior pattern—e.g., what do parents mean by poor peer relations? Others depend on cultural conceptions of what a child is capable of or what is perceived as normal for this period—e.g., do Tahitian parents feel that children between 6 and 12 have a sense of personal, autonomous self-worth? Some Western-defined problems refer to public institutions, such as schools, courts, or welfare agencies, that do not exist in other societies. It is not known, however, which of these or other differences in how troublesomeness may be reported by parents produces differing patterns of behavioral problems in children ages 6–12. Basic comparative research is needed on what parents in other ecocultural environments report in the way of troubles for children in this period. Were we able to replicate Achenbach and Edelbrock's study (1981) in a large, cross-cultural sample, what descriptors of children's troubles would appear? Some items might appear on nearly all lists, some on only one or two, and some in one cluster of societies but not other clusters. In this way, we could begin to disentangle which behavioral problems appear to have some universal recognition and which do not.

The appearance of troublesomeness in children's behavior depends in part on whether parents feel that continuation of the behavior would cause the child to be unable to adapt or survive in his or her niche in the future. The widespread practice of sending children away to other kin or fostering them during the 6–12 age period is sometimes intended to change the child's environment in hopes that the child's troublesomeness will decrease. Although, again, empirical studies are needed, it seems that in general, treatments like sending a child to other kin are usually effective. The 6–12 age period seems to have relatively few children acting out or seriously troubling families, although covert tensions and difficulties with children are certainly present, as is the possibility of pathology (see Korbin, 1981).

Another reason for this apparently lower incidence of problems is the strong, generalized expectable climate of compliance in non-Western families described earlier in this chapter. Deference to adults is expected, as is submission to their requests and commands. Children ages 6–12 participate in training for *learned helpfulness*—expectations to act in a responsible and prosocial manner to others. It is possible that expectable compliance in the home and learned helpfulness among children of these ages may inoculate them against many of the behavior problems described in American parents' reports. Werner and Smith (1982) found that ecological (particularly household personnel) features were most important in accounting for children's troubles during middle childhood in their longitudinal study of the children of Kauai; and they also found that nonmaternal and sibling caretaking played an important role in providing supports for resilient children—those children who were at earlier risk, but without troublesome outcomes.

Every one of these suggestions regarding children's relatively infrequent troublesomeness in non-Western ecocultural contexts needs testing. None has been systematically studied at the present time. Both direct behavioral observation of children and the collection of parents' folk conceptions of troubles need to be obtained. The ecocultural niche differences that may reduce troublesomeness should be studied at the same time as the data on children's problems and troubles are gathered. The transitions from early childhood into middle childhood and from middle childhood into adolescence are certainly not necessarily smooth, and these boundary points also need new, comparative research.

SCHOOLING AND LITERACY

Each cohort of children ages 6–12 over the past two generations, as well as the one to come, is participating in a transformation unique in the history of our species: the spread of formal schooling and literacy around the world. The United States has nearly universal school attendance of children ages 6–12 and has one of the highest rates of literacy in the world; however, formal school attendance is far from universal in much of the world. Indeed, most nations are still in the transition to widespread literacy.

Rogoff (1981) recently published a comprehensive review of the relationship between schooling and the development of cognitive skills, such as perception, memory, classification and concept development, logical problem solving, and Piagetian tasks. When Western task and testing paradigms and materials are used, schooled subjects generally do better on such tests than nonschooled subjects. But Rogoff questioned this research strategy and pattern of results on many grounds and pointed out that the natural experiment created by different formal schooling in different societies has not begun to be exploited by basic researchers.

First, research is needed to investigate the many threats to the generalizability of school-nonschool samples. For instance, parents "who allow or encourage their children to go to school may be wealthier, have more modern attitudes, or hold different aspirations for their children than parents who do not" (Rogoff, 1981:267). Children who are already better on skills assessed by Western tests may have been selected by their parents to attend school. Schooled children may be more familiar with the test materials, testing situations, and the language in which the test is administered than nonschooled children. Tests given in school or based on school-related skills often do not appear to generalize to contexts outside the classroom in any event. Thus the differences between schooled and nonschooled subjects may be, in a variety of ways, an artifact of the tests, selection of children for school attendance, or the context-specificity of school cognitive abilities.

A more telling research need and critique of existing research is the "lack of empirical research studying the mechanism for schooling's presumed effect" (Rogoff, 1981:276). Rogoff suggested four specific aspects of school experience that might be tested for in trying to discover mechanisms underlying the schooling effect (p. 286):

(a) Schooling's emphasis on searching for general rules; (b) the use of verbal instruction out of context from everyday activities; (c) the teaching of specific skills in school, such as memory strategies, taxonomic categorization, and the treatment of "puzzles" in which the answer is to be derived from information in the problem; and specifically (d) literacy, which may allow the examination of statements for consistency or may simply teach some specific cognitive skills.

Scribner and Cole (1981) questioned the generality of literacy effects in particular, and school effects more generally. Their Liberian study of unschooled but literate Vai—literate in an indigenous Liberian Vai script learned in the home—indicates specific transfer effects for specific skills but not a generalized cognitive restructuring traceable either to literacy alone or to schooling.

The challenges for new basic research in this area are of enormous importance. It is only through comparative work with children with different literacy experiences and different formal school experiences that effects of education can be distinguished from maturational and other age-related developmental differences. Educational comparisons (Epps and Smith, in this volume) and cognitive comparisons (Fischer and Bullock, in this volume) between children ages 6–12 need cross-national studies in order to separate the effects of Western mass education and literacy from other influences on development.

Literacy and school skills, in this view, are specific cultural tools, aiding the attainment of localized skills learned in a context in which such skills are needed and valued (see Nerlove and Snipper, 1981). What of other new Western cultural tools looming on the horizon, which go beyond books and literacy, such as the computer? What contextually specific, culturally localized cognitive skills and changes in social-behavioral styles may appear as this new cultural tool continues to spread during the next generation?

SOME COMMENTS ON METHODS

The well-trained developmentalist prepared to study children ages 6–12 is a scholar with a diverse set of research skills packed into a traveling backpack. Depending on the circumstances, this researcher can do participant observation; various kinds of informant interviewing; formal controlled observation, using time and event sampling; experimental manipulations; tests and other kinds of structured tasks; and combinations of these as needed. The location of research work—a school, a middle-class suburb in Chicago, a village in Western Kenya—should not by itself determine the methods to be used. Nor should the substantive problem determine the methods. The study of achievement in children, for example, should never be limited to just a single method (Gallimore, 1981).

Comparative research in human development has used a mix of qualitative and quantitative methods since Tylor (J. Whiting and B. Whiting, 1960). Qualitative, naturalistic research methods have developed a fairly substantial literature with recognized procedures to validate or compare research using these methods (Agar, 1980; Johnson, 1978; LeVine et al., 1980; Pelto and Pelto, 1978; Spradley, 1979; Thomas, 1976). Current research on field-work methods includes: role management in field situations; techniques for notetaking; methods for summarizing and coding field notes; systematic observation of behavior; quantification of field observations; styles and pro-cedures for writing up and presenting ethnographic materials; techniques for informant interviewing; and techniques for analysis and interpretation of texts. Naturalistic field methods will continue to be important in cross-cultural research. The basic research need is for more systematic attention to these procedures. The decision rules for which methods to use, under which circumstances, are particularly in need of attention.

Better specification of the units for analysis would assist cross-cultural and Western work alike. In this chapter, for instance, I have suggested the activity unit (Cole, 1981) or behavior setting (B. Whiting, 1980) as the link between the ecocultural niche variables and individual-level data typical of Western studies. The activity unit consists of an individual, engaged in goal-directed activities, under the constraints of his or her localized niche. Events in such activity settings or units are regulated by others in the setting, by what the actor brings to the situation, and by the environmental cir-cumstances. I believe that methods need to be developed that take the activity unit as the unit of analysis—not the individual actor alone, nor the thought or language of that actor, nor the localized environment. The goal for new basic research should be the development of methods suitable to a comparative theory of activity units.

CONCLUSION

The topics selected for more extended discussion in this chapter (the caretaking roles of children ages 6–12 and children's participation in work for the family; the public and nonindividualistic nature of the self; the possibly reduced troublesomeness of children ages 6–12 in non-Western cultures; and literacy and schooling) are included because each of these issues is an important developmental issue for American children ages 6–12. These certainly do not exhaust the important topics that need new basic research using an ecocultural and comparative approach. Additional topics include, at least, the socialization of emotions and affect; beliefs about temperamental differences of children held by parents in other societies; the effects of urbanization and modernization on children ages 6–12; the comparative phenomenology of childhood—that is, children's own theories of development and accounts of their own behavior; and sex role and gender training. Reviews of these and other topics appear in several recent books (LeVine and Shweder, no date; Munroe et al., 1981; Munroe and Munroe, 1975; Triandis and Lambert, 1980; Werner 1979).

Finally, an ecocultural perspective shows not only the marvelous diversity of children's environments in cultures around the world but also how vulnerable children are to assaults on their safety and subsistence base. Children participate in a world economy; they can be exploited by governments, capitalists, socialists, and terrorists just as adults can. They suffer the consequences of insecticide poisoning, poor food distribution, distorted government, and social policies favoring special interests (see Davis, 1977). The social processes that drive the increasing urbanization, modernization, and exploitation of the weak and the poor in third and fourth world countries are immediate threats to children of all ages. Isolated tribes and regions of great poverty within developed and developing countries deserve special study due to threats to the very survival of some of these peoples.

REFERENCES

Achenbach, R.M., and Edelbrock, C.S.
  1981   Behavioral problems and competencies reported by parents of normal and disturbed children aged four through sixteen. *Monographs of the Society for Research in Child Development* 46(1).
Agar, M.H.
  1980   *The Professional Stranger: An Informal Introduction to Ethnography.* New York: Academic Press.
Bane, M.J., Lein, L. Stueve, A., Welles, B., and O'Donnell, L.
  1978   Child Care in the United States. Working Paper No. 2. Wellesley College Center for Research on Women.
Barker, R.G., and Wright, H.F.
  1954   *Midwest and Its Children: The Psychological Ecology of an American Town.* Evanston, Ill.: Row, Peterson.
Barry, H., III, and Paxson, L.M.
  1971   Infancy and early childhood: Cross-cultural codes 2. *Ethnology* 10:466–508.
Barry, H., Child, I.L., and Bacon, M.
  1959   Relation of child training to subsistence economy. *American Anthropologist* 61:51–63.
Beekman, D.
  1977   *The Mechanical Baby: A Popular History of the Theory and Practice of Child Raising.* New York: Lawrence Hill.
Berry, J.W.
  1976   *Human Ecology and Cognitive Style: Comparative Studies in Cultural and Psychological Adaptation.* Beverly Hills: Sage-Halsted.
  1979   Culture and cognitive style. In A.J. Marsalla, R.G. Tharp, and T.J. Ciborowski, eds., *Perspectives on Cross-Cultural Psychology.* New York: Academic Press.

Blurton-Jones, N.G., and Konner, M.
1973   Sex differences in the behavior of Bushman and London two- to five-year-olds. In J. Crook and R. Michael, eds., *Comparative Ecology and Behavior of Primates*. New York: Academic Press.
Bronfenbrenner, U.
1979   *The Ecology of Human Development: Experiments by Nature and Design*. Cambridge, Mass.: Harvard University Press.
Cole, M.
1981   Society, Mind and Development. Center for Human Information Processing Report No. 106. University of California, San Diego.
Damon, W., and Hart, D.
1982   The development of self-understanding from infancy through adolescence. *Child Development* 53:841–864.
Davis, S.H.
1977   *Victims of the Miracle: Development and the Indians of Brazil*. Cambridge, England: Cambridge University Press.
Dunn, J.
1983   Sibling relationships in early childhood. *Child Development* August 54(4):787–811.
Edgerton, R.B.
1971   *The Individual in Cultural Adaptation. A Study of Four East African Peoples*. Berkeley: University of California Press.
1976   *Deviance: A Cross-Cultural Perspective*. Menlo Park, Calif.: Cummings Publishing Co.
Edwards, C., and Whiting, B.
1980   Differential socialization of girls and boys in light of cross-cultural research. In C. Super and S. Harkness, eds., *Anthropological Perspectives on Child Development*. No. 8. San Francisco: Jossey-Bass.
Gallimore, R.
1981   Affiliation, social context, industriousness, and achievement. In R. Munroe, L. Munroe, and B. Whiting, eds., *Handbook of Cross-Cultural Human Development*. New York: Garland Press.
Gallimore, R., Boggs, J.W., and Jordan, C.
1974   *Culture, Behavior and Education: A Study of Hawaiian-Americans*. Beverly Hills: Sage Publications.
Geertz, C.
1973   *The Interpretation of Cultures*. New York: Basic Books.
Goody, E.N.
1982   *Parenthood and Social Reproduction: Fostering and Occupational Roles in West Africa*. Cambridge, England: Cambridge University Press.
Gottman, J.M.
1983   How children become friends. *Monographs of the Society for Research in Child Development* 48(3). Chicago: University of Chicago Press.
Hallowell, A.I.
1955   *Culture and Experience*. Philadelphia: University of Pennsylvania Press.
Johnson, A.W.
1978   *Quantification in Cultural Anthropology*. Stanford, Calif.: Stanford University Press.
Jordan, C., and Tharp, R.
1979   Culture and education. In A.J. Marsella, R. Tharp, and T.J. Ciborowski, eds., *Perspectives on Cross-Cultural Psychology*. New York: Academic Press.
Katz, M.M., and Konner, M.J.
1981   The role of the father: An anthropological perspective. In M. Lamb, ed., *The Role of the Father in Child Development*. New York: John Wiley & Sons.

Konner, M.
1975   Relations among infants and juveniles in comparative perspective. In M. Lewis and L. Rosenblum, eds., *The Origins of Behavior (Vol. 3). Friendship and Peer Relations.* New York: John Wiley & Sons.
1977   Evolution of human behavior development. In P.H. Leiderman, S.R. Tulkin, and A. Rosenfeld, eds., *Culture and Infancy: Variations in the Human Experience.* New York: Academic Press.
Korbin, J., ed.
1981   *Child Abuse and Neglect. Cross-Cultural Perspectives.* Berkeley: University of California Press.
Lamb, M.E., ed.
1981   *The Role of the Father in Child Development.* New York: John Wiley & Sons.
1982   *Nontraditional Families: Parenting and Child Development.* Hillsdale, N.J.: Lawrence Erlbaum.
Lambert, W.
1971   Cross-cultural backgrounds to personality development and the socialization of aggression: Findings from the six-culture study. In W.W. Lambert and R. Weisbrod, eds., *Comparative Perspectives on Social Psychology.* Boston: Little, Brown.
Lambert, W., Hamers, J.F., and Frasure-Smith, N.
1979   *Child-Rearing Values: A Cross-National Study.* New York: Praeger.
Langness, L., and Frank, G.
1981   *Lives: An Anthropological Approach to Biography.* Novato, Calif.: Chandler and Sharp.
Lee, R.
1981   Politics, sexual and nonsexual, in an egalitarian society: The !Kung San. In G. Berreman, ed., *Social Inequality: Comparative and Developmental Approaches.* New York: Academic Press.
Leiderman, P.H., and Leiderman, G.F.
1973   Polymatric Infant Care in the East African Highlands: Some Affective and Cognitive Consequences. Paper presented at the Minnesota Symposium on Child Development, Minneapolis, Minn.
1977   Economic change and infant care in an East African agricultural community. In P. Leiderman, S. Tulkin, and A. Rosenfeld, eds., *Culture and Infancy. Variations in the Human Experience.* New York: Academic Press.
Levine, H.G., Gallimore, R., et al.
1980   Teaching participant-observation research methods: A skills-building approach. *Anthropology and Education Quarterly* 6(1):38–54.
LeVine, R.
1977   Child rearing as cultural adaptation. In P.H. Leiderman, S. Tulkin, and A. Rosenfeld, eds., *Culture and Infancy. Variations in the Human Experience.* New York: Academic Press.
1980   Anthropology and child development. In C. Super and S. Harkness, eds., *Anthropological Perspectives on Child Development.* San Francisco: Jossey-Bass.
Levine, R., and Shweder, R.
No date   *The Acquisition of Culture.* Manuscript in preparation, Harvard University.
Levine, S.
1979   *Mothers and Wives: Gusii Women of East Africa.* Chicago: University of Chicago Press.
Levy, R.I.
1973   *Tahitians: Mind and Experience in the Society Islands.* Chicago: University of Chicago Press.
Madsen, M.C.
1971   Developmental and cross-cultural differences in the cooperative and competitive behavior of young children. *Journal of Cross-Cultural Psychology* 2:365–371.

Madsen, M.C., and Shapira, A.
1970   Cooperative and competitive behavior of urban Afro-American, Anglo-American, Mexican-American, and Mexican village children. *Developmental Psychology* 3:16–20.
Mead, M.
1961   *Coming of Age in Samoa.* New York: The New American Library of World Literature.
Medrich, E.A., Roizen, J.A., Rubin, V., and Buckley, S.
1982   *The Serious Business of Growing Up: A Study of Children's Lives Outside School.* Berkeley: University of California Press.
Miller, D.
1963   Personality and social interaction. In B. Kaplan, ed., *Studying Personality Cross-Culturally.* New York: Harper & Row.
Minturn, L., and Lambert, W.
1964   *Mothers of Six Cultures.* New York: John Wiley & Sons.
Munroe, R.L., and Munroe, R.H.
1975   *Cross-Cultural Human Development.* Monterey, Calif.: Brooks-Cole.
Munroe, R., Munroe, L., and Whiting, B.
1981   *Handbook of Cross-Cultural Human Development.* New York: Garland Press.
Murdock, G., and Provost, C.
1981   Measurement of cultural complexity. In H. Barry and A. Schlogel, eds., *Cross-Cultural Samples and Codes.* Pittsburgh: Pittsburgh University Press.
Nerlove, S., and Snipper, A.
1981   Cognitive consequences of cultural opportunity. In R. Munroe, L. Munroe, and B. Whiting, eds., *Handbook of Cross-Cultural Human Development.* New York: Garland Press.
Nerlove, S., Roberts, J.M., Klein, R.E., Yarbrough, C., and Habicht, J.
1974   Natural indicators of cognitive development: An observational study of rural Guatemalan children. *Ethos* 2:265–295.
Ogbu, J.
1981   Origins of human competence: A cultural-ecological perspective. *Child Development* 52:413–429.
Pelto, P.J., and Pelto, G.H.
1978   *Anthropological Research: The Structure of Inquiry.* Cambridge, England: Cambridge University Press.
Pleck, J.
1979   Men's family work: Three perspectives and some new data. *Family Coordinator* 28:481–488.
Radin, N.
1982   Primary caregiving and role-sharing fathers. In M.E. Lamb, ed., *Nontraditional Families: Parenting and Child Development.* Hillsdale, N.J.: Lawrence Erlbaum.
Ritchie, James, and Ritchie, Jane
1979   *Growing Up in Polynesia.* Sydney: George Allen and Unwin.
Rogoff, B.
1981   Schooling and the development of cognitive skills. In H.C. Triandis and A. Heron, eds., *Handbook of Cross-Cultural Psychology (Vol. 4). Developmental Psychology.* Boston: Allyn & Bacon.
Rogoff, B., Newcombe, N., Fox, N., and Ellis, S.
1980   Transitions in children's roles and capabilities. *International Journal of Psychology* 15:181–200.
Rogoff, B., et al.
1975   Age of assignment of roles and responsibilities to children. A cross-cultural survey. *Human Development* 18:353–369.

Rohner, R.
1975   *They Love Me: They Love Me Not.* New Haven, Conn.: HRAF Press.
Scribner, S., and Cole, M.
1981   *The Psychology of Literacy.* Cambridge, Mass.: Harvard University Press.
Seymour, S.
1981   Cooperation and competition: Some issues and problems in cross-cultural analysis. In
         R. Munroe, L. Munroe, and B. Whiting, eds., *Handbook of Cross-Cultural Human
         Development.* New York: Garland Press.
Shostak, M.
1981   Nisa: The Life and Words of a !Kung Woman. Cambridge, Mass.: Harvard University
         Press.
Shweder, R.
1981   Beyond Self-Constructed Knowledge: The Study of Culture and Morality. Unpublished
         manuscript, Committee on Human Development, University of Chicago.
Shweder, R., and Bourne, E.
1981   Does the concept of the person vary cross-culturally? In A.J. Marsalla and G. White,
         eds., *Cultural Conceptions of Mental Health and Therapy.* Boston: D. Reidel.
Spradley, J.P.
1979   *The Ethnographic Interview.* New York: Holt, Rinehart & Winston.
Super, C.M.
1981   Behavioral development in infancy. In R. Munroe, L. Munroe, and B. Whiting, eds.,
         Handbook of Cross-Cultural Human Development. New York: Garland Press.
Super, C., and Harkness S., eds.
1980   *Anthropological Perspectives on Child Development: New Directions for Child Development.*
         No. 8. San Francisco: Jossey-Bass.
Super, C.M., and Harkness, S.
1982   The infant's niche in rural Kenya and metropolitan America. In L.L. Adler, ed., *Issues
         in Cross-Cultural Research.* New York: Academic Press.
Thomas, D.H.
1976   *Figuring Anthropology: First Principles of Probability and Statistics.* New York: Holt, Rinehart
         & Winston.
Triandis, H.C., and Lambert, W.W., eds.
1980   *Handbook of Cross-Cultural Psychology.* 6 vols. Boston: Allyn & Bacon, Inc.
Weisner, T.S.
1976   Urban-rural differences in African children's performance on cognitive and memory tasks.
         Ethos 4(2):223–250.
1979   Urban-rural differences in sociable and disruptive behavior of Kenya children. *Ethnology*
         18(2):153–172.
1982a   As we choose: Family life styles, social class, and compliance. Pp. 121–141 in J.G.
         Kennedy and R.B. Edgerton, eds., *Culture and Ecology: Eclectic Perspectives.* Washington,
         D.C.: American Anthropological Association.
1982b   Fathering in egalitarian American families: Shared support and co-equal management.
         Paper presented at American Anthropological Association, Washington, D.C., Decem-
         ber.
1982c   Sibling interdependence and child caretaking: A cross-cultural view. In M. Lamb and
         B. Sutton-Smith, eds., *Sibling Relationships: Their Nature and Significance Across the
         Lifespan.* Hillsdale, N.J.: Lawrence Erlbaum.
Weisner, T.S., and Gallimore, R.
1977   My brother's keeper: Child and sibling caretaking. *Current Anthropology 18(2):169–189.*
Weisner, T.S., Bausano, M., and Kornfein, M.
1983   Putting family ideals into practice: Pronaturalism in conventional and nonconventional
         California families. *Ethos* 11(4):278–304.

Wenger, M.
1983   Gender Role Socialization in an East African Community: Social Interaction Between 2- to 3-Year-Olds and Older Children in Social Ecological Perspective. Doctoral dissertation, Graduate School of Education, Harvard University.
Werner, E.
1979   *Cross-Cultural Child Development. A View from the Planet Earth.* Monterey, Calif.: Brooks-Cole.
Werner, E., and Smith, R.
1982   *Vulnerable But Invincible*: A Study of Resilient Children and Youth. New York: McGraw-Hill.
Wertz, R., and Wertz, D.
1977   *Lying-In: A History of Childbirth in America.* New York: Free Press.
Whiting, B.
1976   The problem of the packaged variable. In K. Riegel and J. Meacham, eds., *The Developing Individual in a Changing World: Historical and Cultural Issues.* Vol. 1. Netherlands: Mouton.
1980   Culture and social behavior: A model for the development of social behavior. *Ethos* 8:95–116.
1983   The Genesis of Prosocial Behavior. In D. Bridgeman, ed., *The Nature of Prosocial Development: Interdisciplinary Theories.* New York: Academic Press.
Whiting, B., and Whiting, J.
1975   *Children of Six Cultures.* Cambridge, Mass.: Harvard University Press.
Whiting, B., et al.
In   *The Company They Keep: The Genesis of Gender Identity.* Cambridge, Mass.: Harvard
press   University Press.
Whiting, J., and Whiting, B.
1960   Contributions of anthropology to the methods of studying child rearing. In P. Mussen, ed., *Handbook of Research Methods in Childhood Development.* New York: John Wiley & Sons.
1973   Altruistic and egoistic behavior in six cultures. In L. Nader and T. Maretzki, eds., *Cultural Illness and Health: Essays in Human Adaptation.* Washington, D.C.: American Anthropological Association.
1975   Aloofness and intimacy of husbands and wives: A cross-cultural study. *Ethos* 3(2):183–207.
1978   A strategy for psychocultural research. In G. Spindler, ed., *The Making of Psychological Anthropology.* Berkeley: University of California Press.

CHAPTER 9

The Status of Research Related to Psychopathology

Thomas M. Achenbach

Several factors make the study of psychopathology of school-age children especially important. First, referrals for mental health services rise rapidly after the age of 5 (Baldwin et al., 1971; Rosen, 1979). Second, mental health problems become closely intertwined with children's functioning in school and their general educational development. Third, mental health problems appear to crystallize into more tenacious patterns during middle childhood than in the preschool years. And mental health problems increasingly extend into the world outside the family, often hindering children's integration into age-appropriate social networks.

Aside from the broad impact of mental health problems and the sharp rise in referrals from the preschool to the elementary school period, what is distinctive about the psychopathology of middle childhood? Unlike major adult disorders, such as schizophrenia and manic-depressive conditions, most disorders of middle childhood involve exaggerations of behavior that nearly all children show in some degree. Many disorders of middle childhood also involve a failure to develop age-appropriate behavior, rather than the decline or deviation from attained levels of functioning often seen in disorders of adolescence and adulthood. And most disorders of middle childhood appear at first glance to be less ominous and more tractable than disorders of adolescence, in which physical size, sexual maturity, suicidal behavior, delinquency, bizarre ideation, and the waning of parental control play larger roles. Whether disorders of middle childhood actually are less ominous or more tractable is an empirical question that can be answered only through longitudinal research.

On one hand, existing longitudinal evidence suggests that many disorders of adolescence are direct outgrowths of childhood disorders rather than emerging de novo (Rutter, 1980; Rutter et al., 1976). On the other hand, some childhood behavior problems that have attracted abundant clinical attention, such as phobias and bed-wetting, may in fact be relatively benign, transitory, and easily treated (see Achenbach, 1982). A major task for research is to distinguish between those childhood problems that are typically self-correcting without intervention, those that are best handled by parents or teachers, and those that require professional help to prevent interference with further development.

As this chapter emphasizes, research on the psychopathology of middle childhood requires a blending of traditional developmental research—with its focus on developmental processes and sequences—and clinically oriented research—with its focus on individual differences. The traditional separation of these contrasting but equally necessary approaches has limited our understanding of the relationships between normal developmental mechanisms and pathological deviations of development.

To elucidate the current status of research related to psychopathology, I first consider two key aspects of recent research: the role of recent research in dispelling myths of earlier eras and some new directions taken by recent research efforts. I then consider the conceptual implications of paradigms that shape the study of child psychopathology. Thereafter, I consider research needs in terms of the prospects for blending clinical and developmental approaches; the methodological and theoretical challenges and contributions of the developmental study of psychopathology; the effects of buffers, prevention, and intervention on the development of disorders; and the training needed to advance developmental research on psychopathology.

IMPLICATIONS OF RECENT RESEARCH: DISPELLING MYTHS

Although there has long been a vast literature on behavior disorders of childhood, little of it was firmly grounded in programmatic research. Instead, it was a potpourri of practitioners' personal experiences, theoretical dogma, and isolated empirical findings, often extrapolated far beyond their original context. The fragility of the research base was reflected in cycles of changing advice about child-rearing and behavior problems. Successive editions of the *Infant Care Bulletin* of the U.S. Children's Bureau (1981), for example, show drastic changes in advice to parents and in the consequences imputed to various practices, despite the lack of data to support either the initial views or the later reversals (see Achenbach, 1982, Ch. 2, for examples).

The research base is still too weak to provide definitive guidelines for understanding, preventing, and treating most behavior disorders, yet the research of the 1970s and 1980s has helped combat certain influential myths. This is an essential step in creating a sounder basis for understanding and treating childhood disorders. As the simple and sovereign assumptions of earlier years give way to a more empirical orientation, there is an increasing need for research methods and paradigms geared specifically to child psychopathology. This section illustrates the role of research in dispelling myths and considers the emergence of new approaches to research.

MBD/Hyperactivity/Attention Deficit Disorder

Throughout the 1960s and 1970s the most publicized behavior disorder of childhood was at first known as MBD, then as hyperactivity or hyperkinesis, and most recently as attention deficit disorder with hyperactivity. This disorder exemplifies the following key aspects of behavior problems of middle childhood:

1. The onset of schooling brings a sharp rise in referrals for the disorder, with a peak at about age 9.

2. The problem behaviors are not blatantly pathognomonic in themselves but rather are exaggerations of behavior that most children show in milder degrees.

3. The problem behaviors do not represent a decline from previously attained levels but rather an impediment to the development of important new behaviors.

4. Clinical referrals are prompted by adults' discomfort with the child's behavior rather than by the child's own requests for help.

Historical Context

During the 1930s and 1940s, Alfred E. Strauss, Heinz Werner, and Laura Lehtinen developed methods for diagnosing and educating brain-damaged children (Strauss and Lehtinen, 1947). Normal children, retarded children with brain damage, and retarded children without known brain damage were compared on various perceptual and cognitive tasks. The behavioral differences that were found between the brain-damaged and other children were interpreted as signs of brain damage.

Strauss's work helped to foster a stereotype of the brain-damaged child. The stereotype featured hyperactivity, impulsivity, distractibility, short attention span, emotional lability, poor performance on perceptual-motor tasks, and clumsiness. Children who showed these behaviors but for whom there was no direct evidence of brain damage were assumed to have subtle brain damage and were labeled with such terms as the following: Strauss syndrome, diffuse brain damage, minimal brain damage, minimal brain dysfunction, and minimal cerebral dysfunction. MBD (minimal brain damage or dysfunction) was soon invoked as an explanation for many forms of problem behavior.

Problems of Diagnostic Criteria

The early attempts to identify children with subtle brain damage soon gave way to an indiscriminate use of MBD as a label for a heterogeneous group who had little in common with the brain-damaged children originally studied by Strauss and his colleagues. Hyperactive behavior, in particular, became virtually synonymous with MBD. The concept of MBD was further broadened to encompass school learning problems. Some people used MBD interchangeably with the terms LD (learning disability) and SLD (specific learning disability; e.g., Ochroch, 1981). Under the assumption that an attention deficit is a core problem in hyperactivity, the official psychiatric nosology eventually adopted the diagnostic category of attention deficit disorder with hyperactivity (American Psychiatric Association, 1980).

During the 1970s a flood of publications on hyperactivity suggested that there was a national epidemic, and American children were diagnosed as hyperactive at 60 times the rate of British children (Weiss and Hechtman, 1979). Yet behavioral ratings by teachers, who often instigate referrals for hyperactivity, showed that American schoolchildren were not perceived as more hyperactive than schoolchildren in Canada, West Germany, or New Zealand (Trites, 1979). The popularity of the diagnosis of hyperactivity in this country, thus, did not appear to reflect significant behavioral differences between American children and those in other Western countries. Furthermore, research on children diagnosed as hyperactive showed that many were not exceptionally or consistently deviant in activity level, although they might be deviant in other ways, such as aggressiveness (e.g., Loney and Milich, 1982).

It seems that the concepts of MBD and hyperactivity had expanded far beyond the phenomena the terms were originally coined to designate. A lack of standardized diagnostic data was partly to blame for the overuse of the diagnosis. Yet even when clinicians were given identical data about putative cases, agreement on the diagnosis of hyperactivity was poor. Analyses of diagnoses made from standardized case materials, for example, showed that individual clinicians differed in the cues they relied on, the way in which they weighted the cues, and their awareness of the diagnostic "policies" guiding their judgments of hyperactivity (Ullman et al., 1981).

Despite individual variations in their use of data, however, the clinicians in the Ullman study generally weighted teachers' and parents' reports of hyperactivity more heavily than data obtained from clinical assessments. Other research also has shown that reports by "significant others" in a child's everyday environment are typically weighted more heavily in clinical diagnoses than are clinical observations of behavior (McCoy, 1976). This suggests that one antidote to the misuse of popular diagnostic concepts is to make better use of data on behavior occurring outside the clinical setting.

Etiological Assumptions

As hyperactivity became a catchall term for a wide variety of problem behaviors, the assumption of an organic etiology remained dominant, but different versions of it were propagated with great conviction. One version was based on the apparent efficacy of stimulant drugs in reducing hyperactivity. In a book written for parents, Wender and Wender (1978:21) state that:

In virtually all instances hyperactivity is the result of an *inborn temperamental difference* in the child. How the child is treated and raised can affect the severity of his problem but it cannot cause the problem. Certain types of raising may make the problem worse, certain types of raising may make the problem better. *No* forms of raising can produce [such problems] in a child who is not temperamentally predisposed to them.

Wender and Wender have argued that hyperactive children have a specific deficiency in the functioning of the neurotransmitter dopamine and that the efficacy of stimulant drugs indicates that they compensate for this deficiency.

Another organic explanation for hyperactivity concerns abnormal sensitivities to foods. The leading proponent of this explanation is the allergist Ben Feingold. According to Feingold, heightened sensitivity to naturally occurring salicylates and artificial colors, flavors, and other food additives causes hyperactivity in many children. Diets free of these substances are said to produce dramatic results (Feingold, 1976:24, 26):

The child who was abusive, disobedient, incorrigible, and disdainful of attention moves toward becoming affectionate, lovable, and responsive to guidance. . . . In [mental] retardation the clinical response may be dramatic, as evidenced by improved behavior, better coordination of both fine and gross muscles, and improved learning ability. All of these gains induce a marked transformation in the patient, whose expression becomes more alert and bright, his social adjustment improves, permitting him to function as a self-sufficient person who does not require one-to-one attention or instruction.

The Wender and Feingold positions reflect widespread assumptions that specific organic abnormalities cause diverse behavior problems labeled as hyperactivity, despite a lack of well-validated diagnostic criteria. The impact of these assumptions on treatment is illustrated by survey findings that stimulant medication was used to treat 85 percent of children whose physicians considered them hyperactive (Sandoval et al., 1980). Parents of other children have joined Feingold associations around the country and attempted to abide by the Feingold dietary strictures.

Research Findings

Although specific causes have not been identified for hyperactivity, research conducted in the 1970s and 1980s has cast doubt on popular etiological assumptions. Diverse studies have shown, for example, that brain damage does not necessarily cause hyperactivity and that most children diagnosed as hyperactive are probably not brain damaged (see Achenbach, 1982, for a review of the evidence). Although stimulant medication has been shown to reduce activity levels and to improve attention, it has the same effects on well-functioning nonhyperactive children (Rapoport et al., 1980). This casts doubt on the assumption that behavioral responses to stimulant medication substantiate neurotransmitter deficits unique to hyperactive children. Furthermore, follow-up studies show that medication alone does little to improve the long-term social or academic functioning of hyperactive children (e.g., Gittelman, 1982).

With respect to Feingold's claims, carefully controlled studies show negligible differences in hyperactivity when children are on Feingold versus normal diets (e.g., Harley et al., 1978; Weiss et al., 1980). If food sensitivities actually play any role at all, it is restricted to a very small proportion of hyperactive children.

Inattentive and overactive behaviors are undoubtedly of concern in their own right since organic abnormalities may well be involved. Yet the assumption of a disease-like entity with a single organic cause seems less fruitful at this point than systematic study of the broader contexts in which the maladaptive behavior occurs. Findings that children treated for hyperactivity vary greatly in activity level and other behaviors and that the different behaviors predict different aspects of outcome call for a stronger focus on overall adaptive patterns.

The Role of Research in Dispelling Myths

Dispelling myths may seem like a prosaic task for research, yet false assumptions about the causes and cures of psychopathology are pernicious and must be unmasked through programmatic research. Only in the last decade has child psychopathology attracted enough serious research to test influential assumptions. Such research is needed to produce the measures, constructs, and basic data for a positive science able to generate valid theories as well as to dispel myths.

Although research on hyperactivity is a key example, some instructive parallels are evident in recent research on a strikingly different disorder: infantile autism, which begins much earlier but typically remains a permanent handicap. The role of research in dispelling myths about autism is especially pertinent because the popular assumptions about autism were the reverse of the assumptions about hyperactivity.

When Kanner (1943) initially described the syndrome of autism, he carefully distinguished it from other disorders, such as schizophrenia. Yet others soon used the term interchangeably with schizophrenia, childhood psychosis, and atypical personality, which they blamed largely on environmental factors, especially parental behavior and attitudes. Despert (1947) and Rank (1949), for example, implicated mothers who were immature, narcissistic, overintellectual, and incapable of mature emotional relationships. Bettelheim (1967) indicted mothers who "wish that [their] child should not exist" (p. 125), and Wolman (1970) cited "parents [who] inadvertently hated one another and use the child emotionally" (p. vii). These claims were buttressed mainly by the authors' psychodynamic interpretations of cases they had seen. An absence of research support did not prevent such claims from dominating the field until the 1970s, with the result that many parents were personally blamed for their child's condition (e.g., Kysar, 1968).

As with hyperactivity, a growing body of research has shown that widely held assumptions about the etiology of autism were not justified. However, in this case, doubt was cast on unsupported assumptions of an environmental rather than an organic etiology. Research on parents of autistic children, for example, shows no evidence that parental personalities or child-rearing practices cause autism but, instead, that certain parental characteristics may be responses to the stress of having an autistic child (see Achenbach, 1982, for a review of evidence). Although research on organic factors has not firmly supported alternative explanations for autism (see Cohen and Shaywitz, 1982), it now seems abundantly clear that it was wrong to blame parents for autism.

IMPLICATIONS OF RECENT RESEARCH: SOME NEW DIRECTIONS

Recent research has not only helped to dispel myths but has also opened new perspectives on the developmental aspects of psychopathology. Although oriented largely toward the study of psychopathology per se, the new approaches invite a closer alliance with the study of normal development, and they may shed more light on developmental processes than traditional clinical research has. To highlight the new directions, I consider research on children assumed to be at high risk for psychopathology, behavioral assessment, and taxonomic research.

Research on High-Risk Children

Major adult disorders, such as schizophrenia, have been intensively studied for decades, but research on people who already manifest such disorders cannot tell us which of their abnormalities are intrinsic to the disorder and which ones might reflect consequences of the disorder, such as rejection of other people, institutionalization, and drug therapies. Experimental manipulation of hypothesized causes would be the method of choice for pinpointing etiologies, but the hypothesized causes cannot ethically be inflicted on people.

As an alternative to studying people who already manifest a major disorder, Mednick proposed longitudinal research on children who are statistically at high risk for developing certain disorders (Mednick et al., 1981). By comparing the developmental course of children at risk who eventually manifest a disorder, at-risk children who do not manifest it, and control children who are not at risk, Mednick hoped to identify specific etiological factors. Mednick applied this strategy to longitudinal research on children who have schizophrenic mothers. Such children are considerably more likely to manifest schizophrenia in adulthood than are the children of nonschizophrenics, although most children of schizophrenics do not become schizophrenic.

Mednick's research began with a cohort of Danish children who had schizophrenic mothers and a demographically matched comparison group whose families were free of mental disorders. Denmark was chosen because it has public health services that can aid in the identification and longitudinal study of groups at risk, plus centralized case registers of mental disorders.

As Mednick's subjects were followed into young adulthood, some manifested severe psychopathology. The findings implicate different precursors of major disorders in males and females. Among males psychophysiological lability was a significant precursor, whereas among females early onset of schizophrenia in their mothers was a precursor (Mednick et al., 1978). Teacher ratings also showed different relationships to later schizophrenia in males and females. Boys who later became schizophrenic were reported by their teachers to behave inappropriately and to present disciplinary problems. By contrast, girls who later became schizophrenic were reported to be poorly controlled, anhedonic, withdrawn, and isolated (John et al., 1982). A further finding was that, among high-risk males who showed psychophysiological lability, those who became schizophrenic had experienced more paternal absences and more institutional care, especially in the first and sixth through tenth years of life (Walker et al., 1981).

In addition to identifying possible precursors of major disorders and sex differences in the precursors, studies of high-risk children have demonstrated the importance of comparing the developmental courses of children who are at risk for different disorders. It has been found, for example, that certain attentional deficits shown by children of schizophrenics are also shown by children of parents having unipolar affective disorders (Harvey et al., 1981). This indicates that abnormalities found in high-risk children are not necessarily unique to the condition for which the children are thought to be at risk. Instead, some abnormalities may reflect a general psychopathology or vulnerability factor. Or they may reveal links among disorders that appear separate in adults.

Behavioral Assessment

Behavioral research has stimulated another type of approach. Several reports of behavioral therapies for children were published in the 1920s and 1930s. There was then a general eclipse of behavioral interventions until the late 1950s. By the 1970s, however, behavioral methods had spawned a large body of literature on case studies and clinical series illustrating particular techniques. Controlled comparisons with other approaches were rarer, but the behavioral emphasis on explicit documentation of problems and outcomes nevertheless yielded a far more objective data base than decades of literature on psychotherapy had.

One of the main rallying points for behavior modifiers was their rejection of traditional assessment in favor of behavioral assessment. By traditional assessment they meant mainly psychodynamic, medically oriented, and personality-trait approaches. A fundamental contrast was drawn between the traditional emphasis on inferences about underlying variables—such as psychodynamic constructs, disease entities, and personality—and the behavioral emphasis on observable behaviors and the environmental contingencies supporting them (Mash and Terdal, 1981).

The behavioral assessment method par excellence is the structured recording of behaviors as they occur in natural settings. From published reports of behavior therapy, we might conclude that direct observations are not only easy and routine for behavior modifiers but also that they somehow avoid all the reliability and validity problems raised by traditional assessment. Such is not the case, however. Because it is seldom practical to have trained observers record problem behaviors for routine clinical assessment, there is often a gap between the idealized model of behavioral assessment and what behavioral clinicians really do (Wade et al., 1979). Furthermore, many problem behaviors, such as stealing, setting fires, and fighting, are unlikely to occur under the watchful eyes of trained observers. And even where exceptionally thorough observations have been done in the homes of very cooperative families, the observed contingencies seem to account for little of the variance in problem behaviors (Patterson, 1980).

The limitations of direct observations under natural conditions and the lack of perfect agreement among various assessment methods have led behavior modifiers to advocate multimethod behavioral assessment (Nay, 1979). For assessments of children the multiple methods include interviews, standardized tests, checklists and log books completed by parents and teachers, observations in natural and clinical settings, and simulation of problem situations.

The advent and broadening of behavioral assessment has greatly enriched the study and treatment of psychopathology by workers of many persuasions. Nevertheless, in dispensing with psychodynamic, disease, and personality constructs, behavioral assessment faces a major problem in "how to reduce the plethora of fine objective behavioral categories into fewer, more meaningful and interpretable categories" (Hetherington and Martin, 1979:154). This raises questions of taxonomy, to which I now turn.

Taxonomic Research

Research on children at risk, behavioral assessment, and most other aspects of psychopathology concerns individual differences. In studies of children at risk, for example, the goal is to identify variables differentiating children having poor outcomes from those having good outcomes. In behavioral assessment the goal is to pinpoint specific behaviors and the environmental contingencies that must be modified to improve a child's functioning. But the study of individual differences must ultimately find a basis for conceptually grouping children according to higher-order patterns of similarities and differences.

A common strategy is to form groups of children whose behavior patterns are similar in the hope that they will be found similar in other important ways, such as the etiology, prognosis, and optimal treatments for their disorders. Grouping children according to behavioral similarities is also necessary for clinical communication, program planning, and the training of clinicians. In short, taxonomies of behavior are fundamental to the study and treatment of psychopathology.

Nosological Approaches

One approach to taxonomy is an outgrowth of traditional medical nosology. This approach assumes that each disorder consists of an underlying disease entity that manifests a distinctive symptom pattern. According to this view, the goal of taxonomic research is to obtain precise descriptions of symptom patterns in order to form groups of individuals who all have the same disorder and to discriminate them from individuals who have different disorders. Once this is done, individuals who have the same disorder can be studied to determine the underlying nature, cause, and optimal treatment of the disorder. Because it is assumed that a specific disease underlies each symptom pattern, the nosological approach puts great emphasis on identifying each disorder in a present versus absent fashion.

The dominant version of the nosological approach to behavior disorders is the Amerian Psychiatric Association's *Diagnostic and Statistical Manual of Mental Disorders* (the "DSM"). The first two editions of the DSM (DSM-I, 1952; DSM-II, 1968) were composed mainly of narrative descriptions and inferred psychodynamics of purported disorders, as negotiated by committees of psychiatrists. The newest edition (DSM-III, 1980) bases the taxonomy of adult disorders on research diagnostic criteria (RDC) that have been evolved for discriminating between long-established taxa, such as schizophrenia and manic-depressive conditions.

In a major departure from the narrative descriptions and inferred dynamics of disorders in DSM-I and DSM-II, DSM-III specifies decision rules for the diagnosis of each disorder. However, the lack of well-established taxa of childhood disorders left the job of specifying criteria for childhood disorders largely to the process of committee negotiations.

Although successive drafts of DSM-III showed improvements in the interjudge reliability of adult diagnoses, there was a decline in the reliability of child diagnoses from early drafts to later drafts (see DSM-III, Appendix F). Furthermore, two studies have shown poorer reliability for DSM-III diagnoses of children than for DSM-II diagnoses, which were themselves not very reliable (Mattison et al., 1979; Mezzich and Mezzich, 1979). The innovations that improved the reliability of adult diagnoses thus seem to have made the nosological diagnoses of childhood disorders even less reliable than before. Better reliability has been obtained for some specific disorders (Edelbrock et al., 1983), and standardized clinical interviews may help improve the reliability of DSM diagnoses in general (Costello and Edelbrock, 1982). However, it remains to be seen whether the DSM categories *validly* discriminate between children whose disorders actually differ in important ways.

Multivariate-Descriptive Approaches

Lacking well-established diagnostic categories, students of child psychopathology turned to statistical methods for empirically identifying behavioral syndromes. After a few rudimentary efforts in the 1940s and 1950s, the advent of electronic computers spawned a host of multivariate studies in the 1960s and 1970s. In most of these studies, ratings of behavior were factor analyzed to identify behavior problems that covaried to form syndromes. Despite differences in the rating instruments, raters, samples, and methods of analysis, there was considerable convergence in the identification of particular syndromes (see Achenbach and Edelbrock, 1978, and Quay, 1979, for detailed reviews). Some of these resemble syndromes that are also evident in nosological approaches, whereas others do not have clear counterparts in psychiatric nosology. Even where the multivariate findings do resemble nosological syndromes, there are some important differences.

1. The nosological syndromes are negotiated formulations of clinicians' concepts of disorders (Spitzer and Cantwell, 1980), whereas the multivariate syndromes are derived statistically from covariation among scores on items rated for samples of children.

2. The nosological syndromes require yes-or-no judgments of the presence or absence of each relevant attribute, whereas multivariate syndromes generally utilize quantitative gradations in the assessment of each attribute.

3. Starting from yes-or-no judgments of each relevant attribute, a nosological diagnosis ultimately culminates in a yes-or-no decision about whether a child has a particular disorder. Multivariate syndromes, by contrast, reflect variations in the degree to which children manifest the characteristics of a syndrome. Thus, a child gets a score that shows how high he or she stands on a particular dimension rather than a yes-or-no diagnosis. However, cutoff points can also be established on such dimensions to discriminate between different groups of children in a categorical fashion, if desired.

4. Although the criteria for nosological diagnoses imply comparisions with "normal" children of the same age, no operational basis is provided for determining how a child compares with normal age-mates. The quantitative nature of multivariate syndromes, by contrast, makes it possible to use a metric derived from normative samples, thereby showing how much a child deviates from normal age-mates.

5. Because the taxa of a nosology are assumed to embody discrete types of disorders, children who show characteristics of several taxa must either receive multiple categorical diagnoses or must be placed in a single category on the basis of preemptive criteria for choosing one diagnosis over another.

The multivariate approach, by contrast, lends itself to a profile format in which a child's scores on all syndromes of the taxonomy are retained, obviating the need for forced choices between categories.

Because multivariate descriptions are neutral with respect to the etiologies of disorders, further research may reveal associations between organic abnormalities and certain multivariate descriptions. For example, if a virus is consistently associated with a particular syndrome, its presence could become one criterion for diagnosis. Yet as pointed out by Shonkoff (in this volume), many diseases having known organic causes cannot be defined exclusively by an etiological agent, because there are major individual differences in the degree and manner of response to the same etiological agent. Even if an organic abnormality is implicated, multivariate approaches may make better use of a larger array of potentially relevant data than hit-or-miss categorical approaches do.

CONCEPTUAL IMPLICATIONS OF TAXONOMIC PARADIGMS

So far, this chapter has viewed recent research on psychopathology largely in terms of efforts to obtain data. However, lurking beneath the surface of all empirical research are conceptual paradigms that shape the questions asked and the answers sought. To link previous research with future research needs, it is important to examine some contrasting tenets of the taxonomic paradigms that may dictate very different research agendas.

Neither the nosological nor the multivariate-descriptive paradigm constitutes a theory of psychopathology designed to explain why particular problems occur. Nevertheless, taxonomic paradigms affect the ways in which disorders are conceptualized and the types of explanations sought.

The Nosological Paradigm

The nosological paradigm implies that each disorder exists as a discrete categorical entity that can be discriminated from other categorical entities and that each disorder will ultimately be found to have a specific cause.

Although categorical nosologies need not necessarily imply organic causes for all disorders, the DSM-III conveys a heavy presumption in favor of organic etiologies by repeatedly referring to disorders as illnesses (American Psychiatric Association, 1980). While organic determinants may eventually be found for some disorders, rigid adherence to a disease model may prematurely impose conceptual categories on children who are not well served by the concept of a specific illness. For example, nosological assumptions promoted the widespread labeling of children as MBD and hyperactive, even though there were no operational criteria for the behavioral phenotype and the children's behavior problems were, in fact, diverse.

More recently, the concept of childhood depression has been cast in a similar role, which has promoted diagnoses of depressive illness despite a lack of well-validated operational criteria diagnosing for childhood depression (Achenbach, 1982, in press; Carlson and Cantwell, 1982). The growing enthusiasm for inferring-depression from many different behaviors prompted one observer to dub childhood depression "the MBD of the 1980s." Other childhood problems that may likewise be prematurely cast into the nosological mold include antisocial behavior, which DSM-III categorizes as "conduct disorders" (e.g., undersocialized aggressive conduct disorder), and school learning deficiencies, which DSM-III categorizes as "specific developmental disorders" (e.g., developmental arithmetic disorder). The nosological categorization of learning deficiencies contrasts with current multidimensional views of even relatively circumscribed reading disorders, which were previously viewed as specific developmental dyslexia (Goldberg et al., 1983).

The Multivariate-Descriptive Paradigm

The lack of satisfactory diagnostic schemas for children's disorders is what initially prompted researchers to apply multivariate methods to the derivation of syndromes. The multivariate syndromes represent a conceptual level roughly analogous to nosological syndromes in the sense that both purport to represent groupings of attributes that tend to co-occur. However, besides being empirically derived and quantifiable, the multivariate syndromes can be cast in a profile format that simultaneously displays a child's standing on each syndrome. Furthermore, profiles can be used as a basis for taxonomy by grouping children according to similarities in their profile patterns. This can be done via multivariate methods such as cluster analysis, which quantifies the degree of similarity between individual profiles and forms groups according to precisely specified algorithms.

Once clusters of similar profiles have been formed, each cluster represents a type of behavioral pattern. The clusters collectively constitute a taxonomy of patterns reflecting children's standings on multiple syndromes, rather than classifying children on each syndrome judged categorically in a yes-or-no fashion. Furthermore, the similarity of an individual child's profile pattern to each profile type can be quantitatively assessed by computing a correlation coefficient between the two. Thus, rather than being constrained by yes-or-no judgments of whether a child fits a particular type, we can systematically determine which children are highly similar to particular types and which children are less similar or not at all similar. (For detailed illustrations of cluster-analytic taxonomies of profiles, see Achenbach and Edelbrock, 1983, and Edelbrock and Achenbach, 1980.)

Implications for Future Research

The nosological and multivariate-descriptive paradigms differ in how they use data to form a picture of the child. A nosology requires the clinician to mentally weigh and combine various kinds of data into a diagnostic judgment; differences in the way individual clinicians obtain, weigh, and combine data contribute to the unreliability of diagnoses.

In the multivariate-descriptive approach, by contrast, data are obtained, weighted, and combined according to standardized procedures that are similar for all cases. The standardization of procedures facilitates comparison of data obtained on a particular case with data obtained in the same fashion by other clinicians and on other cases and normative groups. Typically, the multivariate approach analyzes data from one informant at a time, such as a parent. Data from any informant may be biased with respect to the informant's influence on the child, opportunities to observe particular behaviors, and subjective standards of judgment. Yet this is also true of other approaches to assessing children's behavior. Despite inevitable biases in data from any one source, however, the standardizaton of procedures makes it possible to explicitly compare the pictures of the child obtained from different informants, such as the child's mother, father, and teacher. The reasons for differences in perceptions of the child can then be explored.

The multivariate-descriptive approach can thus contribute standardization, rigor, and reliability to the gathering of data as well as to integrating the data and relating it to norms for a child's age-mates. It has also yielded evidence for patterns of behavior problems that have not been identified through nosological approaches. Factor analyses of behavior problems reported by parents of disturbed 6- to 11-year-old girls, for example, have revealed a syndrome comprised of items such as cruelty to animals, cruelty, bullying or meanness to others, and physical attacks on people, which has been given the descriptive label cruel (Achenbach and Edelbrock, 1979). This syndrome is distinct from a general aggressive syndrome that was found in the same research and is quite similar for both sexes at several age levels. The detection of the "cruel" syndrome among girls may seem surprising, because hurtful behavior toward animals and people is stereotyped in our culture as being more masculine than feminine. Yet empirically derived syndromes reflect the covariation among reported behaviors rather than just their prevalence rates. Thus, although cruelty to animals was reported for more boys than girls, it covaried consistently with a particular set of other behaviors to form a syndrome among disturbed girls but not among boys. Furthermore, cluster analyses of profiles that include the "cruel" syndrome reveal groups of disturbed girls who are more deviant in terms of this syndrome than any other (Edelbrock and Achenbach, 1980).

Regardless of their source, various kinds of data must ultimately be combined into a judgment of what action to take. This requires knowledge of the likely outcome of each disorder under different conditions of intervention and nonintervention, which will be discussed below in the context of research needs.

RESEARCH NEEDS

Developmental research on psychopathology offers rich opportunities for improving our understanding of both development and psychopathology. It also raises methodological and theoretical challenges for combining two enterprises that have differed in their choice of topics, preferred research strategies, research training, reward systems, and consumer audiences. Advancing our knowledge requires people who are well versed in both clinical and developmental issues and who are prepared to ask new questions and forge new approaches that may not win immediate accolades in either field. For this reason, it is worth specifying research needs only if there are researchers who can meet the needs. After considering research needs, I will consider the need for training people to do developmental research on psychopathology.

Developmental Perspectives

Research on psychopathology typically stems from concern for a particular disorder or a particular type of treatment. The ultimate goal is to identify the etiology, course, outcome, and most appropriate treatment of each disorder. Although clinical researchers tend to view these questions in terms of the temporal history of disorders per se, they are developmental questions as well, for the following reasons:

1. The definition of deviance requires a clear picture of what is normal for children of a particular developmental level growing up under particular environmental conditions.

2. Determining which deviant behaviors are maladaptive and which are benign requires longitudinal comparisons of children manifesting the different behaviors over developmentally significant periods in order to determine which ones actually impede development.

3. Assessing the course and outcome of disorders requires longitudinal comparisons with children manifesting other disorders and no disorders, so that variance unique to a particular disorder can be distinguished from variance associated with psychopathology in general and variance associated with normal development.

To answer these clinical-developmental questions, we need more than just a general knowledge of developmental and clinical phenomena. We need research specifically targeted at putative clinical disorders that uses clinically meaningful operational definitions of the disorders and that assesses the same parameters in developmentally similar normative groups.

Such research should take account of cohort, age, and time-of-measurement effects, as emphasized by life-span developmentalists (Baltes et al., 1977). This does not necessarily mean that the elaborate longitudinal-sequential and cross-sectional-sequential designs prescribed by life-span developmentalists offer the only approach to developmental research on psychopathology. In fact, full-scale life-span designs are seldom practical because they require such large numbers of observations on large samples of subjects selected according to complex permutations of age, cohort, and time of assessment. The limited pool of subjects available for longitudinal study of a particular disorder and the difficulty of comparing well-matched subjects who lack the disorder require compromises with the ideal designs.

Furthermore, it now seems clear that the life-span designs cannot disentangle age, cohort, and time-of-assessment effects as fully as had been hoped (Adam, 1978; Horn and Donaldson, 1977). Instead, multiple approaches must be coordinated to answer questions about particular disorders. For example, suppose we want to know whether the surge of diagnoses of hyperactivity in the 1970s actually reflected an epidemic of the disorder, possibly because of an increase in environmental or dietary pollutants; a lowering of adult tolerance for behavior that had previously been more acceptable; a decline in the quality of parenting; or cultural changes that made high activity more incompatible with new demands placed on children.

To find out we would initially need cross-sectional studies to obtain good measures of the behavioral phenotype of hyperactivity under various conditions. Examples of practical measures include devices that directly assess physical activity under standard conditions (e.g., in an experimental playroom situation) and under ecologically representative conditions (e.g., classrooms), plus standardized ratings by the significant others who ultimately decide whether a child has a problem, such as parents and teachers (see Eaton, 1983).

Once we have satisfactory measures of behavior across the target age range (e.g., ages 6–11), children at each age can be compared cross sectionally to see whether there are possible developmental or cohort effects. If there are no significant age differences, any developmental or cohort effects across this particular age span may be negligible. If there are significant age differences, however, it may be worth conducting a longitudinal-sequential study in which children of several cohorts are assessed as they age from 6 to 11 in order to see whether there are uniform changes with age in all cohorts or whether changes occur in all cohorts at the same points in time, regardless of age.

Although feasible for one or two distinctive disorders, such as hyperactivity, this strategy would be impractical for many of the behavior problems that afflict school-age children. Furthermore, because the necessary studies of a specific disorder are not likely to be launched until there is already widespread alarm about the disorder, it would be too late for the most informative comparisons between periods of apparent low prevalence and apparent high prevalence. As an alternative, it would be preferable to have periodic normative-epidemiological assessments of a broad range of behavior problems in large representative samples, as discussed in the next section.

Normative-Epidemiological Research

Developmental research seeks to identify the mechanisms and sequences of development that characterize children in general. Yet developmental studies seldom obtain normative data on representative samples using procedures that are widely replicable. Instead, most developmental studies employ procedures devised to suit a particular conception of theoretical variables, as assessed in samples chosen for convenience rather than representativeness. The practical utility of the procedures and their generalizability to other situations are seldom considered, even though the aim is to derive generalized conclusions.

Clinical research, by contrast, is often spurred by the need for quick, practical procedures that can be readily applied in a variety of settings. This is exemplified by the abundance of procedures for assessing hyperactivity. Few of these procedures, however, are based on normative data that show how individual children compare with representative samples of their peers. Lacking either normative data or a litmus test for the positive diagnosis of disorders such as hyperactivity, we cannot place much faith in the meaning of particular scores.

Both developmental research and clinical research seek conclusions that are generalizable beyond the samples that are actually studied. Yet their research samples and procedures seldom justify generalization of their findings. There is thus a basic need for standardized assessment procedures to provide common denominators across diverse research and practical contexts. It is essential that these procedures be normed on large representative samples of children to provide baselines for comparisons with subsequent research samples and for judgments of how individual children deviate from their peers.

Most previous efforts to obtain normative and/or epidemiological data on children's behavior disorders have used a small number of behavior problem items chosen on the basis of convenience or assumed significance. In some cases the assessment procedures have been severely constrained by the overriding requirements of large-scale surveys, such as the federal government's health examination survey (Roberts and Baird, 1971). In other cases they have been geared to a particular sample of convenience that was selected for ready availability rather than representativeness (e.g., Tuddenham et al., 1974).

Very few studies have obtained data on behavior disorders in representative samples using procedures that could be readily transferred to subsequent research and clinical applications (see Achenbach and Edelbrock, 1981, for a review of studies). However, when this is done, it provides a normative data base with which to compare findings obtained by the same procedures in new contexts. Without such a data base, developmental research on psychopathology tends to be random and noncumulative, unable to relate the findings of one study to those of other studies or to individual children. Periodic repetitions of normative-epidemiological studies at intervals of approximately 10 years would make it possible to reshape the normative data base according to advances in assessment methodology. If certain marker variables were kept standard from one decade to the next, it should be possible to detect major secular changes in behavior disorders.

It is also important to compare data obtained with similar procedures for children of either sex, for children from different ethnic and socioeconomic groups, and for children viewed from different perspectives. For example, despite higher mental health referral rates for school-age boys than girls (Eme, 1979), parents report similar numbers of problems for boys and girls in normative samples. Boys' problems, however, tend more often to involve undercontrolled externalizing behavior, whereas girls' problems tend to involve overcontrolled internalizing behavior (Achenbach and Edelbrock, 1981). Furthermore, teachers report higher rates of school problems for boys than girls in normative samples (Edelbrock and Achenbach, 1984). Where ethnic and socioeconomic differences have been assessed separately, socioeconomic status accounts for much more variance than ethnicity. Parents of lower socioeconomic status, for example, report more problems and fewer competencies than parents of upper socioeconomic status, whereas black and white parents matched for socioeconomic status do not differ much in their reports of either problems or competencies (Achenbach and Edelbrock, 1981).

Psychopathology and Educational Development

During middle childhood, school becomes a central arena for both success and failure (see Epps and Smith, in this volume). Children must master not only academic skills but also diverse social skills. Failure to master either type of skill on an age-graded schedule can lead to a pervasive sense of failure that hampers further development. What may at first be merely a delay or weakness in a specific skill, such as reading, listening attentively, or making friends, can become a source of alienation from the entire education process.

When children do not progress as expected, they are often assigned to bureaucratically defined categories of special services, such as classes for the learning disabled or social/emotionally disturbed. However, by the time special services creak into action, the problems are often multiple, since what begins as a learning problem usually engenders behavioral and emotional problems. Similarly, what begins as a behavioral or emotional problem often impedes learning.

Its central role as a developmental arena during middle childhood and its responsibility for providing appropriate help make the school a key focus for developmental research on psychopathology. Yet not much research has focused on the interactions between children, their families, and their schools that lead to adaptive versus maladaptive development during middle childhood. Recent government funding cuts and legislation that mandates least restrictive environments have combined to curtail the use of special education placements. This further increases our need for understanding the role of school-related variables in healthy development.

One requirement for improving research on relationships between psychopathology and educational development is the type of normative-epidemiological data base discussed in the previous section. Because teachers are well situated to observe behavior problems related to educational development, standardized teachers' assessments of the behavior of representative samples of their pupils can provide a data base on which to build subsequent studies of specific relationships between psychopathology and educational development, as illustrated by the research cited earlier on precursors of schizophrenia (John et al., 1982).

Efforts to form such a data base suggest that teachers apply such terms as *hyperactivity* too broadly to provide much discriminative validity (Edelbrock and Achenbach, 1984). A data base for school behavior must therefore seek more precise discrimination among behavior patterns than is afforded by popular quasi-diagnostic labels. Once a normative data base is available, research can be more finely tuned to the study of such issues as the way particular patterns of children's problems and competencies interact with particular classroom and teaching styles to facilitate or impede development. The role of molar differences between schools can also be studied, as has been done for the impact of secondary schools on juvenile delinquency in Britain (Rutter et al., 1979).

The Role of Specific Risk and Protective Factors

Earlier in this chapter I discussed the study of children at high risk for particular disorders as one of the new directions taken by developmental research on psychopathology. Such studies have mainly sought to pinpoint predictors of major adult disorders such as schizophrenia. However, most childhood risk factors do not lead to such gross deviances. The loss of parents through death, divorce, or abandonment, for example, triggers a variety of reactions falling well short of schizophrenia. Aside from the immediate emotional reactions, the loss of parents can affect adaptive development by altering children's economic circumstances and everyday contacts with adults, including opportunities for modeling of adult behavior. Other environmental changes, such as a move to a new home or school and integration with unfamiliar ethnic or socioeconomic groups, likewise constitute risk factors that trigger diverse reactions. Personal characteristics that conflict with the demands of a particular environment and major illnesses are additional risk factors that can impede development. The long-term outcomes may include school failure, identity diffusion, withdrawal, aggression, and delinquency, which are not necessarily recognized as psychopathology.

The other side of the coin concerns positive adaptive characteristics of both child and environment that facilitate coping with developmental challenges. Under the banners of social competence and the invulnerable child, positive adaptive characteristics have won considerable fanfare in recent years. Despite the popularity of competence as a theoretical construct, however, much remains to be learned about the specific strengths that enable some children to deal constructively with major risk factors that would debilitate other children. Social cognition and peer relations may be especially fruitful areas of study in this regard (see the chapters by Fischer and Bullock and Hartup, in this volume).

To understand both the preexisting competencies that enable children to cope with threats to their development and the competencies that can be fostered by stress or by therapeutic interventions, we need more than a priori notions of competence, such as children's popularity with peers or favorable impressions they make on adults. Instead, we need to study situations likely to be debilitating and to pinpoint the variables that predict good and poor outcomes when children's coping abilities are severely tested. Both the best and the worst outcomes must be analyzed if we are to understand what distinguishes between competence and incompetence and how we might enhance the coping abilities of children who would otherwise suffer poor outcomes.

Evaluation of Prevention and Intervention Efforts

Like the current emphasis on competence, current enthusiasm for prevention rather than treatment of psychopathology reflects a reaction against illness models. Although it is easy to advocate prevention, it is often much harder to carry it out. Even though thousands of tragic deaths are known to be caused by voluntary behaviors (smoking, drunken driving, overeating, the use of guns), for example, massive efforts at changing behaviors have met with little success. Where the specific causes of behavior disorders are unknown, the call for prevention hardly seems more likely to be answered with success. In fact, some of the most ambitious efforts to prevent problem behaviors in children, such as delinquency, seem to have inadvertently increased the behaviors (McCord, 1982; O'Donnell et al., 1979).

Yet prevention is on a continuum with intervention efforts designed to ameliorate problems after they emerge. Secondary prevention, for example, refers to preventing conditions that are evident from causing further harm. Considering the massive outlays for unproven interventions, more priority needs to be given to evaluating the outcomes of efforts to overcome maladaptive development, whether they are called primary or secondary prevention or therapeutic intervention.

Behavioral and drug therapies for psychopathology in middle childhood have been accompanied by more scientific evaluation of outcomes than the previously dominant psychodynamic therapies were. Nevertheless, most outcome evaluations compare the effect of a particular treatment with no treatment or one other treatment on samples of subjects regarded as homogeneous because they manifest particular target symptoms. Unfortunately, such studies cannot detect potentially important interactions between characteristics of the subjects and particular treatments. Thus, if a treatment shows a statistically significant superiority for a group of subjects, it may be wrongly viewed as the treatment of choice for all children manifesting the problem used to define the group.

Yet in the very few studies that have analyzed interactions between subject and treatment variables, interactions with such gross variables as age and socioeconomic status have been found to account for more variance than the main effects of treatment. Love and Kaswan (1974), for example, found that a treatment that was beneficial for upper-class children actually seemed harmful for lower-class children. Exactly the reverse pattern was found for a second treatment. Although controlled evaluations of the outcome of interventions for child psychopathology are difficult, expensive, and lengthy, such evaluations should be mandatory for all efforts at prevention and therapeutic intervention.

Training for Developmental Research on Psychopathology

Developmental research on psychopathology requires skills and interests spanning two areas that have differed in training programs, occupational roles, reward systems, and consumer audiences. Developmental psychologists are mainly trained to carry out research on developmental processes and sequences defined in terms of theoretical and laboratory-based concepts. They are oriented toward academic careers built on scholarly publications intended for an academic audience. Clinicians, by contrast, are trained mainly in the use of clinical assessment and intervention procedures. They are oriented toward the delivery of clinical services in which interpersonal relationships with patients and other practitioners are paramount. Day-to-day coping with practical problems usually takes precedence over abstract research issues.

How can developmentally sophisticated research be used to help troubled children? Because so many different problems remain to be solved, a wide range of personal orientations can contribute. For example, the more theoretically or methodologically oriented researcher can find abundant challenges in devising rigorous assessment procedures for complex clinical phenomena and evolving research designs to untangle interwoven developmental and clinical problems. At the other extreme, the more clinically oriented researcher can find challenges in trying to translate detailed knowledge of individual cases into researchable general questions.

Because not every researcher can be expected to master all the skills relevant to developmental research on psychopathology, it is unrealistic to expect the same people to be expert clinicians *and* statisticians *and* methodologists *and* theoreticians. Furthermore, work with children takes second place to work with adults in most clinical training programs, while clinical research is relatively peripheral to most research training programs. People who want to do developmental research on psychopathology must therefore piece together the necessary training experiences for themselves. As a consequence, potential workers in this field have diverse and checkered backgrounds. The fact that they span two areas having different professional trajectories also necessitates piecing together employment that will enable them to work at the interface of developmental research and clinical services. This can be difficult at all times but especially during a period of scarce funds for both research and clinical services.

The number of people doing developmental research on the psychopathology of middle childhood is small; their employment prospects and research support are tenuous; and they are not sufficiently concentrated in any one place to provide comprehensive training programs. It is, therefore, important to find ways to facilitate research in this area and to train new researchers. Even a small cadre of serious researchers who are able to pursue long-term programmatic research could greatly improve our knowledge and treatment of the psychopathology of childhood.

SUMMARY

During middle childhood, mental health referrals rise rapidly as mental health problems become intertwined with school functioning, crystallize into more tenacious patterns, and hinder integration into social networks outside the family.

Psychopathology in middle childhood typically involves exaggerations of behaviors that most children show to some degree and failures to develop age-appropriate behaviors. A major task for research is to distinguish between childhood problems likely to be self-correcting, those that can be handled by parents or teachers, and those that require professional help to prevent interference with further development.

The study of psychopathology in middle childhood requires a blending of research on developmental processes and sequences with clinically oriented research on individual differences.

Recent research has helped dispell influential myths about the origins and nature of certain disorders, such as hyperactivity and autism. It has also stimulated new approaches to the developmental understanding of psychopathology, as exemplified by studies of children at high risk for psychopathology, by behavioral assessment, and by taxonomic research. The nosological and multivariate-descriptive taxonomic paradigms can lead to very different ways of conceptualizing the psychopathology of middle childhood.

REFERENCES

Achenbach, T.M.
   1982   *Developmental Psychopathology*. Second ed. New York: John Wiley & Sons.
   In   Developmental psychopathology. In M.E. Lamb and M.H. Bornstein, eds., *Developmental*
   press   *Psychology: An Advanced Textbook*. Hillsdale, N.J.: Lawrence Erlbaum.

Achenbach, T.M., and Edelbrock, C.S.
 1978   The classification of child psychopathology: A review and analysis of empirical efforts. *Psychological Bulletin* 85:1275–1301.
 1979   The child behavior profile: I. Boys aged 12–16 and girls aged 6–11 and 12–16. *Journal of Consulting and Clinical Psychology* 47:223–233.
 1981   Behavioral problems and competencies reported by parents of normal and disturbed children aged four to sixteen. *Monographs of the Society for Research in Child Development* 46:Serial No. 188.
 1983   *Manual for the Child Behavior Checklist and Revised Child Behavior Profile.* Burlington: University of Vermont.
Adam, J.
 1978   Sequential strategies and the separation of age, cohort, and time-of-measurement contributions to developmental data. *Psychological Bulletin* 85:1309–1316.
American Psychiatric Association
 1980   *Diagnostic and Statistical Manual of Mental Disorders.* Third edition. Washington, D.C.: American Psychiatric Association.
Baldwin, J.A., Robertson, N.C., and Satin, D.G.
 1971   The incidence of reported deviant behavior in children. *International Psychiatry Clinics* 8:161–175.
Baltes, P.B., Reese, H.W., and Nesselroade, J.R.
 1977   *Life-Span Developmental Psychology: Introduction to Research Methods.* Monterey, Calif.: Brooks/Cole.
Bettelheim, B.
 1967   *The Empty Fortress.* New York: Free Press.
Bradley, C.
 1937   The behavior of children receiving benzedrine. *American Journal of Psychiatry* 94:577–585.
Carlson, G.A., and Cantwell, D.P.
 1982   Diagnosis of childhood depression: A comparison of the Weinberg and DSM-III criteria. *Journal of the American Academy of Child Psychiatry* 21:247–250.
Cohen, D.J., and Shaywitz, B.A.
 1982   Preface to the special issue on neurobiological research in autism. *Journal of Autism and Developmental Disorders* 12:103–107.
Costello, A., and Edelbrock, C.
 1982   Structured interviewing: A progress report on the NIMH Diagnostic Interview Schedule for Children (DISC). Paper presented at the American Academy of Child Psychiatry, Washington, D.C., October.
Despert, L.
 1947   Psychotherapy in childhood schizophrenia. *American Journal of Psychiatry* 104:36–43.
Eaton, W.O.
 1983   Measuring activity level with actometers: Reliability, validity, and arm length. *Child Development* 54:720–726.
Edelbrock, C., and Achenbach, T.M.
 1980   A typology of child behavior profile patterns: Distribution and correlates for disturbed children aged 6-16. *Journal of Abnormal Child Psychology* 8:441–470.
 1984   The teacher version of the child behavior profile. *Journal of Consulting and Clinical Psychology.*
Edelbrock, C., Costello, A.J., and Kessler, M.D.
 1983   Empirical corroboration of the attention deficit disorder. *Journal of the American Academy of Child Psychiatry.*

Eme, R.F.
  1979 Sex differences in childhood psychopathology: A review. *Psychological Bulletin* 86:574–595.
Feingold, B.F.
  1976 Hyperkinesis and learning disabilities linked to the ingestion of artificial food colors and flavors. *Journal of Learning Disabilities* 9:551–559.
Gittelman, R.
  1982 Prospective Follow-up Study of Hyperactive Children. Paper presented at the American Academy of Child Psychiatry, Washington, D.C., October.
Goldberg, H.K., Schiffman, G.B., and Bender, M.
  1983 *Dyslexia. Interdisciplinary Approaches to Reading Disabilities.* New York: Grune & Stratton.
Harley, J.P., Matthews, C.G., and Eichman, P.
  1978 Synthetic food colors and hyperactivity in children: A double-blind challenge experiment. *Pediatrics* 61:818–828.
Harvey, P., Winters, K., Weintraub, S., and Neale, J.M.
  1981 Distractibility in children vulnerable to psychopathology. *Journal of Abnormal Psychology* 90:298–304.
Hetherington, E.M., and Martin, B.
  1979 Family interaction. In H.C. Quay and J.S. Werry, eds., *Psychopathological Disorders of Childhood.* Second ed. New York: John Wiley & Sons.
Horn, J.L., and Donaldson, G.
  1977 Faith is not enough: A response to the Baltes-Schaie claim that intelligence does not wane. *American Psychologist* 32:369–373.
John, R.S., Mednick, S.A., and Schulsinger, F.
  1982 Teacher reports as a predictor of schizophrenia and borderline schizophrenia: A Bayesian decision analysis. *Journal of Abnormal Psychology* 91:399–413.
Kanner, L.
  1943 Autistic disturbances of affective contact. *Nervous Child* 2:217–250.
Kysar, J.E.
  1968 The two camps in child psychiatry: A report from a psychiatrist father of an autistic and retarded child. *American Journal of Psychiatry* 125:103–109.
Loney, J., and Milich, R.
  1982 Hyperactivity, inattention, and aggression in clinical practice. In M. Wolraich and D.K. Routh, eds., *Advances in Behavioral Pediatrics.* Vol. 2. Greenwich, Conn.: JAI Press.
Love, L.R., and Kaswan, J.W.
  1974 *Troubled Children: Their Families, Schools, and Treatments.* New York: John Wiley & Sons.
Mash, E.J., and Terdal, L.G.
  1981 *Behavioral Assessment of Childhood Disorders.* New York: Guilford Press.
Mattison, R., Cantwell, D.P., Russell, A.T., and Will, L.
  1979 A comparison of childhood psychiatric disorders. *Archives of General Psychiatry* 36:1217–1222.
McCord, J.
  1982 The Cambridge-Somerville Youth Study: A sobering lesson on treatment, prevention, and evaluation. In A.J. McSweeney, S.J. Fremouw, and R.P. Hawkins, eds., *Practical Program Evaluation for Youth Treatment.* Springfield, Ill.: Charles C. Thomas.
McCoy, S.A.
  1976 Clinical judgments of normal childhood behavior. *Journal of Consulting and Clinical Psychology* 44:710–714.
Mednick, S.A., Griffith, J.J., and Mednick, B.R.
  1981 Problems with traditional strategies in mental health research. In F. Schulsinger, S.A. Mednick, and J. Knop, eds., *Longitudinal Research. Methods and Uses in Behavioral Science.* Boston: Nijhoff.

Mednick, S.A., Schulsinger, F., Teasdale, T.W., Schulsinger, H., Venables, P.H., and Rock, D.R.
1978   Schizophrenia in high risk children: Sex differences in predisposing factors. In G. Serban, ed., *Cognitive Defects in the Development of Mental Illness*. New York: Brunner/Mazel.
Mezzich, A.C., and Mezzich, J.E.
1979   Diagnostic Reliability of Childhood and Adolescent Behavior Disorders. Paper presented at the American Psychological Association, New York, September.
Nay, R.W.
1979   *Multimethod Clinical Assessments*. New York: Gardner Press.
Ochroch, R., ed.
1981   *The Diagnosis and Treatment of Minimal Brain Dysfunction in Children. A Clinical Approach.* New York: Human Sciences Press.
O'Donnell, C.R., Lydgate, T., and Fo, W.S.O.
1979   The buddy system: Review and follow-up. *Child Behavior Therapy* 1:161–169.
Patterson, G.R.
1980   Mothers: The unacknowledged victims. *Monographs of the Society for Research in Child Development* 45:Serial No. 186.
Quay, H.C.
1979   Classification. In H.C. Quay and J. Werry, eds., *Psychopathological Disorders of Childhood*. Second ed. New York: John Wiley & Sons.
Rank, B.
1949   Adaptation of the psychoanalytic technique for the treatment of young children with atypical development. *American Journal of Orthopsychiatry* 19:130–139.
Rapoport, J.L., Buchsbaum, M.S., Weingartner, H., Zahn, T.P., Ludlow, C., and Mikkelsen, E.J.
1980   Dextroamphetamine. Its cognitive and behavioral effects in normal and hyperactive boys and normal men. *Archives of General Psychiatry* 37:933–943.
Roberts, J., and Baird, J.T.
1971   Parent ratings of behavioral patterns of children. U.S. Department of Health, Education, and Welfare Publication no. (HSM) 72-1010. Washington, D.C.: U.S. Government Printing Office.
Rosen, B.M.
1979   An overview of the mental health delivery system in the United States and services to children. In I.N. Berlin and L.A. Stone, eds., *Basic Handbook of Child Psychiatry*. Vol. 4. New York: Basic Books.
Rutter, M.
1980   *Changing Youth in a Changing Society*. Cambridge, Mass.: Harvard University Press.
Rutter, M., Graham, P., Chadwick, O.F.D., and Yule, W.
1976   Adolescent turmoil: Fact or fiction? *Journal of Child Psychology and Psychiatry* 17:35–56.
Rutter, M., Maughn, B., Mortimore, P., and Ouston, J.
1979   *Fifteen Thousand Hours: Secondary Schools and Their Effects on Children*. Cambridge, Mass.: Harvard University Press.
Sandoval, J., Lambert, N.M., and Sassone, D.
1980   The identification and labeling of hyperactivity in children: An interactive model. In C.K. Whalen and B. Henker, eds., *Hyperactive Children: The Social Ecology of Identification and Treatment*. New York: Academic Press.
Spitzer, R.L., and Cantwell, D.P.
1980   The DSM-III classification of the psychiatric disorders of infancy, childhood, and adolescence. *Journal of the American Academy of Child Psychiatry* 19:356–370.
Strauss, A.A., and Lehtinen, L.E.
1947   *Psychopathology and Education of the Brain-Injured Child*. New York: Grune & Stratton.

Trites, R.L., ed.
  1979   *Hyperactivity in Children. Etiology, Measurement, and Treatment.* Baltimore, Md.: University Park Press.
Tuddenham, R.D., Brooks, J., and Milkovich, L.
  1974   Mothers' reports of behavior of ten-year-olds: Relationships with sex, ethnicity, and mother's education. *Developmental Psychology* 10:959–995.
Ullman, D., Egan, D., Fiedler, N., Jurenec, G., Pliske, R., Thompson, P., and Doherty, M.E.
  1981   The many faces of hyperactivity: Similarities and differences in diagnostic policies. *Journal of Consulting and Clincial Psychology* 49:694–704.
U.S. Children's Bureau
  1981   *Infant Care.* U.S. Department of Health and Human Services. Washington, D.C.: U.S. Government Printing Office. Serial.
Wade, T.C., Baker, R.B., and Hartmann, D.T.
  1979   Behavior therapists' self-reported views and practices. *The Behavior Therapist* 2:3–6.
Walker, E., Hoppes, E., Emory, E., Mednick, S., and Schulsinger, F.
  1981   Environmental factors related to schizophrenia in psychophysiologically labile high-risk males. *Journal of Abnormal Psychology* 90:313–320.
Weiss, G., and Hechtman, L.
  1979   The hyperactive child syndrome. *Science* 205:1348–1354.
Weiss, B., Williams, J.H., Margen, S., Abrams, B., Caan, B., Citron, L.J., Cox, C., McKibben, J., Ogar, D., and Schultz, S.
  1980   Behavioral responses to artificial food colors. *Science* 207:1487–1489.
Wender, P., and Wender, E.
  1978   *The Hyperactive Child and the Learning Disabled Child. A Handbook for Parents.* New York: Cramm.
Wolman, B.B.
  1970   *Children Without Childhood.* New York: Grune & Stratton.

CHAPTER 10

Conclusion:
The Status of Basic Research
on Middle Childhood

W. Andrew Collins

M iddle childhood encompasses a number of distinctive and important transformations in human development. Considerable research now exists to document this conclusion, and the chapters in this volume are attempts to distill from the evidence salient characteristics of development during these years and the major issues facing the future study of middle childhood.

The research that the panel examined in the course of its work is uneven in quality and in the amount of information available from area to area. For the most part, sociological and anthropological studies of middle childhood are few in number. Consequently, additional information is needed on the role of social and cultural structures and influences in middle childhood experiences. The fields of education, medicine, and public health have produced pertinent information, although largely from perspectives that are incidentally concerned with the characteristics of this period of development.

In psychology the amount of information available is relatively large but varies across subareas of the field. Many studies of cognitive development have involved children ages 6–12, but little research addresses the nature of changes in middle childhood in the development of the self and self-regulation. Peer relationships have received a moderate amount of attention, but description of normal socialization practices within the family during middle childhood has been relatively neglected. Considerable evidence has now been accumulated on characteristic behavior problems of middle childhood, but many questions of etiology and the long-term outcomes of both physical and psychological development still urgently need attention.

In all of the fields from which research findings were drawn, it was necessary to reexamine literature traditionally organized under rubrics other than middle childhood. Nevertheless, several distinctive qualities of children ages of 6–12 emerged and are addressed in this chapter. Also noted here are numerous developmental changes that occur during middle childhood as well as individual and group differences that must be recognized as distinctive to the period. Finally, an attempt is made to characterize some general considerations for the future study of children ages 6–12.

THE NATURE AND TASKS OF MIDDLE CHILDHOOD

Any division of human development into age periods is arbitrary from the perspective of current knowledge about developmental change. Nevertheless, some features of middle childhood can be discerned that distinguish it from the early childhood years. At the same time, significant continuities with other age periods can be seen as well as considerable change during middle childhood.

Three general themes emerged from the literature on middle childhood. First, around age 6 or 7, children show skills and characteristic modes of thought and behavior that contrast significantly with typical patterns before age 5. Although no evidence was found that primary elements of functioning emerge de novo in this period, new capacities clearly do emerge. Underlying these contrasts with earlier periods appear to be processes of consolidation, extension, and integration operating on social and personal knowledge, skills, emotions, and modes of response and interaction that were present in similar forms earlier. The concomitants of these changes can be seen in areas ranging from the greater complexity of intellectual problem solving to the capacity for beginning and maintaining intimate friendships.

Second, middle childhood is a time of marked changes in capacities and typical behavior. These years cannot be considered a time of homogeneous functioning, for they are a time during which major transformations in abilities take place. In general, these developments also appear to reflect processes of gradual consolidation and extension of abilities. The intellectual shifts from early to middle childhood are continued, and by age 12 children are capable of applying more flexible, abstract thinking capabilities to a wider range of problems, including those involving the complexities of social relationships. Greater self-regulation of activities and problem-solving skills also occur, and children acquire more extensive repertoires of skills for tasks and more effective techniques for beginning and maintaining social relationships.

Third, although a description of these developmental changes glosses over marked individual differences in the course and outcomes of middle childhood development, it also underscores the continuity of developmental processes in this, as in other, life periods. It is not surprising, then, that development in middle childhood appears to have considerable significance for behavioral orientations, success, and adjustment in adolescence and adulthood. An array of fairly recent evidence supports this conclusion. The strongest indication so far of childhood predictors of adult status and psychopathology comes from this period (see Chapters 6 and 9 of this volume). Early childhood predictors have been much less powerful than measures taken in middle childhood. Behavior disorders appear to become more resistant to change in the course of middle childhood (Chapter 9). Recent research indicates that status as a rejected child also becomes increasingly intransigent in middle childhood; the 5-year stability of rejection in sociometric studies (a standard paradigm for assessing which children are preferred socially by other children) is greater if one starts it at grade 5 than at grade 3. School achievement at grade 12 is more reliably predicted by achievement at grade 3 than by achievement at grade 1.

An issue of special significance, but considerable complexity, is whether middle childhood is a time in which children's personalities, behavioral patterns, and basic competencies become increasingly crystallized into forms that are likely to persist into adolescence and adulthood. It is critically important to understand both the nature and the sources of the consolidations that occur in middle childhood and the implications of crystallizing behavioral patterns.

At this point, many questions remain to be answered. One difficulty lies in the problem of distinguishing increasing stability of behavior and ability from increasing similarity of the measures that can be used for older children and measures of adult characteristics. Similarity also increases between the tasks and settings that are typical of 6- to 12-year-olds and those that adults encounter. These problems make it difficult to sort out the causes of increasing similarity between child and adult indicators during middle childhood. An adequate account for the future of the nature of changing implications of events during middle childhood must include the possibility that the causal direction of influences may change. For example, children's self-concepts of ability affect their academic performance in grade 1, but the pattern is reversed in older children (Entwisle and Hayduk, 1982). The possibility of crystallization and a search for its causes are compelling goals for future research. If additional support is found, the significance of developmental changes in the middle childhood years should become a topic of critical importance.

In summary, although the middle childhood years clearly reflect the continuity of developmental processes, there are distinctive differences that indicate the consolidation and integration of abilities and typical behavior that set the period apart. The sections that follow describe the picture of functioning and the tasks faced by children ages 6–12 that can be drawn from the current literature.

Changing Qualities of Thought and the Growth of Knowledge

Ages 5–7 are universally recognized as a time of significant cognitive changes (Chapters 1 and 8), and considerable research has been devoted to the nature of these changes. At least three developmental transitions can be identified.

First, there is a growing ability to deal systematically with abstract representations of objects and events (Chapter 3). The thought of children younger than 5–7 characteristically involves limitations on the number of objects that can be thought about at one time, and systematic or abstract reasoning is relatively rare. Between ages 6 and 9, most children gain capacities that enable them to reason effectively about increasingly complex problems and circumstances in both the physical and social worlds. Later in the period, another transformation in cognitive abilities is marked by increased abilities for generalizing across concrete instances and problem solving and reasoning characterized by generating and testing hypotheses. This shift to formal-operational thought, in Piaget's terms, has usually been attributed to adolescence, but in Western cultures it typically appears between ages 10 and 12 (Chapter 3). In both transitions, older children's thoughts and problem-solving abilities incorporate elements of functioning that were present in earlier periods but that are combined and integrated in new ways in intellectual performance over the course of the school years.

Second, increasing capacities for planful organized behavior become evident. These "cognitive executive functions" (Sternberg and Powell, 1983) include adopting a plan or goal for activities and subordinating knowledge and actions in the service of the superordinate plan. The ability to monitor one's own activities and mental processes also increases substantially in middle childhood (Brown et al., 1983). Thus, children ages 6–12 often manifest more mature, independent organization of school tasks and other tasks than do preschool children.

Third, and parallel to the first two dimensions of change, middle childhood is a time of pronounced increase in both the opportunity and the capacity for acquiring information and for using new knowledge in reasoning, thinking, problem solving, and action. School is the main formal vehicle for the transmission of knowledge both in academic content and in cultural norms and values (Chapter 7). The general parameters of learning tasks that are effective for school-age children have been studied extensively (Minuchin and Shapiro, 1983; Sternberg and Powell, 1983).

In addition, knowledge in specific topic areas is increasingly being studied in order to specify its role in learning (e.g., Brown et al., 1983; Chi, 1978; Resnick, 1983; Siegler, 1983). We are now gaining valuable information about the ways in which having or acquiring knowledge facilitates the integration and more efficient use of cognitive skills. A major gap in our knowledge, however, continues to be adequate understanding of the social and motivational determinants of effective learning. It is known that these vary considerably among children, according to the degree of economic and educational advantage, but a better understanding is needed of the ways in which the diversity of elementary school pupils can be guaranteed the full benefits of schooling (Chapters 3 and 7).

Informal learning about social systems and relationships and knowledge of social conventions also increases dramatically in middle childhood (Chapters 4, 6, and 8). For example, children ages 6–12 have appreciably greater and more sophisticated knowledge about illness and health than do younger children. Knowledge of behavioral norms and conventions for various settings, recognition of the meaning of dysfunction in others, and an understanding of conception and death are all markedly greater in the middle childhood period than before. Television is a major source of information about social roles, attitudes, and behaviors at all ages (e.g., Collins and Korac, 1982; Comstock et al., 1980; Maccoby and Roberts, 1983), and children ages 6–12, particularly preteen youngsters, spend more time viewing TV than do either younger children or adolescents. Perhaps more significant in middle childhood are increased opportunities to acquire social scripts and concepts from increased exposure to more varied social models and settings.

To date, cognitive research on middle childhood has given us extensive insights into the nature of fundamental changes in cognitive skills and the contributions of knowledge to cognitive performance. Yet many unanswered questions remain regarding cognitive growth and knowledge acquisition in connection with salient aspects of the lives of 6- to 12-year-olds and the implications for later behavior and adjustment. For example, what role does knowledge acquisition—in or out of school, formal or informal—play in the growth of specific competence and performance skills during middle childhood? What characteristics of typical middle childhood environments and experiences are major influences in the growth of knowledge and its effective use? In the long term, what are the implications of learning and development of cognitive skills in this period for adult outcomes such as vocational choice and success? These issues deserve high priority in future research.

Different Functions of the Self

Middle childhood is a time of signal achievements with regard to concepts of self. Major advances occur in the stability and comprehensiveness of self-knowledge, in refining one's understanding of the social world, and in developing standards and expectations for one's own behavior (Chapter 4). Whereas preschool-age children typically couch self-knowledge in terms of concrete, objective attributes and actions, a transition occurs in middle childhood toward descriptions of self that refer to abstract dispositional qualities distinguishing oneself from other persons.

Increasing differentiation of self from others may be fundamental to the consolidation of behavioral orientations during middle childhood. The years from 6 to 12 are typically a time of widening social contacts and experiences, with attendant pressures and opportunities for self-differentiation and self-evaluation. Individuation and self-managed responsibilities appear to be important in most cultures (Chapter 8). In Western societies, however, children face considerable cultural pressures toward individualism, whereas the development of cooperation is given relative emphasis in many other societies (Chapter 8). Children between 6 and 12 in the United States must come to conceive of themselves as distinct from the social system at the same time that they are being socialized to it.

Several processes of developmental change as well as environmental pressures contribute to the salience of self-definition during middle childhood. The growth of cognitive concepts and knowledge of cultural norms and expectations for performance are major influences. In addition, the wider variety of social contexts and the changing relationships encountered by school-age children stimulate comparisons between self and others and provide sources of evaluative feedback about skills and abilities. For example, many Western parents grant more autonomy to the child as a more responsible self becomes apparent, and in turn the child's self-concept is altered as a result of increasingly autonomous control over activities. Cross-cultural evidence indicates that training for coregulation, rather than autonomous self-regulation, is a central socialization goal in this period.

The years 6–12 are a time of social sensitivity in the formation of some aspects of self-concept, such as academic self-concept (Chapters 4 and 7). For example, in the absence of special instructional interventions, school achievement at grade 12 correlates highly with achievement measures taken le 3 but not before (Chapter 7). Correlations between self-perceived :nce and achievement test scores increase from grade 3 to grade 6, a.. re is also greater agreement between teacher ratings of competence and self-perceived competence over this period. Self-perceptions may simply become more realistic during these years, but the causal influence may operate in the other direction as well. Labeling or categorization undoubtedly plays a role, regardless of whether labels are generated by the self or by others. The contributions of these variables to the crystallization of self-concept have not yet been sorted, but they may offer significant clues about the nature of emerging and more stabilized patterns of functioning between the ages of 6 and 12.

Many processes of self-concept formation are still only partially understood. More information is needed on the nature of self-knowledge concerning motives and goals, skills and abilities, emotions, social roles, and the interplay among various domains in which self-concepts are formed (academic, physical, social). These aspects of the self underlie children's abilities to manage their own activities and tasks effectively. They also appear critical to effective social interactions and relationships, including those within the family and the peer culture and to the allocation of effort and choice of activities. The role of self-esteem, although the most frequently studied dimension of self-concept, is still unclear. In particular, the origins of self-esteem that are most significant for 6- to 12-year-olds and their implications for development of individual children need further careful research. The lack of objective criteria against which to calibrate self-esteem is a major impediment to research on this topic.

Changes in Self-Management

Linked to changing concepts of self in middle childhood are greater capacities for self-control and self-regulation. Between ages 6 and 12, impulsivity decreases, capacities for planfulness and other control processes emerge, and skills necessary for regulating one's own behavior and interactions are acquired. Knowledge of the self, emotions, and self-regulatory processes are integral to these self-regulatory capacities, although the processes that link them are not yet understood.

Increasing self-regulation potentially affects many aspects of behavior in middle childhood. Peer group activities are less extensively supervised by adults than they were in early childhood, and more autonomy and independence are expected in tasks at school and at home. Children ages 6–12 are increasingly responsible for interacting with health care personnel and for mastering and acting on information and instructions about medication, specific health practices, and evolving life-style issues with implications for physical and mental well-being. The effect of increasing self-management capabilities may be felt most keenly in the family. Parents' management and control functions are altered when children approach middle childhood, partly in response to the greater self-management skills they evidence (Chapter 5). Although parents do not relinquish control abruptly any more than children abruptly become autonomous, children's self-management skills probably do contribute to a gradual transition from parental regulation of children's behavior to coregulation between child and parent to self-regulation by the child. This transition in turn appears to lay the groundwork for greater autonomy in adolescence and young adulthood.

Several questions deserve attention in the further study of the growth of self-management skills in middle childhood. Self-management and the emergence of coregulation between adults and children may be hastened by developmental changes in cognitive functioning and self-concept, although more information is needed to describe and account for them. For example, are the various components of self-management equally important at all ages? Perhaps as adolescence approaches, some aspects of self-management become more automated, and other tasks, such as reorganizing one's habits to make self-regulation more appropriate to the tasks of adolescence, become dominant. A developmental approach to self-regulation could be fruitfully investigated in the 6- to 12-year-old population. Children's self-knowledge of subjective states, such as motives, goals, emotions, and strategies relevant to self-regulation, may be one avenue to better understanding of this aspect of development.

In Chapter 4 of this volume, Markus and Nurius propose that further research should focus on the social contexts and relationships from which self-concept and capacities for self-regulation grow. For example, studies are needed of changes in parental monitoring with age and the processes by which control is gradually shifted to the child. Research on the contexts that produce shifts in patterns of social regulation also need study. For example, the school's role in management and control of children ages 6–12 appears to have increased in the past two decades, relative to parents' influence. The nature of this change, its impact, and the extent to which it occurs evenly across social strata need to be determined. A source of clues about relevant dimensions of variation in other social contexts may be the differences that have been documented between Western and non-Western cultures (Chapter 8).

Changes in Social Contexts and Relationships

The proportion of time spent at home and with parents is altered in middle childhood, so that 6- to 12-year-olds spend larger amounts of time in settings with other children alone than they did in early childhood. Time with peers is spent in different kinds of social exchanges than typically occur with adults. Children's own differentiations of the two types of relationships are made mainly in terms of the greater extent to which equal-to-equal exchanges are characteristic with peers (Chapter 6). The impact of widening social contexts is often discussed in the literature, but little information is available on several basic questions. For example, what functions are shifted to the peer group as the proportion of time with peers increases between 6 and 12? What are the implications for one system when disruption occurs in the other?

Family and peer relationships themselves undergo transformation in middle childhood. Compared with early childhood, family relationships are characterized by decreased face-to-face interaction and control. Maccoby, in Chapter 5 of this volume, refers to the necessity for more distal processes of control, in which parental monitoring of children's own management of their activities plays a large role. Discipline becomes less physical and less restraint oriented and more directed toward developing internal controls. Children's own concepts of the parent-child relationship move toward notions of mutual caring and responsibility, rather than focusing so extensively on the child's dependency and parents' gratification of the child's needs (Selman, 1980).

Children select friends and associates and accord group status to others on the basis of personal qualities at younger ages, but between 6 and 12 their notions about the qualities that are essential to successful peer relationships and the prerequisites for friendship become more sophisticated. Qualities of individual peer relationships also change. Although the capacity for seeking and forming relationships with others exists in very early childhood, the capacity for maintaining and extending intimate relationships over time is not apparent until late middle childhood. By ages 10–12, children become notably more skilled in using goal-directed planful strategies to begin, maintain, and cooperate within peer relationships. To some degree these patterns undoubtedly reflect the shift in late middle childhood to formal-operational thought, although the growth of knowledge about social conventions, interactions, and specific strategies must also play a role.

These dimensions of peer relationships are known to affect interactions with peers in adolescence. More information is needed, however, on the socializing consequences of close peer relationships during middle childhood and the ways in which the nature and impact of these relationships change as the child develops. In particular, emotional components of peer experiences and peer influences need study. What, for example, is the implication of anxiety in peer relationships for self-concept, self-esteem, harmonious interactions with family, and success in school? The predictive status of poor peer relations for maladjustment in later life makes the study of peer relationships in middle childhood especially urgent and promising.

Characteristic Antecedents of Later Functioning

Much is now known about a variety of events in middle childhood that have potential long-term implications for individual functioning. The most powerful evidence comes from prospective longitudinal studies in which deviant peer relations in middle childhood have been found to predict poor mental health and psychosocial difficulties in adolescence and young adulthood (Chapter 6). Attempts to predict middle childhood outcomes from experiences in early childhood have been less successful (e.g., Richman et al., 1982). Studies of adolescent psychopathology have often revealed roots in middle childhood disorders (Chapter 9). Normative stresses and mundane experiences alike, when they occur in middle childhood, have been shown to have long-term effects. Elder's (1979) analysis of the Oakland and Berkeley Growth Studies indicated that family economic deprivation in childhood affects adult physical health, mental health, and patterning of life decisions such as marriage, and career performance. Correlations are sizable between school achievement and academic self-concept in middle childhood and these same variables measured at grade 12 (Chapter 7).

Most research linking middle childhood events to adult outcomes has focused on psychopathology. Yet a number of interesting questions concern how middle childhood experiences may contribute to a wider range of outcomes. For example, what is the developmental impact of middle childhood experiences on adult health, educational and career achievement, work roles, and productivity? Methodologies recently applied to the study of psychopathology might well be extended to the study of links between middle childhood status and experiences and a variety of outcomes in later periods. Among these are normative-epidemiological techniques (e.g., Rutter, 1982) and multivariate-descriptive taxonomic paradigms (Chapter 9), which are effective in identifying the constellation of characteristics that accurately describe behaviors of interest at different ages. These approaches may lead to additional research in which the operation of risk factors and the immunizing and protective conditions that counteract them can also be fruitfully investigated.

One still troublesome vacuum in our knowledge of middle childhood conditions that have long-term implications concerns school learning problems. The links between chronic learning difficulties and later dysfunction are strongly established, but progress in finding workable approaches to the assessment and remediation of learning difficulties has been slow. Several promising approaches have been devised in recent years (Chapters 2 and

9), including the application of normative-epidemiological research methods (Chapter 9; Rutter et al., 1979). Among other uses, these methods have been applied to the creation of standardized teachers' assessments of pupil behavior. Once such a data base is available, research can be undertaken on differentiated patterns of learning difficulties. In some cases these may be linked to psychopathological conditions that are largely environmentally caused. In others, investigations of neurophysiological conditions may be needed.

At present, however, neither biological science nor understanding of the behavioral and other psychological processes involved in learning are advanced enough to permit definitive conclusions about biological bases for differences in learning. In Chapter 2 of this volume, Shonkoff argues that the applicability of research on biological correlates of cognitive functioning to classrooms and intervention programs requires cooperative interdisciplinary efforts between clinical medicine, education, and basic research. As in the case of psychopathology, it is less likely that the answer lies in devising nosological categories for the diagnosis and treatment of specific clinical entities than in multivariate approaches incorporating notions of risk and protective factors.

Normative development has dominated the research on middle childhood to date in some areas, such as the study of cognitive abilities. In others, like social and personality development, more attention has been given to individual differences and normative changes have been relatively neglected. Both dimensions of variation must become integral to the study of middle childhood development in the future. Individual children negotiate developmental sequences at different rates and along somewhat different trajectories. These alternative paths partly reflect the operation of social structures and other environmental constraints, which must be better specified in connection with developmental studies (see section below on environmental factors). Comparisons of cultures with regard to environmental features that inoculate against, or mark the appearance of, troublesome behaviors in middle childhood would be useful (Chapter 8).

Several dimensions of individual differences in children ages 6–12 deserve special attention in future research. Increased expectations for self-regulation make issues of emotional development and expressiveness, coping capacities, and the various components of self-management skills especially important topics for study. Similarly, individual differences in the development of behaviors relevant to both physical health and satisfactory adjustment to peer and school social systems need special investigation. An appropriate starting point for these investigations is the epidemiological evidence tying adult behaviors and status to specific antecedents in childhood.

Summary

Children in diverse societies enter a wider social world at about age 6 and begin to determine their own experiences, including their contacts with particular others, to a greater degree than previously. Primary questions still to be answered by research concern the interacting influences of individual developmental change and the altered nature and demands of the contexts of middle childhood, including the varied demands, expectations, and options available to children ages 6–12. The long-term implications of middle childhood development, although difficult to assess, may be especially significant, compared with correlates of early childhood functioning. Particularly important gaps exist in three areas.

1. More research is needed on the effects of the rapid acquisition of knowledge on cognitive growth, skill development, and performance, especially the tasks characteristically required of children ages 6–12. The implications of knowledge acquisition and skill and of concept development in this period for smooth transitions into adolescent and adult roles particularly need study.

2. Different trajectories of individual development in the years 6–12 need research attention. Particular study should be devoted to altered concepts of self and the interplay among various contexts (academic, physical, and social) in which self-concepts are formed. The implications of self-concept changes for increasingly autonomous, self-regulated behavior patterns are another topic of considerable importance, as are changes with age in what is required for effective coregulation of behavior between the child and relevant others, especially parents.

3. Middle childhood behavior and performance have repeatedly been found to predict adolescent and adult status, including social and personal dysfunction, more reliably than do early childhood indicators, and this predictiveness increases over the years from 6 to 12. The processes and phenomena of middle childhood that account for enhanced prediction is a topic of considerable importance for additional research.

CROSS-CUTTING ISSUES IN MIDDLE CHILDHOOD DEVELOPMENT

The panel's search for characteristic patterns of children's functioning that distinguish middle childhood from other periods of development began with a review of standard topic areas in developmental study. In the review, however, a set of issues emerged repeatedly across topics. So general are they that the panel believes they should be standard considerations in future research on middle childhood. These issues are not unique to the study of children ages 6–12, but their ramifications for new knowledge are fundamental to a number of high-priority problems for future study.

In addition to methodological issues, which are discussed first, three conceptual issues are fundamental to future research. One concerns the importance and difficulties of specifying environmental constraints and scaffolds for development as an integral part of research on middle childhood. The second pertains to the nature, functions, and interrelationships of social systems in the lives of 6- to 12-year olds. The third addresses the interrelatedness of aspects of development that may be compromised by arbitrary segmentations in the fields of developmental study.

The Problems of Studying Children Ages 6–12

Before discussing conceptual issues, it should be acknowledged that research on middle childhood presents special methodological problems compared with earlier periods of development. Unobtrusive access to information is much more difficult, as the reactivity of participants to being observed increases. Furthermore, settings and problems for children in middle childhood are more complex than those for infants and preschoolers. Many of these methodological difficulties may well be attributable to the relatively small amount of time and energy that developmental scholars have devoted to solving the technical problems of research on this age group. The problems of developing the techniques needed to work with infants and preschool children were seen as formidable in the 1950s, but broad investments of personnel and resources have produced remarkable advances in knowledge about these age periods. Similar investments in the problems of research on middle childhood might well yield quantum increases in our tools for studies of 6- to 12-year-olds. The tools and techniques needed for research in specific problem areas are detailed in the preceding chapters.

Several fundamental problems that face developmental researchers in any given period of childhood or adolescence present considerable difficulties in addressing key questions about middle childhood. One is the problem of measuring functionally similar behaviors at different ages. Differences in the knowledge base and performance skills from one age to another make it difficult to identify reliable and valid tasks that tap the same competencies or characteristics across ages. Recent attempts to address this problem in the areas of social and personality development include longitudinal research by Block and Block (1980) and Sroufe (1977). In this work functionally similar behaviors were identified by analyzing social contexts and issues faced by children of different ages to determine what tasks and abilities were required for optimal functioning. Thus, social competence was actually measured differently at each age studied; acceptable correlations were found among the measures from one age to another for measures of putatively similar behaviors but not for measures of behaviors that were assumed to be functionally different.

Identifying functionally similar measures obviously requires careful psychometric evaluation of the properties of tasks as well as their conceptual appropriateness to the competencies under study. A specific difficulty is the usual increase in literacy skills over this age range. Paper and pencil instruments suitable for children ages 10–12 cannot be used with children 6–8. The youngest children in this age range are the most difficult to include in large-scale studies, yet changes in these earlier years may overshadow later ones.

The potential value of identifying early indicators of later functioning must be given increased attention in research on middle childhood. The importance of this period of development cannot be fully understood without better specification of the ways in which consolidation of personality and skills between ages 6 and 12 is carried forward into other periods of life. Although longitudinal research provides important information on the development of individuals, longitudinal methods are not strictly necessary for analysis of developmental sequences per se. Scalogram analysis of performance should be considered essential for concluding that a sequential pattern has been identified in cross-sectional studies (Chapter 3). More careful attention to psychometric issues in the assessment of developmental patterns is a major requirement for better information about the nature and course of developmental change in the years 6–12.

We now turn to three conceptual issues that must be given attention in future research on middle childhood.

The Nature and the Role of the Environment

The complex issue of environmental influences and constraints on development in middle childhood has repeatedly emerged in the panel's deliberations. Our review has convinced us that a view of middle childhood development as a conjoint function of organismic change and sociocultural demands, constraints, and options available to children in this period is both feasible and essential to the advance of knowledge. However, the nature and impact of environments are rarely specified in research on children ages 6–12.

A fully adequate analysis of relevant environmental supports and constraints in development is relatively rare in the study of children of any age. Even anthropologists have only occasionally produced ethnographies focused on the lives of children in various cultures, and developmentalists have badly neglected ecocultural pressures in their analyses of individual ontogeny and socialization processes (LeVine 1980; Ogbu 1981; Whiting and Whiting, 1975). To date, most of our knowledge of development in children ages 6–12 has been drawn from the capabilities and skills of children observed in a restricted range of situations, such as laboratory experimental tasks and, occasionally, self-reports of activities or observations of discrete units of behavior in less constraining settings. Neither these settings nor more common environments have been as carefully analyzed as the behavior of children within them, however.

A major difficulty is how to specify the characteristics of relevant environments in studies of middle childhood. The most common view of environmental influences on development is the general notion of a local "learning environment" for socialization and intellectual stimulation. In research, environmental features are varied one at a time, as in studies of basic learning processes, or are treated in an undifferentiated global fashion, as when social class is used as a summary indicator for a constellation of social, cultural, and economic variables.

A richer conceptual framework is needed to capture the nature of external forces on the developing child, not only the immediate, ambient sources of stimulation that impinge on children but also the culturally normative responses and the survival pressures that form the context for and give meaning to stimulation. The concept of the ecocultural niche, which was adopted by anthropologists to help account for dramatic cultural variations in non-Western societies, encompasses this broader view (Chapter 8). The term pertains to the cumulative historical, social, and economic structures and experiences that give significance to mundane events as well as to pivotal transitions in a child's life. Such factors as urban versus rural residence, family and domestic group status, parental and nonparental child care arrangements, tasks typically assigned to children, and the role of women in the society have all been demonstrated to affect important dimensions of childhood socialization in Western and non-Western cultures (Chapter 8).

Environments of U.S. Children

Among the significant aspects of niche variation facing children in the United States are those traditionally captured but not well specified by ethnic, subcultural, and socioeconomic variables. Available demographic data (see Chapter 1) indicate that children ages 6–12 from different ethnic backgrounds encounter environments that differ markedly in terms of family constellation, economic advantage, and characteristics of home and community, among other features. Yet the panel repeatedly noted the relative rarity of studies of middle childhood development to which ethnic and socioeconomic variations were integral. Evidence of group differences exists, of course. Studies in education reveal dramatic differences in the adaptation to school of children from different ethnic and subcultural and social-class groups (Chapter 7). In the relatively small number of studies on children's lives outside school, children from different sociocultural backgrounds vary in activity patterns ranging from exposure to television to characteristic leisure-time social involvements. Children also experience different amounts of contact with adults according to sociocultural background, and family settings and parental behavior vary widely as a function of social class and ethnic groups (Chapters 1 and 5). For example, levels of interaction between parents and their school-age children have been reported to be lower in black than in white families (Chapter 5), a comparison that confounds ethnicity and social class.

Although some characteristics of the variables themselves are clearly documented and some correlations with socialization outcomes and children's adaptations to common cultural expectations have been examined, little is known about the significance of ecocultural variations for either short- or long-term outcomes. Models and approaches are needed that can be readily applied to understanding the complex interplay between the developing child and the ecological contexts of development. While the panel does not urge extensive new research on social class and ethnic differences per se, we do believe that much valuable information can come from studies in which discrete dimensions of children's environments are more carefully and systematically examined in terms of their linkages to characteristic experiences and their impacts on individual children. By this we mean giving attention to the tasks created by these environmental variations for the child and the differences in amount and frequency of contacts with adults, responsibilities expected of the child, the availability of resources, and prevailing norms and structures for the control and management of behavior. These aspects of environments are only partially tapped by traditional measures of social class and ethnicity (Chapter 8).

Expectations Regarding Children as an Environmental Indicator

One potentially fruitful avenue is research on subjectively held expectations and cultural beliefs about the behavior of children ages 6–12. A focus on expectations of both adults and children may be our most direct avenue to understanding environmental characteristics and pressures. Recent research in Australia by Goodnow et al. (in press) documents subcultural variations in adults' expectations of younger children. American research (Bugental et al., 1980; Holleran et al., in press) demonstrates the role of adults' expectations in perceptions of and reactions to specific behaviors in children.

A recent example highlights the potential informativeness of studies that include assessments of adult expectations. Entwisle and Hayduk (1982) examined parents' expectations for their children's school performance longitudinally in a multiwave design over a 3-year period from grade 1 to 3. These measurement points encompassed a period from before children's academic skills are ordinarily evaluated to a point at which a number of report cards have been sent home. For both middle- and working-class children, parents' expectations were strong influences on children's first marks. After grade 1, the influence of working-class parents appeared to be considerably less than that of their middle-class counterparts. Absence rates were correlated with working-class, but not middle-class, parents' expectations (Entwisle and Hayduk, 1978). These examples of marked changes in the nature and direction of influence of parental expectations during middle childhood provide models that can be fruitfully extended to other questions. Studies of the expectations normally held by adults in the United States for the behavior and competences of children at different ages between 6 and 12, including subcultural variations, and how these expectations are typically communicated to children and perceived by them may reveal a great deal about the ecocultural niche constraints encountered by children in this age period.

The Child's View of Environments

Research is also needed on children's views of common experiences. The past two decades have seen a proliferation of studies on the development of concepts of universal life events, such as conception, birth, and death (Shantz, 1983). Additional studies are needed on children's concepts of common features of their mundane environments that may be influential in socialization. For example, what are children's concepts of the legitimacy of authority, tasks, responsibility for mundane activities, work, common social practices, achievement, age grading, abnormality, and the like? Recent research on children's understanding of rules and conventions is promising in this regard (see Chapter 6), but further research is needed. Important unanswered questions concern the impact of personal experiences on concepts (e.g., the effect of chronic illness on concepts of disease) and how concepts might be changed to facilitate adjustment. Most studies have focused on questions of children's cognitive competence rather than on the functional significance of variations in pragmatic concepts, and knowledge has largely been drawn from studies of middle-class children. Weisner (Chapter 8) notes that information on cross-cultural variations is likely to be a source of valuable clues to variables of special importance in the study of school-age children's understanding of their circumstances and experiences.

Environmental Supports for Developmental Change

Variation in stable, enduring cultural expectations and adaptations should not be confused with the task and contextual variations in children's behavior that are commonly observed in middle childhood and that pervade the literature of other age periods as well. Task and contextual effects commonly arise in assessments of children's competencies or abilities. In Chapter 3, Fischer and Bullock subsume these findings under the category of supportiveness of the environment. They note that characteristics of some tasks and contexts do not permit successful performance, even when other tasks of similar levels of formal difficulty can be solved. In research on development the problem of task variation is sometimes no more than a problem of sampling tasks adequately to assess the limitations of the child's competence. But as Fischer and Bullock note, task characteristics can also be analyzed for their implications about the role of environmental supports in the acquisition of skill and the fostering of new levels of competence, as when an adult provides aid that enables a child to complete a task successfully. In such cases environmental supports may facilitate task completion at a higher level on subsequent attempts. The relationship between transient task factors such as these and more stable, enduring features of the ecocultural niche need further investigation.

Nature, Functions, and Interrelationships of Social Systems

A focus on the role of the environment in development entails attention to the social relationships and settings that impinge upon children. Both the nature and the function of social systems and the ways in which they are linked to one another are potentially significant factors in research on children ages 6–12.

Social Contexts of Middle Childhood

The study of middle childhood has long included examination of family, peer, and school influences, but societal changes and other factors continue to make salient new issues about which information is needed. For example, the dynamics and influences of family systems have increasingly been receiving more attention from researchers, but much of the information to date concerns families of preschool children. Specific problems of dealing with 6- to 12-year-olds in different family structures would benefit from further research. In two-parent families the role of fathers in children's responses to the challenges of middle childhood is linked to a number of interesting questions of self-concept and its effects, the intensification of cross-sex interactions, and the learning of work roles and life-style practices, but pertinent information is scarce (Chapter 5).

Similarly, the school social system in the late 1950s was alleged to have extensive implications for school achievement and, by implication, for cognitive development and self-concept formation in junior high and high school (e.g., Coleman, 1961). Still, we need to know what features of this system are essential to effects on these potentially significant dimensions of middle childhood experience and how the features operate to produce these effects. Research by Rutter et al. (1979) on high schools provides a valuable model for research on school systems involving 6- to 12-year-olds. Outside school the peer system plays a central role in the socialization and emotional lives of 6- to 12-year-olds. Questions concerning the nature of these experiences and their impact on the child are central to an understanding of middle childhood development, but at present information is sparse and based on indirect assessment of peer influences.

An example of recent research on a developmental change experienced by many children ages 6–12 indicates the importance of social-system influences. Large numbers of children experience the physical changes of pubescence well before their thirteenth birthdays, and much research has now been devoted to the general effects of timing of puberty on trajectories of psychosocial development (Chapter 2). The combination of factors faced by a preteen child who experiences early physical maturation is now being more carefully examined as well. Recent research on the effects of the shift from elementary to junior high school at seventh grade demonstrates that pubertal change, combined with social and achievement pressures from school transitions, heightens the adjustment problems of individual children (Simmons et al., 1979). Research on early dating indicates the complex of social norms and age-graded conventions that contribute to this social pattern for an individual child. These studies compellingly document the interaction between physical, social-structural, and individual factors in development in the latter part of the 6–12 period for many children.

Interrelationships of Social Systems

The interrelationships of social systems and settings also determine pressures on children and their responses to them. We now have fragmentary evidence that consistency between salient social contexts facilitates optimal functioning of children. Most often in such studies the family is one of the two settings involved. Parents' perceived encouragement and facilitation of participation in out-of-school organized activities combined as the single most influential determinant of children's participation (Medrich et al., 1982). Especially in middle childhood, many children depend heavily on parents for transportation, volunteer leadership, and often for knowledge of opportunities. Questions on the relationship of out-of-school activities to the school system are frequently acknowledged, but more information is needed to determine the importance of consistency between these aspects of children's lives.

Despite considerable evidence that disjunctions between family and other settings are inimical to optimal development, the possibility remains that consistency is not an important variable for all children and all situations. In research on school environments, for example, the authority structure of school settings was especially important for children from families that did not emphasize participation in decision making. For other children, variation in classroom organization and teacher's authority style made little difference (Chapter 7). It is possible, as cognitive-developmental theories imply, that moderate inconsistency is sometimes developmentally beneficial. The nature and optimal amount of inconsistency for 6- to 12-year-olds as well as the areas of experience in which consistency and inconsistency are likely to have differential effects are topics about which information is needed. For example, how do children perceive discrepancies in family conventions and expectations and those in other settings? Recent work on the understanding of rules, conventions, and discrepancies between home and school rules (e.g., Much and Shweder, 1978; Nucci and Nucci, 1982) is a useful beginning that should be extended into understanding of other aspects of social systems and structures.

Studies of family and peer influences, especially with regard to shifts in relative influence between early childhood and adolescence, indicate a variety of possible relationships among social systems. The possibility of reciprocal influences has been raised by Youniss's (1980) recent suggestion that children may bring to their families from their peer groups knowledge, expectations, and behavioral tactics that enable their families to adjust to demands of interaction with a rapidly maturing child. Hartup (1979) recently suggested that the family system serves a gating function for smooth, successful peer relationships. This function probably becomes increasingly important in middle childhood. In the future a stronger focus is needed on the varied ways in which family, peers, and other social systems may influence development between the ages of 6 and 12.

Interrelatedness of Developmental Issues

Much of our knowledge about development reflects the long-standing division of the research enterprise into domains of functioning; hence, this report is organized into chapters on cognition, the self, and specific aspects of social experiences (family, peers, schools). Early in its deliberations, however, the panel concluded that an adequate understanding of middle childhood development requires attention to possible interrelationships across these arbitrary boundaries. A compelling example is the implications of cognitive achievements for an emerging sense of self and self-regulatory capacities. As is apparent in Chapters 3 and 4, cognitive and emotional functioning are as integral to one another as they are to self and social relationships. Our reviews of the literature on health, psychopathology, and school affirm the importance of these interrelationships. Nevertheless, research that incorporates these facets of human functioning simultaneously is rare in general and almost nonexistent in the study of middle childhood. For example, simple questions such as the possible influence of boys' height or athletic prowess on self-esteem still need study, but such relationships must be examined in light of other developmental dimensions (e.g., cognitive capabilities) and the social matrix in which the child is embedded.

This deficiency is especially problematic for analyzing children's capacities for coping with circumstances that ordinarily put them at risk for psychopathology and other dysfunctional outcomes. Although we now have extensive knowledge of psychological problems of middle childhood and good tools for learning more about such difficulties, more attention needs to be given to the functioning of children who manage to avoid dysfunctional outcomes. Such work will include, at a minimum, attention to cognitive, social, and emotional components of coping (Garmezy, 1982).

Aspects of middle childhood development about which information is especially needed are emotional understanding and expression and its interrelationships with other domains of functioning. At present, most information about children ages 6–12 in this area pertains to their developing knowledge of emotions and rules for emotional expression, but little is known about the functions of emotional expressions and implications for social relationships, coping, and self-concept. One area in which more information is needed concerns the implications of the emotional character of children's relationships with their teachers to socialization within the school system. Much previous research indicates the importance of warmth and nurturance to teacher-learner relationships of several different kinds, but the specific nature of emotional linkages between salient other persons in middle childhood is not well understood. The effects of anxiety, both positive and negative, and a better, more differentiated understanding of the implications of self-esteem for family, peer, and school experiences are also important topics for investigation. The topic of emotion is now experiencing a resurgence of interest in the social and behavioral sciences, and this renewed attention should be beneficial to the study of emotional functioning in middle childhood development.

CONCLUSION

The study of children ages 6–12 has yielded considerable information about the processes of development. A number of significant questions remain, but the basic research now available is a promising foundation from which new evidence can be generated. New methods will be required in some areas, particularly in those of social relationships and competence, but a number of the required methods for generating new knowledge about this period are now in place.

The most urgent need at present is simply a conviction that the phenomena of middle childhood warrant a commitment of scholarly energies and resources. The panel believes that they do. The panel also believes that the study of any given age period is likely to be most productive when it concerns the distinctive tasks and qualities of the period within the general flow of developmental changes. This approach is well established in the literature on children ages 6–12, and the panel urges its continuation. The complexities of the task notwithstanding, the prospects and benefits of understanding the nature and processes of development in the school years warrant serious attention in the decades ahead.

REFERENCES

Block, J.H., and Block, J.
   1980   The role of ego-control and ego-resiliency in the organization of behavior. Pp. 39–101 in W.A. Collins, ed., *Development of Cognition, Affect, and Social Relations: Minnesota Symposia on Child Psychology*. Vol. 13. Hillsdale, N.J.: Lawrence Erlbaum.
Brown, A., Bransford, J., Ferrara, R., and Campione, J.
   1983   Learning, remembering, and understanding. In J. Flavell and E. Markman, eds., *Handbook of Child Psychology*. Vol. 3 (P. Mussen, General Ed.). New York: John Wiley & Sons.
Bugental, D., Caporael, L., and Shennum, W.
   1980   Experimentally produced child uncontrollability: Effects on the potency of adult communication patterns. *Child Development* 51:520–528.
Chi, M.
   1978   Knowledge of structure and memory development. Pp. 73–96 in R. Siegler, ed., *Children's Thinking: What Develops?* Hillsdale, N.J.: Lawrence Erlbaum.

Coleman, J.
1961   The Adolescent Society. New York: Free Press.
Collins, W.A., and Korac, N.
1982   Recent progress in the study of the effects of television viewing on social development. International Journal of Behavioral Development 5:171–194.
Comstock, G., Chaffee, S., Katzman, N., McCombs, M., and Roberts, D.
1978   Television and Human Behavior. New York: Columbia University Press.
Elder, G.
1979   Historical change in life patterns and personality. In P. Baltes and O. Brim, eds., Lifespan Development and Behavior. Vol. 2. New York: Academic Press.
Entwisle, D., and Hayduk, L.
1978   Too Great Expectations: The Academic Outlook for Young Children. Baltimore, Md.: Johns Hopkins University Press.
1982   Early Schooling. Baltimore, Md.: Johns Hopkins University Press.
Garmezy, N.
1982   Research in clinical psychology: Serving the future hour. Pp. 677–690 in P. Kendall and J. Butcher, eds., Handbook of Research Methods in Clinical Psychology. New York: John Wiley & Sons.
Goodnow, J.
In   Adults' concepts about child development. In M.Perlmutter, ed., Social Cognition: Min-
press   nesota Symposia on Child Psychology. Vol. 18. Hillsdale, N.J.: Lawrence Erlbaum.
Hartup, W.
1979   Two social worlds of childhood. American Psychologist 34:944–950.
Holleran, P., Littman, D., Freund, R., Schmaling, K., and Heeren, J.
In   A signal detection approach to social perception: Identification of negative and positive
press   behaviors. Journal of Abnormal Child Psychology.
LeVine, R.
1980   Anthropology and child development. Pp. 71–86 in C. Super and S. Harkness, eds., Anthropological Perspectives on Child Development. San Francisco: Jossey-Bass.
Maccoby, N., and Roberts, D.
1983   Effects of mass communication. In G. Lindzey and R. Abelson, eds., Handbook of Social Psychology. 3d ed. Reading, Mass.: Addison-Wesley.
Medrich, E., Roizen, J., Rubin, V., and Buckley, S.
1982   The Serious Business of Growing Up. Berkeley: University of California Press.
Minuchin, P., and Shapiro, E.
1983   The school as a context for social development. Pp. 197–274 in E.M. Hetherington, ed., Handbook of Child Psychology. Vol. 4 (P. Mussen, General Ed.). New York: John Wiley & Sons.
Much, N., and Shweder, R.
1978   Speaking of rules: The analysis of culture in breach. Pp. 13–29 in W. Damon, ed., New Directions for Child Development: Moral Development. San Francisco: Jossey-Bass.
Nucci, L., and Nucci, M.
1982   Children's social interactions in the context of moral and conventional transgressions. Child Development 53:403–412.
Ogbu, J.
1981   Origins of human competence: A cultural-ecological perspective. Child Development 52:413–429.
Resnick, L.
1983   Mathematics and science learning: A new conception. Science 29 (April):477.
Richman, N., Stevenson, J., and Graham, P.
1982   Preschool to School: A Behavioral Study. London: Academic Press.

Rutter, M.
    1982   Epidemiological-longitudinal approaches to the study of development. Pp. 105–144 in W.A. Collins, ed., *The Concept of Development: Minnesota Symposia on Child Psychology*. Vol. 15. Hillsdale, N.J.: Lawrence Erlbaum.
Rutter, M., Maughn, B., Mortimore, P., Ouston, J., and Smith, A.
    1979   *Fifteen Thousand Hours: Secondary Schools and Their Effects on Children*. Cambridge, Mass.: Harvard University Press.
Selman, R.
    1980   *The Development of Interpersonal Understanding*. New York: Academic Press.
Shantz, C.
    1983   Social cognition. Pp. 495–555 in J. Flavell and E. Markman, eds., *Handbook of Child Psychology*. Vol. 4 (P. Mussen, General Ed.). New York: John Wiley & Sons.
Siegler, R.
    1983   Five generalizations about cognitive development. *American Psychologist* 38:263–277.
Simmons, R., Blyth, D., Van Cleave, E., and Bush, D.
    1979   Entry into early adolescence: The impact of school structure, puberty, and early dating on self-esteem. *American Sociological Review* 44:948–967.
Sroufe, L.A.
    1977   Attachment as an organizational construct. *Child Development* 48:1184–1199.
Sternberg, R., and Powell, J.
    1983   The development of intelligence. In J. Flavell and E. Markman, eds., *Handbook of Child Psychology*. Vol. 3 (P. Mussen, General Ed.). New York: John Wiley & Sons.
Youniss, J.
    1983   *Parents and Peers in Social Development: A Sullivan-Piaget Perspective*. Chicago: University of Chicago Press.
Whiting, B., and Whiting, J.
    1975   *Children of Six Cultures*. Cambridge, Mass.: Harvard University Press.

INDEX

Ability
  in collaboration approach, 92–93, 131
  and grouping in schools, 286, 321
    cross-racial interactions in, 308
  self-understanding of, 149, 156, 157, 159
Abstract concepts, in cognitive development,
    75, 107, 108, 130, 401
  emotional implications of, 107, 108
Academic achievement, 17, 290, 291–293, 402
  and ability grouping in school, 286, 308, 321
  and behavior problems, 389–390
  in bilingualism, 313–316
  and control beliefs, 293–294, 295, 302, 303
  cultural variations in, 284, 296, 413
  and effects of desegregation, 311–312
  ecological studies of, 287–288
  expectations for, 229, 294
    gender differences in, 297
    parental, 284, 298, 414
    of teachers, 288–289
  in grade 12, compared to middle childhood,
    407
  instructional approaches affecting, 292, 316–
    321
  and intelligence measurements, 292
  parental influence on, 187, 284, 289, 297–
    307, 414
  in maternal employment, 220
  preschool experiences affecting, 291–292
  in reading, 292, 296
  and self-concept, 149, 157, 159, 400, 403
    self-esteem in, 149, 171, 291, 293–295
  socioeconomic variables in, 289, 294, 296,
    298, 402, 413, 414,
  teacher characteristics affecting, 287, 288–289,
    304, 320
Achievement motivation, 118, 157, 402
  in classroom, 294
  cultural studies on, 303, 304–306, 319
  and maternal employment, 220
Acquaintances, interactions with, in friendship
    formation, 248–250
Adoption of children, 346, 360
  of black children by white families, 303
Adrenal hormones, behavioral influences of, 28–
    29, 30
Adrenogenital syndrome, 29
Adult status, childhood predictors of, 400
Aerobic exercises, 42–43, 44
Affective relationships
  parent-child, 188–190, 201–202, 205, 208
    ecocultural patterns in, 357–358
    and peer relations of child, 263
  in school curriculum, 267–268
  between siblings, 225–226

Affiliation motivation, 157
African tribal cultures, comparison of, 341
Age
  and racial attitudes, 309
  of social contacts, 247, 257–258
Aggressive behavior, 21, 200, 203–204, 384
  hormonal influences on, 28–29
  in peer interactions, 242, 243, 245, 246, 247,
    261–262, 268
Alcohol consumption, 47, 48
Alienation from peers, 261, 268–269, 400
Altruism, in peer interactions, 243–244
Amplification, in literate practices, 121, 122–
    123, 132
Androgen secretion
  behavioral influences of, 28, 29
  prepubertal, 28
Anemia, iron deficiency, 46
Anger, between parents and children, 189–190
Antisocial behavior, 203–204, 211, 212
  parental influence on, 265
  in maternal employment, 221
  and peer interactions, 253, 261–262, 265
  and sibling relationships, 226
Anxiety. See Stress and anxiety
Assertiveness, social
  parent-child interactions affecting, 206
  in peer interactions, 242, 262
Assessment of cognitive development, 77–79,
    91, 92–93, 96–103
  environmental influences on, 91, 92, 105,
    106, 125–127
Atherosclerosis, 42, 43
Athletic activities, 43–44. See also Sports activ-
    ities
Attachment, parent-child, 189, 190
  and peer relations of child, 263
  and stress in separation or bereavement, 197
Attention deficit disorders, 372–376, 378. See
    also Hyperactivity
Attraction, social, 245–247
Authority patterns. See Regulation of behavior
Autism
  infantile, 376, 393
  serotonin levels in, 31
Automatization, in continuous change model of
    cognitive development, 82

Behavior
  aggressive. See Aggressive behavior
  antisocial. See Antisocial behavior
  categorization of
    integration of, 93–94
    problems in, 94–95

cognitive development affecting, 72, 75, 78, 81, 94
delinquent. *See* Delinquent behavior
hormonal influences on, 28–30
impulsive, 152, 161, 194–195, 203
in later life, compared to childhood, 400
neurotransmitters affecting, 30–33
peer relationships affecting, 21–22
physical changes affecting, 20
regulation of, 149–151. *See also* Regulation of behavior
Behavior modification, 378–379
in self-regulation, 164–165
in smoking prevention program, 48
Behavior problems, 3, 370–397, 399, 400, 407–408, 418
adult outcomes of, 407
childhood predictors of, 400
behavior assessment in study and treatment of, 378–379, 393
and caretaking system, 360, 374
in chronic illness, 49
compared to adaptive coping behaviors, 390
cultural studies on, 358–361, 408
developmental perspective of, 385–387, 392
DSM categories of, 380, 382
future areas for research on, 384–393, 409
gender differences in, 384–385, 388
high-risk children for, 377–378, 379, 390–391, 393
in hyperactivity and attention deficit, 31–32, 372–376, 383, 389, 393
life-span approach to, 386
normative-epidemiological research on, 387–389, 390, 407, 408
parent-child interactions affecting, 203–204
and peer relationships, 260–261
prevention and intervention in, 371, 391–392, 393
cultural studies on, 358–359
in school, 389–390
self-correcting, without intervention, 371, 393
socioeconomic variations in, 388, 391–392
taxonomy of, 379–385, 393
multivariate-descriptive approach to, 381–382, 383–384, 393, 407, 408
nosological approach to, 380, 381, 382–383, 384, 393
training for research on, 392–393
Bereavement, 197
Bilingualism, 312–316
Biobehavioral research, on vulnerability to illness, 54–55
Biomedical model of health and illness, 35–36
Biopsychosocial approach to health and illness, 36–37
Birth order in family, 172, 173

and affectional relationship with parents, 189
Black families, 6, 8–13, 213, 214
academic achievement in, after desegregation, 311–312
achievement motivation in, 303, 306
adoption of children of, by white families, 303
classroom experiences of children in, 296, 304
education of, 16–17
employment and income of, 13–15, 16
geographic distribution of, 7, 8
home environment of, 7, 8
learned helplessness of, 304
out-of-school activities of, 19
parent-child interactions in, 214–215
population of, 6
self-concept of children in, 154, 172
after school desegregation, 309–311
single-parent, 216
television viewing by, 19
vulnerability of illness in, 55
Bones
age of, and skeletal maturity, 25
sports injuries of, 44
Brain
and behavior relations, 20, 27–33, 95, 112
hormonal influences in, 28–30
neurotransmitters in, 30–33
development of
and cognitive functioning, 95, 110–112, 131
electroencephalography in assessment of, 111, 112
head circumference measurements of, 95, 111, 112
lateralization in, 111
minimal damage of, behavior disorders in, 372–376, 383

Caloric intake, 45
in obesity, 46, 47
Cardiovascular benefits of exercise, 42, 43
Caretaking system, 185, 186–223, 231–232, 337
adoption of children in, 303, 346, 360
in behavior problems, 360
and hyperactivity, 374
cultural studies on, 209, 213–216, 337, 339, 340, 343–351, 357–358, 360
expectations of compliance in, 360
father in, 224–225, 349–350, 416
fostering in, 346, 360
in maternal employment, 220–223, 348–349
parent-child interactions in. *See* Parent-child interactions
and peer relationships, 263–266
polymatric, 346
relatives in, 346

and self-regulation by child, 161–162
  cultural studies on, 357–358
  shared responsibilities in, 345
  siblings in, 337, 343–344, 345–349
  socioeconomic differences in, 207–213, 231
  undercontrol of child in, 203–204
Catecholamine secretion, in stress, 30
Child-rearing practices. *See* Caretaking system
Cholesterol, in diet, 44–45
Chores, household, child responsibility for, 344
Chronic illness, 23, 48–52
  child's view of, 53–54, 110
  cultural studies on, 51–52
  family impact of, 50–51
  health beliefs in, 40, 41
  models of normative development in, 51–52
  prevalence of, 49
Cigarette smoking, 47–48. *See also* Smoking
Classrooms. *See* Schools
Cognitive development, 1, 20, 70–146, 398, 399, 401–403
  abstract concepts in, 75, 107, 108, 130, 401
  assessment of, 96–103
    classification issues in, 77–79
    in collaboration approach, 91, 92–93
    on developmental sequences, 97–101
    environmental influences on, 91, 92, 105, 106, 125–127
    and literate practices, 125–127
    rule-assessment method in, 101–103
    scaling methods in, 97–101, 103, 411
    on speed of development, 100–101
  automatization in, 82
  in bilingualism, 312–313
  and brain changes, 95, 110–112, 131
  caretaking system affecting, 347
  collaboration approach to, 86–93, 95, 96, 113, 119, 131
  concrete operations stage in, 74, 78, 80, 85, 107, 130
  continuous change model of, 81–82, 129–130
  in embedded teaching, 117, 118
  emotional, 93, 94–95, 104–110, 131, 418
  environmental influences on, 20–21, 76, 83–96, 131
  executive processes in, 196–197, 401
  formal operations stage in, 74–75, 80, 85, 107–108, 130
  Freudian processes in, 107, 108–109, 131
  future areas for research on, 103–129, 409
  guided reinvention theory of, 113–116, 117, 118, 119, 132
  and health beliefs of children, 38–39
  hormonal influences on, 29
  individual differences in, 73, 76–79
  information processing model of, 80–81
  integration of theories on, 83, 93–94
  involving relations of representations, 73–74, 107, 130
  and language development, 115–116
  levels of, 72–76
  and literate practices, 119–129, 132
  logic model of, 80, 82–83, 130
  memory in, 80–81, 82–83, 130
  methodological problems in research on, 96
  and moral behavior, 91, 94, 95
  nativist model of, 84, 85, 86
  and parent-child interactions, 114–115, 116, 193–194, 196–197, 206
    maternal influence on, 300
    mutual cognitions affecting, 198–201
  and peer interactions, 244–245
  perspective-taking in, 73, 74, 81
  Piaget on, 4, 70, 73–75, 76, 85–86
  preformed elements in, 84–85
  and problem-solving skills, 401, 402
  processes in, 79–83, 130
  production systems theory of, 82, 102, 130
  reorganizations in, 72–76, 130, 131
    emotional, 106–108, 131
  role-related, 73, 74, 89–91, 107, 193, 402
  and school attendance, 84, 117–118, 283
    cultural studies on, 361–362
  and self-concept, 158–160, 162–165, 174, 175
  sequences of, 97–101, 130
  social, 112–129. *See also* Social cognition
  stages of, 71–73, 76, 80, 129–130
  steps in, 73
  structural and functional approaches to, 70–71, 83
  systems theory on, 86
  universal aspects of, 73, 76–79
Collaboration approach to cognitive development, 86–93, 95, 96, 113, 119, 131
  ability and competence concepts in, 91, 92–93, 131
  problem-solving in, 87
Communication
  and language development, 115–116. *See also* Language development
  literate practices in, 119–129. *See also* Literate practices
  nonverbal, in peer interactions, 244, 245
  parent-child, 202
Comparisons, social
  by black children, 303
  emotional implications of, 107
  and self-concept, 157, 175, 403
Competence, 118, 291
  in cognitive abilities, 206
  in collaboration approach, 91, 92–93, 131
  and coping behavior, 390–391
  cultural studies on, 305–307
  environmental factors affecting measurement

of, 91, 92
parent-child interactions affecting development of, 206–207
in second-language learning and bilingualism, 313, 314
self-understanding of, 149, 156, 157, 169–170
and academic achievement, 294, 295, 404
social, 206
and parent-child interactions, 193–194
Competition, in peer interactions, 244, 273
classroom conditions affecting, 268
in crowding, 255
between friends, 251
in sports, 44
Concrete operations stage of cognitive development, 74, 78, 80, 85, 107, 130
emotional changes in, 107
Conservation tasks in cognitive development, 72, 73, 78, 80, 82, 94
analysis of, 98–99
Continuous change model of cognitive development, 81–82, 129–130
Control of behavior. *See* Regulation of behavior
Cooperation, 21, 403
in parent-child interactions, 191–192, 196–197, 231, 403, 405
in peer interactions, 244, 246, 266, 268, 273
gender differences in, 258
in schools, 266, 268, 308, 318–320
Coping behavior, 390–391, 418
Coregulation of behavior, parent-child, 191–192, 196–197, 231, 403, 405
cultural studies on, 343, 345, 351, 352, 354
Corticosteroid secretion, in stress, 30
Cross-cultural studies. *See* Cultural studies
Crowding, peer interactions in, 255
Cruel behavior syndrome, 384–385
Cultural studies, 1, 2, 5–6, 22, 335–369, 412
on achievement values, 303, 304–306, 319
on adult expectations of children, 360, 413
on African tribes, 341
on behavior problems, 358–361, 408
on black families. *See* Black families
on caretaking system, 209, 213–216, 229, 337, 339, 340, 343–351, 357–358, 360
on child's view of environment, 414–415
complexity of features in, 337–338
on eating patterns, 45
ecocultural niche concept in, 335–336, 412
on employment and family income, 13–15
future areas of, 398
on geographic distribution of population groups, 7, 8
on handicapped children, 51–52
on health behaviors, 34–35, 53
on Hispanic families. *See* Hispanic families
on home environment, 8–13, 338–339
compared to school environment, 305–307

on literate practices, 120–121, 122, 126, 127, 361–362
methodological issues in, 229, 362–363
on out-of-school activities, 19
on peer interactions, 243, 347–348
on regulation of behavior, 150–151, 343–345, 351, 352, 354, 357–358, 405
on schools, 6–7, 16–17, 22, 283–284, 304–316, 361–362
and academic achievement, 284, 296, 311–312, 413
and cooperative learning program, 319–320
after desegregation, 307–312
and second-language learning, 312–316
and teacher-student interactions, 296, 304, 320
on self-concept, 154, 171–172, 351–358, 403, 405
on single-parent families, 216, 220
on television viewing, 19
on vulnerability of certain populations, 364
on Western and non-Western societies, 342

Dating, 222
Defense mechanisms, 109
Delinquent behavior, 203–204, 211, 212
impact of schools on, 390
and maternal employment, 221, 222
peer interactions, 261
prevention and intervention in, 391
and single-parent families, 218
Demographic analysis of middle childhood, 5–19, 336, 357, 412
Depression
in childhood, 383
cultural studies on, 355
Desegregation of schools, 307–312
peer relationships in, 308–309
racial attitudes in, 308–309
self-concept in, 309–311
Diagnostic and Statistical Manual of Mental Disorders (DSM), 380, 382
Diet
cultural studies on, 338
and eating patterns, 44–47
and hyperactivity, 32, 374, 375
in obesity, 46–47
television affecting, 45–46
Discipline techniques, 189–192. *See also* Regulation of behavior
Disease, definition of, 34. *See also* Health and illness
Disembedded teaching, 117, 118, 128
Divorce of parents, 11, 12, 96, 109–110
emotional consequences for children, 109–110, 131, 217
and peer relations of children, 264

and single-parent families, 216–220
Dominance interactions in groups, 254
Drug abuse, 47, 48
    and friendship selection, 248, 253
    peer influence on, 270
Drug therapy
    age-related changes in responsiveness to, 31
    in hyperactivity, 31–32, 374, 375

Eating patterns, 44–47. *See also* Diet
Ecocultural niche, 335–369. *See also* Cultural
        studies
Ecology
    of peer interactions, 225
    of schools, 287–288, 322
Economic status. *See* Socioeconomic status
Education. *See also* Schools
    of parents, and child-rearing practices, 209,
        210, 211, 212
Ego control theories, 160–162
Electroencephalography
    in assessment of brain growth and cognitive
        development, 111, 112
    in attention deficit disorders and learning dis-
        abilities, 32
Embedded teaching, 116–117, 119
    and disembedded teaching, 117, 118, 128
Emotional functioning, 418–419
    and cognitive development, 93, 94–95, 104–
        110, 131, 418
    divorce affecting, 109–110, 131, 217
    family relations affecting, 109–110
    Freudian processes in, 107, 108–109, 131
    self-understanding of, 104–106, 131, 156, 175
Empathy Training Project, 267, 268
Employment
    and child-rearing practices, 209, 348–349
    division of labor in, by age and sex, 336
    and family income, 13–15, 16
    of mothers, 220–223, 348–349
    and stress of unemployment, 227, 264
    and subsistence work cycle, 336, 337, 341
Environmental influences, 7–15, 22, 411–415
    on assessment of cognitive development, 91,
        92, 105, 106, 125–127
    child's view of, 414–415
    on cognitive development, 20–21, 76, 83–
        96, 131
    cultural studies of. *See* Cultural studies
    family in, 8–15. *See also* Family environment
    on health beliefs of children, 39
    on physical maturation, 25, 26
    on self-concept, 403
    on social role knowledge, 89–91
    supporting developmental change, 415
    on vulnerability to illness, 55–56, 364

Epidemiological research on behavior problems,
        387–389, 390, 407, 408
Epinephrine secretion
    behavioral influences of, 31
    in stress, 30, 31
Ethnic studies. *See* Cultural studies
Executive processes, cognitive, 196–197, 401
Exercise
    benefits of, 42–44
    in obesity, 46–47
    risks of, 44
Expectations
    for academic achievement, 229, 294. *See also*
        Academic achievement, expectations for
    and development of self-concept, 150, 151,
        152
    in parent-child interactions, 199, 200
        cultural patterns in, 360, 413–414

Family environment, 1, 8–15, 21, 184–239, 406,
        415–416, 417
    and academic achievement, 297–304
    and achievement motivation, 303
    authority patterns in, compared to school, 302
    birth order in, 172, 173, 189
    child care in. *See* Caretaking system
    chronic illness affecting, 50–51
    cultural studies on, 213–216, 229
    divorce affecting, 109–110
    and eating patterns, 45–46
    emotional climate of, 109–110
    fathers in, 224–225, 349–350, 416
    maternal employment affecting, 220–223, 348
    methodological issues in research on, 227–
        231
    nuclear, 8
    Oedipus conflict in, 107, 109
    parent-child interactions in. *See* Parent-child
        interactions
    and peer interactions, 263–266, 273
    and self-concept of child, 161–162, 172–173,
        175, 416
    siblings in, 8–10. *See also* Siblings
    single-parent, 11, 12, 13, 214, 216–220
    in socialization, 184, 185, 186–192, 231, 398
    socioeconomic status affecting, 13–15, 16. *See
        also* Socioeconomic status
    stress in, 56. *See also* Stress, in families
Fathers, roles of, 224–225, 349–350, 416
Financial status. *See* Socioeconomic status
Food. *See* Diet
Formal operations stage of cognitive develop-
        ment, 74–75, 80, 85, 107–108, 130, 410
    emotional changes in, 107–108
Foster care of children, cultural studies on, 346,
        360

Freud, Sigmund, 4
  on self-management, 160
  on socialization, 149
Freudian processes, 107, 108–109, 131
Friends, 250–252, 273
  and acquaintances, 248–250
  average number of, 250
  and cliques, 246, 250, 266
  competition between, 251
  future areas for research on, 251–252
  reciprocity expectations among, 250–251
  role relations between, 107
  selection of, 247–248, 406
    classroom conditions affecting, 266–267
    cultural studies on, 347–348
  and self-concept, 151, 152

Gender differences, 20
  in academic achievement expectations, 297
  in behavior problems, 384–385, 388
  in peer interactions, 258
  in physical maturation, 25, 26
  in racial attitudes, 309
  in role learning, 21, 206, 337
  in self-concept, 154–155
  in social contacts, 247–248, 258–259, 262
  in spatial reasoning tests, 29
  in teacher-student interactions, 296–297
Genetic factors, in physical maturation, 25
Goal-directed activities
  in classrooms, 118
  guided reinvention in, 115–116, 117, 118
Groups, 252–254
  entry into, 256
  formation of, 252
  gender of membership in, 258
  leaders of, 254
  norms governing, 252–253
  observational studies of, 254
  structure of, 253–254
Guided reinvention theory, 113–116, 117, 118, 119, 132
Guilt feelings, 107
Gusii society, self-regulation of behavior in, 357

Handicapped children, 49
  families of, 50–51
  mainstreaming of, 260, 285
Hawaii, early education program in, 306–307
Head circumference measurements, and cognitive development, 95, 111, 112
Health and illness, 22–23, 24–25, 35–57, 398
  biomedical model of, 35–36
  biopsychosocial approach to, 36–37
  children's concepts of, 37–41, 53–54, 110
  and chronic illness, 48–52
  in community, 336, 337

cultural studies on concept of, 34–35, 53
definitions of, 33–34
and eating patterns, 44–47
education programs on, 56–576
future areas of research on, 52–57
and life-style patterns, 41–52
peer influence on, 253, 270
and physical exercise, 42–44
and self-concept, 41–52
self-regulation of, 404
smoking, alcohol, and drugs affecting, 47–48
stress response to illness, 364
  individual variations in, 54–56
  self-induced, 47–48
Helpfulness, learned, 360
Helplessness, learned, by black children, 304
High-risk children, for behavior problems, 377–378, 379, 390–391, 393
Hispanic families, 6, 7, 10, 11, 12, 213, 214
  in desegrated schools, 309, 310
  employment and income of, 13, 14, 15, 16
  parent-child interactions in, 214, 215
  self-concept in, 154, 309, 310
Home environment, 7, 8
  and academic achievement, 296, 298–300, 305–307
  and achievement values, 304, 305
  child care in, 343–351. *See also* Caretaking system
  in ecocultural niche, 338–339
  family interactions in. *See* Family environment
  compared to school environment, 286, 296, 305–307, 417
  and types of dwellings, 7, 9
Homework and studying, time spent in, 19
Hormonal influences, 20, 28–30
  on aggressive behavior, 28–29
  on cognitive development, 29
  on stress response, 30, 31
Hospitalized children, health-related behavior of, 40
Hyperactivity, 195, 372–276, 383, 389, 393
  diagnostic criteria in, 373–374
  diet in, 32, 374, 375
  drug therapy in, 31–32, 374, 375
  etiology of, 374–375
  neurochemical basis of, 31–32
  parent-child interactions in, 199
  research studies on, 386–387
Hypogonadism, 29

Identity. *See* Self-concept
Illness. *See* Health and illness
Imitation, in cognitive development, 114–115
Impulsive behavior, 161
  parental regulation of, 194–195, 203

self-regulation of, 152
Income of family, 13–15, 16. *See also* Socioeco-
     nomic status
Individuation and individualism, 403
     cultural studies on, 352–354, 356
Information processing
     and cognitive development, 80–81
     and self-concept, 158–160
Input-output analysis of schools, 285–286
Instructional methods in schools, 316–321, 322
Integration of schools, 307–312
Intelligence measurements, and achievement,
     292
Intervention in child psychopathology, 391–392
     cultural variations in, 358–359
Iron deficiency anemia, 46
Isolation, social, 261, 400
     social skills training in, 268–269

Kamehameha Early Education Program, 306–307
!Kung families
     father-child interactions in, 350
     public character of life in, 355

Labeling, in parent-child interactions, 198–200
Labor force participation, 13–15, 16. *See also*
     Employment
Language development, 115–116
     guided reinvention approach to, 115–116
     literate practices in. *See* Literate practices
     maternal influence on, 300
     and peer interactions, 244, 273
     and second-language learning, 312–316
     and self-descriptions, 155
Latchkey children, 222
Lead, and attention-deficit disorders, 32
Learning, 402
     and academic achievement, 291–293. *See also*
          Academic achievement
     brain growth measurements related to, 111
     in disembedded teaching, 117, 118, 128
     in embedded teaching, 116–117, 118
     of helpfulness, 360
     of helplessness, 304
     of roles. *See* Role learning
     problems in, 383, 389, 407–408
          DSM categories of, 383
          neurophysiological mechanisms in, 31–33
          testing situations in, 91
          and self-concept, 149, 157
          social, 112–114. *See also* Social cognition
Life-style, 22, 24, 41–52
     in chronic impairment, 48–52
     eating patterns in, 44–47
     exercise in, 42–44

privacy in, 354–357, 358
and self-induced vulnerability to disease, 47
Literate practices, 19, 119–129, 132, 292, 296
     aliterate conditions, compared to, 123–125
     amplification in, 121, 122–123, 132
     cognitive effects of, 120–122
          assessment of, 125–127
     cultural studies on, 120–121, 122, 126, 127,
          361–362
     definitions of, 120–122
     and home environment, 299, 300, 301, 306
     nonlocal integration in, 121, 123–124, 126
     parental influence on, 300, 301
     range of, 120, 121, 122–125
     readiness for, 292
     representational system in, 121–122, 124–125,
          126, 132
     and school attendance, 122, 283, 284, 286
     and second-language learning, 312–316
     systemic analysis in, 121, 124–125, 126, 132
Logic model of cognitive development, 80, 82–
     83, 130

Malnutrition, 46
Marijuana use, 48
Marital status of parents, 10–13
     divorced. *See* Divorce of parents
     and single-parent families, 11, 12, 13, 214,
          216–220
Mastery learning techniques, 292, 293
MBD (minimal brain damage), 372–376, 383
Memory
     capacity of, 73, 74, 196
     in cognitive development, 80–81, 82–83, 130
     short-term, 80, 81, 83
Menarche, 26
     physical activity affecting, 44
Mental health problems, 370–397
Methodological problems in research, 410–411
     on cognitive development, 96
     on ecocultural niche, 362–363
     on families, 227–231
     on peer interactions, 271–272
     on self-concept, 173–174
Minority group studies. *See* Cultural studies
Modeling
     in peer interactions, 261
     by school personnel, 297
     and self-regulation by child, 163
     in social learning, 114, 268
Moral development
     assessment of, 100
     and cognitive development, 91, 94, 95
     and parent-child interactions, 205
     and peer interactions, 262–263, 267
     in school curriculum, 267

and self-regulation, 152, 161
Motivation
  for achievement. *See* Achievement motivation
  for affiliation, 157
Multivariate-descriptive approach to behavior disorders, 381–382, 383–384, 393, 407

Nativist theory of cognitive development, 84, 85, 86
Neurobiology, developmental, 27–33
Neuromaturation, 27–33
Neuromodulation, 27–28, 32, 35
Neuropsychology, 32, 33
Neurotransmission, 20, 27–28, 30–33, 35
Nonlocal integration in literate practices, 121, 123–124, 126
Nonverbal communication, in peer interactions, 244, 245
Norm(s), 21
  in peer interactions
    conformity to, 265
    among friends, 250–251
    in groups, 252–253
    in school, 270–271
    in social tasks, 256
  of school, compared to home environment, 296
  and self-concept development, 150, 151, 152
Normative-epidemiological research on behavior problems, 387–389, 390, 407, 408
Nosological approach to behavior disorders, 380, 381, 382–383, 384, 393
Nutrition. *See* Diet

Obesity, 46–47
  cultural studies on, 34–35
  definition of, 46
  disorders associated with, 46
  and relationship between childhood and adult weight, 47
Objective self, 155
Occupation. *See* Employment
Oedipus conflict, 107, 109
Ojibwa Indians, self-concept of, 353
Open education, 266–267, 316–318

Parent-child interactions, 21, 184–239
  and academic achievement, 187, 284, 289, 297–307, 414
  and achievement motivation, 220, 303
  affection in, 188–190, 205
    variations in, 201–202, 208
  amount of time spent in, 186
  anger in, 189–190

and antisocial behavior in child, 203–204, 211, 212
attachment in, 189, 190, 197, 263
in autism, 376
for behavior control, 185, 186–201, 231, 405, 406
and cognitive development, 114–115, 116, 193–194, 196–201, 206, 300
collaboration in, 87, 88
and competencies in child, 206–207
education of parents affecting, 209–212
embedded teaching in, 117
expectations affecting, 199, 200, 413–414
fathers in, 224–225, 337, 347–350
health-related, 39–40, 53
and language development, 116, 300
life-cycle changes affecting, 300
maternal employment affecting, 220–223, 348–349
methodological issues in research on, 227–231
and moral development in child, 205
mutual cognitions in, 198–201
observational studies on, 230
openness of communication in, 202
and out-of-school activities, 417
parent-centered, 203
and peer relationships of child, 263–266, 273
and prosocial behavior in child, 205–206
role transmission in, 193, 209
scaffolding in, 87, 88
and self-concept of child, 172, 194, 204–205
and sibling relationships, 226, 227
in single-parent families, 216–220
socioeconomic differences in, 13–15, 16, 207–213, 231
stereotyping and labeling in, 198–199, 200
stress affecting, 210, 217, 219, 227
Peer interactions, 3, 21–22, 240–282, 398, 406–407, 416, 417
  acquaintances in, 248–250
  activities in, 242–243, 255
  age of contacts in, 247, 257–258
  aggression in, 242, 243, 245, 246, 247, 261–262, 268
  competition in, 244, 251, 255, 268, 273
  cooperation in, 244, 246, 258, 266, 268, 273
  and coping behavior, 390
  cultural studies on, 243, 347–348
  and family environment, 263–266, 273
  friends in, 247–248, 250–252, 273, 406
  gender differences in, 258
  in groups, 252–254, 256
  maternal employment affecting, 222
  methodological issues in research on, 271–272
  and moral development, 262–263, 267
  mutual cognitions affecting, 200

norms governing. *See* Norm(s), in peer interactions
observational studies of, 271–272
poor, 400
  and maladjustment in later life, 260–261, 406–407
  social skills training in, 268–269
prosocial behavior in, 242, 243–244, 261, 265, 268
race of contacts in, 248, 259–260, 268
  in desegregated schools, 308–309
racial attitudes and behaviors in, 308–309
romantic involvement in, 259, 262
in school, 242, 247, 254, 259, 260, 266–271
  in tutoring peers, 268, 269–270
and self-concept, 151, 152, 156, 159, 166, 261
self-regulation of behavior in, 404, 406
settings of, 254–255
sex of contacts in, 247–248, 258–259, 262
situational components of, 240–241, 254–260
smoking in, 48, 253, 270
social attraction in, 245–247
social context of, 240, 241–254
social skills acquired in, 194
in social tasks and problems, 255–257
socialization in, 240, 271
stress in, 56, 406
teasing in, 256
time spent in, 242
Perspective-taking, in cognitive development, 73, 74, 81
Physical development, 2, 20, 25–27, 416
  attractive appearance in, associated with social attractiveness, 245, 246
  brain changes in, and cognitive development, 110–112, 131
  in chronic illness, 48–52
  eating patterns affecting, 44–47
  exercise affecting, 42–44
  future areas of research on, 52–57
  and health issues, 33–57
  neurologic, 27–33
  reproductive maturation in, 25–26
  and self-image, 41–52, 53, 154, 155, 156
  skeletal maturation in, 25
  smoking, alcohol and drugs affecting, 47–48
Physical education programs, in schools, 43–44
Physician-child patient relationship, in chronic illness, 54
Piaget theories on cognitive development, 4, 70, 73–75, 76, 85–86
Play activities
  and cognitive development, 72
  composition of play group in, 337, 346
  parent-child interactions concerning, 187
  in peer interactions, 242, 243, 255
  physical exercise in, 42–44

self-regulation in, 165–166
sports in. *See* Sports activities
Polymatric caretaking system, 346
Popular children, characteristics of, 245–247
Population of children
  geographic distribution of, 7, 8
  number of, 6–7
Power-assertive methods of discipline, 192, 195, 205, 206–207
Preformist approach to cognitive development, 84–85
Prevention of child psychopathology, 391–392
Private self, 354–357
Problem-solving, 399, 401, 402
  collaborative cycle in, 87
  development of skill in, 196
  rule assessment of, 102
Production systems theory of cognitive development, 82, 102, 130
Prosocial behavior
  and caretaking patterns, 347, 351
  and learned helpfulness, 360
  and parent-child interactions, 205–206, 265
  in peer interactions, 242, 243–244, 261, 265, 268
  and sibling relationships, 226
Psychoanalytic approach to emotional development, 108–109
Psychological aspects, 4, 23
  in biopsychosocial approach to illness, 36–37
  in emotional functioning. *See* Emotional functioning
  in health-related beliefs of children, 36–37, 38, 49, 50
  in neuropsychological assessment techniques, 32, 33
  in obesity, 46, 47
  pathological deviations in, 370–397. *See also* Behavior problems
  research on, 398
Psychopathology, 370–397. *See also* Behavior problems
Psychopharmacotherapy, age-related changes in responsiveness to, 31
Puberty, 20
  onset of, 25–26
  physical changes in, 416
Public self, 354–357, 358
Punishment, in discipline, 188, 190, 231
  cultural studies on, 215, 357–358
  and self-esteem, 205
  and self-regulation by child, 162–163
  verbal rationale with, 163

Race of social contacts, 248, 259–260, 268
  and cross-race friendship selections, 248
  after school desegregation, 307–312

Racial studies. *See* Cultural studies
Reading. *See* Literate practices
Reciprocity norms, in friendship, 250–251
Recreation activities. *See* Play activities
Regulation of behavior, 2, 185, 188, 189–192, 201, 205, 406
  and academic achievement, 205, 293–294, 302, 303–304
  and competencies in children, 206–207
  cultural patterns of, 150–151, 215, 340, 343–345, 351, 352, 354, 357–358, 405
  for face-to-face control, 192, 231
  for impulsive behavior, 161, 194–195, 203
  maternal employment affecting, 221–222
  for out-of-sight control, 192, 231
  parent-child coregulation of, 191–192, 196–197, 231
  power-assertive methods in, 192, 195, 205, 206–207
  reasoning and explanation in, 163, 192, 202
  school in, 302, 303, 405, 417
  and self-concepts of child, 194, 204–205
  self-system in, 147–183. *See also* Self-regulation of behavior
  in single-parent families, 218
  social cognition affecting, 193, 196
  socioeconomic differences in, 207–213
  strictness of, 202
  and undercontrol of behavior, 203–204
Reinforcement of behavior
  parents in, 185
  in peer interactions, 261
Rejection, social, 261, 268–269, 400
Reorganizations, in cognitive development, 72–76, 130, 131
  emotional, 106–108, 131
Representation(s), relations of, in cognitive development, 73–74, 107, 130
Representational system, in literate practices, 121–122, 124, 125, 126, 132
Reproductive maturation, 25–26
Reputation, social, and social attractiveness, 245, 246
Research, 398–421
  on cognitive development, 96, 103–129
  on emotions, 109–110
  future areas for, 23
  health-related, 52–57
  methodological problems in, 410–411. *See also* Methodological problems in research
  neurobiological, 28, 29, 30, 31, 32–33
  on peer interactions, 271–272
  on psychopathology, 384–393
    training for, 392–393
  on schools, 321
    problems in, 290–291
  on self-concept, 173–174

on tasks of middle childhood, 399–409
  theoretical views in, 3–5
Responsibility for behavior, assumption of. *See* Self-regulation of behavior.
Rewards, in self-regulation of behavior, 164
Role learning, 402
  in cognitive development, 73, 74, 89–91, 107, 193, 402
  emotional consequences of, 107
  environmental influences on, 89–91
  gender differences in, 21, 206, 337
  and health-related beliefs, 38
  in parent-child interactions, 193, 209
  peer relationships in, 21
  in pretend play, 72
  school experiences in, 22, 295–297
  and self-concept development, 151, 158
Rule assessment of cognitive development, 101–103

Scaffolding surrounding children, 336, 339
  in parent-child interactions, 87, 88
Scaling of cognitive development, 97–101, 103, 411
Schemas, of self, 158–159
Schizophrenia, 260, 376
  high-risk children for, 377–378, 390
Schools, 1–2, 3, 15–17, 22, 283–334, 402
  ability grouping in, 286, 308, 321
  academic achievement in, 17, 291–293. *See also* Academic achievement
  affective education in, 267–268
  behavior problems in, 389–390
  behavior regulation in, 302, 303, 405, 417
  caretaking system affecting experiences in, 347
  class size in, 288
  and cognitive development, 84, 117–118, 283, 361–362
  cooperative environment in, 266, 268, 308, 318–320
  cultural studies on. *See* Cultural studies, on schools
  desegregation of, 307–312
  early intervention programs in, 318
  ecological studies on, 287–288, 322
  environment of, 285–289
  functions of, 283
  health education in, 56–57
  home environment compared to, 286, 296, 305–307, 417
  hyperactive children in, 372, 373, 389
  input-output analysis of, 285–286
  instructional approaches in, 316–321, 322
  learning difficulty in, 407–408
  literate practices in, 119–129, 132
  mainstreaming of handicapped children in, 260, 285

mastery learning technique in, 292, 293, 320
moral education in, 267
norms governing behavior in, 270–271
open and traditional classrooms in, 266–267,
    316–318
parent-child interactions concerning, 187
parental involvement in, 301–302
peer interactions in, 242, 247, 254, 259, 260,
    266–271
physical education and exercise activities in,
    43–44
physical maturation affecting performance in,
    26–27
private, number enrolled in, 16–17
productivity studies on, 290
public, number enrolled in, 15
racial and ethnic composition of, 259–260,
    268, 304–316
    problems in research on, 290–291
role learning in, 22, 295–297
second-language learning and bilingualism in,
    312–316
social interactions in, 117–118
social skills training in, 268–269
social system variables in, 286–287, 416, 417
socialization in, 284, 296
socioeconomic influences on experiences in,
    322
stress in, 56, 295
teacher-student interactions in. *See* Teacher-
    student interactions
tutoring in, 292, 293
    by peers, 268, 269–270
Scoliosis, 35
Second-language learning, 312–316
Seizure disorders, 34
Self-concept, 147–183, 403–405, 418
    and academic achievement, 149, 157, 159,
        293–295, 400, 403–404
    and achievement motivation, 157
    active self in, 156
    and affiliation motivation, 157
    behavior modification theories on, 163–165
    biases in, 159–160
    child's description of, 153–156, 358, 403
    and cognitive development, 158–160, 162–
        165, 174, 175, 418
    component models of, 165–166
    cultural studies on, 154, 171–172, 351–358,
        403, 405
    ego control theories on, 160–162
    emotions in, 175
    expectations of others affecting, 151, 152
    family environment affecting, 161–162, 172–
        173, 175, 416
    formation of, 21
        universal problems in, 353–354

variables influencing, 168–173
individuation and individualism in, 352–354,
    356, 403
inferiority feelings in, 149, 158
and information processing, 158–160
integration of theories on, 166–168
multiple views in, 152
objective self in, 155
parent-child interactions affecting, 172, 194,
    204–205
and peer interactions, 151, 152, 156, 159,
    166, 261
perceptions of others affecting, 149
physical development and health affecting,
    41–52, 53, 154, 155, 156
physical self in, 156
potential ideal self in, 157
private and public selves in, 354–357, 358
psychological self in, 156
research on
    future areas for, 409
    methodological issues in, 173–174
school desegregation affecting, 309–311
self-awareness in, 168–169
self-confidence in, 157
    and self-criticism, 158, 175
self-esteem in, 149, 156–157, 158. *See also*
    Self-esteem
and self-presentation, 169–170
self-regulation as function of, 147, 160–168.
    See also Self-regulation of behavior
self-schemas in, 158–159
self-understanding in, 147, 174, 175. *See also*
    Self-understanding
social class affecting, 170–171, 175
social comparisons affecting, 157, 175
social learning theories on, 162–163
as social object, 148–149, 169
and social roles, achieved and ascribed, 158
social self in, 156
social system influencing, 174, 175
sports programs affecting, 44
subjective self in, 155
tasks related to, 151–153
Self-confidence, 157
Self-consciousness, 169
Self-contemplation, cultural studies on, 355–356
Self-criticism, 158, 175
Self-descriptions, 153–156, 158, 358, 403
Self-esteem, 156–157, 158, 404
    and academic achievement, 149, 171, 291,
        293–295
    assessment of, 95
    in chronic illness, 49, 51
    cultural studies on, 172, 356, 357, 358
        after desegregation, 307, 309–311
    internalized standards affecting, 152

parent-child interactions affecting, 204–205
and popularity, 246
socioeconomic influences on, 171, 175
teacher behaviors affecting, 295
Self-expression, ecocultural patterns in, 355–356, 357
Self-managed sequencing of activity, 344
Self-presentation
    enhancing impression, 169
    as handicapping behavior, 169–170
Self-regulation of behavior, 21, 22, 147–183, 399, 403, 404–408
    and academic achievement, 295, 302, 303–304
    adult-based theories on, 167
    cognitive/behavior modification theories on, 163–165
    commitment or choice in, 167
    component models of, 165–166
    cultural studies on, 340, 343–345, 351, 352, 357–358, 405
    ego control theories on, 160–162
    habit reorganization in, 167
    health-related, 41
    impulse control strategies in, 152
    integration of theories on, 166–168
    modeling in, 163
    in open education programs, 316, 317
    parent-child interactions affecting development of, 190–192, 195, 196–197, 198, 205, 206
        in maternal employment, 221–222
    problem recognition in, 167
    research on, 160–168
    social learning theories on, 162–163
    social system affecting, 149–151
Self-understanding, 147–183, 403
    cultural studies on, 352, 353, 356
    of emotions, 104–106, 131, 156, 175
    and language development, 155
    research on, 153–160
    and self-deception, 155
    of skills and abilities, 149, 156, 157, 159
    terms used in description of, 154
Separation from parents, stress of, 197
Serotonin levels, in autism, 31
Sex of social contacts, 247–248, 258–259, 262
Sexual behavior, 259, 262, 271
    cultural studies on, 355
Siblings, 21, 225–227
    child care by, 337
    cultural studies on, 343–344, 345–349
    of chronically ill child, 50–51
    number of, 8–10
Single-parent families, 11, 12, 13, 214, 216–220
Skeletal maturation, 25

Skills and abilities, self-understanding of, 149, 156, 157, 159
Smoking, 47–48
    peer influence on, 48, 253, 270
    prevention programs for, 48
Social cognition, 21, 73, 74, 107, 112–129, 131–132, 402
    and antisocial behavior, 204
    collaboration approach to, 113, 119
    and coping behavior, 390
    development of, 93, 94, 399, 400
    environmental influences on, 89–91, 105, 106
    guided reinvention theory of, 113–116, 117, 118, 119, 132
    hierarchy in, 113–114, 119
    imitation in, 113, 114–115
    and language development, 115–116
    measurement of, 410–411
    and parent-child interactions, 193–194, 196
    and peer interactions, 243, 244, 261, 268–269, 406
    role-related, 193. *See also* Role learning
Social interactions, 1, 2, 405–407
    age of contacts in, 247, 257–258
    in biopsychosocial approach to health and illness, 36–37
    in chronic illness, 51–52
    and cognitive development, 112–129, 131–132. *See also* Social cognition
    collaborative cycle in, 86–88
    comparisons in. *See* Comparisons, social
    convergence rate hierarchy in, 113–114, 119
    embedded teaching in, 116–117
    emotions in, children's conceptions of, 105–106
    and language development, 115–116
    norms in, 21. *See also* Norm(s)
    parent-child. *See* Parent-child interactions
    peers in. *See* Peer interactions
    and public self, 354–357, 358
    race of contacts in, 248, 259–260, 268
    regulation of behavior in, 21, 149–151, 404, 405
    and self-concept, 148–149, 174, 403, 404, 405
    self-presentation in, 355
    sex of contacts in, 247–248, 258–259, 262
    support systems in, 56, 337
    teacher-student. *See* Teacher-student interactions and voluntary social activities, 344
Social learning theories on self-regulation, 162–163
Social systems, 415–419
    variations in, 168, 170–173
Socialization
    coregulation of behavior in, 150

family environment in, 184, 185, 186–192, 231, 398
Freud on, 149
peer context in, 240, 271
schools in, 284, 296
Socioeconomic status, 13–15, 16, 22, 209–211, 413
  and academic achievement, 289, 294, 296, 298, 402, 413, 414
  and behavior problems, 388–389, 391–392
  and child-rearing practices, 207–213, 231
  and health beliefs, 40
  and physical maturation, 25, 26
  and school experiences, 322
  and self-concept, 170–171, 175
  of single-parent families, 216, 219, 220
  and social attractiveness, 245
  and vulnerability to illness, 55–56
Sports activities, 43–44
  competitive pressures in, 44
  injuries in, 44
  peer interactions in, 243
  and self-concept, 159
  sex segregation and integration in, 248, 259
  time spent in, 18, 19
Stereotyping
  in parent-child interactions, 199
  sex role related, 206
Stress and anxiety, 197–198, 210
  in chronic impairment, 49, 50
  coping behavior in, 390–391, 418
  in families, 56
    and child-rearing practices, 210
    and peer relations of child, 263–264
    single-parent, 217, 219
    in unemployment, 227
  hormone secretion in, 30, 31
  in peer relationships, 56, 406
  in school, 295
  in separation from parents, 197
  and vulnerability to illness, 54–56
Studying and homework, time spent in, 19
Subjective self, 155
Support systems
  of single-parent families, 219–220
  and vulnerability to illness, 56
  for women, 337
Systemic analysis in literate practices, 121, 124–125, 126, 132
Systems theories
  of cognitive development, 86
  of family relationships, 223–224
  of health and illness, 36–37

Tahitians, self-concept of, 352–353
Tasks of middle childhood, 399–409, 415

peer interactions related to, 255–257
on self-concept, 151–153
Taxonomy of behavior disorders, 379–385, 393
  multivariate-descriptive approach to, 381–382, 383–384, 393, 407, 408
  nosological approach to, 380, 381, 382–383, 384, 393
Teacher-parent interactions, 301
Teacher-student interactions, 287, 288–289, 418
  and academic achievement, 287, 288–289, 304, 320
  authority style in, 417
  compared to parent-child, 271
  gender differences in, 296–297
  racial differences in, 296, 304, 320
  and self-esteem of students, 295
Teasing, 256
Television viewing
  and eating patterns, 45–46
  and health beliefs, 40, 53
  and language development, 115
  and social learning, 402
  time spent in, 17, 18–19
Temper trantrums, 189
Testing situations, collaboration of environment and cognitive development in, 91, 92
Testosterone levels, and aggressive behavior, 28
Tobacco use, 47–48. *See also* Smoking
Training
  for psychopathology research, 392–393
  on social skills, 268–269
Troublesomeness in children, 358–361. *See also* Behavior problems
Tutoring in schools, 292, 293
  and academic achievement, 320
  by peers, 268, 269–270

Unemployment, family stress in, 227, 264
Universal aspects of cognitive development, 73, 76–79
Urban population of children, 7, 9
  physical maturation of, 25, 26

Vulnerability to illness, 364
  individual variations in, 54–56
  self-induced, 47–48

Western societies, compared to non-Western, 342–343
Work. *See* Employment
Writing. *See* Literate practices